A COMPANION TO FILM COMEDY

A COMPANION TO
FILM
COMEDY

Edited by Andrew Horton and Joanna E. Rapf

WILEY Blackwell

This paperback edition first published 2016
© 2013 John Wiley & Sons Inc.

Edition History: John Wiley & Sons Inc. (hardback, 2013)

Registered Office
John Wiley & Sons Ltd, The Atrium, Southern Gate, Chichester, West Sussex, PO19 8SQ, UK

Editorial Offices
350 Main Street, Malden, MA 02148-5020, USA
9600 Garsington Road, Oxford, OX4 2DQ, UK
The Atrium, Southern Gate, Chichester, West Sussex, PO19 8SQ, UK

For details of our global editorial offices, for customer services, and for information about how to apply for permission to reuse the copyright material in this book please see our website at www.wiley.com / wiley-blackwell.

The right of Andrew Horton and Joanna E. Rapf to be identified as the authors of the editorial material in this work has been asserted in accordance with the UK Copyright, Designs and Patents Act 1988.

Library of Congress Cataloging-in-Publication Data
A companion to film comedy / edited by Andrew Horton and Joanna E. Rapf.
        p. cm.
   Includes bibliographical references and index.
   ISBN 978-1-4443-3859-1 (hardback : alk. paper)
   ISBN 978-1-1191-6955-0 (paperback)
   1. Comedy films–History and criticism. 2. Comic, The. I. Horton, Andrew. II. Rapf, Joanna E.
   PN1995.9.C55C675 2012
   791.43′617–dc23

                                                                                2012023048

A catalogue record for this book is available from the British Library.

Cover image: Charlie Chaplin as the Little Tramp © Bettmann / Corbis, from the Archives of Roy Export Company Establishment. Banana skin © leeavison / iStockphoto

Typeset in 11 / 13pt DanteMTStd by SPi Global, Chennai, India.

1 2016

Contents

Part VI International Comedy

Part VII Comic Animation

Notes on Editors and Contributors

Editors

Andrew Horton is the Jeanne H. Smith Professor of Film and Media Studies at the University of Oklahoma, an award-winning screenwriter, and the author of 24 books on film, screenwriting and cultural studies, including *Laughing Out Loud: Writing the Comedy Centered Screenplay* (University of California Press, 1999). His films include Brad Pitt's first feature film, *Dark Side of the Sun* (1988), and the much-awarded *Something In Between* (1983, Yugoslavia, directed by Srdjan Karanovic).

Joanna E. Rapf is a professor of film in the English Department at the University of Oklahoma. Periodically, she also teaches at Dartmouth College. Her books include *Buster Keaton: A Bio-Bibliography* (1995), *On the Waterfront* (2003), and *Interviews with Sidney Lumet* (2005). Recent publications in the area of comedy have been on Roscoe Arbuckle, Harry Langdon, Fay Tincher, Marie Dressler, Jimmy Durante, Jerry Lewis, and Woody Allen.

Contributors

Kristen Anderson Wagner received her Ph.D. in critical studies from the University of Southern California School of Cinematic Arts. Her dissertation, *Comic Venus: Women and Comedy in American Silent Film*, explores the often overlooked work of silent-era comediennes.

Suzanne Buchan is Professor of Animation Aesthetics and Director of the Animation Research Centre at the University for the Creative Arts in the United Kingdom. She is also a curator, a festival advisor, and the editor of *animation: an interdisciplinary journal* (Sage). Recent publications include *The Quay Brothers: Into a Metaphysical Playroom* (University of Minnesota Press, 2011).

Celestino Deleyto is Professor of Film and English Literature at the Universidad de Zaragoza (Spain). He is the author of *The Secret Life of Romantic Comedy* (Manchester University Press, 2009).

Maria DiBattista teaches English and Comparative Literature and film at Princeton. She is the author of *Fast Talking Dames*, and, most recently, *Novel Characters: A Genealogy*.

Roberta Di Carmine teaches film studies at Western Illinois University. She received her Ph.D. in comparative literature from the University of Oregon (2004) and a master's degree in foreign languages and literatures from West Virginia University (1996). In September 2011, Peter Lang publishers released her first book, *Italy Meets Africa: Colonial Discourses in Italian Cinema*.

Mark Eaton is Professor of English at Azusa Pacific University, where he teaches American literature and film studies. He is co-editor of *The Gift of Story: Narrating Hope in a Postmodern World* (2006), and a contributor to *A Companion to the Modern American Novel, 1900–1950* (2009). He is currently at work on a book about religion in contemporary American fiction.

Lucy Fischer is a distinguished professor of English and film studies at the University of Pittsburgh, where she serves as Director of the Film Studies Program. She is the author of eight books including *Jacques Tati* (1983), *Shot/Countershot: Film Tradition and Women's Cinema* (1989), *Cinematernity: Film, Motherhood, Genre* (1996), and *Designing Women: Art Deco, Cinema and the Female Form* (2003). She has held curatorial positions at The Museum of Modern Art (New York City) and The Carnegie Museum of Art (Pittsburgh), and has been the recipient of both a National Endowment for the Arts Art Critics Fellowship and a National Endowment for the Humanities Fellowship for University Professors. She has served as President of the Society for Cinema and Media Studies (2001–2003) and in 2008 received its Distinguished Service Award.

Dan Georgakas is on the editorial board of *Cineaste* and is director of the Greek American Studies Project of the Center for Byzantine and Modern Greek Studies at Queens College, City University of New York (CUNY). He has published on film in academic and popular journals in the United States and abroad. He has taught film at New York University, Columbia University, the University of Oklahoma, Empire State College, and Queens College. His film books included co-editing *The Cineaste Interviews, In Focus: A Guide to Using Film, Cineaste Interviews 2*, and *Solidarity Forever*, a work based on the film *The Wobblies*. His most recent work is compiling the Greek film entry for the new Oxford University Press On-Line filmography, coediting an issue on Greek film for the *Journal of the Hellenic Diaspora*, and preparing a Greeks of Hollywood issue for the annual *Journal of Modern Hellenism*.

Leger Grindon is Professor of Film and Media Culture at Middlebury College. He is the author of *Shadows on the Past: Studies in the Historical Fiction Film* (1994), *Knockout: The Boxer and Boxing in American Cinema* (2011) and *Hollywood Romantic Comedy: Conventions, History, Controversies* (2011).

Tamar Jeffers McDonald is Senior Lecturer in Film Studies at the University of Kent. She is the author of *Romantic Comedy: Boy Meets Girl Meets Genre* (2007), *Hollywood Catwalk: Exploring Costume and Transformation in American Film* (2010), and the forthcoming *Doris Day Confidential: Hollywood Sex and Stardom* (2012).

Henry Jenkins is the Provost's Professor of Communications, Journalism, Cinematic Arts and Education at the University of Southern California and the former director of the Comparative Media Studies Program at the Massachusetts Institute of Technology (MIT). He is the author or editor of 15 books on media and popular culture, including *What Made Pistachio Nuts? Early Sound Comedy and the Vaudeville Aesthetic* (Columbia University Press), *Classical Hollywood Comedy* (Routledge), and *Convergence Culture: Where Old and New Media Collide* (New York University Press).

Catherine A. John is an associate professor in English and film and media studies at the University of Oklahoma. She has published *Clear Word and Third Sight: Folk Groundings and Diasporic Consciousness in African Caribbean Writing* (Duke University Press in 2003), and she is currently writing *The Just Society and the Diasporic Imagination*. She hopes to produce a book-length text on black film comedy.

Rob King is an assistant professor at the University of Toronto's Cinema Studies Institute and Department of History, where he is currently working on a study of early sound slapstick and Depression-era mass culture. In addition to *The Fun Factory*, he is the co-editor of the volumes *Early Cinema and the "National"* (John Libbey Press, 2008) and, with Tom Paulus, *Slapstick Comedy* (Routledge, 2011).

Frank Krutnik is Reader in Film Studies at the University of Sussex and has written *In a Lonely Street: Film Noir, Genre, Masculinity* (1991) and *Inventing Jerry Lewis* (2000), co-authored *Popular Film and Television Comedy* (1990), and co-edited *Un-American Hollywood: Politics and Film in the Blacklist Era* (2007).

Charles Morrow is a librarian at the New York Public Library for the Performing Arts at the Lincoln Center, where he catalogs moving image material for the Theatre on Film and Tape Archive. He writes essays on the arts, and contributed entries to *Broadway: An Encyclopedia of Theater and American Culture*.

Claire Mortimer teaches film and media studies at Colchester Sixth Form College and has written Romantic Comedy (2010) and co-authored *AS Media Studies\emdash The Essential Introduction* (2011).

Joshua B. Nelson, a Cherokee Nation citizen, is Assistant Professor of English at the University of Oklahoma. His current project, *Progressive Traditions: Cherokee Cultural Studies*, explores the potential of adaptive, traditional dispositions. His work has appeared in the *American Indian Culture and Research Journal* and *Studies in American Indian Literatures*.

Jane Park is a lecturer in gender and cultural studies and the US Studies Centre at the University of Sydney. Along with her first book, *Yellow Future: Oriental Style in Hollywood Cinema* (Minnesota Press, 2010), she has published in *World Literature Today*, *Global Media Journal*, and *Asian Studies Review*.

William Paul is a professor of film studies at Washington University in St. Louis. He is the author of *Ernst Lubitsch's American Comedy* and *Laughing Screaming: Contemporary Horror and Comedy*. He is currently writing *Self-Actuated Romances*, a book about contemporary romantic comedy.

Najat Rahman is Associate Professor of Comparative Literature at the University of Montreal. She is author of *Literary Disinheritance: Home in the Writings of Mahmoud Darwish and Assia Djebar* (2008) and co-editor of *Exile's Poet, Mahmoud Darwish: Critical Essays* (2008). She also managed the production of the documentary *Ustura (Legend)* (1998).

Frank Scheide is a professor in the Department of Communication at the University of Arkansas, where he teaches film history and criticism. He has co-edited a series of books on Charles Chaplin, and has been co-chair of the annual Buster Keaton Celebration in Iola, Kansas since 1998.

David R. Shumway is Professor of English, and Literary and Cultural Studies, and Director of the Humanities Center at Carnegie Mellon University. His most recent book is *John Sayles* (University of Illinois Press, 2012).

Kevin W. Sweeney is a professor of philosophy at the University of Tampa. He has published an anthology of interviews with Buster Keaton, *Buster Keaton: Interviews* (2007). He has also published in *Film Criticism*, *Film Quarterly*, *The Journal of American Culture*, *Literature/Film Quarterly*, *Post Script*, and *Wide Angle*.

Paul Wells is Director of the Animation Academy, Loughborough University, UK. He has published widely in the field of animation studies, including *Understanding Animation* (Routledge), *Re-Imagining Animation* (AVA Academia), and *The Animated Bestiary* (Rutgers University Press). He is also an established writer and director for radio, TV and theater, and conducts workshops and consultancies worldwide based on his book *Scriptwriting* (AVA Academia). He is chair of the Association of British Animation Collections (ABAC).

Comic Introduction
"Make 'em Laugh, make 'em Laugh!"

Andrew Horton and Joanna E. Rapf

Make 'em laugh

Make 'em laugh

Don't you know everyone wants to laugh?

Donald O'Connor as Cosmo in Singin' In The Rain (1952)

We need laughter more than we need a sheriff.

Larry Gelbart, Laughing Matters

Our goal is simple: we hope that our readers' enjoyment of worldwide comedy will be enriched by insights offered in these essays. Comedy is important, as Preston Sturges reminds us in the conclusion to *Sullivan's Travels* (1941), when Sullivan gives up his desire to make the serious Depression drama *O Brother, Where Art Thou?* and is ready to return to Hollywood and once more make comedies: "... there's a lot to be said for making people laugh ... did you know that's all some people have? It isn't much ... but it's better than nothing in this cockeyed caravan ... "

Given the universality of film comedy, and its importance as a genre to the development of the motion pictures and as a reflection of social, political, and cultural trends, it was a natural subject for our anthology. It has been argued that all genres can be conceived in terms of dialectic between cultural and counter-cultural drives where, in the end, the cultural drives must triumph. But between the inevitable "fade in" and "fade out," screen comedy has been free to

A Companion to Film Comedy, First Edition. Edited by Andrew Horton and Joanna E. Rapf.
© 2013 John Wiley & Sons, Inc. Published 2016 by John Wiley & Sons, Inc.

work its complex and often subversive purpose, revealing and commenting on the preoccupations, prejudices, and dreams of the societies that produce it.

Our collection celebrates both the variety and complexity of international film comedy from the "silent" days to the present. We are well aware that it is by no means comprehensive. There are huge gaps; we do not cover queer comedy, for example. But the genre is so vast, drawing on human behavior in its many and manifold forms, that our selection of essays can only touch on some areas, while ignoring others. Since Gerald Mast's second edition of *The Comic Mind* (1979) went out of print with his lively and provocative "opening up" of cinematic comedy's diverse nature and characteristics, there has been no complete history of comic film, and again, this *Companion* does not provide that. Like Geoff King's *Film Comedy* (2002), ours is only a selective analysis of the genre, but it does ask us to take it seriously. Comic films raise questions that have no easy answers and explore social and personal problems that have no easy resolution. In short, they expose folly and present no cure, for folly is an incurable human disease for which, as Beckett wrote in *Waiting for Godot*, there is "nothing to be done."

There are other useful anthologies, such as Andrew Horton's *Comedy/Cinema/Theory* (1991), Kristine Karnick and Henry Jenkins' *Classical Hollywood Comedy* (1995), and Frank Krutnik's *Hollywood Comedians* (2003), but our collection embraces not just American cinema, including Native American and African American, but also the comic films of Europe including Britain, France, Spain, Italy, Germany, the Middle East, and Korea. Hopefully, this anthology will begin to map out some of the myriad ways in which comic films have helped to reflect and influence history, culture, politics, and social institutions globally.

There are many fine studies on specific film comedy topics including Neale and Krutnik (1990), Jenkins (1992), Harvey (1998), Dale (2000), on slapstick in American movies, and Glitre (2006), to mention just a few, along with recent studies by some of our contributors: Claire Mortimer's *Romantic Comedy* (2010), Tom Paulus and Rob King's *Slapstick Comedy* (2011), and Leger Grindon's *Hollywood Romantic Comedy: Conventions, History, Controversies* (2011). These works will be cited throughout this volume and referenced in the authors' lists of suggestions for further reading.

As an overview of the significance of this wonderfully complex topic and of some of the myriad ways of approaching it, we want to lay out six of what could easily be dozens of observations on comedy in general that go beyond film, television, theater, books, or the Internet. Some of these were initially discussed in Horton (2000: 1–16).

1. *Comedy is a way of looking at the universe, more than merely a genre of literature, drama, film or television.* Scientists and psychologists all agree that each of us tends to have or to lack a "comic" view of life, which is in part genetically determined. Furthermore, studies have shown that laughter can often be a

healing factor in life as Norman Cousins (1979: 43) found in helping to cure his cancer through watching Marx Brothers' films and other comedies. "I made the joyous discovery that ten minutes of genuine belly laughter had an anesthetic effect and would give me at least two hours of pain free sleep." Those who laugh more live longer. As Allen Klein (1989: xx) notes, "humor helps us cope because it instantly removes us from pain."

2. *Comedy is a form of "play" that embraces fantasy and festivity.* As part of the larger category of "play," comedy shares what Huizinga (1950) and others have pointed out is a form of activity in which individuals (*Homo ludens*) do not feel threatened because all forms of play have their boundaries that must be followed while in the "game." The festive and fantasy level of comedy as celebrated in communities around the world also points to the spirit of *carnival* during which participants have "fun" and do not feel threatened as they act out fantasies. As Mikhail Bahktin (1968: 7) has written about carnival, it "is not a spectacle seen by the people: they live in it, and everyone participates because its very idea embraces all the people." In this carnivalesque spirit, we can better understand the Greek origin of the word "comedy" as *komos*, which meant a drunken chorus in the Dionysian spirit, singing, drinking and calling out insults while dressed in costumes that Aristophanes' comedies suggest could be frogs, birds, angry women, and more. There is also the Latin origin, in Comus, the playful and lecherous god of springtime revelry, emphasizing that there is in comedy the essential idea of "rebirth" and "renewal."

3. *Comedy and tragedy are near cousins whose paths often cross.* Plato's *Symposium* ends as Socrates and Aristophanes agree that comic and dramatic moments often come very close to each other in life. This observation helps us better appreciate so many comedies including Frank Capra's *It's A Wonderful Life* (1946) in which George Bailey (James Stewart) wishes to commit suicide on Christmas Eve but is saved by Clarence (Henry Travers), a gentle angel sent from Above, who not only saves George, but his family, the town, and the Spirit of Christmas in a festive "happy ending." But comedies differ from tragedies in their emphasis on the social rather than on the individual. Indeed, as Kathleen Rowe (1995: 45) has rightly observed, "comedy often mocks the masculinity that tragedy ennobles." In a similar vein, we can observe that comedies are seldom simply "comedies," but are often a mixture of genres, moods, and implications. Many would call George Roy Hill's *Butch Cassidy and the Sundance Kid* (1969) a western comedy but others would label it a western with comic moments, while it can also be called a "buddy film," and even a "loosely biographical" film as William Goldman's script is based on real outlaws.

4. *Comedy implies a special relationship with and to its audience.* Whether directly or indirectly, comedy through the ages has delighted in breaking down the "fourth wall" so that the actors can see and communicate with the

audience, thus acknowledging the sense of "play" or gamesmanship that comedy creates. In many of Aristophanes' comedies, characters talk to and even walk into the audience to make a point. Similarly, when a comedian such as Woody Allen faces the camera and thus "us," the audience, in *Annie Hall* (1977), he is directly involving us in the laughter that is generated. This was a common technique in even early "silent" comedies, where Roscoe Arbuckle, for example, gestures to the camera (and thereby us) to look away as he is undressing in films such as *The Knockout* (1913) or *Little Band of Gold* (1915). Drama and tragedy, on the other hand, depend on being complete narratives that do not acknowledge the presence of an audience.

5. *In the world of the truly comic, nothing is sacred and nothing human is rejected.* Comic filmmakers, like comic writers and performers throughout history, have had to deal with censorship in many cultures for political, social and religious reasons, yet within the spirit of carnival and the truly comic, everything and everyone is potentially "on camera" for laughs, be it satire, parody, or an open celebration of sex and life itself. Certainly this celebration of "nothing is forbidden" from laughter helps us appreciate and enjoy films such as Luis Buñuel's *Phantom of Liberty* (1974) and Monty Python's *The Life of Brian* (1979), which take on religion with much outright humor, or *Sweet Movie* (1974), directed by Dušan Makavejev of the former Yugoslavia, which looks comically at sexuality and the horrors of real warfare as we witness cross-cutting between an orgy of group sex in a vat of sugar and documentary footage of digging up the bodies of hundreds of Polish officers murdered by the Russians in World War II.

6. *Comedy is one of the most important ways a culture talks to itself about itself.* No study is needed to underline that people in every nation enjoy laughing and that, even if festival awards such as Oscars tend to go to "serious" and/or "art" films, the box office in each country reflects the popularity of comedy. And sometimes the awards and popularity do cross paths. Danis Tanovic's dark comedy about the Bosnian War, *No Man's Land* (2001), for example, won the Best Foreign Film Oscar in 2001. It begins with one soldier asking another, "Do you know the difference between a pessimist and an optimist?" The soldier answers, "A pessimist says things are as bad as they can be and the optimist says they can always be worse," and throughout the film, everything does get worse. The point is that in many ways one can learn as much or more about the Bosnian crisis in this comedy made by a young Bosnian who had been through the war himself as through a traditional TV documentary.

Comedy is obviously a slippery genre, as is the language used in describing it. "Comedy" and "humor" are often seen as interchangeable, although etymologically the words have quite different meanings, with "comedy" coming from the Dionysian *komos*, as described above, while "humor" has its origin in the ancient idea that the body is made up of four "humors" – black bile, yellow bile, phlegm, and blood – which control a person's temperament. Categories or types of comedy overlap. Romantic comedies can contain slapstick elements and they often deal with gender, for example. Because of this element of pastiche or mélange, readers may wonder why some of the chapters in this volume fall under one heading and not another. Some headings are clear. We begin at the beginning, with "Comedy Before Sound," and the development of the slapstick tradition as it carried into the sound era in the American slapstick short. We end with "Animation," another obviously distinct category, and one that is perhaps growing in significance in our digital age. In between, there is a certain amount of fluidity, although the titles of the chapters identify the focus.

Beginning with French audiences laughing at the Lumière Brothers' *The Gardener and the Little Scamp* (1895), cinema has created comedies that have made the world laugh. In France, George Méliès was making trick films and Max Linder became the first internationally known comic film star at the turn of the century, while in the United States, the Biograph Company was soon turning out one-reel comedy shorts. Although D.W. Griffith is sometimes said to the "the father of film," at least in the United States, it might well be argued that it was in the area of comedy that film experienced its most spectacular growth and popularity worldwide, as Frank Scheide's chapter covering key performers in Europe and America during the so-called "silent era" from 1895 to 1929 clearly suggests. Like other chapters in this volume, Scheide talks about the tradition of the *Commedia dell'Arte*, and he emphasizes some of the early comic films before the heyday of Max Sennett and the Keystone Kops, with sections on Max Linder, Bert Williams, Flora Finch, John Bunny, and Mr. and Mrs. Sidney Drew; he ends with Charlie Chaplin. Kristen Anderson Wagner also discusses Finch and Drew, but her chapter, "Pie Queens and Virtuous Vamps," is a more complete look at many of the largely neglected women comics who were so popular in those early years.

Donald Crafton and Tom Gunning have identified the "pie" along with the "chase," the gags that disrupt the narrative, as defining elements of early slapstick. Rob King, writing on early sound shorts, such as those produced by Hal Roach and Educational Pictures, looks at the waning "pie tradition" as sound begins to dominate. He traces the distinction between speech and noise in these films – speech aligned with sophistication and culture, noise with the "lower" aspects of life and suggestively argues that "the history of film comedy might finally be said to have 'begun again' with sound … sundering once again standards of 'low' versus 'sophisticated' comedy that it was the legacy of the silent era to have mediated and reconciled."

Representing the kind of comedy defined by Steve Seidman (1981) as "comedian comedy," four essays discuss comedy in the era of sound with the Marx Brothers, Jacques Tati, Woody Allen, and Mel Brooks, although Jacques Tati, of course, does not rely on dialogue, as the others do, but is a master of sound (noise). Kevin

Sweeney identifies the pattern of repetition in his gags – gags that help us to see the comic in the mundane. Influenced by Mikhail Bakhtin, Frank Krutnik puts the Marx Brothers in the anarchistic tradition of carnival, quite different from Tati, and explores a critique of hegemonic orthodoxy that bubbles beneath their fun. Seeing Woody Allen as a modern incarnation of Charlie Chaplin, not in his style of comedy but in the fact that he writes, directs, and stars in his films, David Shumway examines two fairly distinct Allen personae: "the Nebbish," more characteristic of his earlier films, and the "Artist," predominating in his later, more realistic comedies. With Mel Brooks, Henry Jenkins uses J. Hoberman's concept of "vulgar modernism," a style of comedy he sees emerging after World War II across a range of media, to look at how Brooks plays different media against each other for comic effect. He centers his discussion around a close analysis of *Silent Movie* (1976).

Romantic comedy, as opposed to comedian comedy, obviously involves comic pairs and it tends to be narrative oriented rather than episodic. Celestino Deleyto's essay deals with this sometimes uneasy balance between comic moments and narrative in three films, *The Smiling Lieutenant* (Lubitsch 1931), *The Palm Beach Story* (Sturges 1942), *Man's Favorite Sport* (Hawks 1964), his remake of *Bringing Up Baby* (1938), and *Green Card* (Peter Weir 1990), noting changes in the genre as it developed through evolving social, cultural, and political climates, and how the comic moments he analyzes are also narrative in nature and contribute to the overall structure of the films. Romantic comedies are founded on what may be an irrational belief in the ability of human beings to transform a drab reality into a "utopian scenario." Drawing on this idea, Leger Grindon takes this genre from the twentieth century into the twenty-first with two films from 2004: *Before Sunset* (Richard Linklater) and *Eternal Sunshine of the Spotless Mind* (Michel Gondry). Celestino Deleyto has called *Before Sunset* a romantic comedy "on the margins" (Deleyto 2009: 157–74), but Grindon explores them specifically as comedies of infidelity, portraying doubts about romance without abandoning completely something of the utopian vision seen in their predecessors.

The chapters by Tamar Jeffers McDonald and Lucy Fischer both look at variations of romantic comedy from a male perspective. Jeffers McDonald identifies what she calls the "Homme-com Cycle," comedies that center on the humorous misadventures of a male pair or ensemble but preserve an allegiance to the generic tropes of romantic comedy, such as *I Love You, Man* (John Hamburg 2009) and which feature what is known as the Man Cave or the Lair, and she makes a distinction between them. Lucy Fischer, on the other hand, gives an in-depth reading of *Flirting with Disaster* (David O. Russell 1996), a comedy about the search of a young man (Ben Stiller) for his birth parents. The search becomes fertile ground for a good deal of topical humor on race, religion, and politics. Fischer observes that although adoption comedies are rare, in recent years they have proliferated on that harbinger of what is new and important: *YouTube*.

Like Celestino Deleyto, Charles Morrow also examines the *Smiling Lieutenant*, and his essay might seem to belong, at least in places, under the category of "Romantic Comedy," but he is more specifically concerned with a unique genre he calls "Ruritanian Comedy" – comedies about mythical kingdoms that flourished between World War I and the years of the Great Depression. Some of these comedies, such as Harold Lloyd's *Why Worry* (1923) are gag-oriented, while others, such as Lubitsch's *Love Parade* (1929) are indeed romantic comedies. Morrow gives us an invaluable survey of this genre, through the 1920s and 1930s, including Will Rogers in *Ambassador Bill* (Sam Taylor 1931), W.C. Fields in *Million Dollar Legs* (Edward Cline 1932), and, of course, the Marx Brothers in *Duck Soup* (Le McCarey 1933). Morrow speculates on some of the reasons for the fascination with these fantastic places, and like William Paul in his essay on *You Can't Take It with You* (Frank Capra 1938), sees the need for escapism during the dark years of America's Depression. Paul's essay might fall under the category of "Romantic Comedy" too but it is specifically "topical" in its concern with what he calls an "aesthetics of escapism," seeing romantic comedy not simply in terms of Deleyto's "utopian scenario," but as a way of engaging with the real world.

The "real world" emerges vividly, darkly, and comically in Ernst Lubitsch's wartime farce, *To Be or Not To Be* (1942). Maria DeBattista's detailed analysis of this film that she calls a "totalitarian comedy" is deliberately "disquieting." As other essays in the *Companion* suggest, laughter can sometimes be the best way of saying something about dictatorship, the slaughter of civilians, the repression of individual freedoms, all kinds of human atrocities. Totalitarian comedy, she writes, is a modern marriage of "the not-serious and the dreadful." They are comedies that "refuse to silence their insolent wit or suspend their unruly farces just when they are most needed and least tolerated – during reigns of unfreedom." Such a comedy is *To Be or Not To Be*. In conclusion she cites both Renoir's *Rules of the Game* (1939) and Stanley Kubrick's *Dr. Strangelove* (1964) as two other films that show totalitarianism as vulnerable to farce, and it is Kubrick's film, along with some of the work of the Coen Brothers, that concludes this section in our volume on "Topical Comedy, Irony, and *Humour Noir*" in the essay by Mark Eaton.

Using André Breton and Matthew Winston to define what is known as *humour noir*, Eaton distinguishes it dramatically from romantic comedy, for example, in its unsentimentality, and its emphasis on the fantastic, the surreal, the grotesque, its shattering of expectations, and the way it disturbs our sense of moral certainty. These characteristics, he argues, made it a natural form of comedy for that period of antiauthoritarian upheaval, the 1960s and early 1970s, as antiwar protests proliferated. In this context, he looks specifically at such films as *Dr. Strangelove*, *M * A * S * H* (Altman 1970), *Catch-22* (Mike Nichols 1970), and *Slaughterhouse Five* (George Roy Hill 1971). To illustrate the re-emergence of dark comedy over 20 years later, but with less political emphasis, he focuses on *The Big Libowski* (Coen Brothers 1998). Eaton concludes with some reflections on the state of the post-9/11 world, with the "war on terror," and other wars in

Iraq and Afghanistan, and wonders why they seem incompatible with the moral disturbance of black comedy. He cites *Four Lions* (Christopher Morris 2010) but, as pure farce, that film may fall more into a genre of "escapism" than social critique.

We offer three essays touching on comic perspectives regarding race and ethnicity. Catherine John writing on African Americans and film comedy builds on Mark Reid's innovative study, *Redefining Black Cinema* (1993) with three objectives as she examines how white stereotypes of African Americans continue, how Tyler Perry's films have opened a variety of truly Black levels of comedy, concluding with a close-up analysis of Spike Lee's *Bamboozled* (2000) and Tim Story's *Barbershop* (2002). Joshua Nelson similarly notes the past Hollywood stereotypes, in this case of American Indians including John Ford's films up through more contemporary films such as *Dances With Wolves* (Kevin Costner, 1990), and he explores how, as he explains, "Indian comedic film takes aim at mainstream misrepresentations and their tried-and-true caricatures of Indians," using examples such as Chris Eyre's *Smoke Signals* (1998) and Sterlin Harjo's *Four Sheets to the Wind* (2007). Dan Georgakas focuses on Greek Americans appearing in American film comedies covering *My Big Fat Greek Wedding* (2002), of course, and also others. It is important that he emphasizes that "Genuine cultural patterns only emerge by looking at how they manifest themselves over a very long period in a multitude of films," an observation that clearly could be used in taking on many other immigrant identities in American film comedy.

Film comedy is so much a part of every nation's cinema, as we have noted, and while the majority of our essays focus on American film comedy, we include a selection on international comedy. Claire Mortimer treats us to insights about the comic ambiguity between myth and reality reflected in the Ealing Studio comedies such as *Whisky Galore* (1949) and *The Ladykillers* (1955), directed by the Scottish American director Alexander Mackendrick who, as she observes, "brought a sensibility to Ealing Studios which reflected the fractured times in the wake of the Second World War, with shifting populations having lost their roots and connections." Jane Park introduces us to film comedy that developed in Korea after the Korean War and a period of censorship. She gives a close reading of two comedies, *301,302* (1995) and *200 Pounds Beauty* (2006), focusing on how urban Korean women are portrayed. Roberta Di Carmine takes on comedy "Italian style," explaining how comedies between the 1930s and 1970s were able to be both satirical and supportive of social and cultural changes that Italy was experiencing during and after World War II. Her analysis of Mario Monicelli's *I soliti ignoti* (*Big Deal on Madonna Street*, 1958) allows her to depict clearly the double vision of such a comic style, which, as she observes, "although inclined to provoke laughter," also "offers a dark portrayal of the illness of society."

Finally, in our international section, Najat Rahman clearly depicts how recent Palestinian films have made constructive use of comedy in taking on the difficult realities of the Middle East. Building on film scholars of Middle Eastern cinema such as Hamid Naficy who observes that Palestinian cinema is " … one of the rare cinemas in the world that is structurally exilic … made either in … internal exile in an occupied Palestine or under the erasure … of displacement and external exile," he provides insight to the surprising humor of films such as Rashid Mashrawi's *Laila's Birthday* (2008), Elia Suleiman's *Divine Intervention* (2002), and Abou Assad's *Paradise Now* (2005). Rahman's conclusion touches on how multifaceted film comedy can be to a nation that continues to endure a complex reality. As he states, "the films discussed in this essay push through humor and beyond humor to reconfigure the assault on senses and lives delivered by occupation and by discourses that maintain it, to an aesthetic that neither harmonizes the violence into a simple effect of the beautiful nor falters on its innovative possibilities."

Our volume concludes with a section on "Comic Animation." Paul Wells reminds us that, while animation does share many techniques of comic construction with other kinds of comedy, it also offers "particular and distinctive forms of visual and verbal 'gags'," and his chapter, along with Suzanne Buchan's, illustrates this uniqueness. Wells discusses early animation in the United States, from *Gertie the Dinosaur* (1914) to productions at Disney and Warner Brothers during the golden era between 1928–45. But he also emphasizes animation elsewhere, in Canada, Japan, Poland, Eastern Europe – notably the Estonian animator, Priit Pärn, and the innovative work done in this area by women such as the Czech animator Michaela Patlatova and the English animator, Joanna Quinn. Suzanne Buchan covers some of the same ground as Wells with the early years but her approach is more theoretical, using Henri Bergson, Freud, and even James Joyce to illuminate some of the comic techniques animation exploits. A primary feature of animation's film form is its unique ability to express metamorphosis, and a wonderful example of this is *Porky in Wackyland* (Bob Clampett 1938). She discusses the figures in this film as "visual portmanteaus" that can be compared to the way James Joyce uses language. Tex Avery's *King-size Canary* (1947), she argues, utilizes ideas of Freud and Bergson, while also suggesting some of the grotesque characteristics of black comedy and surrealism. The idea of the surreal and the dark are integral to her essay as she quotes from Samuel Beckett's *Watt* (1959) where he describes the *risus purus* as the highest laugh in the world, "the laugh that laughs at the laugh, the laugh at that which is unhappy." Tex Avery, Chuck Jones, Bob Clampett, and others covered in her essay, were all masters of this *risus purus*, exploiting a range of comedy as only animation can do, from the silly to the absurd, from the whacky to the dark recesses of *humour noir*. Her essay, along with Wells' international perspective, reveal how varied and provocative animation can be, and how, like its human forms, it points to new ways of seeing the world. Today sources of laughter include everything from video games to cell phone gimmicks but especially the comic websites and worlds offered on the Internet including the ever-increasing number of *YouTube* films. Perhaps there may well be a *Companion to YouTube* down the line (and online too!). But in the meantime, cinematic laughter has offered audiences everywhere, and will continue to offer them, a chance to escape and transcend the often harsh failures, losses, disappointments, fears and despair in the huge gaps between the ideal and the real. Since movies began, filmmakers from Hollywood to Hong Kong and everywhere else have been working and playing hard to "make 'em laugh." As we have been suggesting, comedy that celebrates the human capacity to endure rather than to suffer, is, as François Truffaut once said, "by far the most difficult genre, the one that demands the most work, the most talent, and also the most humility." We hope this *Companion* will help to illuminate that difficulty, expose that talent, reveal that humility, and celebrate our capacity to endure.

References

Bakhtin, M. (1968) *Rabelais and his World* (trans. Helene Iswolsky), MIT Press, Cambridge, MA.

Cousins, N. (1979) *Anatomy of an Illness*, W.W. Norton, New York, NY.

Dale, A. (2000) *Comedy is a Man in Trouble*, University of Minnesota Press, Minneapolis, MN.

Deleyto, C. (2009) *The Secret Life of Romantic Comedy*, Manchester University Press, Manchester.

Glitre, K. (2006) *Hollywood Romantic Comedy: States of the Union, 1934–1965*, University of Manchester Press, Manchester.

Grindon, L. (2011) *Hollywood Romantic Comedy: Conventions, History and Controversies*, Wiley-Blackwell, Oxford.

Harvey, J. (1998) *Romantic Comedy In Hollywood: From Lubitsch to Sturges*, Da Capo Press, New York.

Horton, A. (ed.) (1991) *Comedy/Cinema/Theory*, University of California Press, Berkeley, CA.

Horton, A. (2000) *Laughing Out Loud: Writing the Comedy Centered Screenplay*, University of California Press, Berkeley, CA.

Huizinga, J. (1950) *Homo Ludens: The Study of the Play Element in Culture*, Beacon Press, Boston, MA.

Jenkins, H. (1992) *What Made Pistachio Nuts? Early Sound Comedy and the Vaudeville Aesthetic*, Columbia University Press, New York.

Karnick, K. B. and Jenkins, H. (eds.) (1995) *Classical Hollywood Comedy*, Routledge, New York, NY.

King, G. (2002) *Film Comedy*, Wallflower Press, New York, NY.

Klein, A. (1989) *The Healing Power of Humor*, Penguin Putnam, New York, NY.

Mast, G. (1979) *The Comic Mind: Comedy and the Movies*. 2nd edn, University of Chicago Press, Chicago, IL.

Mortimer, C. (2010) *Romantic Comedy*, Routledge, New York, NY.

Neale, S. and Krutnik, F. (1990) *Popular Film and Television Comedy*, Routledge, London.

Paulus, T. and King, R. (2010) *Slapstick Comedy*, Routledge, New York, NY.

Rowe, K. (1995) Comedy, melodrama, gender, in *Classical Hollywood Comedy* (eds. K. B. Karnick and H. Jenkins), Routledge, New York, NY, pp. 39–59.

Seidman, S. (1981) *Comedian Comedy: A Tradition in Hollywood Film* UMI Research Press, Ann Arbor, MI.

Further Reading

Bermel, A. (1982) *Farce: A History From Aristophanes to Woody Allen*, Simon & Schuster, New York, NY.

Cavell, S. (1981) *Pursuits of Happiness: The Hollywood Comedy of Remarriage*, Harvard University Press, Cambridge, MA.

Denby, D. (2007) A Fine Romance: The New Comedy of the Sexes. *The New Yorker*, July 23, 58–65.

DiBattista, M. (2001) *Fast Talking Dames*, Yale University Press, New Haven, NJ.

Gehring, W. (1996) *American Dark Comedy: Beyond Satire*, Greenwood Press, Westport, CT.

Gelbart, L. (1998). *Laughing Matters: On Writing M*A*S*H, Tootsie, Oh, God! And A Few Others*, Random House, New York, NY.

Kerr, W. (1967) *Tragedy and Comedy*, Simon & Schuster, New York, NY.

McDonald, T. J. (2007) *Romantic Comedy: Boy Meets Girl Meets Genre*, Wallflower, New York, NY.

Sikov, E. (1994) *Laughing Hysterically: American Screen Comedy of the 1950s*, Columbia University Press, New York, NY.

Vineberg, S. (2005) *High Comedy in American Movies: Class and Humor from the 1920s to the Present*, Rowman & Littlefield Publishers, New York, NY.

Part I

Comedy Before Sound, and the Slapstick Tradition

1

The Mark of the Ridiculous and Silent Celluloid

Some Trends in American and European Film Comedy from 1894 to 1929

Frank Scheide

Fred Ott's Infectious Sneeze (1894)

Throughout its history silent film comedy was affected by the technology with which it was produced, the culture and mindset of the filmmakers, and the intended audience's desires. When Thomas Edison expressed interest in combining moving pictures with his phonograph in 1888, other inventors around the world were already experimenting with sequential imaging. Edison's approach to inventing was to encourage his "muckers" (technicians, machinists, and engineers) to come up with new ideas by "playing" with state-of-the art resources at his lab (Spehr 2008: 75–82, 649).

Edison Kinetoscopic Record of a Sneeze/Fred Ott's Sneeze, the studio's nineteenth film, was produced from January 2 to 7, 1894. Fred Ott was an engineer credited with making major contributions to Edison's early Kinetograph movie camera, but most film historians remember him for sneezing in an early motion picture. Initially considered a comic novelty for the way it used technical innovation to make much ado about nothing, the title of this film succinctly informs us of its content. The filming of an entire action from conflict to resolution, although only a few seconds in duration, gives the movie a kind of narrative structure. One reason this documentary is associated with comedy is that the subject's loss of bodily control, a condition that theorist Henri Bergson described as "something mechanical encrusted upon the living," makes Fred Ott a comic figure characterized by the "mark of the ridiculous" (Bergson 1956: 92).

A Companion to Film Comedy, First Edition. Edited by Andrew Horton and Joanna E. Rapf.
© 2013 John Wiley & Sons, Inc. Published 2016 by John Wiley & Sons, Inc.

In his *Poetics* of 330 BC, Aristotle identified a comic character as someone who bears a "mark of the ridiculous," which enables the observer to feel superior to this individual. Where the "tragic flaw" of the dramatic hero suffers real pain that brings about the ruin of this protagonist and his followers, the ludicrous condition of the mark of the ridiculous " ... may be defined as a mistake or deformity not productive of pain or harm to others; the mask for instance, that excites laughter, is something ugly and distorted without causing pain" (Aristotle 1962: 194). Ott's mark of the ridiculous was not as pronounced as a physical deformity but the loss of control during his sneeze was considered comically incongruous by the filmmakers. As a consequence the playful Fred Ott is not remembered for his accomplishments as an Edison engineer but for being human. According to silent film historian Luke McKernan, "in later years Ott was happy to claim that he was the first ever 'film star,' which in a way was true"(McKernan 1996).

A Plot Underfoot: The Lumière Brothers' *L'Arroseur arrosé* (1895)

L'Arroseur arrosé (*The Hoser Hosed*) (1895), produced by Louis and Auguste Lumière, is credited with being one of the first comic sketches in the history of the cinema. The sons of a French manufacturer of photographic plates, the Lumière brothers were already versed in imaging technology when they sought to develop an alternative to the Edison Kinetograph. Using Edison's invention as a model, Louis Lumière perfected a workable lightweight camera in 1895 that could also be converted to develop and project the footage. International recognition was achieved on December 28, 1895 when ten Lumière motion pictures, including *L'Arroseur arrosé*, were projected on a big screen to a paying audience in a rented Paris basement.

While *L'Arroseur arrosé*, like *Fred Ott's Sneeze*, is primarily a cinematic depiction of a gag, there is enough of a rudimentary plot to characterize this film as a comic narrative. Because the gardener possesses a "mark of the ridiculous" – an incapacity for ascertaining why a hose might not function, the capacity for becoming curious, and the capability to peer foolishly into a nozzle that can douse him with water – he is susceptible to becoming the victim (comic butt) of a practical joke. When the boy (comic wit) recognizes the gardener's mark of the ridiculous he exploits this deficiency by stepping on the hose, which sets the comic narrative into play. The incongruity of the loss of control suffered by the gardener while sprayed – something mechanical encrusted upon the living – makes this situation humorous.[1]

L'Arroseur arrosé has been identified as one of the first film narratives, but the Lumières would primarily be associated with non-fiction film during their short career as pioneer producers. The documentary would, in fact, be the prevalent form of motion picture until early filmmakers determined how to use the new medium for storytelling. In the meantime some of the most effective motion picture comedies were documentaries of comic routines already perfected for the stage.

Documentary of a Slap Shoe Hero: *Little Tich et ses "Big Boots"* (1900)

Shortly after the Lumières developed motion picture technology to compete with Edison's, the French inventor and entrepreneur Léon Gaumont attempted the same. Gaumont was able to devise a workable camera/projector by 1897, and his secretary, Alice Guy-Blaché, became the company's chief film producer from 1897 to 1906. Among the hundreds of films produced by the world's first important female film director is the delightful Gaumont comic short *Little Tich et ses "Big Boots"* (*Little Tich and his Big Boots*) (1900), perhaps the best motion picture documentation of a major turn-of-the-century English music-hall act and one of the most interesting early novelty films surviving. The renowned French comedian Jacques Tati claimed that *Little Tich et ses "Big Boots"* is "a foundation for everything that has been realized in comedy on the screen" (Anthony 1996).

A comedian with a physical "mark of the ridiculous" similar to the type of deformity associated with Aristotle's definition, the diminutive 4 foot 6 inch Little Tich was born with five fingers and a thumb on each hand and web-like flesh between these digits. While our operational definition argues that the "mark of the ridiculous" is not "productive of pain or harm to others," Harry "Little Tich" Relph was painfully self-conscious of his. Despite this sensitivity regarding his appearance, Little Tich's comic portrayal was that of a "grotesque," "eccentric," "red-nosed," or "baggy-pants" comedian similar to those that fellow English-born comics Charlie Chaplin, Stan Laurel, and Fred "Pimple" Evans performed on stage and later brought to the screen (see Figures 1.1 and 1.2). Tich's comedy contrasted his agility, wit, pronounced musical talents, and proficiency at mime with his incongruous physical appearance and dress. Little Tich was particularly famous for his humorous yet graceful performance in specially modified slap shoes.

Since slap shoes had been around for centuries, Little Tich literally expanded upon an old idea when he made his comic footwear longer in the 1880s. Through trial and error Tich discovered that when he lengthened his slap shoes to 28 inches he could arch his body, lean forward at a 45-degree angle, balance himself on their tips, and rise to the height of six feet, ten inches. More than a valued documentary of a unique novelty act, the 1900 film *Little Tich et ses "Big Boots"* reveals how this gifted performer projected a playful attitude in his work while exhibiting a self-conscious but convivial rapport with his audience. The fact that this French film featured an English vaudeville comedian underscores the international cross-fertilization in popular culture of this time. As is true of previous motion pictures discussed, *Little Tich et ses "Big Boots"* was filmed entirely in one shot.

Figure 1.1   A frame enlargement from *Little Tich et ses "Big Boots"* of the popular music hall comedian doing the finale of his famous routine (producer, Clément-Maurice Gratioulet).

Figure 1.2   Charles Chaplin's famous screen persona doing a variation of Little Tich's big boots routine in his 1919 film *A Day's Pleasure* (producer, Charles Chaplin).

Little Tich et ses "Big Boots" begins with the performer walking on stage from the wings and making "eye contact" with the camera/audience, which he intermittently continues throughout his performance. By looking directly at the camera Little Tich gives the impression that he is singling out and inviting each viewer to become involved in a mutually shared experience. Tich's interaction with the audience confirms that he knows the situation is silly as he cheerfully takes off his regular shoes, puts on his big boots, and does comic business with his hat. Through his glances Tich checks to see if he is still being watched and encourages the onlooker to enjoy his playful antics. A tight long shot enables the observer to appreciate the performer's body language and facial expression while documenting this music-hall act. The action is filmed on a stage comparable to those where this comedian usually performed, and the tempo of this documentary is associated with the music synchronized to the image. Little Tich plays directly to the camera in a manner similar to the way he related to live music-hall audiences. His intent in both instances was to sell himself and his act by engaging viewers in this event and his playful attitude. At the end of the performance Tich leaves the stage and then returns to take his bow.

Comic appearance and technique aside, it should be noted that it is the engaging personality of Little Tich that sells this picture to the viewer. It should also be noted that one must be careful when making assumptions concerning the role of any surviving film in the evolution of silent film history. *Little Tich et ses "Big Boots"* is an example of a turn-of-the-century motion picture that explored filmmaking techniques that were set aside before becoming standard practice several years later. It uses an experimental synchronized sound process that would be discontinued after 1908, so the emphasis on having the performer directly address the camera while responding to indigenous music would not be commonly employed in motion pictures until the coming of the talkies in 1926–7. Tati's claim that this film is "a foundation for everything that has been realized in comedy on the screen" does not mean that filmmakers and critics have always recognized *Little Tich et ses "Big Boots"* as a model throughout film history despite its prototypical qualities.

Little Tich's music hall talents translated exceptionally well to the screen, but he preferred making direct contact with a live audience. It would be left to other artists to modify established forms of popular culture to fit the new film medium. Few were more successful at making stage adaptation cinematic than the magician turned filmmaker, Georges Méliès.

Georges Méliès, "Fantasist Filmmaker" (1896–1902)

The 500 motion pictures that Georges Méliès made between 1896 and 1913 include examples of every film genre known at this time and most of them featured Méliès as a principal performer. Many of his earliest pictures focused upon Méliès doing magic tricks. This interest in magic led to experimentation with cinematic special effects that resulted in Méliès becoming known as "the father of trick photography." In his biography of Emile Cohl, "the father of animated film," Donald Crafton cites a 1900 critic of caricature, Adolphe Brisson, as postulating that there were " ... four kinds of humorist: the caricaturist proper, the parodist, the satirist, and the fantasist ... The fantasist 'obeys no other rules besides his own caprice. He invents, he combines, he suggests' " (Crafton 1990: 307). This could be said of Georges Méliès.

While not exactly a comedian in the sense of a Little Tich, Georges Méliès' playfulness as a magician, his love for fantasy, and capacity for whimsy gave his films a comic atmosphere that can still be appreciated today. The 1902 trick fantasy film *L'Homme á la tête de caoutchouc* (*The Indian Rubber Head*) is literally one of hundreds of Méliès motion pictures with this comic touch. Filmed in one shot, Méliès plays an inventor who has created a very animated bodiless rubber head, also performed by Méliès, which is inflatable when connected to a bellows. When the proud inventor demonstrates his expanding and contracting rubber head to an observer, the spectator insists upon operating the bellows himself which results in the head exploding. This troublemaker is literally kicked out of the room by the distraught inventor who is left weeping as the film ends.

Comedy, like Méliès' stage magic, is based upon incongruity – an awareness of a condition outside the accepted norm, a reversal of usual expectation, a situation or development different from what one ordinarily assumes or anticipates. While early film technology impressed viewers with its ability to document "surface reality," this particular cinematic record consisted of silent two-dimensional black-and-white moving images that were inherently incongruous when compared to the "real world." Besides being a master of cinematic special effects, Méliès was a pioneer in identifying how the film medium could distort "reality." Some of the earliest film comedies exploring distortion versus documentation were produced in England.

Fantasist Filmmaking in Britain (1900–1901)

The 1900 Hepworth film *How it Feels to be Run Over* employs rudimentary trick photography to create an effect very different from Méliès' achievement in *L'Homme á la tête de caoutchouc*. Initially appearing to be a nonfiction picture, *How it Feels to be Run Over* opens on a quiet country road filmed opposite from where a horse and carriage, seen in long shot, eventually pass. Through the dust of the departing buggy the viewer is made aware of an approaching horseless carriage. Rather than follow the path of the preceding horse drawn vehicle, the occupants of the car wave for the viewer to get out of their way. The automobile continues to advance towards the camera until, at the "point of impact," the vehicle is replaced with a black frame. Hand etched question marks and exclamation points appear on this black background followed by a succession of individual words that make up the sentence "Oh! Mother *will* be pleased." By giving the impression that it might be a documentary, *How it Feels to be Run Over* suggests that movie audiences already expected certain cinematic conventions from their motion pictures by 1900. This film challenges the expectation that it is a documentary, and comically attempts to make the relationship between the viewer and screen subject more interactive, by trying to give the appearance that a car has run over the camera. The director of this picture recognizes that trick photography can modify the supposed reality of a documentary record and transform a "real" environment into something as "unreal" as the fantasy world of Georges Méliès.

Fascination with this new medium resulted in some early self-reflexive comedies relating to the motion picture experience itself. One example is R.W. Paul's *The Countryman and the Cinematographe* (1901), which deals with an unsophisticated film viewer on stage reacting to various movies appearing on the screen next to him. At one point this "rube" gleefully mimics a dancing showgirl only to discover that she has been replaced by an oncoming train. In keeping with the myth that early audiences were afraid they would be run over when viewing the 1896 Lumière picture *L'arrivée d'un train en gare de La Ciotat* (*Train Coming into a Station*), the countryman dashes away from the advancing projected locomotive.

James Williamson's 1901 *The Big Swallow* is a particularly bizarre comedy about subject/camera/viewer relationships and the filmmaking process. *The Big Swallow* begins with the subject, played by comedian Sam Dalton, agitated but not quite directly addressing the camera. This point of view abruptly shifts as Dalton's mouth approaches the "viewer" and then the perspective changes again when camera and cameraman are seen being swallowed by the irate Dalton. The offending camera and cameraman now removed, Dalton more cordially acknowledges the "viewer" as he steps back and resumes his business even though this exchange with the audience is still being conveyed through a camera. Besides demonstrating a much more complicated exploration of the cinematic experience than *How it Feels to Be Run Over*, *The Big Swallow* suggests that some people were considering the movies as something less than a novelty by 1901, since the idea of a cameraman as paparazzi is already being addressed. Williamson's comedy verifies that the insatiable appetite of movie audiences for more interesting product would continue to propel experimentation with the medium. One way to increase audience interest was by telling stories using more than one shot.

Cut to the Chase (1907–1909)

Directed by Lewin Fitzhamon for the Hepworth Manufacturing Company in England, *That Fatal Sneeze* (1907) is one of many early silent films employing macabre humor in an attempt to satisfy the fickle movie audience's demand for something different. The "different" in this case was turning Fred Ott's sneeze into a cataclysmic affliction. *That Fatal Sneeze* begins with an uncle dumping pepper on his young nephew's dinner to make him sneeze. The boy retaliates by going into the uncle's bedroom to shake pepper on his hairbrush and clothing. The next morning the uncle is so affected by the pepper that his room shakes, and his sneezing escalates after leaving home. One sneeze knocks over a table smashing some china pots in front of a store, which results in the owner and some passersby giving chase. The man eventually sneezes so intensely that the whole world trembles and he blows up.

As film historian Simon Brown noted in his analysis for the British Film Institute, *That Fatal Sneeze* incorporates three concepts that were popular in film comedies by 1907: the practical joke (*L'Arroséur arrosé*); " ... the trick film, in which the capacity of the camera to show the seemingly impossible is exploited for comic or dramatic effect [*L'Homme á la Tête de Caoutchouc*];... [and] the chase: each time the old man sneezes, causing havoc to a shop owner or a passer-by, that person joins the ever-growing crowd pursuing him" (Brown 2003–2010). Directors began using chase scenes in their films almost as soon as they started telling their stories with more than one shot. Multiple shots freed film characters from the limitations of a single setting and a chase could be particularly effective for increasing the tempo of a picture as an action built to its climax.

Louis Gasnier's *Le chaval emballé* (*The Runaway Horse*) (1907), produced for Pathé Frères, is often cited as a well executed French chase comedy. The horse in *Le chaval emballé* finds an opportunity to eat someone else's oats while his driver is making a delivery. Rather than pay for this grain, the horse and driver flee. Havoc escalates during the ensuing chase as the horse knocks over people and destroys more property until the miscreants find refuge at their stable. According to the verbal commentary provided by the British Film Institute in their video release, "The basic idea was copied by D.W. Griffith in *The Curtain Pole* [1909]."

The Curtain Pole begins with future slapstick legend Mack Sennett, playing the part of "Monsieur Dupont," rushing to replace a curtain pole he broke while visiting a home. Numerous people join in a chase after this frenzied "Frenchman" accidentally hits them with his replacement pole. Upon his return Dupont learns that his chaotic venture was for naught because the broken pole was quietly replaced during his absence. The film ends with a medium close-up of Dupont chewing his unwanted curtain pole in frustration. According to film historian Tom Gunning, "*The Curtain Pole* seems to predict the future of American film comedy by situating Sennett at the center of the film's mayhem, prophetically announcing the blend of Griffith's editing tempo with comic anarchy that Sennett concocted later at Keystone" (Gunning 1991: 132). Both directors would polish their skills at perfecting the chase and Sennett would soon replace the French as the world's pre-eminent producer of film slapstick.

Reflecting the accomplishments of Méliès and others in creating fantasy worlds on screen, the distanced camera placements in *That Fatal Sneeze* emphasize the setting more than the characters. Given that the "star" of many of the earliest films was the environment, the movie frame was treated as a kind of "picture window" featuring everything in long shot. However, as demonstrated by the medium closeup of Monsieur Dupont in *The Curtain Pole*, the people in these films also deserved attention. Audiences wanted to see engaging personalities on the screen and the actions of these performers impacted what motion pictures communicated and how. One early film star who particularly influenced new approaches to cinematic communication was Max Linder, the screen personality upon whom Mack Sennett's "Monsieur Dupont" was based.

Silent Super Star: Max Linder (1905–1912)

Born Gabriel-Maximilien Leuvielle in 1883 to a well-to-do family of wine growers in Saint-Loubès-Gironde, France, "Max Linder" first appeared in films at Pathé in 1905 after pursuing a career in theater. Linder's comedy focused upon the inventive and often absurd manner in which his screen character "Max" coped with problems and embarrassments triggered by his particular mark of the ridiculous – the personality of a playful, and sometimes jealous, incurable romantic. Where other early film comics portrayed bizarre-looking characters wearing exaggerated costumes and grotesque makeup, Linder's appearance was impeccable. Max's elegant dress and polished body language were in stark contrast to the absurd situations that this character's foolish behavior helped create.

Linder introduced his famous dapper and debonair man about town in the 1907 film *Les débuts d'un patineur* (*Max Learns to Skate*). Another early Linder film of historical note is *Au music-hall* (*At the Music Hall*) (1907), in which a drunken Max's interaction with some bad music hall acts ends with a comic boxing match between this inebriated audience member and one of the performers. This film was actually an unauthorized adaptation of English music-hall producer Fred Karno's sketch *Mumming Birds*, which, when performed on stage, was a self-reflexive parody of English vaudeville itself. *Au music-hall* is believed to be the first film challenged for copyright violation in English jurisprudence, but *Mumming Birds* continued to be a popular stage attraction long after Karno lost this case and the film was forgotten. *Mumming Birds* was called *A Night in an English Music Hall* when Charlie Chaplin played the comic drunk in American vaudeville between 1910 and 1913. It would also be an inspiration for Chaplin's 1915 Essanay picture *A Night in the Show*, and the 1929 short comedy *Only Me*, which featured Lupino Lane playing all the roles.

Growing popularity allowed Linder greater control as a filmmaker. By 1909 the opening credits for *Max et la doctoresse* (*Max and the Lady Doctor*) proclaimed: "*Scène de Max Linder, Jouée par l'auteur*" (directed by Max Linder, starring the author). In this comedy of manners Max is embarrassed when the lady doctor in question asks him to remove clothing for an examination. Despite this awkward introduction, Max and the doctor marry and have a child. Later, when Max visits his wife's office, he goes into a rage when she asks other gentlemen to disrobe. Linder also incorporated fantasist elements in his comedies. In *Max et son chien Dick* (*Max and His Dog*) (1912), the canine hero phones his master at work to bark a message that Max's wife is entertaining a lover.

Separating "reality" from fantasy is something of a challenge when viewing the 1913 Linder comedy, *Max toréador*. Max demonstrates his penchant for bullfighting at the beginning of the film when passing bicyclists are treated like bulls charging his cape. To perfect his bullfighting skills Max brings a cow, with calf, to his apartment for practice. This scene shifts to a huge outdoor arena with thousands of spectators. Max fights a real bull with ease and the excited crowd carries him on its shoulders. In one version of this film Max falls out of bed to discover it was all a dream.

Max toréador is especially fascinating for the way it incorporates documentary footage of Linder's visit to Barcelona in 1912 into a fictional narrative. Linder accepted the challenge of performing as an actual matador, and his athleticism is demonstrated in the expert manner by which he dispatches the bull. The scene of Max being carried through the streets is also documentary footage of the real Linder's reception in Spain – evidence of his popularity as one of the first internationally recognized movie stars. The bedroom footage identifying Max's experiences as a dream is not included in the French version of *Max toréador*, which concludes with a very different narrative perspective involving the triumphant matador being carried away by a crowd. David Robinson found the final subtitle in the alternative German version of this motion picture of particular interest. After falling out of bed Max gets to his feet and says, " 'That is the best dream of my life … And a great idea for a film.' He then retires again and pulls the sheets over his head as the film comes to an end" (Robinson 2008: 194). By identifying the waking figure as the director rather than the film character, this caption further blurs the distinctions and raises questions concerning how one is to separate Max Linder from his screen persona.

It is interesting to contrast Linder's work with that of the English filmmaker Fred "Pimple" Evans, a music hall performer and fantasist comedian who began making motion pictures in 1910. The character of "Pimple" was introduced in Evans' seventeenth film in 1912, and would be featured in a series of nearly 190 films made through 1918. Pimple, like Little Tich's character, wore the ill-fitting clothing of the working-class "grotesque" as opposed to the middle and upper class attire of Linder, French comedian Andre' Deed's "Boireau", and Ferdinando Guilliaume's "Tontolini" in Italy. The humor of the Pimple pictures, in keeping with the rowdy nature of the English music hall, is also rather brash when compared with the whimsical French and Italian comedies. Reflective of a British film industry that was putting too little money in its films, the modest production values of these comedies are particularly glaring when compared to French and Italian pictures. A notable example of his many burlesques, *Pimple's The Whip* (1917) is a parody of the popular 1909 horse racing play *The Whip*, which also was made into an American feature in the year of the Evans production. The dramatic feature focused upon real horses, an actual racetrack, and an impressive train wreck while the Pimple film accentuated lack of same.

Particularly tacky pantomime horses represent the mounts while the train is portrayed by cardboard cutouts repeatedly pulled back and forth across the stage at odd times because the stagehands miss their cues (Hammond 2000: 64–5). To compensate for the lack of props and workable sets the actors throw themselves into the situations with an exuberance that is as absurd as the pantomime horses are unconvincing. It is not known if the "mounts" from *Pimple's The Whip* inspired

King Arthur's prancing horseless knights with clacking coconut shells in *Monty Python and the Holy Grail* (1975), but the later motion picture suggests that there is a long tradition for this type of humor in British film comedy (McKernan 2000: 7).

Ethnic Comedy and the American Character (1900–1916)

The comedy of Max Linder and Pimple was based, in part, on contrasting their incongruous characters with the French bourgeoisie and English working class. In comparison, according to Constance Rourke, a unique aspect of the character and culture of the United States is that "as a people, the Americans are said to have no childhood, and the circumstance has been shown to contain pathos as well as loss." Without a sense of cultural evolution or memory other than the "old country," which many Americans purposely left behind, humor became "a fashioning instrument in America ... Its objective – the unconscious objective of a disunited people-has seemed to be that of creating fresh bonds, a new unity, the semblance of a society and the rounded competition of an American type" (Rourke 1931: ix, 8, 9). Given the lack of a recognizable overall culture for this nation of immigrants, it is not surprising that American humor of the nineteenth and twentieth centuries often focused upon ethnic and racial stereotypes as marks of the ridiculous – negative American associations with the old country, if you will.

As vaudeville historian Douglas Gilbert verified, "Irish acts predominated [in the 1880s], blackface ran a close second, and Dutch, or German dialect made an important third." The propensity for the dominant "American stock" "to rib the Irish, the German or the Negro was to thrust at a minority[,] which generally took the jibes good-naturedly" (Gilbert 1941: 61–2). Frequently associated with "pathos and loss," and often painful to see today, it was and continues to be debatable just how harmless or harmful this comedy was. Humor can lessen social tensions as well as inflame them and, equally paradoxically, the comedy of this time could work towards social advancement while perpetuating injury. Even as middle-class media habitually treated aliens and racial groups with derision, some ethnic performers used the same stereotypes to challenge misconception and draw attention to social injustice. By laughing at themselves a few ethnic comedians of the early twentieth century American "melting pot" invited outsiders to come to know and appreciate members of their group as people. Tensions would continue, but shared laughter might foster the recognition of a common humanity that encouraged appreciation and tolerance. A case in point is the great black American comedian Bert Williams (1874–1922).

An urbane, articulate, intelligent, and sensitive man, Bert Williams spoke perfect English, but the comic conventions of the day compelled him to perform in blackface and speak in dialect when playing a melancholy loser who could evoke an audience's sympathy while generating laughter. His salary as a Ziegfield headliner equaled that of the President of the United States, but Bert Williams had to take a freight elevator while on tour when allowed to stay in the same hotel with the rest of his troupe. "In truth, I have never been able to discover that there was anything disgraceful in being a colored man," Williams was to reflect. "But I have often found it inconvenient – in America" (quoted in Forbes 2008: vi).

Bert Williams made three motion pictures: *Dark Town Jubilee* (1914), believed lost, *A Natural Born Gambler, Fish*, both produced in 1916. While his two surviving films are considered disappointing when compared with his brilliant stage performances and popular audio recordings, Williams' famous pantomime of a poker game in *Natural Born Gambler* is evidence of his talent. In jail for participating in an illegal poker game, the addicted card player mimes that he is dealing himself a wonderful hand. Far from a poker face, Williams' countenance exhibits delight at his clearly desirable cards. Williams registers shock, dismay, and then determination when an invisible opponent appears confident about his own hand. In the end our doleful player pushes his chips towards the victor. This woebegone eternal loser cannot win even in his dreams. W.C. Fields remembered Bert Williams as "The funniest man I ever saw and the saddest man I ever knew. I often wonder whether other people sensed what I did in him – that deep undercurrent of pathos" (quoted in Forbes 2008: 298).

Many other American comedians got their start performing ethnic and racial stereotypes – Buster Keaton (Irish), Eddie Cantor (blackface), Groucho Marx (German), Chico Marx (Italian), and Harpo Marx (Irish) being examples. Audience and performer needed a shared context initially to relate to one another, but ultimately the great humorists achieved fame by tapping into some universal aspect of the human condition that transcended comic stereotypes. While Mack Sennett's Keystone Film Studio would become famous for its unique comic personalities, it is not surprising that *Cohen Collects a Debt* (1912), *Riley and Schultz* (1912), and *Pedro's Dilemma* (1912) were some of the earliest Keystone titles (1912).

Mack Sennett's *Commedia dell'Arte* (1912–1917)

Mack Sennett left Biograph to make film comedies for his newly formed Keystone Motion Picture Company in the latter part of 1912, the same year that Max Linder was mobbed by adoring fans when visiting Spain. According to Lewis Jacobs, Sennett's Keystone comedies were known for "chases which defied the laws of gravity" in "a world of vulgarity and violence, with movement, speed, nonsense and improvisation as the chief elements of his style." This fantasist humor, "known as 'slapstick,' … springs essentially from the film medium" (Jacobs 1939: 212, 213). An art form whose importance to the advancement of screen humor should not be minimized, Mack Sennett's slapstick has become so associated with silent film comedy that there is a perception that this director provided the foundation for its origins – an idea very much disputed by the cinematic precedents identified in this chapter and Sennett himself.

Since Sennett's comedy was not based upon long recognized American cultural practice, even though it burlesqued current social values and featured some ethnic stereotypes, another gauge is needed to assess the characters of the Keystone comedies of 1912–1917. Italy's sixteenth-century *Commedia dell'Arte* is a potential model. Literally translated as "comedy of professional actors," *Commedia dell'Arte* was the product of improvisation and choreography rather than the written work of playwrights, and focused upon standard plots and comic situations involving thwarted lovers, petulant masters, and rascally servants (see DiCarmine in this volume). By 1530 nomadic Italian players had introduced *Commedia dell'Arte* to France, where its characters were given different names and greater comic range.

The stock comic characters of the *Commedia dell'Arte* were identified by special masks, costumes, stylized movements, and behavior that characterized their marks of the ridiculous. The thwarted lovers did not conceal their faces and dressed in the contemporary apparel of their upper class society. Sometimes the female lover was assisted by her loyal servant Columbina, who was not faithful in love. Carefree and capable of holding her own in rough-and-tumble situations, Columbina was often defined by a sexual craving as bawdy as that of her male counterpart, Arlecchino (Ducharte 1929: 278). The robust slapstick of the *Commedia dell'Arte* centered largely upon Arlecchino's lechery, doltish behavior, crude pranks, bumbling attempts at thievery, and agile grace.

A coarse and cloddish servant and thief, Arlecchino spent much of his time lusting after the female characters. Arlecchino wore a mask of animal fur in keeping with an earthy personality, and his costume was made up of patches. In contrast to his stupidity, shabby appearance, and lecherous behavior, Arlecchino was capable of performing astounding feats as an acrobat and tumbler. His costume and personality changed dramatically over the years, particularly in France. By the seventeenth century the patches on Arlecchino's clothing had merged into a symmetrical pattern and his mask was a black strip. Now called "Harlequin" and "Columbine," the former servants had become the lovers. Their lusty animal desires having been replaced with romantic yearning, Harlequin and Columbine were now associated with magic, fantasy, and romance rather than low comedy. At this time another *Commedia dell'Arte* Italian servant dating back to the 1500s was undergoing a transformation in both character and name. By the early nineteenth century the simple, awkward, and honest "Pedrolino" became famous in France as the wistfully tragicomic figure called "Pierrot."

Mabel's Dramatic Career (1913) is one of many Keystone films that can be compared with the *Commedia dell'Arte*. In this picture, a rural bumpkin (Mack Sennett) has asked the serving girl (Mabel Normand) to marry him. In keeping with Arlecchino's sexual dalliances, mere minutes after giving Mabel a ring Mack is attracted to a city girl visiting their home. Encouraged by his mother, Mack boorishly breaks off their engagement. Mabel reacts violently to his rude rejection and loses her job. Mack immediately recognizes his mistake when the city girl rejects him, but Mabel is gone and he has no idea where to find her. Unbeknownst to Mack, Mabel has found employment at the Keystone film studio.

Years later Mack stumbles into a theater and discovers that Mabel has become a movie star. After interacting with the motion picture characters on the screen in a manner reminiscent of the rube in *The Countryman and the Cinematographe*, Mack seeks out the villain (Ford Sterling) who had been harassing Mabel in the film. Mack somehow traces Sterling to the actor's home and learns, while looking through a downstairs window, that this "villain" is the father of three little children and he has married Mabel. Doused with water from an upstairs window, the unhappy lover departs as the picture ends.

Like the audiences of the *commedia dell' arte* and the Max Linder comedies, viewers came to the Keystone pictures with preconceptions about the major players. Instead of wearing masks, the Keystone men, as Lewis Jacobs noted, "were all distinguished by some preposterous make-up and abnormal individual characteristics" (Jacobs 1939: 212, 213). The young women usually wore contemporary dress and cosmetics that enhanced their attractiveness. The circumstances and setting might vary from picture to picture, but familiarity with the performers influenced audience expectation. As was true of the early Harlequin and Columbina, it was no surprise seeing Mack and Mabel play a rowdy couple whose relationship was affected by Mack's boorish behavior and sexual infidelity.

The concept of Mabel's unappreciated servant blossoming into a movie star anticipates a "Cinderella" theme that Lewis Jacobs identified in American feature films made after 1916 (Jacobs 1939: 277). The premise of an aspiring female actor becoming a star is the focus of Beatrice Lillie's *Exit Smiling* (1926), Colleen Moore's *Ella Cinders* (1926), Marion Davies' *Show People* (1928), and many other pictures. A particularly intriguing reversal of the "Cinderella transformation" can be seen in Alice Howell's delightful film short *Cinderella Cinders* (1920), produced by Reelcraft Pictures Corporation. Unlike some of her counterparts this pert celluloid daughter of Columbina is not oppressed. Cinderella is comfortable with herself so she does not seek an opportunity to blossom.

Reflecting someone who never would allow a "bad hair day" to get her down, Cinderella Cinders' mark of the ridiculous is an incredibly unkempt coiffure that looks like the victim of severe electrical shock. Cinderella is fired from her job at a greasy spoon after inadvertently flipping pancakes in her clients' faces, but finds new employment almost immediately because the wealthy Doughbill family desperately needs a cook for a party that very evening. Miss Cinders' "Cinderella moment" occurs after the Doughbills ask her to impersonate their special guest, the Countess De Bunco, who is unable to attend. When the camera unveils our new "countess" the emblematic Cinderella transformation does not transpire. Cinderella is wearing a different dress but her makeup and trademark hair have not changed. This is not someone who has undergone a metamorphosis but the Cinderella Cinders of old. By finding satisfaction with current circumstance instead of seeking more, Cinderella is much happier than Mack at the end of their respective pictures.

Cinderella Cinders gave no indication of changing, but comic working-class portrayals were disappearing in Hollywood films by the late teens and twenties. After World War I a growing middle-class movie audience resulted in an increased production of sophisticated comedy, which influenced Mack Sennett to his detriment. Far from a new development in 1917, American middle-class film comedy had been evolving during the same period as Sennett's slapstick.

American Comedy Gets Some Manners: Flora Finch, John Bunny, Mr. & Mrs. Sidney Drew (1908–1917)

Max Linder became a model for other filmmakers around the world, including D.W. Griffith in America. Besides being the inspiration for Mack Sennett's "French" character in *Those Awful Hats* and *The Curtain Pole*, Linder influenced the "Jones family" comedy series which Griffith directed at Biograph in 1908 and 1909 (Bitzer 1971: 71). According to Tom Gunning:

> The comic structure of the Jones films revolves around the proper domesticity of a bourgeois household, with Mr. Jones' infractions of propriety providing the narrative disequilibrium. The middle-class setting differentiated the series from Griffith's broad farces such as *Monday Morning at Coney Island Police Court* (August 7), *Balked at the Altar*, or *The Deceived Slumming Party* (May 27, July 14), which drew on earlier film chases and farces. It also signaled Biograph's wooing of middle-class family audiences with a form of comedy unlikely to offend their sensibilities with slapstick rowdiness. (Gunning 1991: 141)

An English-born actress named Flora Finch performed in the Jones family series. Her first film was a 1908 Biograph drama, directed by Griffith, entitled *The Helping Hand*. The next Finch picture, *Mrs. Jones Entertains*, was the second of the Jones comedies and is noteworthy for having Mack Sennett and Mary Pickford in its cast. *Those Awful Hats*, the actress's fourth film, featured Sennett's first Max Linder impersonation. After making 15 motion pictures Flora Finch left Biograph in 1910 to work at Vitagraph, where she was eventually teamed with one of the first internationally famous American film comedians, John Bunny.

In keeping with Aristotle's discussion of the comic mask "that excites laughter" by being "something ugly and distorted without causing pain," John Bunny's round and animated face was particularly capable of conveying his thoughts and feelings when reacting to the moment. Very much a physical comedian, Bunny's humor was based more on comedy of manners than slapstick. In the handful of surviving pictures from the 174 he made, Bunny sometimes plays a likable and sympathetic character despite his flaws. The nature of Bunny's performance also affected how his films were presented. Medium or tight long shots framed Bunny's body language to best advantage, and were held long enough for the comedian to convey his facial reactions to a given situation adequately. This resulted in an intimate narrative with a moderate tempo very different from the rapid pacing of a chase filmed in more distancing long shots.

By 1911 Bunny's stout figure and round expressive face were comically contrasted with the thin and sometimes dour countenance of the physically plain Flora Finch, who was frequently cast as his wife. *A Cure for Pokeritis* (1912) begins with an exhausted and disheveled George Brown (Bunny) departing a loser from a poker game. Returning to his middle-class home Brown is confronted by his wife (Finch), and vows never to play poker again. But Brown talks in his sleep and his wife's suspicions are aroused. Mrs. Brown asks her cousin Freddie to follow Brown to his Wednesday night "meeting," and it is confirmed that her husband is still playing poker. Freddie persuades members of his Bible study group to don police uniforms and stage a raid. The wives of the miscreants are informed and once the game has been disrupted the pseudo-police withdraw, leaving the poker players to confront their spouses. Relieved that he is not going to be arrested, the film ends with Brown and his wife in a loving embrace.

Mr. and Mrs. Sidney Drew were two other American performers who brought comedy of manners to silent film. A member of the distinguished Drew-Barrymore theatrical family, Sidney Drew, began film acting at Vitagraph on a regular basis in 1913. Drew, like Max Linder, played a charming and witty man whose properly fitting clothing and polished demeanor suggest a respected member of middle- or upper-class society. Sidney Drew's mark of the ridiculous reflected a sudden loss of control due to falling in love, a misunderstanding, or some absurd situation. Instead of playing a shrew, Mrs. Drew portrayed a charming young woman who had won Sidney's heart. Sometimes they are unmarried and Drew struggles, often ridiculously, to win her acceptance. At other times they are a loving couple whose relationship has been disrupted by Drew's ineffectual attempts to avoid something.

An enjoyable example of their work is *Fox-Trot Finesse*, released on October 1, 1915. Ferdie Crosby (Drew) is ecstatic when his mother-in-law goes home after a long visit, but life continues to be complicated because his young wife (Mrs. Drew) wants him to dance the foxtrot constantly. The exhausted Ferdie reads about a famous performer who must give up dancing for several months due to an injury and he feigns the same. After observing her husband walking perfectly without his crutch, Mrs. Crosby shows Ferdie a letter she has written asking her mother to come visit until he is better. Ferdie sees an apparition of his mother-in-law and turns on the phonograph. The picture ends with Ferdie tearing up the letter while fox-trotting.

Goodness Gracious (released on February 7, 1914) is not typical of the later comedies that starred Sidney Drew with his second wife, even though it highlights this actor's usual refusal to take himself seriously and trademark charm. Featuring the 51-year-old Drew as a "youth" in love with Carol Kimball Young, *Goodness Gracious* is a parody of overacting and absurd situations in film and stage melodrama that anticipates the clichés of every lampoon of the silent film made since 1914. The plots for the previous described Bunny and Drew comedies do not bring to mind the silent movie clichés of *Goodness Gracious*, nor does it take much imagination to envision how these stories might be adapted for film and television today. The quality motion pictures made between 1908 and 1917 are testaments to their filmmakers' talents given that studios and audiences were expecting them to produce literally hundreds of physically and often emotionally demanding 10- and 20-minute movies in a very short time. One must also wonder if those films that are not so good might be manifestations of the pressure of production rather than lack of talent. Besides trying to cope with production deadlines, comedians were typecast while being expected to keep their comedy fresh and funny. Once the novelty wore off the silent comedians had to find new approaches to keep the incongruity in their comedies incongruous if they were to continue working.[2]

John Bunny and Sidney Drew died in 1915 and 1919 respectively, and the film careers of most of their European contemporaries had peaked or ended by the close of 1918 – a reflection of the economic devastation resulting from World War I. Hollywood profited from this loss of competition and gained an international advantage that it kept for the remainder of the twentieth century. Silent comedy would continue to be made in other countries, but the most notable films and filmmakers tended to be associated with America after 1918. Though Mack Sennett's Keystone had gone out of existence the year before, his studio had produced a quintessential silent comedy icon comparable to Harlequin and Pierrot who was continuing to evolve.

The "Mark of the Ridiculous" of Charlie Chaplin's "Pierrot" (1914–1918)

The son of English music-hall entertainers, Charles Chaplin's earliest years were spent in middle-class comfort. Circumstances took a dramatic turn after Charlie was six, when Charles Chaplin Sr. refused to support his family and ill health prevented Mrs. Chaplin from earning a living. A show business career would reverse financial misfortune but Charles Spencer Chaplin, who became a master at producing comedy based upon painful autobiographical experience, was forever affected by his Dickensian childhood. Nine years after his father died from alcoholism, Charlie Chaplin gained success playing the comic drunk in the aforementioned Fred Karno sketch, *Mumming Birds*. Acutely self-conscious of the ragged and ill-fitting clothes he sometimes wore as a child, Chaplin later tapped into his embarrassment when garbing his famous "tramp." By this time Chaplin was an immigrant in the United States. Whether the instigator of antisocial behavior or society's victim, Chaplin's screen character was also an "outsider" in virtually every film in which he appeared. Prior to the appearance of his "Little Fellow," Chaplin was conflicted by Mack Sennett's approach to filmmaking.

Although he had no film experience, Charles Chaplin left vaudeville in 1913 to work for Sennett as a featured comic. Upon arriving at the studio Chaplin remembered Sennett telling him, "We have no scenario. We get an idea, and then follow the natural sequence of events until it leads up to a chase, which is the essence of our comedy." Chaplin was not delighted. "I hated chase. It dissipates one's personality; little as I knew about movies, I knew that nothing transcended personality" (Chaplin 1964: 146). It is not surprising that Chaplin's first Keystone, a chase picture entitled *Making a Living*, was a disappointment. As would be true at other times in his life and career, Charles Chaplin used his art to confront a personal problem. Chaplin's second picture, *Kid Auto Races at Venice*, directly addressed the challenge of making Keystone movies.

Steve Massa has observed, "A key element of the Sennett legend is that he always took advantage of any event that was happening near the studio – an auto race, an oil-well fire, or even the draining of a lake–sending his clowns with a cameraman to cavort in the proceedings" (Massa 2008: 198–9). On January 10, 1914, Sennett decided to use a "soap box derby" as a backdrop for an improvised comedy. As Fred Karno used his music hall sketch *Mumming Birds* to parody the music hall, *Kid Auto Races* satirized the filmmaking process. This comedy features Chaplin, in his famous costume for the first time, mugging in front of a "documentary filmmaker's" camera that prevents him from "recording" the event. Chaplin claimed to have been intimidated by the filmmaking process when producing his first film, but his tramp displays no such concern. The Chaplin character of *Making a Living* conformed to external rhythms, but the brazen tramp dominated the frame while dictating the pace and narrative progression in *Kid Auto Races at Venice* and every motion picture he appeared in thereafter.

Arguably a variation of the comic "grotesque" that Little Tich and Chaplin had performed in the English music hall, the tramp was particularly cinematic given his mark of the ridiculous – an erratic way of walking. Numerous filmmakers including Sennett have used the motion picture medium's ability to alter reality for comic effect. What makes Chaplin's tramp a quintessential silent comedy character is that his jerky gait is a self-reflective parody of the motion of early "movies." The tramp's awkward movement harkens back to the motion picture inventors' challenge of eliminating the flicker that prevented the first films from looking "real." Where the incorrect registration or physical deterioration of other people's motion pictures can make their work look unintentionally ludicrous, such issues are less jarring with Chaplin comedies because they bring to mind the comic essence of the tramp's locomotion.

Chaplin's "Little Fellow" is now associated with pathos and tragicomedy but, as was the case of Harlequin, the personality that initially became popular was a brash, earthy, crude, lecherous, and unkempt figure capable of astounding physical grace. Chaplin said of his Keystone character:

> His brain was seldom active then-only his instincts ... But with each succeeding comedy the tramp was growing more complex. Sentiment was beginning to percolate through the character. This became a problem because he was bound by the limits of slapstick ... The solution came when I thought of the tramp as a sort of Pierrot. With this conception I was freer to express and embellish the comedy with touches of sentiment. But logically it was difficult to get a beautiful girl interested in a tramp. This has always been a problem in my films ... The girl in *City Lights* is blind. In this relationship he is romantic and wonderful to her until her sight is restored ... I did not have to read books to know that the theme of life is conflict and pain. Instinctively, all my clowning was based on this. (Chaplin 1964: 224, 226)

Mack Sennett's post-Keystone comedies lost their vitality, in part, because a growing middle-class audience encouraged a change in approach and content that this filmmaker's art could not effectively address. Chaplin's silent comedy remained vital because he played off the dialectical and often painful encounters the tramp had with a society of which he was not a part. The "Little Fellow" was able to function as long as he performed in a world without speech. Chaplin held out longer than any other silent filmmaker, but he stopped making nontalking pictures with the tramp after releasing *Modern Times* in 1936.

The Mark of the Ridiculous and American Middle Class Silent Comedy of Manners (1915–1929)

Charles Chaplin was able to combine a music hall grotesque with fantasist film slapstick to produce an iconic silent screen character that became recognized as a symbol of irrepressible humanity. By sharing insights into the human condition, the tramp proved that a ridiculed figure could become recognized as sublime. Quoting Henri Bergson, Rourke noted that "The comic comes into being just when society and the individual freed from the worry of self-preservation, begin to regard themselves as works of art" (Rourke 1931: 12–13). Still a nation of immigrants in the 1910s, and made up of many types of people, America's middle class identified itself as "the" social standard and Hollywood comic artists responded in kind.

A particularly notable middle-class comic model was introduced to film in 1915, when Douglas Fairbanks appeared in a movie entitled *The Lamb* as the likable but ineffectual all-American boy he performed in the Broadway play *The New Henrietta*. In this play and subsequent films, the Fairbanks character, in a male equivalent of the "Cinderella moment", transcends his mark of the ridiculous by performing a heroic task that results in his being taken seriously

as a man. By the age of thirty-eight Fairbanks chose to star in such adolescent tales as *The Three Musketeers* (1921), *Robin Hood* (1922) and *The
Thief of Baghdad* (1924) rather than continue playing an arrested adolescent.
Others would perform this character. When MGM decided to make an
actual film version of *The New Henrietta* in 1920, Fairbanks suggested that
Buster Keaton, who played a comic grotesque in Roscoe "Fatty" Arbuckle's
slapstick comedies, be cast in the Fairbanks role. Harold Lloyd profited
from Fairbanks' example in 1917, when he stopped playing grotesques to
concentrate upon a white-collar character whose trademark glasses falsely
implied weakness. Often portraying a youth bent at succeeding in business, Lloyd's comic character also triumphed heroically when the occasion
demanded.

With the shift away from the comic grotesque and slapstick for slapstick's sake,
the mark of the ridiculous of American comedy in the teens and twenties became
associated more with a "mistake" relating to attitude and personality than physical
"deformity." Instead of concentrating upon a fantasist capacity to distort the real
world, these silent comedies explored how one might cope with it. For example,
while treating real cowboys and Indians as if they were living in an American frontier comparable to his obsessive fantasy, Douglas Fairbanks' eastern "buckaroo"
Jeff Hillington in *Wild and Wooly* (1917) experiences an embarrassing revelation
when he learns they are not. Chaplin's tramp elicits laughter and heartbreak in his
encounters with society as he teaches his adopted son to become streetwise in *The
Kid* (1921). The perils of advertising are appreciated by Harold Lloyd's character in
Safety Last (1923), when he is forced to change places with a "human fly" that he
hired to climb a skyscraper for a department store promotion. Pragmatism and a
pronounced work ethic enable a misunderstood southern engineer to overcome
seemingly unbeatable obstacles in Buster Keaton's Civil War comedy *The General*
(1927), while single-handedly retrieving his beloved locomotive from the north
after it has been stolen by Yankees.

Comedy of manners was on the increase in the 1920s but fantasist humor continued to be produced. Their comedy often did not lend itself to trends or imitation
but the cartoon-like slapstick of Larry Semon and the surreal clowning of Snub
Pollard produced notable screen moments. Where the mark of the ridiculous of
Fairbanks, Lloyd, and Keaton can be linked to arrested adolescence, Harry Langdon's character was an infant inhabiting a man's body. Some comic heroes shared
insight through clever solutions to complex and even life-threatening problems;
Langdon's clown was overwhelmingly bewildered by objects and situations that
most children would ignore much less take on as crippling enigmas. The sublime
comic personalities of Laurel and Hardy, Raymond Griffith, and Charlie Chase
must also be acknowledged with the recognition that mere mention does not do
them justice.

Proceeding with Henri Bergson's observation that it is one thing for a "society and the individual to begin to regard themselves as works of art," it is another

thing for those outside this society to feel the same. Judging by Lev Kuleshov's 1924 comedy, *Neobychainye priklyucheniya mistera Vesta v strane bolshevikov* (*The Extraordinary Adventures of Mr. West in the Land of the Bolsheviks*) at least two American comic figures were recognized as works of art in Russia. In this film Mr. West, who resembles Harold Lloyd's glasses character, and his sidekick Jeddy, who acts like Jeff Hillington's "buckaroo" in *Wild and Woolly*, visit Russia. Their pre-existing attitudes about communism, and cowboy Jeddy's propensity for over-reaction, create some interesting intercultural comic conflicts. The Russians are patient with these Americans, and Kuleshov claims that there is mutual understanding when the picture ends.

The principal innovative trend in silent comedy during the latter part of the 1920s, was the type of sophisticated humor found in Ernst Lubitsch's *The Marriage Circle* (1924) and *Lady Windemere's Fan* (1925). René Clair's *Un chapeau de paille d'Italie* (*An Italian Straw Hat*) and *Les Deux timides* (*Two Timid Souls*), both made in France in 1928, underscore that this trend in comedy of manners was international. The clever subtitles and pronounced interpersonal engagement of the witty characters in Lewis Milestone's American feature *Garden of Eden* (1928) "screamed" for the addition of sound, and it is not surprising that this genre continued with the coming of the talkies. But even as this form of comedy manners benefited by finding a voice other types of silent comedy, and numerous popular comedians, would be "silenced" by sound.

Conclusion: The Loss of Silents

In 1926, 36 years after Edison suggested the possibility of combining his phonograph with a sequential motion image device, Warner Brothers released the feature film *Don Juan* with a synchronized musical score. Between 1927 and 1932 Hollywood and other national cinemas made the transition to sound, with most American silent filmmakers having tested their luck with the new medium by 1929. Recording both image and sound shifted the focus from *motion* pictures to *talkies*. Nonverbal communication in the cinema was never totally lost but the new technology fundamentally changed both the evolution and content of cinematic expression. The early talkies centered upon a variety of verbal "foreign" languages, so silent film comedy had been more universally accessible. Silent film's dreamlike aura was replaced by a more realistic depiction of a subject seen with indigenous sound. Incongruous fantasist effects were a thing of the past and some of the comic magic was gone. But before its passing silent comedy had become less associated with slapstick for slapstick's sake, and was increasingly identified with the exploration of social attitudes and the nature of humanity as found in the work of artists like Chaplin and Keaton. This was not a bad foundation for the future of film comedy.

Notes

1. Donald Crafton (1990), in his biography of animation pioneer Emile Cohl, identifies
    three different comic strips with scenarios similar to *L'Arroseur arrosé* – evidence that
    this film not only anticipated future film slapstick but was influenced by humor from
    other media of the period. Crafton cites Georges Sadoul as claiming that *L'Arroseur
    arrosé* was similar to a "picture story by Herman Vogel in an 1887 Album Quantin,"
    and reproduces both A. Sorel's "Fait Divers," *La Caricature*, March 12, 1887, and
    "Un Arroseur public," in the *Le Petit Français Illustrê*, August 3, 1889, by Christophe
    (Georges Colomb), as illustrations to confirm the duplication of this gag. It is
    Crafton's belief that the Christophe cartoon "was certainly Lumiére's direct source."
2. The author wishes to thank film historian Robert Arkus for bringing *Goodness Gracious*
    to his attention.

References

Anthony, B. (1996) *Who's Who in Victorian Cinema, Little Tich: British Music Hall Performer*,
    www.victorian-cinema.net/tich.htm (accessed May 18, 2012).

Aristotle (1962) Poetics, in *Comedy: Plays, Theory, and Criticism* (ed. M. Felheim), Harcourt,
    Brace & World, Inc., New York, NY, p. 194.

Bergson, H. (1956) Laughter, in *Comedy* (ed. W. Sypher), Doubleday & Company, Garden
    City, New York, p. 92.

Bitzer, G.W. (1971) *Billy Bitzer: His Story*, Farrar, Straus & Giroux, New York, NY, p. 71.

Brown, S. (2003-2010) *That Fatal Sneeze*, BFI Screenonline, www.screenonline
    .org.uk/film/id/974449/ (accessed May 18, 2012).

Chaplin, C. (1964) *My Autobiography*, Pocket Books, New York, NY, pp. 146, 224, 226.

Crafton, D. (1990) *Emile Cohl, Caricature, and Film*, Princeton University Press, Princeton
    NJ, pp. 252–3, 307.

Duchartre, P.L. (1929) *The Italian Comedy*, George G. Harrap & Co., Ltd., London, p. 278.

Forbes, C.F. (2008) *Introducing Bert Williams: Burnt Cork, Broadway, and the Story of America's
    First Black Star*, Basic Civitas Books, New York, NJ, pp. vi, 298.

Gilbert, D. (1941) *American Vaudeville: Its Life and Times*, Whittlesey House, McGraw-Hill
    Co., Inc., New York, NY, pp. 61–2.

Gunning, T. (1991) *D.W. Griffith and the Origins of the American Narrative Film: The
    Early Years at Biograph*, The University of Illinois Press, Champaign, IL, pp. 41–4,
    132, 141.

Hammond, M. (2000) "Cultivating Pimple": performance traditions and the film comedy
    of Fred and Joe Evans, in *Pimple, Pranks and Pratfalls: British Film Comedy Before 1930* (eds.
    A. Burton and L. Porter), Flicks Books, Trowbridge, pp. 64–5.

Jacobs, L. (1939) *The Rise of the American Film: A Critical History*, Teachers College Press,
    New York, NY, pp. 212, 213, 268, 277.

Massa, S. (2008) Keystone revisited. *Le giornate del cinema muto*, 27 (4-11 October), 198-9,
    www.cinetecadelfriuli.org/gcm/ed_precedenti/edizione2008/Catalogo2008.pdf
    (accessed May 18, 2012).

McKernan, L. (1996) *Who's Who of Victorian Cinema, Fred Ott: American Mechanic*,
    www.victorian-cinema.net/ott.htm (accessed May 18, 2012).

McKernan, L. (2000) How to make *Ben Hur* look like an epic, in *Pimple, Pranks and Pratfalls: British Film Comedy Before 1930* (eds. A. Burton and L. Porter), Flicks Books, Trowbridge, p. 7.

Robinson, D. (2008) Max revisited, *Le giornate del cinema muto*, 27 (4-11 October) 193–194, www.cinetecadelfriuli.org/gcm/ed_precedenti/edizione2008/Catalogo2008.pdf (accessed May 18, 2012).

Rourke, C. (1931) *American Humor*, Harcourt, Brace and Company, New York, NY, pp. ix, 8, 9, 12, 13, 99.

Spehr, P. (2008) *The Man Who Made Movies: W.K.L. Dickson*, John Libbey Publishing Ltd, New Barnet, pp. 75–82, 649.

Further Reading

Agee, J. (1949) Comedy's greatest era, *Life*, September 5, 1949, pp. 70–82, 85-6, 88. Reprinted in Agee, J. (1958) *Agee on Film*, Vol. 1, Grosset & Dunlap, New York, NY, vol. 1, pp. 105–22. Written by one of America's greatest film critics, James Agee, this classic essay was instrumental in fostering the scholarly recognition and rediscovery of America's foremost silent comedians during the second half of the twentieth century. A must read.

Blesh, R. (1966) *Keaton*, Macmillan, New York. Rudi Blesh's engaging biography is an excellent guide for better appreciating this remarkable artist and his work. While much of the same information can be found in Keaton's *My Wonderful World of Slapstick* as told to Charles Samuels (1960), New York: Doubleday, this autobiography does not poetically intertwine the comedian's life with his art to the same degree as Blesh's absorbing assessment.

Kerr, W. (1975) *The Silent Clowns*, Alfred A. Knopf, New York, NY. This thoughtful, perceptive, and loving analysis by Walter Kerr remains one of the best overall examinations of America's major silent film comedians and some of its "lesser clowns."

King, R. (2009) *The Fun Factory: The Keystone Film Company and the Emergence of Mass Culture*, University of California Press, Berkeley, CA. Rob King's notable study examines how Sennett and the Keystone films reflected working class society and its entertainments. *Mack Sennett's Fun Factory: A History and Filmography of His Studio and His Keystone and Mack Sennett Comedies, with Biographies of Players and Personnel*, by Brent Walker (McFarland, Jefferson, NC 2010) is also particularly useful for its historical data on Sennett and Keystone.

Lahue, K. (1966) *World of Laughter: The Motion Picture Comedy Short, 1910-1930*, University of Oklahoma Press, Norman, OK. An overview of silent comedy that helps put the work of John Bunny, Flora Finch, and Mr. and Mrs. Sidney Drew in historical context. Additional scholarship on these significant film comedians is needed.

Linder, M. (1992) Max Linder était mon père (*Max Linder Was My Father*), Flammarion, Paris. This book documents a daughter's search to learn more about a father who died in a double suicide with her mother when the author was a baby. While this biography was never translated into English, Maud Linder's fascinating 1983 documentary *L' Homme au Chapeau de Soie (The Man in the Silk Hat)*, was released on VHS in English. Mme. Linder's work underscores the creativity and importance of this major artist and verifies that additional research on Linder is long overdue.

Robinson, D. (1985) *Chaplin: His Life and Art*, McGraw-Hill, London. David Robinson was the first film scholar to be given access to Charles Chaplin's personal papers and this work, which was revised for a 2001 Penguin edition in Britain, is considered the comedian's definitive biography.

Robinson, D. (1993) *Georges Méliès: Father of Film Fantasy*, British Film Institute, Museum of the Moving Image, London. David Robinson's monograph, which was written to accompany the British Film Institute's major Méliès retrospective at the Museum of the Moving Image in 1993, provides excellent historical insights into how this filmmaker's background as a magician influenced his motion pictures. As indicated by the title, Elizabeth Ezra's *Georges Méliès: The Birth of the Auteur* (Manchester: Manchester University Press, 2000) further isolates Méliès' importance as an artist. Paul Hammond's *Marvellous Méliès* (St. Martin's Press, New York, 1975) also gives an interesting overview of this innovative filmmaker and his work.

Tibbetts, J.C. and Welsh, J.M. (1977) *His Majesty the American: The Cinema of Douglas Fairbanks, Sr.* A.S. Barnes, South Brunswick, NJ. One of the first books to explore Fairbanks' "All American boy," this appraisal is notable for suggesting a number of critical approaches for analyzing this important comedian and his films.

Tich, M. and Findlater, R. (1979) *Little Tich: Giant of the Halls*, Elm Tree Books, London. A contemplative examination of a unique English music hall personality and his involvement in the variety entertainment where so many early British film comedians learned their craft. The foreword was written by Jacques Tati.

2

Pie Queens and Virtuous Vamps

The Funny Women of the Silent Screen

Kristen Anderson Wagner

In 1949, the film critic James Agee published his influential essay "Comedy's Great-est Era," in which he recounts the golden years of silent comedy and proclaims that the genre's "four most eminent masters" were Charlie Chaplin, Buster Keaton, Harold Lloyd, and Harry Langdon (Agee 2001: 15). In the years since this essay was published, film historians and scholars have similarly canonized a few more silent-era comics, including Roscoe "Fatty" Arbuckle, Charley Chase, John Bunny, and Stan Laurel and Oliver Hardy. Conspicuously absent from this list are Mabel Normand, Louise Fazenda, Alice Howell, Constance Talmadge, Colleen Moore, Clara Bow, and numerous other talented and successful silent-era comics. While male comedians have been celebrated, analyzed, and fondly remembered through each passing generation, female comedians have largely been forgotten, by audi-ences and academics alike, despite the fact that they were some of the most popular performers to work in silent film. Certainly, countless other popular performers from the silent era have similarly been neglected and finally forgotten, but the disparity between who has been remembered and who has been forgotten is par-ticularly egregious in the case of silent comedy. While numerous male comedians from the silent era are known the world over, silent comediennes have been virtu-ally erased from the public memory.

There are a variety of reasons for this. Perhaps the most significant is the fact that an alarmingly high percentage of silent films have been lost over the years. The Library of Congress estimates that 90 percent of feature films from the 1910s and 80 percent of features from the 1920s no longer exist. The survival rate is even lower for short films, including the one- and two-reel comedies that made up the bulk of silent-era comedies. The silent films that were saved were often the ones thought by collectors and archivists to be somehow "important," a distinction that generally didn't include comedies, which were widely considered to be lowbrow

A Companion to Film Comedy, First Edition. Edited by Andrew Horton and Joanna E. Rapf.
© 2013 John Wiley & Sons, Inc. Published 2016 by John Wiley & Sons, Inc.

entertainment. With so few silent comedies surviving today, it makes sense that so few silent comedians, male or female, would be remembered.

The lack of availability of films featuring silent comediennes has certainly contributed in a significant way to their current obscurity, and yet it is clear that this is not the only reason for their continued neglect. Also a factor is the longstanding and deep-rooted cultural bias against women performing comedy. The idea that femininity is incompatible with humor dates back to before the nineteenth century and lingers to the present day. Traditionally, women are thought to be too emotional, too passive, and too morally pure to engage in, or even enjoy, comedy, which has the potential to be raucous, rebellious, and antagonistic. Women have historically been placed in the position of society's moral guardians, a position that further excludes them from comedy. They are thought to bear the responsibility of keeping civility and order, while "men were left free to play, to joke, knowing the women would pull them into line soon enough" (Walker 1988: 42). From this dynamic comes the stereotype of the nag, a woman whose sole purpose is to spoil men's fun. Comedy is also seen as appealing to the intellect, a trait diametrically opposed to stereotypically feminine qualities such as empathy, sentiment, and intuition. It follows, then, that "those who deny woman the sense of humor thus have begun by denying her the capacity for logical thought" (Walker 1988: 82). French philosopher Henri Bergson made this same point in his 1900 essay "Laughter," arguing that "laughter has no greater foe than emotion … [H]ighly emotional souls, in tune and unison with life, in whom every event would be sentimentally prolonged and re-echoed, would neither know nor understand laughter" (Bergson 1956: 63). Given the stereotype of women as "highly emotional souls," this line of thinking leaves little room for them to participate in comedy.

The unruly and aggressive nature of comedy is also seen by many as a reason why women are incapable of having a sense of humor. The nineteenth-century feminine ideal was demure and passive, a gentle soul who was quietly submissive to her husband (Welter 1966: 158). Although women today are, generally speaking, no longer expected to be subservient to men, the idea of women as subordinates has not entirely disappeared. Comedy, on the other hand, can be bold, assertive, and above all transgressive. It can be used to question authority, to upset the status quo, to deflate the powerful, and to challenge the social order. In short, as Regina Barreca (1988: 14) says, "Comedy is dangerous; humor is a weapon. Laughter is refusal and triumph." Women who engage in comic performances have the potential to subvert the social structures that keep them oppressed; by poking fun at those in power, especially men, women have the ability to expose their weaknesses and challenge their authority (Walker 1988; Gray 1994; Rowe 1995). It's not surprising that "the fairer sex" would be considered too delicate to engage in such behavior. Adding to this is the fact that comedy can be literally aggressive and even violent. Standup comedians often interact with their audiences directly, hurling barbs along with jokes. Slapstick films, particularly silent

comedies, are particularly violent, with everything from pies to the actors themselves being thrown about in wild brawls. This behavior is certainly at odds with
perceived notions of how proper women should behave, and the resulting contradiction contributes to the idea that women are not suited for comedy.

The idea that women were too morally upright, too emotional, and too passive
to enjoy comedy was deeply engrained in American thinking by the beginning
of the twentieth century, and the result is a general perception that women are
not as funny as men. This prejudice continues to the present day and almost certainly plays a role in the continuing neglect of silent comediennes. This is especially
true when coupled with the loss of so many of the films that feature these funny
women, as audiences who are already primed to question whether women are
capable of performing comedy aren't able to see films that might change their
opinion. Even comediennes' extant films are rarely seen; what scant attention is
paid to silent comedy by academics, historians, festival programmers, book publishers, and DVD distributors is almost exclusively focused on the works of male
comedians such as Chaplin, Keaton, Langdon, Lloyd, and Arbuckle.

Despite the fact that they have largely been forgotten today, female comedians were quite popular during the silent era. They appeared in shorts and feature
films from the birth of cinema through the advent of sound including slapstick and
light and romantic comedies. Fans read stories about their favorite comic actresses
every month in magazines such as *Photoplay* and *Moving Picture World*, and flooded
the mailboxes of stars such as Clara Bow, who was said to receive an average of
35 000 letters a month – twice the amount of any other star in Hollywood (Clara
Bow Got $50.00 per Week in First Role 1927; Color Biography of Clara Bow 1932).
Funny women were active behind the camera as well, as writers, producers, and
directors. A number of comediennes, including Constance Talmadge, Fay Tincher,
and Gale Henry had their own companies so that they could exert greater control
over their projects, and screenwriters such as Anita Loos and Frances Marion and
directors such as Alice Guy and Mrs. Sidney Drew turned out hundreds of films.
These women were doing more than just making people laugh; they were challenging conventional notions of femininity. Their presence and power both on and
off screen meant a great deal of visibility as they broke boundaries and redefined
what it meant to be a woman.

In the nineteenth and early twentieth centuries, concepts like "femininity" and
"womanhood" were in flux. As women increasingly moved from the private to
the public sphere the traditional definition of women as the keepers of hearth and
home began to seem outdated. The figure of the active and independent New
Woman embodied the zeitgeist, as women in greater numbers began working
outside the home, attending college, and championing women's suffrage.
Comediennes both reflected and played a part in the societal reconceptualization
of femininity by challenging cultural expectations for women and providing
audiences with an alternative to the ubiquitous stereotype of women as
demure, passive, well-behaved, and above all, humorless. Slapstick comediennes

transgressed gender boundaries by performing the type of rough physical comedy that many contemporaneous observers felt should be reserved for men, while flappers and light comediennes often incorporated brazen sexuality into their films. Actresses who were too fat, too tall, too homely, or too awkward to be considered conventionally attractive embraced their excessiveness and positioned themselves outside of the narrow and restrictive boundaries of traditional femininity. Certainly, these performances were complicated by the fact that they were often self-deprecating, providing audiences with the opportunity to laugh at, rather than with, the comediennes, and their reliance on misogynistic clichés, such as the awkward spinster or the battleaxe wife, ran the risk of reinforcing, rather than challenging, those stereotypes. Still, regardless of what type of comedy they performed, when comediennes appeared on stage or on screen they were visibly refuting the idea that femininity was incompatible with a sense of humor and proving that women could be aggressive, assertive, bawdy, and, most importantly, funny.

Pioneers of the Pie: Early Silent Comediennes

Funny women have appeared on film since moving pictures were invented. One of the first films to be commercially released, *The Kiss* (Edison 1896), features stage comedienne May Irwin and John C. Rice, her co-star from the stage comedy *The Widow Jones*, in a prolonged onscreen kiss.

One of the most popular of the early comediennes who made their mark onscreen was Flora Finch. Born in England in 1867, Finch worked onstage, in legitimate theater, vaudeville, and music halls, before making her first film appearance in 1908. She signed with Vitagraph in 1910 and was paired with John Bunny, eventually making well over 100 short films with him. After Bunny's death in 1915 Finch continued to work in film, but she never regained the success she had known earlier in her career, despite starting her own company, Flora Finch Films. She continued to work steadily throughout the 1920s and 1930s in increasingly smaller roles, and eventually ended up as an extra and bit player with MGM. Her last film was *The Women*, released the year before her death in 1940.

Tall, skinny, and angular, with sharp features, Finch provided a visual counterpoint to Bunny's rotund figure and boisterous personality. The comedy in her films often centered on her appearance, with her homeliness serving as a visual punch line. In *Stenographers Wanted* (Vitagraph 1912), for example, a pair of businessmen are planning to hire an attractive young woman as their stenographer when their wives go behind their backs to hire Finch, knowing that their husbands will not be tempted by her. A review of a similar film, *The New Stenographer* (Vitagraph 1914), describes how, upon meeting Finch's character, her new bosses "narrowly escape apoplectic attacks at the sight of her face" (Kelly 1914: 8). Finch was part of a long tradition of comediennes who based their comedy on their appearance. This tradition included tall and thin comediennes such as Charlotte Greenwood and Fanny Brice, as well as overweight women such as Marie Dressler, Trixie Friganza, May Irwin, and Sophie Tucker, who sang a song titled "Nobody Loves a Fat Girl." In their acts, these women embraced traits that were not considered conventionally attractive – their excessive height or weight, their awkwardness, their unusual features – and highlighted them to elicit laughter. While this is certainly self-deprecating to some extent, it can also be read as a celebration of non-normative femininity and a rejection of society's demands that women conform to dominant beauty standards.

Finch would often play a nagging wife who had to bring her wayward husband, usually Bunny, into line, as in *A Cure for Pokeritis* (Vitagraph 1912), in which Finch's character hatches an elaborate scheme to prevent her husband from playing poker. She played suffragettes in several films, including *The Pickpocket* (Vitagraph 1913) and *A Trap to Catch a Burglar* (Vitagraph 1913) – not surprising given the popular stereotype of suffragettes as unattractive and unfeminine. The comedy in her films was generally situational rather than physical, based on misunderstandings and sight gags rather than the boisterous and anarchic gags found in slapstick comedy.

Another popular comedy team at Vitagraph was Sidney Drew and Lucille McVey, known as Mr. and Mrs. Sidney Drew. McVey was born in 1890, and worked onstage before marrying Sidney Drew, who was an established comedian in vaudeville and on the legitimate stage, in 1914. The Drews were known for their domestic comedies, which relied on situational, rather than slapstick, comedy, much like the films of Flora Finch and John Bunny. In fact, the press was quick to point out that Mrs. Drew did not lower herself to do physical comedy; an article from 1920 let readers know that "Mrs. Sidney Drew, during all the time she has been making comedies, has not once thrown a pie, run along the edge of a skyscraper, been caught in the wrong bedroom, or resorted to trick photography" (Tinee 1920: D2), while another writer said simply that her "comedies are of the polite type, and questionable situations and slapstick action are taboo" ("From the Screen Shops"). After Sidney Drew's death in 1919 Lucille McVey Drew continued to work sporadically as an actress but she increasingly focused her attention on writing and directing, until her death in 1925. She co-wrote and co-directed the comedies she starred in with her husband, and after his death was the sole director on several films, including *The Emotional Mrs. Vaughn* (Pathé 1920), in which she starred; *The Stimulating Mrs. Barton* (Pathé 1920), and *Cousin Kate* (Vitagraph 1921), starring Alice Joyce.

Mrs. Drew was one of a number of women who directed comedies during the silent era. Alice Guy was undoubtedly the most prolific female director of the silent era, directing approximately 1000 films from 1896 to 1920 in her native France and in the United States. Born in 1873 in Paris, Guy divided her childhood between Switzerland, Chile, and France. In 1894 she was hired as a secretary by Léon Gaumont, and within three years was made head of film production for the newly formed Gaumont Film Company. Guy moved to the United States in 1907, and in 1910 opened her own studio, the Solax Company, with her husband, Herbert Blaché, where she worked as a writer and director and oversaw all production. She had difficulty finding work in the 1920s, and was largely forgotten by the 1950s, when Léon Gaumont's son Louis brought renewed attention to her contributions to film history. In 1955 the French Government awarded her the *Légion d'Honneur*, and two years later she was honored by the Cinémathèque Française. Alice Guy died in 1968.

While Guy directed films in a range of genres, comedy was an important element in her films throughout her career. She often dealt with women's issues, and a number of her comedies deal with the themes of equality between sexes and gender inversion. In *Matrimony's Speed Limit* (Solax 1913), a young man breaks his engagement with his fiancée after losing all of his money in the stock market. The fiancée, who is an heiress, sends him a fake telegram informing him that a distant relative has left him a fortune but to inherit it he must be married by noon on that same day. The young man frantically tries to find a wife, proposing to strangers on the street, before finally tracking down his ex-fiancée who, anticipating his proposal, has gone out to secure a minister. After they're married he discovers the ruse and is initially angry but they reconcile and end in an embrace. Although the woman in *Matrimony's Speed Limit* manipulates her fiancé to marry her, and although she has more money than he does, the film shows that this seeming imbalance in their relationship is ultimately meaningless, as they are clearly emotionally suited to one another. Guy similarly explored the idea of gender equality in several other films, including *Hubby Does the Washing* (Solax 1912) and *A House Divided* (Solax 1913). She addressed gender inversion in a number of films that involve role reversal, as in *Algie the Miner* (Solax 1912), and cross-dressing, as in *Officer Henderson* (Solax 1913).

The "Rough Gals" of Slapstick

The most popular form of comedy through the 1910s was slapstick, with its emphasis on chaos, anarchy, thrills, and gags. Whereas situational comedy of the type performed by Flora Finch and John Bunny and Mr. and Mrs. Sidney Drew was considered "clean," "respectable," and "polite," slapstick was decidedly lowbrow, crass, and often violent, with pies, dishes, furniture, and actors being used as projectiles, and entire companies running amok in chaotic chases. Slapstick comediennes could be seen as exhibiting an especially deviant image of femininity, then, as they rejected traditional feminine qualities such as passivity and diffidence and instead took part in wild brawls alongside their male co-stars. While many comedians, both male and female, wore heavy makeup and bizarre costumes to create instantly identifiable characters and to get easy laughs from the audience, a few comics performed with no character makeup or costumes, instead relying on skillfully performed physical gags for their comedy.

Figure 2.1   Mabel Normand's films showcased her daring stunts as well as her lively personality and girl-next-door beauty.

One of the most popular and successful comediennes of the silent era was Mabel Normand (see Figure 2.1). Normand appeared in over 200 films in the 1910s and 1920s, and although it's difficult to determine exactly how many she directed, there's evidence that she was the director or co-director of somewhere between 15 to 20 of her films (Martin and Segrave 1986: 87; Fussell 1988; King 2009: 305). Her appeal lay in the juxtaposition between her pert beauty and her willingness to engage in even the most violent rough and tumble comedy. Born in 1892 in New York, Normand started her career as an artist's model before making her first film in 1910. She was with Vitagraph for a year (and made at least one film with Flora Finch and John Bunny), and then went to Biograph, where she met Mack Sennett. Normand joined Sennett when he started his own production company, Keystone Studios, in 1912, and it was during her years at Keystone that she had her greatest success, starring in one- and two-reel films co-starring comedians such as Roscoe "Fatty" Arbuckle, Charley Chase, Ford Sterling, Chester Conklin, and Charlie Chaplin. In fact, legend holds that Normand discovered Chaplin when he was performing onstage with a comedy troupe and convinced Sennett to sign him at Keystone. While that story is likely apocryphal, it's widely understood that Normand taught Chaplin a great deal about filmmaking and performing for the camera, and she is known to have directed several of his early films, including

Mabel's Strange Predicament (Keystone 1914), perhaps the first film to feature Chaplin's Little Tramp character (Martin and Segrave 1986: 88).

Normand set up her own company, the Mabel Normand Feature Film Company, in 1916, which produced the feature film *Mickey* in 1918. That same year she signed with Goldwyn, with whom she made 16 features before returning to Mack Sennett's company in 1921. Unfortunately, around this time her name was linked to several scandals, including the murder of director William Desmond Taylor (although she was not implicated in his murder, she was the last person to see him alive). In the late 1920s she made a series of short films for Hal Roach, but by that time years of scandals, drug abuse, and ill health had taken their toll, and she was unable to recapture her earlier success. Normand died from tuberculosis in 1930, at the age of 37.

Normand didn't hesitate to engage in the type of rough-and-tumble slapstick that Keystone specialized in. A typical film might find her throwing punches, being dragged through the mud, driving recklessly, and generally taking part in violent and anarchic gags. In fact, Normand is credited with throwing the screen's first custard pie, at co-star Arbuckle (Unterbrink 1987: 21). In *Mabel's Dramatic Career* (Keystone 1913), Normand plays a small-town girl in love with a boy played by Mack Sennett. When she catches Mack with another girl, Mabel goes berserk, chasing the two around the yard, beating them with a stick, and wringing her rival's neck. Mabel is driven out of town and ends up at the Keystone Studio, hoping to find work, and when she sees the violent action taking place on set she knows she has found her new home. Other films find Normand hitting a prospective suitor (*Barney Oldfield's Race for a Life*, Keystone 1913), shooting her husband (*He Did and He Didn't*, Keystone 1916), and taking part in a wild food fight (*The Ragtime Band*, Keystone 1913). Not all of her comedy was based on these types of gags, of course; she also displayed a vivacious, often flirtatious personality in her films, and a daring athleticism that allowed her to dive from cliffs, race horses, and, in one film, escape a hot-air balloon by sliding down a rope (*Mabel's New Hero*, Keystone 1913).

While many slapstick comediennes donned heavy character makeup and unflattering costumes in their films, Normand's natural beauty was an important element of her persona, and the juxtaposition of her beauty and her daring, violent stunts is what set her apart from many other silent comediennes. It also could create a disjuncture for viewers, because Normand embodied a traditional image of femininity in her appearance but sharply deviated from that image in her onscreen behavior. As Rob King argues, Normand's "screen persona thus offered a heterodox merging of elements typically perceived as incompatible: at once 'classical' (in her beauty) and 'grotesque' (in her slapstick), Normand's screen image unsettled the binarism that sought to contain the spectacle of female comicality" (King 2009: 223).

Normand's feature films, including *What Happened to Rosa?* (Goldwyn 1920), *Molly O'* (Mack Sennett-Mabel Normand Productions 1922), and *The Extra Girl*

Figure 2.2 Louise Fazenda, the "Queen of Screen Comediennes," was known for her rough-and-tumble slapstick.

(Mack Sennett Comedies 1923), blend situation-based comedy with slapstick, and although she is good with light comedy, the physical sequences are where she truly excels.

For a period of more than 25 years, from the 1910s through the 1930s, Louise Fazenda (see Figure 2.2) reigned as one of the funniest and most popular comedians, male or female, in American film. During this period she made well over 200 films, both dramas and comedies, and successfully transitioned from silents to talkies. In 1927 she was described in the press as the "Queen of Screen Comediennes" (Louise Fazenda, Queen of Screen Comediennes, to Play Opposite Will Rogers, ca. 1927), and by the late 1930s she was considered one of the more successful of the silent stars who were making sound films. Louise Fazenda was born around 1896 in Lafayette, Indiana, and raised in Los Angeles, where her family owned a grocery store. She began her film career after graduating from high school in 1913, working first as an extra in westerns for Universal, and soon after playing in Universal's "Joker" comedy unit. In 1915 she signed with Mack Sennett's Keystone Company where, over the next seven years, she was in approximately 50 films, appearing with Arbuckle, Ben Turpin, Mae Busch, and Charlie Murray, and co-starring with Mack Swain in a series of "Ambrose" films. Fazenda's early career was defined by knockabout slapstick roles but by the 1920s she was increasingly moving away from that type of film, although she continued to appear in comedies. Throughout the 1920s she played a wide variety of comedic roles, both lead and supporting, in shorts as well as features. She played flappers and wisecracking chorus girls in a number of films, and at the same time she continued to play her well known farm-girl role in a number of films, including a 1928 remake of *Tillie's Punctured Romance* co-starring W.C. Fields for the Christie Film Company. Fazenda was mostly a supporting player in the 1930s, although she had leading roles in a number of B movies. She retired from the screen in 1939, and died in 1962.

Fazenda's on-screen persona varied throughout her career, but she was primarily known for playing awkward country-bumpkin types with names like Lizzie or Daisy or Tillie. While she was with Keystone she developed a costume that consisted of an ill-fitting gingham dress and pantalettes, with her hair pulled tightly back from her forehead and twisted into wild pigtails – which Mack Sennett insured for $10 000 – and a large curl in the center of her forehead. She wore a guileless deadpan when presented with difficult situations, and her response to romantic entanglements was generally either giddy flirtation, or clocking the unlucky suitor with a blunt object. She would also occasionally appear onscreen without her character makeup. While working for Keystone Fazenda was a physical comedienne, engaging in the knockabout slapstick that was the studio's trademark. In 1918 *Photoplay* dubbed her the "Pie Queen" (Squier 1918), and her reputation for roughhousing followed her throughout her career. A 1938 article described her in terms usually reserved for heavyweight champions:

> Ever since she started out in Mack Sennett comedies away back when a custard pie in the face was a mere love tap, she has been building up a reputation as a quality bruiser … The movie public has come to regard her as an unpredictable cross between Mother Hubbard and Strangler Lewis – the sort of full-rigged female who, if she happened to stand up all of a sudden in a crowd, you couldn't be altogether sure whether she was going to start a community sing or offer to wrastle any guy in the place for $5. (Crowther 1939)

Fazenda's use of character makeup and costumes was typical for slapstick comediennes at this time. Unlike Mabel Normand, whose attractiveness created dissonance when paired with her physically violent routines, Fazenda's costumes and makeup complemented her actions onscreen. In some ways she, and other comediennes whose onscreen personae were defined by homeliness, were confirming the stereotype that held that femininity and a sense of humor were incompatible because their exaggerated features and unruly performances removed them from the ideal conception of femininity to such a degree that critics who argued that women couldn't be funny could feel safe when watching them. At the same time, by donning outlandish costumes and makeup, they were, in a sense, challenging the notion that women would even want to conform to conventional femininity in the first place. While comediennes like Flora Finch made jokes about their actual appearance, for Fazenda it was her *character's* appearance that elicited laughter. When Fazenda and others, including Polly Moran, Alice Howell, and Gale Henry, put on bizarre costumes and makeup to perform physical comedy, they were making a conscious choice to deviate from society's expectations for women in both their looks and their actions.

Like Louise Fazenda, Polly Moran was known for her outlandish costumes and characterizations and her performance of rough-and-tumble slapstick. Born in Chicago in 1883, Moran dropped out of high school to join a touring opera company, but within a few years left opera for vaudeville. In vaudeville she worked as a singing comedienne, building her solo act around comic songs, wisecracks, stories, and, most of all, her personality. With its emphasis on wisecracks, personality, and audience interaction, Moran's act was perfectly suited to the demands of vaudeville in the first decades of the twentieth century, which favored fast-paced, assertive comedy. While many comedians, both male and female, used physical comedy on stage, Moran relied primarily on verbal comedy in her act. Around 1913 Moran moved to California and began appearing in silent films, ultimately signing with Keystone, where she starred in a series of films as Sheriff Nell, a boisterous law woman charged with maintaining order in the Wild West. These films were very successful and by 1917 Moran was the highest paid comedienne at Keystone. As slapstick gave way to light comedy in the 1920s Moran's popularity began to fade, and she spent much of the decade playing small supporting roles until she was paired with Marie Dressler in the 1927 MGM feature *The Callahans and the Murphys*. Although this film was famously pulled from release due to widespread outrage over its unfavorable portrayals of Irish characters, Moran and Dressler remained as partners in a series of shorts and features until 1932. Afterwards, Moran worked sporadically, primarily in character parts, until her death in 1952.

Early in Moran's film career it's clear that she and the studio had not yet settled on her image but by 1917 she had established her new persona as a knockabout comedienne. During her years at Keystone she became known for her demanding and dangerous stunts, especially in the Sheriff Nell series of one-reel comedies from the late 1910s and early 1920s. A 1917 magazine article described the types of gags and stunts she performed in her films:

> She rides a horse with the reckless abandon that would make Bill Hart look like a nursery jockey. Upstairs, downstairs, over cliffs, from one towering ledge to another – that's the sort of horse tricks she executes. And she can wield her fists as fast and as effectively as any man you ever saw. She has no aversion to leaping head foremost into a crowd of some twenty gangsters and then cleaning out the entire set. And she can handle a lariat with dexterous skill. Does she rope one object at a time? She does not! She ropes twenty and thirty with one movement, and just to demonstrate her strength, she pulls them all through the city streets and lodges them in jail. (Polly Moran ca. 1917)

Soon after embarking on her film career she began billing herself as "Polly" rather than the more elegant sounding "Pauline," an indication that she was fully embracing her lowbrow wild woman image. In her films with Marie Dressler, Moran's characters were designed to complement those played by Dressler, as Moran plays a string of disagreeable women whose stubbornness and selfishness create problems that Dressler's long-suffering characters are forced to rectify. These films combine physical and verbal comedy, with the two actresses verbally sparring and playing off of one another as well as taking plenty of pratfalls. In these films "Polly's comeuppance would be in the form of slapstick indignities – a cake in the face, a plunge in a mud bath, and so on. She supplied the low laughs, while Marie provided the heart in such films" (Martin and Segrave 1986: 99).

Marie Dressler was a major star on Broadway and in vaudeville in the late nineteenth and early twentieth centuries, known as much for her broad physical comedy as for her homely appearance. Born in 1869 in Cobourg, Ontario, Canada, Dressler was a self-described "ugly duckling," with a large figure and a plain face. She began touring with various theatrical troupes as a teenager, and then moved on to music hall and vaudeville, where she learned how to incorporate physical comedy into her routines. In 1914 Mack Sennett asked Dressler to star in a loose adaptation of her Broadway play *Tillie's Nightmare*. The film, *Tillie's Punctured Romance* (Keystone 1914) was, at six-reels long, the first full-length slapstick comedy ever filmed, and was a tremendous success for Dressler and her co-stars, Mabel Normand and Charlie Chaplin. Dressler made two sequels to *Tillie's Punctured Romance*, *Tillie's Tomato Surprise* (Lubin 1915) and *Tillie Wakes Up* (Peerless 1917), and then founded her own company, the Marie Dressler Motion Picture Company, which produced four films for her to star in in 1917 and 1918. Dressler's career foundered in the early 1920s for a variety of reasons, including her support of a contentious actors' strike in 1919, which may have caused her to be blacklisted among theater owners, and because her brand of broad physical comedy was falling out of vogue. She had difficulty finding a job on stage or in films for several years, but she enjoyed a resurgence beginning with 1927's *The Callahans and the Murphys*, co-starring Polly Moran. Her comeback was complete by the early 1930s, when she was one of the top-grossing box office stars in Hollywood and ultimately won an Oscar for Best Actress for her performance in *Min and Bill* (MGM 1930). After this career resurgence, Dressler remained extremely popular until her death in 1934. Her films feature a great deal of physical comedy, made even more remarkable by her excessive size. She was surprisingly agile given her weight, and had a remarkably expressive face. While in her earlier slapsticks she relied heavily on pratfalls and mugging, in her later films, including those she made with Polly Moran, she infused pathos into her performances.

Stan Laurel once referred to Alice Howell as one of the greatest comediennes of all time (Slide 1998: 79). Born in New York in 1888, Howell was an established performer in musical comedy and vaudeville, where she had an act with her husband.

She signed with Keystone in 1914 and appeared primarily in supporting roles, often in Mabel Normand vehicles. In 1915 Howell moved to L-KO where she was made a leading lady; she later signed with Century Comedies, Reelcraft, and Universal. By the 1920s she was mostly seen in cameos in feature films, and, having never really enjoyed film work, retired in the mid-1920s and died in 1961. While working at L-KO Howell developed a scrubwoman character that she used in many of her slapstick shorts. Her costume consisted of a long skirt and large, unflattering blouse, with well-worn boots and a mass of fizzy blonde hair piled high on her head. She was generally unflappable in her films, keeping a blank stare or a vacant smile through whatever chaos was occurring around her. In *Cinderella Cinders* (Reelcraft 1920), she plays a cook working for a wealthy family. When the family discovers that the Count and Countess they've invited to a party they're throwing have to cancel at the last minute, they decide to pass off the cook and the butler (played by Howell's husband, Richard Smith) as the honored guests. The counterfeit Count and Countess do their best to imitate high society, even after getting drunk on some spiked punch. Howell remains stiffly formal and completely unfazed throughout the ruse, even when she is having difficulty staying on her feet. She is similarly unflappable in *One Wet Night* (Universal 1924), playing a middle-class wife throwing a dinner party. When the house becomes inundated with water due to a torrential rainstorm, she still remains imperturbable, maintaining a cheerily vacant expression throughout. Described as a "rough gal" in the press, Howell was known for willingly taking part in even the most wild and anarchic physical comedy (*She's a Rough Gal* 1917).

Born in Bear Valley, California, Gale Henry (1893–1972) moved to Los Angeles as a teenager and began a career in comic opera and musical comedy. Henry signed with Universal's Joker Comedy unit in 1914, where she frequently appeared in films alongside Louise Fazenda. In 1915 she starred in the popular *Lady Baffles and Detective Duck* series, produced by Powers Comedies, and in 1918 she opened her own production company, Gale's Model Comedies. Henry worked as a writer, director, and producer at various points throughout her career, and acted in films throughout the silent and early sound eras, making her last film in 1933. Tall and lanky with an elastic face, she specialized in awkward, gawky types, often spinsters or shrewish wives. In *The Detectress* (Model Comedies 1919), Henry plays Lizzie, an amateur detective who sets out to uncover a crime ring, and along the way gets involved in madcap chases, fights, and pratfalls. *Her First Flame* (Model Comedies 1920) is similarly broad. The film is set in the futuristic world of 1950 when women and men have exchanged roles, with, as a title card tell us, "the women earning the bacon while the men take care of the offsprings." Henry plays Lizzie Hap, an excitable woman running for fire chief. After fixing the election, Lizzie wins, but she is too busy romancing her boyfriend, Willie, to fight fires. When Lizzie's rival locks Willie in a burning building, Lizzie and her team of female firefighters come to the rescue, and although Lizzie is thoroughly incompetent in the face of an emergency, her fire brigade saves the day and she is reconciled with her sweetheart.

Henry's typical costume was a long skirt and a blouse or jacket with sleeves that were too short, making her arms look longer, hair pulled back into a tight bun to emphasize her long face, with soap caked in her bangs to make them stick out (Webster 1920). Although Henry's costumes and makeup are not quite as excessive as Fazenda or Howell, they were deliberately chosen to emphasize her tall, angular frame, and her exaggerated, gawky movements. Her pairing with smaller leading men, served the same purpose.

There were numerous other slapstick comediennes working during the silent era, such as Alice Davenport, Phyllis Allen, Blanche Payson, and Dot Farley, who engaged in knockabout comedy and pratfalls. By performing this type of comedy these women were resisting the cultural imperative that women should be passive and demure, and instead embracing unruliness. However, the fact that many comediennes either based their comedy on their own deviance from conventionally defined beauty standards, while other comediennes made themselves up to be homely onscreen, somewhat mitigated their transgressiveness, as they were to some extent acceding to the notion that comedy and traditionally defined femininity were incompatible. This is especially evident when these comediennes are contrasted with Mack Sennett's Bathing Beauties, a group of women that appeared in numerous Keystone films beginning in 1916. The primary purpose of the Bathing Beauties was to look pretty, leaving the comic heavy lifting to the comedians, both male and female. The introduction of the Bathing Beauties does seem to reinforce the stereotype that women could be either funny or pretty, but not both. While some slapstick comediennes, such as Mabel Normand, refuted that stereotype, others seemed to confirm it, and yet, either way, these comediennes were pushing boundaries to varying degrees, and proving that women could be funny.

Flappers, Flirts, and "Polite" Comedy

While slapstick was an extremely popular form of comedy, it was looked down upon by many as coarse and lowbrow, labels that many women, including comediennes, naturally wanted to avoid. Furthermore, gag-driven films, which had been popular since the very beginnings of cinema, seemed dated by the late 1910s. As films grew longer, and narrative supplanted attraction-based cinema, slapstick gave way to light comedy, also described as "refined" or "polite" comedy. This type of comedy was based around situations rather than gags, and physical comedy was used sparingly, if at all. Writer Anita Loos, who wrote screenplays for numerous films starring Fay Tincher and Constance Talmadge, among others, advocated for light comedy that would be "a comedy of ideas," in which "the action grows naturally out of the thoughts and emotions of the main characters" (The Coming Film Comedy of Ideas 1919). Of course, slapstick didn't go away entirely, and filmmakers such as Mack Sennett continued to make knockabout physical comedies throughout the 1920s. Even in feature-length light comedies slapstick would occasionally appear, although the gags were incorporated into the narrative, rather than being the entire purpose of the films. As light comedy began to gain prominence, a new breed of comediennes cropped up, some of whom had never appeared in slapstick, and some of whom were only too happy to put their rough-and-tumble days behind them and move on to polite comedy.

Constance Talmadge, the youngest of a trio of sisters who appeared in silent films, was one of the most popular light comediennes of the time. While her older sister Norma Talmadge was the tragedienne of the family, Constance preferred comedy (the middle sister, Natalie, appeared occasionally in films and was married to Buster Keaton). Born around 1897 in New York, Constance entered pictures after her sister Norma's star was already on the rise. Both sisters started with Vitagraph, but soon moved to Los Angeles and signed with D.W. Griffith, where Constance gained fame as the Mountain Girl in Griffith's *Intolerance* (Triangle 1916). In 1919 she formed her own production company, the Constance Talmadge Film Company, and proceeded to make a string of slightly racy comedies, many of which were written by the husband-and-wife team of Anita Loos and John Emerson. Both Constance and Norma retired from film after the advent of sound, and Constance died in 1973.

Constance Talmadge's appeal lay in her lively personality and high energy. The comedy in her films was almost all situational and plot driven, with very little slapstick. Young and pretty, with blonde hair and large brown eyes, Talmadge played characters who were playful, energetic, and flirtatious. Many of her comedies were bedroom farces where sex was suggested, but Talmadge's characters were always good girls at heart and their relationships with men never progressed beyond innocent flirtation. The title of her 1919 film, *A Virtuous Vamp* (Constance Talmadge Film Company) captures her onscreen persona perfectly, as a good-bad girl who flirts with men but insists on marriage. In *The Duchess of Buffalo* (Constance Talmadge Film Company 1926) she plays a dancer who is first seen on stage in a Salomé-inspired dance involving dropping veils from her costume one at a time. The film cuts to the men in the audience leering at her through binoculars, eagerly waiting for her to remove the last veil but, before she can, her boyfriend rushes backstage and stops her. He apologizes to her for interrupting her act, explaining that he just got excited, and she responds "You must pardon me, dearest – for having excited you." The double entendre here is not subtle, but Talmadge's wide-eyed delivery confirms for the audience that, despite her racy dance, she is actually quite innocent. While a sexually knowing woman may have been viewed as threatening by audience members who clung to the idea of female purity, Talmadge's threat is mitigated by the fact that she flirts with, but never quite arrives at, illicit sexuality.

Like Constance Talmadge, Colleen Moore (1899–1988) primarily starred in light comedies as a flirtatious but innocent ingénue (see Figure 2.3). Moore's film career began in 1917 when D.W. Griffith signed her to his Triangle-Fine Arts studio as a

Figure 2.3 Colleen Moore's carefree flapper—with her trademark bobbed hair—appeared in films as a "good little bad girl."

favor to her uncle, who was the managing editor of the *Chicago Examiner*. Moore's early films were mostly dramas and light comedies, and, because of her youth, which was accentuated by her long, Mary Pickford-esque curls, she often played children, including the title role in *Little Orphant Annie* (Selig 1918). Throughout the late 1910s she had mostly supporting roles in films with Fox, Universal, and Famous Players-Lasky, and then, deciding that she needed to learn how to play comedy, Moore made several films for the Christie Film Company starting in 1919. In 1923 Moore cut her hair to what would become her trademark style, a Dutch bob with thick bangs, to play the flapper lead in the drama *Flaming Youth* (First National 1923). With her new haircut and her new persona as a vivacious flapper, she followed *Flaming Youth* with a string of films that emphasized her comic abilities and her youthful, carefree personality. She alternated between comic and dramatic features throughout the 1920s, and made a few early sound films before retiring in 1934.

In Moore's comedies she plays irrepressible young women who have a difficult time containing their excessive energy. Her characters are frequently working girls, and the comedy in the films often stems from class issues as she's thrust into high society. In *Her Wild Oat* (First National 1927), she plays a lunch truck owner who spends her savings to vacation at a posh resort. Once there, she contrives to pass herself off as a duchess in order to fit in with the wealthy vacationers, performing a working-class version of upper-class manners. Similarly, in *Irene* (First National 1926), she plays a department store worker who is chosen to appear in a society fashion show. She almost succeeds at passing herself off as a high-class model but is exposed when her decidedly low-class family crashes the fashion show. In these films, and in others, Moore's boundless energy is presented as a welcome antidote to stuffy high society. Her comedies, like Constance Talmadge's, are based on situation and personality rather than slapstick, although there are occasionally sight gags and some physical comedy in her films. In *Ella Cinders* (John McCormick Productions 1926), for example, Moore plays Ella, a small-town girl who longs to be a movie star. Prompted by a book on movie acting, Ella practices "the art of expressing every emotion with the eyes," starting with "Flirtatious" and "Love." When the book suggests that actors should be able to look cross-eyed, Ella crosses her eyes, and then – with the help of a split screen – each eye dances wildly around, independent of the other, in an amusing visual gag. Gags such as these occur throughout Moore's films, along with the light comedy that she was known for.

While some light comediennes, such as Constance Talmadge and Colleen Moore, played flirtatious but innocent "good little bad girls," Clara Bow played characters who were unapologetically sexual. Bow was born in a Brooklyn tenement in 1905 to an absentee father and a mentally unstable mother. Longing to escape into the world of movies, in 1921 she entered the Fame and Fortune Contest, a competition run by *Motion Picture* magazine to discover new talent. Bow won the contest and was awarded a bit part in a feature film, a part that ended up on the cutting room floor. She had some difficulty finding a second job after this film, but eventually landed a supporting role in *Down to the Sea in Ships* (Whaling Film Corp. 1922), which earned her positive notices and led to more work, and in 1923 she signed with B.P. Schulberg Productions. For the next few years she played a variety of flappers, vamps, and other sexualized, free-spirited types in dramas and comedies for Schulberg and a number of other production companies, until signing with Famous Players-Lasky/Paramount in 1926. Her career-defining role came in *It* (Famous Players-Lasky 1927), in which she played Betty Lou Spence, a vivacious shopgirl in love with her boss. Bow was dubbed "The 'It' Girl" after this film, "It" referring to a quality of unselfconscious, uninhibited sexual charisma that Betty Lou – and Bow herself – was said to possess. She made a number of sound films, with her last appearance in 1933, and died in 1965, at the age of 60.

There are few sight gags and almost no slapstick in Bow's comedies; instead the comedy is entirely derived from situations, title cards, and Bow's effervescent personality. Her frank sexuality was foregrounded in her films, setting her apart from other light comediennes, but like other light comediennes, sex for Bow's characters was always lighthearted and fun. In *It*, when Betty Lou first spots her boss, her eyes fill with desire and she pleads, "Sweet Santa Claus, give me *him*!" She then sets in motion a plan to win her boss, and succeeds, in large part due to her sexual

Figure 2.4 Although she starred in numerous dramas throughout her career, Marion Davies was a gifted comedienne. She is shown here in a still from *Tillie the Toiler* (producer, Cosmopolitan Production)

attractiveness. In other comedies, such as *Mantrap* (Famous Players-Lasky 1926) and *Hula* (Paramount Famous Lasky Corp. 1927), Bow plays characters who are similarly determined to conquer the objects of their desire. Her energy onscreen is electrifying; she is constantly in motion, unable to hold still for even a moment. The implication that she is controlled by her body rather than by her mind or heart adds to her erotic appeal and makes her performances all the more transgressive, as a woman who was comic as well as unapologetically sexual could be especially threatening to those who were already uncomfortable with women who didn't adhere to traditional gender roles.

Although the majority of Marion Davies' (1897–1961) films were dramas, she starred in several light comedies in the 1920s and 1930s (see Figure 2.4). She began her career as a model and chorus girl in Broadway revues, including the Ziegfeld *Follies*. Davies met newspaper magnate William Randolph Hearst in 1917, and shortly thereafter Hearst formed the Marion Davies Film Corporation to produce films for her to star in. She starred in a variety of dramas, romances, costume dramas, and comedies throughout the 1920s for Hearst's Cosmopolitan Production as well as MGM, and continued making films after the introduction of sound, overcoming a slight stammer that she had since childhood. Her sound films were not very successful, and she made her last film in 1937, a comedy titled *Ever Since Eve*.

Contemporary audiences are most likely familiar with Davies because of her 34-year relationship with Hearst, and she is often conflated with the character of Susan Kane from *Citizen Kane* (Mercury Productions 1941), the untalented wife of Charles Foster Kane (a thinly veiled depiction of Hearst) whom he tries to set up as an opera star. While Hearst did in fact support Davies' career, and financed most of her films, she was an accomplished actress and an especially talented comedienne in her own right. In later years Orson Welles, the writer and director of *Citizen Kane*, acknowledged as much, saying that he "shares much of the blame for casting [a] shadow" on Davies' career, and proclaiming that "Marion Davies was one of the most delightfully accomplished comediennes in the whole history of the screen. She would have been a star if Hearst had never happened" (Welles 1975). Indeed, Hearst's efforts to bolster Davies' career may have done more harm than good, as his newspapers' relentless publicity likely caused both fans and critics to question whether she could be a star in her own right, and his insistence that she star in turgid dramas and staid period pieces failed to make use of her considerable comedic abilities.

Despite Hearst's efforts to make Davies a dramatic star, her forte was clearly light comedy, as is evident in films such as *Show People* (MGM 1928), *The Patsy* (Cosmopolitan 1928), and *The Cardboard Lover* (Cosmopolitan 1928). In *Show People*, she plays Peggy Pepper, a naive Southern belle who comes to Hollywood expecting to become a great dramatic actress but ends up starring in slapstick shorts. Peggy eventually graduates from comedy to high-class dramas, and in the process loses her sense of fun and vivacity, as the lively Peggy Pepper becomes the snooty Patricia Pepoire. Davies' slapstick scenes, involving thrown pies, seltzer water in the face, chases, and pratfalls are expertly done, and her portrayal of Patricia Pepoire – which bears more than a slight resemblance to silent star Gloria Swanson – is a skilled send up of highbrow culture. Davies' gift for impersonation, which is seen in *Show People*, is on full display in *The Patsy* (which also stars Marie Dressler). As a mousy girl named Pat, she decides that she needs to acquire a personality, and so she attempts to imitate several stars, including Lillian Gish, Mae Murray, and Pola Negri. Each impersonation is spot on, and this scene, along with other scenes in which Pat tries to cultivate a personality using self-help books, is an excellent showcase for Davies' comic talents.

Like many other silent stars, Fay Tincher (1884–1983) began her career on the stage, playing in vaudeville and musical theater before starting in motion pictures in 1913. Her first notable role was as a vamp in the D.W. Griffith drama *The Battle of the Sexes* (Majestic 1914), but after making a few more dramas she settled upon comedies. Beginning in 1914 she starred as Ethel, a gum-chewing stenographer in the popular "Bill the office boy" comedy series for Komic. In an attempt to create an eye-catching costume for her Ethel character, Tincher decided to outfit her entirely in black and white stripes, a look that soon became closely identified with both Ethel and Tincher, who became known as "The Girl o' the Stripes" (Fay Tincher 1918). She appeared in a variety of slapstick shorts and light comedies with several companies, including Keystone and Christie, in the 1910s, and formed her own company, "Fay Tincher Productions, in 1917, releasing her films through the World Film Corporation. From 1923 to 1938 she starred as Min Gump in a series of films based on the comic strip "The Gumps." Tincher blended physical and situational comedy and although Ethel's look was highly stylized it was tame compared to the deliberately unattractive costumes used by Fazenda, Henry, Howell, and other character comediennes. In *Rowdy Ann* (Christie 1919), Tincher plays Ann, a cowgirl growing up on her father's ranch out west. Fearing that she's too rough around the edges, Ann's father sends her to boarding school to become more refined. Initially Ann resists the school's attempts to civilize her, at one point wearing cowboy boots and bringing a pistol to a classical dance class. Even though she is eventually outwardly reformed, she still has enough of the Wild West in her to thwart a con man who is attempting to swindle her friend. Tincher uses some physical comedy in this film – including outboxing a cowhand in a bar, and, on a train, shooting at a porter whom she mistakes as a suitor – but for the most part the laughs stem from situations rather than slapstick.

Dorothy Devore (1899–1976) was one of several women, including Bebe Daniels and Fay Tincher, who were vocal in their disdain for knockabout slapstick in favor of what was termed "polite comedy." Devore made it clear in the press that she was not interested in engaging in the wild, anarchic comedy that had been popular in the 1910s, and yet she often incorporated physical comedy into her films. In *Hold Your Breath* (Christie 1924), Devore plays Mabel, a newspaper reporter who runs madly about the city in pursuit of a story. After a complicated turn of events she ends up chasing a monkey who has stolen a valuable bracelet as it scales the side of a building. Devore did most of her own stunts in this film, including crawling along a ledge several stories high, and swinging from a broken awning far above the street. Still, Devore was primarily a light comedienne, often appearing in romantic comedies or farces.

Conclusion

Given the large numbers of women who were performing comedy in the silent era, and their tremendous talent in both slapstick and light comedies, it is astonishing that almost every one of them has been forgotten. The fact that so many silent films have been lost over the years accounts for some of this neglect, but it is likely that longstanding misogynistic stereotypes about women's inability to perform comedy are a significant reason why these women have been excluded from the canon of great silent comedians. Women in the silent era engaged in all types of comedy, from knockabout slapstick to polite comedy, and were some of the most popular and successful stars of their time. The advent of sound brought new opportunities for funny women onscreen, as stars such as Katharine Hepburn,

Myrna Loy, Mae West, Jean Harlow, Carole Lombard, and Jean Arthur excelled in spoken comedy, spouting one liners and verbally sparring with their male co-stars. Television similarly created an outlet for comediennes, from Lucille Ball, Gracie Allen, and Eve Arden in the 1950s, to Mary Tyler Moore, Carol Burnett, Roseanne Barr, and Tina Fey in later years. Whether appearing in movies, television, or on stage, later comediennes owe a debt of gratitude to those who appeared in silent film. Silent comediennes showed that women were capable of being funny, that femininity was not antithetical to a sense of humor. Hopefully, as their films are rediscovered and find a new audience, the work of these boundary-breaking women will finally be recognized and appreciated.

References

Agee, James (2001) Comedy's greatest era, in *The Film Comedy Reader* (ed. Gregg Rickman), Limelight Editions, New York, NY.

Barreca, Regina (ed.) (1988) *Last Laughs, Perspectives on Women and Comedy*, Gordon & Breach, New York, NY.

Bergson, Henri (1956) *Laughter, in Comedy* (ed. Wylie Sypher), The Johns Hopkins University Press, Baltimore, MD.

Clara Bow Got $50.00 per Week in First Role (1928) Unidentified clipping, Clara Bow clipping file, Academy of Motion Picture Arts and Sciences (November 4).

Color Biography of Clara Bow (1932) Clara Bow clipping file, Academy of Motion Picture Arts and Sciences (July).

Crowther, Bosley (ca. 1939) Ladeez and Ge'men, in this Corner. Unidentified clipping, Louise Fazenda clipping file, New York Public Library.

Fay Tincher (1918) *Motion Picture Classic*. Fay Tincher clipping file, New York Public Library (February).

From the Screen Shops (1919) *New York Times* (July 6), p. 40.

Fussell, Betty (1988) The Films of Mabel Normand. *Film History*, 2 (4), 373–91.

Gray, Frances (1994) *Women and Laughter*, University Press of Virginia, Charlottesville, VA.

Kelly, Kitty (1914) "Silent Comedy" is put on Movie Films. *Chicago Daily Tribune* (14 August), p. 8.

King, Rob (2009) *The Fun Factory: The Keystone Film Company and the Emergence of Mass Culture*, University of California Press, Berkeley, CA.

Louise Fazenda, Queen of Screen Comediennes, to Play Opposite Will Rogers (ca. 1927) Unidentified clipping, Louise Fazenda clipping file, New York Public Library.

Martin, Linda and Segrave, Kerry (1986) *Women in Comedy*, Citadel Press, Seacaucus, NJ.

Polly Moran (ca. 1917) Unidentified clipping, Polly Moran clipping file, New York Public Library.

Rowe, Kathleen (1995) *The Unruly Woman: Gender and the Genres of Laughter*, University of Texas Press, Austin, TX.

She's a Rough Gal (1917) *Photoplay* (August), p. 133.

Slide, Anthony (1998) *Eccentrics of Comedy*, The Scarecrow Press, Inc., Lanhan, MD.

Squier, Emma Lindsay (1918) Pies is Pizen! *Photoplay Art* (September), Louise Fazenda clipping file, New York Public Library.

The Coming Film Comedy of Ideas (1919) *The Christian Science Monitor* (November 4), p. 16.

Tinee, Mae (1920) Right Off the Reel. *Chicago Daily Tribune* (April 4), p. D2.

Unterbrink, Mary (1987) *Funny Women: American Comediennes, 1860-1985*, McFarland & Company, Inc., Jefferson, NC.

Walker, Nancy A. (1988) *A Very Serious Thing: Women's Humor and American Culture*, University of Minnesota Press, Minneapolis, MN.

Webster, Dorothy Faith (1920) The Bear Facts About Gale Henry. *Photoplay* (January), n.p., Gale Henry clipping file, New York Public Library.

Welles, Orson (1975) Foreword to Marion Davies, *The Times We Had: Life with William Randolph Hearst*, Ballantine Books, New York, NY.

Welter, Barbara (1966) The cult of true womanhood: 1820-1860. *American Quarterly*, 18 (2:1), 151–74.

Further Reading

Glenn, Susan A. (2000) *Female Spectacle: The Theatrical Roots of Modern Feminism*, Harvard University Press, Cambridge, MA. This excellent book includes a discussion and analysis of female comics working on stage in the late nineteenth and early twentieth centuries.

Louvish, Simon (2003) *Keystone: The Life and Clowns of Mack Sennett*, Faber & Faber, Inc., New York, NY. An accessible and entertaining history of the Keystone Studio.

Massa, Steve (n.d.) Alice Howell and Gale Henry, Queens of Eccentric Comedy. *Griffithiana* 73/74, 95–139. Provides detailed information about the careers of Howell and Henry, including a complete filmography for both.

McMahan, Alison (2002) *Alice Guy Blaché: Lost Visionary of the Cinema*. Continuum, New York, NY. A biography of the director with a discussion of her films and a complete filmography.

Moore, Colleen (1968) *Silent Star* Doubleday & Company, Inc., Garden City, New York, NY. Moore's autobiography is a lively account of the comedienne's years in silent films.

Stenn, David (2000) *Clara Bow: Runnin' Wild*, Cooper Square Press, New York, NY. A fascinating biography detailing the life of the silent film star.

Sturtevant, Victoria (2009) *A Great Big Girl Like Me: The Films of Marie Dressler*, University of Illinois Press, Urbana, IL. Provides a thoughtful analysis of Dressler's persona and film career.

Wagner, Kristen Anderson (2011) "Have women a sense of humor?" Comedy and femininity in early twentieth-century film. *The Velvet Light Trap*, 68, 35–46. This offers a discussion of debates surrounding comedy and femininity around the turn of the century.

3

"Sound Came Along and Out Went the Pies"

The American Slapstick Short and the Coming of Sound

Rob King

"To put it unkindly": Sound and the Historiography of Film Comedy

The story of sound's impact on the American slapstick tradition has traditionally been framed as a decline – a falling off, as it is often framed, from the beauties of silent pantomime toward the blunt physicality of, say, the Three Stooges. "To put it unkindly" – James Agee wrote in his famous 1949 *Life* essay, "Comedy's Greatest Era" – "the only thing wrong with screen comedy today is that it takes place on a screen which talks" (Agee 1958: 4). The explanatory framework is one familiar from classical film theory, pitting the putative realism of sound at loggerheads with an idea of art and judging sound an obstacle to the artistic possibilities of comic performance. It is a perception that Charlie Chaplin clearly shared, declaring in 1929 that talkies were "ruining the great beauty of silence" and famously avoiding synchronized dialogue until his 1940 Hitler parody, *The Great Dictator* (Lynn 1997: 321). And it is a position that critic Walter Kerr would strike decades later, in his landmark 1975 study *The Silent Clowns*, in language frequently echoing the work of film theorist Rudolph Arnheim. "Logically, art begins in a taking away," Kerr argued, continuing, "Each limitation on the camera's power to reproduce reality … [paved] the way to an exercise of art" (Kerr 1975: 3, 25). Compare Arnheim's 1933 *Film as Art*, which argued that cinematic artistry depends on "robbing the real event of something" – on withholding color, three-dimensionality, and sound – and

A Companion to Film Comedy, First Edition. Edited by Andrew Horton and Joanna E. Rapf.
© 2013 John Wiley & Sons, Inc. Published 2016 by John Wiley & Sons, Inc.

that silent film therefore "derives definite artistic possibilities from its silence" (Arnheim 2004: 330, 331). For slapstick, Kerr suggested, this distance from reality became the very foundation of the form's achievement as fantasy: the appeal of the silent clowns rested not merely in their silence, but in their broader liberation from the laws of the ordinary physical world. "None of the limitations of the silent screen ... seemed limitations to its comedians. Rather, they seemed opportunities for slipping ever more elaborately through the cogs of the cosmic machinery, escaping the indignities of a dimensional, hostile universe. Fly through the transom when a policeman locks the door? Why not?" (Kerr 1975:48).

The argument that sound killed the art of slapstick has been a hugely prevalent one, and there can be no doubt that comic filmmakers experienced this transition as a challenge of the first order. What can be queried, however, are the terms through which that challenge was originally understood and experienced. Recognizing Arnheim's influence on Kerr, for instance, immediately exposes the historical limitations of the latter's perspective; for it assesses comedy according to a notion of "art" (itself historically circumscribed) to which few comedians and comic filmmakers of the era would have subscribed, and, as such, brackets off entirely the standards and goals by which those filmmakers were, for the most part, guided. Similarly, while Agee's nostalgic evocations of the "dreamlike beauty" of the great silent pantomimists finds some confirmation in Chaplin's claims to the "beauty of silence," it remains the case that Chaplin was somewhat of a pretentious exception within the field of American slapstick; and that pantomime, when it was discussed by these comedians, was typically approached in practical terms as a matter of *action*, rather than as an issue of *beauty*. Indeed, amidst the great complexity of slapstick filmmakers' transition to the production of talking pictures, three facts about the aesthetic implications of sound technology stand out. First, with very few exceptions, those filmmakers were primarily preoccupied not with an idea of *art* – the concern of later critics such as Agee and Kerr – but instead with sound's implications for comic pace and tempo. Second, in the case of those exceptions, it was sound – particularly *dialogue* – and not silence, to which the concept of art was most commonly attached. Third, and finally, the impact of sound was ultimately to reinforce and invigorate longstanding distinctions separating slapstick comedy from more "sophisticated" comic styles, as each approach came to be codified through a different use of sound technology. Accordingly, this chapter will reconstruct the challenges of sound as they appeared to comic filmmakers at the time rather than view those challenges with the critical distance of hindsight; and it focuses its analysis, not on the well-known feature-length comedians, whose great stardom tended to generate idiosyncratic pathways into the new era, but on the product that provided American screen comedy with its foundations: the one- and two-reel slapstick short.

"The artistry of the Actor in Delivering the Spoken Lines": Playlets and the Uses of Dialogue

Writing in March 1930, the *Exhibitors Herald-World*'s Broadway columnist, Peter Vischer, offered a witty description of developments in short-subject comedies since the coming of sound. "Sound came along and out went the pies," Vischer began:

> No longer was it possible for the average American male mind, aged 14, to enjoy the spectacle of features emerging from a gouey [*sic*] crust or to project himself, figuratively, into the person who was giving the other person, usually a Mr. Milktoast, a lusty boot in the slats. No, sound had come in and the day of the [vaudeville] act arrived.
>
> Mr. Picture-Goer, for his comedy entertainment, had to watch a vaudeville actor play the banjo and sing songs that should have been burned years ago ...
>
> Then came another change. Producers woke up to the fact that acts were not exactly hot; that what might be considered the novelty of sound was no excuse for bum vaudeville. They began to put into the production of their short subjects the same happy robustness that marked them before the microphone reared its trembling magnet before the stuttering player.
>
> Pies actually came into use again. Now you can hear them plop, as well as see them squash. Not that pies are prevalent today; but the spirit that prompted them is. Short comedies have retrieved their schoolboy virility. They are alive, brusquely humorous and often broad. They are productive of belly laughs rather than wan smiles. And that's what they should be. (Vischer 1930: 18)

"Sound came along and out went the pies": Vischer's thumbnail sketch productively recasts the challenge confronted by slapstick filmmakers of the early talkie era. What in retrospect has appeared to later critics as a linear teleology of decline – from silent art to talkie realism – is presented here as a restructuring of what Pierre Bourdieu would have called the "field" of film comedy production. The notion of "field" is, in fact, quite relevant to the present analysis; for, as developed by Bourdieu, it encourages consideration of how any sphere of cultural endeavor comprises a structure of individuals and groups, for example, filmmakers and studios, "placed in a situation of competition for legitimacy" (Bourdieu 1995: 214). Reading Vischer through Bourdieu, the innovation of sound can thus be seen as introducing a new axis across which struggles for legitimacy were waged, bringing about the "day of the vaudeville act" in talkie shorts that, at least temporarily, threatened to dethrone slapstick as the dominant format of comedy shorts. Accordingly, any analysis of sound's impact on short comedies must start from an assessment of that threat. What were the industrial forces that spawned the "day of the vaudeville act"? How precisely did filmed acts reconfigure the terrain of legitimacy – of cultural worth and value – within the field of the short subject?

As it was in shorts that sound was initially introduced, these are questions that lead in the first instance to the studio that most successfully spearheaded the talkie revolution: Warner Bros. With its first program of sound-on-disc Vitaphone shorts accompanying *Don Juan* on August 6, 1926, Warners had initially sought to impress by appealing to traditional highbrow standards: the overture from Wagner's *Tännhauser*, performed by the New York Philharmonic; tenor Giovanni Martinelli's aria from *I Pagliacci*; sopranos Marion Talley and Anna Case performing music by Wagner, Dvořák, and Beethoven – with only Roy Smeck's solo on the Hawaiian guitar offering lighter musical fare. But the company abruptly shifted gears with its second program (October 7) – which showcased performances by Al Jolson, George Jessel, the comedy team of Willie and Eugene Howard, and songstress Elsie Janis – inaugurating a policy of Broadway-style variety that would continue to dominate Warners' Vitaphone output in the years to come. Music from the leading big-band orchestras; monologues and two-acts performed by big-time vaudevillians; comic and dramatic sketches; and a wide assortment of novelty performers, such as Baby Rose Marie, a five-year-old torch singer, and Sol Violinsky's simultaneous playing of the violin and piano – these were now the preferred performance types, and, for the 1928–1929 season, Warner Bros. refurbished its Brooklyn production stages (the old Vitagraph studios) the better to tap the Broadway talent pool.

It would be a mistake, however, to assume that this change in emphasis can be straightforwardly characterized as a shift across the axis from "high art" to "popular" standards, since the very notion of Broadway-style entertainment to which the Vitaphone shorts appealed was a symptom of the collapse of those very distinctions. As a number of historians have noted, early-twentieth-century Broadway's ethos of conspicuous display and extravaganza had encouraged an alternative interpretation of cultural distinction than that through which the older genteel classes had sought to police the boundaries of culture: the cabarets, nightclubs, and lobster palaces of the 1910s and 1920s thus became occasions for conspicuous extravagance wherein Victorian ideals of restraint and self-culture ceded to the taste for luxury, publicly displayed (Erenberg 1981). Similarly, performers captured by the Vitaphone belonged not to the realm of what had once been working-class variety or cheap vaudeville, but to the showy firmament of musical revues that had emerged from the pioneering efforts of nightlife entrepreneurs like Florenz Ziegfeld and Jesse Lasky to repackage variety for a newly expressive middle class. The emphasis in the marketing of the Vitaphone shorts was, accordingly, on notions of urbane exclusivity and sophistication ("Vitaphone links your theater to Broadway … Broadway – Mecca of millions now round the corner resort of all America thanks to Vitaphone!" – quoted in Jenkins 1992: 160), establishing a strategy of appeal that spread swiftly throughout Hollywood during the early sound era. Indeed, a majority of the major studios that made the move into sound for the 1928–1929 season included some short subject series in the Broadway style, emphasizing big-time vaudeville performers after the Vitaphone template: MGM, for instance, had its "Metro Movietone Acts"; Universal its "vaudeville novelties"; and Paramount an in-house series of "Paramount Talking Acts"; among many others.

Nor was it only through canned vaudeville acts that the Broadway ethos left its mark. Also significant were a number of dialogue-oriented shorts adapting theatrical playlets for the screen, and here, too, Warners was at the forefront. For its 1928–1929 season, the company launched a new series of "Vitaphone Playlets" – two-reel, all-talking adaptations of refined comic and dramatic sketches, of a style commonly featured on the big-time variety stage – and, in the process, established a new and influential template of respectability within the field of early sound comedy. Immediately following suit was the Christie Film Company, a short-subject producer that entered talkie production in late 1928 with a prestigious distribution deal through Paramount. Long associated with the sophisticated, plot-based "situation" style of screen humor, the Christie studios soon began emulating the Vitaphone playlet as a way of distinguishing its first talking comedies from more rough-and-tumble slapstick fare. As indicated by early publicity, the Christie talking shorts would comprise "short features adapted from stage plays" by well-known Broadway playwrights, produced under a policy of "cast[ing] them with stars from both stage and screen" (32 Talking Films 1928: 36; January Brings Christie Talking Plays 1929: 44). Scripted dialogue, on this conception, was to provide the royal road for a style of comedy that would forego the vulgarities of physical humor. As studio head Al Christie himself explained in an interview on the "new style" of dialogue comedy:

> The field of comedy type of entertainment was limited before. After all, there were just so many different ways in which a man could be knocked down or lose his trousers and I think myself movie audiences were getting pretty fed up on this kind of striving for laughs … [By contrast,] the new style of entertainment holds the audience interest far more. It has always good construction to get the interest of the audience by promising something and then working up to it. This can be done far better with the addition of good dialogue. (Sound Places Shorts 1929: 128)

Christie's bid for cultural distinction was further reflected in the series' titling, which conspicuously – and pretentiously – avoided the word "Comedies" to promote the films as "Christie Talking Plays."

More-or-less identical discursive strategies were in play in the promotion for another series of talking playlets: Educational Pictures' six two-reel Coronet Comedies featuring Edward Everett Horton, which commenced release in January 1929. "Today, the all-talking Short Feature comedy has virtually brought a re-birth of humor on the screen," declared publicity for the bedroom farce, *The Right Bed* (April, 1929), describing the films as "farce playlets similar to the one-act plays seen for years in vaudeville" (Short Talking Comedies 1929: 2). "Screen comedy for the past two decades has been a thing of fast action, broad situations and physical 'gags,'" the exhibitors' press sheet for Coronet's *Prince Gabby* (September 1929) disparagingly asserted, continuing: "The new talking picture permits of subtlety of expression through … clever dialogue and the artistry of the actor in delivering the spoken lines" (Subtle Humor 1929: 3). Elsewhere, promotional material for the Coronet films expressed ideals of metropolitan cultural dissemination echoed throughout Hollywood during this period, harping continuously on the filmmakers' Broadway credentials (including the Coronet series' two directors, Hugh Faulcon and Leslie Pearce, both former theatrical producers). Similarly, although Horton himself was no stranger to two-reel comedy (having appeared the previous season in a series of starring shorts produced by Harold Lloyd's Hollywood Productions), Coronet publicity chose to emphasize *not* his previous film successes, which went unmentioned, but his theatrical background and experience. Producers who introduced the style of the talking playlet were, in other words, actively asserting their superior legitimacy, and they used slapstick as a foil for defining a new and theatrical conception of comic artistry. Theatricality was evident, too, in the films' visual design, which, with proscenium-like staging, multiple-camera shooting, and unbroken interior spaces, was seemingly designed to accentuate, rather than mask, the films' stage sources: a representative instance, *Ask Dad* (February, 1929) – the second in the Coronet series – takes place entirely in a secretary's office, with "action" limited to characters' entrances and exits, and an editing rate sluggish even for the early sound period (average shot length 20.7 seconds, compared to an industry-wide average of 10.8 for the period 1928–1933) (O'Brien 2005).

"The Funniest Sound Effect Yet Recorded": Slapstick and the Uses of Noise

Not all short comedies strove for the same theatricality, of course, and what is striking is the degree of resistance with which this style of sophisticated dialogue humor was greeted by the filmgoing public. Certainly, no other feature of early sound comedy drew as much specific comment from exhibitors, who remained adamant in their complaints about tempo and excessive dialogue: "There is a lot to be desired in the quality of the two-reel subjects that are coming through with sound," observed one Indiana exhibitor. "The directors are depending too much on dialogue and not getting enough action in the two-reelers" (Voice of the Industry 1931: 72). "And then there's comedy," lamented another showman. "Here's where sound has had the most stultifying effect" (A Showman Discusses 1932: 49). Lending his voice to the chorus, Jules Levy, head of film booking for RKO theaters, summarized the consensus opinion of his exhibitors, declaring that audiences want "straight hokum comedy": "As far as dialog is concerned there is only one answer," he continued. "That answer is that they want action not words" (Climb Hollywood

Wall 1930: 43). The move toward a Broadway style of dialogue-oriented short subject comedy was, then, an inconsistent one, met by counter-pressures seeking a return to the knockabout physicality and rapid tempo of silent-era slapstick. *Return* is, however, the operative word; for, insofar as the talking playlet had claimed for itself the mantle of innovation and distinction, slapstick filmmakers were forced to play a more conservative, even defensive, game of reaffirming established comic principles, which is one reason, no doubt, why slapstick came to be considered somewhat déclassé – if not, in fact, dated – in the move to sound. This idea is again informed by Bourdieu, who notes how any innovation invariably constructs a new polarization – what might be called "rehierarchization" – within a given cultural field, such that formerly dominant forms, like slapstick, are downgraded through a process of "social ageing" (Bourdieu 1995: 254). Indeed, in the case of slapstick, this social ageing was immediately apparent as trade press articles began to ask questions like "Is old-fashioned slapstick to vanish?" virtually from the moment of sound's initial popularization (Speaking Briefly of Comedy 1929: 40).

One gets a sense of this essentially conservative approach by briefly considering how slapstick filmmakers tackled the question of comic pace and tempo during the transition. For few was this so pressing an issue as for Jack White, a producer who had built a reputation for "fast-action" slapstick during his long tenure at Educational Pictures' Mermaid Comedies and who may thus serve as a useful case study. The transition to sound not only saw White's return to the director's chair for the first time since 1922 – for a series of five "Jack White Talking Comedies" – it also entailed the challenge of reworking his "fast action" approach within new formal and technological parameters. The challenge, as White saw it, was that of using dialogue and sound effects to create functional equivalents for the techniques of his silent productions. As he put it in a press release:

> Fast action ... has come to mean something entirely different since talking pictures arrived. Where in the silent comedies it meant visually fast action, it now means the speedy introduction of characters, fast development of plot and rapidity in establishing situations. This means that dialogue for these comedies must be very carefully edited and pruned of all superfluous words, just as fast-action silent comedies were trimmed of unnecessary actions and gestures. (Jack White Uncovers New Entertainment 1929: 2)

More was at issue here, however, than simply the timing and trimming of dialogue scenes. During the silent era, comedies would typically be projected at a notably faster speed than used during shooting (with a shooting rate ranging anywhere from twelve to twenty frames per second, with variation for effect, and a projection speed closer to the sound film ratio of twenty-four frames per second); yet with the coming of sound, the demands of synchronization and a stable sound pitch led to the standardization of motorized cameras and projectors, eliminating the stylization of action that hand-cranked equipment had allowed

(Brownlow 1980). The stabilization of filming and projection speed meant that filmic time was no longer a flexible value, ensuring a regularization of tempo that mitigated against many of the undercranking effects on which silent comedy had depended. White seems to have recognized this problem and claimed in later years to have patented a device that would have allowed variable shooting speeds without altering sound pitch. "I had an invention that had to do with speeding up or slowing sound," he recalled. "I had an electrical engineer draw the plan up whereby I could change speed without making the sound squeak, affecting only the tempo. I thought maybe everybody would use it, but nobody cared for it, so I was out $100 to the lawyer and nothing came of it" (Bruskin 1990: 132).

Whether or not White ever actually developed such a device is unclear. What the anecdote does testify to are the lengths to which slapstick filmmakers often – doggedly – sought to assimilate the new techniques of sound cinema to more familiar knockabout principles. One sees the same process in Mack Sennett's first season of sound films, where, much like White, he returned to regular directing duties for the first time in years for a series of "Mack Sennett Talking Comedies," also released through Educational. Press releases from Educational's publicity offices may have emphasized Sennett's excitement at the possibilities of comic dialogue – "Dialogue," he was reported as saying, "opens to the producer of the heretofore 'silent' pictures, the immense field of verbal humor" – but, to judge from available evidence, it was the use of sound *effects* that interested him more, creating new avenues for punctuating and accentuating the slapstick gags and burlesque melodramatic thrills that had long defined his comic style. "Every comedy situation," Sennett insisted, "can be immensely improved by proper sound effects, such as the roar of lions, the rumble of an approaching train or the crash of breaking dishes" (Mack Sennett Sees Sound as Big Help 1929: 2). Film after film from Sennett's first season was promoted in terms of the capacity of sound effects, not fundamentally to alter the principles of comic cinema, but rather to "Enhance the Effectiveness" (as one promotional article put it) of Sennett's knockabout stock-in-trade: "the sound of a starting motor, the crack of a stick over a comic's head, music or the roar of a speeding train" – all now produced results "better than any comedy creation that the stage or screen has seen heretofore" (Sound Enhances Effectiveness 1929: 3).

Programmatically, Sennett's first sound short, *The Lion's Roar* (December, 1928, working title *Peace and Quiet*) was, from the very start of the scripting process, unrepentantly conceived as a picture about noise, and lots of it. As described in the earliest written draft (and followed more or less closely in the finished film):

> Open up on title: PEACE AND QUIET ... lap-dissolve to ...
> Close up of an old automobile going along a cobblestone street, with one rear tire off and running on the rim, making a terrific rattle ...
> Lap to shot of a big concrete mixer in noisy action ...
> Lap to a workman or electric riveter on new building ...

Lap to a general shot of busy city street, with usual noises – street car bells, auto horns, newsboys shouting papers, etc. from which –
Lap dissolve to …
INTERIOR: CLARENCE'S ROOM IN CITY (DAY). (Peace and Quiet 1928: 1)

For the rest of the film, Clarence (Johnny Burke) flees the bedlam of urban life to spend a weekend in the country with his beloved (Daphne Pollard), only for his "peace and quiet" to be shattered when he finds himself trapped up a tree during a hunting trip, perched above a bellowing mountain lion. The gag here, of course, is that the country is ultimately no less free of din and disturbance than the city; but at a deeper level, Sennett was simply using sound to cock the same snook that he had been pulling for close to twenty years, creating a carnival of aural cacophony as a straightforward sonic equivalent for his trademark visual chaos.

Needless to say, Sennett was hardly alone in appropriating sound effects to established knockabout procedures. It was, in fact, the increasingly widespread use of such effects that provoked Harold Lloyd, who had just completed production on the silent feature *Welcome Danger* (1929), to reshoot the entire film for sound. As he recalled:

> Sound was just coming in, and inconsequential things were getting tremendous laughs – like frying eggs and ice tinkling in a glass. They'd howl at that. So I said, here we're working our heads off trying to get funny ideas, and they're getting them from these sound effects. I said that maybe we had missed the boat and should make *Welcome Danger* over. (Maltin and Bann 1992: 84)

The foundation for such an effects-laden approach had, in fact, already been firmly established by silent-era musical practice, when various noise-making devices – called "traps" – were commonly used in film accompaniment, especially in comedies. Originating in live performances like vaudeville, the "trap drummer" had been responsible for supplying sound effects in sync with the onscreen comic action throughout the silent period, using an assortment of noisemakers for this purpose, from simple coconut shells to more baroque devices (Bottomore 1999; Altman 2004: 236–40). (A cue sheet compiled for Sennett's 1927 silent short *Smith's Modiste Shop* suggests how elaborate such effects could be, including cues for the sound of a boy's sling shot, a smashed ink bottle, and a meat chopping machine) (Altman 2004: 385). The practice also – at least by the 1920s – created significant distinctions according to cultural value, whereby "low" cinematic genres like comedy or animation were permitted a kind of anti-illusionist, nonrealist sound accompaniment (e.g., a slide whistle to accompany a slip) that would have been considered the height of vulgarity in the case of "serious" drama.[1] Thus, whereas Sennett's *The Lion's Roar* had built its soundtrack almost entirely out of *realist* diegetic effects (city noise, and so on), the idea of integrating more illusion-destroying, "trap"-style noises was a predictable next step – first assayed, perhaps, in Laurel and Hardy's fourth sound short for Hal Roach, *Perfect Day* (August, 1929), when, endeavoring to repair a malfunctioning automobile, Ollie hits Stan on the head with the car's clutch. As the clutch smacks Stan's cranium, a loud, hollow clanging noise on the soundtrack underscores the emptiness of his skull – an effect that the *Exhibitors Herald-World* judged "the funniest sound effect yet recorded" (Skretvedt 1987: 173).

Undoubtedly the best known early sound comic series to use nonrealist sound in this way were those produced a few years later by Columbia's short subjects division, launched under the supervision of Jack White's brother, Jules, in 1932. Under the stewardship of sound-effects man Joe Henrie, Columbia's shorts developed an elaborate grammar of knockabout clamor – nowhere more effective than in the Stooges' shorts – translating the stylization of silent-era comic action into a unique sonic expressivity: face slaps accentuated by the crack of a whip; eye-poking by two plunks of a ukulele; ear twisting by the turning of a ratchet; head bonking by a wooden tempo block; blows to the stomach by the sound of a kettledrum, and so forth (Okuda and Watz 1986: 42–3).

Yet the legacy of the trap drummer provided only one set of possibilities for slapstick filmmakers during the transitional period. Different approaches emerge from a closer consideration of the early sound output of the Hal Roach Studios, which entered the talkie era in early 1929 with four short-film series – Laurel and Hardy, Charley Chase, Our Gang, and the Roach All-Stars – with distribution through Loew's-MGM exchanges. Initially, as exemplified by *Perfect Day*, the approach to sound considered at Roach resembled that of the slapstick filmmakers already discussed, emphasizing effects over dialogue and seeking to sustain fast-paced pantomime within the inflexible temporality of sound filmmaking. Commenting at the time on the addition of synchronized sound to his output, Roach outlined his vision for talkie comedies by distinguishing carefully between dialogue and effects: "The art of pantomime is as old as amusement itself and there isn't the slightest chance that dialogue ever will entirely displace pantomime on the screen. Dialogue can't possibly take the place of pantomime in causing laughs … [By contrast,] sound effects in pictures are going to find a definite niche in the market. There is no doubt about that" ("Pantomime Won't Die" 1929: 57).

The previous year, studio manager Warren Doane had expressed similar concerns to Roach in an internal memo in which he recommended that the studio's filmmakers continue to emphasize silent pantomime for their first sound productions, reserving dialogue only for close-up shots to be edited into the picture for narrative clarity (Doane 1928). Something close to this was in fact codified in the early "Our Gang" talking shorts, where initial dissatisfaction over the child actors' spoken delivery in their first sound production, *Small Talk* (May, 1929), led to drastic dialogue pruning for their second, *Railroadin'* (June, 1929).

At the same time, however, a more distinctive approach was being assayed at Roach's Charley Chase unit, which not only pushed in the direction of more

musical formats – including singing and musical numbers in its early sound
productions – but also downplayed the anti-illusionist trap effects employed
in, e.g., *Perfect Day*, in favor of a more diegetically grounded, verisimilar range
of sounds (often originating from Chase's body; hiccups, sneezing, and the
like). Crucially important in this connection was the legacy of the Hal Roach
Studio's trademark "refined" slapstick style, which, ever since Harold Lloyd's
first "glass character" shorts in 1917, had sought to hybridize the gag-based
aesthetic of slapstick with the plot-based situation style, reining in crude and
frenetic knockabout in favor of narrative values and middle-class situations. By
the late 1920s, the Chase unit was the most notable flag bearer for that legacy,
and, for its first all-talkie productions, sought a similarly tempered approach to
the comic possibilities of sound – striking a balance somewhere between the
"Broadway style" of sophisticated dialogue comedies and the more boisterous,
effects-oriented approach evident at Sennett and elsewhere.

The pattern was set in Chase's first talkie production, *The Big Squawk*
(May, 1929) (see Figure 3.1), which can thus serve as an outline of the various
strategies for incorporating sound into the unit's initial all-talking shorts. Most
fundamentally, Charley here plays the role of a musician – in this instance, a
cabaret saxophonist, although subsequent releases would make use of Chase's
fine singing voice by casting him as a crooner (e.g., *Leaping Love*, June, 1929; *The
Snappy Sneezer*, July, 1929; *Stepping Out*, November, 1929; *Great Gobs*, December,
1929). Such an emphasis on music and song was, of course, broadly characteristic
of the early sound period, when the Hollywood studios exploited the new
technology by including songs in an unexpected variety of genres, including even
westerns and melodramas. But what makes for the comedy in the Chase films is
the way these musical performances are amusingly compromised by the narrative
situations in which Charley finds himself. At the beginning of *The Big Squawk*,
for instance, Charley is repeatedly distracted from his playing by his sweetheart,
Mary (Nina Quartero), who is flirting with another man; unable to concentrate,
Charley repeatedly blows sour notes from his saxophone, much to the irritation
of the bandleader. An early story outline establishes sound as a source of comedy
beginning with Chase's very first close up:

> Close shot of Charley in orchestra. He is burnt up and just finishing this note. He
> takes it himself apologetically to the orchestra leader who is greatly irritated. The
> dancers also give it a sour reaction. We see that Nina is slyly enjoying the situation,
> and, taking pains to see that Charley can see her, flirts again with George, where-
> upon we see Charley burn up again, and again blow the sour note. He again takes it
> apologetically to the orchestra leader who is more irritated by now, and the dancers
> also react to it. Nina is obviously getting a big kick out of it all. This same action is
> repeated again and the number comes to a close. Just as it does, Nina angers Charley
> again so that on the final note of the number, as the dancers are stopping, the note
> rings out loud and clear again. The reactions this time are more violent and the leader
> tears his hair. (Story for Charley Chase 1929: 1)

Figure 3.1   A distracted Charley Chase struggles to play the saxophone in *The Big Squawk* (May 1929; producer, Hal Roach). Courtesy Academy of Motion Picture Arts and Sciences.

Similar scenes of failed musicianship recur in several of Chase's early sound shorts, although these typically involve him singing rather than playing an instrument – for example: *Leaping Love*, his second talkie, when Charley vainly tries to sing – again at a cabaret – after swallowing alum; *The Snappy Sneezer*, his third, in which a hay fever-induced sneezing fit interrupts his song; or *Stepping Out*, his fifth, when a drunk Charley hiccups his way through a tune, once more at a cabaret. In all instances the impulse is both to *naturalize* and to *narrativize* the use of comic sound – that is, to derive comic sound effects internally (from narrative situations) rather than externally (from nondiegetic traps), and to reinforce verisimilitude by localizing those effects in relation to Charley's body. The same principles shape the climax to *The Big Squawk*, which translates into sound the famous finale to his silent short *Mighty Like a Moose* (July, 1926), in which Charley pretends to be two people in front of his wife. In the earlier film, Charley seeks to restore his spouse's affections by staging a "fight" with himself – a feat accomplished by running in and out of a room, each time altering his physical appearance so that he seems to be beating another man around the house. Yet what *Mighty Like a Moose* achieves visually – by Charley's use of a set of false teeth and a change of clothes – is accomplished in *The Big Squawk* in terms of speech and dialogue alone. Here, in order to arouse Mary's jealousy, Charley contrives to make it seem that he is being seduced by a "big blonde" while (he believes) Mary is eavesdropping; only once again, there is only Charley, "using his own voice to represent himself, and a high pitched voice to represent the supposed blonde" – a situation that becomes doubly comic by the fact that his wife is in fact elsewhere, and the eavesdropper is a spinsterish older woman (Gale Henry) (Story for Charley Chase 1929: 3).

The point to be made here is not simply that this sequence provides another example of the comic use of Charley's voice; more substantively, the scene illustrates how narrative *depends* upon the voice as a source of comedy in these films, such that Charley's falsetto ventriloquizing becomes intrinsic to the comic situation. The comedy of sound thus functions neither by means of noisy effects, nor simply in terms of the refinements of spoken witticisms; but, steering a course between the two, produces a third possibility: *voice as comic noise*.

"They Love it in the Small Towns": Early Sound Slapstick and the Short-Subject Market

At the foundation of slapstick's development into the sound era was, then, a fundamental dichotomy between speech and noise, a dichotomy that was also a matter of cultural hierarchy; speech was legitimate sound, noise was not. The coming of sound can thus be seen to have marked an intensification in long-standing hierarchical divisions separating traditions of sophisticated humor from the sensationalism of "low" comedy traditions, divisions that, with the transition to sound, were aligned with alternative uses for the new technology – sophistication with the refinements of dialogue in scripted playlets, slapstick with the noisy immediacy of sound effects, while Hal Roach characteristically steered a course between these poles.[2]

It is, in fact, possible at this point to see precisely how the later aesthetic readings of slapstick's decline offered by Agee and Kerr go wrong. For they radically misperceive how the idea of "art" was located within contexts of production and reception at the time. The coming of sound was not primarily experienced as a shift *away* from comic artistry – away, that is, from the formal beauties of silent pantomime, as critics like Kerr would later argue. If anything, as publicity for the talking playlets makes clear, sound could be and was promoted as enabling a shift *toward* art, toward the *theatrical* artistry of "clever, subtle comedy" as exemplified by dialogue humor in Broadway-style farces. Correspondingly, what was feared to have been lost with sound was not "art," but its opposite – that is, the broad, popular style of slapstick in which producers like Sennett and Jack White had formerly specialized and which they sought valiantly to sustain in the new era. Exhibitors who lamented the impact of sound thus typically spoke not of artistry, nor of the decline of pantomime, but more straightforwardly of the need for a return to "good old-fashioned" or "dandy old-fashioned slapstick" (What the Picture Did for Me 1933a: 49; What the Picture Did for Me 1933b: 46) The appropriate dichotomy for comprehending sound's impact on short-format comedy – at least as it was experienced by filmmakers and audiences at the time – thus has very little to do with the Arnheimian division of art versus realism; rather it is the hierarchical gulf that Gilbert Seldes identified in a 1932 essay in which he divided America's comic sensibility into sophisticated vs. populist modes (Seldes 1932).

Seldes's is, in fact, an important perspective within these developments, not only because he described them with greater proximity than either Agee or Kerr, but because of his reputation as one of his era's most astute interpreters of the popular arts. Well known for his essays on jazz, Mack Sennett, and George Herriman's "Krazy Kat," as assembled in his 1924 collection, *The 7 Lively Arts*, Seldes had long seen in popular cultural forms the cadences of a genuinely American vernacular (Seldes 1957). But by the time of his 1932 essay – titled simply "American Humor" – Seldes was forced to confront a widening division in the nation's comic sensibility, increasingly split between, on the one hand, an ascendant sophisticated and urbane mode (which he associated with literature and the impact of the *New Yorker*; that is, with writers like Robert Benchley, Donald Ogden Stewart, and others) and, on the other, a now faltering populist and "provincial" mode (associated with the radio and cinema, with the *Amos 'n' Andy* show and Jimmy Durante) – a split he tentatively attributed to urbanization, the growth of new nationwide circuits of cultural distribution, and their attendant dissemination of metropolitan values. One may discount Seldes's rather strained attempt to assign these different modes to different forms of cultural expression – sophistication with literature, populism with radio/cinema – without dismissing his more fundamental insight. For the divisions Seldes spoke of were themselves abundantly manifest *within* the early sound short subject, providing the framework within which sound's comic possibilities were first identified and refined. Indeed, it is well to note how members of the "*New Yorker* school" hardly limited their urbane creativity to the written word but, in some instances, themselves crossed over to perform witty monologues in filmed short subjects during this period, including Stewart (in a pair of one-reelers for Paramount, in 1929) and, more durably, Benchley (at Fox, 1928–1929; MGM, 1935–1939; and Paramount, 1941–1945).

In effect, what was taking place was a breakdown of processes that had shaped film comedy's evolution as a mass or cross-class form during the silent era – as though the twin poles of slapstick and sophistication that the great silent-era comedians had sought, in varying ways, to mediate were now, with few exceptions (e.g., Roach's Chase unit), posed against one another anew.[3] Nor, moreover, did the uses of sound provide the only symptom of the growing division;

a further index came in the virtually immediate disappearance of an entire roster of "high-hat" slapstick artists – Johnny Arthur, Jerry Drew, Phil Dunham, Raymond Griffith, and others – whose silent shorts had fused knockabout physicality with the upper class settings and character typology of the situation style. Indeed, to the extent that upper class characters continued to appear as comic leads in early sound two-reelers, they typically did so in dialogue-heavy playlets or musical shorts, abandoning the field of physical comedy to a gallery of assorted "low" or "average" character types and clowns – the tattered grifters Clark and McCullough (at RKO, 1930–1935), the henpecked husband Edgar Kennedy in his "Average Man" shorts (also at RKO, 1931–1948), the "hick" comedian Andy Clyde (at Columbia, 1934–1956) and, of course, the Three Stooges (also at Columbia, 1934–1958), to name only a handful.

It is further significant, in this respect, that the most prestige-minded of the vertically integrated majors – Paramount and MGM – both more or less abandoned the field of the live-action slapstick short during the mid- to late 1930s. Beginning with the 1935–1936 season, Paramount neither produced nor distributed a single slapstick short for the remainder of the decade. MGM's involvement in live-action comedy closely followed suit when, in 1938, Hal Roach ended his arrangement with the company to focus on feature-length production. The market for short-subject slapstick had, by this point, shrunk significantly, as Depression-struck theater owners began embracing double features as a way to boost attendance. With a dual bill consisting of two features and, usually, a news-reel, exhibitors simply had little room for live-action two-reelers. "The average two-reel comedy, they say, will be passed up for a one-reel cartoon," reported *Motion Picture Herald* in 1935, "which can be shown in less than 10 minutes" (The Hollywood Scene 1935: 57).[4] As early as 1931, in fact, it had been reported that lowered rentals due to increases in double featuring were forcing slapstick producers to pare budgets, with "the average spent on a two-reeler ... around $25 000" – a drop of about $10 000 compared to pre-Depression prices (Most Trade Leaders Denounce 1931: 32). Independent producers of live-action shorts responded to these changes either by moving into the feature-film market (like Roach) or simply closing shop (e.g., Sennett and Christie in 1933), while the major studios largely followed Paramount and MGM's lead by curtailing live-action shorts in favor of cartoons and newsreels.

Indeed, those majors that *did* remain in the knockabout game – notably, RKO and Columbia – now found success chiefly by targeting their output at tradi-tionally "down-market" publics, such as the small-town and hinterland markets where slapstick remained a reliable box-office draw. As several film historians have noted, this perception of an alliance between slapstick comedy and small-town tastes had long been a term of Hollywood practice – as indicated by Seldes' own reference to the "provincial" orientation of popular comedy – but it was not until the early years of the Depression that such assumptions were fully implicated into patterns of film industry production and distribution (Jenkins 1990: Jacobs

2008: 79–126). A case in point would be the comedies of actor Edgar Kennedy, whose talkie-era comic persona swiftly evolved from his frequent appearances as an irascible Irish city cop at the Hal Roach Studios to the small-town patriarch of RKO's long-lasting "Average Man" series, beginning in 1931. According to Louella Parsons, author Sinclair Lewis claimed that the "Average Man" series was based on the character he had penned in his novel *Babbitt* (1922) – although the series' comic focus was less business and social life, as in the Lewis novel, than domestic frustrations in the suburbs, as supplied by Kennedy's wife and mother-in-law (initially, and most iconically, played by Florence Lake and Dot Farley). "RKO-Pathé believes that daily happenings in the life of the ordinary citizen will furnish enough comedy for a series of short subjects," wrote Parsons; and the series' very first installment, *Lemon Meringue* (1931), signaled the intent to do so in the vein of throwback slapstick, culminating in a pie fight (Cassara 2005: 124, 128). Such comedies, however, were tailored less to the supposedly "sophisticated" tastes of metropolitan audiences than to what was considered the conservative, even old-fashioned, sensibilities of the heartland, where, according to Kennedy biographer Bill Cassara, these films played best (Cassara 2005: 193). The same was also true of Columbia's Three Stooges, whose early reputation and success was almost entirely defined in terms of their popularity with the heartland audiences to which Columbia, lacking its own theater chain, had long targeted its output. Of a film like the Stooges' *Hoi Polloi* (August, 1935), the manager of the Niles Theatre in Animosa, Iowa, thus described the trio's comic style as "knock down, drag-'em-out" slapstick, adding that "They [i.e., audiences] love it in the small towns on Saturday night," while an exhibitor in Lincoln, Kansas, praised the Stooges for finding "more ways to make people laugh than a farmer has coming to town" (What the Picture Did for Me 1936: 72; What the Picture Did for Me 1938b: 60). Children, in particular, responded favorably to the Stooges' shorts, making the pictures a particular boon for small-town and neighborhood exhibitors dependent on the family trade. "Hard to get the kids out as they want to see [the Stooges] two or three times," commented theater owner E.F. Ingram from Ashland, Alabama (What the Picture Did for Me 1938a: 78).

A final reference to Bourdieu may be instructive in this respect, since the processes outlined above testify to the operations of what he terms "banalization" as a corollary to cultural rehierarchization. As developed in his *The Rules of Art* (1995), banalization refers to the way in which cultural forms are devalued as their relation to their public changes: any innovation within a cultural field – and sound's impact on film comedy certainly counts as such – has the effect, Bourdieu notes, not only of generating new forms and styles invested with superior cultural capital, but also of consigning once-popular forms – say, slapstick – to marginalized publics (Bourdieu 1995: 254–5). Slapstick's waning fortunes were thus multiply overdetermined – the product of what might be called an "internal" movement (linked to sound's impact as a catalyst for the production of new styles of short-subject comedy), of an "external" development (linked to slapstick's deteriorating position within broader discourses of cultural value), and, finally, conjoining the two, of market forces (consigning short-subject slapstick to those studios catering to "downmarket" audience segments), each serving to reinforce the form's final pathway toward the déclassé.

"You Don't have to Speak Funny Words to Make Things Funny": Charlie Chaplin versus the Three Stooges

Here we cannot detail every symptom of these processes, but we can end by comparing two sharply contrasting careers in 1930s' slapstick to see how these questions of status were negotiated in practice through the uses of sound. We can also use the opportunity of a conclusion briefly to broaden our purview and assess the greatest of feature-length slapstick comedians, Charlie Chaplin, whose uses of sound stand in productive difference to those most emblematic of short-subject comics, the Three Stooges.

In his provocative history of film sound, *Film, A Sound Art* (2009), Michel Chion categorizes the "Three Steps into Speech" through which Chaplin made his transition into talking pictures, each step represented by a single feature film. The first is *City Lights*, commenced at the transitional moment between the silent and talking periods, but completed only in 1931 – a film that uses the soundtrack to provide musical accompaniment and sound effects, but with no audible dialogue whatsoever; as Chion puts it, "a manifesto in defense of the art of silent film" (Chion 2009: 21). Next is *Modern Times*, released five years later – a film that while "still essentially a silent film" now includes more noticeable incursions of realistic sounds, including, for the first time, sporadic moments of dialogue (Chion 2009: 22). Two types of voice make their presence felt here. On the one hand, there are a number of voices that pass through some media apparatus: the proto-videophone that the factory director uses to communicate to the workers, the gramophone that plays the recorded text of the worker-feeding machines, the radio that the tramp listens to in jail. Yet there is also the unmediated voice of the tramp himself, when, after much suspense, he finally sings his nonsense song, "Je cherche après Titine," consisting only of incomprehensible, if vaguely suggestive, syllables and fragments of words (e.g., "Tu la tu la tu la wa" and "Voulez-vous le taximeter?") – an appropriately contrary gesture for Chaplin's reluctant abandonment of the tramp's silence. The third and concluding step comes with *The Great Dictator* (1940), a full-fledged talkie that completes the transition, bringing Chaplin's speech from nonsense to meaning, and from comedy to seriousness. A series of doubles serve here to resolve the dilemmas that Chaplin had faced since the advent of sound film, the most notable being the comedian's decision to play two characters, the paranoid dictator Adenoid Hynkel and the nameless Jewish barber. As Chaplin explained in his autobiography, the former permitted him to indulge in nonsense dialogue, the other to exercise his pantomimic talents. "As Hitler I could harangue the crowds in jargon and talk all I wanted to. And as the tramp I could remain more or less silent" (Chaplin 1992: 387). Also relevant, however, is a doubling in the very structure of the film, in which Hynkel's mangled speech near the beginning of the film – a scene that seemingly picks up the baton of the nonsense song that ends *Modern Times*–is ultimately answered by another public speech at the close, when, in an infamous scene, the Jewish barber takes Hynkel's place to deliver the pacifist message with which the film ends. A brief excerpt from this near four-minute speech captures the tone:

> You the people have the power, the power to create machines, the power to create happiness. You the people have the power to make life free and beautiful, to make this life a wonderful adventure. Then in the name of democracy, let's use that power; let us all unite … Let us fight to free the world, to do away with national barriers, do away with greed, with hate and intolerance. Let us fight for a world of reason, a world where science and progress will lead to all men's happiness. Soldiers – in the name of democracy, let us all unite!

Comic incomprehensibility thus yields to sincerity and meaning in a culminating speech that finally treats the sound cinema as, in Chion's words, "the depository of a text, a bottle in the ocean" – the vehicle, that is, of a message in which the technologies of sound cinema are no longer a laughing matter (Chion 2009: 26).

Chion's is a perceptive analysis, albeit insulated from any broader consideration of sound's particular implications for *comic* film. Certainly what needs to be added here is how this three-step process – basically, from silence to sound effects to nonsense to dialogue – maps directly onto the topic of cultural hierarchy discussed earlier, such that Chaplin's slow progression to speech and sincerity charts a step-by-step abandonment of the auditory logic of low comedy. If, as has been suggested, *The Great Dictator*'s final sequence is to be considered Chaplin's solution to the aesthetic challenge of progressive politics, then, crucially, it is a solution that depends upon spoken discourse as its medium of articulation – as though Chaplin's own long-standing pretensions as a "serious" artist could no longer be nourished at the level of pantomime alone, pushing him instead toward the oft-remarked speechifying of his subsequent films, such as *Monsieur Verdoux* (1947) and *Limelight* (1952) (Maland 1991: 176–7).

Yet what is found, if we turn now to the Stooges, is almost an exact inversion of this movement; a reversal of the polarities of speech versus nonsense as these pertain to the Stooges' trademark violent slapstick. The Stooges are, of course, often considered quintessential products of the sound era, comedians whose style really depended upon the possibilities that sound afforded – not, of course, because of any notably witty repartee or dialogue humor, but rather because of their dependence on *noise*. The use of "trap"-style effects to accentuate their violent humor has already been touched upon; equally important to their noisy style, however, was the kind of guttural idiolect developed by Curly, with his characteristic "woo woo woos" and "nyuk nyuk nyuks." Even when they speak, words exist for the Stooges more as raw sounds than as signifiers; characteristic here is the joke, again usually in Curly's mouth, that treats quasi-homonyms (words sounding similar to one another) as synonyms (words meaning the same thing) – as in "Are you casting asparagus on my cooking?" from the short *Busy Buddies* (March, 1944).[5] As Moe later put it, glossing the Stooges' characteristic emphasis on noise (and violence) over significance and speech: "You don't have to have words, to speak funny words, to make things funny. Even to the point where many times, if we did something and then the thing wouldn't get a laugh, we found a way to either hit Curly in the stomach and have a barrel noise or grab him by the nose" (Cox and Terry 2006: 32).

But it is not only their general reliance on noise that counts here; for the essential dynamic of the Stooges' comedy, within each short, is itself typically premised on the repudiation and deconstruction of spoken discourse. One short out of dozens will serve as a case study, *Three Sappy People* (December, 1939), the Stooges' forty-third for Columbia. The plot offers a basic variation of their trademark formula: somebody – usually a figure of class authority – seeks some professionals for a job, but by a series of coincidences ends up hiring the Stooges instead. Only here matters are given a psychoanalytic spin: the wealthy Mr. Rumsford needs a therapist to cure his insane wife, but ends up contacting three phone repairmen by mistake – Moe, Larry, and Curly – who decide to take the job for themselves. Characteristic, moreover, is the way sound here reinforces the plot's basic dichotomies: upper versus lower class, order versus chaos, even sanity versus insanity – these antinomies are given a precise sonic dimension in terms of the difference between communicative speech and meaningless noise.

The Stooges' status as agents of verbal misrule is immediately identified in an opening scene in which they try to repair a switchboard, a communications technology that, thanks to their incompetence, now fails to communicate at all (Figure 3.2a). The pattern thus set, the film proceeds through a series of set pieces in which the Stooges repeatedly explode formal discourse into nonsense. Upon arriving outside their patient's home, for instance, they mistakenly begin a medical investigation of Mr. Rumsford – instead of his wife – which swiftly segues into an *a cappella* chorus of "aahs," in turn provoking Mrs. Rumford to burst into uncontrollable hysterics and run off toward the house, shouting "Last one in is a Republican!" (Figure 3.2b). What next ensues is some fairly typical Stooge-ing: Moe, Larry, and Curly have arrived on their new patient's birthday and turn the formal party thrown in her honor into a chaotic food fight. Notable, though, is the way in which the climactic food fight fully inverts the path taken by Chaplin in his sound films; for, whereas Chaplin's trajectory was to ascend from nonsense to speech, the Stooges' comedy progressively breaks down the formal discourse of

(a)

(b)

(c)

Figure 3.2 (a) In *Three Sappy People* (December 1939; producer, Jules White), the Stooges are first introduced dismantling a telephone switchboard, which they transform into a device of *mis* communication … (b) Later, upon arriving at the Rumsford mansion, they turn a medical examination into an impromptu *a cappella* chorus … (c) Finally, spoken discourse is broken down altogether as a dinner party becomes a food fight.

the well-heeled and well-spoken partygoers, reducing them to babbling incoherence; to shrieks, grunts, and hysterics. Put another way, communicative speech becomes impossible when every open mouth has a cake flung into it (Figure 3.2c).

At this point, we can see the lines of cultural distinction drawn most sharply – the dichotomy between the trajectory of a Chaplin who, by ascending from slapstick to speech, sought to secure his critical standing at a time when physical comedy was increasingly déclassé, and, on the other hand, the comic movement of the Three Stooges who, by refusing speech for noise, seemingly reinforced their own critical and cultural marginalization.[6] It is in the figure drawn through this chiasmus that we find once more the fundamental distinction between speech and noise that this paper has been tracing, the former aligned with ideals of cultural pre-eminence, the latter with illegitimacy. There is then, finally, a way in which the history of film comedy might be said to have "begun again" with sound, in the sense that the new technology provided a criterion for breathing life into and resetting comic cinema's foundational dichotomy, sundering once again standards of "low" versus "sophisticated" comedy that it was the legacy of the silent era to have mediated and reconciled. Unlike in previous decades, however, slapstick comedians of the sound era were not successful in transcending those distinctions. Or at least not in shorts.

Notes

1. As early as 1911, *Moving Picture World*'s music columnist had commented on the distinction, noting: "Much liberty is allowable in comedy pictures … but in the straight dramatic pictures sound effects should be made to imitate as nearly as possible the real sounds which would naturally be heard in a real scene such as the picture portrays." Quoted in Altman (2004: 238).
2. On divisions between sophisticated and popular humor, see Jenkins (1992: 26–58). Slapstick's association with noise was nothing new: slapstick comedy derives its very name from a noise-making device, in the form of the *battacio* from the *Commedia dell'Arte*, a club-like object – literally, a slap-stick – that emitted a smacking noise when used in comic beatings.
3. On slapstick's development as a mass form, see King (2009: 105–79).
4. For a superb analysis of changes in the short-subject market during this period, see Ward (2005: 62–98).
5. It is worth noting in this connection that Moe Howard's own Hitler impersonations – in a trio of war-themed comedies, *You Nazty Spy* (January 1940), *I'll Never Heil Again* (July 1941), and *They Stooge to Conga* (January 1943), the first appearing nine months *before The Great Dictator*–remain limited to nonsensical verbiage, and never resolve into sincere speech in the manner of Chaplin's film.
6. In this respect, the Stooges should be distinguished from the Marx Brothers, whose comedy fused comic "noise" (Chico's Italianate mispronunciations, Harpo's ever-present taxi horn) with far more sophisticated patterns of verbal byplay (Groucho's puns). Although some observers of the time equated the two comic teams, the fact remains that the Marxes' features, at least through *A Day at the Races* (1937), maintained a prestige appeal that the Stooges never enjoyed.

References

32 Talking Films of Christie Firm to be Prereleased (1928) *Exhibitors Herald-World* (December 15), p. 36.

Agee, J. (1958) Comedy's greatest era, in *Agee on Film*, vol. 1, Perigree Books, New York, NY, pp. 2–19.

Altman, R. (2004) *Silent Film Sound*, Columbia University Press, New York, NY.

Arnheim, R. (2004) The making of a film, in *Film Theory and Criticism: Introductory Readings* (eds. L. Braudy and M. Cohen), 6th edn, Oxford University Press, New York, NY, pp. 326–31.

A Showman Discusses the Short-comings of the Short Feature (1932) *Motion Picture Herald* (April 23), p. 49

Bottomore, S. (1999) An international survey of sound effects in early cinema. *Film History*, 11 (4), pp. 485–98.

Bourdieu, P. (1995) *The Rules of Art: Genesis and Structure of the Literary Field* (trans. S. Emanuel), Stanford University Press, Stanford, CA.

Brownlow, K. (1980) Silent films: What was the right speed? *Sight and Sound*, 49 (3), 164–167.

Bruskin, D. (1990) *The White Brothers: Jack, Jules, and Sam White*, Metuchen, NJ: Scarecrow Press.

Cassara, B. (2005) *Edgar Kennedy: Master of the Slow Burn*, Bear Manor Media, Boalsburg, PA.

Chaplin, C. (1992) *My Autobiography*, Penguin, London.

Chion, M. (2009) *Film, A Sound Art* (trans. C. Gorbman), Columbia University Press, New York, NY.

Climb "Hollywood Wall," Learn Public Wants, Says Jules Levy (1930) *Exhibitors Herald-World* (October 18), p. 43.

Cox, S. and Terry, J. (2006) *One Fine Stooge: Larry Fine's Frizzy Life in Pictures*, Cumberland House, Nashville, TN.

Doane, W. to Roach, H. (1928) (November 27.) Files - 1930s. Hal Roach Collection, University of Southern California.

Erenberg, L. (1981) *Steppin' Out: New York Nightlife and the Transformation of American Culture, 1890-1930*, Greenwood Press, Westport, CT.

Jack White Uncovers New Entertainment in Talkies (1929) *Hunting the Hunter*, press sheet, New York Public Library for the Performing Arts, p. 2.

Jacobs, L. (2008) *The Decline of Sentiment: American Film in the 1920s*, University of California Press, Berkeley, CA.

January Brings Christie Talking Plays and Cohen Negro Stories (1929) *Exhibitors Herald-World* (January 5), p. 44.

Jenkins, H. (1990) "Shall we make it for New York or for distribution?" Eddie Cantor, *Whoopee*, and regional resistance to the talkies. *Cinema Journal*, 29 (4), 32–52.

Jenkins, H. (1992) *What Made Pistachio Nuts? Early Sound Comedy and the Vaudeville Aesthetic*, Columbia University Press, New York, NY.

Kerr, W. (1975) *The Silent Clowns*. DaCapo Press, New York, NY.

King, R. (2009) *The Fun Factory: The Keystone Film Company and the Emergence of Mass Culture*, University of California Press, Berkeley, CA.

Lynn, K. S. (1997) *Charlie Chaplin and His Times*, Aurum Press, London.

Mack Sennett Sees Sound as Big Help (1929) *The Bees' Buzz*, press sheet, New York Public Library for the Performing Arts, p. 2.

Maland, C. (1991) *Chaplin and American Culture: The Evolution of a Star Image*, Princeton University Press, Princeton, NJ.

Maltin, L. and Bann, R. (1992) *The Little Rascals: The Life and Times of Our Gang*, Three Rivers Press, New York, NY.

Most Trade Leaders Denounce Double Features as a Menace (1931) *Motion Picture Herald* (November 21), pp. 13, 32–3.

O'Brien, C. (2005) Multiple language versions and national films, 1930-1933: Statistical analysis, part I. *Cinéma et cie*, 6, pp. 45–52.

Okuda, T. and Watz, E. (1986) *The Columbia Comedy Shorts: Two-Reel Hollywood Film Comedies*, McFarland, Jefferson, NC.

"Pantomime Won't Die in Talkers" Says Hal Roach (1929) *Exhibitors Herald-World* (November 16), p. 57.

Peace and Quiet (1928) Script, working draft. *The Lion's Roar*. Mack Sennett Collection, Academy of Motion Picture Arts and Sciences.

Seldes, G. (1932) American humor, in *America as Americans See It* (ed. F. J. Ringel), Literary Guild, New York, NY, pp. 347–360.

Seldes, G. (1957) *The 7 Lively Arts*, Sagamore Press, New York, NY.

Short Talking Comedies are Rapidly Becoming Favorites (1929) *The Right Bed*, press sheet, New York Public Library for the Performing Arts, p. 2.

Skretvedt, R. (1987) *Laurel and Hardy: The Magic Behind the Movies*, Moonstone Press, Beverley Hills, CA.

Sound Enhances Effectiveness of Fun in Mack Sennett Film (1929) *The Bees' Buzz*, press sheet, New York Public Library for the Performing Arts, p. 3.

Sound Places Shorts on Feature Plane, Says Al Christie (1929) *Exhibitors Herald-World* (June 15), p. 128.

Speaking Briefly of Comedy (1929) *Exhibitors Herald-World* (February 9), p. 40.

Story for Charley Chase – C21 (1929) *The Big Squawk*. Hal Roach Studios Collection, Academy of Motion Picture Arts and Sciences.

Subtle Humor in New Series of Talking Films (1929) *Prince Gabby*, press sheet, New York Public Library for the Performing Arts, p. 3.

The Hollywood Scene (1935) *Motion Picture Herald* (October 5), p. 57.

Vischer, P. (1930) Broadway, *Exhibitors Herald-World* (March 15), p. 18.

Voice of the Industry (1931) *Motion Picture Herald* (May 2), p. 72.

Ward, R.L. (2005) *A History of the Hal Roach Studios*, Southern Illinois University Press, Carbondale, IL.

What the Picture Did For Me (1933a) *Motion Picture Herald* (June 17), pp. 45–9.

What the Picture Did For Me (1933b) *Motion Picture Herald* (September 9), pp. 42–8.

What the Picture Did For Me (1936) *Motion Picture Herald* (April 18), pp. 67–73.

What the Picture Did For Me (1938a) *Motion Picture Herald* (January 29), pp. 75–9.

What the Picture Did For Me (1938b) *Motion Picture Herald* (February 26), pp. 55–61.

Further Reading

Bruskin, D. (1990) *The White Brothers: Jack, Jules, and Sam White*, Scarecrow Press, Metuchen, NJ. Bruskin's oral history offers a unique perspective on the development of silent- and sound-era slapstick, as told by some of its most notable short-subject producers.

Jenkins, H. (1992) *What Made Pistachio Nuts? Early Sound Comedy and the Vaudeville Aesthetic*, Columbia University Press, New York, NY. A landmark cultural history of film comedy, Jenkins' study examines the influence of the "vaudeville aesthetic" on feature-length comedies of the early sound era.

Kerr, W. (1975) *The Silent Clowns*, DaCapo Press, New York, NY. One of the seminal overviews of American silent slapstick, *The Silent Clowns* is a readable and perceptive critical study informed by classical film theory.

Seldes, G. (1932) American Humor, in *America as Americans See It* (ed. F.J. Ringel), Literary Guild, New York, NY, pp. 347–60. Often overlooked in favor of Seldes's more well known essay on Mack Sennett (in *The Seven Lively Arts*), this 1932 piece assesses the impact of metropolitan literary humor on American comic traditions.

Ward, R.L. (2005) *A History of the Hal Roach Studios*, Southern Illinois University Press, Carbondale, IL. The most comprehensive industrial history of the Hal Roach Studios to date, Ward's study provides superb context about the changing marketplace for short-subject comedy in studio-era Hollywood.

Part II

Comic Performers in the Sound Era

4

Mutinies Wednesdays and Saturdays

Carnivalesque Comedy and the Marx Brothers

Frank Krutnik

Monkey Business (1931) features a scene between Groucho and Chico Marx that provides a good illustration of the team's deconstructive play with logic, history, and language. After the Marx Brothers smuggle themselves on board a liner bound for the New World, Groucho and Chico lock the captain in his cabin. Donning the captain's hat and jacket, Groucho then engages in a comic masquerade that pits his Americanized wise guy against Chico's mock-Italian immigrant. "How dare you invade the sanctity of the Captain's quarters!" he barks at Chico, in mocking imitation of the captain. Groucho's counterfeit captain then proceeds to treat Chico's ersatz lower-class Italian with puffed-up condescension as he subjects him to a lesson in history (see Figure 4.1):

CHICO: My father was a partners with Columbus. Well, what do you think of that, huh?

GROUCHO: Your father and Columbus were partners?

CHICO: You bet.

GROUCHO: Columbus has been dead 400 years.

CHICO: Well, they told me it was my father.

GROUCHO: Well, now just hop up there, little Johnny, and I'll show you a few things you don't know about history. [*Chico sits on desk*] Now, look – there's Columbus. [*Groucho draws circle on globe*]

CHICO: That's Columbus circle.

GROUCHO: Would you mind getting up off that flypaper and giving the flies a chance?

CHICO: Ah, you're crazy – flies can't read papers.

GROUCHO: Now, Columbus sailed from Spain to India looking for a short cut.

A Companion to Film Comedy, First Edition. Edited by Andrew Horton and Joanna E. Rapf.
© 2013 John Wiley & Sons, Inc. Published 2016 by John Wiley & Sons, Inc.

Figure 4.1   Groucho's ersatz captain subjects Chico to a lesson in history (*Monkey Business*; producer Herman J. Mankiewicz).

CHICO: Oh, you mean strawberry short cut.

GROUCHO: I don't know. [*Takes off Captain's hat in exasperation*] When I woke up, there was the nurse taking care of me.

CHICO: What's the matter, couldn't the nurse take care of herself?

GROUCHO: You bet she could, but I found it out too late. Well, enough of this. Let's get back to Columbus. [*puts hat on again*]

CHICO: I'd rather get back to the nurse.

GROUCHO: So would I. But Columbus was sailing along on his vessel–.

CHICO: On his what?

GROUCHO: Not on his what – on his vessel. Don't you know what vessel is?

CHICO: Sure, I can vessel. [*whistles*]

GROUCHO: Do you suppose I could buy back my introduction to you? Now, one night Columbus' sailors started a mutiny–.

CHICO: Nah, no mutinies at night. They're in the afternoon. You know, mutinies Wednesdays and Saturdays.

GROUCHO: [*takes off hat again*] There's my argument – restrict immigration.

Groucho and Chico here conspire together in playing out a scenario that parodies hegemonic orthodoxy, with Groucho appropriating not merely the captain's vestments of command but also his privileged status as a white American. The moral of the narrative he tries to impart is that, although Columbus is the symbolic figurehead of the colonization of America by white Europeans, a lowly descendant such as Chico has no claim on his legacy. The (real) captain is reprising Columbus's journey by steering the ship from Europe to the United States, but as a servant of the moneyed elite he polices access to the New World. As Groucho's final line makes only too plain, the captain is responsible for screening out undesirables such as the Marxian refugees. But the belligerent "immigrant" continually outwits the "WASP official," with Chico's interjections frustrating the telling of a story that subordinates his own role as a poor "Italian" within the broader trajectory of American ascendancy.

The scene's satiric import goes beyond this explicit insurgency, however, to erode further the foundations of language, meaning, and identity that are necessary for the establishment of social authority. The agent of an insurrectionist energy that comes from below, Chico's immigrant strips the hierarchical order of its conceptual scaffolding until the edifice collapses about him. He disempowers the fake captain by jamming the channel of communication through which the latter strives to assert command, deforming and redirecting the meaning of Groucho's words. Chico's trademark specialty is the excruciating pun – "Columbus circle," "strawberry short cut," "vessel"/whistle, "mutinees"/matinees, and so on – which functions as an aggressive form of anti-wit, particularly when delivered with such unsmiling pugnacity.

This scene from *Monkey Business* exemplifies many characteristics of the carnivalesque, as theorized by Mikhail Bakhtin in his book *Rabelais and his World*. For Bakhtin, the carnival festivities of Medieval Europe provided an important safety valve within the regimented social order of feudal Europe. Offering a designated space for the disruption of official culture, carnival allowed both an imaginative overthrow of institutional power structures and the ascendancy of the popular body (Bakhtin 1984: 18–21). Carnival days permitted peasants to mock their social superiors and the authority of the Church, on the understanding that everything would snap back into its conventional alignment the following day. As Bakhtin (1984: 10) puts it, carnival "celebrated temporary liberation from the prevailing truth and from the established order; it marked the suspension of all hierarchical rank, privileges, norms, and prohibitions. Carnival was the true feast of time, the feast of becoming, change and renewal. It was hostile to all that was immortalized and completed."

The liberation from order may have been temporary, but it nonetheless articulated alternative modes of social consciousness and popular imagining. In this regard, carnivals represented "the second life of the people, who for a time entered the utopian realm of community, freedom, equality, and abundance" (Bakhtin 1984: 9). A key feature of the carnivalesque is what Bakhtin (1984: 19–20) terms "grotesque realism," an aesthetic regime characterized by "degradation, that is, the lowering of all that is high, spiritual, ideal, abstract; it is a transfer to the material level, to the sphere of earth and body in their indissoluble unity." Combining crudity and utopianism, carnival grotesquerie frees the human body from social delimitation, releasing the lower bodily stratum (belly, genitals, and anus) from its subjection to the intellect and the spirit and parading bodies of exaggerated proportions, unquenchable sensuality, and revolting assertiveness (Bakhtin 1984: 21). Within the framework of the carnivalesque, liberation of the unruly body takes on a positive force of renewal that has "a cosmic and at the same time an all-people's character." As Bakhtin (1984: 19) sees it, there is a fundamental synergy between this figuration of the body and the broader social utopianism of the carnivalesque, as the "material bodily principle is contained not in the biological individual, not in the bourgeois ego, but in the people, a people who are continually growing and renewed. This is why all that is bodily becomes grandiose, exaggerated, immeasurable."

Bakhtin's account certainly suggests immediate and enticing affinities between the dynamics of carnivalesque and the Hollywood comedian film.[1] The latter similarly provides a context for the imaginative overthrow of social convention, by locating the comic protagonist as an outsider or underdog who consciously or unconsciously upsets hierarchies, institutions and codes of propriety. Carnivalesque narratives of this kind include the Marx Brothers' *Monkey Business* and *A Night at the Opera* (1935), the Dean Martin and Jerry Lewis vehicles *The Caddy* (1953) and *Living it Up* (1954), and the Adam Sandler comedy *Happy Gilmore* (1996). Tellingly, these examples all have an explicit class dynamic, with the comic protagonists battling against the prejudice and opposition they encounter as a result of their lowly social status. Besides offering a playful critique of pomp, pretension, prejudice or hypocrisy, the comic protagonist's dissonant hi-jinks often serve a more inclusive and utopian agenda. Their eventual triumph is not just individual victory, as it symbolizes possibilities for a more equitable social order.

Some performers – particularly Chaplin and Lewis – lace their comedy with explicit sentiment, inviting the audience to identify with the comic outsider's desire for recognition and acceptance. In films such as *The Kid* (Chaplin 1921), *City Lights* (Chaplin 1931), *The Geisha Boy* (Lewis 1958) and *Rock-a-Bye Baby* (Lewis 1958) the beleaguered comic misfit possesses the emotional insight, compassion and selflessness lacking elsewhere in the diegesis. Within these films, the comic figure embarks on a self-sacrificial love relationship that provides a positive counterpoint to the competitive and judgmental society that spurns them. Such films use sentiment to invite the audience to bond with the comic protagonist, based on the special awareness they are granted of his emotional and social integrity. More generally, the carnivalesque unification of comedian and audience is achieved via the festive force of laughter – which is, obviously enough, a prime rationale of the comedian film. The affective release of laughter transforms the cinema audience from an assembly of individual viewers into members of a provisional community, who are able to enjoy the same experiences and respond to them as one. This scenario may be at a far remove from the market squares of Medieval Europe but, temporarily, in the darkness of the cinema, something of the same populist spirit is reignited as individuals find they can laugh together at the folly of mankind and thereby share momentarily in the transcendent promise of community.

The comedian film also continues the carnivalesque fascination with the grotesque or unruly body. Although some comedians – Harold Lloyd and Danny Kaye, in particular – essay relatively naturalistic personas, performers as diverse as Ben Turpin, Charles Chaplin, Laurel and Hardy, The Three Stooges, W.C.

Fields, Mae West, the Marx Brothers, Jerry Lewis, Jim Carrey and the Marx Brothers have cultivated an exaggerated physicality. As in Bakhtin's theory, their grotesque bodies resist cultural discipline and are identified with spontaneity, creative renewal, and egalitarianism. The extremely stylized self-presentation of such comedians, in costume, movement or behavior, underscores their resistance to accommodation within verisimilitudinous fictional frameworks. Whether they are incapable of conforming to the dictates and decorous bounds of the fictional worlds they inhabit, or are unwilling to do so, the physical disjuncture of such figures testifies to an explicit or implicit hostility towards conformist options. A further manifestation of physical grotesquerie occurs when the comedian's body exhibits a capacity for impossible, cartoon-style gags that reject physical laws in favor of surrealistic deformations – as happens frequently, for example, with Harpo Marx, Jerry Lewis, and Jim Carrey. Besides foregrounding the comedian figure's alienation from or resistance to everyday social codes, the comedy of the grotesque body also displays the comedian's creative dexterity as a performer, whether through the development of a trademark style (for example, the distinctive walks and costumes of Chaplin or Groucho Marx) or the agility of their physical responses (for example, Chaplin and Jerry Lewis). A further manifestation of the grotesque body is the rebellious display of unconstrained appetite – for food, for sex, for pleasure of all kinds – which liberates physical gratification from any subjugation to the intellect or propriety. Harpo Marx demonstrates this principle in its most uninhibited manner, as in the scene in *A Night in Casablanca* (1946) where he invades Groucho's office and steals the latter's lunch, wolfing down not just the food but also a candle, coffee cup and saucer.

Although many comedian films articulate carnivalesque processes through their narratives, the carnivalesque can also emerge through a formal resistance to narrative. Some theorists identify the carnivalesque as an oppositional mode that inherently opposes Hollywood's integrative representational norms, particularly the organization of realism, time and causality. Robert Stam (2000: 262), for example, argues that: "The problem-solving mode of the classical narrative, in which highly motivated characters work toward clear and realizable goals, instantiates an anti-carnivalesque, individualist, and competitive *weltanschauung*. Dominant cinema aesthetics relay time as a linear succession of events related through cause and effect, rather than conveying an associative time linked to rituals and festivals."

Comedian films often share affinities with this kind of carnivalesque textual practice, exhibiting numerous deviations from standard Hollywood protocols regarding characterization, narrative development and fictional hermeticism. This is partly due to the way comedian comedy mediates traditions of live entertainment spectacle. As Steve Seidman (1981: 19–57) discusses, comedian films seek to approximate the interactive dynamic of entertainment traditions by working against the effacement associated with classical Hollywood style. Whenever possible, they interrupt the narrative to display performative specialties or to indulge in self-reflexive gags that disrupt the fourth wall: examples include Groucho Marx in *Horse Feathers* (1932) advising the cinema audience to visit the lobby so they can escape Chico's piano interlude, and the direct-to-camera monologue that opens Woody Allen's *Annie Hall* (1977). Such tendencies vary in intensity from comedian to comedian, and from era to era, but the genre provides a space where the dislocation of classical narrative unity is not just accepted but also expected.

While it may have real potential for illuminating key operations of the comedian film, Bakhtin (1984: 51–2) cautions against applying selected features of the carnivalesque to later modes and practices. In particular, later entertainment forms segregate performers from their audiences. For Bakhtin (1984: 7), the Medieval carnival was shaped by collective action: it "does not acknowledge any distinction between actors and spectators ... Carnival is not a spectacle seen by the people; they live in it, and everyone participates because its very idea embraces all the people." The professionalization of entertainment need not eradicate carnivalesque processes, but it certainly transforms them by offering the audience more vicarious forms of participation.

Serving as both emissary and scapegoat for the unruly energies of the crowd, the screen comedian incarnates and acts out counter-cultural impulses. Playing with social codifications of, for example, gender, sexuality, the body, identity, class and ethnicity, comedians such as the Marx Brothers, Mae West and Jerry Lewis can inspire a disorderly rewriting of normative protocols. In this sense, they are the contemporary equivalents of the medieval clowns and fools, who, Bakhtin (1984: 8) suggests, were "the constant, accredited representatives of the carnival spirit in everyday life, out of the carnival season." More than merely comic actors, Medieval fools and clowns were liminal figures who lived on, and spoke from, the margins of orthodox society: "they stood on the borderline between life and art, in a peculiar mid-zone as it were" (Bakhtin 1984: 8). Comedians of the modern age provide a modified version of this traditional role. By comparison with other performers, for example, there is a strong assumption that the comedian's performance is more integrally rooted in lived reality than is the case with other actors. Eliding distinctions between persona and biographical individual, popular discourse on, and by, comedians is rife with psychobiographical speculation about the dark compulsions, dysfunctions or neuroses that provide the wellspring for their comedy (see Shumway on Woody Allen in this volume, for example). This pervasive popular philosophy has two mutually reinforcing implications: first, is the idea that the comedian is compelled to seek laughter to compensate for real life deficiencies; second, is the idea that suffering is the price the individual must be willing to pay to achieve success as a comedian. This psychobiographical mythos locates the comedian as an interstitial figure who, like the earlier clowns and fools, occupies a place of privilege (as truth teller, social commentator, carnivalesque prankster) but who is also at the same time stigmatized as an eternal outsider who never fully belongs to the culture he/she serves and critiques.

The relationship of the comic figure to the community is one of the key drivers of various forms of comic practice. In an essay on stand-up comedy, Lawrence E. Mintz (1987: 89–90) suggests that the embrace of marginality is crucial to the work of comedians, as it allows them to play out a fascinating ambivalence. On the one hand, the comedian can be a *negative exemplar* who embodies socially unacceptable traits that the audience is invited to ridicule, laugh at, repudiate, and symbolically "punish." Such traits may include stupidity, cowardice, effeteness, hypochondria, egotism, vanity, stinginess, neurosis, drunkenness, boorishness, and so on – most of which are exemplified by W.C. Fields' comic persona. On the other hand, as a *comic spokesperson* the comedian also provides insights into human behavior, social convention, injustice, political hypocrisy, and so on. In this regard, the comedian plays a quasi-anthropological role in articulating, mapping and mediating culture (see Koziski 1984: 57–76 and Mintz 1987: 90). By embodying socially unacceptable character traits, Mintz (1987: 89) suggests, the comedian may not so much exorcise them as invite the audience to "identify with his [*sic*] expression or behavior [and] secretly recognize it as reflecting natural tendencies in human activity if not socially approved ones, or publicly affirm it under the guise of 'mere comedy,' or 'just kidding.' " The experience of comedy can be fascinating for the very hesitation it sets up between these interpretative paradigms, creating uncertainty about the comedian's intentions and how the audience is "supposed" to respond. The particular relations established between negative exemplification and comic advocacy will vary from comedian to comedian, and from performance to performance, but it is the potential oscillation between the two, and the obliteration of clear-cut distinctions between them, that lends comedy its character and edge.

Unaccustomed Laughter

With its integral relationship to popular entertainment, the comedian comedy genre is inherently amenable to the carnivalesque. The early sound era, however, triggered an especially intense explosion of carnivalesque comedy onscreen – with the films of the Marx Brothers providing perhaps the most famous examples. While cinema had enlisted vaudeville, music-hall and Broadway entertainers from its early days, comic forms that relied on speech, song or sound eluded the silver screen until the late 1920s. Once this technological barrier was lifted, Hollywood could mine a rich seam of audiovisual comedy that had hitherto been restricted to live theatrical contexts. The Marx Brothers were part of large cohort of stage-trained comic talent recruited to the movies during the transitional sound era, along with Mae West, Winnie Lightner, Charlotte Greenwood, Marie Dressler, Joe E. Brown, Joe Cook, George Burns and Gracie Allen, Bert Wheeler and Robert Woolsey, Bobby Clark and Paul McCullough, Ole Olsen and Chic Johnson, and many others. With two decades of vaudeville experience to their credit, as well as hit Broadway shows, the Marx Brothers were particularly attractive to Hollywood at a juncture when it was seeking a rapid redefinition and expansion of cinematic attractions. Hollywood's massive investment in stage-trained performers was also motivated by an aggressive expansionist strategy. As Henry Jenkins (1992: 159) suggests, "ambitious studio executives saw sound as a means of broadening their entertainment empires and bringing Broadway and vaudeville under their corporate control."

The Marx Brothers were signed by Paramount Pictures, which would build a strong specialization in performer-centered comedy films in the early 1930s (Barrios 1995: 266). The first four films they made for the studio from 1929 to 1933 were phenomenally successful with critics and audiences alike.[2] With the disappointing reception accorded their fifth screen venture, *Duck Soup* (1933), Paramount subsequently refused to renew their contract, and the team was absent from cinema screens for two years. Producer Irving Thalberg then signed them to MGM and sought to broaden the comedians' appeal by, as Groucho Marx (1976: 121) puts it, "making us warm and nice, sort of, and giving our films more production values." The reboot paid instant dividends, with their first MGM release, *A Night at the Opera* (1935), proving a triumphant commercial and critical success. The team remained with MGM until 1941, but their screen vehicles became increasingly formulaic and lacked the polish of their studio debut.

Over time the Marx Brothers have ascended from being a mere comedy team to becoming the subjects of a powerful and widespread cult, fueled by countless revivals of their films in repertory cinemas, colleges and on television, as well as a seemingly endless flow of biographies, autobiographies and devotional appraisals. The cult of the Marx Brothers has its roots in early responses to the team. For example, in 1932 Antonin Artaud, *enfant terrible* of French theater, greeted them as surrealistic and poetic revolutionaries who had returned to comedy "its sense of essential liberation, of destruction of all reality in the mind" (Artaud 1977: 142). The originator of the concept of "theatre of cruelty" saw in the comedians' antics an intoxicatingly dangerous comedy that "leads toward a kind of boiling anarchy, an essential disintegration of the real by poetry" (Artaud 1977: 144). Stumbling into a London cinema to seek refuge from the rain, the English novelist, dramatist and essayist J.B. Priestley was confronted by the Marx Brothers capering onscreen in their first feature film, *The Cocoanuts* (1929). "A fantastic character entered," he later enthused, "and, without speaking a word, took the letters from the rack and casually tore them up, drank the ink, and began to eat the telephone. I sat up, lost in wonder and joy" (Priestley 1949: 36–7). From that moment on, Priestley was a diehard fan of these "inspired zanies" who "have worked out comic routines that may be regarded one day as a saga of satire, Rabelais caught on celluloid" (Priestley 1949: 38).

Marx Brothers fever caught on across the Atlantic, too, in their hometown of New York. Born into poverty to German-Jewish immigrants, these former Yorkville residents became the toast of the literati in the mid 1920s. In a typical accolade, Alexander Woollcott (1925: 44) raved about the stage version of *The Cocoanuts*: "I cannot recall ever having laughed more helplessly, more flagrantly and more continuously in the theatre than I did at the way these Marxes carried on last evening. In this response your correspondent was not alone, for the old Lyric shook with unaccustomed laughter ... *The Cocoanuts* is so funny it's positively weakening."

The Marx Brothers provided an experience unlike any other such smitten dignitaries had witnessed on stage or in films. Over and again, early commentators testify to the insurrectionist energy of the team, their ability to surprise with a rapid-fire barrage of gags, and their continual assault on convention, propriety and order of all kinds. For Artaud and Priestley, in particular, the Marx Brothers dispensed something more than mere entertainment: their comedy was revelatory, liberationist, and subversive. With subsequent admirers greeting their comedy in similar terms, the Marx Brothers would become enmeshed in an increasingly unquestioning cult of personality. Endlessly quoted, ceaselessly imitated, and championed as countercultural idols, the Marx Brothers, like their contemporary Mae West, have become fossilized as popular culture icons. So difficult is it to approach their films with eyes unclouded by the smokescreen of myth that, by comparison with the legions of more popular commentators, few scholars have dared grapple with the Marx Brothers.

Henry Jenkins rightly complains that the Marx Brothers cult often impedes adequate understanding of their films and of the contributions that writers, film studios, the vaudeville tradition, and the other performers made to screen comedy of the late 1920s and early 1930s (Jenkins 1992: 6–10). His 1992 study *What Made Pistachio Nuts: Early Sound Comedy and the Vaudeville Aesthetic* explores the broader formal and institutional negotiations that shaped the performer-centered comedy of this era. Jenkins locates the Marx Brothers as part of a much broader cycle of comedian comedy that flourished in the late 1920s and early 1930s, which he terms "anarchistic comedy." The structural and stylistic similarities between the films of the Marx Brothers and those of contemporaries such as Wheeler and Woolsey and Olsen and Johnson can be explained, he suggests, by the shaping influence of the vaudeville aesthetic. Anarchistic comedies reject the narrative ambitions of the silent features of Chaplin, Lloyd, and Keaton, which sought to integrate gags within representational contexts, in favor of more loosely structured entertainment packages that are organized around the presentation of relatively self-contained scenes of performance. They also shun the genteel comedy, sentiment and credible characterizations favored by the major 1920s' clowns (Jenkins 1992: 5).

The formal disruptiveness often celebrated in the Marx Brothers' Paramount films, Jenkins suggests, cannot adequately be ascribed to the influence of a particular set of performers but derives from the film industry's broader attempts to weld together the distinctive aesthetic regimes of classical Hollywood narrative and vaudeville performance. As Jenkins (1992: 278) puts it, an "aesthetic based on heterogeneity, affective immediacy, and performance confronted one that had long placed primary emphasis upon causality and consistency, closure and cohesiveness." The collision of these two opposing paradigms produces a peculiar and unstable hybrid that is "neither fully contained within the classical Hollywood cinema nor fully free of its norms" (Jenkins 1992: 24). The incorporation of the vaudeville aesthetic may have had a destabilizing effect on conventional Hollywood structural protocols, but it is worth stressing that contemporary US audiences for these films would recognize in them the co-presence of two highly familiar entertainment regimes. Lacking such immediate familiarity with vaudeville, later audiences, and audiences outside the United States – including such high cultural devotees as Artaud and Salvador Dali – may be more inclined to read the qualification of classical Hollywood protocols as an inherently subversive act.

Jenkins' scrupulously researched history has much to teach us about the contexts and conventions that shaped screen comedy in the late 1920s and early 1930s. But I am not convinced that he provides a fully satisfactory explanation of why the Marx Brothers in particular have attracted such attention and adulation, and continue to do so. I doubt that the films of, say, Wheeler and Woolsey would have engendered equally intense responses had they received the same level of dissemination.[3] While Jenkins is right to warn of the dangers of cultism and overexposure, the Marx Brothers' films remain fascinating and highly productive examples of comic practice that merit reasoned reappraisal. The value of Jenkins' work is that it provides the foundation for a more contextually informed appreciation of this particular team as well as of their often-overlooked contemporaries. As he illustrates, the early sound era was a period of unparalleled experimentation and innovation in screen comedy. Anarchistic comedy itself challenged the assimilationist trajectory of classical film narrative in both ideological and formal terms. As Jenkins puts it (in Balio 1995: 263), these early sound comedies "often celebrate the collapse of social order and the liberation of the creativity and impulsiveness of their protagonist."

Plurality Humor

It is tempting to read the Marx Brothers as lower-class immigrant insurgents who invaded the privileged universe of mainstream entertainment to wreak havoc on its orderly procedures and hegemonic privileges. Such interpretations are common currency within the popular cult of the Marx Brothers, which depicts the comedians as impulsively creative *agents provocateurs* whose inherently anarchic personalities provoke them to rebel at the slightest whiff of order and constraint. As Jenkins suggests, such highly romanticized accounts confuse the agency of the comic performers with the formal and ideological strategies of the films in which they appear. In actuality, their films and Broadway shows were complexly mediated constructions that derived from a collaborative tension between diverse cultural registers, traditions and practitioners. Tino Balio (1995: 263), for example, describes anarchistic comedy as combining together influences from vaudeville, silent-era slapstick, Broadway musical comedies, and the urbane comic writing that flourished after World War 1 and reveled in wordplay and absurdity.[4] In particular, the mainstream success the Marx Brothers enjoyed as stars of Broadway and Hollywood, and the exceptional status they attained as entertainers, owe a great deal to the alliance between these veteran vaudevillians and an elite group of New York intellectuals.

When they first hit cinema screens in 1929, the Marx Brothers had amassed over 20 years' experience touring a succession of sketch-based acts around US vaudeville circuits – such as *Fun in Hi Skool, Mr. Green's Reception, Home Again,* and *On the Mezzanine.* These shows allowed the team's members to develop and refine their trademark personas, and the routines they would deploy in later showcases – such as Harpo's mime gags, Chico's Italian immigrant routine, Groucho's wise guy monologues and eccentric dancing, and the musical interludes of Chico and Harpo. Vaudeville equipped them with a varied repertoire of musical and comedy specialties that would stand them in good stead in later years. For example, the Orpheum Circuit program for their sketch *N' Everything* notes that, "The Marx Brothers introduce a variety of amusements, indeed it is hard to find a theatrical accomplishment they do not excel in that is not incorporated in their performance" (Marx 1976: 33). As a family unit, moreover, the various members of the team – Groucho, Chico, Harpo, Gummo, and, latterly, Zeppo – developed a singular on-stage rapport that enabled them to read one another intuitively and to know how far they could push each other in improvising around set routines.

The Marx Brothers were an attractive prospect for Hollywood not merely because of such vaudeville experiences but because of the manner in which they adapted their style to the Broadway stage, and in the process attracted the acclaim and patronage of influential tastemakers. After a disastrous attempt to crack Broadway with the 1919 musical comedy *The Cinderella Girl,* the team gambled again a few years later with the revue *I'll Say She Is!* (Mitchell 1996: 127). Described by Groucho Marx (1976: 40) as "a conglomeration of old gags and routines," the show proved a huge success, drawing rave notices and playing on Broadway for nearly two years. *Variety* (1924: 16) called it the "best burlesque show ... of the season," noting that Groucho and Harpo "had the house in an uproar, not once, but a number of times." Reviewing the show for the *New York World,* esteemed critic Alexander Woollcott (1924: 103) praised the team as "talented cutups," nominating Harpo as one of the all-time great comic clowns and Groucho as "a crafty comedian with a rather fresher and more whimsical assortment of quips than is the lot of most refugees from vaudeville." Other contemporary critics described the show as "the riot of the Summer season," "The greatest show I've seen in 25 years," and – from Charlie Chaplin – "the best musical comedy revue I've ever seen" (in Marx 1976: 48).

The success of *I'll Say She Is!* made the Marx Brothers the toast of Broadway, bringing them the support of such distinguished litterateurs as Woollcott, Percy Hammond, Franklin P. Adams, George S. Kaufman and George Jean Nathan (Adamson 1974: 62). Nathan's response to the team offers insights into why this particular group of entertainers may have resonated so powerfully with these elite cultural voices. A distinguished theatre critic, Nathan stamped his presence on the New York cultural scene through prolific reviews for various newspapers and journals. He also collaborated with H.L. Mencken on the influential literary magazines *The Smart Set: A Magazine of Cleverness* and *The American Mercury*. Nathan covered a range of dramatic forms, performers and playwrights during his career, but had a special fondness for the burlesque comedians he encountered during his boyhood in the 1890s (see Nathan 1915, 1917, 1918, 1919a, 1919b, and 1943). For Nathan, low comedians possessed a vigor and authenticity lacking in more respectable theatrical forms. His most elaborate defense of low comedy can be found in his 1919 essay "The national humor," which is worth quoting at length for Nathan's almost Bakhtinian reading of burlesque-derived comedy as the defining humor of the age:

> The national humor of America … is in the main its lowest and most vulgar humor … [It] is obviously enough the humor not of the few, but of the mass – the plurality humor. [T]he representative humor of the American people is, I believe, the humor of the cheap vaudevilles and the burlesque show … The national humor is the low, broad, easy, vulgar humor that appeals alike to the Elk and the member of the Union Club, the motorman and the owner of a Rolls-Royce, the congressman and the chiropodist, the YMCA superintendent and the brothel keeper, the artist and the shoe clerk: the humor that tickles alike the ribs of ignoramus and intellectual, of rich and poor, of rowdy and genteel, of black, white and tan. And where other than in burlesque do we find this humor in America? Whether spoken humor or physical humor, this burlesque humor regularly graduated to the more legitimate popular stage, to the popular magazines, to the popular songs and books and moving pictures, and so given a thorough national circulation is more often than any other form of American humor successful in amusing the generality of the American people. This burlesque humor, further, is of typical American accent and expression, as the burlesque show itself is a typical American product: one will not find the like of it anywhere in the world. (Nathan 1919b; 239–46)

For Nathan, this is an inherently leveling and democratizing humor that does not depend on or reinforce social distinctions. It is a laughter that transcends artificial divisions of class, education and refinement, its specifically American vernacular dynamism serving as a liberatory tool of cultural unification. In his review of *I'll Say She Is!* Nathan suggests that the Marx Brothers resurrected the raw exuberance of this vital, authentic and quintessential American humor:

> In such low comedians as they, we get again the sweet and fragrant rosemary of the old American burlesque show, beyond a doubt the funniest thing in the music

show line that the stage of any nation has ever seen. The Marxes stem directly from Watson, Bickel and Wrothe and the various other comic teams that adorned the burlesque stage thirty years ago when it was at its zenith and before it started on the sharp decline that was to land it, and lose it, in the second-hand costumes and settings of lately deceased Broadway musical comedies. (in Marx 1976: 50)

Unlike such enthusiasts as Artaud and Priestley, Nathan's assessment of the team is grounded in his intimate familiarity with the broader contexts of US entertainment culture, both high and low. Moreover, when the Marx Brothers took Broadway by storm there were plenty of other comic performers to compare them to. In October 1924 a *Time* magazine article identified the Marx Brothers as part of a much larger cohort of vaudeville-trained comedians who were currently playing key roles in Broadway productions. "The musical comedy and revue season in Manhattan is fast becoming a laughing matter," the *Time* scribe (The Theatre: Loudest and Funniest. The Comedians are Coming 1924) commented. "No matter where you go, you run into a lot of crazy comedians ... With the few inevitable exceptions, every great comedian we have will be winter-quartered in Manhattan." Other names mentioned in the article include Ed Wynn, Eddie Cantor, Joe Cook, James Barton, W.C. Fields, Raymond Hitchcock, Charlotte Greenwood, Fanny Brice, Robert Benchley, Clark and McCullough, Leon Errol, Fred Stone, Jack Hazzard, and Frank Tinney – many of whom would, like the Marx Brothers, be enlisted for talking pictures a few years later.[5]

They were by no means the only crazy comics to progress from vaudeville to more upmarket showcases, but the Marx Brothers certainly had no peers when it came to securing the patronage of New York's influential tastemakers. Woollcott was so excited after seeing *I'll Say She Is!* that he rallied his Algonquin cronies to do the same (Mitchell 1996: 247).[6] One of his acquaintances, George S. Kaufman, proved crucial in the subsequent development of the Marx Brothers' career. Described by Groucho Marx (1976: 55) as "the wittiest man I ever knew," Kaufman was a successful playwright, theater director and *New York Times* drama critic who befriended Harpo Marx via Woollcott. Producer Sam Harris persuaded Kaufman and illustrious songwriter Irving Berlin to devise a musical comedy for the Marx Brothers as a follow up to *I'll Say She Is!* The resulting show, *The Cocoanuts*, opened at the Lyric Theatre in December 1925 and was a great success, playing 377 performances before embarking on a national tour (Mitchell 1996: 58). This was followed by another hit musical comedy, *Animal Crackers*, written by Kaufman and New York poet-dramatist Morrie Ryskind, who had contributed rewrites to *The Cocoanuts*.[7]

While their breakthrough Broadway success was a direct product of vaudeville's entertainment culture, the comedy disseminated through the Marx Brothers' films was shaped by a creative alliance between vaudevillians and New York *litterateurs*. As Stefan Kanfer (2000: 98) comments, "Unquestionably, the bedrock of their style was formed by the Marxes and only the Marxes in their vaudeville years. But it was Kaufman who furnished the polish and professionalism they lacked until *The Cocoanuts.*" These two very different cultural constituencies were brought together through a shared love of the carnivalesque. As contemporary reviews testify repeatedly, these urban intellectuals were thrilled by the Marx Brothers' distinctively realized comic insurgency, which, as George Jean Nathan rejoiced, channeled the raw vitality of less restrained and more assertively popular low comedy traditions. The Marx Brothers' exuberant desecration of propriety, order and rationality clearly appealed to critical palates that were jaded by the more polite appetizers of Broadway drawing room and musical comedy. They may not have been the only practitioners of crazy comedy during the 1920s, but the Marx Brothers offered such an intoxicating entertainment experience that New York's finest cultural advocates wanted not just to enjoy it but also to join in with it. And when the Marx Brothers made the leap from stage to screen, their comedy was available to much larger audience both within the United States and across the world. The final section of this chapter will explore the carnivalesque dynamics of the Marx Brothers' comedy in more detail, focusing on their 1931 Paramount film *Monkey Business.*

Rabelais on Celluloid

Where *The Cocoanuts* (1929) and *Animal Crackers* (1930) were slightly modified transpositions of their Broadway hits, *Monkey Business* was the first Marx Brother film written specifically for the screen. It was also the first film they made in Hollywood, as their previous screen comedies were shot at Paramount's Astoria Studios in Queen's, New York – an arrangement that allowed the team to continue their Broadway engagements. The *Monkey Business* project took the Marx Brothers out of their comfort zone as it required them to perform material they had not already tested onstage. Aiming to replicate the creative alliances that fed their Broadway success, the team enlisted as their initial screenwriters former cartoonist Will B. Johnstone, who had written the book for *I'll Say She Is!* and highbrow scribe S.J. Perelman, a Brown University alumnus, essayist and cartoonist. Just as Groucho had been impressed by Kaufman's wit, so, too, he was drawn by the puns and absurdities of Perelman's prose (Kanfer 2000: 139). A disastrous first reading of the script led to many other contributors being drafted in for a lengthy rewriting process, including drama critic Arthur Sheekman and law student and gag-writer Nat Perrin – who would both work for the team on future projects. The Marx Brothers also interpolated routines they had developed elsewhere (Adamson 1974: 135–8).

Perelman and Johnstone originated the idea of casting the Marx Brothers as stowaways on an ocean liner (Adamson 1974: 122), a scenario that places them immediately as outsiders who are smuggling themselves into a world of privilege. The film opens with Groucho, Harpo, Chico and Zeppo hiding in their

Figure 4.2   The Marx Brothers in their kippered herring barrels (*Monkey Business*; producer Herman J. Mankiewicz).

individual kippered herring barrels in the hold of a ship bound for the New World (see Figure 4.2).[8] Besides identifying the Marx Brothers as creatures from the lower class, their hiding place also hints at a theme that would play across this and other Marx Brothers films – their status as ethnic outsiders within a WASP universe. Herrings are strongly associated with the cuisine of the Ashkenazi Jews of Central and Eastern Europe, a fact that could hardly have escaped either the comedians or the film's almost exclusively Jewish writing personnel.[9]

At the same time as the comedians are introduced in the herring barrels, the soundtrack presents them harmonizing on Richard H. Gerard and Harry W. Armstrong's barbershop quartet standard "Sweet Adeline" (1903), a nostalgic and wistfully sentimental paean to bucolic Americana, with its imagery of nightingales, brooks, clouds and sunshine. The incongruity between the ballad and the herring barrels juxtaposes two vastly opposed regimes of cultural possibility – the sweet-smelling American pastoral and a far less fragrant European otherness. When the Marx Brothers finally reveal themselves, their grotesquery further invalidates the cozy sentiments of "Sweet Adeline." Groucho, Chico and Harpo have become such iconic figures that it is easy to forget the shock of their otherworldly stylization. With the exception of in-house straight man Zeppo, the Marx Brothers belong together because they do clearly belong anywhere else. Their costumes, their movements and their speech (or lack thereof) identify them as creatures from an alternative universe.

Monkey Business has a clearly defined two-part structure: the first deals with the disorderly adventures of the stowaways on the ship, while the second charts their hi-jinks at a high-class party in the United States. In each case, these underclass insurgents assault the protocols of elite society. What qualifies the comedy as carnivalesque, however, is the fact that the attack on an exclusionary social order is accompanied by an emphasis on alternative values of community and solidarity.[10] For example, the scene with the herring barrels, where the Marx Brothers join together in vocal harmony, introduces them as an eccentric yet coherent social unit. Throughout the film they operate as a community of resistance that is unified by a shared hostility towards established formulations of social position, language, and identity.[11]

In his book *American Laughter*, Mark Winokur (1996: 137) suggests that the introduction of synchronized sound to cinema "enabled a Bakhtinian dialogism in which a multiplicity of voices compete for attention and primacy." Such heterogeneity is inscribed as a key principle of the Marx Brothers team, which combines the linguistic arabesques of Groucho's wise-guy hucksterism, the deadpan aggressivity of Chico's faux Italian discourse, and Harpo's very refusal of speech. Alternatively competing against and colluding with one another, these eccentric linguistic styles repeatedly confront formalized discourse – such as the politesse of social elites, or the rhetoric of romance, or the clichéd argot of the movie hoodlum (in *Monkey Business'* parodic gangster subplot). The sound film also enabled the vernacular profiling of ethnically marked voices, accents, dialects and identities to become a key part of the texture of comedy. Thus, C.P. Lee (1998: 168) can read the team's linguistic comedy as an implicit struggle against assimilation, suggesting that "the English of the Marx Brothers is that of a dominant tongue filtered, mediated and regurgitated through the consciousness of an essential ethnicity of perception." Joel Rosenberg (in Hoberman and Shandler, 2003: 163) concurs, arguing that "The zany, anarchic energy of the Marx Brothers, their subversive wordplay and dizzying non-sequitur, suggest a kind of Melting Pot meltdown."[12]

Winokur situates the Marx Brothers within an extended history of negotiation between ethnic identity and the mainstream, in both American cinema and the broader culture. They demonstrate, he suggests (Winokur 1996: 126), how ethnic dynamics can make a revitalizing contribution to the host culture without being accommodated within or subordinated to it.[13] To describe the operational logistics of their comedy, Winokur (1996: 129) invokes the concept of *landsmannschaft*, an organization formed of individuals from the same village that sought "to maintain a recognizable bond apart from sanctioned identities; as an attempt to help the immigrant fit in, it emphasized a memory and history separate from American memory and history." Beyond establishing *landsmannschaft* relations among themselves, the Marx Brothers also seek through their comedy to include the audience within this alternative community dynamic (Winokur 1996: 135–6).

By siding with the comic resistance of the Marx Brothers onscreen, the audience is encouraged to participate vicariously in the overturning of established structures, hierarchies and protocols and to side with the oppositional communal alliance they embody. This transaction is achieved via distinctive carnivalesque strategies, which include rejecting singular conceptions of cultural identity in favor of multiplicity, satirizing desires for upward mobility, and disrupting the self-sufficiency of both language and fiction (Winokur 1996: 143). To conclude this chapter I will briefly consider how such comic practices operate in characteristic scenes from *Monkey Business*.

Delirious Abandon

After being discovered in the hold, the four stowaways are chased round the decks by the ship's officers. Immediately, we see them refusing to behave in a manner consistent with their illicit and subordinate social status: instead of seeking to hide from their pursuers, these upstarts flaunt themselves in delirious abandon. They aim not simply to evade authority, but to outfox it, to belittle it, and to mock its very jurisdiction through acts of interactive pranksterism. A suite of scenes near the start of the film clearly outlines such carnivalesque aspirations. Groucho runs into the ship's captain (Ben Taggart) as the latter is attempting to impress a bevy of young women with the boast that he'll have the stowaways "in the brig before long." Groucho dismisses the women and then launches into one of his absurdist "word cascades," which, as Siegfried Kracauer notes, undermines "the spoken word from within":

> [H]is impossible delivery, both glib like water flowing down tiles and cataclysmic like a deluge, tends to obstruct the sanctioned functions of speech ... Silly and shrewd, scatterbrained and subversive, his repartees are bubbling self-assertions rather than answers or injunctions ... [His utterances] disrupt the ongoing conversation so radically that no message or opinion voiced reaches its destination. Whatever Groucho is saying disintegrates speech all around him (Kracauer 1997: 108)

The exasperated captain makes several ineffectual attempts to restore sanity, but Groucho transforms their encounter into an assaultive monologue:

GROUCHO: Are these your gloves? I found them in your trunk. You girls go to your rooms – I'll be down shortly.
CAPTAIN: Who are you?!
GROUCHO: Are you the floorwalker of this ship?
CAPTAIN: Floor-?
GROUCHO: I want to register a complaint.
CAPTAIN: Why, what's the matter?
GROUCHO: Matter enough. Do you know who sneaked into my stateroom at three o'clock this morning?
CAPTAIN: Who did that?
GROUCHO: Nobody. And that's my complaint. I'm young. I want gaiety, laughter, ha-cha-cha. I wanna dance! [*dances and sings*] I wanna dance 'til the cows come ho-o-ome!

CAPTAIN: Just what do you mean by this!

GROUCHO: Another thing – I don't care for the way you're running this boat. Why don't you get in the back seat for a while and let your wife drive?

CAPTAIN: I want you to know that I've been Captain of this ship for twenty-two years.

GROUCHO: Twenty-two years, eh? If you were a man, you'd go in business for yourself. I know a fellow started only last year with just a canoe. Now he's got more women than you can shake a stick at ... if that's your idea of a good time.

CAPTAIN: One more word out of you, and I'll throw you in irons! [*Groucho sits in deckchair*]

GROUCHO: You can't do it with irons; it's a mashie shot. It's a mashie shot if the wind is against you, [*stands up again*] and if the wind isn't I am. And how about those barrels down below?

CAPTAIN: Barrels?

GROUCHO: Yeah, I wouldn't put a pig in one of those barrels.

CAPTAIN: Now, see here you –

GROUCHO: No, not even if you go down on your knees. And here's your gloves. [*Offers gloves to Captain, then snatches them away*] You would take 'em, wouldn't you?

CAPTAIN: Why you. –

GROUCHO: [*enters the chart room*] And keep away from my office.

During this exchange Groucho runs rings around the captain, stripping him of his capacity to exert command by reversing the polarity of hierarchical relations. Instead of acting like a cowering miscreant, Groucho hurls a series of insults and complaints at the flummoxed officer in a tone of affronted authority. He talks so speedily, moreover, that the captain can hardly get a word in – and when he does manage to do so, the impudent stowaway ignores him or brusquely cuts him off. Groucho also delights in rapidly rerouting the direction of discourse so the captain is unable to predict where things are heading – as when he pretends offense at the prospect of an intruder in his cabin, only to twist the grievance round to mean its opposite. In a characteristic piece of Marxian linguistic sabotage, Groucho tosses in a pun that further strips the captain of his ability to wrest control of the situation: he transforms "irons" from a marker of incarceration into a signifier of play (the 'mashie iron' golf club). In characteristic fashion, the Marx Brothers' comedy exploits the ambiguity of language, exposing its unreliability and instability.

As played by Ben Taggart, the captain is a pretty easy target. Totally oblivious to the fact that he is in a comedy, this excessively inflexible straight man fails to perceive the evident absurdity of his adversary and the crimes he perpetrates against language and logic. Taggart remains stiff and immovable throughout the scene, while the comedian is continuously in motion – stepping back and forth, twisting and turning, breaking into dance, gesticulating wildly with his cigar, sitting in and rising rapidly from the deckchair. In opposition to such unbending emissaries of law, authority and privilege, the Marx Brothers reveal themselves as spirited, quick-witted and protean forces of nature. The encounter with the captain is followed by the scene discussed at the start of this chapter, which relocates the axis of conflict between Chico's ersatz immigrant and Groucho's pretend captain. When the ship's first mate, Gibson (Tom Kennedy), enters the chart room, Groucho and Chico retreat under the table. With an external threat once more entering their sphere of operations, they break into broad smiles and beam at one another in reaffirmed solidarity. When Gibson leaves, Chico and Groucho make their way to the captain's cabin, where they proceed to steal his dinner. The strategic dislocations they have just deployed against one another – insults, wisecracks, puns, and twisted logic – are now redirected at a bona fide representative of the ruling elite, unifying Groucho and Chico against their common foe.

Although Groucho may seem to have the worst of it in the mock history lesson he delivers to Chico, he repeatedly signals his distance from the role he is playing. For example, when asked to identify himself as he calls the galley to order food, Groucho looks inside his purloined hat and declares: "Who am I? I'm the Captain." This bit of business implies that authority, and indeed identity, may be little more than a dress code. This is one of numerous gags in the Marx Brothers' films that expose the concept of inherent and unified identity as a fiction. Other notable examples include the sequence in *Duck Soup* where both Chico and Harpo try to pass themselves as Groucho's mirror image, and the scene in *Monkey Business* where the four stowaways try to persuade immigration officials that each of them is Maurice Chevalier, by brandishing the French singer's passport and embarking on a rendition of his song "You Brought a New Kind of Love To Me." Their patently absurd impressions make little effort to construct a convincing simulation of the dapper Frenchman: Chico sings in his heavily accented Italian voice, Groucho retains his moustache, and Harpo tops the sequence by relinquishing speech in favor of a pantomime enacted to a phonographic recording of Chevalier's song. With a gramophone strapped to his back, Harpo comes unstuck when the disc spins at the wrong speed. This joke is directed not only at early sound-on-disc film systems but also at the phantasmic wholeness of the represented self in early sound cinema, an illusion based on concealing the split between recorded image and recorded voice. Similar jokes abound in the pseudo-satiric account of Hollywood's transition to sound presented by *Singin' in the Rain* (1952), but the scene in *Monkey Business* perhaps more insistently exposes the fictional identity of the sound film itself.

Monkey Business presents a further brisk example of deconstructive identity gaming in the scene where Groucho flirts with bored wife Lucille (Thelma Todd) in her stateroom, and finds himself confronted by her mobster husband, Alky Briggs (Harry Woods). To dumbfound his inflexible opponent, Groucho zips through a dizzying succession of rapid-fire impersonations – including an outraged Southern colonel, a housewife, a quizmaster, a young boy, and a flirtatious girl. This sequence also allows Lucille to join in the fun. Rather than treating her as the object of lecherous pursuit, or as the butt of insults – as happens with the Marx Brothers' regular foil, Margaret Dumont – Groucho engages Lucille as a convivial sparring partner who participates in his madcap frolics. An agile and experienced comedienne, as well as a former beauty queen, Thelma Todd brings considerable panache to her playing of Lucille Briggs, providing a rare opportunity to extend the Marx Brothers' dissident *landsmannschaft* beyond its usual boys' club boundaries.

While *Monkey Business* does feature a plot of sorts, involving the rivalry between mobsters Alky Briggs and Joe Helton (Rockliffe Fellowes) and the kidnapping of the latter's daughter, Mary (Ruth Hall), the film refuses to develop it coherently. The final scenes present the Marx Brothers outwitting the kidnappers and rescuing Mary, but this is accomplished in a flamboyantly mocking and ramshackle manner. Rather than aiming to resolve its plot intrigues, the film simply stops – which is, or course, perfectly consistent with its denarrativizing, carnivalesque trajectory. In lieu of a conclusion, I would like to wrap up my consideration of the Marx Brothers by briefly drawing attention to the implications of this chapter's title, plucked from the Chico-Groucho exchange quoted at the beginning.

In what would later become a clichéd rhetorical move in discussions of the team's comedy, J.B. Priestley (1949: 38) observed that "Karl Marx showed us how the dispossessed would finally take possession. But I think the Brothers Marx do it better." Priestley's comparison between the great socialist philosopher and the American entertainment team is, of course, playfully opportunistic. But at the same time, the two do arguably share more in common than their surnames, and the German-Jewish heritage this connotes. If not actual revolutionaries, the Marx Brothers did work a peculiar alchemical magic that transformed entertainment (matinees) into a carnivalesque festival of aesthetic insurrectionism (mutinees). Over a century after they first trod the boards, and long after they have passed from the land of the living, these comic lords of misrule continue to entice and dazzle audiences with their strangely compulsive liberationist revelry. The "anarchistic" frolics of the Marx Brothers may not presume to transform society but, like the medieval carnival, their enlightened and enlightening laughter does tease productively with alternative ways of thinking about relations between individuals and the social order.

Notes

1. Writers on film comedy influenced by Bakhtin's work on carnival include Paul (1994), Rowe (1995), Krutnik (2000) and many contributors to Horton (1991).
2. *Variety* listed the Marx Brothers' fourth film, *Horse Feathers* (1932), among the top-grossing films of its year (Balio, 1995: 405), and it was also celebrated in a *Time* magazine cover feature (*Time* 1932).
3. In keeping with his canon-busting project, Jenkins restricts scrutiny of the Marx Brothers to attributes they share in common with other contemporary

comedians – although his position is somewhat compromised by the decision to adorn the cover of *Pistachio* with an image of Groucho Marx!

4. For more on such literate crazy humor, associated with Stephen Leacock, Donald Ogden Stewart, Robert Benchley and others, see Weales (1985: 57–60).

5. *Time* may have been right to spot a current trend, but comedians had played central roles in Broadway productions since much earlier. Ethan Mordden identifies the star comic as the oldest ingredient in musical comedy. Comedian-centered shows, he suggests, persisted as an alternative to the book musicals pioneered by Oscar Hammerstein and Jerome Kern, with such performers as Cantor, Wynn, Bert Lahr and Bobby Clark frolicking "in a storyless vacuum at a time when the musical was emphasizing story." Apart from Clark, he notes, the comedians who came to dominate the Broadway shows of the 1910s and 1920s were all Jewish (Mordden 1983: 58, 63).

6. The wits of the Algonquin Round Table adopted Harpo Marx as something of a mascot, and he developed a close friendship with Woollcott that lasted till the latter's death in 1943 (see Marx with Barber 1981: 169–81).

7. Ryskind adapted both *The Cocoanuts* and *Animal Crackers* for the screen, collaborated with Kaufman on the screenplay for *A Night at the Opera*, and wrote the team's awkward 1938 RKO comedy *Room Service* (Marx and Anobile 1976: 128–43).

8. This is the only film in which the Marx Brothers are not given fictionally specific character identities, but are credited simply as Groucho, Chico, Harpo and Zeppo. In what follows, I generally use these names to refer to what the Marx Brothers do onscreen, without implying any broader extra-filmic agency.

9. A nutritious food that conformed to Jewish dietary laws, herrings have been a popular part of the diet of the Ashkenazi Jews since the Middle Ages, with Jewish merchants coming to dominate the European trade in the fish. Salted or pickled herrings became a staple food of the poor in Eastern Europe because of their low cost and long shelf life (Marks 2010: 262–3). Kippered herrings themselves appear to be associated more with émigré Jewish communities in the United States.

10. While acknowledging similarities between the comedians and Bakhtin's conception of the grotesque body, Jenkins (1992: 223) dismisses carnivalesque interpretations of their work because "the Marx Brothers' films embrace a conception of expressive individualism that would contrast sharply with the communalism Bakhtin identifies in Rabelais." He underestimates, however, the degree to which their stylized eccentricity identifies the Marx Brothers as a community of outsiders, as well as their frequent affiliation with actual outsider communities, such as the shipboard immigrants in *A Night at the Opera* and the poor African American community in *A Day at the Races* (1937).

11. Bakhtin (1984: 11–12) regarded hostility as a key feature of carnival's festive laughter: "this laughter is ambivalent: it is gay, triumphant, and at the same time mocking, deriding. It asserts and denies, it buries and revives. Such is the laughter of carnival."

12. For further analysis of the forms and ramifications of linguistic play in the Marx Brothers comedy, see Mellencamp (1983) and French (2001: 44).

13. To enjoy the liberatory antics of the Marx Brothers onscreen, it is not essential to identify them, or to identify with them, as either Jewish or as immigrants. Groucho Marx himself (1976: 21) suggested that "we Marx Brothers never denied our Jewishness. We simply didn't use it. We could have safely fallen back on Yiddish theatre,

making secure careers for ourselves. But our act was designed from the start to have a broad appeal." Hoberman and Shandler (2003: 159) note that "No other American performers have engendered more wide-ranging speculation on the Jewish origins of their art than the Marx Brothers" Such claims, they suggest, may be fed more by "the range of observers' own notions of ... [Jewish] culture" rather than illuminating the Jewish roots of the team's comedy.

References

Adamson, Joe (1974) *Groucho, Harpo, Chico and Sometimes Zeppo: A History of the Marx Brothers and a Satire on the Rest of the World*, Coronet, London.

Artaud, Antonin (1977) The Marx Brothers, *The Theatre and its Double*, Calder, London, pp. 142–4.

Bakhtin, Mikhail (1984) *Rabelais and His World*, Indiana University Press, Bloomington, IN.

Balio, Tino (1995) *Grand Design: Hollywood as a Modern Business Enterprise, 1930–1939*, University of California Press, Berkeley, CA.

Barrios, Richard (1995) *A Song in the Dark: The Birth of the Musical Film*, Oxford University Press, New York, NY.

French, Tony (2001) I wonder whatever became of me? *CineAction*, 55 (July), 41–9.

Hoberman, J. and Shandler, Jeffrey (eds.) (2003) *Entertaining America: Jews, Movies, and Broadcasting*, The Jewish Museum/Princeton University Press, New York, NY.

Horton, Andrew (ed.) (1991) *Comedy/Cinema/Theory*, University of California Press, Berkeley, CA.

Jenkins, Henry (1992) *What Made Pistachio Nuts: Early Sound Comedy and the Vaudeville Aesthetic*, Columbia University Press, New York, NY.

Kanfer, Stefan (2000) *Groucho: The Life and Times of Julius Henry Marx*, Penguin, London.

Koziski, Stephanie (1984) The standup comedian as anthropologist. *Journal of Popular Culture*, 18 (2), 57–76.

Kracauer, Siegfried (1997) *Theory of Film: The Redemption of Physical Reality*, Princeton University Press, Princeton, NJ.

Krutnik, Frank (2000) *Inventing Jerry Lewis*, Smithsonian Institution Press, Washington DC.

Lee, C.P. (1998) "Yeah, and I used to be a Hunchback": immigrants, humor and the Marx Brothers, in *Because I Tell A Joke or Two: Comedy, Politics and Sexual Difference* (ed. Stephen Wagg), Routledge, New York, NY, pp. 244–72.

Marks, Gil (2010) Herring, *Encyclopedia of Jewish Food*, John Wiley & Sons, Inc., Hoboken, NJ, pp. 262–3.

Marx, Groucho (1976) *The Groucho Phile: An Illustrated Life*, Galahad Books, New York, NY.

Marx, Groucho and Anobile, Richard J. (1976) *The Marx Brothers Scrapbook*, Star Books, New York, NY.

Marx, Harpo with Barber, Rowland (1981) *Harpo Speaks!* Coronet, London.

Mellencamp, Patricia (1983) Jokes and their relation to the Marx Brothers, in *Cinema and Language* (eds. Stephen Heath and Patricia Mellencamp), University Publications of America, Frederick, MD, pp. 63–78.

Mintz, Lawrence E. (1987) The standup comedian as social and cultural mediator, in *American Humor* (ed. Arthur Dudden), Oxford University Press, New York, NY, pp. 85–96.

Mitchell, Glenn (1996) *The Marx Brothers Encyclopedia*, Batsford, London.

Mordden, Ethan (1983) *Broadway Babes: The People Who Made the American Musical*, Oxford University Press, New York, NY.

Paul, William (1994) *Laughing, Screaming: Modern Hollywood Horror and Comedy*, Columbia University Press, New York, NY.

Nathan, George Jean (1915) The cream of low comedy. *The Smart Set*, 45 (1), 451–7.

Nathan, George Jean (1917) Slapsticks and Rosemary, *Mr. George Jean Nathan Presents*, Alfred A. Knopf, New York, NY, pp. 97–8.

Nathan, George Jean (1918) It's comedians, in *The Popular Theatre*, Alfred A. Knopf, New York, NY, pp. 114–20.

Nathan, George Jean (1919a) Harry Watson Jr., in *Comedians All*, Alfred A. Knopf, New York, NY, pp. 76–8.

Nathan, George Jean (1919b) The national humor, in *Comedians All*, Alfred A. Knopf, New York, pp. 236–49.

Nathan, George Jean (1943) Laugh, town, laugh, *The Theatre Book of the Year, 1942–3: A Record and an Interpretation*, Alfred A Knopf, New York, NY, pp. 11–17.

Priestley, J.B. (1949) *Delight*, Heinemann, London.

Rowe, Kathleen (1995) *The Unruly Woman: Gender and the Genres of Laughter*, University of Texas Press, Austin, TX.

Seidman, Steve (1981) *Comedian Comedy: A Tradition in Hollywood Film*, UMI Research Press, Ann Arbor, MI.

Stam, Robert (2000) Alternative aesthetics: introduction, in *Film and Theory: An Anthology* (eds. Robert Stam and Toby Miller), Blackwell, Malden MA, pp. 257–64.

The Theatre: Loudest and Funniest. The Comedians are Coming (1924) *Time* (October 20), http://www.time.com/time/magazine/article/0,9171,769093,00.html (accessed May 18, 2012).

Cinema: *Horse Feathers* (1932) *Time* (15 August), http://www.time.com/time/magazine/article/0,9171,744191,00.html (accessed May 18, 2012).

Variety (1924) New Plays Produced Within Week on B'Way: *I'll Say She Is!* (May 28), pp. 16–17.

Weales, Gerald (1985) *Canned Goods as Caviar: American Film Comedy of the 1930s*, University of Chicago Press, Chicago, IL.

Winokur, Mark (1996) *American Laughter: Immigrants, Ethnicity, and 1930s Hollywood Film Comedy*, Macmillan, London.

Woollcott, Alexander (1924) Harpo Marx and Some Brothers: Hilarious Antics Spread Good Cheer at the Casino. *New York World*, 20 May; reproduced in Marx, Groucho and Anobile, Richard J. (1976) *The Marx Brothers Scrapbook*, Star Books, New York, NY, pp. 103–4.

Woollcott, Alexander (1925) Laughter at the Lyric, *The Stage* (December 31), p. 44.

Further Reading

Karnick, Kristine Brunovska Karnick and Jenkins, Henry (eds.) (1995) *Classical Hollywood Comedy*, Routledge, New York, NY. A robust anthology of original, largely historically focused essays on Hollywood comedy from leading scholars in the field, with indispensible work on romantic comedy, comedian films, and the relations between gags, performance and narrative.

Krutnik, Frank (2000) *Inventing Jerry Lewis*, Smithsonian Institution Press, Washington, DC. A multifaceted exploration of the work and significance of controversial Hollywood comedian Jerry Lewis, which examines his hugely successful partnership with Dean Martin, his work as a solo performer, his hotly contested achievements as a total filmmaker, and his work on the MDA Telethon.

Krutnik, Frank (ed.) (2003) *Hollywood Comedians: The Film Reader*, Routledge, London. A critical anthology that gathers together seminal scholarship on Hollywood comedian films from the silent era to the present, featuring contributions from Steve Seidman, Henry Jenkins, Mark Winokur, Joanna Rapf, Kathleen Rowe and many others.

Mellencamp, Patricia (1983) Jokes and their Relation to the Marx Brothers, in Heath, Stephen and Mellencamp, Patricia (eds.) *Cinema and Language*, University Publications of America, Frederick, MD, pp. 63–78. A lively and thoughtful interrogation of the linguistic operations of the Marx Brothers' comedy, drawing on the theories of Sigmund Freud and Jacques Lacan.

Rowe, Kathleen (1995) *The Unruly Woman: Gender and the Genres of Laughter*, University of Texas Press, Texas, TX. Rowe uses and qualifies Bakhtin's work on the carnivalesque in this fascinating feminist exploration of the trope of the unruly woman, which tackles screwball romantic comedy, Roseanne Barr, Miss Piggy, Mae West and other female performers.

Seidman, Steve (1981) *Comedian Comedy: A Tradition in Hollywood Film*, UMI Research Press, Ann Arbor, MI. An agenda-setting work of scholarship on the dynamics of Hollywood comedian films from the silent era to the 1970s, which explores the formal negotiations between performance and fiction as well as the tension between social conformism and counter-cultural impulses.

Winokur, Mark (1996) *American Laughter: Immigrants, Ethnicity, and 1930s Hollywood Film Comedy*, Macmillan, London. An ambitious, wide ranging and original study that situates the comedy of Chaplin, the Marx Brothers and the romantic team of William Powell and Myrna Loy in relation to broader negotiations in American culture between ethnic identity and the mainstream.

5

Jacques Tati and Comedic Performance

Kevin W. Sweeney

Although recognized as one of cinema's great writers and directors of film comedy, Jacques Tati is remembered by most film enthusiasts as a comic actor, most famously incarnated on the screen as the character Monsieur Hulot.[1] Tati introduced the character of Monsieur Hulot in his second feature-length film, *Les Vacances de M. Hulot* (1953) (*Mr. Hulot's Holiday*) (see Figure 5.1). The first scene in which the viewer can closely observe Hulot's comic actions shows him arriving at his seaside holiday hotel and unloading his bags and vacation paraphernalia such as a butterfly net from his dilapidated old convertible, an Amilcar. Bags in hand, Hulot enters the hotel, and right away his bodily deportment and lurching gestures catch the viewer's eye. His behavior is comic in its jerky assertiveness and mechanical rigidity. Hulot stands in the hotel's doorway, legs straight, arms akimbo, upper body bent stiffly forward, with a pipe rakishly cantilevered out of the side of his mouth. His facial expression shows no self-consciousness, annoyance, or even joy at being on vacation, only a mild curiosity at his surroundings. Approaching the hotel's reception desk, he leans forward and mumbles his name. The hotel clerk has to take Hulot's pipe out of his mouth so that he can emphatically pronounce his name, "Hulot." He gives no first name, and none is ever mentioned in any of the Hulot-character films Tati directed.

Having registered, Hulot sees some hotel guests nod to each other in greeting. Then, he too imitates their formal ritual, acknowledging one guest after another with a bow. Hulot moves around the room by propelling himself forward step-by-step, springing forward from one ball of his foot to the next. He occasionally catches himself in mid-step and freezes his forward motion by anchoring his weight on the ball of one foot. As he bows to someone, Hulot bends stiffly forward at the waist, keeping his legs and upper torso both straight and rigid. He does not display the same relaxed manner shown by other hotel guests;

A Companion to Film Comedy, First Edition. Edited by Andrew Horton and Joanna E. Rapf.

Figure 5.1 Jacques Tati as Monsieur Hulot (*Les Vacances de M. Hulot*; producers, Fred Orain and Jacques Tati).

his bows are forced and awkward. He approaches every hotel guest he sees, acknowledging them with the same stiff and mechanical bending at the waist. With each successive bow, Hulot's actions take on an increasingly comic quality, his repeated bows becoming a comic routine.

The humor in this scene comes in part from a tension between Hulot's desire to act in conformity with the middle-class norm of greeting people and his stilted way of acting in accordance with it. However, these repeated bowings are humorous in a way that goes beyond simply reflecting the tension between Hulot's desire to respect a norm and his awkward way of fulfilling it. The tension could have been shown with just a couple of bows, but Hulot's repeated action creates a further comic effect. By Hulot's act of repeatedly bowing, Tati introduces a form of comedy, a gag type, which creates humor by serially repeating an action. I will refer to this distinctive gag type that features the repetition of an action as a "repetition gag." Of course, the repetition gag is not the only form of comedy Tati uses in his films; he uses many different gag types and kinds of comic business. Yet the repetition gag, I believe, occupies a distinctive place in Tati's innovative approach to film comedy.

His use of repetition gags is distinctive for several reasons. First, these gags are a natural outgrowth of Tati's comedic performance style as the character Monsieur Hulot. Tati's style of mimed performance, which accents Hulot's quirky actions, lends itself to the development of this form of comedy. Second, in highlighting his distinctive style of comic performance, the repetition gag shows Tati to be an innovative creator and performer of film comedy. His repetition gags are innovative in part because they challenge the Bergsonian theory about why people find something funny. That is, Tati's performance style, particularly in the repetition gags, undercuts Bergson's social correction theory about why we laugh.

In his book, *Laughter* (1900), Henri Bergson offers an account of why we find some human behavior to be funny. He argues that we find human behavior to be funny when it exhibits the lack of a vital awareness of the surrounding environment. For Bergson, people show this lack of awareness by adopting fixed attitudes or rote behaviors. He believes that we find such behavior to resemble the functioning of a machine. He claims that people's machine-like obliviousness to what is taking place around them produces a hilarious response in observers. Bergson's two terms for this nonconscious machine-like way of acting are "absentmindedness" and "mechanical inelasticity." "What life and society require of each of us," Bergson insists, "is a constantly alert attention that discerns the outlines of the present situation, together with a certain elasticity of mind and body to enable us to adapt ourselves in consequence" (Bergson 1980: 72).

Bergson thinks that machines in themselves are not funny; however, people who behave like machines are funny, especially when they exhibit both obliviousness to their surroundings and a lack of vitality in their actions. In identifying what he thought were the sources of comic behavior, Bergson adopts the common view that we laugh only when we set aside our sympathies for others and their calamities. He claims that when we find the falls and mishaps of others to be funny, we are *laughing at* them rather than sympathetically *laughing with* them. Bergson believes that by laughing at the inattentive and rotelike behavior of others, we are adopting the position of social critics. In laughing we are finding fault with others' absentmindedness and rigidity of action, failings that led to their falls or mishaps. He claims: "Society will therefore be suspicious of all *inelasticity* of character, of mind and even of body, because it is the possible sign of a slumbering activity as well as of an activity with separatist tendencies, that inclines to swerve from the common centre round which society gravitates: in short, because it is the sign of an eccentricity" (Bergson 1980: 73).

For Bergson, comedy is a generic form that encourages an audience to notice social failings and by laughing to engage in acts of social correction. Yet, in laughing at eccentricity of mind and body, Bergson opens his theory up to an appropriation by those who represent the ascendant values and attitudes of the society. Laughter serves the interests of those who would insist on conformity to the dominant norms of the society. It lends itself to enforcing the values of the *bourgeoisie*. "Laughter," Bergson claims, "must be something of ... a sort of *social gesture*. By the fear which it inspires, it restrains eccentricity ... " (Bergson 1980: 73). Although Hulot's repeated actions appear mechanical, they valorize eccentricity rather than encouraging audience scorn. In their unusual social character, as we shall see, they offer a critical yet humane perspective on modern life. Nevertheless, unlike Bergson's corrective theory of comedy, Tati never prescribes a specific social alternative to what he identifies as humorous.

The repetition gags are also innovative because they challenge the incongruity theory of humor, the dominant formal theory about what makes something funny. By using repetition gags, Tati shows that the incongruity theory is at least incomplete as an account of the humorous. With these gags Tati proposes that repetition, and not just a contrasting incongruity, can be funny. Championed by Kant and Schopenhauer in the eighteenth and nineteenth century and forcefully defended by theorists such as John Morreall and David H. Monro in recent years, the incongruity theory holds that we laugh at situations in which we have adopted one psychological attitude or expectation only to have that attitude or expectation overturned. The incongruity theory claims that psychologically incongruous elements are funny. Why does a child laugh if you were to put a shoe on your head? The incongruity theorist would answer that the child laughs because the child knows that a hat goes on your head and shoes go on your feet. You have done the incongruous thing of putting a shoe on your head. The incongruity theory proposes that we laugh at things we find to clash with our expectations.

Tati appears as M. Hulot in only four of his six feature-length films. After the character is introduced in *Les Vacances de M. Hulot*, he successively reappears in *Mon Oncle (My Uncle)* (1958), then *Play Time* (1967), and finally *Trafic* (1971). Before appearing as M. Hulot, Tati appeared in his first feature, *Jour de Fête (The Big Day)* (1949), as François the postman, a role he adapted from the postman he plays in an earlier short film he directed, *L'Ecole des facteurs (School for Postmen)* (1946). In his final feature made in Sweden, *Parade* (1974), Tati again forsakes Hulot. He plays the circus ringmaster, Monsieur Loyal, and includes in the film some of his mimed routines from his early days on the variety stage.[2] For the most part, these mimed skits show people playing various sports. For example, Tati mimes being a soccer goalie, a tennis player, and does a hilarious routine as a badminton player. These routines have their roots in Tati's early adult interest in sports. After his first appearance as Hulot in *Les Vacances de M. Hulot*, Tati was asked many times to continue to play Hulot in other films. Hollywood was especially keen to produce these "Hulot" films, but Tati refused, insisting that the resulting films would be studio products. If he were to work on these proposed films, he would compromise his artistic independence and vision. He would end up merely exploiting the character of Hulot. Instead, Tati came to believe that the character of Hulot was a means to comedic innovation.

It is difficult to separate Tati, the performing artist who brought to life the character of the enigmatic M. Hulot, from the cinematic artist who created the wonderful gag structures and other comedic devices of his films. However, the character of M. Hulot is so distinctive – as recognizable as Chaplin's little tramp with his cane-twirling shuffle or Groucho with his cigar-tipping, low-centered saunter – that there is a natural curiosity about this peculiar character with his stiff bodily comportment, arresting gestures, and puzzled reactions to objects, machines, and other characters. With these quirky characteristics, M. Hulot resists being pigeonholed as a traditional comedic character or clown. From his very first appearance in *Les Vacances de M. Hulot*, Hulot seems to be a character that exhibits his own set of comic characteristics – ones that Tati expended considerable effort in exploring. Developing the character of Hulot encouraged Tati to introduce some innovative comic forms, chief among them the extended gag forms that I have earlier referred to as his "repetition gags."

Jacques Tati was born in the outlying Parisian suburb of Saint-Germain in 1907 as Jacques Tatischeff.[3] "Tati" was used only as a stage or professional name; he never abandoned "Tatischeff" as his last name. His father was the illegitimate offspring of a French woman and a Russian aristocrat assigned to Paris as a military attaché. In 1903, Tati's father married a Parisian woman of Dutch and Italian ancestry. They had two children, Jacques and an older daughter, Odette Nathalie. Although as a child he learned to speak a little Dutch, and he later learned to speak some English, Tati never learned to speak any Russian. "Throughout his life," David Bellos (1999: 5) writes, "Tati seemed to others and to himself as French as garlic sausage; when asked, as he often was, what difference his Russian ancestry made, he would usually just shrug his shoulders, and pass on to the next question." In keeping with his French identity, Tati created the character of Hulot as unmistakably French. Nevertheless, following World War II Tati became an enthusiastic participant in the expanding international film culture with its many festivals.

A shy boy, Tati would spend hours alone in his bedroom, making faces in front of a mirror and miming different characters. He was a mediocre student, and he left school at sixteen to work in his parents' upscale picture-framing business in central Paris. Yet, as a teenager, Tati showed himself to be a natural athlete, and he developed into a superb horseman. His equestrian skills were noticed, and in 1928 he was drafted by the French Army to serve in a local cavalry regiment for his year of compulsory military service. After serving in the army, he visited England where he learned to play rugby, and on his return to France he joined an amateur rugby club, Racing-Club de France.[4] Although he was not a star rugby player, he won the hearts of his fellow team players by doing postgame imitations of their individual performances on the field. He was soon inventing skits that mimed people playing other sports. The popularity of his skits before live audiences soon established that mime was his comedic *forte*. Repeatedly, when explaining his particular style of mime, Tati stressed that his mimed skits were based on observation of people he saw around him.[5] Tati tried to accentuate the quirkiness, even the minute details, of how people acted in various social situations. He wanted to draw attention to how they performed daily tasks or appeared in what in the twentieth century was the new middle-class leisure pastime of engaging in sports such as tennis or being spectators of sports such as cycling or boxing. Tati's most famous ensemble of mimed sketches was called *"Impressions sportives"* (Sporting Impressions), which he introduced in 1931.[6] The goalie and tennis routines that Tati later used in *Parade* were originally included in this ensemble. With the success of his amateur mimed skits, Tati in the early 1930s became a professional vaudevillian, appearing on the variety stage not only in his native France but also all over Europe.

For almost a decade prior to World War I, French clowns from the circus and comedians from the vaudeville stage had begun appearing in film comedies. French film studios such as Pathé, Gaumont, and Éclair produced many series of short comedies, each featuring a noted clown or comedian. These series, starring, for example, Roméo (Roméo Bosetti), Rigadin (Charles Prince), Boireau (André Deed), Calino (Clément Mégé), Onésime (Ernest Bourbon), Léonce (Léonce Perret), and the greatest of them all, Max Linder, were very successful. David Robinson has described this period of French cinema as "an enchanted seven-year flowering of comedy, which greatly contributed to ... [French cinema's] world dominance in those years" (Robinson 2010: 63).

The ravages to French society brought on by World War I put an end to this "flowering." The eclipse of French comedy was also helped along by the trans-Atlantic appearance and popular appeal of Hollywood slapstick, particularly the universally acclaimed films of Charlie Chaplin. Following the war, Max Linder left France and went to Hollywood to make his films (see Scheide in this volume). His suicide in 1925 further inhibited a revival of French comedy in the 1920s. Nevertheless, the success of this early comedic tradition provided a precedent for promising French clowns and variety comedians to look to film as a natural medium to exhibit their talents. It's little wonder that Tati, even in the Depression years of the 1930s, should want to make the jump from the variety stage to the screen, and he was not alone. Fernandel (Fernand Contandin), a star of vaudeville in the 1920s, made his first film in 1930 and went on to have a very successful career as a film comedian and director. While Tati did play several bit parts in dramatic films, his interest was clearly in film comedy. He also realized that if he wanted to maintain control over the presentation of his comic ideas and his personal style of comedy, he would not only have to write his own material – or more importantly, not let anyone else script his comedy – but he would ultimately have to direct his own films. One of Tati's comedic idols, Buster Keaton, had lost control over his distinctive style of comedy in 1928 when he gave up control over production of his films and went to MGM.

The singularity of the character of Hulot, as well as Tati's earlier film roles and his mimed characters from his variety stage acts, provide a performative context for understanding the comedic dimensions of the Hulot character. Photographs of Tati performing on stage as a mime show him dressed in loose white trousers and white shoes.[7] His stage costume has led some critics to see Tati as a contemporary *Commedia dell'Arte* character, like Pierrot. For example, Lucy Fischer has noticed this connection between Tati's performing as a mime and Pierrot; she even thinks that there are similarities to Hulot's character. She says, "Hulot has much the sense about him of a nineteenth-century Pierrot clown: his identification with the spiritual order, his distanced infatuation with women, his affinity for small children ... [H]e is also strongly identified with the spirit of play ... " (Fischer 1983: 31). One could even point out that in keeping with the *commedia* tradition, he shows an interest in *lazzi* or gags that poke fun at the foibles of contemporary society. Perhaps the closest relationship Tati has to *commedia* mime is his emphasis on physical comedy that eschews dialogue. Certainly his character of Hulot conveys most of his humor without the use of dialogue. In this respect, Tati also has a close connection with the Hollywood tradition of "silent" film comedy.

Although Tati in his variety stage costume alludes to the white costume of Pierrot, in his film roles Tati's characters' costumes do not hearken back to any earlier comedic traditions. He avoids linking his costume as Hulot – and this is true of his other screen roles – with costumes associated with vaudeville or the circus. Other film comedians did maintain such a link. Buster Keaton in his baggy pants, tight-fitting vest, and pork-pie hat wore the long slap shoes of a circus clown or vaudeville comedian. As Hulot or as characters in his other early films, Tati adopts the work or leisure clothes that would have been worn by the people he plays in character. As François the postman in *L'Ecole des facteurs* and *Jour de Fête*, he wears the outfit of a rural postman. Playing the character of a farmhand in *Soigne ton gauche* (1936, dir. Réne Clément) (*Watch Your Left*), Tati wears clothes that one would expect a contemporary French farmhand to wear. His costume is not significantly different from the clothes worn by other farmhands in the film. Tati's interest in his early films in sports also requires him to have his characters dress in a contemporary way.

Three of the short film comedies that Tati appeared in during the 1930s center on sports. Tati's first such role was in a comedy about tennis, *Oscar, Champion de tennis* (*Oscar, Tennis Champion*) (1932), which, if it was ever completed, unfortunately is no longer extant. In another sport film, *On demande une brute* (*Wanted: A Brawny Wrestler*) (1934), Tati plays a witless bumpkin, Roger, who has to confront a prize-winning wrestler in the ring. A slightly similar scenario establishes the narrative line for Tati's short film about boxing, the earlier mentioned *Soigne ton gauche*. Tati plays a farmhand, again named Roger, who is persuaded to be the boxing champion's sparring partner after the champ knocks out all of his regulars. The champ's manager sees Roger shadow boxing when he should be moving bales of hay and quickly hustles him into the ring where the champ seems destined to knock him out too. Roger tries to pick up some quick instruction by looking at the illustrations in a boxing manual left open at ringside, but in concentrating on imitating the jabs and feints he sees in the book he fails to pay attention to the champ's punches. Trying to get some further pointers, he mistakenly looks at a fencing manual and adopts the poised sword stance of a fencer. He even imitates the behavior of a fighting rooster that he sees in the farmyard. Roger's different ways of responding to the champ in the ring form a comic series. Although the series is not a repetition gag – the same action is not serially repeated – it does prefigure Tati's later repetition gags.

Although Roger is unable to respond effectively to the onslaught of the champion's blows, coincidence saves him. A telegram-delivering postman enters the ring and is mistakenly punched by the champ, whereupon the postman complains to some nearby farmhands who enter the ring intending to beat up the champ and avenge the postman. A general melee ensues, which causes the ring built up on a platform to collapse. Roger picks up a board, positions it so that it swings around like a windmill, and knocks out the champ. Roger is victorious, although he is then slapped by the woman who is his boss on the farm after she discovers he has been neglecting his farm work.

As a young farmhand who fantasizes he is a boxer, Roger is quite a different comedic character from the early middle-aged Hulot of Les Vacances, who appears with his open collar to be a man of leisure on vacation. Yet, despite the difference in their apparent ages and social class, there is a significant similarity in the comic performances of both characters. Both are interested in sports, yet neither one has any true proficiency in the sport he takes up. Coincidence also plays a role in the eventual outcome of both characters' efforts.

Both characters exhibit a lack of true understanding about how a sport should be played. Roger enters the ring and relies on the fixed poses he finds in the boxing and fencing manuals discovered at ringside. He adopts a particular boxing or fencing position without any regard to how those stances will make him better able to defend himself or attack his opponent. Roger holds to a rigidity of posture rather than developing a fluid response to a changing situation. In Les Vacances, Hulot takes to the tennis courts relying on a similar rigid model of how he should handle his tennis racquet. He just follows the motions demonstrated by the elderly shopkeeper – she is no tennis pro – who sold him the racquet: she thrusts the racquet forward, raises it up, and slams it down. In Tati's 1961 revision of Les Vacances, Hulot aces every serve, winning every match he plays.[8] By repeating the same peculiar serve, he creates a gag sequence, and his actions become funnier and funnier.

Roger's boxing and Hulot's tennis playing strike us as funny because they are fixed and rigid ways of facing an opponent in the ring or serving a tennis ball. There is none of the fluidity and grace shown by the accomplished athlete. They do not seem sensitive to the respective situations they face and, by maintaining their rigid form, seem unresponsive to the constant changes that occur while playing a sport. In holding to their rigid ways of boxing or playing tennis, they exhibit an oblivious attitude that prevents them from questioning the appropriateness of their actions in the ring or on the court.

Their rigid patterns of behavior and oblivious attitudes call to mind Henri Bergson's theory of humor and comedy, which had an extensive influence outside of narrow academic circles in the early twentieth century.[9] One certainly finds rigidity and mechanical inelasticity, as well as a failure to understand or to grasp the significance of what is taking place, in both Roger's boxing and Hulot's tennis playing. Yet, I do not believe that the intent of Tati's comedy is to promote a Bergsonian socially corrective perspective about rigid behavior or absentmindedness. Tati has a broader range of comic interests than merely presenting his characters for mockery. In exhibiting rigid behavior and obliviousness, they do not provoke laughter simply because they lack the skills necessary to conform to established social norms. Rather than an aesthetic intended to encourage conformity, Tati's comedy is a celebration of eccentricity. He sets up the predicaments his characters face in order to establish a tension between a character's attempts to conform to social expectation and that character's behavior, which, while it appears eccentric, is no less vital in being peculiar and even sometimes disruptive.

Certainly, in *Les Vacances* Hulot at times seems oblivious to what is happening around him. On the beach, sitting in his kayak he appears to be painting or water-proofing his boat. He holds a paint brush in his hand and dips it into a pail that he has placed in the sand right next to him. A wave comes up, and the pail floats back with the receding water. Several times the waves move the pail back and forth, and one time waves even move it to the other side of the kayak; however, Hulot does not notice the pail's peregrinations, and he still keeps on dipping his brush into the pail and painting. Sometimes one's obliviousness to a situation does not make much of a difference.

At other times, however, inattention to one's surroundings can create problems, as shown in *Mon Oncle*. Hired to work in Monsieur Arpel's pipemaking factory, Hulot is told to monitor a machine that is making red plastic tubing, in order to ensure that the machine is functioning properly. Not paying attention, Hulot fails to notice that the machine is malfunctioning and is repeatedly crimping the tubing at short lengths. The resulting tubing looks like a long length of red sausages. In that particular example, inattention does cause a problem.

Not only can Hulot be absentminded, but he frequently displays a rigid posture and bodily comportment. Earlier I described his rigid behavior in *Les Vacances* as he bows to the other hotel guests. His awkwardness comes in part from attempting to respect the middle-class norm about greeting people. There are other instances in *Les Vacances* of Hulot trying to observe accepted protocols of behavior and yet having trouble in doing so. For example, after arriving at the hotel, Hulot becomes romantically interested in Martine (Natalie Pascaud), a young woman staying at a boarding house adjacent to Hulot's hotel. When Martine's aunt arrives to join her, Hulot offers to carry Martine's aunt's luggage up the steps to their boarding house. The gag of his making a circuitous run with the luggage through the house, then around the building, and back to the front porch is another comic instance of Hulot's desire to conform to social expectation and his haphazard way of fulfilling that expectation.

The quick run through and around the house also has a choreographed character. So too do Hulot's repeated bows. In their quick execution, the bows seem like a bodily reflex. Yet, as Hulot repeats the gesture, his bows form an ensemble of actions that take on a choreographed character. In the same film there are other examples of Hulot engaging in what appears as a choreographed ensemble of poses and movements. Wearing an equestrian outfit, Hulot waits for Martine in the downstairs lounge of her boarding house. They have made a date to go horseback riding. As he waits, he circles the room gazing at pictures and other ornaments. In his riding outfit, he carries himself in a different way from his stiff attitude at the hotel, at times bending back at the waist. As he steps and leans back to gaze at a picture while waiting for Martine, his riding crop, which he holds tucked under his arm, moves the picture behind him out of balance.

An animal skin rug is on the floor in the center of the room. It's a fox skin which still has the fox's head attached. As Hulot moves around the room, one of his riding spurs becomes caught in the fox's mouth. It looks as if the animal has bitten him and is gripping his ankle. At first Hulot does not notice that he is pulling the rug around behind him, just as he has not noticed that he has pushed the pictures out of balance with his riding crop. Then, startled at seeing what could be an animal attacking his foot, he does a quick turn around the room trying to shake off what is clinging to his boot. As he does so, Hulot's footwork is prominently on display, lending a choreographed aspect to this gag ensemble.

In *Mon Oncle*, one finds Hulot again displaying footwork and postures that look choreographed. There is a walkway that leads from the gate through the garden to the Arpel's modernist villa; it consists of flat stones set in a grassy bed. In walking between the gate and the house, people usually walk along the path trying to keep on the stone steps and avoid the grass. At the Arpel's garden party the guests are standing on the walkway, and Hulot, who is attempting to walk along the path, has to navigate around and between the people, all the while trying to step just on the stones. In his careful stepping and weaving to avoid grass and people, Hulot looks like he is dancing. He shows some elaborate footwork as he maneuvers around different people who seem to be his successive partners in the changing figures of the dance.

Hulot's fast footwork as well as his ability to react quickly contrasts with his deliberate actions and lingering pauses on other occasions. One finds a precedent for these rapid turns in Tati's postman character, François, who first appears in *L'Ecole des facteurs* and later in the feature-length expansion of that film, *Jour de Fête*. In both films Tati's postman character actually does dance. In his critical analysis of Tati's films, David Bellos claims that in his early films "Tati plays characters defined by stupidity ... [they] are variants on a single comic theme, that of the dimwit" (Bellos 1999: 12). I think that what Bellos perceives as stupidity is actually provincialism and François having had little if any formal education. This lack of sophistication makes Tati's postman an easy mark for others' jokes. François is a rube, but he is not without imaginative resources. He is a skillful cyclist exhibiting quite an acrobatic flair in the way he handles his bicycle. He has the ability to ride at break-neck speed, and in *Jour de Fête* he is shown breezing past a cycling team out practicing for a race. His skill on a bicycle allows him to do more than just pedal furiously and zoom past other cyclists. While riding along making his rounds as a postman, he demonstrates his expertise at handling his bicycle by attaching it to the back of a truck as it speeds down the road. He then uses the lowered back flap of the truck as a table on which he stamps and cancels posted letters.

It is not only with his skill on a bicycle that François shows a quick-wittedness that belies his being taken for a simpleton. Called upon to supervise the raising of the maypole in the town square which will mark the start of the festival, François instructs a man holding one of the maypole's stabilizing ropes in how to hold the rope and keep it taut as the pole is raised. As the rope slackens, François quickly turns around; in so doing he demonstrates how to wrap the loose rope around his body and keep the rope taut. It is a deft and quick twirl of his whole body. Though he illustrates the move several times, François is unable to teach the athletically challenged rope holder how to perform it. François has much better luck in getting a cross-eyed villager with a big mallet to pound in a stake that will keep the maypole in place. Because of his eyesight, the mallet swinger always misses by striking to the side of the stake. François figures out how to trick him so that he strikes the stake and pounds it in. François positions a second stake to the side and tells the man to aim for that one. Of course, the man takes aim and ends up pounding in the first stake exactly as François wanted.

Despite his success with the maypole, François is still a rube. He is easily duped into drinking cognac by the two men with the travelling merry-go-round. François had only thought that he was drinking a small glass of white wine. As a result of downing the cognac, he stumbles around in a drunken stupor, making a fool of himself. An especially funny sequence has François on one side of a split rail fence holding onto his bicycle, which is on the other side of the fence. As he pushes his bike along, he tries to clamber onto the bike with the fence still between him and the bike, of course with no luck at all.

The character of Hulot also exhibits some of François's athletic skill and quick wittedness. In *Les Vacances*, perhaps the scene in which Hulot most clearly shows his athletic ability is the one in which the viewer glimpses him playing ping-pong at the hotel. No shot shows the whole ping-pong table, Hulot's opponent, or both players volleying back and forth. Instead, the viewer sees only Hulot prancing back out of the ping-pong table room, wielding his paddle right and left as he returns his opponent's slams, then prancing back on the attack towards the room with the table. This scene shows Hulot to be a man of energy who is able to engage in a furious sustained ping-pong volley. It is a wonderful example of physical comedy.

In one of the most famous gags in the film, Hulot is on the beach talking to Martine's aunt while Martine changes in one of the small wooden changing cabins. Hulot glances down the side of the changing cabin and thinks he sees a man peeping in to watch Martine change. In a quick reaction, Hulot delivers a swift kick to the man's rear end, only to realize when he delivers the kick that the man was not peeping but was instead getting ready to take a snapshot of his family. Hulot makes a hasty getaway. This very short sequence shows Hulot again moving very quickly, both to deliver the kick and to make his retreat. The sequence is a sight gag in which Hulot and the film spectator share the same view of the man who appears to be a voyeur. After the kick, Hulot and the viewer realize that they have been mistaken in their perception. It is a classic misperception sight gag so familiar from silent comedy.[10]

In *Play Time*, Hulot is shown having that same ability to react quickly. In an early scene in the film, he arrives at a glass-enclosed office building in order to keep an appointment with someone. The doorman tells Hulot to wait while he summons the person. That person, M. Giffard, soon arrives carrying a blue folder, and they greet each other in the building's entrance way; however, by a series of coincidences they soon become separated. Hulot desperately tries to find Giffard. He goes up an escalator where he gazes down on a broad space containing an expansive checkerboard maze of enclosed office cubicles. Catching sight of Giffard with his blue folder walking through the maze, Hulot quickly hurries down and tries to navigate through the maze, sprinting to intercept him. Although he moves very quickly, Hulot always misses finding him. The near misses and failures of the two men trying to find each other create an integrated but drawn out comic sequence. This lengthy piece of comic business is preceded by another lengthy comic sequence centered on Hulot.

This earlier gag has no fast movement but shows Hulot waiting for his appointment in a stark glass-enclosed lounge. He enters the waiting room dressed in his sports coat and slacks with brushed suede shoes. Since he is not on vacation, he wears a bowtie along with his three-quarter length overcoat, umbrella, and brimmed hat turned up in the back and down in the front. Dressed in these casual clothes, Hulot presents a contrast to the men in dark business suits going in and out of the building, the uniformed doorman, and the office staff women dressed in uniforms that resemble those of flight attendants. In the stiff manner reminiscent of his arrival at the hotel in *Les Vacances*, Hulot haltingly moves around the waiting room exploring his minimalist surroundings. He propels himself forward step by step, springing forward with each step from the ball of his foot. Sometimes he catches himself in mid-step; other times he moves forward with little quick steps. When something catches his eye or startles him, he suddenly swivels around to look at it. Rather than thinking about his appointment, he seems caught up in the moment, looking at and reacting to whatever he sees. Perplexed by the "whooshing" sound that the foam chairs make when he presses them, he sits down in one to examine it further. When another man in a business suit enters the room and sits down, also apparently waiting for a business appointment, Hulot acknowledges his presence, but there is no formal greeting between the two men. They don't speak to each other. The waiting room environment seems to have the effect of rendering them mute.

Hulot's encounter with the waiting room forms an extended sequence, drawn out far beyond its serving any narrative utility. As a gag sequence, it humorously foregrounds the eccentricity and rigidity of Hulot's behavior. Yet, it also has the effect of defamiliarizing the modernist environment of the waiting room, rendering it humorous by Hulot's strange interaction with it. This gag sequence is one of many in *Play Time* that shows Hulot having to engage with a strange new aspect of Parisian modernity. However, Hulot is not presented as a simpleton for failing to take in stride the depersonalized urban world in which he finds himself, although he does exhibit a touch of provincialism. Through his eyes and through the humor of his physical reactions, viewers see the clash between a modernist sensibility expressed by the glass office buildings and Hulot's more humane yet provincial attitudes. Thus, in a way that counters Bergson's social-corrective view, Hulot's eccentricity is not mocked but provides a humorous perspective on the emerging modernist Parisian milieu.

Tati's humor should not be taken to be adamantly prescriptive. He is not proposing adopting an alternative milieu to the modernist setting of *Play Time*. I believe this resistance to a Bergsonian prescriptivism is revealed in the film's final scene when Hulot buys Barbara (Barbara Denneke) a present as she prepares to leave Paris by bus. In her seat on the bus, Barbara opens the gift which is revealed to be a spray of real flowers, lilies of the valley. In a point of view sequence, Barbara looks at the flowers and then looks out the bus window at the modernist street lights, which have exactly the same shape as the flowers. It's a humorous comparison, but it is not one that suggests that contemporary Paris is completely lacking in natural qualities. David Bellos also notices that Tati's humor is not focused on mockery. "*Playtime*," he writes, "is not fundamentally or essentially a satire of high-rise architecture: it is more a celebration of the beauty of large edifices, and an expression of wonderment at humankind's ability to create" (Bellos 1999: 250).

The extended sequence of Hulot moving around the waiting room in which he repeats his characteristic lurches and reactions forms a comic routine that I have earlier described as a "repetition gag." In Tati's hands, prompted by Hulot's behavior, the repetition gag assumes an innovative character. Of course, earlier comedians had employed extended gag sequences. Buster Keaton extensively used "enchained" gag sequences. In *Sherlock Jr.* (1924), Buster, as the world famous detective, careens around on a motorcycle's handlebars encountering an extended set of obstacles.[11] The humor comes from the amazing way Buster is able to overcome the obstacles, maintain his balance, and continue with the ride. The Three Stooges also made use of gags that serially repeat an incident. In *Men In Black* (1934), they travel around a hospital's hallways knocking into things. They smash into a glass door, and it shatters. A maintenance person replaces the door, but the Stooges break it again. Again it is replaced, and again they break it. This continues several more times in the film. The humor comes from, and is in keeping with, their anarchic destructiveness. They destroy not just the glass door, but almost everything they touch in the hospital. However, the innovative nature of Tati's repetition gags lies in the way they challenge what we take to be humorous, specifically challenging the incongruity theory of humor. As I explain more fully later, the incongruity theory encourages a rather short or economical presentation of a gag. In constructing a gag, one should first set up an expectation in the viewer, and then one should demolish it. Tati's repetition gags do not conform to this model of economical gag presentation, and because of this they challenge what is widely held to be humorous.

To be sure, one also finds Tati's interest in innovative comedy extending to other gag types. For example, he introduces some formally innovative sight gags. In *Play Time*, at the Royal Garden restaurant a plastic tile in the center of the dance floor has come loose and sticks to the shoe of the *maître d'hôtel*. Out in the kitchen, he gets help peeling the tile off his shoe, and then sends a waiter out with the tile to re-cement it into place on the dance floor. A shot shows the waiter in the background applying the cement to the tile, placing the tile in position, and then tapping it in place. In the foreground of the same shot, another waiter, using almost the exact same hand motions used by the tile-attaching waiter, simultaneously shows some diners how the chef prepares one of his special dishes. It's a hilarious moment. It's also a sight gag within a single shot.

Although Tati in his films is innovative in many ways, repetition gags occupy a special place in his comedic aesthetic because they hearken back to his original interest in miming people's behavior. They exhibit his comic interest in observing people's ordinary actions. Tati believed that people's ordinary behavior when watched carefully can be seen as humorous. One of the ways of observing people in this way is by framing their behavior as an extended sequence so as to call attention to their actions and to bring out the humor in them. In *Play Time*, having Hulot in the waiting room watching the other man's ordinary but quirky behavior as he waits for his appointment makes that man's behavior seem peculiar and funny. Over time, his nervous bodily twitches and little movements with his hands, accompanied by sounds such as the "whooshing" sound as he sits down, the clicks of his ballpoint pen, and the closing of his briefcase, take on a comic character.

Watching people's actions for an extended time – not to give them a quick glance but to look at them carefully – Tati believed brings out the humor in them. An example of this extended observation is the scene in *Les Vacances* of the little boy buying two ice cream cones from the beach vendor. After buying the cones, and with a cone in each hand, he starts climbing the steps – big steps for a little boy – up to the hotel. He must then open the front door by turning the door knob, give a cone to the little girl in the chair, and finally get up on his own chair while holding his cone. There is some suspense about whether he will be successful, or whether he will drop one or both of the cones. Some people might dispute whether this not very unusual behavior of the little boy with the ice cream cones is funny; however, I believe that the extended nature of the scene contributes to its being taken as a comic scene. By framing the sequence of the boy's behavior as an extended series, Tati makes the viewer linger in observing the actions. The viewer comes to see them not as just the practical activity of carrying ice cream cones. The boy's activity becomes defamiliarized, a bit peculiar, and because of that humorous. Also, the tension the viewer feels about whether or not the little boy will drop a cone has a heightening effect on one's humorous reaction.

Another motivation for developing the repetition gags comes from Tati's lack of interest in plot development and his desire to introduce comedic digressions. If, in *Les Vacances*, Tati had included only a short shot of Hulot arriving at the hotel and bowing to a guest, such a shot might not have been humorous. However, the extended sequence of Hulot's repeated bowing as he navigates around the lobby lounge does strike one as humorous. And, if we are inclined to laugh at the repetition of Hulot's bowing, we are also likely to laugh at Hulot's repeated serves in playing tennis. Hulot's behavior in these extended scenes becomes the comic precedent for finding other extended scenes to be funny, especially when they are framed as comedic digressions.

Nevertheless, in introducing some prolonged scenes of people's quirky behavior, Tati sometimes challenges the viewer to accept the sequence as funny. In *Les Vacances*, we see Hulot drawing attention to the repetition of an action. A food vendor at the beach has a large piece of taffy hanging from a hook at the side of his cart. The taffy slowly sinks down and looks like it will eventually fall off the hook and onto the ground. Periodically in the film, Hulot sees that the taffy is about to fall off the hook, rushes up, and hangs the taffy back up on the hook. Because Hulot's rescue of the taffy occurs many times, his actions are linked, even though they are not continuous, into a repetition gag. We take Hulot's actions to be humorous because they exhibit the same quirky character as was witnessed when he arrived at the hotel.

Another repetition gag in the same film is comically even more challenging. An older couple is looking at the rocks on the seashore at low tide. The woman picks up a seashell, excitedly exclaims over it and hands it to her husband to look at it. He immediately throws it away without taking any interest in it. This same pair of actions is repeated over and over again; it is a sequence that is framed as repeated behavior. If the viewer were to see the couple doing the pair of actions only once, the event would most likely not be funny; however, with each repetition the scene takes on a greater absurd and hence humorous character. In its peculiarity, the repeated actions become just as humorous as Hulot's repeated peculiar behavior. Viewers have been prepared to see humor in such a series of repeated actions because Hulot's repeated actions have been accepted as humorous.

Tati uses repetition gags in all of his Hulot films. In *Mon Oncle*, a street sweeper who is just about to start sweeping is interrupted and starts a conversation with someone. Consequently, he doesn't start to sweep. Similar interruptions follow, and because of the repetition of these many interruptions, the street sweeper never gets to work. In *Play Time*, at the Royal Garden restaurant, a platter of a specially prepared fish dish is brought to the table of a dining couple. In preparation for serving the fish to the couple, a waiter immediately starts spooning some sauce over the fish, grinding some pepper, and sprinkling some salt over it. Then the waiter walks away. A little later, another waiter arrives, performs the same actions, and again walks away. The same actions are repeated by a third waiter who then also walks away. Finally a waiter arrives and takes the platter away so that the couple is never served the fish. *Trafic* also has repetition gags. In the drive to Amsterdam, Hulot's van stops at a gas station. After paying for the gas, each customer is shown being given a plaster bust of a famous personage. The first such gift seems peculiar, but after many customers receive these gifts, the repeated gift giving becomes absurd and as a result quite funny.

The humor claimed for these repetition gags might be open to the following challenge. One might deny that the repetition gags are funny just because they are extended. According to this view, humor demands brevity of presentation. By repeating an action and drawing out the sequence, Tati has lessened rather than increased the humor. If the repetition gags are funny, a critic might say, it is not because they are extended but because they present an event that encourages an initial expectation and then in the following events challenges that expectation. For example, in *Les Vacances*, when the little boy buys the ice cream cones, the viewer expects that he will drop them. When he does not drop them, our expectation is not met, and we laugh. In this frustration of an expectation, there is the conjunction of two incongruous elements. The challenge is that the repetition gags in their being extended run afoul of the incongruity theory. In one of theory's classic statements, Immanuel Kant in 1790 claimed that laughter is "an affect that arises if a tense expectation is transformed into nothing" (Kant 1987: 204). As perceivers, we laugh because we undergo a psychological transformation; we start out with a particular expectation or cognitive stance – a tense one, Kant says – and then we are presented with something that evaporates that expectation. When we laugh we have to undergo a cognitive shift in attitude, Kant claims, but he emphasizes that the original stance must disappear in order for one to perceive the humor. Later incongruity theorists such as John Morreall also insist that humor requires a psychological shift. In emphasizing such a shift, incongruity theorists would seem to prefer shorter two-part gag sequences that clearly set out the incongruity between the gag's elements. Of course, one should point out that Tati sometimes uses gags in his films that do depend on an incongruity of elements for their humor. The misperception sight gag in *Les Vacances* in which Hulot kicks the man he takes to be a voyeur is such a gag.

One of the innovative aspects of Tati's repetition gags, I believe, is that in their repeating similar elements these gags do challenge the incongruity theory's proposal about humor. The repetition gag's humor lies not in presenting an initial expectation that is then challenged, but in the repetition of an event similar to the initial one, again and again. Instead of just turning our initial expectation into nothing, the gags work – we find them humorous – because they fulfill an expectation that the response will repeat. This fulfillment of expectation that repetition gags elicit also runs counter to later Incongruity theories that emphasize the mismatching of gag elements.[12]

Tati's repetition gags do not present comic business in a traditionally comic way. They present comedic sequences in a way that challenges a more traditional conception of humorous incidents, one that the incongruity theory purports to describe. Because of the innovative comic nature of his repetition gags, Tati recognizes that he must include materials in his films which teach or alert viewers about the comic nature of these nontraditional extended gags and encourage viewers to respond appropriately. Tati does this with his own comic performance as Monsieur Hulot. By having extended sequences that draw attention to and accentuate Hulot's distinctive behavior, Tati encourages viewers to see other extended sequences, particularly those which repeat an action, as being humorous. Thus, there is a clear connection, I believe, between Tati's distinctive performance style as Hulot and Tati's achievement as an innovator of film comedy.

Unlike Chaplin, whose films spawned many imitators of the Little Tramp, Tati's effect on later film comedy, especially the legacy of his comedic innovations, is not quite as obvious. However, one can see Tati's influence in the films of the French comedian Pierre Etaix, and one can also observe his influence in Rowan Atkinson's humorous television sketches of Mr. Bean. Many critics have also found Tati's influence at work in Atkinson's *Mr. Bean's Holiday* (2007). Recently, one of Tati's screenplays served as the basis for Sylvain Chomet's animated feature film, *The Illusionist* (2010) in which an animated M. Hulot is one of the major characters. Perhaps there have not been many other notable influences because of the challenging nature of Tati's comedy. Ultimately, Tati creates a narrative world in which ordinary actions and events take on a comic character. In his essay on Tati, André Bazin explores the nature of Tati's comedic world:

> Like all the great comics, Tati – before he makes us laugh – creates a universe. A world is created from his character ... He [Hulot] can be absent personally from the most comic gags because M. Hulot is only the metaphysical incarnation of a disorder which endures after he has passed by ... [T]he very lightness of M. Hulot's touch on the world will be the cause of all the catastrophes because it is never applied according to the rules of propriety and social efficacy. M. Hulot has the genius of gratuitousness, but that is not to say that he is gauche and awkward. On the contrary, M. Hulot is all grace; he is the Angel Hurluberlu, and the disorder that he introduces is that of tenderness and freedom. (Bazin 1983: 151)

Tati, especially through the "gratuitous" agency of Hulot, creates a comedic world – a world of people – that due to its "disorder" does not conform to familiar social principles. In Tati's comedic world, the viewer is charmed into finding humorous even the most mundane actions and situations. Through the character of Hulot, then, the viewer learns to accept this world as a humorous one, but, as Bazin says, also one of "tenderness and freedom."

Notes

1. In his authoritative biography of Tati, Bellos (1999) gives a full account of how Tati came to make his films and how the character of Hulot evolved in them.
2. The critical analyses of Tati's films are legion. For an overview and appraisal of criticism of Tati's films written during his lifetime, see Fischer's (1983) valuable annotated bibliography.
3. In recounting Tati's personal history, I have relied extensively on Bellos's (1999) biography of Tati.
4. Bellos (1999: 30) points out that Tati was most certainly an amateur rugby player. There were no professional rugby teams in France in the early 1930s.
5. See Bellos (1999: 34–5). Fischer (1983: 28–9) gives several examples of Tati crediting observation as a source for his comedy.
6. See Bellos (1999: 40–1).
7. See the illustrations in Gilliatt (1976: 12–13, 18–19).
8. In her article on *Les Vacances*, Thompson (1988: 96) discusses the changes to Hulot's tennis playing in the different versions of the film.
9. Some other commentators have also used Henri Bergson's ideas to discuss Tati's comedy. In her book on Tati, Fischer (1983: 26, 31) uses Bergson's views to make some different points about Tati's comedy.
10. For further discussion of sight gags, see Carroll (1991).
11. For further discussion of Keaton's gags in the film, see Sweeney (1991).
12. For accounts of the incongruity theory, see Monro (1963) and Morreall (2009).

References

Bazin, A. (1983) Mr. Hulot and Time, in *Jacques Tati: A Guide to References and Resources* (ed. L. Fischer), G.K. Hall, Boston, MA, pp. 149–53.

Bellos, D. (1999) *Jacques Tati: His Life and Art*, Harvill Press, London.

Bergson, H. (1980) Laughter, in *Comedy* (ed. W. Sypher), Johns Hopkins University Press, Baltimore, MD, pp. 59–190.

Carroll, N. (1991) Notes on the sight gag, in *Comedy/Cinema/Theory* (ed. A. Horton), University of California Press, Berkeley, CA, pp. 25–42.

Fischer, L. (1983) *Jacques Tati: A Guide to References and Resources*, G.K. Hall, Boston, MA.

Gilliatt, P. (1976) *Jacques Tati*, Woburn Press, London.

Kant, I. (1987) *Critique of Judgment*. W.S. Pluhar (trans.), Hackett Publishing Co, Indianapolis, IN.

Monro, D.H. (1963) *Argument of Laughter*, University of Notre Dame Press, Notre Dame, IN.

Morreall, J. (2009) *Comic Relief: A Comprehensive Philosophy of Humor*, Wiley-Blackwell, Malden, MA.

Robinson, D. (2010) Comici francesi/French Clowns 1907–1914, A–Z, in *Le Giornate Del Cinema Muto Catalogue 2010*, Cinemazero, Pordenone, pp. 63–84.

Sweeney, K.W. (1991) The dream of disruption: melodrama and gag structure in Keaton's *Sherlock Junior*. *Wide Angle*, 13 (1), 104–20.

Thompson, K. (1988) Boredom on the beach: triviality and humor in *Les Vacances de Monsieur Hulot*, in *Breaking The Glass Armor*, Princeton University Press, Princeton, NJ, pp. 89–109.

Further Reading

Bellos, D. (1999) *Jacques Tati: His Life and Art*, Harvill Press, London. The authoritative biography of Jacques Tati, which also contains insightful critical analyses of Tati's films.

Bergson, H. (1980) Laughter, in *Comedy* (ed. W. Sypher), Johns Hopkins University Press, Baltimore, MD, pp. 59–190. Bergson's classic theory of humor and comedy as social critique. He claims that we find humorous people behaving absentmindedly and exhibiting signs of "mechanical inelasticity."

Chion, M. (2006) *The Films of Jacques Tati*, Guernica, Toronto. A critical analysis of Tati's films and comedic performance by a French critic and filmmaker.

Fischer, L. (1983) *Jacques Tati: A Guide to References and Resources*, G.K. Hall, Boston, MA. The most complete reference work to publications about Tati and his films during Tati's lifetime. The resource also contains valuable critical analyses of Tati's films.

Gilliatt, P. (1976) *Jacques Tati*, Woburn Press, London. Gilliat offers many insights into Tati's views on mime and physical comedy.

Monro, D.H. (1963) *Argument of Laughter*, University of Notre Dame Press, Notre Dame, IN. One of the best statements and sustained arguments for the incongruity theory of humor.

Morreall, J. (2009) *Comic Relief: A Comprehensive Philosophy of Humor*, John Wiley & Sons, Inc., New York, NY. A recent clear and cogent statement and defense of the incongruity theory of humor.

6

Woody Allen

Charlie Chaplin of New Hollywood

David R. Shumway

Charlie Chaplin was the greatest international icon of Hollywood's silent era, yet he achieved that status by playing a character he invented for himself, the "Little Tramp." Chaplin wrote and directed all of his own films beginning with his thirteenth short for Keystone in 1914, but the public at large was not much aware of Charles Chaplin as an auteur. They knew and loved the Tramp, a character who first appeared in the second film in which Chaplin appeared, *Kid Auto Races* (1914). And while Chaplin made several acknowledged masterpieces after the advent of sound and eventually created new speaking parts for himself, he remains the "Little Tramp" in the public mind. Chaplin's invention and development of the Tramp is largely responsible for judgments like this one, by Andrew Sarris in 1998: "Charles Chaplin is arguably the single most important artist produced by the cinema, certainly its most extraordinary performer and probably still its most universal icon"(Sarris 2006: 45).

Chaplin was by almost any standard the most successful silent film comic, but he was hardly the only one to appear primarily as a single character. Harry Langdon, Buster Keaton, and many others were also largely unchanged from role to role. In the sound era, comic performers like Laurel and Hardy, Abbott and Costello, the Three Stooges, W.C. Fields, and the Marx Brothers continued to appear in films as the same characters. But unlike the great silent comics, they did not direct the films in which they appeared, although in some cases they wrote them. And, with the possible exception of the Marx Brothers, these sound comics were never regarded as being major artists the way Chaplin and Keaton were. During the golden age of Hollywood sound film, the great icons were mostly dramatic actors, or performers, like Cary Grant and Katharine Hepburn, equally at home in comic or dramatic roles.

A Companion to Film Comedy, First Edition. Edited by Andrew Horton and Joanna E. Rapf.
© 2013 John Wiley & Sons, Inc. Published 2016 by John Wiley & Sons, Inc.

There was no successor to Chaplin as director, writer and star of his own comic films until Woody Allen. And like Chaplin, in his early films, *Take the Money and Run* (1969) through *Love and Death* (1975), Allen invented a more or less consistent character for himself, known as either the "Schlemiel," or the "Nebbish."[1] But this character is not the only one Allen has portrayed on screen. Just as Chaplin began to make more serious films later in his career, Allen, with *Annie Hall* (1977), began to play a more realistic character – someone who was much more like the person we imagine the real life Woody Allen to be. The familiarity of the earlier role made it hard for audiences and critics to see the change, especially since the "Nebbish" does not disappear entirely, recurring in somewhat different guises in *Zelig* (1983), *Broadway Danny Rose* (1984), *Manhattan Murder Mystery* (1993), *Small Time Crooks* (2000), *The Curse of Jade Scorpion* (2001), and perhaps a few others.[2] It is my argument that we need to recognize that Allen has invented two more or less consistent screen characters, the second of which I call the "Artist." Allen plays this distinctly different character in *Annie Hall* (1977), *Manhattan* (1979), *Stardust Memories* (1980), *Hannah and Her Sisters* (1986), *Husbands and Wives* (1992), *Deconstructing Harry* (1997), and, in a more minor role, *Everyone Says I Love You* (1996). Allen's public persona, then, developed as an amalgam of both the screen characters and off screen publicity, which became especially significant after his relationship with Soon Yi Previn became public in 1992. My concern in this chapter is to analyze not the larger persona, but the two repeating screen characters, the first in films from *Take the Money and Run* (1969) to *Love and Death* (1975), and the second in the 20 years between *Annie Hall* and *Deconstructing Harry*. I will be concerned only with films which Allen directed and in which he acted.

Allen achieved an autobiographical effect in the Artist films, which, despite his denials, was clearly intentional, not only by using details from his own life, but by inventing filmic equivalents to the discourse of prose autobiography. These autobiographical conventions together with the fact that Allen's films repeatedly borrow details from his life, have led viewer to confuse his on screen characters with the person he is off screen. While it is probably obvious to most that the "Nebbish" he has played in films could not be the same person who has been a successful comic, writer, actor, and filmmaker, there is a much more plausible consistency between the artist and that person. As Allen puts it, people think he's just playing himself because "unlike Charlie Chaplin, say, who puts on a moustache and a hat and a coat and a cane, and looks totally different than the Charlie Chaplin who shows up at the studio to direct a film, I dress in real life the way I dress, 'cause I play a guy from New York" (Schickel 2003: 125–6).

The Nebbish

The Yiddish words "schlemiel" and "nebbish" have long been applied to Allen's onscreen characters. Virgil Starkwell, whom he plays in *Take the Money*, is called a "schlemiel" by a "witness" (Louise Lasser), who also calls him an "idiot" and a "nothing," which are partial synonyms. "Schlemiel" and "nebbish" are similar in meaning, but they have somewhat different connotations and contexts of usage. According to the Yiddish dictionary online, *nebbish* means "a person who is inept, ineffective, shy, dull, a nerd; a loser," while *schlemiel* means a "bungler, ineffectual person, inept person; a person who is easily victimized." The *Oxford English Dictionary* defines "nebbish" as "An insignificant or ineffectual person; a nobody; a nonentity" (one of the quotations mentions Woody Allen as an example), and schlemiel as "an awkward, clumsy person, a blunderer; a 'born loser'; a 'dope' or 'drip.'" The word "schlemiel" has a possible Biblical origin in Shelumiel (Numbers 1: 6) "said in the Talmud to have met with an unhappy end," and was perhaps influenced by the name of the eponymous hero of Adelbert von Chamisso's *Peter Schlemihls wundersame Geschichte* (1814). Irving Howe calls attention to another way in which term was used, describing Allen as "a reincarnated Menashe Skulnik, quintessential schlemiel of the Yiddish theater" (Howe 1976: 571). A vaudeville comic, Skulnik is said to have influenced not only Allen, but also many Jewish comedians, including Sid Caesar, Lenny Bruce, Billy Crystal, and Jerry Seinfeld (Howe 1976: 570). Yet, none of these others has been so consistently identified as a schlemiel. Both words represent, of course, negative identities, characters Jewish mothers warned their sons not to become. In part because the word "schlemiel" has stronger resonances with earlier performers, I'm going to use "nebbish" to refer to the character Allen created in his first films.

As Allen himself observed, the best comics developed their own characters they played in stand up (Lax 2007: 11, 64). Their jokes are not just collections of random gags, but rather depend on a persona the audience understands to be both the source and, to a large extent, the object of them. Allen developed a character first in his stand-up performances, but his early films recreated it while retaining key elements. Allen's appearance in stand up – his horned-rimmed glasses, his college-professor-casual clothes, his nervous ticks – all become part of the onscreen Nebbish. But physical humor became part of the Nebbish to a degree that it could not be in the stand-up character. That humor was directly influenced by the silent comedies of Chaplin and Buster Keaton (Schickel 2003 95–103).[3]

Critics complained that *Take the Money* and *Bananas* consisted of series of gags strung together by a plot designed merely to serve that purpose, which was, of course, also true of much of the great comedy of the silent era. What strikes one today about those early films, and Allen's, is how good the physical comedy is. In *Take the Money*, a pseudo-documentary where Allen plays a career criminal named Virgil Starkwell, consider the escaped chain-gang sequence in which a group of men chained together escape from a truck. The idea for the escape is Virgil's, a point that illustrates an important trait of the Nebbish: he is, unaccountably, often a leader. Later in the sequence, Virgil will be one who gets someone to let the escapees into her house, and who remains in charge of their effort not to be discovered. The beginning of sequence is played as a silent film, accompanied by music but no dialogue, a technique Allen will use often up through *Love and Death*. The humor comes not only from the idea of a group of men still chained together trying to escape by running across an open field, but from the fact that they actually succeed even though the guards do eventually give chase. The first scene of sequence concludes with Virgil repeatedly trying and failing to get over a relatively low wall that all of the other escapees have apparently negotiated with ease. The longer the group can remain at large under these circumstances, the more preposterous the gag becomes. The fact that none of them even tries to find a way to remove their chains may not even register with viewer.

Virgil's inability to climb the low wall illustrates one of the Nebbish's most salient characteristics: his physical ineptness. There is a sense in which the Tramp could be said to have also had this characteristic. Consider his inability to negotiate the escalator in *The Floorwalker* (1916). Yet there is an important difference between the Tramp and the Nebbish in that the former, whatever his physical failings, always seems graceful, and sometimes he demonstrates amazing physical prowess, as is in the fight scene with Henry Bergman in the same film. The Nebbish's ineptitude is much more complete, and is never graceful. This fact is related to another of the Nebbish's characteristics: klutziness. Ineptness and klutziness are distinguishable because the former involves physical weakness or the inability to perform ordinary tasks, while the latter involves not physical weakness or lack of skill, but an extreme gracelessness including the propensity to screw up any task, regardless of its physical requirements. When in *Love and Death* the Nebbish named Boris is unable to march in step, or to get his sword out the scabbard during military drills he is inept, but when in the same film at the opera where every time Boris bows, his scabbarded sword comes up behind him and gooses a bystander, he is a klutz. The Tramp is sometime inept, but he is never a klutz.

In addition to their physical difficulties, each of the roles Allen plays in his first four films – Virgil, Fielding Mellish in *Bananas*, Miles in *Sleeper*, and Boris – are all born losers, though like the Tramp, Fielding and Miles overcome that designation to become heroes of a sort. Since *Take the Money* is a mockumentary giving us Virgil's life history, we learn that he has been losing ever since he was born. Some of his misfortune is utterly beyond control, but much of it seems to derive from his unbelievably bad choices, starting with the decision to find a career in crime. Early on, we see him being intimidated by much bigger and tougher kids, who, among other things, take his glasses and stomp on them. In *Bananas*, Fielding goes to Latin America to escape a bad relationship and ends up in the middle of a revolution. In *Sleeper*, Miles wakes up 200 years after his body had been cryogenically preserved only to find himself in a future where the United States is ruled by an Orwellian dictatorship. Boris is executed at the end of *Love and Death* for the attempted murder of Napoleon, a murder that his moral scruples would not allow him to commit. In each case, the character's luck is cosmically bad.

Figure 6.1   Miles (Woody Allen), disguised as a robot, does battle with a pudding in *Sleeper* (producer, Jack Grossberg).

Take the Money's comic premise is to some extent parallel to that of *The Gold Rush* (1925) in that this character is so utterly unsuited for the role in which we find him. This has to do with his lack of ability to intimidate, not only because of physical weakness, but also because of his failure to act intimidating. In the famous bank robbery scene where his hold-up note is illegible and the employees debate what it says, ("I have a gub?" "What's a gub?"), he becomes more interested in defending his penmanship than in demanding cash. As a criminal, Virgil can do nothing right and almost seems to be an illustration of the truism that criminals as a group are not very bright. The same comic premise exists in the other three films as well, even if it is less exhaustively established.

The Nebbish, like the Tramp, is essentially a clown, and the films Allen wrote for this character are built around sight gags as much as one-liners. Allen may be his most clownish in *Sleeper*, where he plays much of the film in whiteface or in various odd costumes. Miles, who in the 1970s owned a health-food store in Greenwich Village, finds himself treated as a dangerous alien and to avoid capture, he disguises himself as a robot, applying whiteface, dressing up in tails, and sticking a sort of speaker in his mouth (see Figure 6.1). This renders him a silent clown, who shuffles his feet in order imitate the gait of the other robots. He finds himself delivered to Luna's (Diane Keaton) house, where is asked to prepare and serve food for a party. Not knowing how the kitchen of the future works, he pours instant pudding into a pot, and it immediately begins to expand over the sides of the vessel. After admitting the guests (who are dressed like the cast of *A Clockwork Orange*–Stanley Kubrick, 1971), taking their coats and, by mistake, putting them in the trash disposal, he returns to the kitchen to find the pudding on the floor, now having become animate and advancing upon him. Miles tries to subdue it with broom, which he finally does after much effort. He then is asked to pass "the orb," a silver sphere that produces a contact high. Miles is affected despite his gloves, and begins to hold on to the orb rather than allow the guests to take it. Loosing his inhibitions, he ends up in the lap of one of guests, taking the speaker out his mouth, and biting her neck. None of the stoned guests seems to notice that the robot is behaving strangely.

As a robot, Allen is to some extent out of character, since the distinctive voice and speech pattern are absent and the facial expressions much reduced. Later, after Miles has escaped from the robot with Luna as a sort of hostage, he tries to get her to eat some crackers he has found in her car. Allen plays the scene as a Jewish mother trying to get her child to eat. He whines and pleads with her, and a close up on his face, still somewhat white from his disguise, focuses our attention on his extravagant facial expressions – the eyebrows that jump to punctuate each point, while the lips convey both vehemence and distress. When the camera pulls back for a two shot, we see the same emphasis portrayed in Allen's hand gestures. Meanwhile, Luna screams hysterically, just like a toddler. Luna's inability to cope with even the slightest bit of discomfort – "I haven't had bath in seven hours" – has the ring of social commentary, carrying over from the debauched party guests and her early remark to one of them that she can't understand why there should be an underground, since "this world is so full of wonderful things." Luna's shallowness and ignorance are played off against Miles's wisdom, which he brings from an earlier time – one that actually seems to date from before the 1970s. These two personality types will be opposed again much more realistically in the characters played by Allen and Keaton in *Annie Hall*.

If *Sleeper* presents the Nebbish at his most clownish, *Love and Death* presents him at his most cerebral and neurotic. Allen told Schickel that, while in *Sleeper* the gags didn't violate the reality of the story, *Love and Death* is more like earlier films, in that "the jokes violated anything we wanted" (Schickel 2003: 95). Of course, as the sci-fi premise of *Sleeper* allows its reality to be almost anything Allen wants it to be, while *Love and Death's* historical setting carries its own, predetermined reality. Physical humor certainly plays a role in this film, and there are clownish sequences, but most of the jokes revolve around the two ideas named in the title and allusions to Russian literature, especially Tolstoy. In this film there is a somewhat smaller gap between character and role, reminding one more of Bob Hope than of Chaplin. In his interview with Schickel, Allen said, "Bob Hope was the biggest comic influence on my performing," and he contrasted Hope to Groucho Marx, who "was a clown, and you can never picture Groucho in a realistic situation … Hope gets away with these lines and behavior in a real context – he can play a real person, a love interest, a guy posing as a private detective … and his work is wonderful" (Schickel 2003: 81). Schickel observes that the combination of cowardice and lechery in Allen's early roles derives from Hope. Allen says that *Love and Death* in particular involves a catalog of mannerisms and gags borrowed from Hope. He mentions as an example the scene in which Boris meets the Countess Alexandrova (Olga Georges-Picot), and then invites him to her bedroom. Like Hope, Allen says Boris is posing as a hero, though we know he is not (Schickel 2003: 82). In the bedroom he reels off a string of Hope-like one liners with the Countess playing straight woman. The situation is certainly reminiscent of Hope's films, and yet with Allen playing the part, the hero pose becomes not merely comic, but absurd. Compare Hope finding himself engaged to the princess (Dorothy Lamour) in *Road to Morocco* (David Butler 1942), where the comic can't quite believe his good fortune, but he isn't the least bit worried about taking advantage of it.

The Nebbish's absurd behavior and the comparison with Bob Hope both suggest that a character is entirely apolitical, distinguishing him from Chaplin's Tramp, who was beloved of many because he was understood to represent the downtrodden. But the Tramp was never associated with organized political activity (except by accident in *Modern Times*), while it is worth noting that each of these early Allen films deals with some sort of resistance or opposition to an established order. While that order in *Take the Money* remains politically unidentified, the film assumes, in its pseudo-documentary narration, the 1960s' view of social inequality that inspired the War on Poverty. *Bananas* seems to make oppression a kind of cultural trait of Latin America, the rebel leader becoming just another dictator once he has gained power. Still, even here, Fielding joins the rebels, and he returns to the United States an enemy of the state. It is significant that the Nebbish always finds himself on the outside of power. The Tramp, of course, is also always on the outside, but his character is defined as a member of the subaltern. The Nebbish's roles are not usually so low on the social order, but he ends up being much more active in the opposition to the political status quo than the Tramp.

This kind of humor certainly derives to some extent from the 1960s, and the failure of its movements to produce the revolutionary change they often claimed as their goals. The Nebbish's failures might in relation be understood as a kind of consolation, making such an outcome seem inevitable rather than the fault of the revolutionaries, or they could be a way to make us laugh at our overreaching. In either case, the ultimate message would not be revolutionary, even though the value of resistance is not entirely negated. Miles's success in *Sleeper* is undermined by his concluding warning to Diane Keaton that the rebels' leader, Erno, is going to turn into a despot just like the one they have successfully removed. "Political solutions," says the Nebbish, "don't work ... It doesn't matter who's up there. They're all terrible."

The Nebbish would seem to be as unsuited to the role of lover as he is to role of revolutionary, but this is the one area where he has some degree of success. In each film, the Nebbish manages to maintain some kind of long-term relationship, including marriages in *Bananas* and *Love and Death*. The Tramp also is often presented, also seemingly without rational explanation, as successful with women. The Tramp's relationships, however, usually involve a good deal of pathos, as he seems not to be able to understand the unlikelihood of the woman's interest in him. This is illustrated by the New Year's Eve party in *The Gold Rush* to which no one comes. The Nebbish, because his social status is not so obviously displayed in his wardrobe, is less a pathetic lover than an unbelievable one. Like the Tramp, his ambitions in this area know no bounds, but unlike the Tramp, these ambitions are explicitly sexual. Adam Gopnik has observed that Allen in his stand-up routines and film characters beginning with Victor in *What's New Pussycat* (Clive Donner and Richard Talmadge, 1965, which Allen wrote) was a lecher, whose "mildly predatory desire" pointed toward the ideal of "the *Playboy* life style" (Gopnik 1993: 92).[4] The Nebbish's outsized desires and claims to sexual athleticism are funny because they are so at odds with every other aspect of his character. That is true *because* women are attracted to him, and he does manage to fulfill his desires. In romance, the Nebbish is not a loser. He gets the girl in the end in both *Bananas* and *Sleeper*, suggesting that these early films give us a somewhat more innocent view of relationships than we will find after *Annie Hall*. Yet audiences seem to have responded to this romantic and sexual success much as they did to Tramp's occasional successes, by finding them the most improbable thing about him.

Gopnik's reading of Allen captures the lecherous aspect of the Nebbish, but it misses another side of that character, one that will grow larger in the Artist. Even in *Take the Money and Run* and *Bananas*, Allen's character is interested in more than just sex. These films are among the first American movies to make "the relationship" an explicit concern, as Bogart's (Jerry Lacy) comment in *Play It Again, Sam* (Herbert Ross, 1972, adapted from Allen's play) shows: "Relationship? Where did you learn that word? From one of those Park Avenue headshrinkers?" In *Take the Money*, Virgil's relationship with Louise (Janet Margolin), is improbable, but it is nevertheless described in detail, the voice over giving us an analysis. Allen both makes fun of an emergent way of thinking about love and courtship, while at the same time his very use of it helped to disseminate it and give credence to it. That Virgil and Louise so obviously aren't right for each other is the joke, but the film suggests that their difficulties aren't so different from many other couples whose mismatch may be less obvious but just as real.

Still the implausibility of Virgil and Louise's relationship largely deprives it of emotional impact. In *Sleeper*, we begin to get scenes in which the Nebbish's feelings are meant to be shared by the audience. Miles's frustration with Luna's refusal to help him is the premise for outlandish interaction between them, but it is also understandable. Later, after Miles and Luna have become lovers, Allen has them play battling spouses. The camera tracks in front of them as they walk down a long corridor arguing about the mission they are there to undertake, the abduction of the Leader's nose. The conversation begins with Miles telling Luna to act naturally, while she observes that he is "Shaking like a leaf." He responds, "How do you want me to shake?" She says, too emphatically, "everything is going to be fine," prompting him to ask, "then how come you're shaking?" She replies that he is making her nervous, and he responds, "Don't blame me." Miles then brings up Erno, the revolutionary leader with whom Luna is also involved, making jealousy an explicit issue. Their exchange gets nastier as it continues, and the absurdity of the complaints is typical of a long-married couple rather than young lovers. At the end of film, Luna stops Miles philosophizing about politics, saying, "I think you really love me." Miles responds, "Of course I love you. This is what this is all about." Allen's character will have virtually identical lines at the end of *Manhattan*, when Tracy asks him if he loves her. These scenes in *Sleeper* can be regarded as transitional moments in the development of Allen's onscreen characters, previewing the kind of character he will fully portray starting with *Annie Hall*.

Finally, a major difference between the Tramp and the Nebbish is that while the former seems to lack any particular cultural identity, the latter is distinctly Jewish. That is true despite the fact that the characters Virgil Starkwell and Boris are not Jews. The Nebbish's Jewish identity is defined both by the audience's foreknowledge of Allen, but also by his speech patterns and accent which remind one that he is a New York Jew. Perhaps most important, however, are the gags that derive from Jewish life in general and from Jewish humor in particular. In *Bananas*, for example, the dictator has an argument with one of his cabinet about rebel uniforms they have had made in order to make their murder of Fielding look like a rebel atrocity. The argument is over the quality of tailoring, and whether a different tailor should have been chosen. It's funny, of course, because it is an anachronism in this Latin American location, but the joke depends on a sense of the tailor as a familiar figure, something true mainly of urban Jewish neighborhoods earlier in the century. There's a tailor joke in *Sleeper* as well, where the tailors are robots, but speak and behave like they were programmed on the Lower East Side in the 1940s. As Gopnik has observed, Allen's jokes often depend on familiarity with the lives and habits of a community that ceased to exist (Gopnik 1993: 92). The Nebbish's ethnic identity may have to some extent interfered with audience identification, but as a clown, this character does not require close identification for audiences to respond appropriately with laughter and sympathy.

The Artist

Chaplin's influence on Allen is mainly visible in the four Nebbish films I've discussed so far, but there is one work of Chaplin's that seems to have had more lasting impact. Allen told Richard Schickel that "when I saw *City Lights* I realized what a deep filmmaker he was, 'cause I felt that that film ... said more about love than so many purportedly serious investigations of the subject in either books or films" (Schickel 2003: 98). What Allen says he responded to in Chaplin (but which he found lacking in Buster Keaton) was that "he got pathos in a genuinely moving way – the extreme example being the end of *City Lights*" (Schickel 2003: 99). *City Lights* tells the story of the Tramp's love for a beautiful blind girl, whose eyesight is restored in an operation he managed to pay for by hook and crook, landing him jail. When he gets out, and she sees him for first time, she recognizes that he is not the rich man she thought he was, and his hopes are shattered. While *City Lights* is a comic version of a story worthy of nineteenth-century melodrama, its combination of comedy and the pathos of lost love provides the basic pattern for Allen's artist films.

Allen's artist, however, is even farther from the Tramp's everyman than was the Nebbish. Allen's cultural identity is more of an issue when he plays the Artist, who is someone of a particular ethnicity, a distinct level of social status and income, living in an actual, contemporary American city, and producing a recognizable art. The Artist is always Jewish, though the significance of his Jewishness varies from film to film. *Annie Hall* makes a point of Jewish difference by comparing holiday meals with Annie's and Alvy's families, but there is barely a reference to Gabe's Judaism in *Husbands and Wives*. Besides being Jewish, the type is urban and intellectual as revealed by the content of the characters' conversations. Some of the same traits read differently in the Artist than they do in the Nebbish, in part because the former's worldly success makes him seem less deserving of our sympathy. Both the Nebbish and the Artist are neurotic, and their neuroses, while not identical from film to film, are repeated without regard to which character Allen is playing. Yet in the Nebbish, the neuroses seemed themselves to be jokes, since they were embodied in a clown. While I think that some of the neurotic traits – paranoia, feeling victimized – are less obvious in the Artist, all of them become more serious when they are part of that character. The neuroses are no longer merely comic, but become genuinely troubling to the character and to the audience. The Artist becomes a "difficult" character, someone whom the audience may not necessarily like. According to Freud, we are all more or less neurotic, and Allen's films depend for their appeal on this insight. The various neurotic traits Allen's characters exhibit are ones many in the audience doubtless share. And yet, people who don't see the world through a psychoanalytically informed lens may perceive the neurotic as Other. That the character is a New York, Jewish intellectual simply confirms the otherness. The Nebbish was meant to be a – harmless – Other; the Artist, on the contrary, demands a deeper identification.

Beside their neuroses, there are a number of other consistencies between the Nebbish and the Artist. The horned-rimmed glasses have remained trademark throughout Allen's career, as have the repertory of facial expressions. Allen's wardrobe – which consists of ordinary, casual clothing typical of the post-1960s when the business suit became largely restricted to business executives – is pretty much the same in *Take the Money* and *Bananas* as it is in *Annie Hall* and *Manhattan*. Maybe most important, the speech patterns, accent, and even the vocabulary of the two characters remain remarkably similar. This consistent manner of speaking links Allen with the stars of Hollywood's past, whose speech was so distinctive that they could be evoked by an impressionist in as little as sentence. Radio played a major role in making the voices of comics such as Hope, Jack Benny, and George Burns intimately familiar to audiences in the 1930s and 1940s.

An entire branch of entertainment depended on such distinctive speech of movie and radio stars, which did not change from role to role. It is hard to think of another star from the 1970s on who is so clearly identified by his or her voice. Allen's vocal patterns are as distinctive as Cary Grant's or John Wayne's, and like those, his include accent, vocabulary, and cadence. He also adds verbal ticks that they did not have, and which would have been *verboten* for any role other than a fool or a clown. There is, for example, the way in which he often can't quite get his most emotionally loaded sentences to come out until he has made several stabs at beginning. It's like a stutter, but the repeated syllable is more clearly articulated, a kind of hesitation, akin to saying "um," but more expressive and distinctive – for example, in Ike's indictment of Yale in *Manhattan* where each new accusation requires several tries (see below). The accent is recognizably New York, yet not identifiable with a particular borough or neighborhood. Allen's sentences sometimes bear traces of Yiddish, with the verb coming at the end. And there is a distinct cadence, in which strong emphasis is made on predictable words or syllables. The pattern is so much attached to Allen, that when Kenneth Branagh imitated it in *Celebrity* (1998) it sounded to many people more like an impression than acting. While it has been argued on the basis of performances like Branagh's that Allen's "persona" has been played by others, I would argue that Branagh's example proves the opposite (Rivet 2001: 23). We respond differently to Branagh or Larry David in *Whatever Works* (2009) because their screen personas and performance styles produce distinct characters. Allen can create similar roles for other actors, but his screen characters are unique to him. Consider Gil, Owen Wilson's writer in *Midnight in Paris* (2011), whose much gentler behavior and more ingenuous attitude distinguish him radically from Woody's Artists despite the fact that we can easily imagine Allen in this story had it been made when he was young enough to fit the role.

The fact that the Nebbish and the Artist share significant features accounts not only for the fact that many people fail to distinguish the two characters, but also that they don't make a distinction between Allen on screen and off. The confusion is further encouraged because these films obviously borrow from Allen's life off screen and they make use of the conventions of autobiographical narrative. Yet these autobiographical comedies, from *Annie Hall* through *Deconstructing Harry*, are about far more than just Woody Allen. Indeed, Allen's comedies from this 20-year period (1977–97) are arguably the most revealing comedies of manners in late-twentieth-century film. They significantly revise the conventions of comedy as a dramatic form, usually dispensing with the happy ending. These films explore how intimate relationships have changed in the wake of the sexual revolution and second-wave feminism. In this sense, Allen's films dealt with widely shared aspects of contemporary life, and several of his films were significant box-office successes.[5]

The films in which the Artist appears may be taken together to be a prime example of what I have argued elsewhere is a new genre, the relationship story (Shumway 2003). Where the typical Hollywood love story is the tale of an obstructed but ultimately successful courtship, Allen's films are about how people "relate" to each other after they have gotten together. In his world, marriage is significant, but it is no longer the only kind of socially acceptable sexual relationship. Thus, Allen's films and the genre they represent reflect a new discourse of love, the discourse of intimacy. This discourse emerged in the second half of the twentieth century and now coexists with the discourse of romance. It is the discourse of intimacy that gives us the term "relationship," which as Anthony Giddens observes, has only recently come to mean "a close and continuing emotional tie to another" (Giddens 1992: 58). Where Hollywood romance traditionally equated marriage with "happily ever after," the discourse of intimacy depicts relationships as inherently complex and difficult. In its nonfictional form, it explains how relationships can be made to work. Allen's use of the discourse strongly suggests that they cannot. The films I'm discussing here, with the exception of *Hannah and Her Sisters*, make use of a transformed version of the generic romantic plot. Instead of "Boy gets girl, boy loses girl, boy gets girl back," Allen gives us "Boy loses girl, boy finds another girl, boy loses her too." If marriage has long been assumed by the culture to be the normal state for adults, Allen's films present a world where being single is the norm.

The opening of *Annie Hall* provides good examples of both Allen's use of autobiographical conventions and of the Artist's analytical stance. The first shot presents Woody Allen, the co-writer, director, and leading man of the film addressing the camera. It thus violates one of the most basic conventions of Hollywood, and invokes instead a documentary convention. The shot defines what follows as the confession of the film's protagonist, Alvy Singer, but we do not know that it is Alvy speaking until later. Audiences thus are seemly encouraged to read this opening as autobiographical, since it seems to be Woody Allen stand-up comic who is talking. But even as Alvy's monologue it remains a confession, an instance of one of the chief forms of autobiographical discourse. *Annie Hall* is Alvy Singer's autobiography. What Alvy has to say, however, is not merely a confession; it is also an analysis. The monologue is an attempt to explain Alvy's difficulties in his relationships. It thus distances him and the audience from the events of the film's narrative to follow, which is in part why this finally unsuccessful love story can remain comic.

The narrative of *Annie Hall* focuses on the rise and fall of one relationship, a story that is set against the background of Alvy's prior life history. While that film and *Husbands and Wives* are similar in their more explicit use of autobiographical conventions, *Manhattan* and *Husbands and Wives* are closer in their content. They tell more-or-less the same story in different styles, tones, and outcomes. Or to put it more accurately perhaps, the films pose the same problems for a similar group of characters, but they are understood from a different perspective. Each movie features a writer (played by Allen himself) who becomes romantically involved with a "girl" – Tracy (Mariel Hemingway) in *Manhattan*, Rain (Juliette Lewis) in *Husbands and Wives*– less than half his age.[6] In each, the writer is a friend of another couple whose marriage is in trouble. In each, a third party – Mary (Diane Keaton) in *Manhattan*, Michael (Liam Neeson) in *Husbands and Wives* – becomes involved with two of the protagonists. Each film features a woman who is "too cerebral" – Mary and Sally (Judy Davis) – and one who is more emotional – Tracy in *Manhattan*, Judy (Mia Farrow) in *Husbands and Wives*. Like all of the Artist films, they deal with the intimate struggles of upper middle-class, more-or-less intellectual New Yorkers who find that their intimate relationships do not live up to the expectations they have of them.

But if the Artist (and most of his friends) is nearly always unlucky in love, he is not in other respects unsuccessful. Alvy Singer, Ike Davis, Sandy Bates, Mickey, Gabe Roth, and Harry Block are not born losers, but highly accomplished and creative professionals. Alvy is a successful stand-up comic. Ike is a writer of hit TV show, Sandy a film director so famous he besieged by fans, and Mickey is an accomplished TV producer. Gabe is a lauded novelist and teacher, while Harry is also a famous fiction writer. They are neither *klutzes* nor inept, although they may worry about being these things. Indeed, the physical comedy that is so important in the earlier films in largely missing from those where Allen plays the artist. The humor becomes almost entirely verbal – or, perhaps we should say, verbal and gestural, as Allen's facial expressions and bodily movement are strongly connected to what he says. While the performance of most successful screen comedians involves this connection, Allen's are more extreme and therefore more distinctive despite the fact that they are often borrowed from other comics such as Chaplin and Hope. While the expressions and gestures are fairly consistent throughout both of his onscreen characters, their meaning differs. When the Nebbish performs them, they are predominantly comic; with the Artist they may reveal more serious emotions, making the humor of these films often troubling. In the case of *Husbands and Wives*, many viewers felt they had lost all comic force.

As comedies of manners, there is a realism to be found in Allen's relationship stories that is missing from the earlier comedies. Much of this realism derives from the way Allen performs. He often says lines that might well have been spoken by the Nebbish but, by saying them more conversationally, they no longer seem like gags. Consider the line Ike utters in the first scene of *Manhattan*, when, after raising the question, would one when crossing a bridge and seeing a man drowning in the water below have the courage to jump in and try to save him, he quips, "I, myself, never have to face this question because I can't swim." It's a remark worthy of Bob Hope, revealing a cowardice at odds with what we thought the moral problem he posed was supposed to illustrate. And yet here, it is just a joke among friends, said with just a slight arch of the brow.

Because of their greater realism, the roles Allen has written for himself as Artist are more three dimensional and individualized than those he wrote for himself as Nebbish. Alvy, Ike, and Mickey are fundamentally sympathetic characters, with whom the audience is encouraged to identify, while Sandy, Gabe, and Harry, are less likeable. Allen has said that he had wanted to call *Deconstructing Harry* "The

Meanest Man in the World," and had hoped to find someone else to play the part (Hirschberg 1997). In all of these roles, Allen's character has difficulties in his love life and is worried about death. Beyond that, each psychological profile of each role differs somewhat. Alvy, for example, suffers from anhedonia, a psychoanalytic term for the inability to experience pleasure. Anhedonia was the film's original title. Ike, on the contrary, famously gives us a list of aesthetic objects that make life worth living and which represent different pleasures, while the film itself asks us to take pleasure in its picture of the city and George Gershwin's music. Gabe treats others well, but gets nothing in return. Harry treats others badly, and gets more or less the same result.

But these roles also have a great deal in common besides that fact that Woody Allen plays all of them. In each case, Allen plays someone who is engaged in some kind of intellectual quest. In *Hannah and Her Sisters*, for example, Mickey's quest is to find a religion that can provide answers to his questions about the meaning of life and ease his fear of death. The quest is comic, of course, but it is also nearly tragic as it brings Mickey to the verge of suicide. Moreover, its lack of success is not trivial. For Allen, no religion can solve these problems. In the end, Mickey will be rescued from his unhappiness by a women's love, making this film an out-lier. It is also unusual in that there are three characters who embody different traits we normally find in Allen's artist: the painter Frederick (Max von Sydow) embodies his hostility and antisocial characteristics, while Eliot (Michael Caine), a financial adviser, is the one who undergoes a romantic adventure. But Mickey, like all of the Artist roles, is an intellectual in the sense that he turns his intelligence upon himself to try to understand his own problems. But that understanding is not merely idiosyncratic or personal, but implicitly reflective of commonly shared dilemmas. The joke that opens *Annie Hall* is meant not just to character-ize Alvy's view of life, but also to make us wonder whether it isn't true: "Two elderly women are at a Catskill mountain resort, and one of 'em says, 'Boy, the food at this place is really terrible.' The other one says, 'Yeah, I know, and such small portions.' "

Annie Hall is about Alvy's living this paradox, which, as the film's final joke suggests, is only possible through the imagination or art: "This guy goes to a psy-chiatrist and says, 'Doc, uh, my brother's crazy. He thinks he's a chicken.' And the doctor says, 'Well, why don't you turn him in?' And the guy says, 'I would but I need the eggs.' "

The joke parallels the film's end, where we see Alvy watching actors reading his new play in which his relationship with Annie comes out the way he wanted it to.

While the Nebbish is usually caught up in circumstances beyond his control, the Artist is capable of action to change his situation. Alvy moves from stand-up comic to playwright. Ike leaves his job as a writer for a successful *Saturday Night*-like TV show to write a book. Gabe resists Rain's seduction, while Harry manages to find people to see him honored by his old college. None of these actions is heroic, and sometimes, as is the case with Harry, they do not achieve the desired goal. But even Harry, in the end, despite the ceremony in which he was to be honored being cancelled on account of his arrest for kidnapping his son, is redeemed by art. The film ends with his fictional characters convening to honor their creator. Taken together, Allen's Artist films reveal a modernist faith in the value and power of art and artists that the filmmaker shares with many of the authors, painters, musicians, and directors his characters self-reflexively discuss.

The most important distinction between Nebbish and Artist is that the latter, however funny he may be, demands to be taken seriously. His problems are not mainly odd idiosyncrasies, but neurotic patterns that are widely shared and yet consistently misrecognized. These problems tend to recur throughout the different roles. One of them is articulated in the second joke Alvy tells in the opening monologue of *Annie Hall*:

> The – the other important joke for me is one that's, uh, usually attributed to Groucho Marx, but I think it appears originally in Freud's *Wit and its Relation to the Unconscious*. And it goes like this – I'm paraphrasing: Uh … I would never wanna belong to any club that would have someone like me for a member. That's the key joke of my adult life in terms of my relationships with women.

The way joke is told makes it clear that Alvy wants us to understand it as more than a joke. The dual attribution is an intellectual's habit, not a comedian's. What the joke illustrates here is a problem that many men – and a significant number of women – have in forming relationships. It will be illustrated by the Artist's behavior in most of the other films, as in *Manhattan* where Ike drops young Tracy, who adores him, to pursue Mary, whom he met when she was his friend Yale's mistress. It will be renamed or redefined in both *Stardust Memories* and *Husbands and Wives* as desiring women whom the Artist knows will be bad for him, while he is bored by those who are good to him. As Gabe's friend Jack puts it, Gabe was always attracted to "crazies" because at some level he knows these relationships will not work out. Advice books – and Stephen Frears's film of Nick Hornby's *High Fidelity* (2000) – attribute this behavior to a fear of intimacy, but Jack believes it comes either out Gabe's need to punish himself or from having grown up on "movies and novels where doomed love was romantic." Gabe himself attributes his desire for the love of his life, Harriet, a woman who ended up in a mental hospital, to his attraction for "kamikaze" women, who are not only self-destructive, but who destroy their lovers in the process. In his novel, Gabe's narrator wonders if men are simply driven by reproductive instincts to seek new partners, while Rain quotes *Time* magazine as claiming that passion only lasts four years.

The paradoxical quality of the Artist's behavior – of wanting what you know is bad for you because it is bad for you, or wanting what is logically impossible (to join a club that won't have one) – is at some level funny. It is a place where funny "strange" and funny "ha ha" meet. Such behavior is indicative of the power of the unconscious and the difficulty that the conscious mind has in breaking out of deeply ingrained psychic habits. It is precisely Freudian psychoanalysis that has brought these psychic patterns to light, and psychoanalysis is almost always mentioned, if not actually represented, in these films. For some viewers, the Artist's self analysis is offputting, rendering him precisely strange or neurotic and, perhaps, threatening, since such thinking may call into question one's own motives or assumptions. For others, it makes him admirable in his willingness to understand and accept the difficult workings of his own mind. Know thy self, Socrates told us, and the Artist is one who takes this injunction seriously.

Besides his quest to know himself, the Artist is also admirable for his moral scruples. He is not always able to live up to his morality, but, with the possible exception of *Deconstructing Harry*, he strives to do so. Adultery figures as an explicit concern in *Manhattan, Hannah and her Sisters,* and *Husbands and Wives,* but *Allen's* character is not guilty of it. He worries in both *Manhattan* and *Husbands and Wives* about the morality of being involved with much younger women, and in the latter, resists the temptation to do so. In both of those films, his character is depicted as more upright than his friends Yale and Jack, both of whom cheat on their wives. The Artist drinks, but refuses to take drugs. Even though he is portrayed as successful and financially well off, there is little evidence of extravagance, Sandy's Rolls Royce in *Stardust Memories* being perhaps the major exception. Those people familiar with the cost of Manhattan real estate may recognize that the apartments the Artist occupies are beyond the means of even the upper middle class, but that does not make them extravagant by the standards of most Americans who in fact have more space.

The Artist's morality is connected to his propensity to criticism and judgment. One of the things the Artist does in every film is to express his opinion, especially about other artists and their works. Such judgments are both positive and negative, but, with the exception of *Manhattan*, the negative ones are more common and more memorable. We remember Alvy's judgment about Los Angeles in *Annie Hall*, as a place "where the only cultural advantage is that you can make a right turn on a red light." His inability to ignore the loud-mouthed professor in line at the movie theater ends in the famous gag where Allen produces Marshall McLuhan to refute the offending party. Judy, Gabe's wife in *Husbands and Wives*, repeatedly complains that he is too critical. She chooses to show her poems to Michael rather than to her writing-teacher husband, because she's afraid of his judgment. Sandy Bates's judgments about the fans of his work led many to conclude that Woody Allen was demeaning his audience in *Stardust Memories*. These judgments are often quite persuasive, and, if we believe that judgment itself is a valuable intellectual endeavor, the Artist's use of it is also likely to endear him to us even if we don't always share his views. For example, the Artist is famously hard on rock & roll, making his tastes seem dated, especially by the late 1970s when the dominant tastes included an appreciation of the best work in all forms, high and low. Yet this very quality of refusing to change his views to suit changes in popular opinion is also evidence of strength of character.

The Artist, then, commands our identification, and not only because he is the clear protagonist in most of the films. But that does not mean that Allen intends us to accept the Artist as infallible or a model to be imitated. It is clear, for example, that Harry Block's philandering and whoring – indeed, his treatment of women in general – is not something that Allen is celebrating. *Deconstructing Harry*, however, is unusual in the degree to which the Artist appears unsympathetic. But even in the other Artist films, there are moments where the Artist's views or behavior are called into question. Several of the best examples occur in *Manhattan*, where Ike may be the protagonist, but Tracy is the film's moral center. Ike says throughout roughly the first half of the film that he needs to get out of his relationship with Tracy, who is only seventeen and still in high school. We, of course, tend to agree with this sentiment, yet when Ike breaks up with Tracy, our assumptions are challenged by the couple's conversation. While Ike insists that she can't possibly be in love with him, since "You're a kid. You don't know what love means. I don't know what it means. Nobody out there knows what the hell's going on," Tracy replies with a simple yet utterly compelling definition: "We have laughs together. I care about you. Your concerns are my concerns. We have great sex." When a few lines later, Ike tells her "Don't be so precocious, okay? I mean don't be so smart," he's conceding her the argument even as he persists in following his desire to be free of her to pursue Mary.

If this instance is a fairly obvious rebuke of the Artist, a later scene is more complicated and subtle, but also more revealing of the way in which the Artist character is presented in the whole series of film. When Mary tells Ike that she has started to see Yale again, Ike marches – as the up-tempo music (Gershwin's "The Land of the Gay Caballero") suggests – over to the building where he is teaching, and motions for him to step out of class to speak with him. They duck into an empty anatomy classroom where a hominid skeleton is mounted in the front facing the class, while several other skeletons hang off to each side in the background. Allen frames his own character standing next to this creature, while Yale stands against the left wall to Ike's right (see Figure 6.2). The scene opens as a two (or three) shot, with the skeleton in between the men, emphasizing the distance between them. After the conversation begins, Ike walks toward the hominid, and the rest of the scene is edited in what would be a traditional shot / reverse shot pattern except that the camera is not in either case placed over the shoulder the listener, but slightly askew, so that as we look at Ike and the hominid, it is almost as if we are sitting in the classroom.

Ike clearly does have the moral high ground as the scene opens. Yale had encouraged him to see Mary after their initial affair had ended, and he now has started to see her again behind Ike's back. A superficial reading of the scene, then, might simply assume an identity between Ike's views and the filmmaker's. A careful analysis, however, shows the scene to be more ambiguous. To begin

Figure 6.2 Ike (Woody Allen) berates his friend Yale while the skeleton looks on in *Manhattan* (producers, Charles H. Joffe and Jack Rollins).

with, we need to recognize that both men are simply defending their own actions and interests, so neither one can be seen as objective. And if Ike has obviously been wronged, what Yale has done to him is not so different from what he did to Tracy. The visuals are not designed to allow us to accept Ike's tirade at face value. Not only is Ike mocked by having to share the screen with the hominid, whose short stature, and wide skull's eyes make it resemble Woody Allen, but also the extremity of his claims and his gestures ultimately helps create some sympathy for Yale's perspective. After apparently catching Yale in a lie about the extent of his renewed relationship with Mary, Yale responds, "Well, I'm not a saint, okay?" Ike then launches into an attack, talking with both arms, his eyebrows arching wildly:

> But you – you're too easy on yourself, don't you see that? … You're not honest with yourself … . you wanna write a book, but – but, in the end, you'd rather buy the Porsche, you know, or you cheat a little bit on Emily [his wife], and you play around with the truth a little with me, and – the next thing you know, you're in front of a Senate committee and you're naming names! You're informing on your friends!

Yale's response is dead on: "You are so self-righteous, you know. I mean, we're just people, we're just human beings, you know. You think you're God!" Ike's reply is funny, but it also seems to concede Yale's criticism, "I – I gotta model myself after someone." Moreover, Allen's earlier actions – not only toward Tracy, but also having tried to hit his ex-wife's girlfriend with a car – show that his behavior has been less than God-like. The conversation puts us emotionally on Ike's side, but its content favors neither character.

While each of the various roles entails some change over the course of the film, there are no major transformations. For example, in *Manhattan* it is clear that Ike learns he made a mistake when he dumped Tracy for Mary, but it is much less clear that he has learned the film's central lesson, which Tracy articulates in the film's last line: "you have to have a little faith in people." Ike's smile – in the moment that in Allen's work comes closest to the end of *City Lights* – suggests that maybe he gets it, but it's not clear whether he is emotionally capable of such faith. Change itself is often represented as something to be avoided. Ike is worried that if Tracy goes to London to study acting, "that thing about you that I like" will change. Gabe tells Judy in *Husbands and Wives* that change equals death. But perhaps more important, the Artist is defined by patterns of thought and behavior he knows are unsuccessful but which he cannot change. The Freudian concept that seems to explain the most about this character is the compulsion to repeat. While the Artist often makes professional progress, he seldom makes emotional or psychological progress, as Alvy explicitly complains about his own analysis. This means that we are asked to identity with a character who consistently will fail to do what he knows he should. We can't just laugh at this problem, because by implication it is one we may share. The Artist, thus, makes us uncomfortable in ways in the Nebbish does not.

Still, the Artist films depend heavily on building an emotional connection with the audience despite the fact that the Artist is a difficult, flawed character. Allen asks us to find pathos in the Artist's inability to find love and happiness despite professional and material success. As Sandy argues in connection with *The Bicycle Thief* in *Stardust Memories*, if you don't have enough to eat "the issues become very clear-cut." But if you're living in a more affluent society the issues are more complicated and "your problems become, how can I fall in love, or why can't I fall in love, more accurately, and um, why do I age and die ... " Allen's Artist is clearly better off materially than the Tramp in *City Lights*, but he is no more capable of realizing his most important dreams.

There are of course limits to what these Artist films can do. They depict a fairly narrow range of American lives, those of the white, urban middle-class who usually work in the culture industry, while the Artist himself is defined by his geography, ethnicity, and profession. This narrowness reflects changes in the film industry and its audience. Chaplin's Tramp was an everyman for a time when film had a genuinely mass audience, but Allen's films are a product of the niche marketing of films, as revealed by the fact that his movies since *Hannah and Her Sisters* have in general remained profitable because of a dependable European audience. This is fitting because Allen styled himself after such great postwar European directors as Bergman, Truffaut, and Fellini. His films are aimed at the kind of people who cared about the more abstract or intellectual problems that had always interested him. The result is an extraordinarily rich body of work that deserves comparison not only with the work of the greatest filmmakers, but also with that of contemporary literary artists, from Samuel Beckett to John Updike and Phillip Roth. Allen's Artist character was essential to this aesthetic achievement. Contrary to prejudices that privilege impersonation, acting in which the actor strives to disappear into each different role, over personification, in which actor's persona remains consistent from role to role, the examples of Chaplin and Allen suggest that in comedy personification allows for more complex development of character because the development can take place over the course of many films. If personification may seem unrealistic in a drama, it is much less a problem in comedy, where the codes of realism are routinely violated. This tends to turn comic actors into clowns, as Allen observed of Groucho (Schickel 2003: 81). But Allen managed to solve the problem of realism by resorting to conventions of autobiography, giving the Artist a sense of referentiality lacking in the personas of most movie stars. These innovations allowed Allen to produce films that were at once deeply serious and very funny.

Notes

1. See, for example, Pinsker (2006) and Fallon (2001).
2. Most critics treat Allen's onscreen character as consistent throughout his career, despite the general recognition that, with *Annie Hall*, his films became much more narratively complex and sophisticated. See Gopnik (1993); Curry (1996); Librach (1996); Rivet (2001); and Pinsker (2006). Allen himself refers to his screen character in the singular in interviews with Lax (2007: 65, 149), but its not clear from these remarks whether this a simple shorthand, accepting the interviewer's term, or an actual assertion of a consistent single character.
3. Still, this influence has sometimes been overstated, as in Pogel (1987) and Curry (1996: 7), who asserts that "Allen's little-man figures [are] based on Charlie Chaplin's little tramp."
4. While Gopnik's reading is legitimate given the era in which Allen was working, the Nebbish's lechery is very similar to what we see in Hope as early as 1940 with *Road to Singapore* (Victor Schertzinger).
5. According to imdb.com, *Annie Hall* earned a US gross of $38 251 425 on an estimated cost of $4 million, and was the seventh highest grossing film of the year. *Manhattan* grossed $39 900 000 and *Hannah and Her Sisters*, $40 084 041. Each of these films provided significant return on investment.
6. The Artist has some kind of relationship with a younger woman (usually much younger) in each of the films except *Hannah*, and in these relationships he usually acts as her teacher, even though *Husbands and Wives* is the only film where the Artist is employed as teacher. See Shumway (2001) for an extended discussion of Allen's treatment of these relationships.

References

Bjorkman, S. (1993) *Woody Allen on Woody Allen*, Grove, New York, NY.

Curry, R.R. (1996) Woody Allen: The artist as worker, in *Perspectives on Woody Allen* (ed. R.R. Curry), Hall, New York, NY, pp. 3–18.

DeCurtis, A. (1993) Woody Allen: The *Rolling Stone* Interview. *Rolling Stone* (September 16), pp. 45–50+.

Fallon, L. (2001) The nebbish king: Spiritual renewal, in Woody Allen's *Manhattan*, in *Woody Allen: A Casebook* (ed. K. King), Routledge, New York, NY, pp. 47–54.

Giddens, A. (1992) *The Transformation of Intimacy: Sexuality, Love, and Eroticism in Modern Societies*, Stanford University Press, Stanford, CA.

Gopnik, A. (1993) The Outsider. *The New Yorker* (October 25), pp. 86–93.

Hirschberg, L. (1997) The Two Hollywoods. *NY Times Magazine* (November 16), http://www.nytimes.com/1997/11/16/magazine/the-two-hollywoods-the-directors-woody-allen-martin-scorsese.html?scp=6&sq=WoodyAllen&st=nyt&pagewanted=6 (accessed May 18, 2012).

Howe, I. (1976) *World of Our Fathers*, Harcourt, New York, NY.

Lax, E. (2007) *Conversations with Woody Allen: His Films, The Movies, and Moviemaking*, Knopf, New York, NY.

Librach, R.S. (1996) A portrait of the artist as a neurotic: studies of interior distancing in the films of Woody Allen, in *Perspectives on Woody Allen* (ed. R.R. Curry), Hall, New York, NY, pp. 158–76.

Pinsker, S. (2006) Woody Allen's lovable anxious schlemiels, in *The Films of Woody Allen: Critical Essays* (ed. C.L.P. Silet), Scarecrow, Lanham, MD, pp. 1–12.

Pogel, N. (1987) *Woody Allen*, Knopf, New York, NY.

Rivet, M.-P. (2001) Woody Allen: The relationship between the persona and its author, in *Woody Allen: A Casebook* (ed. K. King), New York, Routledge, pp. 23–34.

Sarris, A. (2006) The most harmonious comedian, in *The Essential Chaplin* (ed. R. Schickel), Ivan R. Dee, Chicago, IL, pp. 45–58.

Schickel, R. (2003a) *Woody Allen: A Life in Film*, Ivan R. Dee, Chicago, IL.

Schickel, R. (2003b) Introduction: Woody in the afternoon. In *Woody Allen: A Life in Film*, Ivan R. Dee, Chicago, IL, pp. 5–70.

Shumway, D.R. (2001) Woody Allen, "the Artist," and "the Little Girl," in *The End of Cinema as We Know It: American Film in the Nineties* (ed. Jon Lewis), New York University Press, New York, NY, pp. 195–202.

Shumway, D.R. (2003) *Modern Love: Romance, Intimacy, and the Marriage Crisis*, New York University Press, New York, NY.

Further Reading

Gopnik, A. (1993) The Outsider. *The New Yorker* (October 25), pp. 86–93. A lucid attempt to come to terms with Allen's cultural significance in the wake of the Soon Yi scandal.

Lax, E. (2007) *Conversations with Woody Allen: His Films, the Movies, and Moviemaking*, Knopf, New York, NY. A collection of interviews conducted over the course of Allen's career.

Rosenblum, R. and Karen, R. (1986) *When the Shooting Stops… the Cutting Begins: A Film Editor's Story*, Da Capo, New York, NY. An account of how Allen learned his craft from an experienced film editor. See the chapters on *Scenes from A Marriage* and *Annie Hall*, the latter being especially revealing.

Schickel, R. (2003) *Woody Allen: A Life in Film*, Ivan R. Dee, Chicago, IL. Schickel's introduction is the most perceptive single piece of writing about Allen's films. The interview is among the richest of the many Allen has given.

Shumway, D.R. (2003) *Modern Love: Romance, Intimacy, and the Marriage Crisis*, New York University Press, New York, NY. Reads some of Allen's "Artist" films in the context of other contemporary relationship stories and the history of discourses of love and intimacy.

7

Mel Brooks, Vulgar Modernism, and Comic Remediation

Henry Jenkins

What is it? A Musical? A Love Story? A Western?
Studio Chief (Sid Caesar) to Mel Funn (Mel Brooks), Silent Movie *(1976)*

By the time Mel Brooks directed his first feature film, *The Producers*, in 1968, he had already enjoyed a long and distinguished career as a comic working across a range of media. Brooks began as a Tummler (master entertainer) at various Catskills resorts, where he honed his skills at telling jokes and doing impersonations. He was hired as a comedy writer for television in the late 1950s, most famously as part of the team behind *Your Show of Shows with Sid Caesar* (NBC, 1950–1954), where he also sometimes performed (and which, as we will see, informed much of his subsequent comedy practices). His intense and vivid personality inspired the character of Buddy Sorrell (Morey Amsterdam) when co-writer Carl Reiner became the creator of *The Dick Van Dyke Show* (CBS 1961–1966). Brooks himself went on to co-create *Get Smart* (NBC 1965–1969; CBS 1969–1970) with Buck Henry. Meanwhile, Brooks and Reiner reunited as a comedy duo in 1960 on *The Steve Allen Show* (NBC 1956–1960; ABC 1961; syndication, 1962–1964), a gig that ultimately led to a series of five hit comedy albums, which foregrounded the character of the 2000 Year Old Man. Alongside his work on stage, television, and records, Brooks provided the stream-of-consciousness commentary for an Ernest Pintoff cartoon, *The Critic*, which won the Oscar for Short Subjects, Cartoons in 1963.

No wonder, then, that Mel Brooks describes his entry into making film comedies as a relatively arbitrary decision, one more movement across media in a career defined by his ability to entertain in almost any context. In the *Making*

A Companion to Film Comedy, First Edition. Edited by Andrew Horton and Joanna E. Rapf.
© 2013 John Wiley & Sons, Inc. Published 2016 by John Wiley & Sons, Inc.

Of video on the 2002 DVD release of *The Producers*, Brooks explains how he was struggling with which medium might best contain a story he wanted to tell about a larger-than-life showman he had met during the early phases of his career:

> It started as a book – too much dialogue, not enough action. Okay, it's a play. I started writing it as a play, showed it to some friends of mine, and they told me too many scenes, too many sets. So, I said 'what is it?' and they said it was a movie. Dialogue, lots of different places. I never wrote it as a movie, but they said write it. So I wrote it as a movie.

In an anthology focused on "film comedy," it may be difficult mentally to recover that moment when Brooks asked "what is it?" about his work in progress, yet in this chapter, I want to shift our frame to consider what it might mean to think of Brooks in the context of a more expansive understanding of "media comedy." Expanding the frame of our analysis not only allows us to trace connections among Brooks' work in a range of different media. Specifically, talking about "media comedy" allows us to think about Mel Brooks in relation to broader trends J. Hoberman (1991) described as "vulgar modernism," in a highly influential essay he published in *Artforum* in 1982 and revised for publication in a 1991 book of the same title. "Vulgar modernism" refers to a style of comedy that emerged in the postwar period and linked together developments on film, television, comics and humor magazines, animation, and recorded sound. Because of these constant border-crossings between media, Brooks shows a consistent consciousness about the properties of the medium in which he is working, often playing different media against each other for comic effect. Finally, I will focus this consideration of Brooks as a "media comic" around a close analysis of sound-based and sight gags in *Silent Movie* (1976). *Silent Movie* is neither Brooks' best comedy nor his most popular, but it is the film where his awareness of his medium is most pronounced. In short, Brooks is not only a clown who works across media, but also someone who clowns with the properties of media.

The Last Gas(p) of Vulgar Modernism

Calling Mel Brooks a "vulgar modernist" may invite us to focus on his intentional deployment of references to bodily functions. After all, Brooks may well have been the person who introduced fart and erection jokes into the repertoire of American screen comedy (pushing against taboos at a time when censorship standards in Hollywood were in flux). A spoof of Hitchcock's *The Birds* (1963) in *High Anxiety* (1977) involves a flock of pigeons chasing Brooks down the street, pooping on him again and again. A major plot point in *History of the World, Part I* (1981), a segment depicting the French Revolution, focuses on a piss bucket. Current and future generations of critics may not be eager to forgive him for what he unleashed on the screen.

Brooks is known for soliciting broad comic performances, which often involve various degrees of human degradation. Consider, for example, Charlie Callas in *High Anxiety* as a mental patent convinced he is a family dog. Callas not only bounces around on the floor and barks but also masturbates against Mel Brooks' leg and pretends to urinate against a wall. Or for that matter, think about the spectacle of the dignified Ron Moore in *The Twelve Chairs* (1970) being pushed by his con-man compatriot to pretend to have an epileptic fit, foaming at the mouth, and thrashing about in the dirty streets of Moscow.

For those who don't like Mel Brooks, and there are many who fall into this category, these scatological references and over-the-top performances account for much of the distaste: he has a reputation for low comedy that inspires pleasure or displeasure depending on the audience's own sense of humor, and one can feel both, moment by moment. When Brooks remade the classic romantic comedy *To Be or Not To Be* (1942) in 1983, critics complained that he had replaced the nuanced "Lubitsch touch" with the Brooks knee-slap. Bits of witty banter from the original screenplay co-exist in the same scene with sexy Anna Bronski (Anne Bancroft) wiping the drool off the face of a lustful Nazi officer.

Often, this sense of "vulgar," as in "distasteful," comes coupled with another sense of "vulgar" as in coming from the "vulgar" classes, as having relatively low cultural status. Of course, the issue of cultural status is historically variable as was suggested when Barack Obama awarded Mel Brooks the Kennedy Center Award, alongside actor Robert De Niro, rocker Bruce Springsteen, jazz musician Dave Brubeck, and opera singer Grace Bumbry, as people who have "transformed the arts in America."

These various associations with vulgarity have been part of the concept of the clown throughout the ages (Jenkins 1992: 221–30). Our modern word "clown" is derived from two Old German terms, Klonne, meaning "clumsy lout, lumpish fellow, a countryman, rustic or peasant" and Klunj, meaning "a clod, clot or lump." The clown is a liminal figure, an outsider, a social vagrant or conversely, a representative of the lowest orders of the social hierarchy ("a rustic or peasant.") In either case, the clown is a "lout," poorly assimilated into the social order that his or her antics constantly disrupt. Secondly, the clown is "lumpish," a "clot" of contradictory meanings and associations, a "clump" of opposing cultural categories, a "clod" of irreconcilable impulses. Historically, the clown was someone who enjoyed the "comic freedom" to defame those in power, who debased the sacred (Heib 1972: 163–95). Ritual clowns throw excrement at funerals as a cosmological statement on the links between order and disorder, purity and dirt. At least Brooks uses fake excrement! Dom DeLuise functions as this kind of clown as the Emperor in *History of the World, Part I*, scratching his balls and belching throughout a state dinner. Read from that perspective, of course, Mel Brooks is vulgar – that's part of his job description. The modern comedian is a secularized version of the classic clown, now stripped of its ritual function, now seeking to entertain rather than to instruct, but still lumpish, loutish, and above all, vulgar.

Brooks often couples issues of class and taste with those of ethnicity (in this case, Jewish-ness), race (often in terms of the blackness of some of his co-stars) and sexuality (persistent references to queer identities and desires). Brooks uses his "low" humor and clownish status to speak about other forms of marginality and exclusion in American culture, a practice that made his films, especially those of the 1960s and 1970s, more pointed and topical than they might seem to contemporary viewers.

He clearly courts vulgarity in *The Producers*' "Springtime for Hitler" sequence: the showmen are staging a sure flop play, written by a neo-Nazi, staged by a flaming queen, performed by a drugged out hippie, which they are sure is going to offend their audience. The stagecraft is loud, excessive, and what we'd now call "politically incorrect," with goose-stepping chorus girls dressed in Heimlet-themed scanties and jokes that evoke but do not acknowledge the horrors of the Holocaust. Brooks dares us to be shocked, while also hoping that we will be sophisticated to be inside the joke in much the same ways that R. Crumb and others in the underground comics of the period amplified and spoofed racist and sexist stereotypes to shatter cultural taboos. Brooks deploys faggy stereotypes in his depiction of the play's drag-queen director – decorating their apartment with Greek statuary with their rumps turned towards the camera and showing Gene Wilder's shock when his hand accidentally lands on one of the statue's backsides or Zero Mostel's discomfort in being crammed together with the director's "roommate," with his leather jacket and mascara, in an overly confining elevator. We could read these jokes as homophobic, but they are also making fun of the homophobic responses of the protagonists, suggesting a solidarity that exists in his early films between queers, blacks, and Jews. Mel Brooks' comedy is vulgar – on a mission.

All of this has to be on the table from the start if we are going to write an appreciation of Brooks' contributions to American comedy. But, in describing Brooks as a vulgar modernist, I am trying to link him to Hoberman's essay mentioned above, where he examines a range of popular artists who were seemingly locked out of the canon on the basis of their low cultural status, even as their work continued to influence a broad range of modern and postmodern artists. Hoberman (1991: 33) describes "vulgar modernism" as "the vulgar equivalent of modernism itself. By this I mean a popular, ironic, somewhat dehumanized mode reflexively concerned with specific properties of its medium or the conditions of its making." According to Hoberman (1991: 33), this "sensibility [...] developed between 1940 and 1960 in such peripheral corners of the 'culture industry' as animated cartoons, comic books, early morning TV, and certain Dean Martin/Jerry Lewis comedies." Hoberman devotes the core of his essay to individualized discussions of animator Tex Avery, director Frank Tashlin, cartoonist Will Elder, and television performer Ernie Kovacs, yet his introduction makes clear that the concept more broadly describes a historically specific relationship between popular culture and high art. My own work extends the category to include the sound comedy of Spike Jones or the graphic humor of Basil Wolverton, which share many traits with the others on Hoberman's list (Jenkins 2011). Brooks has not been previously discussed as a vulgar modernist. A focus on his film comedies would position him far outside the historical period on which Hoberman focuses, yet a multiple media perspective allows us to see Brooks' approach to comedy as taking shape during the high water period of vulgar modernism.

Any list of 1950s' comic texts that includes Ernie Kovacs but excludes *Your Show of Shows* (NBC, 1950–1954) is clearly incomplete, since Kovacs and Caesar existed side by side as the hallmarks of sophisticated comedy in the first decade of American television, the high against which one defined the low of Milton Berle. *Your Show of Shows'* team of writers included not only Reiner and Brooks, but also Neil Simon, Woody Allen, Mel Tonken, and many others who would define comedy on big screens and small ever since. *Your Show of Shows* was more performance centered, Kovacs more gag-centered, but both relied heavily on parody and spoofs of the culture around them, including targets, such as silent movies, operas, and foreign films, too high brow for most of today's comedy shows.

Brooks' subsequent work – from the ongoing spoof of James Bond and other Cold War thrillers in *Get Smart* to the parodies of specific genres (the western in *Blazing Saddles*), film series (Universal's 1930s' monster movies in *Young Franken-stein* (1974)), films (*Star Wars* in *Spaceballs* (1987)) and directors (Hitchcock in *High Anxiety*) – relied on equally sophisticated plays with the audience's familiarity with other forms of popular entertainment. Mock interviews – often involving Carl Reiner as a reporter questioning Sid Caesar as the Professor with the always flexible range of expertise – were a staple of *Your Show of Shows*, providing Caesar with an excuse to do "double talk," fusing English with mock versions of different international languages. The Professor sketches were the prototype for the later comedy albums where Reiner again plays interviewer to Brooks who also shows a capacity to mimic different accents and argots as they parody such topics as Madison Avenue, self-help books, beatnik poets, and international film festivals.

Modernism operates in Hoberman's argument as a very broad and loose signifier of twentieth-century high art. What links these popular artists to "modernism" for Hoberman is their interest in foregrounding the materiality of their medium and the conditions of its production and reception, their embrace of reflexivity and intertextuality. See, for example, his description of what Will Elder brought to early *Mad Magazine*:

> His best pieces are collage like arrangements of advertising trademarks, media icons, banal slogans, visual puns, and assorted non-sequiturs […] As *Mad*'s leading formalist, Elder allows internal objects to tamper with the boundaries of a panel,

breaks continuous vistas into consecutive frames, offers visually identical panels with wildly fluctuating details, and otherwise emphasizes the essential serial nature of his medium. (Hoberman 1991: 37)

Hoberman is interested in these popular artists' refusal to produce a coherent, consistent, or classically constructed world, openly displaying their own authorial interventions. Hoberman, most likely, was inspired by *Screen's* attempt to generate a Brechtian mode of film theory in the 1970s and by the French rediscovery of Frank Tashlin and Jerry Lewis, both of which rested on arguments that self-reflexivity and intertextuality shattered the codes and conventions of classical cinema.

The Critic, the animated short that represented Brooks' first screen venture, depends on a literal juxtaposition between vulgarity and modernism. Brooks provides voiceover, as a cranky Jewish old man trying to make sense of Ernest Pintoff's abstract, experimental animation: "What the hell is this? Must be a cartoon." Over the course of the three minutes, he expresses curiosity and outrage, trying to interpret the action through a series of metaphors and analogies (from birth and sex to cockroaches), dismissing the abstract art as "dirt," "trash," "junk," and "filth," grumbling about how much he paid for his tickets and about whether the artist could find a more productive way to earn his living, but never quite resolving what it is he is watching. The cartoon played both to sophisticated filmgoers who can feel superior to those who lack the training to engage with *avant garde* works and to those who think that the emperor has no clothes.

Be a Clown!

In his classic formulation, Steve Seidman (1981: 15) stresses what he calls the "extrafictional" nature of comedian-centered films, calling attention to: "anything that interrupts the smooth exposition of a fictional universe or anything that intrudes upon the depiction of a 'real' fictional universe to give the sense that 'it's only a movie.'"

For Seidman (1981: 15), though, this self-consciousness is closely associated with "the comedian who assumes a particular narrational stance that allows the articulation of these features."

Brooks' comedies certainly include an army of comedians, starting with Brooks himself, but extending to his ensemble casts (including recurring partners such as Gene Wilder, Madeline Kahn, Dom DeLuise, Sid Caesar, or Marty Feldman), and secondary performers (Ron Carrey, Harold Gould, Fritz Feld, Howard Morris) who may appear to perform in only one gag or bit. *Silent Movie*, for example, includes a sequence where a giant fly soars off the top of an exterminator's truck and into Henny Youngman's soup, playing off his long-standing association with "waiter, there's a fly in my soup" gags; or another where Harry Ritz of the Ritz Brothers minces and prances as he models a "half off" suit. Brooks taps into the classical iconography of the clown, with characters defined through their appetites and pleasures (sooner or later, everything goes into DeLuise's mouth), their neurosis (Wilder clinging to his "blanky" in *The Producers*), or their deformities (Feldman's bulging eyes and shifting hump in *Young Frankenstein*).

The comedian in Seidman's formulation – a modern, secularized variant on the clown, defined as much through personality as through desires – is someone who refuses to or is unable to conform to social expectations and thus becomes a disruptive force in the story world, his disruptions extending to include the capacity to destabilize the film's construction of reality (for example Bob Hope and Bing Crosby call attention to the Paramount icon as part of the background in their *Road to …* comedies (1940–1962)). But, Brooks' films already exist in a landscape littered with gags and the disruption of film language simply becomes part of this broader logic.

Of all of Brooks' films, *Silent Movie* may be the most clearly focused around a central team of disruptive comedians (Brooks, Feldman, DeLuise). When they court various Hollywood stars in the hopes of convincing them to appear in their movie, the stars may initially be read as figures of order against which we read their clownish disorder but the stars end up very much part of the physical comedy and very much enjoying the pleasures of comic performance, whether it is the narcissistic Burt Reynolds finding the comedians in his shower, the prankish Paul Newman trying to race them in a motorized wheelchair around the hospital grounds, Hollywood royalty Liza Minnelli laughing at their bungling dressed as knights in armor, or Anne Bancroft who relishes becoming part of their nightclub performance as a mariachi band. The stars cannot resist trying their hands at slapstick comedy, and this is how they get suckered into joining the troubled film production. The decentering of the comic performers into a comic universe might link Brooks' films back to that vulgar modernist classic, *Hellzapoppin'* (1941), where any and every performer has the ability to freeze the frame, reverse the motion, or otherwise manipulate filmic conventions. (By the way, *Hellzapoppin'* also prefigures Brooks in its depiction of a stage show where everything goes wrong but becomes so funny that it becomes a hit, a central plot point in *The Producers*).

Yet, there are gags here that do not rest at all on comic performance, such as a toss-away bit where the comedians drive past a Szechuan eatery and see smoke pouring out of the patrons' mouths. Many gags rest on the comic deployment of signs, such as the chart on the wall of the studio executive's office which shows that revenue declines have been so steep that the line runs off the poster and onto the sofa below it, the words carved into the marble bathroom of the Engulf and Devoir corporate headquarters, which read "Our toilets are nicer than most people's homes," and the company's logo which promises, "our fingers are in everything." Here, the gags are etched onto the *mise-en-scène*, become part of the background, and in many of these cases, the comic performers do not even react to their presence.

Figure 7.1   An example of "Chicken Fat" humor in *Blazing Saddles* (producer, Michael Hertzberg).

Chicken Fat and Blackouts

Mad's Will Elder, a certified Vulgar Modernist, used to call such stand-alone gags, often stuck in the background of an already cluttered environment, "chicken fat," explaining "chicken fat is the part of the soup that is bad for you, yet gives the soup its delicious pleasure." Brooks embraces such "chicken-fat" strategies when he implants comic elements in the settings of his films and lets his camera slowly pan across them. Consider, for example, the wall-sized photographs hanging at the psychologists' convention in *High Anxiety* – Freud, Jung, Adler, and Dr. Joyce Brothers. Similarly gag-encrusted signage abounds in the cartoons of Tex Avery who may sometimes have gag signs that comment on gag signs or the comics of Basil Wolverton, where they are often coupled with his play with slang. Such jokes are buried in plain sight; there if we spot them, suggesting a world where gags are so plentiful that we may not notice all of them on first viewing.

The use of "chicken fat" as a metaphor for this kind of humor is hardly accidental – a recurring form of "chicken fat" humor involved the introduction of Yiddish phrases and Jewish references as a new generation of Jewish comics refused to accept the erasure of ethnicity that, as recent historians have suggested, represent the efforts of Jewish studio executives to court waspish respectability in Hollywood's construction of America (Gabler 1989). Mel Brooks similarly made a cameo in *Blazing Saddles* as an Indian chief who calls a wagon train full of African American settlers "*schwartza.*" The opposite of assimilation, "chicken fat" humor refuses to remain hidden in the background.

In many cases, Brooks couples "chicken-fat" gags with "blackout" sketches, short gag sequences, often comic because of their abruptness and their lack of clear integration to the narrative logic of the film. Such "blackout" sketches were one of the hallmarks of Ernie Kovacs' television comedy, where the rapid succession of sight gags, each building towards simple and disposable punch lines, helped to fill the gaps between larger sketches (Horton 2010: 51–72). The sequence where the fly lands in Henny Youngman's soup is a classic example of a blackout gag – in this case, it builds from a larger chase sequence but it is a distraction or digression from the unfolding plot. In some cases, Brooks could construct an entire sequence of nothing but blackout gags, as in the prehistoric sequence of *History*, which depicts the first artist and first critic, the discovery of fire, the invention of music, and so forth. Each short segment involves the build up and pay-off of a specific joke – so the first critic scratches on his beard and demonstrates his disdain by urinating on the cave painting.

A running gag in *Silent Movie* involves a newspaper stand owner who is being bullied by the newspaper delivery team. Here, the newspaper functions as a narrational device, a classic way of encapsulating the action, but it becomes something more as the newspaper headline also describes what just happened at the news stand, "newspaper vendor struck down by Bundle of Papers again," and later in the film, the headlines become a series of nonsensical spoofs of *Variety*'s distinctive argot, "Pix Tix Nix Mix" or "Boff Noff Toff Roff."

"Chicken fat" disrupts constructions of space, "blackouts" constructions of time, but both break with the larger structures of the films. In both cases, they constitute a form of comic excess, when read against traditional notions of classical film construction which emphasize economy and clarity. Taken to extremes, as was often the case in early *Mad*, the background overwhelms the foreground, as we are encouraged to pay attention to elements that are unconnected with the overall experience of the work. Regular readers took great pleasure in the tug-of-war over our attention being conducted by artist Will Elder and writer Harvey Kurtzman. There's a blackout gag in *Silent Movie* which works very much in this same way: in the foreground, a distracted nurse reads a pulpy romance, while in the background, a row of monitors show desperate patients, in various states of distress and discomfort, signaling for help, both cutaways from the central action which involves the protagonists walking through the hospital lobby to visit a patient.

The introduction of the town of Rock Ridge in *Blazing Saddles* demonstrates how chicken fat and blackout gags can work together to shape the comic climate. As the camera tracks along the streets, we see a traditional country store juxtaposed with a much more contemporary looking Howard Johnsons, complete with a sign promising "1 Flavor," perhaps anticipating a future where many more options will be on offer. Inside the local saloon, cowboys playing poker are overrun by their cows and the barkeeper, who "always kept things nice and clean," spits and polishes a mug. The peaceful scene is disrupted by "a pack of murderers and thieves" riding through the streets – shooting hats full of holes, knocking people into puddles, ripping down scaffolding from under a worker, beating up an old woman (who turns to the camera to protest the "cruelty"), and knocking aside a shower stall to leave a soap-sudsy man clutching at his privacy. The scene then introduces the whitewashed church where the townspeople have gathered to discuss their plight as they sing, as a hymn, that "there's no avoiding this conclusion – our town is turning into shit."

The church service introduces a series of running jokes: the townspeople all seem to be named Johnson ("Howard," "Van," "Olsen," "Dr. Samuel"), an old prospector mumbles "authentic frontier gibberish" that no one else can understand and the random harrumphing noises made by the background extras. In three or four minutes time, Brooks has introduced a range of throwaway gags, in some cases setting up recurring patterns which he will play with throughout the film, many of which disrupt the coherence of the diegesis (through various incongruous and anachronistic jokes), without slowing down the exposition. At the same time, the scenes establish the setting and set up the need to hire a new sheriff, an action motivating the rest of the film's action.

Or consider the sequence later in *Blazing Saddles* where the scheming Hedley Lamore (Harvey Korman) issues a help wanted poster to recruit "heartless villains" to destroy Rock Ridge, a post which includes an affirmative action statement. The next shot pans along the line as we move from rustlers and desperadoes, Nazi soldiers, Mexican banditos, motorcycle gang members, Arabs on camel back, and finally, the Ku Klux Klan, whose hoods upon closer inspection display yellow smiley faces and urge us to "have a nice day." Each new element tops what came before, until we laugh at the accumulation of details, much as we might anticipate in a page from "Sooperdooperman," "Ping Pong," "Starchy," or another classic Elder-Kurtzman comic.

Brooks' choice of the western as the target of his first major film parody was surely no accident, given that 1950s, the heyday of vulgar modernism, was also the golden age of the television and film western. Kurtzman, for example, turns his attention to the adult western in "Compulsion on the Range," part of the 1959 *Jungle Book* anthology. Billed as "a gripping tale of Schizophrenia on the sage-brush and paranoia on the prairie," Kurtzman made fun of the psychological turn in 1950s' westerns. In the course of this gag-stuffed story, we encounter a fast-draw protagonist who never hits what he shoots at, who falls in love with a chief's daughter only to discover that she's a cigar-store statue, who trades insults with the "fat sergeant" from *Zorro* (ABC 1957–1959), only to discover that it's actually the overweight and overaged swashbuckler himself, and who ends up surrounded by "Indians" in old Calcutta.

Ernie Kovacs staged another western spoof for his television series, which made fun of how the sheer repetition of basic genre elements given the proliferation of westerns was forcing producers to try new visual effects, to add psychological realism, or to combine the western with horror and science fiction elements reminiscent of *The Twilight Zone* (CBS 1959–1964). Kovac's comedy characteristically played around with visual conventions, representing the essence of the meta-discourse Hoberman saw as characteristic of vulgar modernism. Neither of these example yields, pardon the pun, a smoking gun which explicitly links *Blazing Saddles* back to these earlier parodies, yet it is hard to imagine Brooks, who helped to script so many spoofs for Sid Caesar and Imogene Coco, and who has an encyclopedic memory of cornball gags, did not have some of these classic parodies in mind when he sat down with Richard Pryor and Andrew Bergman to craft the script. *Blazing Saddles* may have felt fresh and original to the younger generation for whom his challenges to the purity of classical Hollywood had just the right taint of adolescent rebellion but it was also a throwback to the 1950s.

Bodily Eruptions and Generic Transformations

At roughly the same time that Hoberman was discovering vulgar modernism and Seidman was writing about the extratextual aspects of comedian comedy, John G. Cawelti (1979) greeted the release of *Chinatown* (1974) with an essay on the "generic transformation" of the American cinema. Cawelti references Brooks – alongside Robert Altman, Sam Peckinpah, Arthur Penn, and Roman Polanski, among others – as part of a larger movement questioning and deconstructing the building blocks shaping previous decades of popular cinema. Their works, Cawelti (1979: 191) writes, "set the elements of a conventional popular genre in an altered context, thereby making us perceive these traditional forms and images in a new way." Cawelti identified four different strategies for debunking or transforming classical genres – "humorous burlesque, evocation of nostalgia, demythologization of generic myth, and the reaffirmation of myth as myth" – of which, not unexpectedly, he mostly associates Brooks with "humorous burlesque." Cawelti singles out two key moments from Brooks' films as illustrations of the ways parodies rewrite genre mythologies:

> A situation that we are ordinarily accustomed to seeing in rather romanticized terms can be suddenly invested with a sense of reality … [In *Blazing Saddles*,] the cowboys sit around a blazing campfire at night, a scene in which we are accustomed to hearing mournful and lyrical cowboy ballads performed by such groups as the Sons of the Pioneers. Instead, we are treated to an escalating barrage of flatulence. Anyone who knows the usual effect of canned wilderness fare is likely to be delighted at this sudden exposure of the sham involved in the traditional western campfire scene.
>
> This type of burlesque is even more effective when the inverted presentation actually seems to bring out some latent meanings that were lurking all the time in the original convention … In his *Young Frankenstein*, the monster attacks Frankenstein's fiancé Elizabeth – a moment of tragic violence in the original novel – and the result is complete sexual satisfaction on both sides, something most of us had suspected all along. (1979: 192)

For Cawelti, in the campfire scene in *Blazing Saddles*, the innocence and romanticism of the western gives way to something much earthier, while the seduction in *Young Frankenstein* represents a moral inversion where what seemed horrifying in the original becomes desirable in the parody. Consistent with Cawelti's focus on mythic analysis, both examples rest upon the level of the story and its meaning, yet Brooks was also noted for disruptive narrational strategies.

It would have been a toss-up at the time when the film was first released whether the farting around the campfire or the final brawl that extends beyond the western town and across the sound stages and the studio canteen would have been the most transgressive element in *Blazing Saddles*.

Cawelti may describe the farting scene in terms of its reintroduction of realism into a mythic structure, but it is also a joke that evokes shifting standards of movie censorship, which sanitized classic westerns and now allowed a much more open acknowledgement of the body's sounds and processes. The closing moments of *Blazing Saddles* call attention to the means of production and consumption especially when the protagonists seek to escape the movie itself but finding themselves entering Grauman's Chinese Theater where *Blazing Saddles* is being projected, having a gunfight that leaves Hedley dying on the hand prints outside, and has the Sheriff and his sidekick eating popcorn back in Rock Ridge. The sequence also questions the walls between genres as the western brawl crashes into the staging of a Hollywood musical, leaving the cowpokes slugging it out with some rather prissy chorus line dancers. These scenes penetrate the Fourth Wall and keep battering that fragile barrier until nothing is left. These closing moments are, of course, consistent with other gags throughout which center on the characters' awareness of the stars and conventions of classic westerns: when the townspeople talk "battling dicks" they mean Richard Dix; Hedley Lamarr's name keeps getting turned to Heddy, much to his growing frustration; and Randolph Scott's name is spoken with awe.

New media theorists Jay David Bolter and Richard Grusin (2002: 5) might see the two sequences as illustrating the "double logic of remediation," the complex interplay between immediacy and hypermediacy: "Our culture wants both to multiply its media and to erase all traces of mediation: ideally, it wants to erase its media in the very act of multiplying it." In talking about the farting around the camp fire, Cawelti is linking the gag to what Bolter and Grusin are calling immediacy – a sense that what we are seeing is less mediated and less sanitized than the classic westerns it is spoofing. This recognition comes through implicit if not explicit comparison with other media representations. The film's final sequences, by contrast, might be described as "hypermediacy." As the camera pans up and out from the streets of Rock Ridge, revealing the town to be a set, and showing both the Warners' back lot and the city of Los Angeles beyond, we are invited to re-engage with all of the apparatus we know has gone into making the movie but which we have been encouraged to forget for its duration. Bolter and Grusin use the term "remediation" to describe any of the processes whereby one medium seeks to reproduce or comment upon the devices and processes of another, sometimes seeking to gain prestige through analogies to some legacy medium, sometimes trying to signal its improvement on the old. Such moments are ripe for parody.

Jokes about cinematic representation abound in Brooks' films. The lush romantic music that accompanies the sheriff's ride across the desert in *Blazing*

Saddles turns out to be coming from Count Basie and his Orchestra who for inexplicable reasons are jamming in the wasteland. Brooks repeats the gag in *High Anxiety* where suspense music turns out to be coming from the Los Angeles Orchestra, which is driving past the protagonist in a bus. In *High Anxiety*, a forward tracking shot calls attention to the camera when it smashes through a glass door, interrupting the characters, or when a camera pulls back and splinters wooden walls at the end of the film. In a spoof of a famous sequence from *Notorious* (1946) involving a glass tray and an iridescent glass of milk, a conversation in *Anxiety* is shot looking up through a glass table but keeps getting blocked as the characters set down various plates, glasses, and trays in the course of sharing afternoon tea. The opening sequence from *To Be or Not To Be* involves Mel Brooks and Anne Bancroft singing "Sweet Georgia Brown" in Polish, before the narrator interrupts the film to explain, "In the interests of clarity and sanity, the rest of this movie will not be in Polish." Brooks and Bancroft look around confused trying to locate the sound's source but clearly relieved not to have to carry the burden of this level of cultural and historical accuracy. Each of these jokes rests as much on how screen reality is being constructed as they do with any of the specific narrative or thematic content.

In other cases, Brooks calls attention to the nature of cinema as a medium through his pastiches of famous moments from other movies – for example, the attempts to copy the sets and sparky apparatus Kenneth Strickfadden designed for the original Universal movies, not to mention the expressionistic lighting and canted camera angles in *Young Frankenstein* or the return to key settings from *Vertigo* (1958), *Spellbound* (1945), *North by Northwest* (1959), and other Hitchcock movies in *High Anxiety*. In that same film, Brooks duplicates many specific shots from the shower movie montage which Saul Bass designed for *Psycho* (1960), rendered silly by using Brooks' hairy leg rather than Janet Leigh's sleek limbs or showing Brooks being attacked by a hotel worker brandishing a newspaper. The flaming titles and whiplashes in the title sequence for *Blazing Saddles*, especially coupled with the deadpan presentation of John Morris's anthem by longtime western singer Frankie Laine, amplify some of the already hyperbolic conventions of the B-western.

This coupling of broad physical humor with precise reconstructions of visual conventions may be part of what Brooks inherited from his time on *Your Show of Shows*, which was noted for its spoofs of contemporary television programs and films. As Woody Allen recalls on *The Sid Caesar Collection–The Buried Treasures* (2004): "When he did a silent movie, it looked like a silent movie. It wasn't some dopey little sketch … where you knew everything was fake. It was beautifully executed. And that air of verisimilitude made the comedy very funny."

In this same sequence, Brooks notes that the group often went to the art cinema or galleries after work, shared experiences that in turn folded back into their parodies. *A Streetcar Named ???* tries to capture and comment on the quirks of method acting, while *Gallapacci*, a parody of Japanese samurai movies, lovingly

Figure 7.2 Carl Reiner, Imogene Coca, and Sid Caesar in self-reflexive skit from *Your Show of Shows* (producer, Max Liebman), where Mel Brooks honed his skills.

creates the frontality, the exaggerated facial expressions, and ornamental style which scholars of Japanese cinema have identified in the works of Kenji Mizoguchi and Akira Kurosawa.

Silent movie parody *A Drunk There Was* makes extensive use of the iris in focusing attention on meaningful details, introduces the characters through vignettes, uses fixed camera positions, follows inter title conventions, and otherwise shows a sophisticated understanding of the language of silent cinema, while also playing around with the melodramatic gestures and postures found in early D.W. Griffith shorts. The closing sequence of this spoof, on the other hand, borrows shot by shot from *Stella Dallas* (1937), as the disgraced father stands outside in the rain watching his upwardly mobile daughter get married through a half-open window. *Your Show of Shows* may have made fun of classic and international films, yet it also showed tremendous respect for the craftsmanship and emotional power of these works, displaying an attention to detail that respected the audience's own intelligence and knowledge. Similarly, *Mad*'s parodies of Madison Avenue often required Elder to design well executed ads according to the era's graphic and branding conventions.

Throughout Brooks' work, we find recurring gags which center on media technologies or acts of remediation. Many of the most memorable gags in Brooks television series, *Get Smart*, focused on the outlandish technologies we associate with 1960s spy movies, including Smart's telephone shoe and the Cone of Silence, both gags about communication devices. In the hospital sequence in *Silent Movie*, Feldman and DeLuise transform the studio chief's life-support system into a game system, playing Pong, as their boss thrashes about in the bed and twists his tongue. Such physical comedy was well suited to Sid Caesar who was noted for his rubber faced reaction shots on *Your Show of Shows*. In a sequence shot but not included in *Young Frankenstein*, the deceased reads his will to the bereaved "in my own voice" via a phonograph record. The recording is warped and scratched, includes passages unintentionally recorded, needs to be flipped over mid-reading, and starts skipping and repeating a particularly inappropriate passage. The sequence foregrounds the limitations of old phonograph records as a means of preserving and replicating the human voice down through the ages. Key plot points in *High Anxiety* require us to pay particular attention to the properties of photography, including an extended darkroom sequence inspired by *Blow-Up* (1966).

Perhaps the most persistent reference point, though, running through Brooks works is to theatricality, with almost all of his films featuring some form of live performance including circuses (*Twelve Chairs*), nightclubs (*Silent Movie, High Anxiety*), saloons (*Blazing Saddles*), Broadway stages (*Producers*). Even *Young Frankenstein* includes a sequence where the monster tap-dances and sings "Putting on the Ritz" in front of a gawking and sometimes frightened audience. And many of these scenes are as obsessed with the audience's responses to the performance as with what's taking place onstage. In *The Producers*, the neo-Nazi playwright seeks to discipline an audience that is laughing inappropriately by claiming he "outranks" them. Both *Silent Movie* and *Blazing Saddles* show the process of buying tickets and entering a theater. Brooks uses such sequences, in part, to comment on his own troubled relationship with his audience, depicting people in anoraks waiting outside a screening of *Young Frankenstein* in *Silent Movie* as if they were shamed patrons at a porno house. In turning his camera onto the audience, Brooks may have again been hearkening back to classic sketches on *Your Show of Shows*, such as "This is Your Story," a parody of *This Is Your Life* (NBC 1952–1961) which involves a reluctant and actively resisting guest being pulled out of the audience, or "At the Movies," where Reiner and Coco play a quarrelling couple whose drama of jealousy, lust, and aggression victimizes an innocent bystander (Caesar) who is simply trying to watch a movie romance. Turning the lens on the audience may be the ultimate act of reflexivity, inviting the spectator to think not about the film but about their own presence in the cinema house.

Sound Gags and Silent Movies

Without stretching a point, Brooks' decision to make a silent comedy represents another shout back to his time on *Your Show of Shows*, a tribute made all the more explicit by his casting of his former boss, Caesar, as the studio executive. As Lynn Spigel (2008: 188) notes, performers such as Caesar, Kovacs, and Red Skelton featured recurring pantomime segments, as well as numerous spoofs of silent movies, in their television variety series, another way of showcasing their own virtuosity as performers and also playing upon the sophisticated cultural knowledge of early television viewers. Silent films were enjoying a revival of

Figure 7.3   The mime, Marcel Marceau, speaks in *Silent Movie* (producer, Michael Hertzberg).

interest on late night television as the Hollywood studios sold off their film libraries, much as Mel Brooks would later be able to assume familiarity with classic genre movies that were being released in the thriving retro house circuit in the 1970s. Kovacs had hoped to produce a feature-length silent comedy starring his Eugene character, plans cut short by his death. Spigel (2008: 192) also notes that the spoofs of silent cinema on early television were not in any simple sense silent comedies, since, while they contained no spoken dialogue, they often relied on complex synchronizations of sounds and images that could only be achieved through recorded sound and an awareness of the absence of sound which came from making silent entertainment at a time when it was no longer the norm. In that sense, they may compare more closely with Charlie Chaplin's *Modern Times* (1937), a silent film made in the sound era, and deploying carefully selected bits of recorded sound for comic effect.

The opening of *Silent Movie*, for example, plays upon audience expectations about the nature of silent film, continuing for several minutes in total silence, before adding music and sound effects. In another early sequence, a secretary tries to tell the studio chief that Funn has a drinking problem by pantomiming an uplifted bottle, but her boss remains confused, wondering if she's trying to say that he sucks his thumb, a joke that rests on the difference between the guessing games we play at charades and the expressive gestures of silent cinema. Chaplin uses speech in *Modern Times* only through recordings, radio, television, and in the end, a nonsense song, all devices that call attention to the mediation of sound. Brooks allows only one spoken word into his silent comedy – in this case, uttered by world famous mime, Marcel Marceau. Brooks builds to this moment through close-ups on Marceau's telephone which rings in French, "*sonnez ... sonnez*," restaging some of his classic "walking into the wind" bits to heighten our awareness of the traditions from which he comes, and then having him aggressively growl "no" when asked if he wants to be in a silent film, a response which Mel Funn claims not to have grasped, "I don't understand French!"

As Andres Lombana Bermudez (2010) reminds us, sound-image relations have long been fundamental to the slapstick comedy tradition. The term, slapstick, refers to a prop that made an amplified and stylized thwacking sound when it was slapped against the rump of a performer during *commedia dell' arte* or the head of a puppet in Punch and Judy shows. From the start, performers knew that physical aggression did not seem as real or as threatening in a world where bonking people's heads together made coo-coo sounds rather than producing screams of pain. As Lombana writes:

> What I call sounds of the slap-of-the-stick are different sounds that have been used across media to enhance comic routines, adding acoustic physicality to them, exaggerating – even more – the violence and disruption, and materializing the grotesque movements and the mockery and abuse of the body. Visual impacts such as pratfalls, pie smashes, blows, collisions, squashes and stretches turn into points of synchronization where the sounds of the slap-of-the-stick are heard. The perfect synchronization of the sounds and visuals finally creates the comic effect of meeting elements of different natures. (2010: 33)

Sid Caesar, in *Silent Movie*, pays tribute to this aspect of silent comedy: having declared slapstick dead, he flips his chair backwards, goes sliding across the room, and slams his head, accompanied by the sound of a bell ringing. As Lombana notes, much of the humor comes from the implausible or unlikely match of sound and image, which helps to create a comic climate for the gag.

Many of the *Silent Movie*'s gags depend on such careful synchronizations, as in a sequence where Feldman is tossed about by the crowds trying to exit various elevators to the sounds of a pinball machine. Brooks returns to his old standby, the confusion of diegetic and nondiegetic sounds, when a peppy samba number turns out to be coming from the exercise room for geriatric patients in the hospital who tap their walkers with the beat. The Studio Executive makes cash-register sounds when he anticipates the revenue from Funn's movie, while the greedy villain snarls like a dog. Bernadette Peters swings her hips, accompanied by a clashing symbol, and sends tables and chairs flying. Funn's heart throbs rhythmically as he witnesses her sensuous performance, or at least we think it is his heart until he pulls an oversized frog from his shirt pocket.

There are certainly many sight gags in *Silent Movie* (such as a light bulb glowing behind Funn when he gets an idea), even gags about sight as when a blind man coming out of a restroom gets the wrong dog, and is dragged screaming and kicking through a park at the leash of a hyperactive pooch. But many more of the jokes are really sound gags, which depend on our anticipation of sounds. Brooks uses intertitles, for example, to convey doorbells and ringing telephones in a way that calls attention to the noises they are not making more than conveying information necessary for clarity. In one sequence, a flunky whispers to his boss, which reads on the intertitle as "whisper … whisper … whisper," but when the boss doesn't understand him, he shouts, which gets represented in all caps, "YOUR FLY IS OPEN!" When James Caan tries to speak through a boxer's mouth guard, the intertitle reads "Farl - Tarl - Barl- Sharl." Such gags were certainly possible in film comedies of the silent era but they were not common, as each signals the limitations of intertitles as a way of representing the soundscape. If *A Drunk There Was* is any indication, we did not see these kinds of sound-focused games in the intertitles in the silent movie parodies found on *Your Show of Shows*: here, the intertitles function much more according to silent cinema conventions, often the source of humor but more because of their verbosity or pomposity ("lips that have touched liquor shall never lick my company's stamps!").

If the gags in *Silent Movie* often play upon audience consciousness of the absence of sound, the gags in Brooks' comedy records often hinge on the absence of vision. Many of the gags in *In the Coffeehouse*, a 1962 routine spoofing beatnik culture, work only if we cannot see what is happening but form expectations based on what we are hearing. Reiner interviews a patron (voiced by Brooks) who is "depressed" because he's not "pretty." When Reiner reassures him, "you're a good looking man, sir," the humiliated Brooks responds, "I am not a man – I'm a woman." Confusions over identity and appearance continue as another Brooks' character is described as looking like "a cross between Marlon Brando and Joanne Woodward." Asked if he is an actor, Brooks responds that he is a "lesbian." Reiner encounters a painter, but gets confused between the artist's work and his lunch, the air-conditioning unit, and some dead flies he has pasted onto his canvas. In each case, the absence of visuals, our reliance on Reiner's uncertain narration, allows us quickly to revise our impressions. Some of the other segments in this routine rest entirely on sound, such as a series of jokes about a protest singer whose songs all sound the same and who can strum only one note on his guitar. Here, again, Brooks couples jokes that call attention to the properties of his medium with gags which spoof the nature of art and of mediated experience more generally.

"Hey, It Worked in *Blazing Saddles*"

In discussing Brooks' comedy, I am finding myself inventorying gags and the ways they disrupt the narrative logic and diegetic coherence of the genre formulae that characterized the classic Hollywood era. This, far more than characters and plots, or even performances, is the basis upon which Brooks' comedy is going to be remembered. Unfortunately, a gag-centered comedy works only as long as the gags are funny.

From the start, Brooks' fans had to have a high tolerance for gags that didn't produce laughter and for slapstick stunts that, well, fell flat. At his best, Brooks gags were bold, aggressive, slaps in the face and jabs to the ribcage. His jokes were never subtle but, often, nevertheless highly precise in their parody of genres, films, and artists of the previous era and in calling out their silences about race, sexuality, ethnicity, and the body. At their worst, they were loud and dumb, in your face and willing to do anything to make us laugh, even if they weren't really all that funny. His comedy's strengths and weaknesses were more or less the same – Brooks would go lower than his predecessors and hit harder than his contemporaries. Brooks was open in his affection for old movies, his passion for kitschy musical numbers, and his respect for the elders of American comedy.

Brooks forged a bridge to the "vulgar modernists" of the 1950s, to *Your Show of Shows* and early *Mad* in particular, which had mastered a particular style of blunderbuss parody that opened fire at all aspects of contemporary commercial culture. Caesar had provided Brooks with a training ground, sharpening skills he had acquired in his Catskill days, and preparing the way for his subsequent work in television, animation, sound recording, and finally feature-length motion pictures. Brooks is not the only member of *Your Show of Shows'* writing staff to incorporate forms of parody into his subsequent work. Woody Allen's early comedies (sometimes known as the "funny ones") spoofed everything from *War and Peace* (*Love and Death* 1975) to *Looking Backwards* (*Sleeper* 1973). Carl Reiner more often directed romantic or character-driven comedies, yet he turned his attention to the parody of film noir with *Dead Men Don't Wear Plaid* (1982) and of B-movie science fiction with *The Man with Two Brains* (1983). Even Neil Simon wrote the script for *Murder by Death* (1976), a spoof of classic whodunits. Yet, of his contemporaries, Brooks became most associated with parody.

Brooks' emergence as a film comedy director and performer in the 1970s and 1980s seemed perfectly timed: a fascination with reflexive humor ran through film criticism, as witnessed by the close proximity in time of the publication of Hoberman's "Vulgar modernism," Cawelti's essay on genre transformation, and Seidman's dissertation on comedian comedy, each of which offered ways of connecting Brooks to larger shifts in Hollywood practice. Brooks emerged at a moment when the meaningfulness of old genre formulas was being questioned, old censorship standards were increasingly being challenged, and a film school trained generation was seeking to display its familiarity with and superiority to the classical Hollywood tradition. Brooks was, as I have suggested here, a "media comedian" in two senses of the word – in that he worked across many different media in the course of his career and in the sense that he constantly called attention to the nature of remediation across his works. Yet, he was also a film comedian whose parodies of classic genres marked a moment of transition between classical and postclassical cinema.

By 1993, when Brooks directed *Robin Hood: Men in Tights*, his comedy no longer seemed shocking or original. In his final films, he had fallen into a formula. One can read the cast of his swashbuckler spoof as simple replacements for the casts we had enjoyed in his earlier works: Dave Chappelle standing in for Cleavon Little, Tracey Ullman for Cloris Leachman, Richard Lewis for Harvey Korman, Carey Elwes for Gene Wilder, Amy Yasbeck for Teri Garr, and so on. Perhaps most pathetic of all, there was Mel Brooks standing in for himself. They lacked the chemistry that made Teri Garr, Marty Feldman, and Gene Wilder so much fun to watch together in *Young Frankenstein*.

Brooks' strategy of chasing gags wherever he could find them left him without the straight man roles Carl Reiner so ably performed in the comedy albums and without the emotional core Gene Wilder provided in *The Producers*, *Blazing Saddles*, and *Young Frankenstein*. When Wilder left to make his own comedies, such as *The Adventures of Sherlock Holmes' Smarter Brother* (1975), something essential went out of Brooks' comedy, even though it would take him and us a while to realize it. Anne Bancroft would provide some of that magic in her cameo in *Silent Movie* and her performance in *To Be or Not To Be*. There was a pleasure in watching Brooks and his offscreen wife play against each other, given how much they both clearly enjoyed each other's company. But, even so, Brooks would aim for yucks and deliver only impatient snorts. There would only so many times Brooks could trot out "walk this way" jokes and make us chuckle about their repetition and predictability.

By the end of *Robin Hood: Men in Tights*, Brooks himself seemed ready to acknowledge he had nothing new to say. When King Richard (Patrick Stewart) kisses Maid Marian, Brooks' Rabbi Tuckman smirks and says, "It's good to be the king," a wink towards a catchphrase Brooks had used in *History of the World, Part I*. When the people of Rottingham object to the King's decision to name Chappelle's Ahchoo their sheriff, the hip black comic turns to them and says, "Hey, it worked in *Blazing Saddles*." Yes, it did. But not any more. Not again. Please, God, not again.

In more recent years, Brooks has gone Broadway with both *The Producers* and *Young Frankenstein* updated as stage musicals and *The Producers* remade as a screen comedy (2005). This process is bringing new audiences to Brooks' comedy, audiences who may well not fully appreciate what these films meant when they first came out but who may also be in a position to read them without regard to the later failures which left a bitter taste in the mouth of many of his first-generation fans. My hope is that this chapter has offered some ways of understanding why Brooks' films mattered then and why they may matter now.

References

Bolter, J.D. and Grusin, R. (2002) *Remediation: Understanding New Media*, MIT Press, Cambridge, MA.

Cawelti, J.G. (1979) *Chinatown* and generic transformation in recent American films, in *Film Theory and Criticism: Introductory Readings* (eds. G. Mast and M. Cohen), 2nd edn, Oxford University Press, New York, NY, pp. 559–79.

Gabler, N. (1989) *An Empire of Their Own: How the Jews Invented Hollywood*, Anchor, New York, NY.

Heib, Louis A. (1972) Meaning and mismeaning: towards an understanding of the ritual clown, in *New Perspectives on the Pueblo* (ed. A. Oritz), University of New Mexico Press, Albuquerque, NM, pp. 163–95.

Hoberman, J. (1991) Vulgar modernism, in *Vulgar Modernism: Writing on Movies and Other Media*, Temple University Press, Philadelphia, PA, pp. 32–9.

Horton, A. (2010) *Ernie Kovacs and Early TV Comedy: Nothing in Moderation*, University of Texas Press, Austin, TX.

Jenkins, H. (1992) *What Made Pistachio Nuts? Early Sound Comedy and the Vaudeville Aesthetic*, Columbia University Press, New York, NY

Jenkins, H. (2011) "I like to sock myself in the face": reconsidering "vulgar modernism," in *Funny Pictures: Animation and Comedy in Studio-Era Hollywood* (eds. D. Goldmark and C. Keil), University of California Press, Berkeley, CA, pp. 153–74.

Kurtzman, H. (1959) Compulsion on the range, in *Harvey Kurtzman's Jungle Book*, Ballantine Books, New York, NY, n.p.

Lombana Bermudez, A. (2010) Lunacy at Termite Terrace: the slapstick style of Warner Bros. animation. *Cinephile*, 6 (1), 33–8.

Seidman, S. (1981) *Comedian Comedy: A Tradition in Hollywood Film*, UMI Research, Ann Arbor, MI.

Spigel, L. (2008) *TV By Design: Modern Art and The Rise of Network Television*, University of Chicago Press, Chicago, IL.

Further Reading

Goldmark, D. and Keil, C. (eds.) (2011) *Funny Pictures: Animation and Comedy in Studio-Era Hollywood*, University of California Press, Berkeley, CA. This important recent collection explores issues of gags, stereotypes, genre, mode of production, and authorship by examining points of intersection between comedy and animation.

Hoberman, J. (1991) Vulgar modernism, in *Vulgar Modernism: Writing on Movies and Other Media*, Temple University Press, Philadelphia, PA, pp. 32–9. Hoberman first introduced the idea that "vulgar modernism" might be a discrete school within the larger history of American popular humor – one that emerged after World War II among artists working in a range of different media (including film, television, comics, and live performance).

Parish, J. (2007) *It's Good to Be the King: The Seriously Funny Life of Mel Brooks*, John Wiley & Sons, Inc., Hoboken. This recent critical biography traces the performers' career across media, suggesting continuities in his style and persona, despite shifts in his production contexts.

Seidman, S. (1981) *Comedian Comedy: A Tradition in Hollywood Film*, UMI Research, Ann Arbor, MI. Seidman defined the comedian comedy as a distinct genre – one that foregrounds issues of performance and one that explores the tension between creative disruption and social integration as a core thematic across the work of a diverse array of movie clowns and comedians.

Yacowar, M. (1984) *Method in Madness: The Comic Art of Mel Brooks*, Comet, New York, NY. Long the definitive book on Brooks' screen comedy, this book includes the close reading of many of his major works.

Part III

New Perspectives on Romantic Comedy and Masculinity

8

Humor and Erotic Utopia

The Intimate Scenarios of Romantic Comedy

Celestino Deleyto

Comedy has often been said to pose a challenge to narrative. Jokes, gags, and comic moments tend to resist integration into larger structures. Yet from Aristophanes to Hollywood's recent spate of "homme-coms" (Jeffers McDonald 2007: 108–9), history also abounds in examples of the fruitful marriage between comedy and narrative. Without wishing to deny the anarchic impulses of gags and jokes (Karnick and Jenkins 1995) or to underplay the contribution of comedian comedy to the history of the genre in the cinema (see, for example, Krutnik 2003), I would like to argue that narrative comedy, and specifically its most popular manifestation in the cinema, romantic comedy, is inconceivable without the presence of humor, laughter, and the comic. Indeed, I will be suggesting that the centrality of jokes, gags, and other comic moments in this genre may help us understand narrative differently and find alternative methods to explore its workings, moving away from teleology and the tyranny of the thus-far all-powerful ending, and noticing instead the complexity and cultural import of isolated segments. If, as I have argued elsewhere, romantic comedy is less a narrative of the heterosexual couple with a happy ending than a particular type of story about interpersonal affective and erotic relationships, the comic moments that abound in these stories constitute privileged sites for the exploration of such cultural conventions and protocols, instances that are often more telling and significant than the endings (Deleyto 2009: 18, 30).

Andrew Horton (1991: 7) has provided a definition of comedy based on the uneasy balance between humor and narrative in the genre. For him, a comedy is an interlocking sequence of jokes and gags that either places narrative in

A Companion to Film Comedy, First Edition. Edited by Andrew Horton and Joanna E. Rapf.
© 2013 John Wiley & Sons, Inc. Published 2016 by John Wiley & Sons, Inc.

the foreground or uses narrative as an excuse to highlight the individual comic moments. This draws attention to the fluidity and versatility of the "contract" between the two and suggests that, rather than two types of comedy, we might consider the existence of a continuum with different emphases depending on the individual comic narrative. It also allows for at least a third possibility, somewhere between Horton's two, which would fit romantic comedy: the genre as sequences of jokes and gags that use narrative conventions such as plot and character construction in order to construct comic scenarios of love, sexuality, and intimate matters. From this perspective, romantic comedies would be not so much, or at least not only, tales of the consolidation of a heterosexual couple as series of narrative events representing assorted forms of desire within particular historical contexts.

The view of narrative as not governed by a single movement towards the end but as composed of interlocking comic scenes also connects with new ways of seeing films in which fragmentation and repetition of selected moments take preeminence over uninterrupted viewings of films from beginning to end. Fast-changing home-entertainment technology, including DVD, Internet downloads and the sharing of files in social networks, as well as the viewing protocols prompted both by these technologies and cultural habits, increasingly privilege this form of spectatorship. The special place held by jokes, gags and comic moments within comic narratives places this genre in a particularly potent position to adapt to changing patterns of reception. On the other hand, the ways in which spectators have experienced narrative films in the past may not be very distant from present ones: is, for example, the whole narrative structure of *When Harry Met Sally* (Rob Reiner 1989) more historically important – not to mention better remembered – than the reaction of a patron at the restaurant where Sally (Meg Ryan) is faking an orgasm for Harry (Billy Crystal) – "I'll have what she's having"? Or, to use another instance from the same period, after innumerable viewings of *Pretty Woman* (Garry Marshall 1990), do we derive more comic pleasure from the Cinderella narrative with a (slightly postmodern) happy ending or from Vivian's (Julia Roberts) second visit to the exclusive boutique in Rodeo Drive where she had previously been humiliated, now loaded with purchases from other shops in the famous street, to tell the snooty assistant: "Big mistake!"? Even the filmmakers seem to confirm the claims of the latter when they have Roberts's character in the more recent *Valentine Day* (Garry Marshall 2010) relive the moment in the post-final credits sequence. Of course, these comic moments derive their significance from the narrative context in which they are inserted, outside of which they would not make any sense, but at the same time they stand out on their own as complex repositories of cultural meaning while enriching the films in which they are placed and the history of the genre. Given their overall impact in comic narratives, these moments are deserving of more critical and theoretical attention than they have been given so far. My aim in this chapter is to suggest, through the close analysis of a selection of individual scenes, gags and comic motifs, that romantic comedies are much more than their happy endings and the monologic intimate imagination with which they have often been identified.

We begin our journey with Ernst Lubitsch, for many a crucial player and decisive influence in the formation of the Hollywood comedy of the sexes (Babington and Evans 1989: 45–7; Harvey 1998: 3). More specifically, and although he had already directed comedies both in his German and Hollywood periods, he was the first to envisage the potential of sound for the consolidation of romantic comedy in Hollywood, a genre that took off and enjoyed its first golden period as a direct consequence of the new technology. He started his exploration of the possibilities of sound for the genre with a series of musical comedies, based on European operettas. In them he developed his peculiar style and, in spite of the remoteness and exoticism of the Ruritanian plots, managed to convey the sexual vibrancy and strong libido that characterized his characters' experience of desire, and that would later be explored in his nonmusical romantic comedies (Paul 1983: 12).

The Smiling Lieutenant (1931, screenplay by Ernest Vajda and Samson Raphaelson) was the third of these films, after *The Love Parade* (1929) and *Monte Carlo* (1930). Its plot revolves around a smile (from the smiling lieutenant) and a wink, addressed to one woman but unexpectedly intercepted by another (see Charles Morrow's chapter in this volume for another discussion of this film). Through these two gestures, and the story constructed around them, Lubitsch explores a volatile sexual scenario which, at the time of the film's release, spoke to a series of transformations, anxieties, and pressures in US intimate matters, the same that according to Stanley Cavell (1981), Charles Musser (1995), Tina Olsin Lent (1995), and others, provided the cultural framework for the birth of the comedy of remarriage, De Mille's earlier divorce comedies and the screwball cycle.

To provide a brief narrative context, Niki (Maurice Chevalier), a lieutenant in the Austrian army, and Franzi (Claudette Colbert), a violin player in an all-girl band in Vienna, meet, fall in love at first sight and spend the night together. The next morning, the king of the neighboring country of Flausenthurm, Adolf XV (George Barbier), and his daughter Princess Anna (Miriam Hopkins) arrive in Vienna on an official visit. Niki stands at attention leading the guard while Franzi, who has just left the barracks, stands across the road, smiles and blows a kiss at her new lover. Niki, still standing at attention, his erect saber in his hand, smiles back and winks at her, but at that very moment the royal chariot happens to pass by and Anna catches the smile and the wink and assumes that they were meant for her. Already incensed and humiliated because the Emperor has not come to receive them personally and, what is worse, in his telegram has spelt Flausenthurm without the "h," the two visitors feel that the young princess has been made the laughing stock by the sophisticated soldier and in general by the arrogant Austrians, and demand an explanation. Enlightened as to the meaning of the smile and the wink by the handsome lieutenant ("when we like somebody we smile but when we want to do something about it we wink"), with whom she immediately falls hopeless in love, Anna, who is ridiculously and comically inexperienced in sexual matters, builds all her expectations for the incipient relationship around that wink. The wink becomes an affair of state and Niki is forcefully separated from his beloved Franzi and his equally beloved Vienna: he has to travel to Flausenthurm (which he at least can spell correctly – "what a speller!" as one of the princess's ladies-in-waiting admiringly trills) and marry Anna. Which takes us to the wedding night.

Once inside the royal bedchamber, Niki, who has no intention of spending the night with his bride, says "Good night, dear" to Anna. When she shows her surprise and disappointment at his behavior, he pretends not to understand, arguing that both "good night" and "dear" are perfectly fitting expressions for the circumstances (it is 9.30 in the evening and they are married, so "dear" is an appropriate form of address). Then, with the camera tracking in to a medium close-up of Anna for emphasis, she winks at him, in order to convey what she expects from the wedding night and to save herself the embarrassment of saying it in words. Niki now pretends that he finally understands what she means and the following dialogue ensues:

NIKI: Oh, no! Oh, no! Married people don't do that.
ANNA: They don't?
NIKI: Oh, no!
ANNA: Married people don't wink?
NIKI: Yes, they wink, but not at each other.
ANNA: Well, what's the use of getting married?
NIKI: All the philosophers, for three thousand years, have tried to find that out.
            And they failed. And I don't think we'll solve that problem tonight.
            Good night.

The wink is such an obvious metaphor for sex that even naive Anna grasps it immediately but the narrative importance of the gesture and the sexual, romantic and social meanings suggested by its comic deployment in the film go well beyond its pre-Hays Code explicitness and its easy categorization as part of the "Lubitsch touch." Anna's wink reveals that her principal reason for wanting to get married was to have sex with Niki, or that her love for him is inseparable from her sexual attraction. In the film's intimate unconscious there is no workable difference between love and sex. In this, *The Smiling Lieutenant* is part of the long process of sexualization of love that according to Steve Seidman (1991: 4–5) took place in the course of the first half of the twentieth century, a process whereby sex and sexual satisfaction gained increasing weight within the conceptualization and experience of romantic love. The exchange prompted by Anna's wink speaks to the social insecurities and anxieties surrounding the institution of marriage.

On the one hand, marriage is sexualized through Anna's eagerness and the role of sex in married life is presented as central for the wellbeing of the couple – in fact, as its only reason for existing. On the other, the oft-repeated Lubitschean theme of marriage as both the end and motor of desire (for somebody else) is given a hilarious summary in Niki's reply: winking is part and parcel of the experience of marriage, but only as long as married partners wink at somebody else. The suggestion that infidelity is not something to be banned from marriage but, on the contrary, a central ingredient of the institution, a practice to be encouraged, even an obligation of married people, is given predominance over the sexual satisfaction within marriage by being uttered by Niki, the more experienced and sophisticated of the two. But we can also feel the weight of the textual ideology behind Anna's candid reply – "what then is the point in getting married" – an awareness of both the pleasures and contradictions of sexualized coupledom. As a consequence of these two confronted views the spectators get a sense of the complications of marriage and the debates then being articulated about an institution in search of a new definition and even a new reason for existing.

But we would be wrong to infer from this comic exchange no more than a manifestation of cultural anxiety, an expression of the impossible contradiction at the heart of the institution, or only the presence of a pessimistic mind at work behind the comic brilliance of the jokes. Neither is the comic perspective here, as has often been argued about comedy in general, a way of "pulling the punches," or papering over the contradictions and trivializing the problems (King 2002: 5–18).

Lubitsch may suggest in his films, as James Harvey (1998: 43) has argued, that strong, passionate feelings are the surest road to ending up alone, that intensity of emotion means eventual isolation and loneliness, but underneath this pessimism lies a deep-seated belief in the power of comedy to lift us, as well as his characters, above our drab existence, and the power of desire to make our lives, as well as theirs, special and worth living. When Niki, whose love for Franzi has been cruelly and summarily repressed, returns some of that cruelty and teases Anna and finally leaves the room, and when desperate Anna awkwardly winks at her husband begging him to stay, the comic dialogue conveys not only the textual abhorrence of a marriage not founded on mutual desire but also the exhilaration of the sexual game. The dénouement will later on level out the desires of the two characters, but even now, when the distance between them is enormous, producing frustration and even anger, the comic situation is based on a certain openness towards the representation of sexual attraction, complete with sadistic and masochistic impulses, that conveys the feeling that sex is exciting and worth fighting for.

As Freud (1961:428–9) argued, humor is liberating and uplifting. Through it, the ego refuses to suffer, and turns drawbacks and disappointments into an occasion for laughter, drawing pleasure from potentially distressing experiences. For Freud not everybody is capable of enjoying humorous pleasure. Humor is a rare and precious gift that is only bestowed on a minority (Freud 1961 [1927]: 433). At a time of doubt and a certain degree of disorientation in sexual matters and, more specifically, with respect to the institution of marriage (not to mention profound economic and social crisis), Lubitsch's film turns anxiety into an occasion for joyful experimentation and exploration of the contradictions. The humor in the scene is addressed at those happy few who understand and believe in the beneficial impact of strong sexual desire, a drive that not only keeps us alive and full of energy but also makes us better individuals.

In his account of Shakespearean comedy Stephen Greenblatt echoes sixteenth-century physician William Harvey's view (in Greenblatt 1988: 89) that men and women are never more pleasant, sprightly and beautiful than when about to have sex. Greenblatt argues that since the beauty of sexual arousal and fulfillment could not be directly represented on the stage in Elizabethan England, dramatists developed a method to suggest it indirectly. That method was romantic comedy and, particularly, its witty banter and verbal friction between prospective lovers. In *The Smiling Lieutenant*, the dialogue between Niki and Anna, beyond using their differences as an opportunity to amuse the audience, isolates them as members of a privileged community that appreciates the value and the beauty of desire, its importance in the construction of modern life and in the reconstruction of the institution of marriage. Niki and Anna may not be about to spend the night together but the comic articulation of their disagreement turns the latter into an indirect representation of a compatibility that is being cemented around their shared views on the importance of desire. Those spectators who manage to identify with the characters, to see their comic friction as a metaphor of their sexual compatibility, may also share the Freudian view of humor as an opportunity to turn potential dissonance into pleasure.

The film will eventually bring these two characters emotionally and sexually together, marriage being, in this case, the preamble to rather than the culmination of desire, and it will also unexpectedly drop Franzi out of the equation, suggesting through her plight that love can also bring about suffering and disappointment. In the meantime, however, the wedding-night scene and the dialogue between the newly married partners stand on their own and, to some extent, function independently as a reflection of contemporary anxieties about the proper fit between sex and marriage in the wake of the cultural convulsions brought about by the first wave of feminism, but also as a celebration of the power of sexuality to make people happier and even to contradict social etiquette, a discourse that was then starting its unstoppable climb toward cultural prominence.

My second example comes from *The Palm Beach Story* (1942, written and directed by Preston Sturges – see Figure 8.1), a film in which Claudette Colbert's luck has most definitely (and deservedly) changed, from rejected lover to being the object of desire of the husband she has halfheartedly dropped, an aspiring and very rich lover and, less seriously, all the members of the Ale and Quail Club, who adopt her as their protégée during a train trip to Florida. Only 11 years have passed since Lubitsch's film but in terms of the history of romantic comedy the distance seems much greater. Harvey places what he calls "the Lubitsch era" and "the Preston Sturges era" respectively at the beginning and end of the great

Figure 8.1   Enchantment and the philosopher king: Claudette Colbert's face encapsulates the romantic vision of Preston Sturges' *The Palm Beach Story* (producers, Paul Jones and Buddy G. DeSylva).

period of the genre in Hollywood, the 1930s. For him, the Sturges era heralds its decadence after the variety, sophistication and artistic triumph of the preceding decade (Harvey 1998: 405). The 1940s, however, still had a lot to offer, including the dazzling series of seven comedies written and directed by Sturges in the space of five years at the beginning of this decade.

These films, as a whole, cannot be defined as romantic comedies, and even when romantic comedy predominates in them, they are very impure instances of it. Still, romantic comedy almost always has an important presence in their generic structures. *The Lady Eve* (1941) and *The Palm Beach Story* present particularly acerbic views of marriage, which in these films, unlike in those of Lubitsch, does not seem have much to offer men and women except ample opportunities for embarrassment and ridicule. At the end of *The Lady Eve*, its male protagonist, who since his wedding has undergone all sorts of humiliations (including abundant pratfalls), just about knows that he is married but not who he is married to. *The Palm Beach Story* starts and ends with two rather absurd and arbitrary weddings, which bracket a story in which marriage is seen as an impediment to freedom or, at best, as the pastime of eccentric millionaires.

Eccentricity is at the heart of Sturges's approach to comedy in general, with groups of odd characters often stealing the limelight from the protagonists and taking the narratives in unexpected directions. *The Palm Beach Story* has more than its share of eccentrics, from the raucous dozen or so members of the Ale and Quail Club, who threaten to wreck a whole train with their violent celebrations, to the absurdly affluent siblings that aspire to break the marriage of the protagonists and turn them into their own spouses. Here, as in the other films, these characters provoke situations and express views that force us to see the fictional world in alternative ways, often shaking us out of our complacency and acceptance of received opinions and patterns of behavior. Sturges, who is invariably constructed as an eccentric in biographies and accounts of his career (see, for example, Henderson 1986), brought these secondary characters to the fore as embodiments of the comic spirit, the protagonists, if they were lucky, learning from them the values of hilarity, ironic detachment and irresponsible conduct.

Not all of the members of the Sturges troupe have something to say about romantic love, desire or intimate matters because not all the comedies are centrally concerned with these issues, but when they do it is often a good idea to pay attention to them, in spite of their frequent flippancy or eccentricity. Since most of these characters only feature intermittently or sometimes hardly at all in the plots, they appear to contribute little to the narrative structures and therefore tend to become invisible in teleological analyses of the genre. For this reason, the scenes in which they do appear are particularly amenable to the kind of analysis proposed here, the cinema of Preston Sturges in general excelling in the comic impact of such isolated moments. One such character in *The Palm Beach Story* is the Wienie King (Robert Dudley), a sausage tycoon and inventor of the Texas Wienie ("lay off them, you'll live longer"), who appears twice in the movie and has two hilarious dialogues, first with the female protagonist, Gerry (Claudette Colbert), and then with her husband Tom (Joel McCrea), and twice solves their financial problems by the simple method of handing them a wad of money without even bothering to ask for anything in return. Here I would like to focus on the first of these two exchanges, which takes place at the beginning of the movie, immediately after the hectic credit-cum-wedding sequence.

Five years have passed since the unexplained wedding, and now Gerry and Tom are in economic difficulties. These five years have affected their relationship and will soon bring Gerry to make the decision to leave her husband and become an "adventuress." More urgently, however, they have failed to pay the rent of their Park Avenue apartment as a result of which the agency has put it back on the market. The Wienie King and his wife (Esther Howard) have come with the manager (Franklin Pangborn, one of Sturges's regulars) to look at the property while Gerry is still at home. The Wienie King is hard of hearing, but we suspect rather that he hears what he chooses to hear, and neither his wife nor the manager appear to have anything to say that would induce him to make an effort. In their conversation they both appear exclusively concerned with social etiquette, economic solvency, and middle-class privilege. The Wienie King, on the other hand, likes birds (whatever he may mean by that), does not mind a little noise and dirt, and is not particularly fond of his wife or, as he soon discovers, the manager.

When they go into the apartment, there is an interesting movement of the frame. The camera that has so far focused on the three characters, moving with them along the outside corridor, now pans and tilts up to the upper floor where Gerry is coming out of her bedroom in a glamorous dressing-gown that hardly matches the dire financial straits in which she and her husband appear to be. A reverse shot in high angle frames the other three from her perspective as they start moving off the frame, maybe in the direction of the kitchen. The Wienie King, however, inexplicably walks in a different direction and goes up the stairs towards where Gerry is standing. Even though he has not seen her, and the other two never become aware of Gerry's presence in the house, it is as if the moment she appears he immediately feels her presence and "naturally" gravitates towards her. The vertical configuration of the space, with the two *alazons*, to use the Aristotelian terminology, below and the representative of the younger generation above, openly establishes the textual system of values and its reversal of social hierarchies. Far from being the representative of the older generation that in the New Comedy is initially there to repress and then be replaced by the younger characters at the center of the social structure, the Wienie King aligns himself with the young couple and becomes their protector, not only in financial terms.

About Gerry, Harvey has said that she is surrounded by enchantment from the beginning, and while the rest of the eccentric characters that she meets later in the narrative also contribute to the creation of the magic atmosphere that confers her specialness as a desiring woman and as a romantic lover, it is her contact with this first eccentric that starts her charmed existence in the film (Harvey 1998: 601). The Wienie King has probably been a ruthless businessman who, at the end of his life, thinks that there is nothing more important than a woman's beauty and clear voice.

In his practical, no-nonsense style, he immediately becomes the emotional and ideological center of the narrative, constructing a magic circle around Gerry and defining her as the romantic heroine of his comic utopia. This comic utopia is characterized by the combination of *carpe-diem* lyricism and humorous awareness of his physical decay that he displays in his dialogues. Looking at her face and hearing her voice (if they were married he'd hear almost everything she said, he assures her), he breaks into poetry: "Cruel are the hands of time that creep along relentlessly,/destroying slowly but without pity that which yesterday was young./Alone our memories resist this disintegration and grow more lovely with the passing years." To which he adds: "That's hard to say with false teeth." The lines have to be taken seriously because of the earnestness of the unlikely poet, as coming straight from his heart, the final rejoinder on his false teeth working not as a deflating comment but as a way of framing his pseudo-Shakespearean speculations on the passing of time and beauty within the realm of comedy. Our smile or laughter will not detract from the power of the poetic lines but rather protect them from accusations of banality or superficiality through our humorous awareness of the Wienie King's pragmatism and sincerity. His old age confers credibility to his words, and his ability to blend insight with humor wins our admiration and respect. He is indeed the metaphorical king, the provider of the comic romantic universe that is about to unfold in front of our eyes. The Wienie King directs our vision and marks the outlines of a comic world of which he is too old to be part. A few seconds later, when he is warning Gerry that it will all be over before she knows, the film gives us a closeup of Claudette Colbert, in which the glamour of her young beauty is mixed with her compassion for the philosopher king, her growing understanding of his call to romantic action and, simultaneously, her incipient awareness of the state of her relationship with her husband. As he then proceeds to lavish on her the money that will provide the means for a new beginning for her, Gerry emerges from the encounter with the aura of enchantment that Harvey notices and will last her for the rest of the story. From then on, surrounded by characters, including her husband, who do not understand the importance of desire, she will carry with her the aura bestowed on her early on by the king.

Other eccentrics that will cross her way in the course of her journey will reassure her that, despite appearances to the contrary, she will remain protected in this enchanted world. Her aura is no different from the comic atmosphere that surrounds the lovers of other romantic comedies, but *The Palm Beach Story* allows the spectators an insight into its origin. In Preston Sturges, this origin of the comic world is closely connected with the moments of eccentricity, those isolated instances, apparently sterile from the point of view of narrative development, in which the amused perspective of the distorted look at society transforms our vision and gives us unexpected wisdom.

Tom's later reaction to the news that a strange old man has given his wife a lot of money for no apparent reason shows that, for the moment, he is still not one of the chosen ones. This fact justifies her decision to leave him and go to Florida. Even though she takes him back at the end, *The Palm Beach Story*'s peculiarity as a romantic comedy lies in its focus on the female protagonist, whose lovers do not measure up to much, but who, in herself, embodies the centrality of desire in our lives and the importance that humor has in its artistic articulation in the genre. Much more than in the ups and downs of her relationship with Tom or with the other eccentric millionaire, J.D. Hackensacker III (Rudy Vallee), it is in her encounter with the Wienie King that she shines as a privileged representative of the genre's utopian world, his comic wisdom and generosity with no bounds and her receptivity to his influence encapsulated in the closeup analyzed above.

Preston Sturges's success as a Hollywood comedy director was as short lived as Howard Hawks' was prolonged. A practitioner of most classical genres, Hawks' comic genius managed to spill over from his comedies onto most of the other films he directed. A *film noir* like *The Big Sleep* (1946) or a western like *Rio Bravo* (1959) are comic masterpieces even though they are not usually described as comedies. He contributed centrally to the success of screwball comedy in the 1930s and early 1940s and continued to make comedies in that mould for two more decades even when the cultural and industrial conditions had changed in Hollywood. Films such as *I was a Male War Bride* (1949), *Monkey Business* (1952) or *Man's Favorite Sport?* (1964) reflect the persistence of the conventions and the worldview of screwball within new contexts. Part of the interest of these later films lies in what could be described as their cultural and historical hybridity: they are simultaneously screwball comedies outside their temporal frame (approximately 1934–1942) and films of their own time, collapsing to some extent the differences between different comic trends. To be more precise, these three films trace the gradual increase in the visibility and explicitness of sex and talk about sex in a genre that, as Brian Henderson and Andrew Sarris famously argued (more or less at the same time), had always been predicated on its exclusion (Henderson 1978; Sarris 1978).

Man's Favorite Sport? (screenplay by John Fenton Murray and Steve McNeil), Hawks' remake of *Bringing Up Baby* (1938), has often been discarded by critics as a pale imitation (Wood 1983: 138–9), but, because of Hawks' screwball origins, it is particularly illuminating about the process through which sexual desire was gradually incorporated into the notion of heterosexual romance within the history of the genre. In this sense, its screwball origins, and Hawks' amusing description of himself as self-plagiarist, should not blind us to the simultaneous fact that the movie is one more entry in the popular Doris Day and Rock Hudson sex comedy cycle, and Hudson's performance in it as Roger Willoughby is an interesting combination of the victimized male at the mercy of the overwhelming woman of *Bringing Up Baby* and other Hawks' comedies and the man pretending to be somebody else of the sex comedies (Babington and Evans 1989: 206; Krutnik 1990; Jeffers McDonald 2007: 38–58). Our third example comes from the beginning of this movie.

"Screwy story," says the police officer to Roger Willoughby after the latter's weak attempt to explain why he is trying to move somebody else's car from a parking space. This meta-cinematic reference to the cycle of comedies in which Hawks played a central part verbalizes the similarities that the knowing spectator had already noticed between the first encounters of the protagonist couples of *Bringing Up Baby* and *Man's Favorite Sport? Bringing Up Baby* is a particularly representative example of the indirect approach taken in the genre towards the representation of desire and sexuality. In his analysis of the film, Stanley Cavell (1981: 116–17) argues that the constant sexual references (without there once being an explicit reference to sex) that the spectator finds in it are what the film is ultimately about, yet at the same time we are never sure how hard to press those references. Although Cavell's impression works by accumulation and through the spectators' gradual elucidation of the text's metaphoric pattern, it also applies to the impact of individual scenes and moments, which, while providing hilarious sexual images, also work to convey comic perspectives on the social and psychological dynamics between men and women. When, in one of the funniest and most popular scenes of the film, Susan Vance (Katharine Hepburn) and David Huxley (Cary Grant) leave a restaurant walking in perfect time with David standing right behind Susan after he has inadvertently torn her dress, we immediately acknowledge the potent visual metaphor of sexual compatibility and joy, but the comic moment also works as part of the war of the sexes between

Figure 8.2   The power of metaphor: Roger Willoughby struggles to introduce his massive body inside Abigail's diminutive car in Howard Hawks' *Man's Favorite Sport?* (producer, Howard Hawks).

the two protagonists. Such moments integrate both social and sexual dynamics with psychological patterns of aggression and humiliation, as if there were no separation between them. But we can only feel comfortable with this integration if we accept that everything else can be reduced to sex in the film's fictional world and that a film of the late 1930s could so brazenly be putting forward such a proposition under the reportedly attentive eyes of the PCA.

Man's Favorite Sport? (see Figure 8.2) continues this trend two-and-a-half decades later, at a moment in which the barriers to the representation and discussion of sex on the Hollywood screen were beginning to be lifted under cultural pressure and, as Henderson (1978) has explained, the change was threatening to tear romantic comedy at the seams. Some of this tension can be discerned in Hawks' return to what might be described as the metaphoric explicitness of the earlier film. The first few shots after the credits reverse the setup of the restaurant scene from *Bringing Up Baby*: Roger Willoughby, star shop assistant at a sporting goods store in downtown San Francisco, is driving to work in his smart, large black convertible, with Abigail Page (Paula Prentiss) following him ridiculously close in a much smaller, fashionable yellow car. The scene does not make much narrative sense: they do not know each other and although they are going to the same place no explanation is offered for Abigail's behavior. Beyond the pleasure afforded by its visual absurdity, the gag makes sense perhaps only as an ingenious reference to the earlier film: the man and the woman walking in unison out of the restaurant now become two cars, comically marked as masculine and feminine, following one another, except that now the positions have been reversed. The reference to *Bringing Up Baby* underlines the amusing sexual overtones of this duo drive through the attractively filmed streets of San Francisco. The gender reversal that Hawks' other comedies carefully trace in the course of the narrative development is here simply and economically visualized, as if, rather than a stage that the man and the woman have to reach on the road to romantic happiness, it had by now become a normal fact of life, something not be explored or narrativized but matter-of-factly and amusingly stated.

The motorized "persecution" makes even more comic sense within the context of sex comedies such as *Pillow Talk* (1959) and *Lover Come Back* (1961), in which Hudson plays the sexual predator constantly chasing after women while always remaining in control, even as his sentimental education at the hands of the female protagonist gets under way. The unexplained reversal announces the inevitability of immediate changes in sexual politics in the following years but, as in the metaphoric structure of *Bringing Up Baby*, it does so by "reducing" everything to sex and, within the spirit of utopianism of the genre, cueing the spectators to sit back and take pleasure in the upcoming changes. For the comic text there is obviously much to enjoy and celebrate in bringing the male predator down to size even though this is achieved precisely by exaggerating his considerable size.

When the two cars finally arrive at their destination – the car park where Roger leaves his car every day – and he, following his usual routine, maneuvers to back the vehicle into his allotted space, she neatly beats him to it and drives straight in. He then gets out of the car to explain politely and even shyly that she has taken his space by mistake, to which she responds with the kind of false but seamless logic that turns her into an explicit heir of Susan Vance. By the time she finishes with him he is down on his knees, as if romantically asking her for her hand, as her friend "Easy" Muller (Maria Perschy), who has just joined them, points out they are also closely surveyed by a policeman who threatens to give Roger a parking ticket if he does not move his car. Given the relative sizes of Roger and Abigail's tiny car, being on his knees is the only way he has to get down to the level of her window to speak to her. Before that, however, when he first tries to reason with her, he finds it more comfortable to talk through the opening in her car roof. Hawks underlines the unconventionality of the position by means of a high-angle shot/low-angle reverse shot, with Abigail in close-up and Roger in approximate medium closeup. Here the filmmaker plays with visual expectations, gently contradicting the usual connotations of frame angles: if a character framed in high angle is generally perceived as threatened, overwhelmed or trapped, the high-angle closeup of Abigail finds her perfectly at ease, even enjoying the situation, apparently not bothered by the towering figure looming over her and her little car, and ready to engage him with her verbal acumen. Conversely, the low-angle reverse shot of Roger increases the distance between them and emphasizes the opening in her roof, out of which his head seems de-centered and out of place, his expression one of helplessness at his position as he looks in with some measure of embarrassment. This is probably the most spectacular framing in a movie from a director well known for his no-nonsense use of stylistic and narrative rhetoric and for his dislike of visual flourishes. It perfectly captures the unbalanced nature of the power game that has been established between them as part of this new replay of the war of the sexes. The reversal of the high-angle/low-angle traditional meanings works as a continuation of the earlier car drive and places the spectator firmly in the realm of social utopia and comic redress of a sexual balance long ago upset by patriarchy. At the same time, however, the shot inaugurates a new visual motif, this time in the realm of sexual utopia, which has to do with the metonymic link it establishes between Abigail and the hole in her roof, with Roger first peeping in through the opening, rather scared of what he is going to find, and finally and boldly penetrating the welcoming/threatening space.

No matter how scared he looks in this shot, there must be something there that he finds attractive because once Abigail and Easy have disappeared inside the store he immediately returns to her car and intrepidly goes inside through the opening in the roof. In narrative terms, he is taking up her previous invitation to move her car if he wants to. He decides that he does but since the doors are predictably locked he has no option but to use the hole in the roof. Once he is half way in he realizes how small the inside of the car is compared to his own size and finds himself stuck with his head down and his feet up as the policeman looks on with curiosity. He finally does manage to ease his body completely in, his head now sticking out as he tries to sit down. He then starts to get out again, but when asked for his driving license by the suspicious policeman he has to go down again because the license had predictably fallen on the car floor. When he finally finds it and hands it to the policeman (after two attempts, since he first finds Abigail's) he tries to explain what has happened, unfortunately lacking the verbal dexterity previously exhibited by Abigail. The scene closes with Roger receiving a fine from the law for his transgression. By now, however, the amused spectator knows that the protagonist has transgressed, perhaps not altogether unwittingly, more than one law.

The gag is designed to visualize the embarrassment caused to Roger by a woman he does not even know. Why Abigail chooses to chase him, rather than anybody else, and lightly torture him in this manner the film does not bother to explain. Rather, it seems an arbitrary action, a ritual punishment that she carries out in the name of all women on the sexual predator, an image that Hudson does not exactly elaborate on in this film but that he carries into it from earlier movies. But *Man's Favorite Sport?* is a romantic comedy which identifies itself as such from the very beginning, so the spectators, even those who have not seen the film before, will have a pretty accurate idea that these two characters will end up getting romantically involved. The gag, therefore, offers simultaneously a form of comic retribution on men for the patriarchal abuse of women – the fine – and an ironic and amused look at the mixed blessings of sexual desire and the relative merits of male potency (from both a male and a female perspective) – no matter what the difficulties, desire will have its way, but, when seen from the outside, it does look decidedly ridiculous.

Given the awkwardness of the situation, which could perhaps be interpreted as the awkwardness of sex, Roger would have probably been much better off giving up his parking space for one day and going to park his car somewhere else, yet he feels inexplicably compelled to enter the reduced space of this particular woman's pretty yellow car. This choice is not even his own initiative but an almost unconscious reaction to Abigail's offhand (and also inexplicable) invitation to move her car if he wants to.

If romantic comedy celebrates the compatibility between lovers – the perfect fit – the fit here is ostensibly less than perfect. Hawks makes Hudson look even bigger than he is by setting the ridiculous task for him of slipping in through the apparently inadequate hole. Roger clearly does not fit inside Abigail's car, yet he keeps trying, rocking the flimsy vehicle to and fro, and contorting and wriggling his body until he manages to put it all inside. Once he has fulfilled his task, he does not even have a second to show any sign of satisfaction or fulfillment, because he immediately notices that he is being watched. The policeman is our stand-in in the diegesis and our hilarity increases when Roger notices that what he thought was a private act had been public from the beginning, his awkward struggle and guilty pleasure closely monitored by the representative of the law. The policeman goes on to question his gender identity, suggesting that for all its outward magnificence, his masculinity is in doubt, or perhaps that in following Abigail's casual invitation he has been swallowed by her femininity, a comic version of the male fear of castration and feminization at the hands of the all-powerful mother (Lurie 1980; Creed 1993). Not only has the mission been difficult and awkward but society has not approved, and Roger gets a fine for his transgression of decorum.

As with the whole of *Bringing Up Baby*, it is difficult to know how far to press this gag's sexual references. Yet given its visual power and its relative narrative uselessness, this opening scene makes it equally hard for the viewer to ignore its metaphoric discourse on the joys and embarrassments of sex. The man's determination to push on in spite of the difficulties, even the anatomical difficulties, that the comic text has not lost the capacity to find amusing and slightly ridiculous, are part of the fascination of the exercise, but this determination is here compounded by surrender to the feminine. The gag's combination of the sexual and the social makes this surrender both prescient, in historical terms, and consistent with Hawks' earlier visitations of the genre. For this director, romantic happiness and sexual compatibility are always dependent on the man's debasement, his acknowledgement of the injustice done by patriarchy to women and his ritual humiliation as a form of redress. Male feminization may be resisted by society, its gatekeepers always on the lookout for improprieties, but the romantic lover must learn to ignore social strictures and let himself be carried by the force of his desire. Near the end of his career, Hawks registers current cultural changes and offers his own version of the sexual liberation by deploying the same type of explicit metaphorical displacement that he had learnt to use at the time of screwball. For the comic artist, the laughter at the embarrassments of sex, particularly for the male partner, is part of the joys of desire, and comedy and sex, not necessarily in that order, which make our lives worth living.

The opening gag in *Man's Favorite Sport?* reveals the tensions of a genre trying to adapt to a changing cultural and industrial climate and achieving only limited success. The genre did take a while to adapt but, after a period of relative dearth, romantic comedy came back with a vengeance and, since the mid-1980s, has re-established itself as one of the most popular Hollywood genres, a position that it has not yet abandoned after reinventing itself several times. Peter Weir's *Green Card* (1990) belongs to the second phase of this revival, what Steve Neale has called the New Romances and Jeffers McDonald, the neotraditional romantic comedy, a relative return to traditional views of romantic love within a conservative climate, after the short-lived flourishing of the nervous romances or radical romantic comedies (Krutnik 1990: 62–2; Neale 1992: 287; Jeffers McDonald 2007: 59, 86). According to Jeffers McDonald (2007: 97), the later films seem to lose interest in sex, which is replaced by what she describes as "a vague romantic intensity."

Relaxed censorship in sexual matters has rendered strategies such as those employed in screwball comedy or even *Man's Favorite Sport?* obsolete, but the neotraditional romantic comedies do not have much use for them anyway, because, after the neo-conservative backlash in sexual matters of the 1980s, sex appears to have stopped figuring at the top of the genre's agenda. At the same time, however, the films continue to chronicle the history and the vicissitudes of desire, finding new ways of celebrating it in the face of adverse circumstances and renewed social pressure. *Green Card* is a particularly interesting example of a New Romance that tells a story of immigration in which national difference becomes the engine of desire in the type of unlikely circumstances in which the genre usually revels.

Whereas the other three examples explored in this chapter are taken from films directed by some of the most renowned artists in the history of film comedy, Australian Peter Weir (who wrote, produced and directed the film) is an unlikely player in this genre, and this mostly Australian-French co-production is a some-what unexpected addition to the boom that the genre was experiencing in Hol-lywood in the late 1980s and early 1990s. However, a closer look at Weir's earlier films suggests certain continuities that might be summarized in the creation of particularly rich and intense atmospheres. From the fraught tension emanating from the Australian hinterland in *Picnic at Hanging Rock* (1975) to the exoticized and eroticized war space of Sukarno's Indonesia in *The Year of Living Dangerously* (1982); from the small Amish community of *Witness* (1985) to the ambivalently portrayed Central American jungle of *The Mosquito Coast* (1986), Weir's films tell stories in which the vividly portrayed physical context often becomes as important as the characters. These movies use a variety of genres but they all have in com-mon the creation of complex filmic spaces. *Green Card* introduced a new genre in the director's career while extending his exploration of filmic space through the construction of the Manhattan apartment as the magic space of romantic com-edy. I have argued elsewhere for the importance of this magic space as one of the genre's central conventions (Deleyto 2009: 30–8; 2010: 104–15) and Weir's film is a clear example of its centrality in the celebration of desire and in the articulation of specific ideological discourses.

Brontë (Andie McDowell) and Georges (Gérard Depardieu) are forced to share a dwelling and pretend they are a couple in front of the immigration authorities, who rightly suspect them of having got married to give French Georges residence in the United States. Brontë is not particularly interested in the fate of illegal immigrants and has married Georges only because that is her only way into the apartment she covets. The spectacular greenhouse that has attracted horticulturist Brontë to the dwelling has ambivalent meanings as an expressionistic extension of the female protagonist: it represents a modern urban identity that has lost touch with nature and stages an apparent return to it through what is considered appropriate. Brontë's interest in nature is coded as artificial, barren, and repressive, and her garden becomes an index of her inability to find herself in the midst of her politically correct posturing. On the other hand, however, her beloved green space suggests her potential for change and the strength of her hidden desire.

The romantic comedy uses this urban green world to articulate a protective atmosphere in which what has been repressed will finally find an outlet. As is often the case in the genre, she and Georges are introduced as glaringly incompatible but the way in which the genre throws them together in this magic space anticipates their potential for compatibility and mutual desire. Humor is used to shore up this magic space and to remind us of the pleasures and delights of a world ruled by desire in which other differences and disagreements gradually become irrelevant and even faintly absurd. It is this function of humor as contributing to the magic space that I would like to explore through the analysis of a moment of silent tension between the two prospective but at this point still extremely unlikely lovers.

Shortly after the wedding, two officials from the Immigration Department visit the new couple. When Georges, who has just arrived at the flat at Brontë's urgent request, is unable to direct one of them to the bathroom, they become suspicious and set up a more formal in-depth interview for a few days later, the consequence of which may well be Georges's deportation. Brontë, who thought she would not need to see her husband ever again, has to agree to spend a weekend with him in her apartment in preparation for the interview. The weekend does not start well, their differences seemingly irreconcilable: Brontë proposes to invent a story in case they run into their friends, from whom she would like to keep their marriage secret. She wants him to pretend he is gay but he would prefer to be a terrorist. He is flippant and she is sarcastic. He starts to light a cigarette but she does not allow smoking inside the house. She offers him coffee but he cannot swallow or even recognize her powder decaf as proper coffee. The last sequence of shots in the scene builds on their previous disagreements amusingly, to summarize their relationship and their respective attitudes to one another.

It starts with a re-establishing shot, both characters sitting at either end of the kitchen table. The table is rather small but the frontal framing and the use of the wide angle emphasize the distance between them, their performance and body language confirming the high improbability of the match: Georges slouches on the chair and constantly fidgets while Brontë sits very straight and talks about splitting expenses. Even though both know that they need to work together their postures express the hopelessness of their predicament. Georges's devil-may-care attitude is made worse by Brontë's uptightness, her intolerance and animosity towards his manners increased by his conscious intention to shock her. The following shots are a masterpiece of comic timing, based on the two performances, the comic textual perspective and the accumulation of differences and hostility between them. There are two shots and two countershots in closeup before the end of the scene. In the first two he offers to cook and she looks completely blank at his suggestion. He abhors her bland vegetarian diet and reasonably thinks that his recipes might make the weekend more attractive, but at the same time he knows that the type of dishes that he can offer her, full of unhealthy red meat, will disgust her and go against her numerous politically correct principles. She would probably agree that he is the better cook of the two but would not let that admission interfere with her general sense of righteous superiority. In the next shot, he tries to fill the embarrassing silence looking for something to do with his hands, feeling like a caged animal in her gilded cage. He picks up a cigarette from the table, then realizes that he is not allowed to smoke and puts it down again, picks up the coffee mug and brings it to his mouth and then remembers that the content is her insipid coffee, conveys with a slight grimace that he cannot take it and puts it down again. As he lifts his eyes to her again looking for silent understanding of his plight, the film cuts to her. She looks away and sighs in quiet desperation, still holding onto her own coffee for protection and warmth against the comically threatening other. The scene ends and the narrative cuts to the street where, some time later, they are trying to do the shopping for the weekend.

This brief sequence, only a few seconds long, goes almost unnoticed within the overall development of the narrative yet it stays in the spectators' minds because of the comic way in which it visually articulates differences both in the social protocols that they are both comfortable and familiar with and their general attitudes to living in society. The text wordlessly constructs the two as opposites, emphasizing their national identities, and looks amusingly at their inability and unwillingness to compromise, even as they outwardly attempt to remain civilized. At the same time, however, the comic atmosphere, which, as I have argued, is here a composite of comic perspective, magic location and performance, is operating on them, bringing them together even as the chasm between them grows larger. Part of the spectator's enjoyment of the situation is derived from the certainty that the cultural differences that the characters now feel are so forbidding will be the very engine of the desire that has already started to flow between them. It is not so much that these two specific characters are unconsciously attracted to one another, although they may well indeed be by now, but that the comic text has constructed a *mise-en-scène* of desire based on the strength of their hostility and incomprehension. We identify with the comic text, enjoy its operation, and even feel exhilarated by it because of the way it turns aggression into desire, narrow-mindedness into tolerance, national prejudice into curiosity and harmony. We may laugh at their stubbornness but at the same time smile at the human potential and longing for communication, and at the power of desire to bring people together, grounding its existence precisely on the apparent irreconcilability of their differences.

Romantic comedy generally focuses on historically specific social protocols that, when internalized, become harmful and alienating, but does not stop at criticizing them and warning us against their negative effects. Beyond social surfaces, it looks for the underlying humanity in people's behavior and, in its absolute committal to the power of sexual desire, magically transforms hostility into affinity, or perhaps affirms that hostility and affinity are, if properly managed, part of the same positive feeling, part of the fun of being alive. The general hilarity and sensation of wellbeing produced by the genre is based precisely on this nagging belief in our enormous potential to transform our drab reality into fascinating utopian scenarios governed by the inexplicable laws of desire.

Within the history of the genre, these scenarios are constituted not only by whole films but also by individual moments, gags and comic motifs such as the ones analyzed here. As we have seen, these are all narrative in nature, derive their meaning from the larger narratives in which they are inserted, and contribute to their overall development. But at the same time they enjoy a certain degree of autonomy articulating important cultural meanings as well as providing exciting reenactments of the genre's unflagging attraction to the multifarious scenarios of sexual desire. Comic moments tend to offer less monolithic, more flexible discourses on intimate matters and, in their relative freedom from teleology, determinism and organicism, they may come closer to the more inchoate everyday experience of the spectators while never failing to transform that experience into the stuff of sexual utopia.

References

Babington, B. and Evans, P.W. (1989) *Affairs to Remember: The Hollywood Comedy of the Sexes*, Manchester University Press, Manchester

Cavell, S. (1981) *Pursuits of Happiness: The Hollywood Comedy of Remarriage*, Harvard University Press, Cambridge, MA

Creed, B. (1993) *The Monstrous-Feminine: Film, Feminism, Psychoanalysis*, Routledge, London

Deleyto, C. (2009) *The Secret Life of Romantic Comedy*, Manchester University Press, Manchester

Deleyto, C. (2010) Tales of the Millennium (Park): the happy ending and the magic cityscape of contemporary romantic comedy, in *Happy Endings and Films* (eds. A. Parey, I. Roblin, and D. Sipière), Michel Houdiard, Paris, pp. 103–14.

Freud, S. (1961 [1927]) Humour, *Art and Literature*, Penguin, Harmondsworth, pp. 427–33.

Greenblatt, S. (1988) *Shakespearean Negotiations*, Clarendon Press, Oxford.

Harvey, J. (1998) *Romantic Comedy in Hollywood: From Lubitsch to Sturges*, Da Capo, New York, NY.

Henderson, B. (1978) Romantic comedy today: semi-tough or impossible? *Film Quarterly*, 31 (4), 11–22.

Henderson, B. (1986) Introduction, in *Five Screenplays by Preston Sturges* (ed. B. Henderson), University of California Press, Berkeley, CA, pp. 1–30.

Horton, A. (1991) Introduction, in *Comedy/Cinema/Theory* (ed. A. Horton), University of California Press, Berkeley, CA.

Jeffers McDonald, T. (2007) *Romantic Comedy: Boy Meets Girl Meets Genre*, Wallflower, London.

Karnick, K.B. and Jenkins, Henry (eds.) (1995) *Classical Hollywood Comedy*, Routledge, New York, NY, pp. 63–86.

King, G. (2002) *Film Comedy*, Wallflower, London.

Krutnik, F. (1990) The faint aroma of performing seals: the "nervous" romance and the comedy of the sexes. *The Velvet Light Trap*, 26 (Fall), 57–72.

Krutnik, F. (ed.) (2003) *Hollywood Comedians: The Film Reader*, Routledge, London.

Lent, T.O. (1995) Romantic love and friendship: the redefinition of gender relations in screwball comedy, in *Classical Hollywood Comedy* (eds. K.B. Karnick and H. Jenkins), Routledge, New York, NY, pp. 314–31.

Lurie, S. (1980) Pornography and the dread of women: the male sexual dilemma, in *Take Back the Night* (ed. L. Lederer), William Morrow, London, pp. 159–73.

Musser, C. (1995) Divorce, De Mille and the comedy of remarriage, in *Classical Hollywood Comedy* (eds. K.B. Karnick and H. Jenkins), Routledge, New York, NY, pp. 282–313.

Neale, S. (1992) The big romance or something wild? Romantic comedy today. *Screen*, 33 (3), 284–99.

Paul, W. (1983) *Ernst Lubitsch's American Comedy*, Columbia University Press, New York, NY.

Sarris, A. (1978) The sex comedy without sex. *American Film*, 3 (5), 8–15.

Seidman, S. (1991) *Romantic Longings: Love in America, 1830–1980*, Routledge, New York.

Wood, R. (1983) *Howard Hawks*, BFI, London.

Further Reading

Babington, B. and Evans, P.W. (1989) *Affairs to Remember: The Hollywood Comedy of the Sexes*, Manchester University Press, Manchester. An ambitious and extremely well-written analysis of the most important moments and cycles in the history of Hollywood Romantic Comedy. Selected films and filmmakers range between the canonical (*Bringing Up Baby*), the not so obvious (Bob Hope, Mae West) and the frankly unexpected (Douglas Sirk comedies). Constant links to other genres, media and cultural traditions suggest the importance of romantic comedy both in cultural and psychological terms.

Grindon, Leger (2011) *The Hollywood Romantic Comedy*, Wiley-Blackwell, Malden, MA. The most recent study of the genre to date, the book beautifully frames the most important debates surrounding romantic comedy and its cultural impact, providing a very useful guide for students and experts. The wide selection of films and traditions analyzed in its central chapters give a very accurate idea of the complexity and richness of the genre in the history of Hollywood, and takes the genre up to the present, adding cycles and traditions that prove its continuing relevance and effervescence.

Neale, Steve and Krutnik, Frank (1990) *Popular Film and Television Comedy*, Routledge, London. A general theory of film and television comedy, this book is one of the most influential in later writing on romantic comedy, which here only occupies one relatively short chapter. This chapter, however, frames romantic comedy very firmly as a subgenre within the larger tradition of comedy and is the kernel of later, also very influential incursions of these two authors in the genre during the 1990s.

Jeffers McDonald, Tamar (2007) *Romantic Comedy: Boy Meets Girl Meets Genre*, Wallflower, London. This relatively short book manages to be canonical and polemical at the same time. The author streamlines and clarifies earlier theories of the genres into a consistent whole, while constantly decrying the shortcomings of those texts that, in her opinion, betray and diminish the genre, particularly since the 1980s. The book celebrates romantic comedy as an important instance of popular culture and contains a particularly excellent chapter on the sex comedies and Doris Day.

Karnick, Kristine Brunovska & Jenkins, Henry (1995) *Classical Hollywood Comedy*, Routledge, New York, NY. This edited work brings together many of the most important film comedy scholars and structures their individual studies around the dichotomy comedian/narrative comedy, a particularly influential classification of the genre in the 1990s. Within this structure, only the last, relatively short section, is devoted to romantic comedy, but it contains the groundbreaking essay by Charles Musser on De Mille's divorce comedies as the true origin of the genre in Hollywood cinema.

9

Taking Romantic Comedy Seriously in *Eternal Sunshine of the Spotless Mind* (2004) and *Before Sunset* (2004)

Leger Grindon

The terrain of romantic comedy shifted in 2004. In that year J. Hoberman, Amy Taubin, and Nick James praised *Before Sunset* and *Eternal Sunshine of the Spotless Mind* (along with *Lost in Translation*) as representing a "new romanticism" (Hoberman 2004; James 2004; Taubin 2004: 18). Perhaps Taubin was most explicit in defining the sensibility:

> Time ... is shaped in terms of emotion rather than conventional plotting; characters spend most of their energy trying to sort out their inchoate feelings, desires, and ideas rather than battling external obstacles; the protagonists are attracted to each other as soul mates even more than as bedmates; ... the two people are catalysts for each other's self-discovery, because, paradoxically, they offer each other a chance to get out of their own heads ... These films suggest that beauty is fragile, connections are tenuous, and love, while absolute in principle, is always contingent in practice.

The sensibility aims to invest the lovers with an intense, meaningful attraction and runs counter to the existing trend toward the ambivalent and the grotesque in romantic comedy, represented by hits such as *My Best Friend's Wedding* (1997), *There's Something about* Mary (1998), *Sideways* (2004), and later by *Knocked Up* (2007) (Grindon 2011: 61–6). The emphasis on profound emotion still allows for humor to bind the couple. *Eternal Sunshine* was widely identified as a romantic comedy. The DVD packaging prominently quoted Joe Morgenstern of the *Wall Street Journal* describing the film as "A romantic comedy unlike any other ..." (Morgenstern

2004). Charlie Kaufman (*Being John Malkovich, Adaptation*), the screenwriter who won an Oscar for his script, confessed, "I wanted to write a relationship that I recognized. I didn't want to write a romantic comedy in the conventional sense" (Winter 2004: 20). A.O. Scott and Carol Vernallis associated the film with Harvard philosopher Stanley Cavell's treatise on Hollywood romantic comedy, *Pursuits of Happiness*. Scott wrote of *Eternal Sunshine* that "the film's adherence to the rules of the genre [romantic comedy] is part of its point" (Scott 2004; Vernallis 2008: 292).

Whereas *Eternal Sunshine* wanted to play with the conventions of romantic comedy, *Before Sunset* was seldom identified with genre. Rather, the filmmaker, Richard Linklater (*Slacker, Dazed and Confused, Before Sunrise*), emphasized its presentation in real time, and others praised its natural approach to the extended conversation between the American novelist Jesse (Ethan Hawke) and the Parisian social activist Celine (Julie Delpy). Realism is often thought to be contrary to the formulae of genre, so *Before Sunset*, in spite of a romance laced with humor, eluded being identified as romantic comedy. However, Linklater admitted that *Before Sunrise* (1995) and *Before Sunset* are "technically romantic comedies maybe, but I don't acknowledge the genre stuff too much" (Koresky and Reichert 2004: pt. 2, 1). Celestino Deleyto, in a brilliant analysis, discusses *Before Sunset* as a romantic comedy "on the margins" (Deleyto 2009: 157–74). Both films draw upon the tradition of romantic comedy exploring the infidelity plot variation in which the lovers are tempted to stray from their established mates. Only some infidelity comedies result in the remarriage Cavell highlights in *Pursuits of Happiness*. Others, like *Platinum Blonde* (1931) or *Desperately Seeking Susan* (1985) end with the dissolution of a marriage. *Eternal Sunshine* concludes with the temporary reconciliation of the lovers and fashions its plot in the form of a maze; whereas *Before Sunset* ends with Jesse and Celine turning from their established partners in a mutual embrace and its plot functions as a confession.

Eternal Sunshine and *Before Sunset* opened to strong reviews in 2004 and each enjoyed commercial success. With an estimated budget of $20 million, *Eternal Sunshine* cost less than half the average Hollywood production for 2004 despite featuring major stars, who worked below their normal salaries. The worldwide theatrical box office of $72 258 126 indicated a hit for the modest but challenging film. *Before Sunset* had an even lower estimated budget of $2.7 million, described by Linklater at "to-the-bone cheap" (Koresky and Reichert 2004: pt. 3, 3). The movie earned a solid return of nearly $16 million worldwide (Box Office Mojo website features these figures on budget and theatrical revenue). Both films captured awards on the festival circuit, among associations of film critics and from the entertainment industry. *Eternal Sunshine* won an Oscar for "Best Screenplay Written Directly for the Screen" and the "Best Original Screenplay" award from the Writers Guild of America and from the National Board of Review. Kate Winslet earned an Oscar nomination for "Best Actress," among other honors. The Academy of Motion Pictures and the Writers Guild of America nominated *Before Sunset* for "Best Adapted Screenplay." Julie Delpy won awards for her performance. The National Board of Review honored the film with "Special Recognition" for "excellence in filmmaking." Today the stature of both films has risen. In an international poll of 184 critics, filmmakers and scholars conducted by *Film Comment* magazine in 2010, *Before Sunset* and *Eternal Sunshine* were selected among the 50 outstanding films of the previous decade (*Before Sunset* polled at #20; *Eternal Sunshine* at #32) (A decade in the dark 2010). *Before Sunset* and *Eternal Sunshine* stand at the frontier of romantic comedy at the beginning of the twenty-first century. This chapter aims to analyze both films in relation to the conventions of romantic comedy and in comparison with each other.

Since style informs the content and shapes our experience of a work, the two films establish a sharp contrast. *Eternal Sunshine* presents a convoluted plot based upon a labyrinthine flashback scheme from the perspective of Joel (Jim Carrey), who recently broke up with Clementine (Kate Winslet) after a two-year relationship. The highly self-conscious approach, typical of screenwriter Charlie Kaufman, is filled with doubt, reversals and recrimination. Dense editing of image and sound and a network of repetitions establish a fragmented treatment that struggles to find coherence in a world filtered through human subjectivity. Kaufman has acknowledged that "You're not watching a relationship – you're watching someone's idea of a relationship, and everything that Clementine says to Joel during the whole memory erasing procedure is just Joel talking to himself. I thought it would be really interesting to do another movie which is Clementine erasing the same relationship. It would be a completely different movie" (Winter 2004: 20).

The treatment is further clouded by irony, which splits the message into multiple, even contradictory meanings. For example, when Joel discovers the dent in the side of his car, he leaves a note on the adjacent vehicle reading "Thank You" as a hostile reproach. By contrast, *Before Sunset* strives for a natural simplicity: former lovers meet nine years after their single day together and talk during an afternoon while strolling around Paris. The 80-minute presentation in real time submerges its style while aiming for a spontaneous, convincing portrait of Jesse and Celine. The long takes with the camera following the couple and shot-countershot cutting on dialogue employs a classical style that, without highlighting the cinematic apparatus, makes the viewer an emotional participant. "The goal we [Linklater, Hawke, Delpy] set was for the film to seem like we just turned on a camera and followed them spontaneously," says Linklater. "I wanted both the acting and the style of the film to be unnoticeable – for it to seem that you're encountering an old friend you are happy to see" (Bradshaw 2004: 15). The dual perspective in *Before Sunset* balances Jesse and Celine and the film achieves a rapport between the couple without having one character dominate. As Robin Wood has noted of *Before Sunrise*, this rigorous cultivation of equality is rare in the cinema (Wood 1998: 327, 329). So *Eternal Sunshine* uses a highly edited, self-conscious style emphasizing subjectivity and a postmodern fragmentation. By contrast, *Before Sunset* cultivates unity of time and space in the tradition of Eric Rohmer's conversation films (*My Night at Maud's* (1968), *A Tale of Springtime* (1990)) underlining an objective, realistic, classical approach. On the one hand, a man's skeptical solipsism struggles for emotional renewal; on the other, a disillusioned couple strives to regain a sense of innocence and honesty. Both productions fashion a distinctive style that shapes the relationship between film and audience.

The titles are revealing. *Eternal Sunshine of the Spotless Mind* is strange, and its elusive language introduces the viewer to the labyrinthine tactics at work in the movie. Only after seeing the film does the resonance of the title begin to make sense. The name is constructed around negation and counter meanings: rather than eternal, time is limited; rather than sunshine, the film is set during a cloudy winter; rather than spotless, the couple is soiled in a turbulent conflict; rather than a logical mind, the film emphasizes impulses. The title introduces the comic irony characteristic of the movie. This incongruity fosters the humor at play in the work. Furthermore, the title comes from a passage by the eighteenth-century English poet Alexander Pope. The source was noted in the press book for film critics and many reviewers cited the reference. Mary (Kirsten Dunst) recites the passage to Dr. Howard Mierzwiak (Tom Wilkinson) late in the film. Perhaps Philip French (2004) offers the clearest explanation. He notes that the poem "Epistle of Eloisa to Abelard," is about the famous twelfth-century lovers separated by the church. Eloisa envies chaste virgins who escape the torment of a lost love and therefore enjoy the "eternal sunshine of the spotless mind." The allusion to a classic English poem and an even older legendary romance alerts the informed viewer to the artistic ambition of the film and the cinematic language that aspires to the multivalent quality of poetry.

The title *Before Sunset* presents a lyrical image based on a daily natural event, recognizable to everyone. The name also refers to *Before Sunrise*, the 1995 film that sets the stage for this sequel. The new film was released nine years after the first and portrays Jesse and Celine nine years after their initial meeting in *Before Sunrise*. The Linklater titles pose the common device of a deadline; however the original evoked dawn, the beginning of a new day, whereas the later refers to the end of the day. The first movie portrayed young lovers who had their lives before them; the sequel has them meeting nearly a decade after, when it may be too late for a serious relationship. The title introduces the time motif, which is cultivated throughout the movie. The names *Eternal Sunshine of the Spotless Mind* and *Before Sunset* successfully set the tone for each movie. *Eternal Sunshine* is an elusive, often baffling work, referring to the past to find meaning in its mystery. *Before Sunset* is simple in comparison. The words evoke the routine, the universal, a realistic natural phenomenon; yet despite its unassuming language, the title resonates in multiple directions.

Each film begins with a distinct prelude or introductory passage that deploys the two common opening plot moves of romantic comedy: unfulfilled desire and the "cute meet." Both set up a dynamic of retrospective knowledge whereby episodes and images are established that the viewer will be solicited to remember later in the film. Only on repeated viewing can the spectator understand the implications of these openings in terms of memory and time.

The first image of a film should have rich significance. Director Michel Gondry presents a facial closeup of Joel sleeping and we watch him awaken. This image anticipates the epiphany or emotional awakening of the character that will be the central quest of the film, and is another convention of the romantic comedy genre. *Eternal Sunshine* has an extended precredit sequence on Valentine's Day in which Joel Barish takes a train to the beach at Montauk, Long Island, where he meets Clementine Kruczynski, who aggressively pursues, engages and "marries" the shy man. From the opening a pattern of repetition and reversal is established. The sequence lasts for over 17 minutes and includes approximately ten scenes. Joel's introspective ramblings confirm the film's subjective anchor. The first words are Joel's voice-over expressing his unfulfilled desire: "Random thoughts for Valentine's Day 2004: the day is a holiday invented by greeting card companies to make people feel like crap." The thought motivates the lonely man to change his direction, "ditch work," and hop the train to the beach. "I don't know why. I'm not an impulsive person," Joel muses. The "cute meet" episode provides the humorous tone. Clem appears at a distance from Joel on the beach, eyes him at a coffee shop, flags him whimsically at the train station and finally approaches him on the train: "Do I Know You?" Her determined "come-on" and "blue ruin" hair coloring identify her as a half-crazy, willful heroine, related to "screwballs" like Susan Vance from *Bringing Up Baby* (1938) or Jean Harrington in *The Lady Eve* (1941). But in her orange, hooded sweatshirt Clem is ragged rather than elegant, and her troubles seep through her self-confidence. Rather than being wealthy, she is a "book slave" at a Barnes and Noble store.

After her engaging approach, she becomes contentious when Joel tries "to be nice." When Joel observes that her name means "merciful," Clem counters, "you don't know me ... I'm a vindictive little bitch." She slugs him in the chest as a parting gesture. The flirtation between Joel and Clem takes a step forward when he offers her a ride home from the Rockville station and she invites him up for a drink. She advises him to "Drink up ... It will make the whole seduction part less repugnant." After a few chugs Clem cuddles up announcing, "I'm gonna marry you." Spooked, Joel retreats to his drab suburban apartment and telephones at Clem's request; he assures her he misses her with an "I do" and Clem replies, "I guess that means we're married." The following night she takes him to a frozen rendezvous staring up at the stars from the iced-over Charles River (see Figure 9.1). The winter picnic seals their union, and when Joel drives Clem to her apartment the next morning she has fallen asleep in the car. Her awakening echoes the opening image of the film. She asks Joel: "Can I come over to your house to sleep?" sealing their "marriage" with his consent. When Clem leaves the car to "get my toothbrush," a stranger, later identified as Patrick (Elijah Wood), inexplicably bangs on Joel's car window and asks, "What are you doing here?" The image fades, to emerge with Joel sobbing in his car alone as the credits

Figure 9.1 *Spotless.* Clementine (Kate Winslet) takes Joel (Jim Carrey) to a frozen rendezvous. They stare up at the stars from the iced-over Charles River. The winter picnic seals their union. The repeated stargazing on the frozen Charles River presents a magical locale traditional to romantic comedy, the special place removed from routine that allows repression to fade and love to transform individual identity into the unity of the couple (*Eternal Sunshine of the Spotless Mind*; director, Michael Gondry; producers, Anthony Bregman and Steve Golin).

begin to roll. The change from the happiness of fresh love to tears of desperation uses an emotional reversal to mark an ambiguous time shift. In the precredit sequence the couple meet, date and "marry" before the film proper has even begun. But there would be no romantic comedy without the obstacles that arise to block their union. A strange shifting in tone introduces us to *Eternal Sunshine of the Spotless Mind*.

Before Sunset is largely designed around long takes of an extended conversation; however, the introductory sequence is grounded in editing. The opening takes approximately seven-and-a-half minutes and presents two sequences – a montage of Parisian locales and a scene of the author Jesse Wallace answering questions from an audience about his first novel at the Shakespeare & Company Bookstore. The opening ends when the camera moves outside the bookstore, where Jesse and Celine meet, having agreed to share coffee before his scheduled departure at 7:30 p.m. to catch a plane to New York.

The Parisian locales act as establishing shots, setting the scene on a shady, late summer afternoon around 6 p.m. The sequence presents 11 images at an even tempo. During the montage, brief credits appear identifying the distribution and production companies and the film's title. On the sound track, Julie Delpy sings the opening seven lines of her composition, "An Ocean Apart" ending with "Time goes by, people cry, everything goes too fast." The song refers to the separation of Jesse and Celine that ended *Before Sunrise*. The opening alludes to a similar montage of Vienna near the close of the earlier film. In the 1995 production, the images presented sites that Jesse and Celine had occupied throughout their romance. The locales are presented in the absence of the couple, but with a composition that recalls their presence. The montage evokes for our memory the experiences they have had together.

The sequence is similar to the retrospective flashbacks at the close of *Annie Hall* (1977), *When Harry Met Sally* (1989), and *There's Something About Mary* (1998). Such a sequence has become a cliché of romantic comedy, which Linklater accents with a fresh note by removing the couple from the image and letting the viewer sense them. *Before Sunset* presents another variation. The montage of urban Paris opens rather than closes the film, and, as Jonathan Rosenbaum has noted, anticipates the locales that the characters are going to occupy in the course of events (Rosenbaum 2004). The locales present a reverse chronology beginning with the path into the courtyard of Celine's apartment building, retreating into the busy street outside the courtyard, showing the tour boat on the Seine, the arbor, the café and various street scenes finally leading to the exterior of Shakespeare and Co. bookstore and the sign announcing the reading by Jesse Wallace from his novel *This Time*. The images reverse the montage in *Before Sunrise* by serving as a prelude to presence. Furthermore, they invest the movement of the couple with a sense of destiny. The book's title, the montage and the song cultivate the time motif. *Eternal Sunshine* uses irony to split meaning, fostering a tension within the work that engenders complexity. By contrast, *Before Sunset* employs various devices working in unity to highlight aesthetic intensity.

In the bookstore, the author entertains questions from his audience in shot/countershot. The exchange reveals that Jesse's novel is based upon his romance with Celine portrayed in *Before Sunrise*. While admitting that the fiction arises from his experience, Wallace refuses to reveal whether he ever reunited with the lover portrayed in his novel. His answers prompt flashback images of Jesse and Celine from nine years earlier in *Before Sunrise*. The film accentuates the aging of the couple in the contrast between the youthful American and the successful author. Finally the film cuts from a closeup of the beautiful Celine in Vienna to the older woman looking on from the wings among the bookshelves. After the session ends, Jesse moves to greet her. As Deleyto has noted, a discourse on love is established at two levels: the idealized experience based upon the memories of Vienna and a real relationship arising from the immediate exchange between Jesse and Celine in Paris (Deleyto 2009: 158).

What prompted Jesse to write this novel? Perhaps it was the aesthetic drive to convey powerful emotions. Possibly he wrote as a means of mourning his lost love. Or maybe the incentive was his desire to find Celine, as he had no information with which to contact her. Now, almost magically, she appears. When the questioner asks Jesse whether the couple ever get back together, Jesse replies that it depends upon the attitude of the reader. A cynic will assume that they part forever; a romantic will bring them together. The film affirms its romantic attitude with Celine's appearance, but holds its skepticism in reserve.

Actually, Jesse and Celine had met on one occasion after the close of *Before Sunrise*. Richard Linklater featured them in one episode of his animated daydream film *Waking Life* (2001), where they have a post-coital conversation in bed. After working together again, Richard Linklater, Ethan Hawke and Julie Delpy wanted to continue developing the couple they had created. Afterwards the three exchanged screenplay drafts for a reunion film. "For a year we e-mailed and faxed revisions to each other," Linklater explains. "There were scenes that Julie and I liked that Ethan didn't and vice versa. We'd cut them out. It was still a huge challenge to be natural and realistic and watchable and entertaining." "When we saw each other, we'd lock ourselves in a room and just write," Delpy continues. "Two weeks before the shoot we read through it and we cut out everything that wasn't really entertaining and really interesting" (Verini 2004: E8). Even though the production itself involved only three weeks of rehearsal and 15 days of shooting, the trio had labored for years developing a screenplay that each found to be a convincing treatment of Jesse and Celine as they mature.

Before the interview ends, another question arises: "What is your next book?" Wallace imagines a narrator watching his five-year-old daughter dancing on a table to a pop song, which reminds him of when, at sixteen, after losing his virginity, he watched his girlfriend dance to the same song on top of a car. "He's there in both moments simultaneously. For an instant all his life is folding in on itself," Jess says. "And it's obvious to him that time is a lie; that it's all happening all the time, inside every moment is another moment all happening simultaneously." While uttering these words Jesse notices Celine. Jesse's surprise when he recognizes her throws him off balance, and he experiences the concept he had just explained in a witty "cute meet." Jesse's new novel, like the first one, is about himself; successful but dispirited, he is ready to resume his search for meaning. Suddenly time is no longer sequential, but is collapsing together as the past and its felt associations converge with the present.

Eternal Sunshine and *Before Sunset* initiate their fiction with the lovers' union, which the following episodes disrupt. Romantic comedies portray courtship through the obstacles that the couple strives to overcome. For example, in *A Midsummer Night's Dream* Hermia and Lysander must flee to the wood because Hermia's father objects to their union. Oberon and Titania fight over a child, the Indian boy. Parents still serve as obstacles in contemporary comedies like *Meet the Parents* (2000) or *My Big Fat Greek Wedding* (2002). However, more common obstacles are those of class that divide Peter (Clark Gable) and Ellie (Claudette Colbert) in *It Happened One Night* (1934), or different ethnic backgrounds that divide Alvy (Woodie Allen) and Annie (Diane Keaton) in *Annie Hall* (1977). Constructing the obstacle through dramatic conflict is the task of the next sequence in both films.

The credits in *Eternal Sunshine* are initiated with a shift to Joel in tears at the wheel of his car. Night replaces day. The cause of his distress appears to be an audiocassette, which he throws away as he drives off. A song reports on Joel's troubles rather than the cassette: "I need your lovin" like the sunshine. Everybody's gotta learn some time ... " Here begins the confusion with time. The emotional reversal has no context. Only further confusion ensues: we see

Joel drive home and get out of his car without any evidence of crying. The point of view changes to unidentified characters we later learn to be Stan (Mark Ruffalo) and Patrick, agents of Lacuna, Inc. who observe Joel from their van as he enters his bleak Rockville apartment building. Joel's neighbor Frank (Thomas Jay Ryan) refers to the day as before Valentine's Day. The plot has moved back at least two days. Joel goes into his apartment, immediately gets into new pajamas and takes medication. Soon the operators from Lacuna have entered his room and installed their apparatus on the sleeping man. The shifting emotional tone takes precedence over temporal coherence. The disorientation expresses Joel's psychic trauma.

The postcredit sequence focuses on the science fiction conceit of Lacuna, a service that can erase selected memories for a fee. The technology alters emotion by deleting a disturbing experience. The film poses the conflict between emotion and reason in the struggle between a lovers' bond and their longing to forget when their relationship turns into painful regret. Rather than explaining the device through exposition, *Eternal Sunshine* begins the procedure on Joel, portraying his recollections from the most recent backwards, and only reveals what is happening as the episodes in Joel's mind are being vaporized. As a result, the audience discovers the design of the plot only as the procedure unfolds, expressing Joel's feeling before the logic connecting events becomes apparent. In this way the ascendency of sentiment over coherence becomes embedded in our experience of the film. The temporal jumps within Joel's consciousness feed into the humor of an otherwise distressing experience. Repetition, focal shifts, disjunctive editing, further time cues and a busy sound track continue to orient and/or confuse the viewer as Joel's circumstances unravel his history, even as it is being erased. Joel bemoans his breakup with Clem to Rob and Carrie, married friends whose quarrelsome domestic life makes them unlikely counselors for the lovelorn. Carrie gives nurturing advice ("make a clean break"), while Rob offers a "joint" for consolation before handing Joel a postcard indicating that Clem has used the mysterious Lacuna, Inc. to eliminate any vestige of her recent romance.

Soon Joel finds himself at the Lacuna office. It is an operation that looks like a cut-rate dentist. Their service delivers a mental exorcism guided by portable computers, clumsy paper files and nifty headgear. Joel's skepticism fades and he decides that the best way to avenge himself on Clem is to erase her in turn. "Is there any risk of brain damage?" Joel inquires. "Technically speaking the procedure is brain damage, but it's on a par with a night of heavy drinking," Dr. Howard Mierzwiak explains before instructing Joel that he must collect everything that reminds him of his estranged lover, so the operatives can excise his memories. Soon Joel returns to the office with trash bags filled with the refuse of a romance and signs up for the procedure that will clear up his anxiety as he sleeps. Humor arises from the antiseptic treatment of the anguish of the heart as if it were tooth decay. The flashback mixes dime store science fiction with tacky office furniture and adolescent gizmos that probe into the dark corners

Figure 9.2 *Sunset.* The couple talks for the first time in nine years, walking along the streets of Paris. Celine (Julie Delpy) and Jesse (Ethan Hawke) radiate a mixture of discomfort and joy at their reunion. Their questions, accusations and reversals condense the misunderstandings that plague lovers and make romance humorous (*Before Sunset*; director, Richard Linklater; producers, Richard Linklater and Anne Walker-McBay).

of consciousness. The montage of mementos conjures an intersection of the childlike and the erotic condensed into a coffee-mug photo, potato-head dolls and an inflated skeleton. Joel in pajamas shows up at the Lacuna office watching himself under a domed brain zapper as the rush of time produces a collision between the desire to retrieve and the need to forget. Joel can't decide what he wants and resistance grows even as the erasure continues, until Joel arrives at his last memory of Clem at their breakup. The introduction of Lacuna provides a comic avenue into the contradictory feelings in a relationship while delaying any revelation of the conflicts separating the couple.

Before Sunset portrays the obstacles between Jesse and Celine with greater formal simplicity, but comparable human complexity. Dialogue, performance and a discreetly observant camera keep the tools basic. The couple talks for the first time in nine years, walking along the streets of Paris (see Figure 9.2). Both radiate a mixture of discomfort and joy at their reunion. The conversation unfolds in three settings: the walk to the café, at the café and through the arbor. The couple confronts their obstacles from the past, renew their mutual attraction and finally acknowledge their current relationships.

On the way to the café, the past provokes a comic negotiation. Celine needs to know, "Did you show up in Vienna that December?" She explains that her grandmother died and she couldn't keep her promise to return. At first she laughs with relief when Jesse shakes his head "Nah." Then she is angry that he neglected the rendezvous, only to discover that he politely lied for her benefit. She laughs again realizing that "you must have been hating me all this time." The questions, accusations and reversals condense the misunderstandings that plague lovers and make romance humorous. Jesse teases Celine with a tale about Gretchen, an imaginary rival, only to admit that his trip to Vienna was "awful." He confesses to writing a fictional version in which the woman meets him and they make love for days, but come to realize that they don't get along. "I like that. It's more real," Celine remarks, but the editor believed that "love sells," and so *This Time* ended with a hopeful parting. Celine accuses Jesse of "idealizing the night," but counters that he made "me neurotic." Finally she concedes that reading his novel was "Disturbing ... being part of someone else's memory; seeing myself through your eyes." The contrast, discussed by Deleyto, between ideal and real love becomes the object of humorous incongruity (Deleyto 2009: 159).

In spite of their powerful attraction and good intentions at their first meeting, the lovers come up against common obstacles – distance compounded by time, unexpected circumstances and family obligations, and finally their naïve commitment to reunion rather than a practical exchange of information. Their actions testify to the romantic myth that destiny will guide you to your ideal mate. Now Celine's neuroses amplify love's disappointments rather than its power to transform the ordinary. Jesse, for his part, maintains a comic detachment under the shadow of his heartbreak, kidding Celine with coy deceptions and stories about "Gretchen." He dismisses their botched reunion: "it's no big deal." Once the impasse has been put to rest, he asks, "I wanna know about you ... what're you doin'?"

At Le Pure Café they renew their mutual attraction by keeping the conversation focused on work, values and activities without getting too personal. Celine describes her job at Green Cross, an environmental service organization, and her travels to India, Warsaw and her time in New York. He counters her pessimism about politics with the hope that though shifting fortunes may make life harder, people also get wiser. Their global travel portrays cosmopolitans at ease in an international culture. But he gulps at the realization that they both lived in New York during 1998–9 and never met. He finds her thinner; she notes the deep wrinkle between his eyes. The American talks about the difficulty of "living in the moment," and bums a cigarette as if to prove he has no fear of dying. He speaks about being liberated from desire, but Celine claims that to desire intimacy or a new dress is healthy. He admires her for "putting your passion into action." The talk flows in a stimulating exchange of thrusts and parries that confirms their rapport after the long separation. Compared to Joel and Clementine they are a compatible couple who bridge their differences with wit even as their divergent histories make them attractive to each other. They are "having fun together," as romantic comedy dictates. The exchange of successful profiles appears to reassure them both that the Vienna impasse has been put to rest.

Leaving the café for a walk through the arbor, the conversation becomes more personal. Did we have sex that night in Vienna? He winces when she doesn't remember. She denies and then admits to having sex. Memory shapes our present but the present can also alter our memories. Celine notes that their meeting changes the memory of nine years ago. There is no longer a sad conclusion. The talk continues as they move toward a park bench. Do people have an innate disposition, or is there mystery in life, unaccountable coincidence, luck, magic?

How can we live with death without asking what is important, what should be done right now? Is one's fate shaped by will or circumstance? The flow of opinion leads back toward sex and communication. "To truly communicate with people is very hard to do," Celine declares as she revives the rapport with Jesse that established a standard for intimacy that she has never been able to regain. Just as they seem near an embrace, the Parisian observes, "I read in that article that you're married with a kid." After a description of his family, she replies, "I'm in a good relationship … he's a photo journalist." The unseen rivals qualify the frank conversation and freeze the flirtation. The new conflict, typically arising in the master plot of romantic comedy at its midpoint, punctuates the film and stands between Jesse and Celine (for a description of the master plot of romantic comedy see Grindon 2011: 8–11).

Before Sunset may be the longest continuous flirtation in cinema. Deleyto identifies the film with "the confessional comedy," a trend in independent cinema initiated by *sex, lies and videotape* (Soderbergh 1989); "serious comedies about intimate relationships … which favor word over action and emotion over irony" (Deleyto 2009: 165). These movies, such as *The Wedding Banquet* (1993), *Clerks* (1994), *Walking and Talking* (1997), develop around conversations that gradually reveal greater intimacy and an honest self-understanding, but prefer talking about sex to sex. However, romantic comedy is about delay, the overcoming of obstacles rather than desire fulfilled.

Identification and laughter distinguish between *Eternal Sunshine* and *Before Sunset*. Joel and Clementine are a troubled couple marked by pathos and self-loathing. They embody the attraction of opposites, the shy man and the aggressive woman. Their relationship is distressed, as are the secondary couples – Rob and Carrie, Stan and Mary, Patrick and Clem, Dr. Mierzwiak and his wife. Joel and Clem's extreme behavior, such as stargazing on a winter night in the middle of a frozen river, places the viewer at a distance. We laugh at them. The audience dismisses the conceit of Lacuna as a joke based upon human folly. Rather than being ensnared like Joel in this foolhardy venture, we chuckle at his escapades. On the contrary, Jesse and Celine are an articulate, charming couple. Successful cosmopolitans, he writes novels, she crusades for worthy causes, they are at leisure in glamorous summertime Paris. The viewer wants to be like them. They tease each other as lovers do, they are witty, they laugh together and we laugh with them; we are at their side, a partner to their flirtation. Laughter becomes a product of their erotic excitement. Whereas *Eternal Sunshine* presents a one-sided, subjective male perspective propelled by comic exaggeration, *Before Sunset* portrays a balanced couple unusual in their intimate rapport, which excites our envy. Their stroll appears natural, their chatter impressively fluent, but well within the limits of our imagination. The style and content of *Eternal Sunshine* leaves us detached and dazzled by extremes; by contrast, *Before Sunset* invites us to identify and come closer. Both films, however, following the common pattern of romantic comedy, grow in intensity after their midpoint and move toward a defining crisis.

When Joel's memory erasure brings him to his breakup with Clem ("this is the last time I saw you"), *Eternal Sunshine* takes off into an accelerating complexity. The third act of the film moves between Joel's memories in the process of being zapped and the Lacuna employees in his bedroom attending to the erasure, at first Stan and Patrick, later joined by Mary, the office receptionist, and later still by Dr. Mierzwiak. These two plotlines in the past and the present at first appear distinct and then become increasingly intertwined into an emotional tangle. Roger Ebert identifies *Eternal Sunshine* as "a radical example of Maze Cinema, that style in which the story coils back upon itself, redefining everything" (Ebert 2004).

Joel's consciousness continues its backward trajectory. His anger over his final quarrel with Clem assures him that she deserves to be erased. She returns to his apartment drunk at 3 a.m., having smashed his car and possibly "fucked someone." As Joel's experience streams in reverse, the underlying source of the fight emerges. When Clem suggests that they have a child, Joel backs away from the commitment. Earlier Clem shares her thoughts with Joel, but she is disappointed at his reserve. She feels that he is holding back from intimacy. But soon the conflicts evaporate into dreamy embraces under sun-baked blankets and a return to stargazing on the frozen Charles River. As the memories grow ever more affectionate, Joel cries out, "I wanna call it off." The rupture between the couple dissolves into their love, and Joel takes Clem by the hand to flee from the erasure machine. Clem suggests that Joel take her "somewhere where I don't belong" in order to escape. The flight sends them back to childhood – Clem's fear of being ugly, Joel's humiliation at being bullied, and an infant's bath in the kitchen sink. In a counter ploy Joel's consciousness brings him forward in time to the Lacuna offices demanding that the procedure be halted. The couple find themselves in their bed on a wintry Montauk shore, playfully wrestling on the snow-covered sand and then running to the imposing beach house. Joel's consciousness intermingles memories, his growing resistance and the scuttlebutt between Stan and Patrick. The swirling plot makes the viewer dizzy.

While the erasure is in progress, the film cuts back and forth between Joel's receding memories, and the Lacuna operatives in his bedroom. Patrick confesses to Stan that he fell in love with Clem while they were erasing her brain the previous week. Now he is using his insider's knowledge of Joel's romance to woo Clementine. Stan chides his partner for using a client's confidential information to take advantage. The streams of action increase as Mary arrives to cuddle up with Stan, and Patrick departs to visit Clem. Patrick proceeds to ingratiate himself by using Joel's memorabilia, and Clem tries blindly to revive her forgotten romance by repeating scenarios already played out with Joel. While Joel sleeps under the brain zapper, Stan and Mary engage in inebriated foreplay, but Mary keeps praising Howard Mierzwiak, suggesting a history between the doctor and his clerk. The Lacuna flirtation moves toward a crisis when, after having sex with Mary, Stan realizes that Joel has escaped the surveillance of their machine and panics. A call brings Dr. Mierzwiak to the apartment. His initial attempt to put the erasure back on track is distracted when Stan discreetly leaves, and Mary kisses the doctor. The irony mounts. Even as Joel is taking a cure for the follies of romance, the operatives indulge in behavior they will soon regret.

Michel Gondry keeps the movement between Joel's stream of consciousness and the various subsidiary romances separate in the film's style. Exaggeration, ellipsis, special effects and disorienting sound cues characterize Joel's interiority, which becomes a surrealist combination of dream and reality. By contrast, the scenes at the apartment as well as Patrick's meeting with Clem, that is, the episodes taking place in dramatic time moving forward, are presented in a realistic manner. This distinction in style helps the audience follow the competing plotlines. The move between a fantastic interiority and a bleak social reality makes the imaginary life much more appealing than Rockville's suburban decay. A challenge for *Eternal Sunshine* is to bring love's illumination into the ordinary experience of Joel and Clementine.

Eternal Sunshine uses its subsidiary romantic couples to develop irony and skepticism toward love. Joel first goes to visit Carrie and Rob after Clem dumps him, but we later learn the warring couple facilitated Joel and Clem's first meeting in Montauk. The subsidiary couples also establish parallel romantic triangles: Joel, Clem, Patrick and Stan, Mary, Dr. Mierzwiak. The parallels expose the flaws in the Lacuna system, an apparatus built upon the human limitations of those who created it. Even as its aid for the lovelorn fails, the process offers the opportunity for further abuse. The misunderstandings, deception and quarrels of the subsidiary couples portray a minefield of thwarted desire. The move of Joel and Clem toward reconciliation offers only a glimmer of love in contrast to the pervasive skepticism. By contrast, *Before Sunset* keeps its focus on the principals, which allows them to sustain a more balanced vision.

But this summary of the design of *Eternal Sunshine* can only suggest the rich associations cultivated by the film. Carol Vernallis claims that over 30 motifs are at work and after describing six admits, "It is hard to ascertain fully which kinds of work these motifs accomplish" (Vernallis 2008: 280–3). Clearly some are more coherent than others. Expressive devices, like Clementine's hair color changing from blue to tangerine, project a mood shift from glum to bright. The Montauk beach setting serves as a positive romantic motif and its sumptuous, empty beach house suggests an idyllic shelter inviting the couple to take residence, yet threatening them with a confining domesticity. The repeated stargazing on the frozen Charles River also fulfills the couple's desire. These settings present magical locales traditional to romantic comedy, the special place removed from routine that allows repression to fade and love to transform individual identity into the unity of the couple. *Eternal Sunshine* cultivates a discomforting undercurrent by using winter rather than summer for the season of romance, but these places of the heart still serve well-established convention. On the other hand, some motifs create an ominous tone without allowing us to unravel their mystery. For example, Joel and Clem engage in a sex game, associated with Joel's childhood, of smothering each other with a pillow. The activity conjures a mixture of *thanatos* and *eros*. The skeleton imagery and the hammered bird further link passion with the macabre. See below for a discussion of the flight motif that also expresses an erotic undercurrent. These motifs give the film resonance without grounding the motifs in a coherent theme. Varnallis points to Gondry's background in music video as an influence that expands beyond the limits of narrative into an evocative, mysterious emotional timbre. The expanding maze of *Eternal Sunshine* contrasts with the frank confessions promoting depth in *Before Sunset*.

Journeys in romantic comedy typically move the couple away from ordinary life into a special place where repression is lifted and the lovers can shape a new, common identity as a couple. The journey represents a process of transformation. For example, think of Joe and Jerry's trip from Chicago to Florida in *Some Like It Hot* (1959), Miles and Jack's excursion to the wine country in *Sideways* (2004) or the archetypal night in the wood in *A Midsummer Night's Dream*. In *Eternal Sunshine* the journeys to Montauk and the Charles River take on this special significance, and Joel's journey back in time also serves as a means of transformation. In *Before Sunset* there are two key trips on a smaller scale – the tour boat ride on the Seine and the auto trip from the pier to Celine's apartment building. Here the movement prompts a crisis. The acceleration from walking, to the boat, and then the car, speeds time forward toward the couple's separation, so the movement toward parting gains a rising urgency. The tone shifts from witty flirtation to grim reflection. The sequence is balanced symmetrically with both members of the couple responding to their absent partners, the wife and the boyfriend. Jesse complains about his marriage during the boat ride. In the car Celine's distress at her failed relationships with men becomes the focus. The American confesses to a vapid union, while the Frenchwoman regrets being single. The balance marking the film's design continues into this third act.

During the boat ride Jesse compares writing his novel to the Notre Dame cathedral, "so I wouldn't forget the details of the time we spent together." He admits, "I wrote it ... to find you" and painfully cries, "Why weren't you there in Vienna?" With the beauty of the cathedral in the background, the speed of the passing river emphasizes the flow of time. Celine reflects, "When you are young you believe there will be many people you will connect with. Later in life you realize it only happens a few times." Finally Jesse reports on his passionless marriage. He portrays his wife as "a great teacher, good mom, smart, pretty" but their wedding was a product of convenience and responsibility. Now his feelings have atrophied, *eros* has vanished and he seems to be "running a small nursery with somebody I used to date." Celine consoles him explaining that it's only normal for passion to fade, pressed by childrearing and life's routine. However, during the car trip she unleashes her distress as if prodded by his confession.

The increase of speed in the limo and the closer quarters of the back seat prompt more intimate revelations. Celine accuses Jesse: "I was fine until I read your fucking book." The experience reminds her that their "romantic night took everything away from me … now I don't believe in … love." In all her relationships, "I never felt it was the right man. The idea that we can only be complete with another person is evil. I've been heartbroken too many times." Celine continues, "You come here all romantic to Paris and married – screw you!" Celine's anger competes with Jesse's sorrow. The American replies by explaining that "My life is 24-7 bad, the only happiness I get is when I'm out with my son … [I'm] living in the pretense of a marriage" haunted by painful dreams of you. "I might have given up on the whole idea of romantic love, that day when you weren't there." The confession purges them of the unstated longing that had been diverted by their amusing flirtation. Reflecting now, as they approach middle age, on their one night, they realize it has haunted their dreams and drained the potential from their later relationships. Here the limitations of marriage are matched by the desperation of remaining single. Realism gains ascendancy in the conflict between the romantic and the realistic. As Celine says, "Reality and love are almost contradictory for me." But their insight is also about opportunity lost, as Celine acknowledges, "It's about that time, that moment in time that is forever gone." The confession sets the stage for the ascendancy of love at the close. Jesse and Celine appear to surrender to disillusionment as they prepare to separate. The crisis typical of the romantic comedy master plot has done its work. In the car, they each nearly touched the other listening to the sorrows of their companion. But both hesitate at physical contact. Finally as the car brings Celine to her courtyard, she wants to "try something" and hugs Jesse who responds with apprehension. Then he decides to walk her to her door and the resolution of the film is at hand.

The conclusion of *Eternal Sunshine* shifts its focus to Mary in counterpoint with Joel and Clementine. The ascendancy of the central couple increases in dominance as they approach their reconciliation. The force of memory asserts itself as the triangle of Stan-Mary-Howard breaks apart and the competing threesome has Joel and Clem affirming their union, with Patrick told to "Go away." Finally the couple emerges from the maze of memory.

The reference to the film's title signals the turn toward resolution. Mary recites the passage, "How happy is the blameless Vestal's lot / The world forgetting by the world forgot / Eternal sunshine of the spotless mind / Each prayer accepted, each wish resigned." Her words sound in voiceover as the image cuts to Joel and Clem watching an elephant parade with Clem happily shouting, "I wanna be a great, big, huge elephant." Irony arises from the contrast between the elephant, who proverbially never forgets, and the vestal who, like Mary, has been sheltered from experience. Mary moves toward the attraction seeping through her flawed Lacuna wipe. She kisses Howard, only to be caught when Mrs. Mierzwiak arrives and prods her husband to inform Mary that the recollection of their earlier affair has been erased. In distress Mary goes back to the Lacuna offices to grab her client file and to mail back the confessional interview tapes to all the company's customers. Her confrontation with the past makes her realize that others must do the same. Her hesitant exchange on the street with Stan, hinting at reconciliation, ends her role, and anticipates the final accord between Joel and Clementine.

Intercut with Mary's debacle are the earliest memories of Joel's romance as his erasure comes to a climax. During the closing episodes, he and Clem re-enact their early courtship while acknowledging the Lacuna process, which dissolves the experience. The film moves from the elephant parade to Joel's visit to the bookstore to ask the enticing woman he has met on the beach for "another go around." Then further back, to their initial meeting on the Montauk shore, their adventure in the sumptuous, empty house and the montage of Joel's ride home from the beach party with Carrie and Rob as the excitement of this enveloping passion takes hold.

Finally the film returns to its opening image, the close up of Joel awakening from sleep after Howard has put the final touches on his procedure. The pronounced subjectivity during Joel's erasure gives way to a more realistic approach. A reprise of shots from the film's prologue takes us to the morning when Joel drives Clem back to her apartment, and he waits for her to join him. On the way, Clem picks up an envelope from Mary containing the Lacuna cassette. She innocently pops it into the car player, while, next to her, Joel listens as she speaks of her anger at Joel, foreshadowing the end of a relationship that appears to be just beginning. The circle entwines the couple when, after a quarrel, Clementine returns to Joel's apartment, and hears the tape he made for Lacuna describing his antagonism toward her. How can one maintain an intimacy whose history, like all histories, is twisted by cruelty, is inflated by pride, and fraught with misunderstandings and the flaws that constitute our humanity? The cassettes echo like the cries of lovers struggling to grasp the tenderness that binds them, rather than the barbs tearing them apart. When Clem rushes from the apartment, Joel runs after her, asking her to wait. They say nothing more but pause, finally exchanging an "OK" to each other's faults, peculiarities and affection. "Change your heart, look around you / Change your heart, it will astound you" goes the song as the closing shot watches Joel and Clem chase each other playfully down the snowy beach at Montauk.

The conflicts between Joel and Clem remain. (Will they conceive a child? Maybe. Will Joel's reserve develop into a fluent intimacy? Probably not.) But the couple endures in a tentative, but passionate gaze that acknowledges and embraces each partner's limitations. Like the irony shaping the film's humor, the couple accepts the dissonance that may be inevitable in all but the most blessed of human relationships. The flight motif is a key pattern whose concept arises from the intersection of wordplay and image association. Imagery of airplanes, such as the pajama print Joel wears as a baby, or birds, such as the victim of the child's hammer, floats through the film. Rob disturbs his wife's piece of mind by nailing together his bird cage. Joel and Clem flee from the reach of the erasure machine. At the Montauk beach party where Joel and Clem first meet, Rob flies his model plane over the waves. The color of the plane matches Clem's sweatshirt. The sound of its motor becomes background noise for the opening flirtation between Joel and Clem. The same day, Joel flees when Clem wants to set up house in the empty mansion. The flight motif combines the elation of soaring above common experience with the fear of running from the unusual, the enticing, the forbidden. The motif serves as an amplification of the mix of *eros* and *thanatos* that underlies sexuality. As Joel's last memory fades, he stands ambivalent, caught between ecstasy and humiliation. As the phantom Clem vanishes into the Lacuna machine, like Eurydice, she calls Joel back for a "make-up goodbye." As they bow their heads to kiss, Joel declares "I love you" and Clem whispers an amplified, distorted sound closeup "Meet me in Montauk" – the summons that reunites them in the aftermath of the scientific cure.

Joel's epiphany unfolds in the time reversal. His declaration of love is spoken in the wake of his history reversed, his feelings revealed. The inside-out maze combines detachment with engagement rather than posing these attitudes as distinct, or opposing. *Eternal Sunshine* carries the viewer along into Joel's past, which becomes the present tense of his passion. He wakes with his memories gone, but his abiding love propels him to Montauk. Later when the couple is faced with the bitterness of the tell-tale cassettes, their love, fed by memory, overwhelms their reservations and leaves them on the beach in that special transcendence of the ordinary which is the vocation of romantic comedy. The multivalent fluency in *Eternal Sunshine*, ironic yet deeply emotional, constitutes a rare achievement. The film finds its way through postmodern fragmentation, and molds its cleverness into heartfelt sincerity.

The "sublime" ending of *Before Sunset* reacts against the chatter that has consumed Jesse and Celine (Dargis 2004). Celine's embrace of her companion has thrown the conversation off balance. Jesse has constantly postponed their parting – strolling from the café, hopping onto the boat, offering a car to Celine's apartment. Like an absolution, the hug lifts his spirits and he escorts Celine to her door. With each step forward, reserve grows. At the door of the building, Jesse asks Celine to play her songs for him. "One song, but quickly," Celine agrees. The slow march up a winding staircase with the camera rising above the couple in a long, steady take brings them to the apartment door. Celine holds her cat, maintaining a distance, a brake on the impulse to touch. At the door she gives her pet to Jesse and opens the room. Romantic comedy engineers delay. The retarded tempo and the silence feed our expectation as the couple rises toward another level of intimacy.

Once in Celine's charming studio, a boundary is crossed. For the first time in the film, the couple enjoys privacy. Whereas *Eternal Sunshine* portrays a longstanding sexual relationship and we see the couple often in bed, in the Linklater film there is hardly a touch, never a kiss. The back seat of the limo offers an intermediate locale between public and private. The hug at the entrance to the courtyard signals a move beyond confession. Now the former lovers are alone. The prominent bed underlines the prospect of sex. The hostess offers tea and explains that she has only three songs in English. Jesse wants to hear the waltz.

Two songs organize the close. The couple remains at a distance. Jesse sits on a couch waiting for his tea. With hesitation, Celine takes up her guitar and sits on the bed facing the camera to sing "Waltz for a Night." The lyrics tell of the fond memory of a one-night stand. The song answers Delpy's "An Ocean Apart" from the opening and also presents her reply to Jesse's novel. Celine has written the song to the man who now faces her, and though embarrassed by its directness, she has finally addressed her lyric to the beloved. "I just wanted another try/I just wanted another night/Even if it doesn't seem quite right/You meant for me much more/Than anyone I've met before." Jesse listens with growing excitement, but holds his seat. After the song, he gives Celine a chance to dismiss her overture, "Do you just plug that name in for every guy that comes up here?" "Oh yes, of course," Celine replies with a laugh, "what do you think, I wrote that song about you?" While Celine prepares the tea, Jesse plays a disc, Nina Simone singing "Just in Time." They sigh at the singer's death, acknowledging life's limitation. Celine describes seeing Simone in concert and begins to imitate the singer. Her dance elaborates her final pass, her decision to make love to her guest, as she says in the manner of Simone, "Baby, you're going to miss that plane." The camera cuts to Jesse on the couch and makes a modest dolly in as he smiles in reply, "I know."

In *Before Sunrise*, Jesse departed on a train at the conclusion. The sequel reverses that decision. Faced with the nine intervening years, Jesse remains in the moment; he refuses to be separated from the beloved by his deadline. Jonathan Rosenbaum notes the balance Linklater maintains between "the weight of time" and "the volatile lightness of the dangerous present ... in one of the most perfect endings of any film" (Rosenbaum 2004). Though Jesse wishes the best for his wife, and longs to watch his son grow, here and now he has chosen to realize the desire that has haunted him. The camera withdraws from the romance leaving the audience to imagine its further torments and delights.

Eternal Sunshine and *Before Sunset* are infidelity comedies that unite the couple in their resolution. Joel and Clementine are reconciled; Jesse and Celine abandon their wrong partners for each other. Though a sense of transience marks both endings, the couples embrace. Time shapes and shadows the epiphany. Joel's immersion in his emotional history allows him to recognize his lover's value. Jesse and Celine discover that their attraction was more than a youthful illusion; their passion grew from a genuine rapport that a second meeting has reignited. Whether sorting through memories or confessing one's feelings, *Eternal Sunshine* and *Before Sunset* resist the pull toward the grotesque and the force of ambivalence. Though markedly different in style and tone, these romantic comedies are distinguished by their sincerity; their commitment to love's force even as they play upon its humor. As Manohla Dargis writes, "*Before Sunset* transcends the ordinary in great part because it takes love seriously" (Dargis 2004). In an era when skepticism or fluff dominates popular treatments of love, *Eternal Sunshine* and *Before Sunset* portray our doubts about romance without abandoning a commitment to its fulfillment. The conviction that distinguishes both films allows them to construct their persuasive, comic vision.

References

A decade in the dark: 2000–2009 (2010) *Film Comment*, 46 (1), 16–41, http://www.filmlinc.com/film-comment/article/film-comments-end-of-the-decade-critics-poll (accessed May 18, 2012).

Bradshaw, Nick (2004) Once More, With Feeling, *Time Out London* (July 21–28), pp. 14–15.

Cavell, Stanley (1981) *Pursuits of Happiness: The Hollywood Comedy of Remarriage*, Harvard University Press, Cambridge, MA.

Dargis, Manola (2004) *Before Sunset*: After Nine Years, Did Their Hearts Grow Fonder? *Los Angeles Times Calendar* (July 2), http://articles.latimes.com/2004/jul/02/entertainment/et-dargis2 (accessed May 18, 2012).

Deleyto, Celestino (2009) *The Secret Life of Romantic Comedy*, Manchester University Press, Manchester (especially pp. 157–74).

surEbert, Roger (2004) *Eternal Sunshine of the Spotless Mind*. *Chicago Sun-Times* (March 19), http://rogerebert.suntimes.com/apps/pbcs.dll/article?AID = /20040319/REVIEWS/403190302 (accessed May 18, 2012).

French, Philip (2004) It'll All Come Out in the Brainwash. *The Observer* (May 2), http://www.guardian.co.uk/film/2004/may/02/philipfrench/print (accessed April 19, 2012).

Grindon, Leger (2011) *Hollywood Romantic Comedy: Conventions, History, Controversies*, Wiley-Blackwell, Malden, MA.

Hoberman, J. (2004) Aching Life: *Before Sunrise*'s Gen X Lovers Walk, Talk, and Catch Up in a Romantic Real-Time Sequel. *Village Voice* (June 22), http://www.villagevoice.com/content/printVersion/184245 (accessed April 19, 2012).

James, Nick (2004) Debrief Encounter. Sight and Sound (August), http://www.bfi.org.uk/sightandsound/feature/105/ (accessed April 19, 2012).

Koresky, Michael and Reichert, Jeff (2004) A Conversation With Richard Linklater. Summer, Reverse Shot Online, http://www.reverseshot.com/legacy/summer04/linklater1.html (accessed May 18, 2012).

Morgenstern, Joe (2004) Brilliant Mind Games: While Carrey Loses Memory, *Sunshine* is Unforgettable. *Wall Street Journal* (March 19), http://online.wsj.com/article/SB107965692804159910.html (accessed April 19, 2012).

Rosenbaum, Jonathan (2004) Spur of the Moment. *Chicago Reader* (July 2), http://www.chicagoreader.com/chicago/spur-of-the-moment/Content?oid=915922 (accessed May 18, 2012). See also http://www.jonathanrosenbaum.com/?p=6040 (accessed May 18, 2012).

Scott, A.O. (2004) Film; Charlie Kaufman's Critique of Pure Comedy. *New York Times* (April 4), http://www.nytimes.com/2004/04/04/arts/film-charlie-kaufman-s-critique-of-pure-comedy.html?pagewanted=all&src=pm (accessed May 18, 2012).

Taubin, Amy (2004) Nine years on, Richard Linklater reunites Ethan Hawke and Julie Delpy for another brief encounter in this miraculous real-time sequel to *Before Sunrise*. *Film Comment*, 40 (3), 18–19.

Verini, James (2004) Gee, Long Time No See. *Los Angeles Times* (June 20), pp. E1 and E8.

Vernallis, Carol (2008) Music video, songs, sound: experience, technique and emotion in *Eternal Sunshine of the Spotless Mind*. *Screen*, 49 (3), 277–97.

Winter, Jessica (2004) The Mind's Eye. *Time Out London* (April 21–8), p. 20.

Wood, Robin (1998) Rethinking romantic love: before sunset, in *Sexual Politics and Narrative Film: Hollywood and Beyond*, Columbia University Press, New York, NY, pp. 318–35.

Further Reading

Cavell, Stanley (1981) *Pursuits of Happiness: The Hollywood Comedy of Remarriage*, Harvard University Press, Cambridge, MA. A classic text in which Cavell, a distinguished Harvard philosopher, writes with sensitivity, insight and careful attention to detail about six screwball films: *It Happened One Night* (1934), *The Awful Truth* (1937), *Bringing Up Baby* (1938), *His Girl Friday* (1940), *The Philadelphia Story* (1940), *The Lady Eve* (1941) plus *Adam's Rib* (1949), arguing that these films portray a comic process of the growing maturity and education of a couple that concludes with a "remarriage" on a higher level of mutual understanding.

Deleyto, Celestino (2009) *The Secret Life of Romantic Comedy*, Manchester University Press, Manchester. After discussing genre theory, this fine book presents a theory of romantic comedy addressing the importance of laughter, the function of the mid-plot and the space of romantic comedy. Analyses of influential films on the margins of the genre follows: *To Be or Not To Be* (1942), *Kiss Me Stupid* (1964), *Rear Window* (1954), *Crimes and Misdemeanors* (1989), *Before Sunset* (2004).

Grindon, Leger (2011) *The Hollywood Romantic Comedy: Conventions, History, Controversies*, Wiley-Blackwell, Malden, MA. An excellent survey that explains the conventions of dramatic conflict, plotting, characters, masquerade setting, and humor. The history of the genre since the coming of sound reviews nine distinct cycles and ten key films are analyzed from *Trouble in Paradise* (1932) through *There's Something About Mary* (1998) and beyond. The literary heritage, function of humor and cultural politics of the genre are addressed.

10

The View from the Man Cave

Comedy in the Contemporary "Homme-com" Cycle

Tamar Jeffers McDonald

Introduction

Peter Klaven (Paul Rudd) has met the perfect girl, Zooey (Rashida Jones), and is happily planning his wedding to her. Only one thing spoils his anticipation of the event: he does not have a best man. A lifelong "girlfriend kinda guy," Peter has always been more comfortable around women than men, as scenes set at his office aptly demonstrate: he is at ease sharing details about the proposal with his female workmates; calls each of them by name rather than using the generic, patronizing "darling" employed by another male colleague; and when Zooey has her girlfriends round, he painstakingly makes them all root beer floats, complete with chocolate straws. They assume he is gay. Zooey is not worried, but nonetheless the search begins to find Peter a man to be manly with, and he goes on a series of "man-dates" to find a compatible partner. Eventually he meets Sydney Fife (Jason Segal), a man as laid-back and free-wheeling as Peter is uptight and regulated. In true screwball comedy fashion, each learns to change a little, and the film culminates at Peter and Zooey's wedding, with not only the man and woman exchanging vows, but the men too declaring their feelings, as they proclaim the film's title: *I Love You, Man* (John Hamburg 2009). Hamburg, as I will discuss later, has pushed before at the confining boundaries of the rom-com, and *I Love You, Man* continues this resistance; what I particularly want to focus on at the start of this chapter, however, is the scene when Sydney takes Peter to hang out at his house for the first time.

A Companion to Film Comedy, First Edition. Edited by Andrew Horton and Joanna E. Rapf.

Figure 10.1   Stanley's Man Cave (*I Love You Man*, USA, 2009; director, John Hamburg; producers, Donald De Line and John Hamburg. Dreamworks SKG).

Appropriately, Sydney lives in the Venice beach area of Los Angeles, a cool locale still imbued with the hippy, counter-culture flavor it acquired in the 1960s. His domicile partakes of this coolness particularly in its annex: a detached garage, flanked by scooter, E-bay-bought bumper-car, and miscellaneous other accoutrements.

Sydney proudly shows off the hip recreation room he has created in his garage, an enviable arena he calls "the Man Cave" (see Figure 10.1). This is a space harmoniously divided into zones for various activities catering to male enjoyment, including an area with guitars, bass, bongos and full drum kit, a section with fridge, couch and multiple televisions for video watching and gaming, and a corner supplied with comfy chair, bong and hand cream: "this is where I jerk off." Peter, surprised, specifically focuses on this last locale and asks him what he does with the masturbatory paraphernalia when women are there. Sydney is appalled: "Pete, this is the *Man Cave*, no women allowed in *here*." The Man Cave is thus defined as being out of bounds to women visitors.

Sydney's Man Cave seems emblematic of the space recently aggrandised by male-centered Hollywood romantic comedies, such as *I Now Pronounce You Chuck And Larry* (Dennis Dugan 2007), *Good Luck Chuck* (Mark Helfrich 2007), and *The Heartbreak Kid* (Bobby and Peter Farrelly 2007). I want to examine what a Man Cave symbolizes, and how it links to that older locus, the *lair*, a place found predominantly in sex comedies from the mid-1950s to mid-1960s, which I discuss below. Interestingly, it seems that the view from the Man Cave can not only help provide a perspective on relations between the sexes as evinced in *contemporary* romantic comedy, but can also offer an illuminating site from which to examine this topic in rom-coms from other periods, including the 1950s' sex comedy, the radical films of the genre from the 1970s, and the more traditionalist ones of the 1980s onwards. While this chapter will, then, ask the topical questions suggested by my title – what is the view from the Man Cave? Does the Man Cave differ from the Lair, its older twin, in proposing the exclusion of women from spaces of sexuality and desire; and if it does, what does this bode for contemporary romantic comedy as a genre? – it will also afford the opportunity to contemplate some of the traditional conventions of the romantic comedy as a whole.

Variously hailed as "bromances," "dude comedies" and dick flicks, broad comedies that center on the humorous misadventures of a male pair or ensemble have proliferated at the box office lately. The phenomenal success of Todd Phillips' films, *The Hangover* (2009) and *The Hangover II* (2011), serves as the most visible example of this trend. This large recent group of films shares a resolutely male focus, and contains scenes that highlight the seemingly inevitable concomitant of that perspective, humor derived from sexual and scatological sources. However, amongst this cluster of films I am particularly interested in those such as *I Love You, Man*, which, while maintaining the masculine point of view, also preserve an allegiance to the generic tropes of the romantic comedy, thus contributing to a relatively recent evolution of the genre – what I call the *homme-com* (Jeffers McDonald 2009: 146). The homme-com blends the usual story arc of the romantic comedy – boy meets, loses, regains, girl – with the gross-out of what William Paul has termed "animal comedy" (1995) to produce films that allow themselves to generate humor through sexual problems, physical mishaps and all the emissions of the unruly body, while still starting with a "cute meet" and concluding with a happy ending. Such films as *The Tao of Steve* (Jenniphr Goodman 2000), *Along Came Polly* (John Hamburg 2004), *Wedding Crashers* (David Dobkin 2005), *The 40 Year Old Virgin* (Judd Apatow 2005), and *Blind Dating* (James Keach 2006), all maintain the general rom-com structure but make it new by inflecting it from the man's point of view.

While the heterosexual romance plot forms part of the generic imperative for these films, they tend to share the same rather reductive view of their female characters, who generally occupy underdeveloped "girlfriend" roles as heroines, or, in smaller parts, conform to a number of other limited stereotypes. A regular cast would include the "bitch," the girlfriend's "kooky friend," the "slut," and her older sister, the "cougar." These roles can combine – as in *Along Came Polly* where Roxanne (Missy Pyle) is both Polly's kooky best friend *and* a slut, while Kathleen Cleary (Jane Seymour) in *Wedding Crashers* is both bitch *and* cougar – but remain fixed around their sexual status and perhaps one key personality trait.

Thus is set up a paradox at the heart of the new homme-coms: despite their seemingly liberal foregrounding of sex, the division of females into categories that align with their sexual activity, potential heroine status, and eventual narrative fate, is decidedly conservative, and links the Man Cave to the 1950's Lair. The newer films can be seen to be bringing back Lair-era ideas about "the double standard," which tacitly mandated that having sex before marriage was expected for men but forbidden to all women who wanted to be "respectable." Nice girls *didn't,* and the girls who *did* might be fun to dally with but were not marriage material. The American media became particularly obsessed with this idea after it seemed to be challenged by the release of Alfred C. Kinsey's *Sexual Behavior in the Human Female* (1953). Although it only made claims about his sample of 5940 18 to 30-year-old unmarried white women, the "Kinsey Report" was largely taken to be indicative of *all* single American females; thus his findings that 50 percent of his sample were not virgins was felt as a huge shock, picked up and debated throughout the press and media: seemingly, some nice girls *did*. The Lair films can be seen to be Hollywood's way of exploring and working out the mingled anxiety and excitement caused by the notion of single *respectable* women being sexually willing and desirous.

While the double standard as demonstrated across much literature of the time attempted to downplay notions of female sexual desire and agency, it is noticeable that the 1950's and 1960's films that explore this theme rarely convince on this point.[1] For example, as I have argued elsewhere (Jeffers McDonald 2010), the Doris Day character, Jan, in *Pillow Talk* (1959), is just as desirous of sex with Brad (Rock Hudson) as he is with her, and is prepared to scheme and plot to achieve her sensual goals – just like him. She, however, stops at active lying about her identity, *unlike* him, and it is the discovery of his masquerade, rather than his ulterior motives, that alienates her. Although various commentators, including Al Capp (1962) and Alexander Walker (1968), have asserted that the Day heroine is sex-averse, this is not true: she actually wants sex as much as her male *vis-à-vis*, but within a long-term relationship. It is true, however, that the sex comedy heroine rarely commits any irrevocable act before marriage, and it is this that is emulated by the contemporary homme-com. The implicit division of women into disposable sex partners and more chaste marriage potentials made by the Lair films can be seen repeating itself in the newer group of films. Before considering the ramifications of this division, however, I want to return to the Man Cave and explore its amenities and purposes. Where is the Cave found, and what goes on there? The answers to this indicate the Cave's employment as an emblem, as well as a place of male fantasy.

The Man Cave

The Man Cave is an exclusively male locale, a place inside the domestic arena where the man of the house can go to be himself; and this "self" is outwardly figured as being messy, slobbish, drunken, and obsessed with sports and sex. Amenities for the Cave therefore must include the television, the fridge and bar, and it will never be subject to the same rules of tidiness and cleanliness as the rest of the house. While the "Man Cave" as an appellation seems to date from the mid-2000s, being mentioned in newspaper articles from around that time (see Evans 2004; Collier 2005), examples of Man Caves from film, television, and other media predate this. Further research would be needed to pinpoint the inaugural Man Cave, but a case could perhaps be made for this being Batman's Bat Cave, first seen in the comic book in 1939. Full of gadgets and the "wonderful toys" that Jack Nicholson's Joker exclaims over in the 1989 film version, the Bat Cave is also a place of authenticity. While "millionaire Bruce Wayne" is the outward persona, the *true* identity as well as the secret one is that of the Batman, a haunted vigilante provoked by his parents' murders to mete out justice to wrongdoers. Other Man Caves similarly provide places for the characters that inhabit them to let out their real identities. Doug Liman's *Mr. and Mrs. Smith* (2005) plays with this notion as well as with the gendered binaries of "his and hers," since both John Smith (Brad Pitt) and his wife Jane (Angelina Jolie) have clearly defined areas of responsibility and influence within the home: she has the kitchen, he the garden shed. Humorously, however, these places are *actually* the locales where each, an assassin, can store their arsenals. Jane has a microwave with a false front that reveals arrays of guns and knives, while John's shed hides a subterranean cellar stocked with bombs and banknotes. Jane and John look like a dull married couple, but each has a secret place where they can both let out the real person, the exciting, sexy, dangerous one.

Not only can the Cave suggest something about the character traits of its possessor – it can also reveal points about his cohabiters. In *Juno* (Jason Reitman 2007), the 16-year-old eponymous heroine (Ellen Page) finds herself pregnant and decides to have her baby adopted. She picks childless Vanessa Loring (Jennifer Garner) and her husband Mark (Jason Bateman) as the recipients. Against the advice of family and friends, Juno bonds with Mark and spends a lot of time with him in his version of the Man Cave, his basement. Interestingly, however, Mark has not asked for this space: his wife has caused the Cave to come into being as she will not allow his things – books, music, ephemera – to clutter the rest of her perfect house. Mark's sojourn in the basement is enough to tell the audience that there is trouble in the marriage, even before he makes a semi-pass at Juno and admits he does not want a child. By locating his identity in the basement with his music collection, comic books and guitars, memorabilia from his earlier, college days, Vanessa has unwittingly encouraged Mark to see himself still as a single guy, rather than part of a couple about to have a baby. While the Man Cave usually can be seen acting as a safety valve, then, by allowing mess and sloppy behavior within a single circumscribed zone in the house, in this case the quarantining has the undesired effect of making Mark long for an entire apartment of – and on – his own.

In the homme-com, the Man Cave often expands to embrace the whole domicile, especially when single men are the focal point of the narrative. In *The Forty Year Old Virgin*, Andy Stitzer (Steve Carell) has collections of action figures, giant chairs on either side of a console for video gaming, exercise equipment and cardboard movie character standees enough to rival the contents of Sydney's Cave, but there is a significant difference: he keeps his apartment spotlessly tidy. In Andy's case, his borderline-obsessive neatness correlates with his virgin status: his respect for his own surroundings chimes with his extensive, and distancing, courtesy towards women. As a final example, Ben in *Knocked Up* (Judd Apatow

2007) lives with four male friends in a house that has totally been given over to Cavehood. The guys are shown in an extended montage hanging out, inventing elaborate modes of smoking dope, playing sports, diving in their filthy swimming pool, and dancing; they enjoy sitting on their filthy couch watching porn. It is a sign of an encroaching maturity that Ben eventually moves out of this house and into an apartment on his own; though he can truly be himself in the house with his friends, it is a self he needs to leave behind. While the Man Cave exists as just one room, to be visited occasionally, it can be a safety valve; when it is the only place you live, it threatens to hinder maturity and development.

Sydney's Man Cave, then, is a place for him to be alone, or with other male friends having fun. Its barring of women coupled with its function as a "place where he jerks off" underlines the fact that Sydney goes there to be (and play with) himself, away from appraising or judging eyes. This underlines the Man Cave's function a place of authenticity, identity, where Sydney can afford to let out his true self. It can also be seen as a place of immaturity, since masturbation occurs there and this is a form of sex most frequently associated with youth or youthful behavior, as films as diverse as *American Pie* (Chris and Paul Weitz 1999) and *American Beauty* (Sam Mendes 1999) attest.

The Man Cave in its emphasis on authenticity thus differs from the Lair, which, although similarly a space, like the Cave, harmoniously divided into zones for male enjoyment, is a place catering to, and aspiring to attract, the female. The bachelor of the mid-century Hollywood sex comedies attempts to lure his prey to the Lair, hoping that the combination of *its* powerfully persuasive atmosphere with *his* seductive wiles will be enough to conquer her resistance. Although both Man Cave and Lair thus exist for sex, the Lair is for sex *partnered*, rather than sex *solus*.

The Lair

If the Man Cave symbolizes authenticity and identity, the Lair, by contrast, can be seen as emblematic of performance and spectacle. In film, the Lair is found most often in the sex comedies of the mid-1950s to mid-1960s, but is also sometimes apparent in melodramas of the same period. It seems to owe much to the fantasy apartments conjured up in the pages of *Playboy* magazine, which began publishing in the same year that Kinsey published his "Report" on women, 1953.

From its first issue, *Playboy* sought to underline the primacy of its fantasy space of seduction; while other activities are dealt with in its pages, the magazine is largely given over to instructions on ways to impress, so as ultimately to undress, women: "We like our apartment. We enjoy mixing up cocktails and an hors d'oeuvre or two, putting a little mood music on the phonograph and inviting in a female for a quiet discussion on Picasso, Nietzsche, jazz, sex" (Anon. 1953: 3).

Playboy's articles help instruct the reader on how to lure women to the Lair, and what to do with them once there. It was only a matter of time, therefore, before it also issued guidelines on what this Lair would be like. Across the September and October issues for 1956, it produced outlines for "Playboy's Penthouse Apartment" and these seem to have had a major impact on the Hollywood version of the Lair.[2] The 1956 Penthouse has been carefully designed to provide fluid, open-plan spaces, which can be sculpted into different arenas, depending on the guest or guests being entertained: " … there are two basic areas, an active zone for fun and partying and a quiet zone for relaxation, sleeping *and such*" (italics mine; Anon. 1956a: 65). The plans build in space for gatherings of hi-fi enthusiasts, poker games – both "stag and strip" (Anon 1956b: 60) – and post-theater suppers, as well as the more intimate scenes of seduction. For *these* occasions, the apartment is fitted with carefully placed amenities and discreet push-button devices that will not break the mood or scare off the hunter's prey. Silently, lights dim and curtains draw. Furthermore, the bar is located in the living room so that, when glasses need topping up, there is "No chance of missing the proper psychological moment – no chance of leaving her cosily curled up on the couch with her shoes off and returning to find her mind changed, purse in hand, and the young lady ready to go home, damn it" (Anon. 1956b: 59).

Describing the main living area, *Playboy* notes the construction of spectacle and interest through the presence of different *surfaces*:

The smooth plaster wall is in dramatic contrast to the stone hearth, which has a painting on its right and a raised planter with climbing vine on its left. The apartment's sense of masculine richness and excitement stems in part from such juxtapositions of textures – the smooth wall, the stone, the planter, the cork floor – and for visual impact the unadorned brick wall which closes off the bath and kitchen area. Turn to the window wall. Here's drama and contrast again, a view of the city through casements richly hung with white dacron and slate gray silk shantung overdrapes. (September 1956, 57)

As will be seen, the unadorned brick wall and the picture window are highly visible features of the Lairs in films of the period, indicating how dominant the *Playboy* vision of the bachelor pad became in cinema.

Furthermore, although the whole of the apartment would seem to present its dweller with an urban paradise, the 1956 designs yet insist that such an indoor Eden needs one final facility:

Even a bachelor in his own domain needs a place like our apartment's study, where he can get away from the rest of the house and be really alone, where if he wishes he can leave papers on the desk in seeming disarray … This is the sanctum sanctorum, where women are seldom invited, where we can work or read or just sit and think while gazing into the fireplace. (Anon. 1956a: 70)

I find this paragraph particularly fascinating. What makes this inner sanctum so special? Is it the possibility of permitting clutter in here, as in no other corner of the apartment, since here the Lair owner can leave his papers lying around messily? Or could it be the fact that "women are seldom invited" here? This final zone, providing a space for masculine introspection, underlines the fact that the rest of the apartment is a stage, a place for performance, for the *public* acting out of the seemingly *private* persona *Playboy* has conceived. The Lair itself then requires a 1950s' version of the Man Cave, although, unlike the contemporary Cave with its "jerk-off" station, *Playboy* seems to hold this as the one locale in the apartment where sexualized activity is inappropriate.

Playboy seems thus to anticipate the concept of the Man Cave; furthermore, it foreshadows it not only here in devising an inner sanctuary but also in the interior detail picked up on by George Wagner, when he notes of the first plans: "The primal theme of the male as hunter is further pursued in the decor: 'One entire wall is decorated with bold and vigorous primitive paintings reminiscent of the prehistoric drawings in the caves of Lascaux" ' (Anon., 1956a: 70; Wagner 205). Thus it is possible to suggest that *Playboy* not only popularized the notion of the bachelor Lair, but also of the Man Cave too. While the magazine's siting of the one within the other seems superfluous, it actually attests to the faux-private, actually performative, space of the Lair, which thus still needs the *actually* private locus of the Cave to provide the final amenity.

While this bachelor's paradise is generally confined to romantic comedies, as previously noted, it is occasionally also observed, perhaps as a warning to young ladies, in melodramas. *The Best of Everything* (Jean Negulesco 1959) presents the perfect example of the bachelor lounge: deep-carpeted for noisy or for quiet fun, possessing a picture window revealing the ever-changing city, it also has that wall of plain brick, here hung with plain blocks of contrasting colors. The sensuous overload of this décor, combined with low music and the skilled administration of Dexter, the Lair-owner – perhaps the *Laird*? – has the maiden, April, soon succumbing. Because this is a melodrama and not a romantic comedy, this is generically permissible, and also inevitably punished by her pregnancy and Dexter's betrayal. Women of the lighter genres such as sex comedies who are exposed to such storms of sensual arousal via design are generally either rescued through some third-act revelation, or are not the heroine – and therefore do not matter. Thus the mid-century sex comedies evince a disregard for the multiple disposable women: a disregard that, as will be seen, is also present in the contemporary homme-coms.

Examples of the Lair in the sex comedy stress both its modernity as fully automated and its theatricality as a space of spectacularized seduction. The Lairds do as well as they do with women because of the spaces they own to do it *in*. *Playboy's* contrasting textures and surfaces are found in the apartment of Brad Allen in *Pillow Talk*, as the film employs the plain brick wall used as a contrasting background for Brad's collection of modern art. The apartment is also governed by the active/quiet zone and push-button automation principles cited

Figure 10.2   Horner's Lair (*Under The Yum Yum Tree*, USA, 1963; director, David Swift; producer, Frederick Brisson. Columbia Pictures).

in the magazine: doors lock, a bed unfurls from a couch, and the record player commences to play mood music all at the flick of a switch.

Laird Hogan (Jack Lemmon) in *Under The Yum Yum Tree* (David Swift 1963) goes one musical step further. Where Brad has a switch to make records start to play, Hogan has *violins* emerge from a case and they begin synchronized serenading. His couch is a circular affair sunken in the middle of the room, while the huge waterbed occupies pride of place on a dais, and *everything* is a deep engorged red, including Hogan's socks (see Figure 10.2). In *Come Blow Your Horn* (Bud Yorkin 1983) the lavish apartment belonging to Alan Baker (Frank Sinatra) has the huge picture window of the ever-changing city with which to beguile female guests, as suggested by *Playboy*'s guidelines, as well as different levels to his apartment to reinforce the idea of different zones.

By the time of *How To Murder Your Wife* (Richard Quine 1965), the Lair has become so much a feature of the sex comedy that it is almost acknowledged as a character in its own right. At the start of the film, the manservant of Lair-owner Stanley Ford (Jack Lemmon) proudly takes us on a tour of the place. Addressing himself solely to "gentlemen" because he assumes the title of the picture has frightened their wives into staying away from the picture, butler Charles (Terry Thomas) proudly shows us around the facilities, including the terrace, living room – again with those plain brick walls for contrast – and bathroom. And everywhere there is no taint of the feminine, a point Charles gleefully emphasizes: "Notice if you will the complete absence of a so-called woman's touch, no gay little chintzes, no big gunky lamps … everything masculine *and perfect*. In fact, the sort of place you could have had … ah, if only you'd had the sense *not* to get married!

While, then, the Lair is the stage for the performance of the role of urban bachelor, the Man Cave has no such outward-looking dimensions. It is, by contrast, concerned with privacy and authenticity, with letting the real man out.

Although the 1956 *Playboy* directives might state that its ideal bachelor apartment was a place "styled for a man of taste and sophistication ... *his* place, to fit his moods, suit ... his needs, reflect his personality" (Anon. 1956a: 70), there is very much a sense that most of this space is an arena for the public performance of a persona, for the "reflection" of the bachelor persona for an audience, rather than the sanctum sanctorum, the place where he can go to be alone. For that purpose, *Playboy* recognizes the need for a Man Cave, since this space, whether in a finely appointed bachelor pad, hippy garage or suburban garden shed, is the place the man can go to be himself, although also allowing a more social gathering if the Cave dweller is feeling gregarious. It should be acknowledged, however, that any visitors will be of the same sex as the Caveman – remember that, unlike the Lair, "no women allowed in here" – and having guests of this single-sex seems to mean that he still does not have to put on a performance. One presumes Sydney or other Cave dwellers would not take work clients or a potential boss there; it is a place where he can relax either alone or with men *like him*, men who enjoy playing loud music, drinking beer, expertly plying both bong and games console: men, in other words, who *are* Sydney. While the Man Cave is a place of male exclusivity, then, it is also a place of narcissism.

The Lair therefore connotes the public and priapism; the Cave implies the private and solipsism. I would like to go further and suggest that the Lair can be seen representing "romance" and the Cave "sex." While obviously the goal of the Laird is to lure his prey there *for* sex, the very performance he puts on in order to seduce her, with soft music and lighting, sensuous surroundings, flattering attention, constitutes, *is*, romance. The Cave by contrast provides no seduction: possessing no switches or push-buttons, no artfully contrasting textures to beguile, its paraphernalia is restricted to the condoms openly stocked by Sydney for prolonging his own solitary enjoyment.

It is tempting to conclude the Cave represents the juvenile and the Lair the mature, but I think this would be wrong. *Both* locales are in fact condemned as immature in their various narratives. By their films' conclusions, most of the Lair-Lotharios give up their bachelor pads for the shared home their new couple-status requires, either leaving entirely, as Alan does in *Come Blow Your Horn*, or eradicating the Lair's traces. *Pillow Talk*'s Brad invites Jan to redecorate his apartment, hoping she will realize this is his subtle way of leaving bachelorhood behind and sub-mitting to marriage. Charles' master Stanley Ford also suffers the indignity of having his Lair redecorated by his wife: his is overrun with the gay chintzes and gunky lamps formerly missing. Only Hogan remains unrepentant and *in situ*.

As for Sydney, if he were the central hero of *I Love You, Man* he would be forced to leave his Cave at the film's conclusion, since he would inevitably have gained a partner. As he is the *second* male lead, however, he can enjoy his Cave a little longer. The true hero of the film, Peter, is already mature enough to be sharing his space with a woman. He does not need a Cave, a space for solo sexual activity, because, though he does admit to masturbating on one occasion, it is at home inspired by a photo of his fiancée. Even when she is physically absent, therefore, Zooey is present in image. She is not excluded from the sexualized space, but lives in it all the time. She therefore fares better than the prey of the Laird who is expected to leave after a night of passion.

Both Lair and Man Cave are therefore sites of masculine immaturity, but only the newer version of this macho space seeks to eliminate the presence of women. It fascinates me that both locales appear in concert with a "double standard." Although the newer films admit, as their 1950s' and 1960s' counterparts try both simultaneously to acknowledge and disavow, that women do have sexual urges and experiences, *which women* are allowed in these homme-coms to have sex is a moot point.

Homme-coms

I have been reading the Man Cave as emblematic of the recent cycle in Hollywood romantic comedy, the homme-com. But what made a space that was dedicated to sex in this way necessary? Why did the homme-com itself arise? To answer these questions, a look at the prevailing tenor of the genre before the new cycle's emergence is necessary.

As I have previously suggested (Jeffers McDonald 2007, 2009), from the 1980s, contemporary romantic comedy saw a steady eradication of sex as motor for the humor. Ignoring the use that such 1970s' films as *Annie Hall* (Woody Allen 1977), *An Unmarried Woman* (Paul Mazursky 1978), and *Starting Over* (Alan J Pakula 1979) made of sexual matters for comedy, subsequent films entered a sexual-comic drought. Unfortunately, this dry season also coincided with a new association of the genre with female concerns, stars and audiences. The two trends became inextricably linked: rom-coms appeared both female-centric and sex-free. During this time a sex scene was usually *unseen*, generally because it was not narrativized. If it was, as rarely, permitted, it usually took place in an ellipsis. In *How To Lose A Guy In 10 Days* (Donald Petrie 2003) dueling lovers Andie and Ben spar, fight, connive and generally enjoy being horrid until a sudden moment of tenderness catches them unprepared. While many instances of the lovers behaving badly to each other have been shown, by contrast, once they embrace, the camera pans diplomatically out of the window. This discreet camera operates with equal bashfulness across many other rom-coms of the time. Of course, this coyness is not a complete innovation: the same kind of concentration on courtship and foreplay, and avoidance of actual intercourse, is present in the screwball comedies of the 1930s' also. But the screwballs were made under the Production Code; the new coyness of the rom-coms cannot, by contrast, be attributed to prohibition or legislation.

The *homme-coms*, beginning with Doug Liman's 1996 comedy *Swingers*, set out to reintroduce the sexual element to the romantic comedy after this enforced drought. *Homme-coms* return sex to the romance, allowing the desirous body and its acts and exigencies to become again a source for onscreen humor. However, that this emphasis on sex is clearly linked to a male perspective creates as many problems as it solves. The comedy in these films tends to arise from *male* physiological sources and worries. Premature ejaculation is as frequent as the neurosis that there will be no ejaculation. Besides the humor caused by sexual malfunction, these films also manage to find comic mileage in scatological sources, punishing everyone from ex-boyfriends of the heroine to the hero himself – but never the woman – with ferocious bouts of diarrhea. The women in homme-coms are thus generally blocked from participating in the messy, gross-out moments that make up much of the comedy in these films. Furthermore, just as the women seem above bodily functions for comedy in such films, they also seem above the fulfillment of sexual desire. These contemporary romantic comedies routinely minimize the occurrence and thus the importance of sex to their heroines. By then also minimizing the importance of the women who *do* have sex they also serve to indicate that sexual activity is not a female-appropriate goal, or at least not an appropriate goal for the heroine.

Although happily employing the zeitgeist in other ways, then, the contemporary homme-com cycle can be seen to reintroduce the older double standard in the operating of its sexual politics. Women thus seem either to be placed on a pedestal that reserves them as objects, rather than subjects, of desire, *and* keeps them far away from humor, or are allowed to participate in both the knockabout mess and the sex, but at the expense of narrative importance and longevity, as will be seen in the discussion below. One director who seems to be aware of, and trying to correct, these problems is John Hamburg. As someone closely involved in the writing of his homme-com projects as well in their direction, Hamburg can be considered responsible for their contents. In this chapter I want to highlight another of his films alongside 2009's *I Love You, Man*, exploring how both exemplify the problems and developments in this recent cycle, and suggesting that Hamburg can be seen trying to work towards a parity in sexual matters which means the heroine can be assured equality in desire, fulfillment *and* comedy.

John Hamburg's first foray into homme-com, *Along Came Polly* (2004), has both its successes and failures in trying to overcome the problems outlined above. It does both narrativize and spectacularize Polly's desire, permitting her a sexual past and present without punishing her. But Polly is never the agent of the film's *comic* moments, as a short recap attests.

Brand-new divorcé Reuben Feffer (Ben Stiller) goes with best friend Sandy Lyle (Philip Seymour Hoffman) to an art exhibition and meets a former high school friend, Polly Prince (Jennifer Aniston). Just as Polly and Reuben seem to be hitting it off, Sandy tells his friend they must leave immediately because he has "sharted":

REUBEN: I don't know what that means.
SANDY: I tried to fart, and a little shit came out, I just sharted.

Reuben's response is to tell him: "You are the most disgusting person I have ever met in my life." The narrative ensures he will shortly be punished for this remark: when Reuben takes Polly out to dinner, she picks a restaurant where the food is very spicy. Going back to Polly's apartment, Reuben, who has irritable bowel syndrome, excuses himself to the bathroom and tries to relieve his bowels, but disaster strikes as he blocks the toilet and runs out of paper – just as the alarmed Polly comes in to check on him. This moment of abjection is the film's punishment for Reuben's disgust at Sandy's predicament earlier. While he would often like to forget the fact, the narrative of the film constantly reminds Reuben that he possesses an unruly body, as in another scene where he and Polly begin to have sex and Reuben, over-aroused, climaxes much too quickly.

While this first example of Hamburg's foray into romantic comedy incorporates many well-established tropes of the genre, such as the inevitable public act that heals the equally inevitable (and rather flimsily engineered) break-up, it also secures its place within the new homme-com cycle by focusing on the man's point of view, his desire for true love, his nervousness about everything from contemporary dating rituals to sexual performance with a new partner. *Along Came Polly* also incorporates the moments of gross-out comedy caused by physical outbursts and eruptions that tend to mark the homme-com, reveling in its own display of somatic unruliness.

However, there are clearly two strands to the comedy in *Along Came Polly*. One strand involves Sandy and Reuben, and often ends in gross out, while the other involves Polly and Reuben, often also ending with physical comedy but of a different order, as in the scenes where the two have sex, or attempt to dance salsa. Sandy and Polly are similar characters in that they both are relaxed and freewheeling, in touch with their bodies, their own urges and desires. Both invoke the screwball trope of the more relaxed, wacky partner acting upon, loosening up, the uptight persona here played by Reuben, who has to learn to stop thinking and start feeling. But while both are involved in physical humor, Polly's comic scenes revolve around her bodily control and Reuben's lack thereof, his frequents failures to match her – he can neither dance nor have sex with the same degree of skill. Sandy, by contrast, acts as a watershed, an abject level to which Reuben never sinks even in his lowest moments. Polly is therefore *above* mess and chaos, even if she evokes these things in Reuben, while he, even as he descends into them, never declines as far as the point Sandy inhabits *below* him.

Although *Along Came Polly* is not entirely successful in allowing its lead female to participate in the film's comedy, at least not in the messy moments that provoke much of the loudest laughter, the film does, unlike many other homme-coms, grant Polly some sexual agency and desire. As will now be seen, in this she fares better than many of the other heroines in this new cycle.

Judd Apatow's landmark 2005 film *The 40 Year Old Virgin* subverts some expectations by indicating that it is not its male hero, Andy Stitzer (Steve Carell), who is desperate to lose his innocence. Instead, his experienced work colleagues are the ones who cannot bear his virginity, although eventually they all admit they are saddened at the wasted energies they have devoted to meaningless sex. The film rewards Andy with a sensitive, intelligent and patient woman whom he eventually marries. However, along the way it presents less palatable pictures of female sexuality, one of which especially highlights the homme-com's problems with permitting women sexual desire. Nicky (Elizabeth Banks) is one of Andy's attempted pickups; despairing of his virginity, at the end of the film he finally goes to her apartment. His male friends arrive to prevent him from taking the desperate step, despite having urged it on him all the way through the film, on the grounds that Nicky is "a freak." From her behavior, this freakiness seems to consist solely of being sexually aroused and masturbating. Although the film presents numerous other women throwing up, passing out, taking drugs, being vulgar, and propositioning Andy, its greatest distaste seems to be reserved for Nicky's arousal, allowing the scene of her enthusiastic self-pleasuring to roll on while the men watch in horror.

I Now Pronounce You Chuck And Larry presents Adam Sandler and Kevin James, playing heterosexual fire-fighters who pretend to be a gay couple in order to gain the financial benefits of marriage. The film invokes the masquerade plot of the 1950s' and 1960s' sex comedy, updating it with this *overt* homosexual twist, and introducing a potential love interest for Chuck, the Sandler character, his lawyer Alex (Jessica Biel). Because she believes Chuck is gay, Alex can be totally relaxed with him, letting him see the real her. And because he can't try his usual wiles and patter to seduce her, due to his masquerade, Chuck has time to see her as a person and finally learns how to love. Sex-wise, this is all fine for Chuck and the multiple women he is seen bedding in the early parts of the film, but Alex is not permitted any sexual satisfaction. The explosion of the imposture simultaneously makes him eligible and ineligible – the former as actually straight, but the latter as a liar. Only at the very end of the film does the pair reunite but there are no scenes of their sexual union.

The heroine of *Good Luck Chuck* fares a little better, as she is permitted a single night with her lover during the main narrative trajectory. Unlike the other sex scenes in a film of many sex scenes, however, this is not shown. The audience witnesses the pair's attraction for each other and eventual foreplay but the camera pans coyly to the floor once they get into bed. At precisely the point it has previously started gleefully rolling.

The split between the good girl who *doesn't* and the bad girl who *does* is perhaps made most manifest in the Farrelly Brothers' *Heartbreak Kid*. In this film, Eddie (Ben Stiller) meets and swiftly marries Lila (Malign Ackerman) but discovers after the wedding that she has many disagreeable characteristics she had hidden from him. On his honeymoon, while still regretting his marriage, he meets another woman, Miranda (Michelle Monaghan) who seems perfect, but the film's commitment to farcical action and slapstick mess rather than traditional rom-com closure ensures that, although they love each other, they never manage to get together during the film's running time. The film thus preserves the dichotomy between the for-keeps love-object who gets no sex, and the temporary woman who does.

Forgetting Sarah Marshall (Nicholas Stoller 2008) is interesting in that it challenges the new cycle's convention that the heroine will not have sex with the hero during the narrative running time. However, it maintains the general rule that sex with the significant other will not be played for laughs. When Peter (Jason Segal) and Rachel (Mila Kunis) get together, the scene is narrativized as punishment for Peter's ex-girlfriend, Sarah (Kristen Bell), who is in the hotel room next door, listening, and similarly having sex with her new beau. Sarah perceives this as a challenge and screams, whoops and moans in order to outdo her ex, but this backfires on her: not only does the comedy in the scene come at her expense, underlining her shallow, selfish personality, but her faking alienates her partner who leaves her because of the pretence. The film thus unusually puts the intercourse on screen, but in juxtaposing sex-with-affection between Peter and Rachel with Sarah's sex-as-narcissistic-revenge, it oddly manages to purify the former act.

Thus, few of these exemplar films show the central *romantic* couple engaged in sex, and none in *sex for comedy*. This seems odd when other sexual encounters are permitted such visual and comic emphasis. What these examples indicate is that the new homme-coms have returned to the 1950s' double standard, again judging men and women differently for their sexual behavior. The twenty-first century homme-coms resurrect the double standard and the concomitant dichotomy of female types, their narratives again supplying multiple, disposable women who can be used for sex and comedy, and contrasting them with a lead female, who ensures the generically necessary happy ending but won't be involved in onscreen sex – at least for comic purposes. This leads to the situation in which meaningless sex is shown and played for laughs, but supposedly meaningful sex is rarely shown at all. Like Sydney's Man Cave, the homme-com thus excludes women from the space of desire and sexual agency, as well as from the locus of humor. Not only does this echo the timid way that traditionalist rom-coms handle sex – by discreetly panning away as the couple go into an intimate clinch – but it works to suggest that sexual fulfillment is an inappropriate goal for self-respecting women – just as material from the era of the "double standard" did.

Conclusion

I want to return, in conclusion, to both *I Love You, Man* and to my statement that the Lair connotes romance while the Man Cave means sex. These twin locales can be seen as twin impulses within romantic comedy that need joining; the female-focused side of the hero who indulges in romantic behavior needs to be united with the comic masturbating loner. In achieving this union, *I Love You,*

Man can act as an exemplar text, as it attempts to fuse the two aspects within the homme-com, the romantic and the comically sexual, through its dual males, Peter and Sydney, *and* manages to get rid of the double-standard problem present in so many other homme-coms too.

A scene from the beginning of the film exemplifies this more egalitarian approach to the relations between the sexes. Peter has just proposed to Zooey; in the car driving home she calls her two best girlfriends and puts them, unbeknownst to the pair, on speakerphone. Denise (Jaime Presley) and Hailey (Sarah Burns) react happily to the news, marveling at the fact that Peter has booked for the wedding and reception a place in Santa Barbara where he and Zooey had enjoyed an earlier date. "He is SO romantic!" they agree, before Hailey muses, "That's the place you guys fucked for the first time, right?" Denise and Hailey debate the details of this first encounter, before Hailey affirms, "No ... that was just oral. You had your period in Santa Barbara and you wanted to wait. God, you're so old-fashioned, Zooey!" While the listening Peter is still absorbing the fact that his wife-to-be evidently discusses his sex life with her gal pals, there is more to come. Zooey, trying to turn the conversation from matters sexual, remarks that the wedding is quite soon but – "Who cares?" demands Denise. "Peter's a real doll and he goes down on you like six times a week." "Yeah," endorses Hailey. "Marry him. Don't wait. Lock that tongue down, girl."

From the film's start, then, it is evident that Peter is being held up as the romantic one; he is driven to making the proposal perfect, picking the right location, going down on one knee, choosing an expensive ring, booking the ideal meaningful location for the wedding and reception; and his fiancée and her best girlfriends are the ones who are foul-mouthed, brisk and blatant about sex, pragmatically recognizing the rarity of a man who will give frequent oral pleasure without expecting a quid pro quo. The film provokes laughter at the women for being so outrageously blunt in their appraisals while at the same time forcing audience members to rethink their gender and genre assumptions – are men always the less romantic ones?

The film's characters are more complex than they appear. Sydney, although wealthy and leisured, seems to have as his major achievement the creation of the Man Cave, a space where women may not be. While Sydney seems superficially to have life sorted out, this compartmentalizing attitude to women is eventually shown to be immature. Sydney is not a lifestyle guru, as Peter originally thinks, but a man-boy who inhabits the role of id to the more uptight Peter's ego; like Sandy to Reuben, Sydney is there to mess up Peter's overly tidy life, make him less set in his ways, more spontaneous, but the film does not imply that Sydney has all the right ideas about life and love. His insistence on masturbating wearing a condom – it lasts longer and there's no mess to clean up afterwards, he notes defensively – indicates a form of pathology in his life from which Peter is blissfully free.

In many other rom-coms, Peter, the slightly wimpy, kind, cute, romantic guy would be the "Wrong Partner" in Steve Neale's formulation (1992, 289).

The Wrong Partner is the one who the heroine has at the start of the film, until she meets the Alpha Male with whom she is destined to be. In Hamburg's rom-com universe, however, Peter is permitted to be the Right Partner: Zooey is seen to be better off with a guy in touch with his feminine side who understands and loves her, than an aggressive bully like the one married to her friend Denise.

Not only, then, does *I Love You, Man* happily confound the typical character types of the rom-com – it also subverts the now-established patterns of the homme-com, binding the women more closely into the comedy derived from sexy situations, allowing them to voice their desires and their satisfaction when they are fulfilled. In this way, Hamburg's most recent homme-com sets out to address the problems of the cycle directly. As in his earlier *Along Came Polly*, he admits the female characters are driven by the need for sexual fulfillment just as men are, but here he also binds them more closely into the humor of the film through a clever reversal of expectations. Hamburg takes the ruling principle of the homme-com cycle itself – that men want romance and love and snuggling, worry about dating etiquette and what to wear and when to call, *just like women* – but then supplies the counter-shot to the gaze at the males that has largely been missing in the cycle until now: he shows that women talk dirty, share sex details, are crude and explicit, *just like men*.

There are signs that since *I Love You, Man*, the standard rom-com has started to incorporate sex back into its narratives, without punishing women who "*do*." For example, films that concentrate on the woman's story, such as *The Rebound* (Bart Freundlich 2009), which once would have employed that discreet camera in its intimate scenes, instead resolutely focuses its gaze on the sexual moments in the relationship between Sandy (Catherine Zeta-Jones) and her "manny" (Justin Bartha), and plays them for laughs, such as the scene where they are having sex on the couch, and suddenly realize that her young son is watching with interest. Similarly, *Going The Distance* (Nanette Burstein 2010) permits long-distance lovers Erin (Drew Barrymore) and Garrett (Justin Long) to have sex, talk about sex, attempt phone sex, and then have tabletop sex, all with the blessing of the generic happy ending and without implied disapproval of the woman. *No Strings Attached* (Ivan Reitman 2011) and *Friends With Benefits* (Will Gluck 2011) similarly allow their respective heroines to have sex both for comedy and for keeps.

At the same time as the more traditionally female-focused rom-com has started to reincorporate sexual humor into its mix, the male-centered comedy seems to be sloughing off its more romantic overtones, maintaining the "hard R"-rated language and humor but avoiding entanglement in the emotional issues of its characters with which earlier homme-coms had been preoccupied. *The Hangover 2* (Todd Phillips 2011) supplies the male "Wolfpack" buddies with cipher female partners but maintains the narrative around the boys as they repeat their previous amnesiac adventures, this time in a different country. Similarly, a look at two roles played by one of the frequent actors of the homme-com repertory company can further illustrate this new shift in the male-focused comedy.[3] Owen Wilson played the scheming playboy bachelor in *Wedding Crashers* who eventually ends up looking for true love. In *Hall Pass* (Farrelly Brothers 2011), however, Wilson now finds himself playing a character who tied the knot years ago, and is instead trying to create opportunities for extramarital sex. In this way the distance seems to have been maintained between the male- and female-oriented films, but whereas the *former* once blended sex and romance for comic purposes, now the *latter* often does, and the male-focused films frequently remove the emphasis on romance altogether.

I Love You, Man* may have succeeded so well as a homme-com that it may have killed off its own cycle. With female-centered rom-coms now happy to use sex for comedic purposes, is there still a need for the homme-com? I think there is, as long as there are Beta Males like Peter Klaven who would prefer to be romantic rather than raunchy. In the best possible scenario, there would be movies that speak to both men and women about love and sex, making everyone laugh, and obviating the need for either gender to retreat to a cave where the other sex is not allowed.

Notes

1. As evinced by this sample quotation, taken from *It's Time You Knew*, a guide for High School girls: "In the average, normal girl, [sex] longings come only once in a while, and they are considerably less intense than those with which the average male must contend [and] more easily controlled." (Shultz 1955: 90).
2. Further blueprints for bachelor pads occurred in later issues, as George Wagner (1996: 219) notes: "Between 1956 and 1970, *Playboy* published five commissioned designs for the bachelor's quarters."
3. *I Love You, Man*'s lead actors, Paul Rudd and Jason Segal, can be seen as part of this frequently-used set of actors which seem to belong to the cycle. Others would include Seth Rogen, Jonah Hill, Owen Wilson, Vince Vaughn … perhaps in keeping with the male focus of the cycle, women actors are not featured repeatedly.

References

Anon. (1953) Editorial, *Playboy* (December), p. 3.

Anon. (1956a) Playboy's Penthouse Apartment: A Second Look at a High, Handsome Haven – Pre-Planned and Furnished for the Bachelor in Town. *Playboy* (October), pp. 65–70.

Anon. (1956b) Playboy's Penthouse Apartment: A High, Handsome Haven – Pre-Planned and Furnished for the Bachelor in Town. *Playboy* (September), pp. 53–60.

Capp, Al (1962) The Day Dream. *Stage* (December), 72–3,136–7.

Collier, Joe Guy (2005) Man Cave: A Place to Call His Own. *Seattle Times* (August 10), http://seattletimes.nwsource.com/html/homegarden/2002546811_designmancave08.html (accessed May 18, 2012).

Evans, Roni (2004) Definition of "Man Cave", Urban Dictionary, http://www
.urbandictionary.com/define.php?term=man+cave (accessed May 18, 2012).

Jeffers McDonald, Tamar (2009) "Homme-com," in *Falling In Love Again: Romantic Comedy
in Contemporary Cinema* (eds. Stacey Abbott and Deborah Jermyn), I. B. Tauris, London,
pp. 146–159.

Jeffers McDonald, Tamar (2010) Performances of desire and inexperience: Doris Day's fluctuating filmic virginity, in *Virgin Territory: Representing Sexual Innocence in Film* (ed. Tamar
Jeffers McDonald), Wayne State University Press, Detroit, MI, pp. 103–22.

Kinsey, Alfred C., Pomeroy, Wardell B., Martin, Clyde E., and Gebhard, Paul H. (1953)
Sexual Behavior In The Human Female, W.B. Saunders Company, Philadelphia, PA.

Neale, Steve (1992) The big romance or something wild? Romantic comedy today.*Screen*,
33 (3), 284–99.

Paul, William (1995) *Laughing Screaming: Modern Hollywood Horror and Comedy*, Columbia
University Press, New York, NY.

Shultz, Gladys Denny (1955) *It's Time You Knew*, J.B. Lippincott Company, Philadelphia,
PA.

Wagner, George (1996) The lair of the bachelor, in *Architecture and Feminism* (eds. Debra L.
Coleman, Elizabeth Ann Danze, and Carol Jane Henderson), Architecture Press, New
York, NY, pp. 183–220.

Walker, Alexander (1968) The great American massacre: Rock Hudson and Co., in *Sex in
The Movies*, Penguin, London, pp. 231–51.

Further Reading

Osgerby, Bill (2001) *Playboys in Paradise: Masculinity, Youth and Leisure-Style in Modern
America*, Berg Publishers, Oxford. Examines the playboy ethos introduced into American culture in the mid-1950s.

Sorenson, Deborah (2008) Bachelor Modern: Mid Century Style in American
Film. *Blueprints* (Spring/Summer), http://www.nationalbuildingmuseum.net/pdf/
Blueprints/BachelorModern_BlueprintsSpSu08.pdf (accessed May 18, 2012). A fascinating illustrated article that examines the 1950s' association of "Modern" design,
including furniture and architecture, with the figure of the bachelor or playboy.

Wojcik, Pamela Robertson (2010) *The Apartment Plot: Urban Living in American Film and
Popular Culture, 1945 to 1975*, Duke University Press, Durham, NC. Robertson posits that
the significance of the apartment to many films is sufficient to make "the apartment
plot" a separate movie genre, and investigates various meanings of the apartment
space.

11

The Reproduction of Mothering

Masculinity, Adoption, and Identity in *Flirting with Disaster*

Lucy Fischer

Flirting with Disaster (written and directed by David O. Russell in 1996) adopts a comic attitude toward adoption. This is uncommon in the cinema, which has most often treated the subject within a melodramatic frame. Here one thinks of fiction dramas like *Penny Serenade* (Stevens 1941) about a childless couple's adoption of a daughter who later tragically dies. Or one considers a more contemporary work like *High Tide* (Armstrong 1987) about a woman who has abandoned a child at birth and then accidentally encounters her as a teenager. Other moving dramatic films have been told from the adoptee's point of view; *Secrets and Lies* (Leigh 1996), for instance, concerns a multiracial woman who seeks out her reluctant white birth mother.

Within the documentary realm, there are countless works on the subject that generally embrace a tone of poignancy, sentimentality, or even pathos – whether representing the struggles of adoptive parents, as in *Off and Running* (Opper 2009), or the parental search of the adopted child, as in *First Person Plural* (Borshay 2000), or the relationship between a parent who relinquished a child and the child who later tracks her down, as in *Finding Christa* (Billops and Hatch 1991).

As for feature-length film comedies, the subject of adoption makes a scant appearance. Here one thinks of Charlie Chaplin's *The Kid* (1921) in which The Tramp happens upon a forsaken infant and, being a kind soul, raises the child as his own. Much of the humor, of course, focuses on the mishaps of *male* parenting – thought ludicrous within the frame of 1920s' America. More recently, there is the case of *The Infidel* (Appignanesi 2010), a British movie about a devout middle-aged Muslim man who learns he is adopted only after his parents have

A Companion to Film Comedy, First Edition. Edited by Andrew Horton and Joanna E. Rapf.

died and, in researching his roots, realizes that he is Jewish. Much hilarity ensues as he prepares to meet his elderly birth father by trying to learn how to act Semitic. Currently, industry blogs gossip about Keenan Ivory Wayans' alleged plans to make a so-called adoption comedy[1] tentatively titled *It Takes a Village* about a white woman who adopts a baby from a Pacific Island and must bring the tribal elders home to her gated community in order for them to judge if she is a worthy guardian. Clearly, here, Wayans is satirizing high visibility adoptions from the Third World by white celebrities. Angelina Jolie, for instance, adopted children from Cambodia and Ethiopia between 2002 and 2005, and Madonna from Malawi between 2008 and 2009.

Despite the rarity of adoption as a subject for comedy, *Flirting with Disaster* proves it to be a highly fertile subject (albeit that adoption often results from infertility). Thus, an analysis of the film must proceed on two levels (which frequently intermix): one exploring the work's status as a comedy and the nature of the humor it produces; and another, investigating its insights not only into adoption but into having and being a child.

Flirting with Disaster tells the tale of Mel Coplin (Ben Stiller), a young man who has recently become a father. He has always known he is adopted but suddenly has a need to locate his birth parents, a quest that seems tied to his inability to name his son. (Interestingly, of course, adoption means that an adult legally gives his or her name to a child who has been born with another surname or none at all.) That the film will involve a comic quest for identity is signified in the opening moments as we hear a male voiceover (Mel's) talking, before we have even seen him – leaving the configurations of his person entirely unknown. He fantasizes about who may be his mother as we see images of women on the street that conform to the dimensions of his mind's eye: for instance a rich woman (imperious and smartly dressed), a rich and stupid woman (walking dogs and carrying shopping bags), or a poor and kind woman (toting roses for sale). He also considers who his father might be as we see a montage of different men on the street – though less detail is given in his musings to their specific types. Bringing the two together, he imagines his mother and father "hooking up" to conceive him, at which point we see a series of couples walking along – again from his point of view. This opening sequence sets the tone of the film in that *imagining* a family will prove as important as *having* one – and here Mel literally builds one from scratch. Interestingly, the definition for adoption talks of taking and rearing "the child of other parents *as one's own*."[2] The notion of "*as* one's own" seems to suggest some kind of play acting beyond its legal implications, and is thus consonant with Mel's inventive acts. Furthermore, the word *adoption* is derived from the Latin verb *optare*, which, among other things means "to wish" – again signifying, on some level, a creative impulse.

In Mel's case, the notion of imagining his parents is reality based, since he realizes that he is adopted. But, according to Freud, to some degree all children fantasize about this – even those assured that they know their roots. Early on,

Figure 11.1   Mel (Ben Stiller), Nancy (Patricia Arquette) and unnamed son (*Flirting With Disaster*; director, David O'Russell; producer, Dean Silvers).

Freud comments, "parents are … the only authority and the source of all belief," and the "child's most momentous wish during these early years is to be" them (Freud 1959: 74).[3] Eventually, however, the child "gets to know other parents and compares them with his own, and so comes to doubt the incomparable and unique quality which he has attributed to them." The child then engages in a "phantasy in which both parents are replaced by others of better birth" (Freud 1959: 76). While in most youngsters, this is but a passing stage, in neurotics, it develops into a more extreme version, the "family romance," which "takes over the topic of family relations." For adoptees, however, the "family romance" is not a fancy but a fact of life.

In his search for his birth parents, Mel soon consults the agency that originally handled his adoption and encounters Tina Kalb (Téa Leoni), a doctoral student in psychology who is working there as part of her dissertation research. She locates his birth mother, and the two tell Nancy (Patricia Arquette), Mel's wife (see Figure 11.1).

Mel is hell bent on making a road trip to find his mother and suggests that Tina come along (and document it for her thesis). While Nancy, who is struggling with post-partum weight gain, and doubts about her attractiveness, is immediately wary of chic, svelte, professional Tina, she agrees to the venture. As we learn, Tina's plan for recording events is to film them – which parodies the by-now-cliché video documentary charting an adoptee's parental search. In fact, there was, in 2009, an ABC documentary television show (based on an earlier Australian one), *Find My Parents*, in which "contestants" were filmed during their familial quest.[4] When Mel informs his adoptive parents, Pearl (Mary Tyler Moore) and Eddie (George Segal) Coplin of his intentions, all hell breaks loose. "Oh, my God! Why are you doing this?" Pearl cries, playing the martyr card. We begin to feel that Mel is "flirting with disaster" in two senses – disturbing the equilibrium of his nuclear family by searching for his birth parents, and threatening the health of his marriage by trifling with Tina – creating a bizarre *ménage á trois*. But the disasters to come are not of a melodramatic kind; rather, they are the stuff of farce.

This form of light comedy is characterized by improbable plot situations, exaggerated characters, slapstick elements, sexual misunderstandings and mix-ups (hence the term "bedroom" farce), and broad verbal humor. Derived from the Latin word for *stuffing*, farce signifies a lowly art form that is rather bloated or full of hot air. Already, in the five characters to which we have been introduced, we see the form's propensity for burlesque stereotype. Mel is an urban neurotic with sexual hang-ups and an inability to deal with being a parent until he finds birth parents of his own. In a sense then, *Flirting with Disaster* is a comic form of the *bildungsroman* – a story of a young person (usually male) seeking maturity. The root of the term comes from the word "to build," which reminds us that Mel has fabricated imaginary families in the movie's opening sequence. What is humorous about Mel's situation is that in order to move forward with his life he must move backward – returning not only to a childhood that he has never lived, but to his conception (as this is what determines his biological makeup). As for other stereotypes, Tina is a 30-year-old divorcee "desperate for a baby of her own," looking for an intelligent man to "impregnate her." Pearl and Eddie Coplin are classic, hysterical, smothering, Jewish parents. Pearl can't resist telling Nancy that she needs a support bra after childbirth (despite the fact that she herself has never been pregnant), and when Eddie learns that Mel's trip will take him to California, he immediately warns him about car bumpings in which drivers are mutilated and vehicles stolen. At one point, convinced that Mel is in trouble on his journey, the Coplins follow him uninvited and unannounced to his destination.

The exaggerated characters multiply as Mel launches his search and meets his birth mother, Valerie Swaney (Celia Weston) in San Diego (see Figure 11.2). She is a tall blonde who speaks with a Southern accent and informs Mel that she is of Finnish/Scottish extraction, a total contrast to Mel who is short and dark. She is a WASP conservative: a sketch of Ronald Reagan proudly hangs on her wall, and she brags of being the descendant of a Confederate general named Beauregard. (Later she and Nancy sing "Dixie" to the baby who Valerie calls a cute little "cracker.") When her college-age twin daughters arrive, they are statuesque, Aryan jocks who want to play beach volleyball with Mel. He immediately tries to fit into the family – stating that he intends to review his attitude toward Reagan, and that he will call his son Beau, in honor of the general. The Swaneys see family resemblances in Mel's demeanor: Valerie recognizes "something" in his eyes and forehead and tells him his "daddy was [also] short"; and the girls remark that his nose is like that of their uncle (a sexual pervert).

Soon, however, there is trouble in paradise. While Tina and Mel horse around, they crash into a shelf of glass animal figurines (*a Glass Menagerie*, perhaps); it falls and the contents break. Like a good mother, Valerie refuses Mel's offer to pay for the damage and responds with understanding: "All children break things and all is forgiven," she says, as though he were a child. However, when Valerie

Figure 11.2   Valerie Swaney (Ceilia Weston) photographed by Tina (Tea Leoni) (*Flirting With Disaster*; director, David O'Russell; producer, Dean Silvers).

casually mentions that Mel's birth date is 1963, he acts surprised, stating that he has always known it as 1965. Tina says she will call the adoption agency to clarify the situation and returns with the unhappy news that there has been a clerical error; Valerie is *not* Mel's birth mother. Clearly, this is one of the "improbable situations" for which farce is known. The atmosphere suddenly shifts. Valerie asks (looking at Mel) "Who *is* this man?" and requires that he reimburse her for the shelf.

Aside from slapstick and stereotypical characterization, what is funny in this sequence is what it reveals about the nature of our attitudes toward being parents or children. While Valerie *thinks* that Mel is her son and Mel that she is his mother, both are overcome by the illusion that there are family physical resemblances (while we can see there are none). Due to this narcissistic "will to believe," Mel also shape-shifts to conform to his new family – making us sense that his name relates to the word *meld* (to become merged). In this sense, he is, perhaps, a relative of Woody Allen's Zelig, a chameleon-like figure who changes to fit the historical or social circumstances (a Jew who impersonates a Nazi, a mental patient who impersonates a psychoanalyst).

Though we assume Mel to be an urban liberal (he is raised by New York Jews, after all), he now wants to reconsider his view of Ronald Reagan and takes new-found pride in being related to a Confederate general. Then, at the moment that Valerie and Mel learn that they are *not* related, all sense of connection instantly fades and they become strangers again. Hence, it seems that one's *sense* of being a parent or child is more a state of mind or a matter of faith than a biological fact. In a split second, the very individuals to whom we feel bound are suddenly meddlesome, burdensome, bothersome, aliens.

This process continues when Tina says that she has now found Mel's birth father, Fritz Boudreau (David Patrick Kelly) who lives in Michigan. So the road trip (which started in New York City) proceeds from suburban San Diego to the rust belt near Detroit – showing that the film involves not only a spiritual and genealogical journey but a geographical one as well that maps the entirety of the United States. Fritz is a macho, working-class truck driver and a former Hell's Angel whose first response to Mel's inquiry is to punch him (we suspect he is wanted by the law). When he learns the real reason for Mel's visit he affectionately calls him "turd face" and brags that he "dropped a lot of baby batter" around the time Mel was conceived. Mel immediately shape-shifts again, claiming that he has always wanted to drive a big rig (a fact that shocks Nancy who has never heard him mention it). He gets in the driver's seat ready for Fritz to give him a lesson. Soon, however, as Fritz learns that Mel is a scientist and surveys his appearance, his attitude changes. "You're not a bitch boy?" he inquires, and states that Mel has a "Jew look" about him (strange because, as Mel comments, he was only *raised* by Jews). Suddenly, Fritz recalls that the woman with whom he was involved at the time of Mel's conception ran off with another man who is probably Mel's real father, after all. Shocked, Mel mistakenly puts the car in reverse, steps on the gas, and backs the rig into a local post office. Once more, we have seen two individuals overcome by the *fantasy* of being biologically related – momentarily reconfiguring their lives and natures to fit the mold. Again, however, we see that chimera shattered and with it the feeling of manufactured connection. Of course, the fact that Tina has struck out again – introducing Mel to yet another faux parent – is another instance of the type of dodgy situation for which farce is known.

At this point both the road trip and the comedy take a narrative detour through the introduction of characters that do not further the story of Mel's search for his birth parents (though they do relate to issues of reproduction). Because of the truck accident, Mel is detained at the local police station where he is questioned by detectives Paul Harmon (Richard Jenkins) and Tony Kent (Josh Brolin). As it turns out (yet another implausibility), Nancy realizes that she and Tony went to high school together and the two reunite in warm friendship. Tony seems inordinately interested in the Coplin baby and immediately wants to hold and play with him. Paul gets annoyed at this and it soon becomes clear that the men are lovers who disagree about having or adopting a child themselves. When Nancy reveals that she will travel to New Mexico (at the suggestion of Fritz) to find Mel's birth mother, Josh suggests that he and Paul accompany the group and Nancy seems intrigued by the idea. Mel, however (sensing a past romance between the two) is decidedly not.

It is here that the erotic elements of the comedy (heterosexual, homosexual, and bisexual) begin to percolate – highlighting its status as *bedroom* farce. Even earlier, we have seen intimations of this. When Tina and Mel visit Valerie's home, they go off from the group into another room. Tina's camera lens is dirty and Mel helps her lift her skirt in order to use it as a lens wipe. He needs to bend down to do this in a position that has a distinctly sexual cast to it. Later, after Mel is released by Tony and Paul, Tina and the Coplins spend the night at a precious but suffocating B&B run by a boring, authoritarian, intrusive hostess. That evening, as Mel goes into the hall on his way to the bathroom (wearing only underwear), he encounters Tina who is also half-undressed, and the two share an impulsive, passionate, embrace. In so doing, they once again knock something over (another nod to slapstick) – this time a table, and abruptly part. The problem is, however, that Mel now has a hard-on, which Nancy notices upon his return to their room. He tries to cover over this by pouncing on her to have sex, but she resists, sensing that he cannot even look at her. Here, Mel's imagination veers toward a different sexual partner rather than a fantasized parent.

When Tina and the Coplins get to the airport (to add the Southwest to their geographical tour), they are followed by Paul and Tony, who have decided to come along. Their addition to the group reminds us of such farcical films as *The Pumpkin Race* (Louis Feuillade 1907) in which, as a comic chases progresses, it attracts more and more people, drawn apparently by some inexplicable magnetic force. On the airplane, Tony sits with Nancy and, as she breast feeds, he advises her on avoiding nipple irritation – a strange knowledge base for a childless gay man. Further back in the plane, Mel sits with Tina – jealous of the developing relationship between his wife and her long-lost friend. Paul wanders the plane not knowing where to sit – a fifth wheel. Thus, here, we have a proliferation of (what Paul calls) "illicit couples" to which we might add Valerie and the sire of her illegitimate child (who is *not* Mel) and Fritz and Mel's birth mother.

When the ménage-á-cinq gets to New Mexico, they travel to the home of Mel's *real* birth parents – the Schlichtings – Mary (Lily Tomlin) and Richard (Alan Alda) (see Figure 11.3). Significantly, everyone has problems pronouncing their name, which often takes the form of "Shit Kings" in the mouth of Pearl Coplin. This is additionally ironic, given that a name is what marks one as belonging to a family – be it biological or adoptive. So the group's comic struggles with pronunciation mirror their hapless effort to determine lineage. The use of a scatological pun is also evidence of how farce depends on broad verbal humor – and belongs to the category of low versus high art. To the caricatures (and potential parental candidates) of Southern Belle and White Trash we now must add Aging Hippie. (Thus, Mel is also like the hero of a picaresque novel who encounters people from every social stratum as he moves along.) Mary and Richard are "artists" (he makes bad metal sculptures and she ugly ceramic pots). When Mel gets excited about having creative roots and asks if they support themselves in this fashion, they mention sheepishly that they must "supplement" their income. When Mel asks why they gave him away at birth, they confess that they were in jail for manufacturing LSD. (We later learn that they still produce it in the form of stickers emblazoned with the image of Ronald Reagan who makes his second appearance in the film – now as an object of derision rather than worship.) Concerned about his parents' former drug use, Mel asks Mary if she took LSD while pregnant; she smiles coyly and jokes that she was relieved when he came out of the womb normal. Mel also learns that he has an adolescent brother, Lonnie (Glenn Fitzgerald) who, unfortunately, seems to be a sociopath.

Figure 11.3   Mel meets the Schlichtings (Lily Tomlin, Alan Alda) (*Flirting With Disaster*; director, David O'Russell; producer, Dean Silvers).

He looks like Edward Scissorhands and is inordinately jealous at Mel's arrival. When Lonnie learns that Mel is a scientist and so resembles his chemist father, he gets upset. Mary comforts him by saying: "Even if you were Jeffrey Dahmer we'd love you," and we suspect that he just might be. Lonnie tries to spike Mel's food with LSD but instead (due to another improbable happenstance), the food is served to Paul who sinks into a hallucinogenic morass. Part of the comedy involved in Lonnie's portrayal is that he is the product of living with his birth parents – supposedly the most normal and nurturing circumstance – and the one that might have been Mel's fate. But Lonnie emerges as a maladjusted miscreant, and Mel (raised by adoptive parents) as a reasonably healthy guy – despite his belief that his neuroses stem from being adopted. So much for sentimentalizing the biological family.

While Mel, Tina, and the Schlichtings have dinner, Nancy excuses herself and goes upstairs where she is followed by Tony who suggests that they shower together. After dinner, Mel comes upstairs and realizes that Tony and his wife are behind a closed bedroom doors. Distraught, he goes into Tina's room for comfort where the two begin to kiss. The sexual pairings and re-pairings have come to a head. Later, when Mel barges in on Nancy and Tony, he finds the latter licking his wife's underarm. He fears that the unsettling image will stay with him for the rest of his life.

At this point, the farcical circumstances spin out at a dizzying rate. Paul, emerging from his LSD trip, decides to arrest the Schlichtings for manufacturing drugs, at which point Lonnie knocks him out and Mary and Richard wheel him off into the desert unconscious. The Schlichtings clear out their drug lab and steal Mel's white rental car to escape, putting their paraphernalia in the trunk. Then the Coplins (who have tracked Mel down) arrive in an identical white rental car. As they come to the Schlichting's door, Pearl suddenly has cold feet about barging in on the group. The two return to the driveway but take off in the wrong white car (the one filled with drug gear). Shortly thereafter, the Schlichtings emerge and drive off in the Coplin's car with the goal of travelling to Mexico, thinking the automobile they are driving is the one whose trunk they have packed. Ultimately, the two cars collide (without either couple knowing who the other is). The Schlichtings (afraid of the law) race off leaving the Coplins holding the bag. As Eddie opens the trunk and discovers the bizarre paraphernalia, a police car arrives and we understand what their fate will be.

The next morning, Mel must get them out of jail – explaining to them and the police the strange mixups that have led to their wrongful arrest. Pearl is touched when he refers to them as his "parents." But, indicating that he still remains somewhat tied to the Schlichtings, Mel suggests to Nancy that they name their son Garcia, since his counter-culture birth parents were fans of the Grateful Dead. When the group leaves the jail, they encounter Tina in a heated discussion with Tony and Paul about adopting their own child (so the cycle continues into a new generation). At the close of the film the two Coplin couples plus Paul, Tina, and Tony pose for a group photograph. Then, as the credits roll, we see a series of couples making love: Pearl and Eddie embrace (but are interrupted by their crying grandchild); Mary straddles Richard (with Lonnie looking on) while chanting Tibetan phrases and ringing bells. Mel and Nancy frolic in bed. Thus, the film returns to the potential moment of conception (the genesis of Mel's quandary) – though we realize that only Couple #3 still has the biological wherewithal to initiate the procreative process. Furthermore, here, as in many recent comedies, the narrative "spills over" into the credits.

In sum, the film uses farce and satire to raise a series of complex issues in a humorous fashion. While Nancy Chodorow talked about the "reproduction of mothering," here we might better speak of the "reproduction of parenting."[5] Mel can't be a parent until he "re-produces" his own. In the same way that, at birth, *he* had no name (because he was disowned), he stalls in naming his son. His efforts to find his real parents are sabotaged not only by Tina's flaky research but by his own "will to believe" that he is the child of whomever is sequentially presented to him. The reproduction of parenting has further comic meaning in that the number of potential parents is continually re-produced – first we have Mel's fantasy parents on the street; then we have his adoptive parents; then we have Valerie; then we have Fritz; finally we have Mary and Richard and finally we have Paul and Tony. Expanding the number even further, when Mel calls Pearl from the B&B and its elderly proprietress shouts in the background, Pearl asks: "Is that tyrant your mother?"

As we have seen, the film also turns questions of nature vs. nurture on their head. Mel apparently looks like a Jew because he has been raised by Jews. Much of the comedy derives from the fact that, as he meets parental candidates, he tries to pretend that nature dominates (that he has always wanted to drive a rig, that he likes Reagan more than he had thought, that he is pleased to have been sired by artists), when the truth is that the manner in which he has been nurtured seems to be determinative (he is a liberal, urban, neurotic like the Coplins). The film also provides an ironic view of the "natural" versus "unnatural" family unit. While the Schlichtings, who live with their biological offspring, are dysfunctional, the Coplins have "coped" very well. Furthermore, the film questions traditional gendered views of parenthood. While Mel is a rather perfunctory father, leaving childrearing mostly to Nancy (who breastfeeds, carries the infant, and seems most concerned for his safety), Tony is fully comfortable with the maternal role – pressuring Paul to have a child, and studying up on such things as nursing, and the pros and cons of circumcision. His acceptance of the maternal function stands in strong contrast to Tina, who slaps Mel's face when he says that she reminds him of his mother (evidently the worst insult a woman can receive from a man).

Moreover, the film considers the role of chance in being a parent or child. In the opening sequence, when Mel is selecting strangers on the street as make-believe parents, he muses that, had he been raised by his birth parents, his life might have been totally different – and he might have married another person. Of course, we understand that, from a parental stance, there is just as much chance involved in birthing a child since the genetic combinations of eggs and sperm are endless. Thus, the same couple can breed a Lonnie or a Mel in the game of procreative Russian roulette. Here, of course, an adoptive parent has more power and selectivity in the process than a "natural" one, reminding us that another root of the term *adoption* is "to choose."

Finally, it seems important that in the one scene of the film depicting Nancy at work in a museum, she is preparing a statue of a Neanderthal man for exhibition. Hence, we assume that she (and Mel) are employed at some institution of "Natural History." In fact, in the same scene he shows her a tray of insects that they found on their first field trip together. In a sense, we can view the whole film as an attempt by Mel to chart his own "natural history" through a second "field trip" taken with Nancy. For just as we need to know that the Neanderthal is our ancestor in the "Family of Man," so Mel needs to trace that genealogy to his personal place on a family tree.

In closing, we might note that, while adoption comedies are rare within the feature film category, like all things cutting-edge, they proliferate on *YouTube*, which is, perhaps, the advance-guard of popular culture. Here, there are videos posted of stand-up comics who are adopted, doing bits about their situation. Jack Dee (2008) does one such routine, joking about how his parents did not tell him he was adopted until he was eighteen since they were waiting for Hallmark to produce an appropriate greeting card.[6] Similarly, Asian comic Andy Dawson riffs about being adopted by a Caucasian couple.[7] He jokes with the crowd about not seeing many Asians in the audience, and then says that this is okay because there were not a lot of Asians at home either. Alternately, some stand-up comics who are *not* adopted make jokes about celebrity adoptions. For instance, Robin Reiser does a bit in which she dreams that Brad Pitt and Angelina Jolie fight with Madonna over who will adopt her.[8]

Other videos on *YouTube* are parodies. One depicts Brad and Angelina looka-likes doing a public service announcement promoting Haitian adoption but, in the process, the comics burlesque the actors' own obsession with expanding their family.[9] As "Brad" shows pictures of children to adopt (ostensibly aimed at the viewers), "Angelina" reacts as though she is evaluating them for her own brood, saying about one, "too old," about a second, "too sad," and about a third, "I'll take it" – to which "Brad" responds that this is not an auction. He then claims that she probably can't even remember all the names of their current children, to which she says that she recalls all five (and he reminds her that there are six). Then as she reels off their names, she makes a mistake, calling one of them "Botox." At the end of the routine, she says she is going to India to get "one of those slumdog babies." On a similar note, in another video, British comic Mitch Benn sings a song titled "I want an African baby."[10] Some of its lyrics are as follows:

> I'm just *searchin'* for a third world *urchin'*
> Whose *poor* little life is a drag
> And such a *lovely* shade of brown
> That when I *take* him into town
> He'll *match* my shoes and bag.

In a final video, a potential father is interviewed by an adoption agent. The latter asks the man why he wants to be a parent. When he earnestly responds "I love children," the agent counters: "So – you're a sexual pervert?"[11]

Talk of *YouTube* parodies and stand-up comics reminds us of an old Rodney Dangerfield routine, typical for the comedian who claimed he got "no respect." The joke he tells goes: "When I was a kid my parents moved a lot, but I always found them."[12] While the gag is not meant to voice the complaint of an adoptee, it does so, nonetheless – speaking to the kind of pain felt by all those whose parents (either literally or figuratively) have been missing in action.

Notes

1. Rich, Katey/CinemaBlend (2010).
2. See www.Dictionary.com (n.d.).
3. Freud, Sigmund (1959: 74–8).
4. Bialczak, Mark (2009) or see www.findmyfamily.org/documentary.
5. Chodorow (1978).
6. See http://www.youtube.com/watch?v=4m45CX5LiC8 (accessed May 18, 2012).
7. See http://www.youtube.com/watch?v=xMYYPUyLhCg.
8. See http://www.youtube.com/watch?v=Y-KSMXPUQMs (accessed May 18, 2012).
9. See http://www.youtube.com/watch?v=3nSeS4kbfdY (accessed May 18, 2012).
10. See http://www.youtube.com/watch?v=FmSeK_xz7RY (accessed May 18, 2012).
11. See http://youtu.be/V5XWWM6gml8 (accessed May 18, 2012)
12. Rodney Dangerfield (n.d.).

References

Bialczak, Mark/Syracuse .com (2009) *CNY's Tim Green on TV Tonight with "Find My Family,"* http://blog.syracuse.com/entertainment/2009/11/tim_green_back_on_tv_tonight_w.html (accessed May 18, 2012).

Chodorow, Nancy (1978) *The Reproduction of Mothering: Psychoanalysis and the Sociology of Gender*, University of California Press, Berkeley, CA.

Dangerfield, Rodney (n.d.) *When I was a Kid...*, http://www.quotationspage.com/quote/34017.html (accessed May 18, 2012).

Dee, Jack (2008) *Adoption – Jack Dee Live at the Apollo – BBC Stand-Up Comedy*, http://youtu.be/4m45CX5LiC8 (accessed May 18, 2012).

Dictionary.com (n.d.) *Adoption*, http://dictionary.reference.com/browse/adoption (accessed May 18, 2012.

Freud, Sigmund (1959) Family romances, in *Collected Papers, Volume Five* (ed. James Strachey), Basic Books, New York, pp. 74–8.

Rich, Katey (2010) *Keenan Ivory Wayans Parodying Adoption With His Next Comedy Project*, http://www.cinemablend.com/new/Keenen-Ivory-Wayans-Parodying-Adoption-With-His-Next-Comedy-Project-19680.html (accessed May 18, 2012).

Further Reading

Brodzinsky, David and Schechter, Marshall D. (eds.) (1993) *The Psychology of Adoption*, Oxford University Press, Oxford.

Horton, Andrew S. (1991) *Comedy/Cinema/Theory*, University of California Press, Berkeley, CA.

King, Geoff (2002) *Film Comedy*, Wallflower Press, London.

Russell, David O. (2006) *Flirting with Disaster and Spanking the Monkey*, Faber & Faber, London.

Part IV

Topical Comedy, Irony, and *Humour Noir*

12

It's Good to be the King

Hollywood's Mythical Monarchies, Troubled Republics, and Crazy Kingdoms

Charles Morrow

The Genesis of Ruritanian Comedy

Around the turn of the last century, when the producers, directors, stars, and screenwriters of classic era Hollywood were children, it is a safe bet that most were familiar with the kingdoms of Ruritania, Graustark, and Pontevidro.

It's likely they often visited those places, fictional though they were, for the popular literature and drama of the 1890s and early 1900s represented the pinnacle of Ruritanian romance, lightweight yarns set in imaginary lands, stories of action and adventure that would one day lend themselves perfectly to filming. The kids who grew up to rule the movie capital heard these tales, read them, or saw them dramatized on the stage; as adults they would bring them to the screen, adapt and rework them, and, eventually, play them for laughs, thus creating a new genre of their own Ruritanian comedy. From the time of the Great War through the Great Depression comic filmmakers of every stripe employed the premise of the mythical kingdom or republic. Harold Lloyd, Ernst Lubitsch, Charlie Chaplin, and many of their peers produced comedies set in hazily defined portions of Latin America or the Balkan Peninsula, where palaces are rife with intrigue, Cabinet Ministers plot against the Crown, and the people, more often than not, are on the verge of revolution. Some of these films (such as Lloyd's 1923 *Why Worry?*), were gag-driven romps created simply to make audiences laugh; some (like Lubitsch's 1929 *The Love Parade*) were romantic comedies more concerned with the politics of the royal bedchamber than those of the throne room; while others (e.g. Chaplin's 1940 *The Great Dictator*) satirized actual persons and events, indirectly or otherwise.

A Companion to Film Comedy, First Edition. Edited by Andrew Horton and Joanna E. Rapf.
© 2013 John Wiley & Sons, Inc. Published 2016 by John Wiley & Sons, Inc.

It's easy to understand why comedians were drawn to this genre: make-believe settings allowed them the freedom to poke fun without fear of offending nationalist sentiments – or harming box office receipts – in any particular foreign market. And because the genre demanded the creation of an imaginary *elsewhere* it was possible to satirize American foibles with greater latitude. With the passage of time the tone of these comedies grew ever darker, reflecting an evolving national mood: euphoric after the First World War, gradually more ironic and cynical. The economic and political crises of the 1930s would provoke a wide range of responses, from the escapist (forget about the world!) to the absurdist (the world is a madhouse!) to the heroic (we must save the world!). Ruritanian comedy provided a platform for them all.

Ruritania itself was the creation of Englishman Anthony Hope, whose best-selling novel *The Prisoner of Zenda* (1894) and its follow-up *Rupert of Hentzau* (1898) were set in the quasi-Teutonic republic that would provide a lasting name for the genre. Hope had many imitators, the most successful being his American counterpart George Barr McCutcheon, who in 1901 published *Graustark: The Story of a Love Behind a Throne*. This fanciful tale set somewhere in the Balkans sold so well the author launched a series of Graustark novels spanning the next 25 years. Both Hope and McCutcheon had their works dramatized, but the greatest "Ruritanian" stage-play of them all was Franz Lehár's operetta *The Merry Widow*, which takes place in the Grand Duchy of Pontevidro. The show premiered in Vienna in 1905, and thanks in part to an English-language production it became an international sensation with a cultural impact beyond the theater, inspiring the merchandizing of Merry Widow hats, shoes, dolls, and even such unlikely items as corsets and cigars.

Hope, McCutcheon, and Lehár all lived to see film adaptations of their work. In Hope's lifetime at least five silent versions of his Ruritania books were produced, but he didn't live quite long enough to catch the definitive 1937 version of *The Prisoner of Zenda*. In this highly entertaining escapade Douglas Fairbanks Jr. had the best role of his career – and, it would seem, the most fun of his career – playing aristocratic scoundrel Rupert of Hentzau. In a manner of speaking Doug Jr. was himself a prince of the realm, for his father was a key player in the establishment of the mythical kingdom known as Hollywood. Douglas Fairbanks Sr. was also a primary creator of Ruritanian comedy, so any discussion of the genre must begin with him and the comedies he made during his early years in the movies.

The 1910s: America is Ace High

Although he's best remembered today for his exuberant swashbuckling roles of the 1920s, such as Zorro and Robin Hood, Douglas Fairbanks appeared in some 30 feature-length comedies with contemporary settings between 1915 and 1921. Here the star was usually presented as a likeable young fellow who finds himself in extraordinary situations, tested to the limit of his abilities. In viewing these movies today we find, along with the action sequences, a less expected element of satire aimed at modern attitudes and foibles. Three Fairbanks comedies made during or just after the Great War take place in imaginary republics or kingdoms, and give us a sense of how Americans viewed the fractious world beyond their borders. As producer and primary author of his films, Fairbanks crafted the two basic templates that would be used for this sort of comedy for years thereafter: first, one in which the hero visits an unstable Mittel-European kingdom, as in *Reaching for the Moon* (1917) and *His Majesty the American* (1919), and second, a Latino variation, as in *The Americano* (1916). As the star of these movies Doug, a grinning specimen of healthy American manhood, embodied his era's cocksure optimism but also gave expression to its common prejudices; that is, the prejudices of the white males who were in charge of practically everything at the time.

Most of the action in *The Americano* takes place in the Republic of Paragonia, somewhere in South America. This nation's mines are operated by engineers from the United States but ministers of the Paragonian Cabinet disagree on the issue of the mining concession's future. El Presidente, grave and dignified, wishes to renew the contract, but Minister of War, Salsa Espada, bluntly labeled cruel and ambitious in an intertitle, calls the Americans "pigs" and wants to see them expelled from the country. Despite his anti-Gringo stance Espada's speech is ironically peppered with then-current American slang; it's ironic too that for all his villainy the man's name suggests a zesty table condiment. It comes as no great surprise that the War Minister and his henchmen seize power, imprison the president, and nationalize the mines. But they soon realize that the American-made machinery is too sophisticated for Paragonian workers to understand or operate, a crudely chauvinistic point that is reiterated and underscored heavily. Blaze Derringer, a brash engineer newly arrived from Brooklyn (Fairbanks of course), pretends to collude with the usurpers but eventually defeats them, frees the president, marries his beautiful daughter and, for good measure, is named Paragonia's new Minister of War!

An early work, *The Americano* plays on the level of a comic book and takes pains to flatter a presumed belief in Caucasian superiority on the part of the viewer. It was made during a period of high tension between the United States and Mexico, shortly after Mexican General Pancho Villa, already a legendary figure, had split with the United States, his former allies, and sanctioned raids by his troops in which American mining officials were killed. Regarded in this context the film appears to be a wish-fulfillment fantasy, a rewrite of events in which an American engineer turns the tables on a sinister Hispanic military officer.

In *Reaching for the Moon* Doug plays Alexis, a lowly clerk in a button factory who dreams of hobnobbing with aristocrats. His mother, who died giving him birth, was a refugee from the Balkan kingdom of Vulgaria. When he learns that she was actually a princess who fled a rebellion, Alexis journeys to this volatile land to take his rightful place as King. The film's central joke is soon revealed: it's not so good to be the King after all, because everyone keeps trying to kill you. Much of the film is taken up with our hero's frantic attempts to elude assassination. After Alexis narrowly manages to avoid being poisoned, beaten to death, stabbed, blown up, shot, and thrown off a balcony, the film's funniest moment arrives when one of his treacherous ministers turns to another and remarks: "It is no use, we shall have to resort to violence." Even romance holds no pleasure, for when our unhappy monarch learns that for political reasons he must wed Valentina, princess of a neighboring land, he is crushed to find that she's homely. Finally, in a plot twist that should have been illegal even in 1917, it is revealed that Alexis's misadventure was all a bad dream. He gratefully returns to his job at the button factory, marries his girlfriend, and settles down with her in the suburbs of New Jersey!

Reaching for the Moon was made at the height of the Great War, and is suffused with paranoia about the Old World. Europe, as depicted here, is a crazy slaughterhouse best avoided. The moral? Sensible Americans should buckle down to their work and forget about rubbing elbows with royalty. (After the war, ironically, movie stars like Douglas Fairbanks would do that very thing.) The film was successful at the box office, but it appears that Fairbanks had second thoughts about its theme and denouement, for two years later he set out to make a movie that would rework its central premise, with a bigger budget and a more satisfying conclusion. This time he intended to make an explicit political statement about America's place in the post-war world.

His Majesty the American was the first film released by United Artists, the new production company of which Fairbanks was a co-founder. Doug plays William Brooks, "an excitement hunting thrill hound" who initially hunts thrills in Manhattan. Finding the city too sedate he heads for Mexico to chase after Pancho Villa. (What, again?) Next he journeys to Alaine, somewhere in Europe, a once-peaceful kingdom torn by political turmoil. The aging King wishes to grant self-rule to his people, but is opposed by an ambitious Minister of War (yes, again) who is surreptitiously fomenting unrest so as to seize power in the confusion. Brooks learns, in the course of his visit, that he is heir to the throne, and this time it's no dream, but Alaine proves to be just as volatile as Vulgaria. One grim sequence must have stirred memories in contemporary viewers of the 1914 assassination of Archduke Franz Ferdinand in Sarajevo, the event that touched off the Great War: a Chancellor loyal to the king attempts to address a restless crowd but is shot dead by a sniper, and falls into an open carriage as panic spreads. The heavy sequences are balanced with lighter moments, but the tone is generally sober, for Fairbanks had an agenda. *His Majesty the American* was planned as an endorsement of the newly formed League of Nations, the organization designed to promote international understanding and prevent future wars. This mission was cleared with the White House, and a copy of the script was actually submitted to government officials for approval (Vance 2008: 76–8). Unfortunately, while the film was in production the US Congress voted against American participation in the League. Fairbanks and his colleagues were forced to rewrite their finale in haste. Alaine remains a monarchy and Brooks is crowned King, although it is implied he will grant his people a degree of self-rule (see Figure 12.1). There is

Figure 12.1   Douglas Fairbanks is "an excitement-hunting thrill-hound" who becomes King of Alaine, in *His Majesty the American* (1919; producer, Douglas Fairbanks).

no mention of the League of Nations. Whatever point the producer originally wished to make was overtaken and blurred by real-world political developments, an occupational hazard for purveyors of topical entertainment.

As the 1920s dawned, Fairbanks turned from his modern satirical comedies to swashbuckling adventures with period settings, escapist films that, significantly, were immune to the impact of current events. Doug's mantle as comic-action hero was taken up by others, notably Wallace Reid. Reid was an athletic, classically handsome performer with a flair for understated humor, and all of these traits are on display in *Hawthorne of the USA*, released at the end of 1919. This film closely resembles a Fairbanks vehicle, and for good reason: it was based on a Broadway hit of 1912 in which Doug had starred, prior to his movie career. In this updated adaptation *Hawthorne* captures the American mood of postwar self-infatuation, seasoned with a hearty scorn for old Europe's decadent ways. Reid plays Anthony Hamilton Hawthorne, called "Tony," a dashing young sport who is motoring across Europe. After he wins two million francs at a Monte Carlo roulette table Tony heads for a spa, but he's waylaid *en route* in sleepy, decrepit Oberon, capital city of Bovinia. This kingdom is ruled by Adolphus III, a weakling who bears a disturbing resemblance to Woodrow Wilson. Adolphus and his daughter Irma (Lila Lee) are surrounded by plotters led by Count Henloe, treacherous Minister of War (evidently a recurring motif). Tony attracts the notice of the King's enemies, mainly because of his loot but also because of pointed remarks he made to journalists in Monte Carlo, expressing contempt for monarchies.

Like Doug in *The Americano*, the young American temporarily pretends to collude with the plotters in their plan to seize the government. In the finale Tony deftly escapes a firing squad, saves Adolphus from a torch-wielding mob, and wins the loyalty of the army by distributing the back pay owed to the soldiers. Any further thoughts of rebellion are quickly dispelled by his pledge: "If you'll cut this revolution bunk, I'll put money into this burg." A year passes, and we find that Hawthorne has transformed Oberon into a bustling Chicago-like metropolis, where American slang is common parlance and locals dance the shimmy to the beat of an imported Negro jazz band. Our hero wins the hand of Irma following the King's peaceful abdication, ending the story on a happy note both romantically and politically.

Briskly directed by James Cruze, *Hawthorne of the USA* points up the power of the dollar in postwar Europe, though not without irony. Whenever Tony finds himself in a tight spot a friendly bribe gets him whatever he needs, and his ultimate triumph is clearly based on his deep pockets as much as any perception of American political superiority; note that he quells the revolution with the promise of cash, not voting booths. Even so, and despite the satirical self-awareness, the film's implicit message is that Yankee ideology has won the day. This is made plain when Princess Irma refuses Hawthorne's first proposal of marriage because he has no title. Indignantly he exclaims: "What more do you want? Don't you know an American citizen is ace high any place in the world?" And indeed so it seemed, for a time.

The 1920s: Forbidden Paradiso

Harold Lloyd's output in the 1920s was in some respects a continuation of what Fairbanks had introduced in the 'teens, although in Lloyd's action-comedies the emphasis was decidedly on producing laughs rather than on making topical social or political comments. As a screen figure Harold was a highly representative American type, as energetic and optimistic as Doug but also comically awkward and somewhat dim. In the short feature *Why Worry?* (1923) Lloyd plays a wealthy hypochondriac who travels to Paradiso, "a restful little republic in the tropics," for his health. He is slow to recognize that Paradiso is misnamed. Modern viewers will find the familiar trappings of Hollywood's stereotypical Latin America – sleepy peasants, burros, and sudden outbreaks of violence – firmly in place, although it must be added that, unlike *The Americano*, this portrayal can be read as an intentional parody, given that we're seeing the country through the eyes of a clueless innocent. Harold cheerfully accepts all he sees as quaint and colorful, at first anyway. The rulers of Paradiso are absent, but we do meet a grungy schemer named Jim Blake who plots to seize power by pitting his outlaw gang against federal troops. Blake is an outlaw from the United States, a refreshing twist in villainy that permits us a full measure of satisfaction when Harold outmaneuvers the crook and his gang with the help of a friendly local, who is seven feet tall and mighty strong.

Three years before *Why Worry?* Lloyd starred in a Ruritanian short comedy called *His Royal Slyness*, in which he was an encyclopedia salesman who closely resembles the Prince of Thermosa. The Prince (played by Lloyd's look-a-like brother, Gaylord) is a dissolute fellow who is in the United States supposedly going to school, though actually lounging about with his sultry mistress. At the Prince's behest Harold takes his place and travels to Thermosa where the impersonation fools everyone, even members of the Royal Family. The nobles, courtiers and palace pages are attired in an amusing hodgepodge of English costume styles, ranging from the Elizabethan to the Edwardian, suggesting that the court is an anachronistic holdover from olden times. But the peasants in Thermosa's town square appear distinctly Slavic, and must have looked quite contemporary to audiences of 1920, at the height of the Russian Civil War. It's striking that the nobles are depicted as lazy and drunk, while the villagers are downtrodden victims of oppression. The filmmakers' sympathies are clear, and surprising. No scheming ministers are required to agitate the people, as there is ample justification for an uprising. Harold's impersonation is revealed when the real Prince, dumped by his girlfriend, returns home and has him ejected. Quite by accident our hero finds himself leading the mob as they storm the palace, and he personally fires the cannon that marks the downfall of the monarchy. Harold is promptly made "President," but, in one final twist, we observe that when this new boss issues commands they are quickly and fearfully obeyed. Has the monarchy been replaced by a dictatorship?

Various kingdoms were ruled by Charley Chase, Harry Langdon, and other top comedians of the 1920s, usually in short films crafted for general audiences. But at the same time a more sophisticated style of comedy was emerging in features aimed primarily at adults, a style that would be associated with key directors rather than performers, notably German émigré Ernst Lubitsch. This director's treatment of human foibles, especially those connected with the pleasures and discontents of romantic love, found expression in an idiosyncratic style that critics would christen the Lubitsch Touch. Curiously, this master of sly, understated innuendo began his film career as a slapstick comedian. As he switched from acting to directing, Lubitsch honed his satirical skill in features such as *The Oyster Princess* (1919), in which he drew parallels between the crass behavior of *nouveau riche* Americans and that of royalty. Subsequently he established an international reputation for large-scale historical spectacles that differed from the standard product of the day in a crucial respect: his kings, queens, and aristocrats were not bloodless figures from schoolbooks but human beings with quirks, flaws, and sexual needs. That last element in particular caught the public's fancy, and the success of these epics brought the director to Hollywood, where he would make a specialty of romantic comedies set in mythical kingdoms. Lubitsch, who always contributed to the scripts he directed, would use this genre to explore personal issues, especially power relationships between the sexes.

One of Lubitsch's first Hollywood projects was *Forbidden Paradise*, made for Paramount in 1924 and starring Pola Negri, with whom he had worked in Germany. It was adapted from a play titled *The Czarina*, produced on Broadway two years earlier, loosely based on the life of Russia's Empress Catherine II. The play was a melodrama set in 1730s' Russia, while the film is a contemporary comedy set in an unnamed Slavic kingdom. Modernization permitted Negri to sport current fashions – including, at one point, a man's crisp white military uniform – and to bob her hair, a grooming decision that reduces her ladies-in-waiting to tears. The story is primarily concerned with the Queen's frankly carnal interest in a handsome young officer, Captain Alexei Czerny (Rod La Rocque). They meet when he rushes to the palace to warn her that a rebellion is brewing in the top ranks of the military. She is blithely indifferent to the danger; once the captain has aroused her interest, politics can wait. The love scenes between Catherine and her reluctant conquest are languidly paced and rife with heavily freighted gestures played for comedy, as Alexei becomes a virtual prisoner in the Queen's sumptuous quarters. Her Chancellor (Adolphe Menjou) guards the door, and is not above peeking through the keyhole to monitor progress. Catherine grants her captive a promotion and presents him with a medal, but Alexei learns its true significance at a palace banquet when he sits at a table lined with officers, and discovers that the men all wear medals identical to his own. The inference is plain, and outrageous.

Meanwhile, the simmering military coup threatens Catherine's throne. Disaster is only narrowly averted, information Lubitsch conveys with a sharp visual device. The Queen's Chancellor confronts the mutinous officers. When the rebel leader reaches for his sword a closeup shows his hand as he grips its pommel, threateningly; next, a matching close-up shows the Chancellor's hand reaching for his checkbook and a pen. The rebel leader hesitates, then relaxes his grip. So much for the Revolution! But the director has a more serious message to impart in the final scenes. Catherine mistakenly assumes she's been betrayed and that her enemies are approaching, and dashes about her now-abandoned palace in a growing panic before she finally learns she's safe. The setting of *Forbidden Paradise* is an imaginary pseudo-Russia where no Revolution has occurred, but during the climax viewers might recall the ugly fate of the Romanovs and consider the perils of wearing a crown.

Three years later Lubitsch hammered this point home in his late silent drama *The Student Prince in Old Heidelberg* (1927), a melancholy adaptation of the Sigmund Romberg operetta. This is the tale of the hapless Prince Karl of Karlsburg, a man denied a normal life due to the inescapable obligations of his position. Lubitsch would continue to examine paradoxes of royal power, such as the impotence of the seemingly omnipotent, but in a lighter vein hereafter, utilizing a heretofore unavailable technological resource, sound.

The Talkies: See Sylvania First!

Released in autumn 1929, *The Love Parade* was not only Lubitsch's first talkie but one of the first "story" musicals with songs integrated into the plot. It was a resounding success, greeted with critical hosannas that may seem excessive today. Until, that is, one compares it to the general run of talkies in release at the time, when it becomes obvious that Lubitsch was miles ahead of his contemporaries, impressively adroit in his use of sound and music. Based on a 1905 play called *The Prince Consort*, the story concerns the courtship and marriage of Queen Louise of Sylvania (Jeanette MacDonald) to Count Alfred Renard (Maurice Chevalier). Alfred is Sylvania's military attaché in Paris, but his scandalous love affairs, including one with the wife of Sylvania's ambassador, prompt his recall. Louise, whose unmarried state has been a cause of concern to her cabinet ministers and subjects, reads a dossier on his case and takes an intense personal interest. A whirlwind romance ensues, but once they are married Alfred is dismayed to find that he has been reduced to the status of royal plaything. He must employ all his masculine wiles to reassert himself and, regardless of rank, gain supremacy over his wife.

The central situation resembles that of *Forbidden Paradise*: once again, an officer is ensnared and humiliated by a powerful Queen until he finally, successfully rebels. (In a shared gag, both films feature courtiers who spy on royal lovemaking through keyholes.) But *Forbidden Paradise* was dominated by Pola Negri's man-eating Catherine, who overshadowed her rather colorless co-star. In *The Love Parade* the balance of power tilts the other way, for the director clearly pities Alfred in his plight and expects us to follow suit. As a performer Maurice Chevalier is something of an acquired taste, but it must be said that he more than holds his own opposite MacDonald. Her Louise is formidable but also prim, and implicitly virginal. Alfred meanwhile is an incorrigible tomcat, the type of man who loves women but would never willingly submit to female rule – that is, precisely the sort of man who should not marry a Queen. At the royal wedding Alfred belatedly realizes what he's gotten himself into as he absorbs the wording of the vows, which emphasize his emasculation: "You promise to fulfill Her Majesty's every wish, to execute Her Majesty's every command, and to be an obedient and docile husband?" etc. He manages to follow through, but we know that battle lines have been drawn. Louise, born to rule, can stand up to Alfred before her Cabinet Ministers when he attempts to intervene in state affairs, but when he announces his imminent departure in the privacy of their boudoir she is reduced to whimpering obeisance. Alfred's victory, and the final reprise of the title song, comes only when Louise surrenders and addresses him not as her consort but as "My King!"

This is disquieting material, but Lubitsch maintains a sprightly tone with a steady supply of verbal and visual gags, and lively songs. He also keeps his focus squarely on the boudoir, with no pretense of interest in Sylvania or its people; the kingdom is merely a backdrop to the male-female power struggle that is his primary concern. Whenever Lubitsch ventured into Ruritanian comedy (until *The Merry Widow* in 1934) he would tell the same basic story – that of a man who triumphs over the powerful woman who has dominated him. We can only wonder why the director was so drawn to this plot, but it may be instructive to consider his first days in America. In Germany, Lubitsch had been accustomed to complete control over his work, but when he directed his first film in the United States, *Rosita* (1923), he did so as a hireling of the world-famous Mary Pickford, easily the most powerful woman in Hollywood. She was both star and producer, and had final word on the set. Although he always spoke well of her in public, Lubitsch made it known to intimates that he found the situation humiliating (Eyman 1993: 90 and 95). Is it a coincidence that he challenged this power dynamic repeatedly in his Ruritanian comedies? Perhaps.

The Love Parade was filmed during the summer of 1929. It went into general release a few weeks after the Wall Street crash, in the first uncertain days of the Great Depression. The year 1930 was a transitional one for the nation and for the motion picture industry. It began with hopes that the downturn would be brief, but ended with the realization that recovery would not be swift or easy. In addition to struggling with the economic crisis Hollywood was still adjusting to the sound revolution, to new techniques, personalities, and trends. In the wake of *The Love Parade* musicals flooded the market, followed by gangster movies, horror films, and comedies that relied heavily on the spoken word, often featuring wisecracking comics from the stage. Bert Wheeler and Robert Woolsey were one such team who made the leap from stage to screen in the early talkie era. They were signed to RKO in 1929 and starred in a series of popular features, lightweight vehicles filled with snappy patter, risqué quips, and peppy song-and-dance numbers. After several such efforts something different was attempted: an absurdist Ruritanian comedy with a dark streak of gallows humor, offered to a presumably surprised public in April 1931.

Cracked Nuts concerns the monarchy of El Dorania, where 12 kings have been deposed in 12 months. Not only is the throne up for grabs, but the apparently perpetual "Revolution" is for sale, too. A slimy El Doranian plotter named Boris (Boris Karloff) persuades a rich American dimwit named Wendell (Bert Wheeler) to invest in the latest *coup d'etat*, in return for which he will be named King – a dubious honor, it would seem. Meanwhile the current King plays the roulette table in Monte Carlo, where he wagers his crown as prize. A con artist called "Zup" (Robert Woolsey) wins the crown and thus becomes King. Thereafter Zup and Wendell, who happen to be old friends, affably compete for leadership of the dysfunctional nation. Eventually King Zup alienates the country's top general, who decides to have him eliminated in a novel fashion: he shall be killed before spectators at a public event designated for the purpose. The King is to sit on his throne in the middle of a field, while a plane flying overhead drops bombs on him.

This macabre climax is introduced by a title card reading: "Assassination Day – Never before had an El Doranian Bomb Festival drawn so many fans." Indeed the occasion looks like a football game, complete with hot dog vendors, cheerleaders, and a marching band. In a throwback to silent comedy the plane's pilot turns out to be cross-eyed Ben Turpin, who haplessly misses his target time and again as the crowd jeers. At the last moment Wendell rescues Zup; simultaneously, the detonation of a stray bomb strikes oil. Thanks to this new revenue stream (get it?) the kingdom is wealthy. Zup proclaims El Dorania a republic and names himself its president, and as his first act has the plotters arrested.

We're a long way from Lubitsch Land. Pervasive weirdness notwithstanding, *Cracked Nuts* bears some resemblance to the go-getter comedies of earlier days. Bert Wheeler's Wendell, a moneyed American who triumphs over foreign sharpies, is a dumbed-down version of characters played by Fairbanks and Reid, but the prevalent mood has soured. The euphoria of *Hawthorne of the USA* is gone, for those Yankee pockets are no longer so deep: early on we learn that Wendell has already squandered a chunk of his fortune, so an investment in El Dorania may be his last chance to make good. Moreover, a disconcerting amount of the humor concerns violent death. Regicide is discussed with nonchalance, and its near-realization at a festive sporting event packs a jolt even today. The film's director Eddie Cline was a comedy veteran with an extensive track record. In 1920 Cline had collaborated with Buster Keaton on a short called *Convict 13* in which a prisoner's execution was similarly portrayed as a pageant with vendors, etc., but that event turned out to be a nightmare. Here, we are expected to regard what we're seeing as "real." Even with the last-minute reversal of fortune for our heroes the finale leaves an acrid aftertaste. Critics did not rave over *Cracked Nuts* but, despite hard times, it turned a profit, and thus may have been at least partly responsible for the wave of increasingly wacky Ruritanian comedies that went before the cameras as the Depression worsened. Cline would take another crack at the genre the following year, when he would direct *Million Dollar Legs* with more felicitous results.

In the summer of 1931 Lubitsch returned with *The Smiling Lieutenant*, another Ruritanian musical comedy in his characteristic style. Chevalier was back as Lieutenant "Nikki" von Preyn of the Viennese Imperial Guard. As in *The Love Parade*, our leading man is trapped in a marriage with a woman more powerful than himself; this time he is ensnared by the naïve but willful Princess Anna (Miriam Hopkins) of Flausenthurm, a tiny and irredeemably second-rate kingdom that shares a border with Austria. Their forced marriage, which Anna desires and Nikki resents, is predicated entirely on a misinterpreted signal, for the Princess erroneously believes that Nikki's rakish wink, meant for his girlfriend Franzi (Claudette Colbert), was intended for herself. The situation is a rather distasteful one, but Lubitsch keeps the laughs coming regardless, mostly at the expense of poor, shabby Flausenthurm. The director also explores a favorite theme dating back to his historical epics, i.e. that for the ruling class intimate personal gestures can have magnified and unintended consequences. (For more on *The Smiling Lieutenant* see Deleyto in this volume.)

Three months after this film was released a new Ruritanian comedy called *Ambassador Bill* hit the theaters, this one featuring a leading man who was in many respects Maurice Chevalier's polar opposite. Oklahoma-born Will Rogers came to national attention as a humorist during the 1910s, when his vaudeville act as a cowboy roper evolved into a standup routine based largely on current events. Rogers parlayed his success into an early example of modern mass media superstardom: he wrote a nationally distributed newspaper column, broadcast speeches on the radio, and appeared in dozens of movies. Like Douglas Fairbanks he also hobnobbed with politicians, world leaders, and actual royalty. In 1924 Rogers starred in his first Ruritanian venture, a two-reel silent short for Hal Roach called *A Truthful Liar* in which he played fictional Okie politician Alfalfa Doolittle. In earlier shorts Doolittle had successfully run for office and gone to Congress as a representative; now he is returning home after serving as a diplomat. What unfolds in *A Truthful Liar* represents Doolittle's account of his adventures to the hometown folks, a framework that allows for outlandish exaggeration. Doolittle reports that he was posted to the kingdom of Cornucopia after the murder of the previous ambassador. On his arrival a servant confides: "There isn't much danger, just an occasional riot." The new ambassador bridles at dressing up for official functions and wears cowboy gear when he is presented at court. After Doolittle saves the King from a bomb hurled by an anarchist (and lassos the latter) he is rewarded with the role of royal sidekick, and teaches the monarch to play poker and eat hot dogs. In gratitude the King presents Doolittle with a souvenir, his crown. *A Truthful Liar* is an amusing romp, lighter and more gag-oriented than Rogers' subsequent work in sound features.

In *Ambassador Bill* Rogers plays Oklahoma cattle rancher Bill Harper, who is appointed ambassador to the strife-torn Balkan kingdom of Sylvania – a far cry from the Sylvania of *The Love Parade*. Life has been bleak here since the reins of government were seized by the sinister Prime Minister, Prince de Polikoff. Queen Vanya and her eight-year-old son Paul have acted as figurehead rulers since the forced abdication of Vanya's husband Lothar (played by a very young Ray Milland). Sylvania is torn by near-constant violence while the Prime Minister and his clique enrich themselves and reject all trade agreements with outsiders. Harper's primary task is to negotiate a commercial treaty, despite the opposition of the De Polikoff faction and certain members of the US Senate, who are dubious about investing in such an unstable country.

In its opening sequence, *Ambassador Bill* is almost as harsh in tone as *Cracked Nuts*. Battles rage in the street while officials at the US embassy attempt to ignore the noise. Uniformed servants distribute earplugs, and one blandly explains the unpleasantness to a dignitary in the film's first line: "Just another revolution, sir. It's the first one we've had this week." But as soon as the new ambassador arrives the fighting subsides and the mood changes. Harper eschews court etiquette, exclaiming "Pleased to meetcha!" to the startled Queen as he shakes her hand. He takes an instant dislike to De Polikoff, and is appalled to find an eight year-old boy saddled with duties of state that keep him up past his bedtime. Harper sets out to provide young King Paul with an Oklahoma-style boyhood, giving him cowboy gear and teaching him to play baseball. In the ambassador's opinion the only problem with Sylvania's political situation is that Queen Vanya, who seems like a nice young lady, needs to patch things up with her ex-husband and make a real home for their son; he appears to have no problem with monarchy *per se*, as long as that treaty goes through. In the end, after a violent revolution, which Harper calls "the best one they've had since I've been here," De Polikoff is defeated, Vanya and Lothar are reunited, and their son gets to go fishing with the friendly American he calls Mr. Bill.

Since Ruritania was a natural destination for Will Rogers, *Ambassador Bill* serves as a suitable showcase for his warm personality and seemingly offhand observations. Director Sam Taylor had guided several silent features for Harold Lloyd including *Why Worry?* and knew how to maintain focus on the star and keep things moving. Rogers' topical references (as when he casually drops the names of Senator William Borah or former Vice President Charles Dawes) have inevitably become obscure, but his remarks about Congress, lobbyists, and the economy remain surprisingly current. A number of his barbs are aimed at a fellow American official traveling in Sylvania, Senator Pillsbury, an obese Republican windbag who looks like an editorial cartoon come to life. When Pillsbury sanctimoniously asserts that it's against United States policy to meddle in other countries' affairs, Harper chuckles and murmurs "Tell that to the Marines." For audiences of 1931 this may have called to mind then-recent US military interventions in Nicaragua and China; for modern viewers, sadly, the quip retains its sting.

Despite the worsening Depression, *Cracked Nuts, The Smiling Lieutenant,* and *Ambassador Bill* were all box office successes. At this point Paramount Pictures, the studio hardest hit by the economic downturn, would serve as production head-quarters for Hollywood's best known Ruritanian comedies, two feature films of 1932 and 1933, both box office disappointments in their day, which have grown in stature and are now recognized as classics of the genre.

The Pinnacle: Hail Klopstokia! Hail Freedonia!

In autumn of 1931 Paramount's production chief B.P. Schulberg issued a memo to the studio's staff writers in which he pointed out that the Olympic games would be held in Los Angeles the following summer, and indicated that he wanted a related film ready in time to coincide with the event. Seizing the opportunity, 22-year-old screenwriter Joseph L. Mankiewicz proposed that they eschew the clichés of routine sport films and try something unusual. He had attended the 1928 Olympic games in Amsterdam, and was haunted by the memory of a scrawny

Albanian pole-vaulter who took the field in goatskin shorts. Working with play-wright Henry Myers the young writer came up with a crazy story, initially titled *On Your Mark*, about a woebegone kingdom called Klopstokia. Here all the men are named George and all the women Angela, and everyone possesses super-human athletic prowess. Nevertheless the kingdom is beset with difficulties: the treasury is depleted, spying is rampant, and the King is continually challenged by conniving cabinet ministers who seek his overthrow. But thanks to the intervention of an American brush salesman blessed with the name Migg Tweeny, Klopstokia is saved from ruin through the successful participation of its super-athletes in the Los Angeles Olympic games.

Surprisingly, Schulberg approved this idea with only one proviso: rather than risk offending royalist sensibilities in Great Britain he had the writers change Klopstokia to a republic and its king to a president. The project would be supervised by Mankiewicz's older brother Herman, who had worked with the Marx Brothers and thus knew something about translating crazy comedy to the screen. Eddie Cline, who had guided *Cracked Nuts* with mixed results, was hired to direct and promptly filled the cast with silent comedy veterans, most notably Ben Turpin, who appears as a mysterious cloaked spy. (Turpin, seen briefly in *The Love Parade* and *Ambassador Bill* as well as *Cracked Nuts*, found a new career niche in sound era Ruritanian comedies.) W.C. Fields, whose talents had not yet been properly harnessed in the movies, was selected to play Klopstokia's beleaguered President, while the romantic leads went to Jack Oakie and Susan Fleming. Oakie was known for oafish comic roles, often, ironically, in the collegiate sport programmers Mankiewicz cited as models to avoid, while Fleming was a lovely brunette whose flat delivery of dialogue proved to be an unexpected plus. *Million Dollar Legs* was the title chosen for this farrago, supposedly in reference to wizened Andy Clyde, who portrays Klopstokia's fastest runner. Viewers can be forgiven for assuming the title refers to blonde bombshell Lyda Roberti, unforgettable as *femme fatale* Mata Machree, the Woman No Man Can Resist. The character's name and bizarre pseudo-Swedish dialect suggest a parody of Garbo's Mata Hari, but Roberti's performance, highlighted by her rendition of the torch song "When I Get Hot in Klopstokia," stands on its own as a comic tour-de-force.

The oddball combination of sight gags, non sequiturs, macabre touches, and self-referential Hollywood satire known as *Million Dollar Legs* is bracingly surreal, a mélange of old and new techniques that recalls Mack Sennett's Keystone but also anticipates the later work of Preston Sturges, Ernie Kovacs, and the Zucker/Abrams team. Whether by accident or design the film aptly reflects its historical moment, for when filming commenced in May 1932 the economy was scraping bottom, and national morale was at a perilously low ebb. The downward spiral seemed irreversible despite the country's vaunted political and financial might.

Is Klopstokia, a nation of superathletes somehow reduced to ragtag impotence, a thinly disguised portrait of Herbert Hoover's United States? Along with the

Olympics, *Million Dollar Legs* coincided with the presidential campaign season, a process parodied in the film's ritualized struggle for power, a series of arm-wrestling matches between the President and his main adversary, the Secretary of the Treasury (Hugh Herbert). After one of these contests, Fields seizes Herbert, looks in his mouth, and exclaims, "Just as I suspected. The country's starving, and you with gold in your teeth!" Allusions to the nation's depleted coffers abound, but a triumphant showing at the Olympic games brings financial salvation, thanks to a generous endowment from an unlikely *deus ex machina*, Tweeny's boss, a wealthy American brush magnate named Baldwin (George Barbier) who admires athletes. Klopstokia is victorious on the field but the United States ultimately wins the day, metaphorically anyhow, for in the film's final moments Baldwin proves to be the only man strong enough to best Klopstokia's President. Challenged to a good-natured wrestling match, Baldwin throws the President headlong.

Mankiewicz's freakish brainchild was welcomed by most critics as refreshing and imaginative, yet despite decent business in metropolitan centers the film failed to find an audience in the American heartland, where its quirky humor fell flat. The response in Europe was more gratifying: *Million Dollar Legs* was warmly embraced by Man Ray and his fellow surrealists, who regarded it as a masterwork. A few weeks after its release, Paramount announced a new project along the same lines for The Four Marx Brothers, to be directed by Ernst Lubitsch and titled *Oo La La*. Groucho, Harpo, Chico and Zeppo Marx, vaudeville troupers who rose to Broadway stardom with a combination of clever wordplay, musical skill, and roughhouse comedy, were among the many stage luminaries who stepped before the cameras with the coming of sound. (See Krutnik in this volume.) By 1932 the Marxes' status as movie stars was secure: their summer release *Horse Feathers* was Paramount's top grosser of the year, landing the team on the cover of *Time* magazine. Unfortunately we can only imagine what a Lubitsch-directed Marx Brothers movie might have looked like, for he was not destined to work with the team. *Oo La La* was assigned to the screenwriter/songwriter duo Harry Ruby and Bert Kalmar, who were assisted by a number of contributors at various stages in the project's long gestation period. The title was changed to *Cracked Ice* (shades of Wheeler & Woolsey), then *Grasshoppers* before director Leo McCarey came up with the moniker *Duck Soup*. That one stuck.

While the script was undergoing revisions during the spring of 1933 the brothers were involved in a prolonged salary dispute with Paramount. By the time filming commenced that summer several significant personnel changes had occurred. Paramount itself had gone into receivership, leading to the ouster of B.P. Schulberg and the installation of a new regime. In the world outside the studio newly inaugurated President Franklin D. Roosevelt launched his national recovery programs in an atmosphere of acute crisis. In Germany, Chancellor Adolf Hitler initiated a campaign of terror against Jewish citizens. Given the circumstances it is no surprise to find a consistent emphasis on political turmoil and warfare in every version of the scenario. The setting is Freedonia, a troubled republic at odds with neighboring Sylvania (that name again!). In an early edition of the script Groucho is a salesman for the Eureka Ammunition Company who becomes dictator and cold-bloodedly starts a war for commercial reasons, i.e. to sell his goods. This draft ends with a sequence in which a cheering throng proclaims him King. In response he delivers a most un-Groucho-like speech: "Now is not the time for political temporizing, all interests must be sacrificed to the common weal!" etc. A later draft concludes eerily with the Marxes, having accidentally blown themselves to bits, ascending to Heaven as Harpo strums his harp.

Needless to say, *Duck Soup* as finally committed to film is quite different, but war remains a central theme. Our first impression of Freedonia is of a nation in crisis: the treasury has mismanaged funds loaned by the nation's wealthiest woman, Gloria Teasdale (Margaret Dumont). She demands that the President relinquish his office to that "progressive, fearless fighter" Rufus T. Firefly. Firefly arrives late for his ridiculously elaborate reception ceremony and immediately issues a proclamation in song prohibiting all forms of pleasure, from whistling to telling dirty jokes. Thereafter he spends his time insulting everyone he meets, though reserving special animus for Trentino, Sylvania's ambassador. Freedonia, like Klopstokia, is crawling with spies, including Trentino's hirelings Chicolini and Pinky (Chico and Harpo). Trentino is determined to destabilize Freedonia, while Firefly is equally determined to antagonize Trentino. Why? Because he doesn't like him. Their conflict comes to a head and the result is war, a calamity greeted with an exuberant musical number, a crazed pastiche of military spectacle, hoedown, and gospel jubilee. The war is depicted in a scattershot montage of blackout gags, stock shots, and blatantly unconvincing model work, complemented with a barrage of puns. Firefly and his cohorts, Chicolini, and Pinky (whose loyalties are flexible) survive a siege in an isolated cabin, capture Trentino, and win the war for Freedonia. When Mrs. Teasdale attempts to celebrate victory by singing the national anthem, they pelt her with ripe fruit.

Duck Soup is a sharp political satire whose neatly balanced components support a dark, coherent vision. This is the story of a man wholly unsuited to leadership who is granted absolute power, which he squanders. His childish quarrel with a foreign leader explodes into full-scale armed conflict, which ironically inspires rejoicing by those who have the most to lose. In the fog of war soldiers are killed by "friendly fire." Triumph on the battlefield results not in peace or wisdom but in more fighting. Is it too much to suggest that *Duck Soup* is a 68-minute tutorial in modern world history?

Director Leo McCarey learned his craft at the Hal Roach Studio where he developed a keen sense of timing, as demonstrated here when a petty dispute between Harpo, Chico, and an unfriendly lemonade vendor (Edgar Kennedy) escalates into outrageous acts of reciprocal destruction. This is a largely visual interlude, and so too is the film's most celebrated sequence, the mirror routine in which Harpo, disguised as Groucho, attempts to mimic the latter's every move as they face each other across a threshold. This venerable bit had been performed in the movies by – among others – Charlie Chaplin, Max Linder, and Charley Chase, the latter in a 1924 short called *Sittin' Pretty* directed by McCarey. And although Lubitsch did not guide this project his influence can be detected in the wry musical numbers, the satirical jabs at court protocol, and, above all, in the notion that the petty behavior of rulers can have magnified and sometimes disastrous consequences for the ruled.

Shortly after filming was completed, Harpo Marx set sail for the Soviet Union. He was the first American entertainer to perform there after the United States's diplomatic recognition of the USSR was announced in November 1933. On the set of *Duck Soup* Harpo and his brothers, who were of German Jewish descent, had listened with dread to radio broadcasts of Hitler's speeches. *En route* to Moscow Harpo traveled through Hamburg, and was shocked to observe evidence of Nazi rule: splashed across the windows of boycotted shops were Stars of David and the word JUDE in bright red paint. He wrote in his autobiography: "I got across Germany as fast as I could go" (Marx 1961: 301). In Moscow Harpo discovered that his official escort was a government spy, and that his phone was tapped. It would be interesting to know if, during his travels in Hitler's Germany and Stalin's USSR, Harpo was reminded of Freedonia, where the new boss declared in song: "The last man nearly ruined this place, he didn't know what to do with it/If you think this country's bad off now just wait 'til I get through with it!"

Leaving Ruritania

Contrary to popular belief *Duck Soup* was not a box office failure. It fell short of expectations, but was moderately successful considering the dire economic climate. In this tumultuous period, as Hollywood's producers struggled to anticipate the shifting yet essentially unpredictable demands of a fickle public, it appeared that Ruritanian comedy might still have an audience.

Since the coming of talkies Irving Thalberg of MGM had planned a new version of Franz Lehár's operetta *The Merry Widow*. A silent adaptation in 1925 had been one of the studio's biggest hits. Now, of course, Lehár's famous songs could be sung on screen, with lyrics newly adapted for the sensibilities of 1934. Thalberg hired Lubitsch to direct and granted him a generous budget. Maurice Chevalier and Jeanette MacDonald were reunited to play the leads, and the supporting cast was filled with top character actors. Several hands including Lubitsch himself worked on the screenplay, and their finished product was faithful to the spirit of the 1905 stage original.

In place of Lehár's Pontevidro, our setting is Marshovia, 1885. The kingdom's wealthiest widow Madame Sonia (MacDonald), who has been in mourning for almost a year, decides to resume an active life and leaves for Paris. This reduces Marshovia's King Achmed and his cabinet to a state of panic, for the kingdom depends on Sonia's taxes for income. A special agent must follow the widow, seduce her, and lure her back to Marshovia. For this task Achmed selects Prince Danilo (Chevalier), whom he knows is cuckolding him with his own wife the Queen. Danilo, who is already interested in Sonia but unaware she is the same woman he has been assigned to seduce, goes to Paris, and, after various complications, accomplishes his mission.

Our introduction to the kingdom is pure Lubitsch: we are shown a map of Eastern Europe, but Marshovia is not visible until a hand holding a magnifying glass helpfully reaches into the shot. The director's familiar comic touches are present, as when a military parade is nearly disrupted by unruly cattle; or, later, when King Achmed discovers his wife is unfaithful the moment he fetches a sword-belt from their bedroom, straps it on, finds it too tight, and realizes that it belongs to another man. But beyond the gags, the prevailing tone of *The Merry Widow* is sober compared to the director's previous Ruritanian frolics. The score is treated with more reverence than the cheerful ditties of the earlier operettas, and unusual care is lavished on the dance sequences. Chevalier's Danilo initially appears to be the same smug tomcat we've met before, but after repeated verbal clashes with the witty Sonia he matures convincingly from feckless womanizer to a man in love, and a worthy husband. The finale, an impromptu wedding ceremony conducted in Danilo's jail cell, is both romantic and amusing: what is Lubitsch saying about matrimony?

Despite the film's high quality, moviegoers were not buying, at least not in sufficient numbers. *The Merry Widow* failed to earn back its cost. With this surprise flop the heyday of Ruritanian comedy was over. Box office receipts indicate that audiences of the time preferred the screwball sophistication of *The Thin Man*, the effervescence of Fred Astaire and Ginger Rogers, and even the saccharine cuteness of Shirley Temple to another mythical kingdom farce from the *Love Parade* team. Lubitsch never directed another film set in an imaginary land. It is understandable, too, that other moviemakers did not rush to develop new Ruritanian comedies, given the disappointing financial returns for the releases of 1932–4.

An echo of the genre can be heard, however faintly, in Mervyn LeRoy's *The King and the Chorus Girl*, a tepid 1937 comedy about the deposed monarch of an unnamed country living in comfortable exile in Paris. Alfred VII (Fernand Gravet) is a dissolute playboy, reformed by love for a Brooklyn-born dancer (Joan Blondell). Only four months prior to the film's release England's King Edward VIII had abdicated to marry American socialite Wallis Simpson, and the obvious parallels were widely noted. The link is underscored when Alfred remarks that he once ruled a kingdom of 1000 square miles, and now has only an apartment. "Well there's one consolation," he adds. "As long as I pay the rent they can't force me to abdicate the apartment." The screenplay was co-authored by Norman Krasna and, of all people, Groucho Marx. In the face of criticism, Warner Brothers, the production company responsible, claimed the project was in development long before the abdication crisis. Nonetheless they chose to exploit it with the dubious slogan "Reign, Reign, Go Away, HRH Wants to Play." The film was rechristened *Romance is Sacred* prior to distribution in the United Kingdom, but it sparked anger in England and was denounced in *Picturegoer* magazine as "an outrage on good taste" (Mitchell 1996: 165). In the 1970s, long after the controversy had faded, Groucho belatedly admitted that the fictional Alfred VII was indeed based on the actual Edward VIII (Mitchell 1996: 165).

The year 1937 also saw the release of Hollywood's definitive Ruritanian romance, David Selznick's *Prisoner of Zenda*, a deluxe adaptation, which offered sufficient escapism to help viewers forget ominous current events. Studio executives, wary of hurting lucrative markets overseas, preferred to avoid sensitive political issues; therefore, in contemporary films, the American way of life was touted but other forms of government were seldom criticized. Furthermore, the Production Code that regulated screen morality, strictly enforced since 1934, specifically decreed that the "national feelings" of all countries were entitled to respectful treatment. This applied even to Nazi Germany, particularly since the moguls, most of whom were Jewish, did not want to provoke an anti-Semitic backlash. Only one filmmaker dared to take on Hitler directly, by making what might be considered the last Ruritanian comedy of classic era Hollywood.

Charlie Chaplin, the movies' preeminent comic superstar, had been writing, directing, and producing his work since 1918. During the 1930s he grew increasingly alarmed by political developments in Europe, especially in Germany. Meanwhile, the resemblance between Chaplin's Tramp and Adolf Hitler, an unsettling correlation between beloved clown and despised despot, had not gone unnoticed in the press; it was inevitable Chaplin would use it on screen. Though widely believed to be Jewish the comedian was in fact Gentile, thus in a sense immune to concerns that silenced others. His friend Alexander Korda may have been the first to suggest an anti-Hitler film, but it is likely Chaplin was also influenced by his older brother Syd, a gifted comedian in his own right. Back in 1921 Syd had written and directed a comedy called *King, Queen and Joker* in which he played a dual role. This was the tale of a barber who is a double for the King of Coronia. Rebels kidnap the King and install the barber in his place, forcing him to impersonate the ruler. When the real King regains his throne the barber is sentenced to death, but the Queen helps him escape and resume his former trade. Charlie used elements of his brother's Zenda-like story to create his own political satire, *The Great Dictator* (1940), which would be his first talking picture.

Chaplin's film concerns a Jewish barber from Tomania, wounded in World War I, who spends years in a military hospital suffering from amnesia. He returns home to find that his country has been taken over by an anti-Semitic madman named Adenoid Hynkel, who orders the persecution of Tomania's Jews. Hynkel is an arrogant, uniformed monster who spews pseudo-Teutonic invective, while the barber is a soft-spoken gent who wants only to live and let live. The dictator

Figure 12.2 In *The Great Dictator* (1940; producer, Charles Chaplin) Charlie Chaplin assumes the role of Adenoid Hynkel, ruthless and strangely familiar-looking ruler of a land called Tomania.

orders his troops to invade neighboring Osterlich as a first step toward wider conquest. As the invasion commences the barber is mistaken for the dictator, and vice versa. Hynkel is arrested, and in his place the barber ascends to a podium to deliver a worldwide radio broadcast (see Figure 12.2). Instead of the expected bellicose rhetoric he stuns his listeners with a call for peace and international brotherhood. (See Rob King's chapter in this volume.)

During the entire period of this film's production, from the first draft of the text in 1938 to the first screenings in autumn 1940, a succession of horrific events unfolded. War erupted in Europe, and the Nazis swiftly conquered Poland, Belgium, Holland, and Denmark. Paris fell, and the Battle of Britain began. Under these circumstances how could a Hitler-like ruler be a figure of fun? With his work half-finished Chaplin vacillated, unsure if the project was appropriate. In the completed film this uncertainty can be detected in the final speech, when the comic mask drops and Charles Chaplin – not the Jewish barber – addresses the world. The talk has been criticized as mawkish and artistically incongruous, but ample anecdotal evidence attests that this movie, speech and all, boosted morale and offered hope at a desperate time. Using a genre developed by his close friend Douglas Fairbanks, Chaplin crafted a unique cinematic milestone whose very creation was an act of personal and political courage. "When you are faced by the totalitarian regimes," said writer Ray Bradbury, an admirer of *The Great Dictator*, "courage isn't enough. You have to be able to laugh in their face" (as quoted in Brownlow's documentary *The Tramp and the Dictator* (2001)). Against the odds, in a very dark hour, a funnyman inspired the world to laugh defiantly in the face of evil. What greater service to humanity could comedy provide?

Acknowledgments

I am grateful to Charles Silver, curator in the Museum of Modern Art's Department of Film, for allowing me to screen MoMA's prints of *His Majesty the American* and *Forbidden Paradise*. I would also like to thank Steve Massa and James Bigwood for providing me with copies of other hard-to-find films.

While researching this chapter I frequently consulted the amazing resources of the Billy Rose Theatre Division at The New York Public Library for the Performing Arts. (By a happy coincidence, I work there.) I examined contemporary reviews and other material related to the films I wrote about, as well as reviews of those projects which began life as stage plays, including *Hawthorne of the USA, The Czarina* (which became *Forbidden Paradise*), and *The Prince Consort* (which became *The Love Parade*). I also read the library's copy of *Cracked Ice*, an early draft of *Duck Soup*.

References

Eyman, Scott (1993) *Ernst Lubitsch: Laughter in Paradise*, Simon & Schuster, New York, NY.

Marx, Harpo, with Rowland Barber (1961) *Harpo Speaks!* Bernard Geis Associates, New York, NY.

Mitchell, Glenn (1996) *The Marx Brothers Encyclopedia*, Batsford, London.

The Tramp and the Dictator (2001), film directed by Kevin Brownlow and Michael Kloft, Photoplay Productions.

Vance, Jeffrey (2008) *Douglas Fairbanks*, University of California Press, Berkeley, CA.

Further Reading

Goldsworthy, V. (1998) *Inventing Ruritania: the Imperialism of the Imagination*, Yale University Press, New Haven, CT. The literary antecedents of Hollywood's Ruritanian comedies are examined in this interesting and informative book. The author explores the ways in which Western prejudices concerning the nations of the Balkan Peninsula have been influenced by Western literature of the nineteenth and twentieth centuries. Goldsworthy discusses Anthony Hope's *Prisoner of Zenda* trilogy, Bram Stoker's *Dracula*, and numerous works set in imaginary lands based on Balkan monarchies and republics.

Harvey, J. (1987) *Romantic Comedy in Hollywood*, Knopf, New York, NY. An incisive look at the great romantic comedies of the 1930s and 1940s, key directors such as Lubitsch, Capra, Hawks, and Sturges, and the top stars of the genre, including Carole Lombard, Cary Grant, Irene Dunne, and many others. The films discussed range from iconic classics to overlooked works that deserve more attention. Readers need not agree with all of Harvey's idiosyncratic opinions in order to find his book thought provoking and stimulating.

Sterling, B. and Sterling, F. (1984) *Will Rogers in Hollywood*, Crown, New York, NY. The most comprehensive guide to Rogers' movie career, featuring production data for each film, excerpts from contemporary reviews, and Rogers' own comments about Hollywood and his colleagues.

Tibbetts, J. and Welsh, J. (1977) *His Majesty the American: the Cinema of Douglas Fairbanks*, A.S. Barnes, South Brunswick, NJ. An exhaustively researched study of Fairbanks and his films, with considerable background information about his collaborators, his influences, and his era. *Douglas Fairbanks* by Jeffrey Vance (University of California Press, Berkeley, CA, 2008) is focused primarily on Fairbanks himself, and beautifully illustrated. Also of interest are Vance's *Harold Lloyd, Master Comedian* (Abrams, New York, NY, 2002), written in collaboration with Suzanne Lloyd, and *Chaplin: Genius of the Cinema* (Abrams, New York, NY, 2003). Both offer interesting behind-the-scenes details on Lloyd's and Chaplin's major productions.

13

No Escaping the Depression

Utopian Comedy and the Aesthetics of Escapism in Frank Capra's *You Can't Take It with You* (1938)

William Paul

In the first decade of the twenty-first century there was much journalistic writing about the success of escapist movies, first in response to terrorism and the Iraq war, subsequently, to a bad economy. In a 2008 article, *Variety* asked, "Are people more pumped for escapism thanks to the recession?" and immediately answered, "The summer box office is doing great – against the odds." But perhaps not against odds since the article proposes a kind of equation by quoting a studio executive who claims, "When times get tough, the movie business tends to holdup. More than ever, people want to escape" (McClintock 2008: 1, 58). A writer for *Brandweek* used similar terms to make the same equation in 2009: "When the going gets tough, the tough go the movies. People want their escapism, dammit, so a recession is hardly the death knell for entertainment" (Ebenkampe 2009: 6). When it comes to movies, tough times most often seems to mean a bad economy, so much so that twenty-first-century escapist movies inevitably led journalists to compare them to the era most frequently cited for its escapist cinema, the Great Depression. Central to this perception of escapism in Depression films was a new style of comedy, screwball, because in these films characters seemed free to operate irresponsibly in a period that seemed to call for more sober behavior.

That might sound like a description of Marx Brothers movies, but screwy as they were, they were not specifically screwball, which signified rather a variety of romantic comedy. This is an important distinction: romantic comedy, as opposed to tendentious comic forms such as satire or parody, is inevitably escapist because the overcoming of conflicts and promise of a better future that comes with the union of the couple at the plot's conclusion is fundamentally utopian. As a critical

A Companion to Film Comedy, First Edition. Edited by Andrew Horton and Joanna E. Rapf.
© 2013 John Wiley & Sons, Inc. Published 2016 by John Wiley & Sons, Inc.

category, escapism is problematic because its connotations are entirely negative, seemingly embodying a disavowal of reality. How can we value works whose sole purpose is to make us forget hard times? In what follows, I would like to look at escapism more positively and see in the utopian aspirations of romantic comedy a fuller engagement with the world than might be apparent at first glance. Determining how that engagement with the world might be expressed will enable me to propose a tentative aesthetics of escapism and with it a way of evaluating romantic comedies as something other than pleasant diversions from serious concerns.

Specifically, I will be centering my discussion on Frank Capra's film version of the George S. Kaufman and Moss Hart comedy, *You Can't Take It with You*, a work that in both its forms embraced utopianism. The play was a major critical success, winning the Pulitzer Prize for best drama of the 1936–1937 season. Why such accolades for a seemingly inconsequential work? Certainly the inconsequentiality was itself part of the appeal: a *Chicago Daily Tribune* review defined the play as "irresponsible and impish," noting it appeared at a time when "the stage ... has been overburdened of late with solemnities and serious social meanings" (Collins 1937: 15). A *Time* review reflected much of the contemporary reception; while it saw the plot as "deliberately banal," it lighted on the collection of wacky characters as the play's primary attraction: "the playwrights have conjured a species of dramatis personae which transcends plot, bursts the bonds of the established theatre and mounts into the stratosphere of great literary lunacy" (The Theatre 1936: 33). Why this collection of "lovable loons," as the *Literary Digest* called them, should be so appealing for a contemporary audience was most clearly articulated by Brooks Atkinson in a *New York Times* Sunday think-piece following his review of the premiere (Farcical Antics of Lovable Loons 1936: 22). Countering the "carping" of an imagined "neighborhood intellectual" who complained that "Mr. Hart and Mr. Kaufman had not explained how the Sycamore family could ride their hobby-horses so fantastically in a world dominated by rent, the price of foodstuffs, and raw materials," Atkinson praised Hart and Kaufman for foregoing their usual satirical approach: "They have never before written about such enjoyable people or treated them so tolerantly" (Atkinson 1936: X3). The appeal of the play, then, was that its characters, almost none of whom works for a living, had somehow escaped the demands of the real world, made all the more pointed in the Depression era, much as the play itself had escaped the solemnity of other contemporary productions.

As the contemporary response demonstrates, the escapism of the original play accounts for much of its appeal. Wildly popular escapist fare would seem tailor-made for Depression-era Hollywood, likely the reason the play commanded the record purchase price of $200 000 (Hart-Kaufman Play 1937: 19). Furthermore, with its odd assortment of irresponsible characters, it could seem to fit perfectly into the screwball cycle that had already been recognized with that name by contemporary journalists. The subsequent film was also a critical and popular success: it was nominated for seven Academy Awards, winning for best picture and best direction, an unusual accomplishment for a romantic comedy, and emerging as one of the top-grossing films of the year. This was clearly a work that spoke to 1930s' audiences, and spoke in a way that that seems to correspond to the understanding of Depression-era films most frequently articulated in the popular press. Nevertheless, the escapism of play and film actually works in different ways, with the play oddly coming closer to common conceptions of Hollywood escapism.

The play takes place entirely within one set, the living room of the Vanderhof residence, home to Grandpa Vanderhof and his extended family, a setting that seems almost cut off from the outside world. Providing little sense of the immediate neighborhood, the stage directions make sure we understand the meaning of this omission: " … just around the corner from Columbia University, but don't go looking for it" (Hart and Kaufman 2004: 689). In other words, the setting has only a vague connection to reality. With the exception of Grandpa, who likes to go out occasionally and see what's going on outside his home, and his granddaughter Alice, who works as a secretary, the only family member to hold a job, the rest of the family spends most of their time in this world, which is situated not quite in our world. This place embodies an alternative – and better – reality, or, as a contemporary *Wall Street Journal* review put it, essentially defining the appeal of escapism, "a self-contained world by itself, which spins gallantly and happily like a stray moon at a safe distance from the blinding sun of all our logic" (Bowen 1937: 15).

Even as the play distances itself from reality, there is nonetheless an invocation of an outside world since it is the outside world that intrudes in a progressive fashion and serves to structure the play's narrative: first, tentatively, in the person of an IRS agent, brought in partly to explain the family's apparent freedom from money concerns; then, more central to the plot's development, the snobbish Mr. and Mrs. Kirby, parents of Tony, the young man who wants to marry Alice, and with them the reality of class distinctions in a setting that ignores them; and finally, giving rise to the truly spectacular second act curtain that follows a series on unintentional fireworks explosions, FBI agents, there to investigate suspicions of revolutionary activity. In all cases, these incursions of outside reality are either repelled, as are all the representatives of the government, or, by the conventional logic of romantic comedy, are incorporated into the family, as are Tony and Mr. Kirby. This movement towards incorporation reflects a general pattern of romantic comedy that Northrop Frye has noted:

> As the hero gets closer to the heroine and opposition is overcome, all the right-thinking people come over to his side. Thus a new social unit is formed on the stage … . In the last scene when the dramatist usually tries to get all his characters on the stage at once, the audience witnesses the birth of a renewed sense of social integration … . The freer the society, the greater the variety of individuals it can tolerate, and the natural tendency of comedy is to include as many as possible in its final festival. (Frye 1949: 59–62)

The ideal world of the Vanderhof household becomes a new social unit by the addition of Tony and Mr. Kirby, although this free society is not open to all: Mrs. Kirby is apparently irredeemable in her snobbishness and so left off-stage at the end. Otherwise, all the major characters are folded into the family so that the sense of a utopian sanctuary set off from the outside world is forcefully reasserted at the end of the play. Given this utopianism, it is almost logical that romantic comedy provides the only real sense of forward movement to the *You Can't Take It with You* plot.

In the play, the escapism works by keeping reality at bay. And this is in line with the popular perception of "escapism" as antithetical to "realism," another problematic term because its meanings may be as varied as the number of people who have deployed it. Contra this opposition, I would like to suggest a different understanding: escapism as a narrative mode is not the antithesis of realism for the simple reason that escapism of necessity *inscribes* a reality. This should be clear if we ask two crucial questions, which I think escapist art inevitably prompts us to ask, either implicitly, which is the case with the original Kaufman-Hart play, or explicitly, which is more the case with the film version. What is being escaped from? What is being escaped to? Escapism cannot work as a mode if those two questions are not at the least implicitly addressed because they provide our access to the fantastic world of the fiction. Keeping this in mind, we can see how much the specifics of the play's escapism are a product of its time, and in these specifics we can locate the reality the escapism references, the social order that its comic utopia seeks to counter. Certainly, as we have seen, the Depression is effectively evoked and denied in *You Can't Take It with You* by the carefree living that apparently accompanies unemployment. But there is another dimension here, one that explains the contemporary appreciation lovable loons.

The opening stage directions provide a clue in the description of the setting: "what is customarily described as a living room, but in this house the term is something of an understatement. The every-man-for-himself room would be more like it" (Hart and Kaufman 2004: 121). There is a contemporary context for a world in which everyone gets to do whatever they want, and it is specifically the rise of fascism in Europe, where you get to do only what people tell you to. This "escapist" play, then, is a response to a specific political situation, and it responded with great popular success by celebrating American individualism, even to the point of courting an anarchism that is rendered anodyne only by the innocence of its characters. The union of the couple that ends romantic comedy is never simply about the union of the couple. The promised marriage of Tony to Alice transforms the snobbism of Tony's father and validates a world in which conventional hierarchies are replaced with a radically egalitarian view. In another Sunday think-piece written eight months after the play's premiere, Brooks Atkinson located a previously unnoticed serious core in the Sycamore family's most positive trait, something "even the intellectual should respect":

> They are tolerant people. Although Mrs. Sycamore, the scatter-brained playwright, is not personally interested in fireworks, she recognizes her husband's right to dabble in powder and flame and she inquires charitably after the success of the other hobbies that swoop through her cluttered living-room … in a world which is truculently saying "this is right" to one group of individuals and "this is wrong" to another, it is refreshing to encounter a family so united and charitable that it does not sit in judgment on individual behavior. (Atkinson 1937: X1)

With the Stalinist purges in the Soviet Union, the brutality of the Spanish Civil War (the German Luftwaffe destruction of Guernica in April) and the ascension of General Franco as dictator, the Japanese attacks on China and occupation of Peking in July, and Europe moving closer to continental war, the serious appeal of the play "in a world that is violently on edge," as Atkinson could now describe it, was more apparent. The fact that it took Atkinson so long to recognize it, however, suggests how implicit this content is.

The film works in somewhat different fashion, making its escapism an aesthetic mode for dealing directly with contemporary reality. Part of the changes in the film derives from its following processes of play adaptation that were standard in classical Hollywood. The adaptation process generally involved two interconnected strategies. First, narrative lines were usually simplified because of the much shorter running times of feature films in this period, as well as a sense, especially evident in the 1930s, that films had to move rapidly: there is, for example, an astonishing amount of narrative material presented in the first ten minutes of the film, albeit material not present in the play. Second, since plays in the twentieth-century commercial American theater often operated within fairly restricted settings, as is the case with *You Can't Take It with You*, Hollywood practitioners at the time, drawing on the seemingly infinite possibilities afforded by film, felt that plays had to be "opened up" and the range of settings expanded. This was also seen as a way of simplifying narrative because events in the play that would require extensive exposition might be handled with a few brief shots in the film version.

I want to begin by considering changes to the narrative itself because the film takes an unusual approach in this area. With regards to simplifying the narrative, it is not surprising then that the film drops two prominent characters from the play (the Grand Duchess Olga and the actress Gay Wellington) since this kind of thing happens with some frequency in Hollywood adaptations. But, on the other hand, it adds *four* prominent characters (Mr. Poppins, Mr. Blakeley, Ramsey, and the judge), and then, as if that were not enough, adds to them a host of striking minor characters (the English lord, the jitterbugging kids in the park, Mr. Kirby's business partners, the people in the jail, and the Vanderhof neighbors). As a consequence, contrary to the usual adaptation process, the play seems streamlined, while the movie is densely populated. As one contemporary reviewer of the film emphatically put it, "The story is made up of such a number of side yarns and is so prolix with characters that to go into details would wear me down" (Tinée 1938: 17).

Complementing the much larger cast of characters, Capra and Riskin complicate the play's narrative, although the film does have a shorter running time than the play; this is to say, there is more narrative, but, true to Hollywood style of the period, it generally moves faster. Contemporary reviews took note of the changes and generally regarded the movie as an improvement on the play, both for its richer characterizations and more consequential plot. Narrative complications in the movie come about in two ways. First, Capra and Riskin add a plot element not present in the play by effectively incorporating another genre into romantic comedy: the mortgage melodrama.[1] Commensurately, the film adds two scenes upfront before the point at which the narrative begins in the play; both center on money, a concern largely absent from the play; both are there to set the melodrama plot in motion, and, as a consequence of the "opening-up" process, both move beyond the magical world of the Vanderhof house to the real world of business and politics. Further, while Mr. Kirby in the play is sufficiently a stock Wall Street figure that he does not appear until the middle of Act II, the movie begins with him and his scheme to deprive Vanderhof's neighbors of their homes for his own financial benefit.

From the moment he first appears in the film, Anthony P. Kirby (Edward Arnold) is visually defined as a dynamo, providing a ground against which the Vanderhof-Sycamore loonies will be contrasted: he not only functions in the real world, as they do not, but rather seeks to take control of it. In a period in which antitrust legislation was relatively recent and still had real power, he regards it dismissively, freely claiming of his business, "it will be the largest individual monopoly in the world." Furthermore, what the play invokes implicitly, the film makes explicit when Kirby announces, "with the world going crazy, the next big move is munitions, and Kirby and Company are going to cash in on it." The only craziness in the play resides in the Vanderhof manse itself, and it is always the benign craziness of an egalitarian utopia. The film effectively gives us two kinds of crazy, the less benign version reflecting contemporary events.

By 1938 the world had gone crazier than when the play premiered: with war already underway in Asia, Hitler's annexation of Austria in March made war increasingly inevitable in Europe.[2] In this context, a contemporary audience might well have needed nothing more than Kirby's ambition to monopolize munitions as a sign of moral failing. Nevertheless, the film does offer a different critical view of his aggression in the opening scene. As Kirby recounts his monopolist plans to his assembled factotums, there are two reaction shots of his son, Tony (James Stewart). In the first, Tony rests his head on his hands, only raising his eyes, not his head, when Kirby says, "the next big move is munitions."

The slightness of the gesture seems intended more to undercut Kirby's line than reveal Tony's interest. This is evident when the next shot shows Tony yawning and then examining his nails. As dynamic as Kirby might be, his excitement can't engage Tony, for reasons the film will subsequently make clear.

The business of munitions that the film devises for Kirby is a ingenious extrapolation of something latent in the play. In the play, Grandpa's son-in-law and friends manufacture fireworks in the basement for pleasure. But fireworks are, of course, based on the technology developed for munitions, so Kirby's business in the film sets up an opposition between gunpowder used for realistic – and deadly – purposes and gunpowder in effect used for an aestheticized fantasy divorced from practical application. By beginning with Kirby, the film effectively begins with gunpowder as a prelude to the fireworks of the play, providing a narrative trajectory from purposeful work to a ludic creativity that will be repeatedly echoed throughout the film. While Kirby's attempt to capitalize on the world's craziness with a munitions monopoly does not engage Tony, the crazy family's fireworks will prove as captivating as his romance with Alice. At various points in the film (the dancing children in the park, for example), the romance becomes specifically allied with the spirit of play.

In his monopolistic ambitions, Kirby is always deadly serious, embracing a social Darwinism to turn an attack – "You're no businessman, you're like a lion in the jungle" – into praise: "Yes, and I've got the longest and the sharpest claws, too." As his paterfamilias counterpart in the narrative as well as his counterpoint in philosophy, Grandpa (Lionel Barrymore) specifically rejects all ideology, or as he calls it, "ism-mania," leading off with communism and fascism, the two "isms" dominating Europe. In its place, he recommends "Americanism," an "ism" that denies ideology, or, perhaps we might say that facilitates an *escape* from ideology: "Lincoln said, with malice toward none and charity to all. Nowadays they say, think the way I do, or I'll bomb the daylights out of ya." As a counter to fascism, Grandpa's invocation of Lincoln's Second Inaugural Address might seem an odd opposition. The bulk of Lincoln's address, delivered as war continued to rage, dealt with the issue of slavery as a cause of the war. Why not someone more contemporary actually speaking against fascism? As Grandpa quietly laughs to himself over his last remark, the next shot provides an answer: Rheba (Lillian Yarbo), the black maid, enters the image and, strikingly, for the time, offers advice and commentary to Penny on her writing: she suggests that Penny should go back to her war play because "I liked that one best." There is something like an unconscious logic in this sequencing of shots that moves us from Lincoln and the Civil War to Rheba. Rheba's preference for "your war play" becomes particularly pointed given that Grandpa posits the opposition to Lincoln's generosity as "I'll bomb the daylights out of ya."

As a way of getting at the importance of Rheba, a seemingly minor stock character, I want to consider how the film offers a number of striking qualifiers to the very values it seem to embrace. Because Grandpa in the film is established independently of the house and out in the real world, he always stands somewhat to the side of the oddities of the other characters. The film further reinforces this by making him less eccentric than the play's Grandpa. So, for example, where the Grandpa of the play collects snakes, this more ordinary Grandpa of the film collects stamps. As the most ordinary member of this household, along with Alice, Grandpa becomes something of an ally for the audience, for which reason the film introduces him before any other member of the family. Further, the alliance is repeatedly reinforced by reaction shots that make Grandpa's view of an action or character dominant. Because it sets him so decisively apart from the other characters, one striking moment stresses our alliance with him in a way that undercuts the valorization of wackiness embodied by the other characters.

This runs counter to the play, where Grandpa is always benignly indulgent of all his zany progeny and their equally zany spouses, and is even somewhat zany himself. The moment comes in a scene that shows the various activities members of this extended family may engage in on a given evening. Grandpa is throwing darts, while Donald (Eddie Anderson), Rheba's boyfriend, is setting the table for dinner. Mr. DePinna (Halliwell Hobbes), the ice delivery man who walked off the job to move in eight years previously, has convinced Penny (Spring Byington) to return to her previous artistic endeavor, painting, and resume a portrait of Mr. DePinna as a Roman discus thrower. In need of a discus, Mr. DePinna, without asking, grabs a plate from Donald, who is about to set it on the table. Next Essie (Ann Miller), intent on beginning her dance lesson with Kolenkhov, comes downstairs and walks by the strange sight of Mr. DePinna posing in costume with plate without taking notice. As Essie, her husband Ed (Dub Taylor), and Kolenkhov role up the carpet so she can begin dancing, exposing three backsides to the camera, there is a cut to Grandpa, getting ready to throw a dart, but suddenly taking notice of this strange sight. A cut back to the backsides offers further provocation, which the next shot of Grandpa realizes: he aims the dart towards this most tempting target. Hesitating, he finally drops the dart, pushes his hair back as if to control his impulse, but does take one glance back at the abandoned target with some expression of regret. I have described just enough of what precedes the moment of Grandpa aiming the dart to demonstrate how the film makes us aware of the provocation, namely how very self-absorbed and narrowly focused these people are.

While a contemporary review of the play could implicitly acknowledge a contradictory appeal by describing it as "an evening in an amiable amateur psychopathic ward" (Farcical Antics of Lovable Loons 1936: 22), by the time of the film, the New York Times reviewer could note of the "batty family": "they'd be amusing to visit, but terrible to live with" – an insight likely facilitated by the film itself (Nugent 1938b: X3). With Grandpa's temptation, the film works its most daring transformation on the play: it acknowledges that while these characters might be fun to watch, they could be quite irritating if you actually had to interact with them. In fact, they could be irritating to spend an entire movie with, which is why they must work best as secondary characters whom we get in small doses. As a consequence, with Grandpa's one gesture the film compromises the play's project as a celebration of individualism, making explicit that we clearly value some individuals more than others, much as Grandpa values Alice over his other progeny.

In the larger scheme of this narrative, some characters are meant to be laughed at, while others are meant to be our allies. The play need not make this hierarchy explicit, as the film does, because convention and genre help us understand implicitly that the ultra-conventional romantic couple are the characters we are supposed to feel closest to. In the film, our allies are the characters we might define as "normal," if we can understand normal to mean characters who could function in the real world, which is, after all, where the narrative of the film begins. The chief thing I want to take from the sudden revelation of Grandpa's mischievous desire is that the film offers us an appealing utopian ideal as a counter to a world careening towards war at the same time that it provides the grounds for critiquing that ideal.

This movement in two contradictory directions is perhaps most striking with the characters of Rheba and Donald, fairly conventional racial stereotypes that the film inherits from the play, but also to some degree undermines. I can best get at their overt function in the narrative by posing a simple question: how can this nearly anarchic social group in which everyone is single-mindedly focused on his or her own little obsessions whether making fireworks, dancing, or writing plays, how can such a group function as well as it does? The solution is simple: black help. On his first appearance in the play, Donald announces, "I don't go no place much. I'm on relief" (695). And relief in the play is repeatedly used to reinforce jokes about Donald's laziness as when he complains about the arduousness of collecting relief: "Only thing is you got to go round to the place every week and collect it, and sometimes you got to stand in line pretty near half an hour" (725). With this remark Donald seems to move in the direction of the character type perfected onscreen by Stepin Fetchitt.

This stereotype is undercut from the outset by the casting of Eddie Anderson, who was already well-known in this period as the wily chauffeur Rochester on the "Jack Benny Show," then the most popular show on radio. And while Donald's first line in the film seems to echo the stereotype of the play – "I ain't done nothing, but I'm sure tired" – there are countercurrents. After Rheba initially complains that he is always tired, she puts him to work setting the table, an activity we see him perform a couple of times in the film. Donald's slight needling in his response to Rheba's command, "I don't see why I gotta do your work just cause we're engaged," makes the line sounds a bit like something Rochester might say on the radio show. But it's a line that also serves to point out a salient aspect of his character for the film: he does the job without being employed or recompensed, and his unpaid work will remain a consistent motif. In fact, throughout the rest of the film, we inevitably see Donald perform quite a lot of work for the family and often with more energy than any other character.

In the play, our introduction to the crazy family begins with Penny, as she tries to write her latest play and uses the kitten as a paper weight. I've already indicated that the opening of the play is pushed back to the third sequence of the movie. And even then there's an additional delay because, rather than beginning with Penny and her kitten, the movie begins with Rheba, who is rarely directly involved in the film's action. Nevertheless, her introduction is handled with a striking visual motif that represents an extrapolation and elaboration of a line from the play. Towards the end of Act One, Alice's tells Tony how her grandfather suddenly stopped working: "Thirty-five years ago he just quit business one day. He started up to his office in the elevator and came right down again. He just stopped" (714). Alice has similar dialogue at roughly the same point in the narrative in the film, but it is has been prepared visually in the first two sequences, and then it is made emphatic when Grandpa himself describes his decisive ride on the elevator to Kirby during the jail scene. As the narrative contrives it, Kirby will repeat the same action as a transition to the film's final scene.

The film renders this arriving-departing action as a visual motif of opening and closing elevator doors, established at the very beginning of the movie when Kirby goes up to his office the first time. Much as it provides the lead-in to the first dialogue scene, it serves as a transition linking the second sequence to the third. At the end of the second sequence, Mr. Poppins, an accountant working for Kirby's real estate broker, decides to leave the drudgery of work and accept Grandpa's invitation to stay with him and become a "lily of the field," free of economic necessity. When Poppins runs after Grandpa and joins him on an elevator, the elevator doors close, decisively cutting him off from the world of work. At this point there is a direct cut to the interior of a closed cupboard with a pitcher, salt and pepper shakers, a cruet and dishes in the foreground. The cupboard opens via sliding doors that perfectly mirror the elevator doors of the last shot. A whistling Rheba, who has just opened the cupboard, takes out the pitcher and shakers, while Essie, in soft focus, dances in the background near the stove. As she pours milk into the pitcher, Rheba asks Essie about Grandpa, effectively picking up on the last scene by wondering how many people Grandpa might bring home to dinner. Essie then dances into the living room, at which point we see Penny and her kitten paperweight, the action that opens the play.

As a way of getting at the door imagery, I want to briefly linger over Mr. Poppins because he is the film's most notable addition to the dramatis personae of the play. In accepting Grandpa's invitation, he is not simply leaving the deadening world of business. Rather, he is leaving to pursue his penchant for making cute gadgets, one of which had attracted Grandpa, who tells him, "It seems to me, Mr. Poppins, that this is the kind of work you ought to be doing." Grandpa, then, is not so much advocating a complete rejection of work, but, rather, encouraging a different kind of work. Because the musical toy Mr. Poppins shows Grandpa is attractive – it pulls in his coworkers like a magnet – it is significant that we meet Poppins *before* we see any of the lovable loons from the play. The work of the other "lilies" is generally rendered silly and nonproductive: Essie can't dance, Penny never finishes either her plays or her paintings, Ed prints up flyers solely because he likes running a printing press, Kolenkhov is more sponge than dance instructor, and so on. By using Poppins's creative activity, a counter to his work as an accountant, as an introduction to the varied hobbies of the family, the film places a value on all creative work that is absent from the play even if that work seems of no particular value.

The use of the opening-closing door motif as a transition between these two scenes should suggest a definitive rejection of a world where work is routine and mechanical in order to enter into a world of creative play. But the matter is somewhat complicated by the fact that we begin with Rheba, the one member of the household who actually works *for* the household, something underscored by the fact that she continues to work as she talks to Essie. Since, as we subsequently learn, Essie had been making candy, her positioning by the stove could involve similar work. But, instead, the shot initially creates a contrast between Rheba's purposeful work and Essie's free-form dancing. Rheba's whistling, something that will be picked up on in a later scene, could indicate a pleasure in her work, but it is still in contrast to Essie, who, the shot implies, can indulge her free spirit because there is someone to take care of practical matters. The Vanderhof paradise, then, is not entirely free from work, and it can offer different *kinds* of work.

Beginning the sequence with Rheba as our point of access effectively makes her a member of the family and, by emphasizing the practical nature of her activities, allies her with Grandpa and Alice, who are both more oriented towards the real world. It might seem odd to us now, but the treatment of Rheba along with Donald caused some problem for the film during production in the form of a warning from the Production Code Administration. In a letter to Harry Cohn, dated March 7, 1938, Production Code head Joseph Breen wrote, "Here and elsewhere, showing of the negro characters, Rheba and Donald, care should be taken to avoid objection in Southern sections of this country where the showing of negroes in association with whites has sometimes been subjected to criticism by the public generally and to deletion by political censor boards. Such criticism has been based on the feeling that negroes in pictures have been shown on terms too familiar and of 'social equality'" (History of Cinema 2006: 1938). In his autobiography, *The Name above the Title*, Capra seems to directly challenge the PCA, albeit it after the fact and perhaps unconsciously, by referring to Rheba and Donald as "the Negro branch of the family" (Capra 1971: 243). Furthermore, the film does at times make them family members *visually*, especially in group shots in which they are fully integrated into the group, a truly utopian gesture in this period (see Figure 13.1). Finally, genre gives them a special role in the film since they effectively fall into romantic comedy convention of the second couple, a couple who parallels the main couple, but is always earthier, often funnier, generally more physical – we do briefly see them dance a mean jitterbug as a contrast to Essie's clumsy ballet – and inevitably lower class than the main couple.

Figure 13.1   Family grouping (*You Can't Take It with You*; producer, Frank Capra).

Much as the second couple both parallels but differs from the main couple, there are times when their integration into the family also points to difference, much as Rheba's work is differentiated from Essie's play in the shot that introduces them. Consider the one time the film shows us what is actually going on in the basement. For a film apparently about the joys of not working, it is odd how much time is actually spent at the workplace and on details of work. In the long shot that begins the scene, we see Alice's father Paul (Samuel S. Hinds), De Pinna, Poppins, Ed and Donald each working on his specific task. Following this is a series of four shots that show individuals at work: Poppins carving a figure, De Pinna and Paul separately working on their fireworks, and finally Donald, who is packaging Essie's candy. On the soundtrack is a whistled tune emerging from one of Poppins's carved figure, specifically "Whistle While You Work" from *Snow White and the Seven Dwarfs*, itself a very recent film (December 1937), reiterating the connection between whistling and work made in Rheba's first appearance. The tune might be taken as celebratory, as it is in the source film, where the song helps turn housework into play and the dwarfs themselves engage in jewel mining that is more aesthetic than purposeful. Moreover, the childlike quality of the dwarfs carries over to the way the men are portrayed here.

Nevertheless, the scene actually revolves around an oscillation between criticism and celebration. The criticism is in line with what we see in the play, a sense that the world of conventional work has become deadening even as Americans in the 1930s might have given anything to have one of those deadening situations simply to stay alive. As if often true with this film, the criticism from the play is made more specific. Donald's work does not spring from his own interest, as work does with the other men in the scene. Rather, he is packaging Essie's candies and doing so with the help of an avian assistant, a crow named Jim, who picks up empty packages and brings them to Donald to fill. In presentation the action both evokes and critiques the assembly line, with the worker crow providing something of the critique, suggesting this is work that befits a trained animal. On the other hand, work as configured here is made better because it is connected to creativity, with Mr. Poppins the most wildly creative of the group and commensurately, as the film has it, the most childlike, previously the most deadened by the grown-up world of work and responsibility.

Implicit in this scene, then, is a key opposition: work as drudgery, mechanical and thoughtless, and work as play, fully engaging our creative and imaginative sensibilities. This is what Grandpa has found with his stamp collecting, which helps keeps the family afloat, and it is what Tony, breaking away from his father, seeks in embracing the Vanderhof ethos through his courtship of Alice. But it is also something chiefly available to white male characters in the film. Essie and Penny do engage in creative play, but their creativity is consistently ridiculed as that of the men is not. On the other hand, Alice, Rheba, and Donald are all always engaged in more purposeful work throughout the film. In the "Whistle While You Work" scene, Donald seems to be more of an equal to the other men in that he appears with them in the establishing shot and is granted his own separate shot as are three of the other men. But even if the cutting creates a kind of parallel and Donald's work might be made playful by the use of the crow, the crow also renders it as routine, making it finally less play than work, having the very practical end of getting packages ready for sale. The white characters, then, may engage in purely creative pursuits because there is someone present to do the practical work.

As characters who occupy a special place in the family setting, both in it and not quite of it, Donald and Rheba facilitate the film's access to its most foreign setting, the jail. In the context of an escapist fiction, this sequence, running a full ten minutes, is the most striking because it moves the furthest away from the utopian world to something of a dystopia. Although only briefly talked about after the fact in the play, in the film it is also the sequence that is the true climax of the narrative, ratcheting up all the emotional conflicts that have been simmering under the surface: first the problematic relationship between Tony and his father, the hostility of Mrs. Kirby towards Alice, Grandpa's seemingly disengaged, possibly ironic, but always courteous responses to the Kirbys, which moves finally to an angry outburst against Mr. Kirby. Appropriately, it is the sequence in which the central romantic relationship becomes most imperiled.

Donald and Rheba are separated here as the jail segregates the sexes, but each is given a remark that both allies them and makes clear their familiarity with the setting. The first shot in the jail, a very crowded long shot, is set up in such a way that we initially don't have a clear view of the cell's inhabitants; rather, the *mise-en-scène* directs us to our familiar characters and specifically to Donald, who, alone among these characters, is pushed into the cell with a dismissive gesture by a policeman. After an annoyed look at the policeman, Donald surveys the cell and says resignedly, "Home again." Donald's remark might fit in with the initial "shiftless Negro" stereotype, but since the film has repeatedly overturned the stereotype after first instancing it, and, in this case, we know the arrest is not warranted by events, the line of dialogue can seem dissonant. How much so is made evident when we move to the women's ward. While Penny seems to be having fun recalling their ride in the police van, Mrs. Kirby, outraged, walks away and sits next to Rheba, who offers practical advice: "Better sit on your hands, Mrs. Kirby. It gets kind of cold after you set awhile." Nothing we have learned about Rheba up to this point – she's one of the few gainfully employed people in the film and she is always industrious – could have prepared us for this remark, which indicates not just that she has been in jail before, but that she has been there often enough to have gained this practical knowledge.

How can we make sense of the special role granted Donald and Rheba here? The actual prison population is key: it's appropriate that the sequence begins with Donald recognizing "home" because here we see a range of class and race that exists nowhere else in the movie. And, I should add, it is a demographic we almost never glimpse in any other movie of the period, even those with a prison setting. There is, then, a kind of realism here not evident in works from the period that might be regarded as more realistic. But there is also an implicit attitude towards this population you are also not likely to see: given that we learn both Donald and Rheba have apparently been in prison before, we cannot but question the justness of incarceration for the people that we do see there.

The roles of Donald and Rheba here are also critical because the sequence is truly at the core of the film, both emotionally and thematically. As it combines a kind of sociological realism, broadly extending the class range of the play, with an escapist fantasy, it is key to my argument. Of particular importance is a stylistic strategy employed by the sequence that I can best get at by looking closely at one moment. About a third of the way into this sequence, Kirby, impatiently waiting for his lawyers, lights up a cigar. As he does so, at two different points in the action Capra cuts to different reaction shots of groups of men milling about and looking hungrily at Kirby. The group in the first shot is framed by a black man on the left and a Chinese man in Chinese costuming on the right (see Figure 13.2); in the second, the camera is closer in and the black man, moved to the right of center, is somewhat more prominent. Set against these images of other men's desires, Kirby complains, "Spend a quarter of a million dollars a year for attorneys, and I can't get one of them." Disgusted, he throws the barely smoked cigar to the floor, which prompts most of the men in the cell to dive for possession of it. Into this action, Capra cuts another reaction shot, this time of Paul, who is smoking a pipe, Ed and Kolenkhov as they look at the scramble, clearly struck by what they see. From another shot of the melee, Capra cuts to a medium single of Grandpa, who reacts viscerally to the men's hunger, but then looks up towards Kirby. A medium single of Kirby could initially seem to follow Grandpa's expression, but soon Kirby's face clearly takes on a look of disgust. A return to the shot of Grandpa

Figure 13.2   Prison demographics (*You Can't Take It with You*; producer, Frank Capra).

has him look back at the men, shake his head over their desperation, and then briefly look back to Kirby in a way that suggests he's trying to take in how much this affects the man. This is a remarkably complex piece of filmmaking – one that sets reactions against reactions, with each building on or modifying the other. So, for example, we could possibly see Kirby's reaction as continuing a negative line of development for the character, but not entirely because we also get Grandpa's reaction to Kirby's reaction. The fact that Grandpa responds empathically to Kirby as well has to modify the way we look at him.

The range of responses here functions as a stylistic metaphor for the broad social class spread that is unique to this scene, an opening-up of the play in the most profound sense of that term in that it virtually explodes the insular world of the play's setting. It is as if we have to move outside the bounds of a conventional social order, as well as outside the bounds of genre conventions, to arrive at this reality – or perhaps we need a jail cell in order to contain all the disparate and contentious elements that make up a pluralistic society, elements that could not otherwise be forced to integrate. This moving beyond genre likely accounts for the claim by Frank S. Nugent, in a Sunday column, that "the picture manages to be as funny as the play (when it wants to be) without being entirely a comedy" (Nugent, "Traces" 1938: X1). Other contemporary critics had no trouble seeing the film as a comedy, with many thinking it retained the laugh quotient of its source but improved on its plotting and sense of character. Still, I think it worth lingering over Nugent's categorical hesitation because its source clearly derives from the film's move into melodrama. This move also characterizes Capra's subsequent prewar films, *Mr. Smith Goes to Washington* (1939) and *Meet John Doe* (1941), but in both of those the melodrama progressively outweighs the comedy, with the possibility of an escapist utopia lost as the world became increasingly desperate. The resulting genre conflicts likely accounts for the difficulty Capra had in fashioning an ending for each of the later films.

By contrast, the melodrama of *You Can't Take It with You* itself becomes a comic strategy, facilitating the ebullient return to a utopian vision. Drawing on Henri Bergson's *élan vital*, Suzanne Langer has proposed a way of thinking about comedy and the nature of laughter that is relevant here:

> The pure sense of life is the underlying feeling of comedy, developed in countless different ways … Laughter, or the tendency to laugh … seems to arise from a surge of vital feeling … Real comedy sets up in the audience a sense of general exhilaration, because it presents the very image of "livingness" and the perception of it is exciting. Whatever the story may be, it takes the form of a temporary triumph over the surrounding world. (Langer 1953: 327, 340, 348)

It is precisely the move out into "the surrounding world" that facilitates the "surge of vital feeling" embodied in the triumph of a utopian view. This play between drama and comedy is hardly unique to Capra. One of the most tenacious structural attributes of romantic comedy is the change in dramatic tone that generally occurs before the final movement of the narrative, a point at which the future union of the couple seems most in doubt: a lessening of jokes, a slowing down of pace, a realization that the comic conflicts might have more serious consequences than previously appeared. In Northrop Frye's seasonal view of comedy, which he designates the "Mythos of Spring," this is the wintry section of the narrative (Frye 1957: 171). This section in the Capra–Riskin *You Can't Take It with You* is unusual both for its length and the extent to which it moves out into the real world. Yet the real world as it is conceived here also serves to validate the ideals represented by the film's utopianism.

Even as the jail scene decisively moves the narrative away from the utopian world of the Vanderhof home, the seeds for this scene had been planted earlier by Grandpa in his call for an "ism" that can vanquish all other "isms." By its large cast of characters, ranging widely across the entire social order, the jail scene presents the most evident representation of Grandpa's Americanism. But he initially posited this "ism" comfortably from an easy chair in a middle class living room. Seeing this diversity in actuality in a jail cell makes it something else and possibly undercuts any lingering sentimentality we might attribute to Grandpa's speech. The individualism that Grandpa eulogizes, and the "everyone doing what they want" aspect that the house epitomizes, is turned on end in this scene both by Kirby, who has everything, but still asserting his rights of possession, and by the image of men reduced by economic necessity to fighting over one cigar.

On the other hand, even if we have a sense of confronting the real world here more than anywhere else in the film, there is no doubt the scene is not only escapist, but also ultimately comic in its move towards a possible social reintegration. The first reaction shots of the crowd when they hear Kirby's name raise a suggestion of violence in the potential class conflict. But even as violence remains an undercurrent throughout much of the sequence, by its end the film returns us to a fantasy of good will. When Kirby dismisses the "scum" in the jail cell, Grandpa responds with an extended attack in which he calls him a failure, "failure as a man, failure as a human being, even a failure as a father." The attack clearly stings, and Grandpa regrets his outburst. As a peace offering, having previously urged Kirby to relax a little by playing the harmonica, Grandpa slips a harmonica into Kirby's pocket. At this point, Capra provides the final reaction shot of the sequence: a very close shot of the group of the men, now all smiling in response to this gesture. With this shot, the sequence that gives us the most precise view of a contemporary reality, then, also moves us back towards the film's utopian fantasy, with a crowd as malleable as the crowd in Shakespeare's *Julius Caesar*.

Arguably it is the safety valve of the scene's final escapist gesture that enables us to look so closely at these contending social forces, riven and irreconcilable in reality, most likely, but made whole here by the conventional comic move towards social integration. And it is Capra's stylistic strategy that makes possible our belief in this integration. In managing to give us reaction shots for virtually every character in this scene, ranging from minor individuals to our major characters to shots of the entire crowd reacting, the film sets into motion a range of diverging and converging points of view. More than any other moment in the film, the stylistic complexity of this scene validates the impulses behind the utopian ideal of community that the film embraces.

As Donald and Rheba in the film, from their roles as simple supernumeraries in the play, become characters who actually expand the class range within the family, after the jail sequence they serve to remind us of a world beyond the "every-man-for-himself room" of the play, the world that we have seen in the jail. The way they work in the film is forcefully restated in the last shot, which, at first glance could seem more escapist than the original play. In the play, as I noted, Mrs. Kirby remains off-stage at the end because she is apparently irredeemable. The film, on the other hand, might seem to move towards a more utopian vision as it includes all the major characters in an image so crowded people spill out the edge of the frame. But there are two very important qualifiers here: first, the interaction between Kolenkhov and Mrs. Kirby; second, the placement of Donald and Rheba. After Grandpa tells Rheba to serve the dinner, a two-shot shows Kolenkhov deliver a hearty slap to Mrs. Kirby's back as he says, "Now it is two easy lessons, Mrs. Kirby … " Mrs. Kirby jumps, clearly feeling the sting of the slap, and looks offended until Kolenhov mollifies her by whispering in her ear. Mrs. Kirby's initial response is appropriate to the provocation, having nothing to do with her previous snobbishness, and it serves as a reminder of how annoying these people can be.

The final shot itself reiterates that the hard work of Rheba and Donald is essential for this image of fruitfulness and freedom from want. One of the most

Figure 13.3   The final festival (*You Can't Take It with You*; producer, Frank Capra).

striking things about this image is that, for the first time in the film, both Rheba and Donald appear in formal servant uniform (see Figure 13.3). While Rheba has never worn anything remotely like this earlier in the film, even more puzzling is how Donald might have come by his uniform. While never actually employed by the family, here he has fully assumed the role of servant, an odd discordant note in the image of harmony. The fact that they are chiefly there to facilitate the dinner is underscored by their sudden disappearance from the image before the final fade out. While the film initially seems to follow Frye by including "as many as possible in its final festival," for Rheba and Donald the inclusion must be only partial and temporary. The film effectively ends with a feast, not unlike a wedding, celebrating the union of a couple that brings together two opposing families, but the couple that makes the feast possible is erased from the festivity. As a generic feature, the second couple is always expendable.

Throughout this chapter, I have been trying to sketch out a more positive way of looking at escapism, principally by trying to sever the escapist-realist binary. Realism should not in itself only mean a world in which bad things happen. The kind of self-awareness and emotional complexity I have been arguing for in *You Can't Take It with You* can in themselves signal a kind of realism. Further, the escapism of romantic comedy, as I have been arguing, is inevitably based in a particular reality: every utopian vision represented by the couple's union is shaped by the social and historical context in which it is imagined. What we need to consider in developing an aesthetics of escapism is how forcefully any work is able to artic-ulate that reality and, as a consequence, how effectively it can make us feel the valid emotions that give foundation to escapist desire. What I finally find most compelling about *You Can't Take It with You* is the way the film both retains its escapism and repeatedly reminds us of the source of its appeal: the desire for social harmony in a world made up of fractious desires and behaviors; the desire for a classless social order where all work can become play so long as there is a working class to support it.

Notes

1. An article written while the film was in production noted, "Strengthened in the motion picture manner, the plot has been galvanized by the addition of a mortgage foreclosure device" (Churchill 1938: X3). Grandpa owns his house, so the only actual mortgages are those of his neighbors. But Churchill's observations make it clear that the plot effectively invoked a familiar genre for the contemporary observer.
2. There is evidence the screenplay was still being written in this period. Lionel Barrymore was the first actor to be cast, with an announcement made in the second week of February. Robert Riskin and Capra were working on the screenplay throughout the casting, as indicated by the narrative's offering an explanation for Grandpa's inability to walk. Final casting was completed in the middle of April, and production began April 25 (News of the Screen 1938: 11; Of Local Origin 1938: 16).

References

Atkinson, Brooks (1936) Topsy-Turvydom. *New York Times* (December 20), p. X3.

Atkinson, Brooks (1937) Y–C–T–I–W–Y–. *New York Times* (August 29), p. X1.

Bowen, Stirling (1937) The Theatre. *Wall Street Journal* (January 4), p. 15.

Capra, Frank (1971) *The Name Above the Title*, Macmillan, New York, NY.

Churchill, Douglas W. (1938) Hollywood and Its Little Women. *New York Times* (May 15), p. X3.

Cinema (1938) *Time* (September 12), pp. 42–5.

Collins, Charles (1937) "Can't Take It with You" Is Gleeful Roar. *Chicago Daily Tribune* (February 8), p. 15.

Ebenkampe, Becky (2009) A Hollywood Ending for '08 Makes Case of Escapism. *Bandweek* (January 5), p. 6.

Farcical Antics of Lovable Loons (1936) *Literary Digest* (December 26), p. 22.

Frye, Northrop (1949) The argument of comedy, in *English Institute Essays 1948* (ed. D. A. Robertson, Jr.), Columbia University Press, New York, NY, pp. 59–62.

Frye, Northrop (1957) *Anatomy of Criticism: Four Essays*, Princeton University Press, Princeton, NJ.

Hart–Kaufman Play Bought by Columbia (1937) *New York Times* (January 12), p. 19.

Hart, Moss and Kaufman, George S. (2004) *You Can't Take It with You* in *Kaufman & Co.: Broadway Comedies*, The Library of America, New York, NY.

History of Cinema (2006) Series 1, Hollywood and the Production Code. Selected files from the Motion Picture Association of America Production Code Administration collection, Woodbridge, CT. Microfilm.

Langer, Suzanne (1953) *Feeling and Form: A Theory of Art*, Charles Scribner's Sons, New York, NY.

McClintock, Pamela (2008) H'W'D Gets Bump from Slump. *Variety* (June 30–July 13), pp. 1, 58.

News of the Screen (1938) *New York Times* (April 18), p. 11.

Nugent, Frank S. (1938a) Picking up the Traces. *New York Times* (September 4), p. X1.

Nugent, Frank S. (1938b) These Touching Honors. *New York Times* (September 11), p. X3.

Of Local Origin (1938) *New York Times* (February 9), p. 16.

The Theatre (1936) *Time* (December 28), p. 33.

Tinée, Mae (1938) Movie version of stage hit is just as funny. *Chicago Daily Tribune* (October 8), p. 17. (Using a standard bibliographical listing of last name first obscures that this name is a pseudonym derived from "matinee.")

Further Reading

Sikov, Ed (1989) *Screwball: Hollywood's Madcap Romantic Comedies*, Crown Publishers, New York. Impressively thorough historical research combined with astute critical analysis make this a key text for anyone interested in screwball comedy.

14

The Totalitarian Comedy of Lubitsch's *To Be or Not To Be*

Maria DiBattista

First a disclaimer: in offering up Ernst Lubitsch's wartime farce, *To Be Or Not To Be* (1942), as an example, perhaps the defining and supreme example, of totalitarian comedy, I am not suggesting either his moral idiocy or (I hope) mine. I mean the phrase – indeed the very notion – of "totalitarian comedy" to be a disquieting one. How could it be otherwise? Comedy is a genre that encourages laughter and instills moral as well as formal confidence in "a happy ending" that gratifies the human desire for love and social harmony. Thus it hardly seems "right," much less decent, to suggest that comedy, with its endemic and intractable optimism, can have anything meaningful to say about the outrages of totalitarian regimes: the brutal suppression of dissent; the indiscriminate slaughter of civilians; the campaigns to liquidate entire racial, ethnic, or culturally reviled populations; the fanatical insistence that civilian institutions, habits, and traditions of the everyday conform to a fixed ideological regimen that serves state rather than personal interests.

Nonetheless, there exists a small but hardy and venerable body of opinion, amounting almost to a tradition, which embraces the comic precisely for its power to confront unmitigated atrocities and corral them into the realm of the human, where they are again subject to our imaginative control and correction. One of the more eloquent expressions of this conviction is to be found in the diary that the Polish writer Witold Gombrowicz kept during World War II. "In moments when devastating conditions force us to complete inner transformation," he wrote, "laughter is our last resort. It draws us out of ourselves and allows our humanity to survive independently of the painful changes in our shell ... No nation has needed laughter more than we do today. And never has a nation *understood* laughter's liberating role less" (Gombrowicz 1988:101). Milan Kundera, also familiar with totalitarian assaults on everyday life, not only understands the

A Companion to Film Comedy, First Edition. Edited by Andrew Horton and Joanna E. Rapf.
© 2013 John Wiley & Sons, Inc. Published 2016 by John Wiley & Sons, Inc.

liberating role of laughter amid the devastating conditions imposed by totalitarian states, but celebrates it as a singularly modern invention – "the marriage of the not-serious and dreadful," he calls it (Kundera 1996: 4).

Totalitarian comedy represents the most scandalous offspring of this distinctly modern marriage of the not-serious and the dreadful. This lineage not only explains, but justifies the disclaimer with which I began this chapter: by totalitarian comedy, I do not mean comedies sponsored by, or designed to placate, totalitarian regimes. Such comedies, like the regimes that authorize and promote them, are unremittingly dreadful, and whatever laughter they promote is forced, ghastly, and *very* serious. I mean, rather, comedies that represent totalitarian governments and their ideology in all their dreadfulness, but that do so un-seriously; I mean comedies that refuse to silence their insolent wit or suspend their unruly farces just when they are most needed and least tolerated – during the reigns of unfreedom. We might say, echoing Gombrowicz, that totalitarian comedy is the comedy of last resort for those people, cultures and societies that face annihilation either in the form of physical extinction or in the complete transformation of the conditions and terms of their existence.

Northrop Frye's suggestive remark that the action of comedy entails a movement from a society marked by ritual bondage and arbitrary law to a new or pragmatically free society gives us a vital clue to its singular generic, and, indeed, moral character (Frye 1966: 167–9). Frye is thinking primarily of Shakespearean comedies like *Comedy of Errors* and *A Midsummer's Night Dream*, but this purposeful movement propels the best and sturdiest of classic American film comedies, from *It Happened One Night* (1934), *Bringing up Baby* (1938), *Holiday* (1938), *The Philadelphia Story* (1940), *The Lady Eve* (1941), and some of the other films discussed in this volume – all of which celebrate the self-delighting moments when inhibitions are suddenly shed: getting a piggyback ride (*It Happened One Night*), chasing leopards in Connecticut (*Baby*), performing cartwheels out of sheer physical joy (*Holiday*), or howling naked at the moon, as Tracy Lord is said to have done in her rare moments of unloosed emotion (*The Philadelphia Story*). These moments of unfettered instinctual life not only free comic protagonists from the strictures of their own personality and the repressive social mores that have defined them; they also instill an appetite for happiness that eventually will insist on being satisfied in any subsequent scheme of life. To imagine such schemes of reformed life is the great business of comedy.

Totalitarian regimes threaten this comic understanding of what a liberated personality and renewed society might be like. Totalitarian despots are inspired by their own sick but vital dreams of a "happy ending," one in which the world will be completely remade into a "new society" that will abolish any trace of pragmatic freedom and subdue individual impulse by the strict enforcement of authoritarian law. It is in this respect, and perhaps only in this respect, that totalitarian regimes qualify as comic subjects: in their declared intention not only to redefine our notion of what the good society is, but, more dreadfully, what human beings are and can become. Their main political objective is to subjugate entire populations to ritual bondage, to reduce human behavior to ideological reflex. This explains why, as we will see, a genocidal eugenics is not just an accidental, but necessary and central theme of totalitarian comedy as it is of totalitarian regimes.

No one explored the liberating role of laughter in resisting such totalitarian designs with more confident wit than Ernst Lubitsch, a director primarily identified by the gossamer sophistications of his inimitable "touch," a touch so light that it passed over the objects graced by its visitations without leaving the slightest moral imprint (see also the chapters by Morrow and Deleyto in this volume).[1] That touch was justly celebrated when it wrought its magic on comedies of manners like *Trouble in Paradise* (1932) or musicals set in mythical kingdoms like Sylvania (*The Love Parade* 1929) and Flausenthurm (*The Smiling Lieutenant* 1931). It was tolerated, even applauded in *Ninotchka* (1939), his ebullient satire on the transformative encounter of a Soviet emissary (a divinely androgynous and humorless Great Garbo) with the romantic culture of Paris, which Lubitsch presents as one of the finest yet also the most morally infirm achievements of the beauty- and pleasure-loving Capitalist West. *Ninotchka* is Lubitsch's first foray into the moral minefield of totalitarian comedy but you could hardly tell from his comic assurance in presiding over the wedding of the not-serious and the dreadful. We can see how his "touch" remains as light and as penetrating as ever in the almost throwaway line that exposes the comical element in Ninotchka's fanatical devotion to Soviet ideals. Asked by the comrades who welcome her to Paris how things are at home, she reports – without a flicker of moral revulsion – that "the Moscow trials have been a great success. There will be fewer but better Russians."

The comic temperament that could wring a genocidal joke out of the Soviet purges was hailed in 1939. But it was almost universally denounced in 1942, when *To Be or Not to Be* opened. Not only did the film depict the war and the Nazi occupation of Poland as a tragic theater ripe for farce, but also the recent death of its luminous star, Carole Lombard, in an air crash returning from a tour to sell war bonds, cast a further pall over the film. Unlike Chaplin's *The Great Dictator*, whose mordant satire on the Nazi regime is set in Tomania, *To Be or Not to Be* sets its backstage farce about a troupe of Polish actors called upon to play their part in the Underground movement in a "real" historical time and space – Warsaw just before and after the outbreak of the war. Moreover, Lubitsch doesn't resort, as Chaplin does in the final scene of *The Great Dictator*, to a rousing declamation of the political principles that comedy, in league with a democratic, progressive politics, promotes: prosperity, social harmony, the freedom to make "life free and beautiful, to make this life a wonderful adventure." Lubitsch never permits himself or his actors to "speak" except through the mask of comic imposture.

This decision puts tremendous pressure on Lubitsch to demonstrate that his own comic sense of human nature, particularly as manifested in its sexual behaviors, might not only survive the Nazi horror story unfolding in Europe, but actually be enlisted in the battle against it. Comedy is given to chiding those in charge of the world, but seldom in ousting them; it is always moving forward to a happy time, when marriages are made in a society purged, however temporarily, of dissent and obsession. *To Be Or Not To Be* poses a direct challenge (one that can sound, at times, like a threat) to comedy's moral standing in representing the devastating conditions of totalitarian occupation and world war. The film's title, which at first seems to be no more than a comic wink at Hamlet's more existential and proudly tragic struggle with a corrupt and murderous regime, can also be read as a loaded question about the film's own right to exist. The question may be put this way: should the comic corrective, essentially conservative and humane in regarding history and its agents as subject to reform but never elimination, be *trusted* to comprehend, much less combat the totalitarian assault on the human world?

The film signals its intentions to address momentous contemporary issues in the way moviegoers from that day to this are conditioned to distinguish the "real" from the imaginary world in the movies – through the stentorian voiceover of the newsreel commentator who identifies the places, the people and the significance of the scenes being projected before our eyes. Lubitsch lightheartedly spoofs the documentary authority of such newsreel realism by nimbly composing, in the film's first few frames, an ethnographic montage of storefront signs to be found on the streets of Warsaw (a Warsaw that all too clearly exists on a studio back lot and that we know is Polish only because the storefronts all have names that end in "-ski"!). We are then shown scenes of the city's inhabitants unconcernedly going about their business until they are stopped in their tracks by some unaccountable marvel appearing in their midst. The commentator informs us that the crowd is reacting to the unwonted, unannounced and – even more incongruous – the *unaccompanied* presence of Adolf Hitler on the streets of Warsaw. A quick cut shows us Hitler eyeing the wares of a Jewish delicatessen, commodities verboten on two counts for an anti-Semitic vegetarian, although the commentator reminds us that Hitler often goes off his diet, swallowing whole countries at a time.

Hitler's monster appetite is the first in a menu of food gags, from the ethnically fastidious – "What you are I wouldn't eat!" snuffs the Jewish actor, Greenberg (Felix Bressart); "How dare you call me a ham!" retorts the resident blusterer, Rawich (Lionel Atwill) – to the recurring joke told at Gestapo headquarters and repeated throughout the film about the afterlife of historical figures: "They named a brandy after Napoleon, a herring after Bismarck, and after Hitler – a piece of cheese!" Comedy is interested in food as part of its larger concern with the individual vagaries of human appetite. In wartime this interest becomes a matter of real urgency, since food shortages are one of war's nonpartisan negative creations. The humor surrounding food thus becomes a kind of moral index of the lengths one is willing to go to survive. Food jokes often take on the flavor of gallows humor, like the grim jest directed against the Nazis' gluttony for killing: "You can't have your cake and shoot it too!"

Hitler's renegade appetite may need no explanation, but his surprising presence in Warsaw does. The commentator accordingly translates us to Gestapo Head-quarters in Berlin, promising that there we will find an explanation. There we see Jack Benny, costumed as a Gestapo officer, a sight that reportedly so upset Benny's father that he walked out of the film. Benny is conferring with his adjutant in preparation for an interrogation whose subject is soon ushered in and turns out to be a mere boy. This first sight gag, which introduces a uniformed Hitler youth in the place of the adult subversive we had been led to expect, is the first of may such "conversion downwards" – to use Kenneth Burke's phrase for one form the comic corrective may take – of the targeted enemy (Burke 1984: 43). The comic logic here, hardly tolerated by the reviewers of the film when it opened, is to rely on such tactical visual depreciations to reduce the Hitlerian monster and his breed to unintimidating proportions.

This stratagem was most vehemently disparaged by Parker Tyler, who argued that the film's psycho-political premise – "that, if imaginatively the enemy is underrated, it is easier to defeat him" – was a foolish and even dangerous one (Tyler 1944: 217). Tyler ridiculed the argument that the film's buffoonery would serve as a morale booster for an apprehensive home front audience. Hitler could not be defeated, or even be seen to be vulnerable, Tyler insisted, if he were treated as a cartoon. Numbers, not the deformations of fantasy and propaganda, Tyler predicted in 1944, would determine the final outcome of the war. To envision any other possibility was to capitulate to the "upstart genius of fascism, a philosophy of the great Leader against many scattered groups of small leaders." The reality, Tyler insisted, was that the United States and the British Empire, whose combined territories at that time covered almost two-thirds of the globe, held the advantages over Germany, a much smaller nation by any geographical or demographic measure (Tyler 1944: 217). Tyler's view was not echoed in the more lowly entertainments offered to wartime audiences, however. As Stephen Tifft has shown, Hitler in the early thirties was popularly represented as a cartoon figure in the European dailies and weeklies, most commonly as a "militant edition of Charles Chaplin," as *The Literary Digest* remarked in 1933, but also as King Kong, Jekyll and Hyde, and even as "Adolf-in-the-Box" in Warner Brother's mock-documentary "Nutty News" (1942), a cartoon narrated by the lisping Elmer Fudd (Tifft 1991: 24).

Lubitsch's satire, while animated by the same derisory impulses of popular cartoon culture, stops short of sheer buffoonery (unlike the lamentably misconceived Mel Brooks 1983 remake of *To Be or Not to Be*, which never steps out of the precincts of sheer buffoonery). In fact, the film is partly a reflection on what might constitute the most damaging representation of Hitler and his regime. So much is insinuated in an argument that breaks out between Bronski, an actor in the Polish troupe who will impersonate Hitler, and Dobosh, the director of the company. Dobosh complains that Bronski's physical imitation of Hitler is unim-posing, representing him as nothing more than "a little man with a moustache."

Bronski and the troupe insist that is exactly what Hitler is. Also insistent, Dobosh counters by pointing to what he takes to be an official state portrait hanging in the theater. Bronski, equally insistent, points out that the portrait is of *himself*. (It was he, after all, who had been strolling the streets of Warsaw, fooling the locals into thinking they were being visited by the Führer.) "Then the picture is wrong!" blurts out the unpersuadable Dobosh. Hitler's "reality" exceeds any attempt at either naturalistic imposture or insolent caricature but seems to hover, uneasily, between the two.

Lubitsch, temperamentally averse to extremes, commits himself to a strategy of comic belittlement that burlesques Hitler without for a minute underestimating him. It is a strategy that exposes him to some perils, but whose benefits he knew and relied on, having perfected it in his high society comedies, remarkable for keeping their frank treatment of sex within the bounds of both decency and humor. It is a strategy that ultimately depends in this film on a rhetoric of "little things," from the "little things" that bother that "great, great actor, Joseph Tura" who otherwise would be such a wonderful husband to his wife and co-star Maria ("like that little thing in the second row," as Maria's maid calls her latest admirer) to that "little thing" called a conscience that Maria invokes when offered the protection – and the appetizing rations (three eggs a week) – of the Nazi occupying forces, to the "inkling" Tura wishes he could have of the reasons he must assassinate a Pole turned traitor ("And after I killed him, I would appreciate knowing what it was all about!"). Whether such a strategy estranges us from reality (Tyler's view) or works to keep it in perspective (Lubitsch's position) is what the film, in its defense of the comic attitude toward the world, asks us to decide. Our final judgment will depend on whether we take seriously the possibility Lubitsch offers that Hitler, or any world-historical demon, can be demystified, reduced to his actual human dimension, not so much *to* comic proportions as *by* them.

The comic diminishment of Hitler is augmented, if I might be permitted another paradox in a chapter already plagued by so many, by Lubitsch's refusal to give Hitler and his film surrogates any opportunity for self-magnifying display. The first refusal involves a running gag built upon the quintessential Nazi reflex – the Heil Hitler salute (see Figure 14.1). It was a stock formula in the "lighter" spy thrillers and war satires of the period to ridicule the Nazi salute as a particularly risible and contemporary example of the Bergsonian comedy of automatism (taken to an extreme in Stanley Kubrick's *Dr. Strangelove*, discussed in this volume).[2] Lubitsch seizes upon this Hitlerian reflex not for a quick sight gag but, more tellingly, as a means of comic punctuation, employing it as a panicky end-stop whenever Nazis fear their loyalty might be questioned and, on one notable occasion which I shall soon describe, a comically orgasmic exclamation point.

The other instance of comic refusal is at once so remarkable yet unemphatic that many critics have failed to take proper note of it: that Lubitsch's film deprives Hitler of one of his most potent weapons and most recognizable public attribute

Figure 14.1 Jack Benny, aka Joseph Tura, impersonating Concentration Camp Erhardt, giving the Nazi salute (*To Be or Not To Be*; producer, Ernst Lubitsch).

(outside of his moustache): his flamboyant and incendiary speechmaking. Unlike Chaplin, who debunks Hitler's Nuremburgian performances in Adenoid Hynkel's convulsive orations – the sobs, the breast-beatings, the body twisting itself into a corkscrew of self-enraptured, self-entangling rhetoric – Lubitsch gives us a nearly mute as well as inglorious Hitler. His Hitler is not just a "little man with a moustache"; he is, more to the point, a bit player confined to a walk-on at the end of the film with no lines to deliver. Even within the film, Bronski, the Polish actor who impersonates Hitler both in a play and in the "real-life" drama of an underground plot to blow-up vital Nazi supply depots, is given only two lines "in character." Of these the more inspired is his response to the chain reaction of Heil Hitlers that usher in the Führer at the conclusion of the opening interrogation scene – a matter of fact, blandly self-affirming, "Heil myself."

"Heil myself" confirms and justifies the parodic form of the interrogation scene, prompting the first dramatic countershot in the film: the cut from what we have been told (but hardly believe) are the Nazi headquarters in Berlin, to a filmic and ideological space outside and diametrically opposed to it – the seats of a theater, where we see a man *not* in uniform, obviously a director, overseeing the action being performed on the stage and vehemently objecting to the improvised line because it is not in the script. Not only the filmic space, but aesthetic and ideological horizons expand as we realize that the scene we have been witnessing is actually a play within the film, a piece called *The Gestapo* being rehearsed by a troupe of Polish actors headed by that self-proclaimed "great, great actor, Joseph Tura" (Jack Benny), and Maria Tura, his wife and rivalrous co-star, played with imperturbable comic aplomb by Carole Lombard.

The interrogation room is thus a stage, the Nazis merely players, and personages like Hitler no more than what he looks like when viewed through a comic lens – a little man with a moustache. Parker Tyler snorted that Lubitsch managed the egregious and immoral feat of rendering the invasion of Warsaw as "a sort of *Helzapoppin* version of Pirandello"(Tyler 1944: 219) The gibe is witty, but may have missed the main point of Lubitsch's Pirandellian staging of a play within his movie. The device of the play within the play (or movie), as common to Busby Berkeley musicals as it was to Shakespeare's dramas, permitted Lubitsch not only to lampoon the conventions of dramatic and cinematic performance, but to establish a polarity, essential to the film's comedy as well as its politics, between two megalomaniac spheres – the theater world of prima donnas, ham actors and bit players wanting to enlarge their parts, and the armed regime of the Nazi occupation. "Heil myself" is thus a kind of comic salvo that ricochets between two rival, though adjacent realms of action and representation – politics and theater.

Real and represented worlds, identity and impersonation deliriously interpenetrate as an aesthetic dispute breaks out within the acting troupe about the appropriateness of the line. The director, a strict constructionist, demands it be dropped on the grounds of aesthetic decorum: not only is the line not in the script, but it fatally changes, as well as interrupts, the mood of the play. The actors, however, especially Bronski, the Hitler impersonator, and Greenberg, the spear-carrying extra who longs to play Shylock, like it for precisely that reason: it will get a big laugh. These minor players insist that a laugh is nothing to be sneezed at in the darkest times, a view that is even more vehemently asserted in Preston Sturges's *Sullivan's Travels* (1941). That film's protagonist, a director of slaphappy comedies like *Ants in Your Plants*, must descend into the black hole of crime melodrama to discover that laughter is the spirit's restorative even during the darkest turnings in life's "cockeyed caravan." Against this reasoning, Dobosh, the director, who is clearly *not* a figure for Lubitsch, remains resolutely opposed. He objects both to buffoonery or improvisation, whether of the principled or pandering variety, insisting that he intends to produce a realistic drama, a documentary of Nazi Germany (that he ultimately wins the argument is suggested when the play is later censored by the authorities).

Lombard's first entrance at this critical juncture not only completes the comic company of players but also complicates the charged aesthetic debate. She strolls to center stage and asks the director whether he likes her dress, an exquisite, body-caressing concoction by Irene (stipulated as the designer in Lombard's contract) that at once drapes and reveals the sensuous contours of Lombard's body. He absent-mindedly answers yes, until he realizes that she plans to wear it in the play, where it would be, of course, absurdly, even shockingly out of place. He can't believe, he objects, that an artist could be so inartistic. But Lombard's artistic instinct, which unsurprisingly coincides with her histrionic character, is to defend the dress on the grounds that it would present, as she puts it, a "tremendous contrast" when the lights go on to reveal her as a tortured woman being "flogged in the dark." Lombard's practiced insouciance in the art of contrasts gives her, as the film proceeds to demonstrate with ingenious, often hilarious invention, a particular and decided advantage on the various occasion for sexual play – and politics Lubitsch sends up the shenanigans of his earlier films, like *Design for Living* or *Trouble in Paradise*, as if relegating, even as he is delighting in such things as lovers' (usually adulterous) trysts, the comedy of their stratagems and the giddy wit of their codes, to some vanished belle epoch in human sophistication, of which Lubitsch himself might rightly claim to be the most knowing, as well as most entertaining, historian.

To Be or Not to Be as a title thus seems to signal a crisis in his own career, a crisis that is also the explicit subject of Sturges's *Sullivan's Travels*. Regarded in this light, one can appreciate why Lubitsch resisted the studio's pressure to change the film's allusive title, regarded then as too highbrow, to *The Censored Play*. The studio wanted a title that inserted the comedy within the known precincts of political satire; Lubitsch wanted a title that kept the audience entertained by his own ingenious and varied adaptations of this famous line. Initially, Lubitsch seems to have nothing more than good-natured parody of Hamlet's high doings in making "To be or not to be" the cue for Maria's young admirer, the young Polish flyer played by Robert Stack, to visit her backstage, a lovely absurdity in itself, since, as Ophelia, Maria would have to cut short her backstage dalliance to return to the stage, being the first person Hamlet encounters after his famous soliloquy. Perhaps her dramatic sense of contrasts, and the farceur's eagerness to display her split-second timing, explains her choice of that particular soliloquy.

Certainly Lubitsch's own sense of contrasts determined his pacing of the film. He defended his artistic choices in defending the picture in *The New York Times* of March 29, 1942:

> Drama with comedy relief and comedy with dramatic relief. I had made up my mind to make a picture with no attempt to relieve anybody from anything at any time; dramatic when the situation demands it, satire or comedy whenever it is called for. One might call it a tragical farce of a farcical tragedy – I do not care and neither do the audiences. (Paul 1983: 288)

Lubitsch uncharacteristically assumes a somewhat aggressive posture toward his audience in defending his resolve not to relieve "anybody from anything at any time." But it should also be noted that Lubitsch's resolve not to afford any comic or dramatic relief also makes extraordinary demands on his players, who must be so adept at transitions that they can react to whatever the hapless moment, whether dire or ludicrous, requires of them. This determination not to relieve either audience or players from anything at any time, defines Lubitsch's totalitarian comedy.

Such is Lombard's enhanced importance in the film. The histrionic Mildred Platka who knows how to play up her star persona in *Twentieth Century* (1934, the *annus mirabilis* of talking comedy) and the unaffectedly decent women she brought to life *In Name Only* (1939) or *Vigil In the Night* (1940), peacefully cohabit the psyche of Lombard's Maria Tura, transcendent in her narcissism and her decency alike. As William Paul has noted, Lubitsch delegates the film's most difficult, sudden changes in tone and affect to her (Paul 1983: 233). The first abrupt emotional as well as historical shift in the film the occurs when Maria's flirtation with a young Polish flyer reaches its foreshortened climax when he declares that he will take her away from her complicated life of the stage and give her the simple life on a farm. ("By the way, where was that?" he inquires, recalling a news photo that pictured her behind a plow; "In the Chronicle," she wistfully returns, as if inwardly admiring the effect of that pose and the publicity that has turned her into the most idolized woman in prewar Poland.) Lubitsch has great fun elaborating the premise that the young flyer's main attraction for Maria is, delicately put, her fascination with a man "who could drop three tons of dynamite in two minutes," a line Lombard delivers to suggest both sexual awe and a professional appreciation for such high-octane performances. Of course the conventions of farce not only permit, but revel in dalliances based on the promise of such spectacular sexual powers, which are shown to carry little risk of real and lasting, much less severe penalty. "How does it look?" Maria asks her maid, handing her the note setting the time for her first assignation with her admirer in the second row: "Safe," is the acerbic, knowing and thoroughly approving reply. (With his customary economy, Lubitsch makes quick, but expert use of the convention that dramatically employs the maid primarily as an abettor to sexual intrigue.) So when the besotted flyer actually proposes, upsetting the delicate balance between flirtation and love, she means to enlighten him as to the limits of their sexual play. But before she can do so, war is announced (see Figure 14.2), a reality that does not so much show up or expose the sexual farce as vain and trivial, as suspend it – without, needless to say, any sense of relief. There is no time to protest, much less morally assess the tremendous contrasts Lubitsch achieves in orchestrating the imminent breakup of the sexual intrigue with the outbreak of war.

Lombard is entrusted to manage the transition from the comedy of backstage intrigues to the somber drama of war. When her maid brings in the newspaper announcing the invasion of Poland, Lombard and Stack fill and dominate the screen in a two-shot that suddenly brings them in a stark proximity not yet attempted in the film. Lombard, who literally seconds before the announcement handled her naive and adoring suitor with her customary amatory skill, immediately *responds* to the sudden intrusion of tragic reality into her playhouse world. A sudden gravity overtakes her features when she hears the news, erasing any trace of the histrionic demeanor that had earlier made her face a transparent register of the conscious self-deceptions of the woman of affairs. Although she has been caught off guard ("Without a word of warning," she marvels on seeing the headlines), she instantly understands the import of the appalling, tremendous, and yet simple fact confronting her: "War, it's really war. People are going to kill each

Figure 14.2   "War, it's really war": The first marriage of the not-serious and dreadful in this sudden (but temporary) halt to Lubitsch's backstage farce (*To Be or Not To Be*; producer, Ernst Lubitsch).

other and be killed." The intensifier "really" takes on an unexpected and austere authority in this moment, and accounts for the abrupt plunge into *actual* intimacy between her starry-eyed suitor and herself: "Come back, Stanislaus." These are not the words of dismissal, but parting words infused with a genuine, even tender concern for his fate. And of her own as well, since she too has been forcefully shunted out of the realm of backstage farce into the larger theater of war.

From this point on – and it is still very early in screen time – the consequences of Lubitsch's decision to *keep up* the laughs – that is, not to kill the comedy in respectful deference to grim reality – are magnified exponentially. To play out the farce is to risk being reviled not only as unpatriotic, but inartistic, if artistry is to be understood to exist in *some* relation to the way things so bleakly are. Responding to critics who thought the film tasteless when not outrageous or, in Tyler's view, delusional, Lubitsch defended his farcical representation of Nazi barbarism:

> I admit that I have not resorted to the methods usually employed in pictures, novels and plays to signify Nazi terror. No actual torture chamber is photographed, no flogging is shown, no close-up of excited Nazis using their whips and rolling their eyes in lust. My Nazis are different: they passed that stage long ago. Brutality, flogging and torture have become their daily routine. They talk about it the same way as a salesman referring to the sale for a handbag. Their humor is built around concentration camps, around the sufferings of their victims. (Paul 1983: 233)

Lubitsch's sense of the banality of evil extends to the jokes the Nazis tell, including the one that appalled critics and silenced even Lubitsch's closest associates and unabashed admirers, like Billy Wilder. It is a joke ostensibly at the expense of Joseph Tura's acting abilities, which prompts Concentration Camp Ehrhardt (who Benny will first impersonate and later gull) to propose the morally obtuse analogy: "Oh yes, I saw him (Tura) in *Hamlet* once. What he did to Shakespeare, we are doing now to Poland." Ehrhardt's unidiomatic and pointed inversion "we are doing now" rather than the less conspicuous phrasing "we are now doing," injects into the comparison the possibility that the invasion of Poland came partly as an act of artistic retribution, as if to the demented Nazi there was an obvious link between Tura's butchery of Shakespeare and the Nazis retaliatory moves against his country. Despite almost universal consternation at the line, Lubitsch insisted that the joke be kept, presumably on the grounds that the offensive humor exposed the casualness as well as the pervasiveness of the Nazi passion for destruction.

Lubitsch's vehicle for this outrageous quip is Colonel Ehrhardt. As his epithet "Concentration Camp Ehrhardt" suggests, he is a burlesque-horror version of the *miles gloriosus* or braggart soldier, a remarkably enduring comic figure, from Plautus to Shakespeare's Falstaff, Chaplin's Hitler and most of the military command in Stanley Kubrick's *Dr. Strangelove*. The continued popularity, indeed necessity, of this comic type is due, as Northrop Fry observed, to his spectacular showmanship.[3] The *miles* knows how to draw and please a crowd with accounts of mighty exploits. Colonel Ehrhardt is clearly within this tradition in equating the Nazi's showstopper *blitzkrieg* with Tura's butchered performance. The joke *is* a horrible one, but its very horror expresses in an unpleasantly immediate way Walter Benjamin's more abstract reflection on the degree to which a self-alienated mankind could now "experience its own destruction as an aesthetic pleasure of the first order." This was the situation of politics that Benjamin claimed, "fascism is rendering aesthetic" (Benjamin 1969: 242). Lubitsch, alert to the way the joke can function as an act of self-exposure, offers something like a reverse insight: the joke helps expose the Nazi's evil genius for putting on a *bad* show.

Lubitsch did something more questionable, even more terrifying than underrating the enemy – he took their measure against a human, reliable standard of the morality of everyday life and found them completely habituated to a world in which brutality was not exceptional, but commonplace. In this regard, more troubling than the crude and deadly buffooneries headlining the Nazi theater of destruction may be the sophistication of Nazi evil, as played out in the high comedy of ideological and sexual seduction that calls upon all of Maria Tura's actorly and amatory skills. Lubitsch, master at dignifying the bedroom farce so that it becomes, as In *Trouble In Paradise*, the ultimate standard in human refinement, is equally expert in dramatizing the barbarity of the Nazi's sexual as well as military culture. Maria is summoned to the Hotel Europski (!), by Professor Siletsky, the traitor who the next morning intends to reveal the names of members of the Polish underground to the Gestapo. Lubitsch stages their exchange in a fairly close, though not intimate, shot-counter-shot sequence, as if to bring us as close as comedy is permitted to the moral brinkmanship of collaboration. Siletsky, obviously taken with her beauty, seeks to recruit her to the Nazi cause, appealing to her initially on *professional* grounds. Success in life, as in the theater, he menacingly insinuates, ultimately depends on what role – or sides – one takes. Maria, apparently genuinely interested as well as curious, asks "Which side is that?" "The winning side."

The separate, heightened reality of stage life is compromised once theater is regarded not as a *reflection* on, but as a *preparation for* an historical role one is called upon to play. Maria, who once played a spy – to rave notices! – is asked to "entertain" for the Nazi cause. She will be given the proper surroundings, she is assured, and life will be made very comfortable for her. "Naturally, it all sounds very attractive and tempting," she admits, "but what are we do with my conscience?" Maria puts the question as if it represented an authentic, if minor perplexity, yet it is the mark of her abilities as an actress and her decency as a human being that the line hovers over the rest of the scene. In the diabolic inversions that give their subsequent banter its eerie, yet irresistible rhythms, Siletsky offers his suave reassurances that all the Nazis want "in the final analysis … is a happy world for happy people." Nazism is ingeniously promoted as aspiring to its own version of "totalitarian comedy," whose outcome is envisioned as "a happy world for happy people." In an historical irony that would be exposed in the Nazi-Soviet Non-Aggression Pact of 1939, signed just months before the Nazi invasion of Poland, Stalinist Russia and Nazi Germany had mutual interests and similar aims in remaking the world to conform to their idea of a happy world filled only with happy, acquiescent people. As Andrew Horton has pointed out to me in conversation, Stalin sought to promote his sweeping totalitarian visions of a transformed humanity by encouraging "happy" Communist musicals, among which the 1938 extravaganza *Volga-Volga* (title courtesy of an offhand and hardly serious suggestion of Charlie Chaplin, who enchanted by the folksong in which the phrase appears, made an offhand suggestion to the director Grigori Aleksandrov, who had just sang it to him) was reportedly Stalin's favorite film. Chaplin himself, however, projected a completely different vision of a happy world for happy people in the final speech of *The Great Dictator*.

One reason totalitarian comedies are so disturbing is that they put extraordinary pressure on our sense of what constitutes human happiness. For Chaplin, happiness is a life lived in freedom, beyond the encroachments of greed and the hatred stirred up by nationalism and other ideological creeds. But Siletsky, a professor after all, seems to be playing on the etymological roots of happiness in "hap," that quality that attaches to whatever is found to be *suitable* or *convenient*. Certainly that is the way Maria, in her comic prescience, understands it. She immediately responds to the eugenic pogrom implied in the Nazi's myth of total happiness: "And those who don't want to be happy have no place in a happy world."

Lubitsch complicates his vision of the totalitarian eugenics that would create a happy world by targeting "unhappy" people for extinction by insisting that what renders the Nazis horrifying is not that they are deviants outside the human pale, but very much within it. Lubitsch's insistence that his Nazis are human finds ironic, diabolic confirmation in the case Siletsky makes for Nazi culture: "We're not brutal. We're not monsters. We love to sing. We love to dance. We admire beautiful women. We're human." Song, dance and love, the ebullient staples of comic existence, are summoned as evidence that Nazis have the same "dimensions, senses, affections, passions" as the rest of mankind. The echo here of Shylock's Rialto speech – "Hath not a Jew eyes? Hath not a Jew hands, organs, dimensions, senses, passions" (*The Merchant of Venice*, Act III, Scene i) – is both canny and sinister. But Siletsky's diabolic appropriation and interpretation of Shylock's protestations of his inalienable humanity are effectively countermanded by three strategic recitations of Shylock's speech offered by Greenberg, the film's most vocal advocate of the salutary dramaturgy of the "great laugh." Each time he recites a slightly different *part* of the speech until he delivers the crucial lines: "If you prick us do we not bleed? If you tickle us do we not laugh? If you poison us do we not die? And if you wrong us shall we not revenge?" In the farce staged within the film, the word revenge is the dramatic signal that puts into motion the troupe's plot to create a diversion so that the underground might do its work unopposed and unmolested. Thus it assumes, as does the speech itself, the moral burden of justifying Lubitsch's farcical treatment of history. Siletsky appropriates the Shylockian claims of humanity as an inducement to moral as well as sexual surrender to evil. Greenberg will make them his anthem for moral resistance.

But these clever, morally charged reversals are still to come. Lombard's disingenuous responses to Siletsky's sexual and ideological overtures are so lightly given here that they seem to evaporate even as they are ventured. Her own talent for recognizing the power of "tremendous contrasts" re-emerges at the conclusion of the scene. Calling attention to her present destitute appearance, she asks leave to return home to change, so that she may "present the Polish case in more suitable attire." She initially bids a calm and dramatically unremarkable *au revoir* (her diction in keeping with the decadent cosmopolitanism Siletsky represents) when she is stopped at the door. Siletsky, with undisguised self-importance, informs her that it is harder to get out of Gestapo headquarters than it is to enter. Lombard pretends to be suitably impressed by this fact: "I'm terribly frightened and terribly thrilled. Bye!" We have heard this "Bye"–prompted by and saluting amazing power – before, only earlier it had been inspired by the figure of a man who could drop six tons of dynamite in three minutes. Now Maria's "Bye!" is a way of playing up to Siletsky's inflated sense of his own sexual and political power. By such comic subterfuge, Maria can toy with Siletsky's sexuality while eluding the military and ideological apparatus at his command (see Figure 14.3).

With a comic audacity that has by this point in the film become almost blasé, Lubitsch cuts from Lombard's delicate and diplomatic exit to Benny's stumbling home, where he will find Sobinski sleeping soundly in his bed. The audacity resides in visually as well as narratively asserting that the connection between Siletsky and Sobinski comprehends not only their dramatic significance

Figure 14.3   Affairs of State: Maria Tura in her greatest role—ensnaring the Nazi seducer
(*To Be or Not To Be*; producer, Ernst Lubitsch).

as opposite moral types – patriot and traitor, one an incorruptible, the other a
decadent political being – but also encompasses their *complementary* roles as sexual
rivals. What Siletsky and Sobinski share is their attraction to Maria, which involves
both of them in the illicit pleasures, as well as the indignities of farce. Sobinski's
involvement is at once more noble and cruder. When Joseph Tura decides to
confirm his suspicion that the sleeper is the man who walked out on his great
soliloquy and into his bed, he sequesters himself behind the bed and whispers,
"To be or not to be." The flyer instantly rises, drawn out of his sleep by the lure of
the prearranged sexual signal. Benny's comic outrage at the thought of someone
else slipping into his slippers, then into his bed, is frantic and fine enough, but the
subsisting energy of the scene comes from motif of sexual automatism so central
to the farcical view of human behavior, a view to be fully explored when Maria
returns to complete her sexual and ideological maneuverings with Siletsky.

The second act of Siletsky's blitzkrieg seduction plays more openly with him
as the epitome of the self-regarding decadence underlying Nazi militarism (first
and less elaborately parodied in Bronski's "Heil, myself!"). But where he had
earlier seemed darkly menacing in his blandishments, Siletsky is much more
the erotic stooge in this repeat performance. Lombard returns to his room, as
commentators have noted, in the theatrical gown initially meant to present a
"tremendous contrast" to her scenes in *The Gestapo*, but which the director has
dismissed and disdained as morally and artistically inappropriate. There is no
question of its artistic and strategic value now. Her costume is not only put to
unexpected use in a real life drama, but more importantly, so are the symbolic
associations of the dress with regimes of torture. Military rather than the
theatrical metaphors of their first meeting thus come to dominate the amorous

banter between the potential lover-combatants, Siletsky predictably opting for the proven success of *blitzkrieg*, Maria expressing her personal preference for slow encirclement. Her subsequent actions are perfectly in accord with her declared tactics: she coyly suggests that behind the Professor's beard she detects "a boyish quality," as if finally assenting to his earlier protestations of his essential harmlessness. Then, under the guise of "reading" his masculine character, she maneuvers him into giving her a sample of his signature, which she intends to use to fake a suicide note to cover the death the Underground has planned for him.

These transparent stratagems serve the foolishness of the comic plot, but they also have a more serious function in debunking male potency in its most fatuous, repellent and at the same time most dangerous form – the Nazi seducer. Thus when Siletsky finally takes her into his arms, the canny actress-cum-spy responds with a sublime imposture of sexual rapture, "Heil Hitler!" Her erotic salute triggers in him an answering reflex, although his is in response to a political rather than sexual stimulus. Sobinski, the besotted sleepwalker, finds his farcical and demonic double in the Nazi intellectual, abdicating his will, his reflexes, and finally his sexuality to the compulsions, not of Eros, but of Hitlerian Thanatos.[4] The militant virility that forms such a central part of fascist self-mythologizing is expertly debunked in this ravishing moment of sexual charade. The anarchic exuberance of sexual farce seems not only a licit, but even honorable mode of behavior when compared to the apocalyptic designs of a totalitarian regime lumbering mercilessly and brutally toward its desired end of a happy world for its happy people.

These rival comic regimes, one totalitarian, the other libidinal – both equal though opposite exponents of the Life of Unrestraint – confront each other in the two overtly dramatic set-pieces of the film. The victory in each confrontation goes to the farceurs, since, possessed of trickster's facility in disguise and impersonation, they are better at the instantaneous and credible assumption of a false character. The first showdown brings Siletsky, the suave apologist and seducer, face to face with the husband he intends to wrong – that great, great actor Joseph Tura, now cast in the role of Concentration Camp Ehrhardt. Tura's impersonation fails not because it is essentially facetious – "So they call me Concentration Camp Ehrhardt," he says when Siletsky informs him of the pet name given him by the Berlin High Command–but because he suddenly drops his jovial Nazi mask and becomes seriously offended by Siletsky's initially casual, then calculated sexual allusions to his wife. As William Paul has astutely observed, Siletsky is an anti-comic figure whose political and sexual ambitions mutually re-enforce each other, thus giving him a "wholeness" missing from the other characters. His "wholeness," contends Paul, "is finally beyond the ironies of the actors with their understanding of split reality. The force he represents sitting as close as he does to the top of hierarchy can only be defeated by like force: he must be killed by a soldier, Lieutenant Sobinski, the only character on the side of the good guys who is never ironic" (Paul 1983: 253).

Sobinski's incapacity for irony thus makes him uniquely qualified to commit the only act of personal violence we observe in the film – the shooting of Siletsky on the set of *Hamlet* in the Theater Polski. Yet since this political murder takes place on stage, the killing morally profits by the dramatic ironies supplied by Lubitsch's direction, of which the most cinematically striking is the use of the spotlight as a searchlight, a conflation that signals the collapse of history into theater, the invasion, as Paul himself notes, of the real world into the make-believe world of the stage. The visual identity between searchlight and spotlight also signals the common cause that theater, which is limited in what it can show us, and film, which can visually take us anywhere, share in extruding the totalitarian imagination from their domain. The most dramatically suspenseful moment in the film is the moment when the curtain is raised to show Siletsky, clutching his side and attempting one last Hitlerian salute, falling to his death center stage. This is the most satisfying *spectacle* Lubitsch stages for us, a *coup de théâtre* in which Lubitsch abandons his typical middle distance framing and adopts the only high-angle shot in the film. This elevated perspective insinuates a cinematic transcendence and mastery over both theater, which film can mimic but also outdistance, and history, which it can represent and surpass through the moral scrutiny and compass of its gaze.

Lubitsch reserves one last dramatic irony for the Siletsky plot, a farcical coda to his spectacular death. Tura, who had earlier impersonated Colonel Ehrhardt to entrap Siletsky, now assumes Siletsky's identity to gull the real Colonel, and cracks, by the way, one of the great character jokes in the film when the two actually meet: "So they call me Concentration Camp Ehrhardt, do they?" says the real Colonel; "I thought you would react just that way" responds Tura, in one of his rare moments of professional vindication. His ruse, successfully played out, is jeopardized when Siletsky's corpse is found, setting up the hilarious, tricky, and potentially fatal situation in which there is one Siletsky too many. Tura's battle of wits with the Gestapo again pits two different aesthetic regimes against each other. Ehrhardt, who now suspects that he is dealing with an imposter (and he is!), ushers Tura – as Siletsky into his spacious quarters, leaving him alone to discover the corpse of the "real" Siletsky. If this ruse to catch the conscience of the conspirator fails, Ehrhardt assures his impatient underlings, he will then resort to "physical culture." The word culture signifies and undergoes a double degradation, perversely enlisted as it is here to signify the barbarities of the sadistic Nazi regime, just as earlier it had served as Siletsky's euphemism for the Nazis' genocidal schemes to create a happy world for happy people.

After all this verbal preparation, the dumb show that ensues is farce's remarkably eloquent counter-response to the deviant culture of totalitarianism. This scene is staged to get a great laugh – Greenberg's ultimate test of comic showmanship. In such moments *To Be Or Not To Be* is not far from the surreal antics of Leo McCarey's *Duck Soup* (1933); with a little imagination, one can see (but would not want) Harpo, his power of speech restored, and Groucho double for Benny in the absurdist, eerie pantomime that ensues. We are shown the unsuspecting Tura strolling in the room, unaware of what is starkly visible to us – Siletsky's corpse propped up in a chair. Benny does a speechless double take on spotting the body, assesses the corpse as the prop it has become, and then immediately repairs to the bathroom to regard himself, with actorly rather than narcissistic self-appraisal, in the mirror. A quick though surprisingly suspenseful cut shows him re-emerging, with truly remarkable nonchalance, to confront his tormentors. A farcical stalemate ensues when Tura disarms Ehrhardt's suspicions by pulling Siletsky's beard, which yields to his tug, only to have his beard pulled by Ravitch (the ham actor now taking on the role of commandant), who has arrived with the rest of the troop. In a real-life reprise of their original roles in *The Gestapo*, Ravitch plays a blustering field-officer who affects outrage at Ehrhardt's bungling of the Siletsky plot, which could have been so easily resolved had he only done the obvious theatrical thing–pulled his beard!: "Here was a beard and you didn't even pull it," he bellows in astonishment, blurting out a charge of incompetence that ricochets in two directions at once–rebounding to the credit of the farceurs skilled in all forms of comic effrontery, of which pulling the beard is especially satisfying, and against the Nazis' reputedly efficient political "culture," so inept at unmasking the most obvious impersonator.

All this ludicrous stage business over facial hair, applied, removed or missing, continues the barrage on the Nazi myth of virility, from Hitler's little moustache to the boyishness Maria had detected hidden behind Siletsky's beard. Tura, we must note, will ultimately "lose his moustache," when, headed out of Warsaw, he looks out the car window to witness the bombing that confirms that the Resistance is alive and well. "We now belong to history," proclaims Tura, relinquishing his farceur's role as Gestapo officer and settling back into his seat. As it transpires he has "lost face" too soon, for a beardless, out-of-character Tura cannot retrieve his wife, who awaits him at their apartment. She is detained there in the company of Colonel Ehrhardt, who is trying his luck at seducing her with, among other things, the promise of an extra ration of butter and three eggs a week. So Bronski, still in costume and in character, is dispatched to retrieve her, setting up Lubitsch's penultimate joke at the expense of Hitlerian man. When Bronski opens the door, Maria, capitalizing on Ehrhardt's mistaking Bronski for Hitler, chases after the retreating Bronski crying "Mein Führer! Mein Führer!" As she descends the stairs, we are left with only a closed door in view – but what dramatic wonders can Lubitsch produce with closed doors! – from which issues the sound of a gunshot, followed by its comical aftershock – "Schultz!"

Had the film had ended here, we might have attached to it the same generic markers Tom Chambers (Frederick March), the playwright in Lubitsch's film of Noel Coward's *Design for Living* (1933), formulated for his play, preposterously but suitably subtitled *A Comedy In Three Acts with a Tragic Ending*. The film would have been obliged to return us to history, to actual war that lies behind and beyond what is enacted on screen, a reality we know to be taking place yet unavailable for representation. But such a resolution, while at once realistic and dramatic, would signal the abdication of art before the rule of force. Lubitsch remains as convinced in the ultimate truth of his comical representations as Dobosh, his directorial foil, is committed to the principles of stark realism. Still he has the tact to reinforce the boundaries between the realm of play and the domain of the Actual. He does this through the last great visual and verbal gag in the film. We are shown the plane in which the Polish troupe has flown to England and to freedom, intercut with historical war footage of anti-aircraft fire and parachutes falling from the stricken skies. The camera ultimately alights on a haystack from which emerges a safe, if somewhat disheveled Bronski, still in costume. "First Hess, now him," remarks the unflustered Scottish farmer, rake in hand, who discovers him in a haystack. The joke alludes, of course, to Rudolf Hess's famous "secret" drop into England to negotiate the end of the war. The joke is fine on its own terms, but it also works to remind us that the real Hitler, like real history, is elsewhere.

Yet the joke serves another purpose; it reminds us that totalitarian assaults on reality can never eradicate the comical persistence of human beings in being themselves. Thus when the troupe arrives safely in England and is lionized by the British public for heroic acts of resistance, Tura struts his hour on the stage with his customary bravura. In their meeting with the appreciative British press, Tura, now acclaimed as "the hero of the play" known as history, is asked what he desires. "He wants to play Hamlet," Maria confides, not once but twice, the first time as a matter of information, the second as a knowing commentary on her husband's unchastened actorly megalomania.

Maria's comic vitality proves equally and reassuringly undiminished. The movie ends by returning Tura to his favorite role as the saturnine Dane, taking the stage for his famous soliloquy. This time he scans the audience, sees that Sobinski shows no sign of rising and begins the sonorous intonation "To be or not to be." In the final affirming joke on the comic nature of human sexuality, *both* Sobinski and Tura watch in consternation as an unidentified man, rising on cue, makes his away through the seats presumably on *his* way to a backstage rendezvous. The theatrical coda, which wittily segues from the on-stage tragedy to the resumption of the backstage farce, reaffirms Lubitsch's vision of tragedy and farce as not so much opposed, as simultaneous, intertwined and even reciprocal modes of being and acting in the world.

Lubitsch's provocative, indeed stubborn alignment of history and farce on parallel, often intersecting planes of action and representation establishes him as one of cinema's great moderns. He has not always been thought of and evaluated in such terms. Herman Weinburg, the author *of The Lubitsch Touch*, likened Lubitsch to George Feydeau, "the Shakespeare of the boulevard farce and the greatest comic dramatist after Molière" (Weinberg 1968: 224). I would suggest another figure helped continue and extend this tradition that gave us

Feydeau's farces and Chaplin's *The Great Dictator*: Proust in the final volume of his epic history, *à la recherche du temps perdu*. Strolling the streets of Paris during World War I, the narrator and his childhood companion, Robert Saint-Loup, a soldier home on leave, contemplate the zeppelins that patrol the Parisian skies, "squadron after squadron resembling Valkyrie" (did Coppola have this passage in mind when scoring the helicopter sequence in *Apocalypse Now*?). The narrator tells his friend that "if he had been at home the previous evening, he might, while contemplating the apocalypse in the sky, at the same time watched on the ground (as in El Greco's *Burial of Count Orgaz* in which the two planes are distinct and parallel) a first rate farce acted by characters in night attire." Saint Loup agrees, noting that "The Ritz on those evenings when the Zeppelins are overhead, must look like Feydeau's *L'Hôtel du libre échange*" (Proust 1982: 782).

Only an artist like Lubitsch – or Renoir in *Rules of the Game* (1939, another controversial comic satire that was actually banned both by the French and German governments when it was first released) or, Kubrick (although with less faith in the comic) in *Dr. Strangelove or: How I Learned to Stop Worrying and Love the Bomb* (1964) – would be so inartistic as to transpose apocalyptic history and uncensored farce from their distinct and parallel planes onto the same representational space, where actors might step, gingerly or not, from one mode to another. By showing us totalitarian agents and movements as vulnerable to the intrusions and libidinal correctives of farce, Lubitsch dramatizes the very real difference between the demonic totalitarian lust to remake the world into "a happy place for happy people," and the saving grace of a comedy that works (honorably and hard!) to get not just a big laugh, but the last laugh.

Notes

1. Andrew Sarris has objected to the very notion of limiting Lubitsch's art to such a term, claiming that "To speak of Lubitsch in terms of his 'touch' is to reduce feelings to flourishes." Scott Eyman, his biographer, remarks that Lubitsch himself shied away from the epithet. "'If there is such a thing, I do not know what it is,' he would say. 'It exists only in people's minds. If I were conscious of it, I would be afraid I might lose it.'" See Eyman (1993: 127).

2. In his *Laughter: An Essay on the Meaning of the Comic*, Bergson isolated a certain mechanical inelasticity as the source of comic laughter. "The attitudes, gestures and movements of the human body are laughable in exact proportion as that body reminds us of a mere machine," he writes specifically of comic gestures, gestures in which the mechanical motion has supplanted organic and instinctive bodily movements. The Hitlerian reflex is a sad instance of this totalitarianism comic reflex. See Bergson (n.d.), especially section IV.

3. "The original *miles gloriousus* in Plautus," Frye remarks, "is a son of Pluto and Venus who has killed an elephant with his fist and seven thousand men in one day's fighting. In other words, he is trying to put on a good show" (Frye 1966: 165).

4. As evidence that history is quite permeable to the insolence of farce, take the "curious incident of the dog in Finland who was trained to give a Nazi Salute," as the New York Times headline reported the comically notorious case. According to the historian Klaus Hillenbrand, who discovered what he calls the dog affair in German Foreign Ministry, a pharmaceutical manufacturer named Tor Borg, of Tampere Finland, taught his dog to raise its paw whenever he heard the world Hitler. This canine salute did not amuse the German Vice consul in Helsinki, who, on hearing of the incident, reported it to the Nazi foreign office. NY Times, January 11, 2011.

References

Benjamin, Walter (1969) The work of art in the age of mechanical reproduction, in *Illuminations*, Schocken, New York, NY.

Bergson, Henri (n.d.) *Laughter: An Essay on the Meaning of the Comic*, available online at http://www.authorama.com/laughter-5.html (accessed April 23, 2012).

Burke, Kenneth (1984) *Attitudes Toward History*, University of California Press, Berkeley, CA.

Eyman, Scott (1993) *Ernst Lubitsch: Laughter in Paradise*, Simon & Schuster, New York, NY.

Frye, Northrop (1966) *Anatomy of Criticism*, Princeton University Press, Princeton, NJ.

Gombrowicz, Witold (1988) *Diary Volume*, Northwestern University Press, Chicago, IL.

Kundera, Milan (1996) *Testaments Betrayed*, Harper Perennial, New York, NY.

Paul, William (1983) *Ernst Lubitsch's American Comedy*, Columbia University Press, New York, NY.

Proust, Marcel (1982) *Remembrance of Things Past*, Vol. III, translated by Andreas Mayor, Vintage, New York, NY.

Tifft, Stephen (1991) Miming the Führer: *To Be or Not to Be* and the Mechanisms of Outrage. *Yale Journal of Criticism*, 5 (1), 1–40.

Tyler, Parker (1944) *The Hollywood Hallucination*, Creative Prescience, New York, NY.

Weinburg, Hermann (1968) *The Lubitsch Touch*, Dutton, New York, NY.

Further Reading

Barnes, Peter (2002) *To Be Or Not To Be*, BFI, London. Excellent introduction to the film, including background information on the historical context and contractual terms of the production, Lubitsch's working methods and, of course, how the film wrested comedy out of tragedy. Written by an established dramatist and screenwriter (*Enchanted April*) who personally struggled with the question of whether laughter "is a legitimate reaction to events too terrible to contemplate" in a play called *Laughter* about the horrors of Auschwitz.

Eyman, Scott (2000) *Ernst Lubitsch: Laughter in Paradise*, Johns Hopkins University Press, Baltimore, MD. Standard and thorough biography of the filmmaker.

Smedley, Nick (2011) *A Divided World: Hollywood Cinema and Émigré Directors in the Era of Roosevelt and Hitler, 1933–1948*, Intellect Limited, Bristol. Archival material on Lubitsch's working methods and determination to make an anti-Nazi comedy that flouted the conventions of mainstream Hollywood film. Considers Lubitsch along with Fritz Lang and Billy Wilder.

Thompson, Kristin (2006) *Herr Lubitsch Goes to Hollywood: German and American Film after World War I*, Amsterdam University Press, Amsterdam. Extremely helpful in understanding the roots of Lubitsch's filmmaking and the films that preceded *To Be Or Not To Be*.

15

Dark Comedy from Dr. Strangelove to the Dude

Mark Eaton

Gentlemen, you can't fight in here, this is the War Room! (President Merkin Muffley in Dr. Strangelove *(1964))*

Your revolution is over, Mr. Lebowski. Condolences. (Jeffrey Lebowski a.k.a. The Big Lebowski to Jeffrey Lebowski a.k.a. the Dude in The Big Lebowski *(1998))*

Beginning with the landmark Stanley Kubrick film *Dr. Strangelove; or, How I Learned to Stop Worrying and Love the Bomb* (1964), dark comedy emerged as a genre that allowed filmmakers to develop serious cultural critiques of American politics and society in the guise of comedies. Dark comedy also permitted filmmakers to take on more controversial or serious subject matter at a time when the longstanding strictures of the Production Code Administration (PCA) were increasingly under siege but had not yet been dismantled. Adherence to the Production Code had been largely a matter of self-regulation, but when, for a variety of reasons, box-office revenues declined 43 percent from 1946 to 1961, it was only a matter of time before "someone would break ranks and try to make some money with a movie that defied the PCA" (Lewis 2008: 238). The radical countercultural ethos of the New Hollywood, a period dating from roughly 1965 to 1975, encouraged ever darker and more violent yet comedic treatments of subjects like adultery, suicide, and especially war. Dark comedy played a pivotal and underappreciated role in the transition to a postclassical era in American cinema, when the studios ceded considerable power to maverick film directors.

Influenced by the French New Wave, with its coterie of innovative directors, Jean-Luc Godard and Francois Truffaut foremost among them, and its self-proclaimed auteur theory, or *politique des auteurs*, a generation of young

A Companion to Film Comedy, First Edition. Edited by Andrew Horton and Joanna E. Rapf.

filmmakers in the United States sought to become auteurs themselves, consciously flouting the rules even as they worked within the studio system. Whether or not they went to film school, directors such as Robert Altman, Hal Ashby, Peter Bogdanovich, Francis Ford Coppola, William Friedkin, Norman Jewison, Mike Nichols, Arthur Penn, Roman Polanski, Martin Scorsese, and others make up what is now commonly referred to as the film-school generation. Together they developed a "new realism" and contributed to "a liberalization of Hollywood politics," which allowed for greater permissiveness in portraying sex and violence onscreen, as well as more critical, edgy representations of war (Thompson 1999: 2). According to film historian Jon Lewis (2008: 286), studio executives suddenly realized, if reluctantly, "that an emerging generation of filmmakers making topical movies with a political edge had a much more instinctive sense of what the youth audience wanted to see on-screen than did the executives themselves."

Like so many mutant children born in the aftermath of *Dr. Strangelove*'s nuclear apocalypse, the sheer number of dark comedies that were produced in subsequent years, including *The Graduate* (Mike Nichols 1966), *M*A*S*H** (Robert Altman 1970), *Catch-22* (Mike Nichols 1970), *Slaughterhouse-Five* (George Roy Hill 1972), and *The Last Detail* (Hal Ashby 1973), suggests that Kubrick's film had struck a chord. Given the dark comedy vogue that followed, it is difficult to overstate the influence of *Dr. Strangelove*, which, according to Mark Harris (2008: 25), "went leagues further than any prior studio movie in its near nihilistic savaging of cold war politics." This watershed film showed aspiring filmmakers what could be done with dark comedy, even as it paved the way for more forceful – and more political – representations of sexuality and violence in the coming years.

This chapter traces the development of dark comedy from Stanley Kubrick's masterpiece of the genre in the mid-1960s, through the comic experiments of the so-called New Hollywood in the late 1960s and 1970s, to the revival of dark comedy in the 1990s, most prominently in the work of Joel and Ethan Coen: *Barton Fink* (1991), *Fargo* (1996), and *The Big Lebowski* (1998). The last film in particular, because of the way it invokes the political context of the Gulf War, recalls *Dr. Strangelove*'s use of dark comedy to develop a satirical critique of the US military. Tracing this genealogy from *Dr. Strangelove* to the Dude, then, reveals a tradition of political dissent through dark comedy films that is worth exploring in more detail.

Comic Nightmare

"How did they ever make a movie of *Lolita*?" asked the famous publicity poster for Stanley Kubrick's film adaptation of Vladimir Nabokov's infamous novel, depicting Sue Lyon as Lolita licking a red lollipop in matching heart-shaped sunglasses. The answer to that tongue-in-cheek question, I argue, is that Kubrick exploited the subversive potential of dark comedy. The director shared with Nabokov, as James Naremore (2007: 98) puts it, "a love of chess and a taste for dark humor," and in adapting *Lolita* for the screen, he combined both to push the envelope of what was considered acceptable in the cinema. Kubrick was a savvy player within a studio system that was just beginning to feel the rumblings of a countercultural revolution. While he made certain concessions to the ratings board – the implied age of Lolita was raised from 12 in the novel to about 15 in the film – he boasted that adapting *Lolita* for the screen gave him "an avenue of telling certain types of stories that haven't yet been explored in movies" (Kubrick 1963: 113). That avenue was dark comedy, or what Kubrick (1963: 112) himself called "comic nightmare."

Kubrick's next film project would be about "our failure to understand the dangers of nuclear war," which the director regarded as "too outrageous, too fantastic to be treated in any conventional manner"; it could only be treated as "some kind of hideous joke" (Southern 1995: 140). With *Dr. Strangelove*, Kubrick not only flagrantly violated the Production Code but also perfected his new preferred method of comic nightmare, making him a hero of the counterculture and a darling of younger filmmakers. "Why should the bomb be approached with reverence?" he asked in *Life* magazine. "Reverence can be a paralyzing state of mind" (Wainwright 1964: 15). Such irreverence clearly disturbed some viewers, but others were thrilled by Kubrick's audacity.

Coming five years after his great anti-war film *Paths of Glory* (1957), the timing of *Dr. Strangelove* coincided with heightened tensions between the United States and the Soviet Union. The Cold War looked more and more like it might turn into a hot war. In his Farewell Address of January 1961, President Dwight D. Eisenhower, a former general himself, warned Americans that the "potential for the disastrous rise of misplaced power exists and will persist" unless we "guard against the acquisition of unwarranted influence … by the military-industrial complex." As if heeding that warning, Kubrick went to work shortly thereafter at Shepperton Studios on what is surely his finest cinematic achievement, a film that offers, in Paul Monaco's (2001: 173) phrase, "an unusually compelling combination of parody and serious social criticism."

All comedy is political insofar as it tends to subvert social standards of propriety and taste. Black comedy is even more subversive. When the French surrealist Andre Breton coined the term "black humor" in his *Anthologie de l'humour noir* (1939), he recognized that it was a supremely unsentimental – indeed, *anti-sentimental* – subcategory of satire marked by black or gallows humor, which is what distinguishes this brand of comedy so dramatically from romantic comedy, for example. "Most forms of comedy tend to pull their punches," observes Geoff King. "Satire is comedy with an edge and a target" (King 2002: 93–4). Yet satire goes beyond merely "exposing and castigating" human folly and stupidity, according to Alvin B. Kernin in his classic study *The Plot of Satire* (1965: 11), to become "the expression of a far-ranging moral honesty."

Dark comedy arguably shares something of this moral impulse; but it differs from satire in that dark comedy typically despairs of any possibility for social reform. "Although the black humorist often takes a moralist's or satirist's stance," Mathew Winston (1972: 270) explains, "his perception of inseparable complexities and unresolvable antitheses keeps him from advocating or hoping for any reform. Instead, he attempts to bring his audience into the same position he occupies by threatening or horrifying it and then undercutting its fear by some witty or comic turn." In Winston's helpful formulation, dark comedy is not so much a genre as "an "attitude, a stance, or a perspective" that crosses generic boundaries and forms (Winston 1972: 270). Typically, dark comedy "uses an ironic and biting intelligence to attack sentimentality, social convention... and an apparently absurd universe"; it "favors the fantastic, the surreal, and the grotesque"; and it attempts to "break down complacency" by employing "violent images and shock tactics" (Winston 1972: 270). From this description of key traits, we can easily see why the 1960s' counterculture proved to be a receptive audience for subversive dark comedies that shared its own anti-authoritarian ethos.

Kubrick planned to make a serious film about the Cold War when he bought the screen rights to Peter George's novel *Red Alert* (1958), but he soon realized that the material was so extreme it could only work as comedy. "It occurred to me that I was approaching the project in the wrong way," Kubrick later recalled. "The only way to tell the story was as a black comedy, or better, a nightmare comedy, where the things you laugh at are really the heart of the paradoxical postures that make a nuclear war possible" (Gelmis 1970: 309).[1] Kubrick's shift to dark comedy imbued *Dr. Strangelove* with a fever dreamlike aura that is at once hilarious and historically incisive. As cultural historian Paul S. Boyer (1996: 266) has observed, *Dr. Strangelove* manages to "convey all too accurately the weird logic of deterrence theory, the paranoia of the Cold War, and the nuclear jitters of the early 1960s."

Dr. Strangelove is a dark comedy about the insanity of mutual assured destruction, a policy pursued by both the United States and the Soviet Union during the Cold War in which the buildup of nuclear arms was presumed to be an effective deterrent to nuclear war. If both sides had enough nuclear bombs, the argument runs, then neither side would be stupid enough to use them. But as the telling acronym for that misguided military policy (MAD) hints, it would only require one mad general to trigger a total catastrophe. "This film is the first break in the catatonic cold war trance," wrote Lewis Mumford (1964: 25), "that has so long held our country in its rigid grip."

The terrifying specter of the Bomb dominated US culture in the late 1950s and 1960s. Although anxieties about nuclear war had been the subject of two contemporaneous films, *Fail-Safe* (Sidney Lumet 1962) and *Seven Days in May* (John Frankenheimer 1964), both of them "earnest cautionary tales" (Morrison 2008: 128), Kubrick's approach makes it a very different kind of Cold War film. Peter Sellers had previously shown a gift for accents and caricature in *Lolita*, and he had become a bona-fide movie star in *The Pink Panther* (Blake Edwards 1963), but here, playing not one but three different roles as Group Captain

Lionel Mandrake, President Merkin Muffley, and the eponymous Dr. Strangelove himself, with his involuntary Hitler salutes, faux-European accent, and wheelchair-bound theatrics, Sellers' droll antics seem less gratuitous than central to its biting satire. A European émigré now working for the United States, Dr. Strangelove hints that totalitarianism had come home to roost. Indeed, by pointing to the sublimated presence of fascism within the US military, Kubrick implicitly raises the question, not what might have happened had the fascists won the war, but rather, did they after all?[2]

Dr. Strangelove also implies that a hawkish attitude – learning to Love the Bomb, as the subtitle has it – can help allay our fears. Note that Hawk Films Ltd. is the name of the production company responsible for the film, according to the title card. All this is part of the hideous joke, of course, as if Kubrick took perverse pleasure in provoking even as he parodied public fears about the surreal end game being played out by the Cold War. Thus *Dr. Strangelove* conveys a strong sense of dread – a sense "that it could all turn deadly serious again in an instant," as James Morrison (2008: 129) puts it, "with the slightest shift in angle."

In the so-called War Room sequence, the structural centerpiece of *Dr. Strangelove*, Kubrick imagines a terrifying scenario in which an all-out nuclear war could potentially occur. Apparently, a rogue Brigadier General named Jack D. Ripper (Sterling Hayden) has ordered a full-scale attack on the Soviet Union using B-52 bombers flying at their "fail-safe points." They cannot be recalled from their mission because according to the regulations of "Code Red," all further communications with the planes are cut off. "Part of the complexity of *Dr. Strangelove*," Robert Kolker (2000: 125–6) suggests, "is that it presents its prophecy as comedy, provoking laughter and fear, observing with bemused condescension a situation that reveals to an audience its own powerlessness and potential destruction." No small irony of the scene is how long it is: with only 20 minutes to go until the bombs drop, General Buck Turgidson (George C. Scott) takes up nearly ten minutes briefing President Merkin Muffley (Peter Sellers) on the situation at hand. "That's right, Sir," Turgidson says, putting a stick of gum in his mouth, "And although I *hate* to judge before all the facts are in, it's beginning to look like General Ripper exceeded his authority." "It certainly does," the President intones, matching the general's understated tone.

Another irony is that the actor Sterling Hayden (who plays General Ripper), who had served during World War II in the Office of Strategic Services (OSS; a precursor to the CIA), was an informer during the House Un-American Activities Committee (HUAC) investigations of Hollywood in the late 1940s. Hayden deeply regretted cooperating with HUAC and "suffered from despair over the act" (Kolker 2000: 123). "I was a rat, a stoolie," Hayden told a reporter in 1963, "and the names I named of those close friends were blacklisted and deprived of their livelihood" (Buhle and Wagner 2003: 251). Hayden's cooperation with the investigation renders his character's mad ravings about Communist infiltration even more historically resonant for viewers in on the joke. Consider the moment when

Figure 15.1   General "Buck" Turgidson (George C. Scott) briefs the president and his advisors in the "War Room" at the Pentagon, from *Dr. Strangelove* (1964; director and producer, Stanley Kubrick).

Ripper asks Captain Mandrake, "Do you recall what Clemenceau once said about war?" "He said war was too important to be left to the generals … . But today war is too important to be left to the politicians. They have neither the time, the training, nor the inclination for strategic thought. I can no longer sit back and allow communist infiltration, communist indoctrination, communist subversion and the International Communist Conspiracy to sap and impurify all of our precious bodily fluids." The speech cannot help but recall HUAC or the McCarthy hearings, although it actually derives from a conspiracy theory then being promulgated by the John Birch Society, whose members believed that the US government's plan to fluoridate the nation's water supply was actually a Communist plot.[3]

While General Turgidson comes across as insouciant in the face of imminent disaster, he begins to look increasingly unhinged and even psychotic himself: "Now, *if*, on the *other hand*, we were to immediately launch an all out and coordinated attack on all their airfields and missile bases we'd stand a damn good chance of catching them with their pants down." The General at first shows visible glee at the prospect of a first strike attack against Russia, which then turns into dismay when he learns that Soviet ambassador Alexi de Sadesky (Peter Bull) has been invited to the War Room – "But he'll see the Big Board!" George C. Scott's manic performance as Buck Turgidson arguably steals the scene; he insists matter-of-factly that the United States now faces a choice "between two admittedly regrettable, but nevertheless, distinguishable post-war environments: one where you got twenty million people killed, and the other where you got a hundred and fifty million people killed." "You're taking about mass murder, General, not war," declares Muffley. "Mr. President," Turgidson admits, "I'm not saying we wouldn't get our hair mussed. But I do say … no more than ten to twenty million killed, tops. Uh … depending on the breaks." When collateral damage on the scale of ten or twenty million casualties is likened to getting our hair mussed, we know we're in the upside down world of dark comedy, which as

Morris Dickstein (2007: 97) memorably puts it, "is pitched at the breaking point where moral anguish explodes into a mixture of comedy and terror, where things are so bad you might as well laugh."

"Peace is our Profession," the official motto of Strategic Air Command at the time, keeps appearing onscreen, and nowhere does the irony of the phrase become more apparent than when we see it on a large billboard in the background as soldiers attempt to regain control of the base. In these documentary-like scenes, *Dr. Strangelove* suddenly and without warning turns into a realistic war film, with handheld shots of fierce fighting between US troops and, presumably, General Ripper's rogue forces. This scene allegorizes the assumption on which the policy of mutually assured destruction rests: only by engaging in war can we keep the peace.

Dr. Strangelove premiered at a time when traditional gender roles and sexual mores were changing, as young people challenged the dominant domestic ideologies of the postwar period. Historian Elaine Tyler May (1986: 167) has argued that Kubrick "equated the madness of the cold war with Americans' unresolved sexual neuroses," an attribution that no doubt resonated with those in the midst of a sexual revolution. Viewed as the cause of all kinds of social ills, sexual repression, for Kubrick, seemed somehow at fault for America's military hubris. Jack C. Ripper's name invokes the notorious serial killer who murdered prostitutes in late-nineteenth-century London, giving a somewhat sinister undertone to his bizarre claim that, by withholding "my essence" during "the physical act of love," he will safeguard the purity of certain "precious bodily fluids." The name Dr. Strangelove also lends a note of perversion to his fantasy of a post-apocalyptic society in which there would be "ten females to every male." "I hasten to add that each man will be required to do prodigious service along these lines," Dr. Strangelove declares, "and women will have to be selected for their sexual characteristics, which will have to be of a highly stimulating nature." In the penultimate scene, Dr. Strangelove's involuntary Hitler salute is meant to hint that he cannot control his bodily urges (an unused shot showed him masturbating with his wayward hand). Finally, the missile attack itself is rendered in hilariously phallic terms: Major T.J. "King" Kong straddles a nuclear bomb and rides it like a mechanical bull – wearing his trademark cowboy hat – until it detonates. No wonder James Naremore (2007: 119) sums up the film's predominantly regressive sexual politics as a kind of hyper-masculine "wargasm."

Dr. Strangelove ends with a climactic montage of mushroom clouds, surely the most iconic image of the Cold War, with a pointedly ironic accompaniment of Vera Lynn's song "We'll Meet Again." This ending forms a kind of bookend with the montage of military aircraft having sex in the opening credit sequence, although the dark comedy is considerably *darker* in this final scene than in the sexual sight gags at the beginning. "I found myself at the edge of tears as I watched a series of nuclear explosions fill the screen," wrote singer and songwriter Loudon Wainright in his *Life* magazine piece titled "The Strange Case of Strangelove"

(1964: 15), adding, "This happened at the very end of *Dr. Strangelove* ... [after] I had been laughing wildly for an hour and a half." With its abrupt shifts in tone and its ironic juxtapositions of image and sound – from the black comedy of the War Room to the cinema vérité of the battle scenes, from the documentary footage of mushroom clouds to the bathos of the accompanying music – *Dr. Strangelove* achieves a supremely unsettling affect even as it exudes an effortlessly *cool* aura. Viewers didn't know whether to laugh or cry at what they feared could be the fate of the earth.[4]

Critical Responses; or, The Half-life of Not Getting the Point

The first test screening of *Dr. Strangelove* was scheduled for November 22, 1963, the day President John F. Kennedy was assassinated in Dallas. Concerned that the nation was in no mood for comedy, however dark, Columbia delayed the release of *Dr. Strangelove* until January 1964. The studio also deemed the political climate too sensitive for General Buck Turgidson's uncanny remark when Russian ambassador Alexi de Sadesky throws a pie in President Merkin Muffley's face: "Gentlemen, our beloved president has been infamously struck down by a pie in the prime of life! Are we going to let that happen? Massive retaliation!" (Naremore 2007: 127). To get rid of the line, the pie-throwing scene that originally concluded the War Room sequence was cut. When *Dr. Strangelove* was finally released at the end of January 1964, in any event, audiences flocked to see it. "Despite or perhaps because of its cheeky approach," writes Naremore (2000: 121), "*Dr. Strangelove* became the most popular film in America for seventeen straight weeks."

Dr. Strangelove was in fact a polarizing film, delightfully naughty and perverse to some, offputting or downright offensive to others. It became something of a litmus test for film critics. Bosley Crowther (2006) of *The New York Times*, who later reacted negatively to *Bonnie and Clyde* as well, called *Dr. Strangelove* "beyond any question the most shattering sick joke I've ever come across." With its "brazenly jesting speculation" about "what might happen ... if some maniac Air Force general should suddenly order a nuclear attack on the Soviet Union," he argued, *Dr. Strangelove* "is at the same time one of the cleverest and most inclusive thrusts at ... the folly of the military that [has] ever been on screen." Crowther goes on to question Kubrick's good faith in subjecting such a grave matter as nuclear annihilation to withering black humor. There is "much that is brilliant and amusing, and much that is grave and dangerous," he writes.

> On the other hand, I am troubled by the feeling which runs all through the film, of discredit and even holds contempt for our whole defense establishment, up to an even including the hypothetical commander-in-chief .... The ultimate touch of ghoulish humor is when we see the bomb actually going off, dropped on some point

in Russia, and a jazzy sound track comes in with a cheerful melodic rendition of "We'll Meet Again Some Sunny Day." Somehow, to me, it isn't funny. It is malefic and sick. (Crowther 2006: 141-2)

Clearly to be in on the sick joke, rather than, say, being the butt of it, required a willingness to laugh at matters normally treated with seriousness. Which is to say it required a willingness to appreciate dark comedy. For as Lewis Mumford (1964: 19) insisted, coming to Kubrick's defense, "it is not the film that is sick, what is sick is our supposedly moral, democratic country which allowed this policy to be formulated and implemented without even the pretense of public debate."

Comparing Kubrick's film unfavorably to Charlie Chaplin's *The Great Dictator* (1940), Susan Sontag (1990: 148) provocatively argued that *Dr. Strangelove* had less "political daring" than the "left-liberals" who were so enamored with the film assumed. For Sontag, it satirized the defense establishment "from an entirely post-political, *Mad Magazine* point of view" (Sontag 1990: 149). With its "comic detachment" from "the terrifying" consequences of nuclear war, *Dr. Strangelove* indulged in a kind of "philistine nihilism" that Sontag found objectionable (Sontag 1990: 150). Only from the perspective of nihilism, or worse, "misanthropy" can the "topic of mass annihilation" be viewed as "comic" (Sontag 1990: 150). Sontag's moral censoriousness prevented her from fully appreciating dark comedy, in my view, yet she put her finger on the growing disillusionment of the counterculture when she astutely observed, "nihilism is our contemporary form of moral uplift" (Sontag 1990: 149).

Dr. Strangelove was a Rorschach test that predictably divided along generational lines. The film certainly delighted a number of filmmakers. Warren Beatty was reportedly almost as impressed with the film as he was with himself, and he considered asking Kubrick to direct *Bonnie and Clyde*, which went to Arthur Penn instead (the screenwriters Robert Benton and David Newman also approached both Jean-Luc Godard and Francois Truffaut). The director Norman Jewison left a screening of *Dr. Strangelove* by turns impressed with Kubrick's bravado and depressed that "my life was being wasted on these commercial comedies where everyone ended up happy and went to the seashore" (Harris 2008: 25, 143). And sure enough, Jewison would go on to direct the *Dr. Strangelove*-inspired Cold War black comedy *The Russians Are Coming, the Russians Are Coming* (1966), working with a promising editor Hal Ashby (they also collaborated, a year later, on *In the Heat of the Night* 1967). Ashby, in turn, brought his own eccentric personality to bear on a number of dark comedies he went on to direct in the 1970s, including *Harold and Maude* (1971), *The Last Detail* (1973), and *Shampoo* (1975), the latter starring Warren Beatty. *Harold and Maude* may well be the blackest dark comedy of the period, and *The Last Detail*, from a delightfully vulgar screenplay by Robert Towne, had even greater profanity than Robert Altman's *M * A * S * H* (1970). The existential angst in Ashby's films was symptomatic of the growing disillusionment or crisis of confidence during the early 1970s.

Dr. Strangelove paved the way for directors like Ashby, the inheritor of Kubrick's dark comedic legacy, who like Kubrick both catered to this cynical, highly pessimistic sensibility and captured the cultural zeitgeist. For viewers still coming to grips with JFK's assassination, dark comedy spoke to their disillusionment. As Stanley Kauffmann once remarked about *Strangelove*: "It is so truthful a film, so unsparing, so hopeless in the last pit-bottom depths of that word, that the very blackness has a kind of shine" (Maland 1979: 716). Loudon Wainwright (1964: 15) quipped that the outrage provoked by the film only proved, as he puts it, "the half-life of Not Getting the Point is forever." Suffice it to say that what unnerved Bosley Crowther, who called *Dr. Strangelove* "a bit too contemptuous of our defense establishment for my comfort and taste," was precisely the point (Henriksen 1997: 330). Embedding his critique of the military industrial complex within a seemingly innocuous dark comedy, Kubrick evidently ruffled some feathers, but he also showed the tremendous potential of a genre that appealed to the antiauthoritarian ethos of the period. Dark comedy gave Kubrick the means to insinuate – and furthermore, to demonstrate – that if left to its own devices, the US military had a disturbingly fascist bent.

Charlie Don't Surf

In order to grasp just how bold Kubrick's dark comedy was, it is important to remember that any critique of the military, much less an explicitly anti-war film, was rare in Hollywood. When *Dr. Strangelove* appeared in January 1964, the Vietnam War was not yet "on the political agenda for Hollywood" (Harris 2008: 103). Even after the Gulf of Tonkin in August of that year prompted journalists to devote more attention to what was happening in Southeast Asia, *Variety* magazine observed in 1965: "the war in Vietnam is too hot for Hollywood" (Doherty 1993: 283).

Apart from *The Green Berets* (1968), starring John Wayne, the Vietnam War tended to be "addressed only indirectly in American cinema" until the late 1970s, for instance by focusing on traumatized veterans or on the "culture of violence" at home (Lev 2000: 107; Schulman 2001). Still, Vietnam is the key to understanding virtually any war movie in this period, even if it was ostensibly about World War II. Consider the opening scene of *Patton* (1970). General Patton (George C. Scott) advances to the stage in front of a large American flag and salutes. "All this stuff you've heard about America not wanting to fight, wanting to stay out of the war," he tells us, "is a lot of horse dump. Americans traditionally love to fight. All real Americans love the sting of battle .... That's why Americans have never lost and will never lose a war, because the very thought of losing is hateful to Americans." A thinly disguised dig at the antiwar movement, this dramatic opening scene appears at first glance to support the hawks. Yet Patton's bombast surely undercuts his hawkish stance, and by extension military involvement in

Vietnam. Patton's integrity is further undermined by arrogance and callousness. "Now I want you to remember," he announces, "that no bastard ever won a war by dying for his country. He won it by making the other poor dumb bastard die for his country." The film's portrayal of Patton is decidedly mixed, which helps explain why it "appealed to both pro-war and antiwar audiences" (Lev 200: 108).

Writing in *The New Yorker*, Pauline Kael (1970: 73) speculated that *Patton* "appears to be deliberately planned as a Rorschach test." Was General Patton a war hero or a dangerous megalomaniac? George C. Scott's masterful performance in the lead role was ambiguous enough to support both interpretations. No doubt influenced by Scott's memorable turn in *Strangelove*, viewers could not help but recall the gum-chewing General Turgidson in the War Room, to my knowledge Scott's only previous role in a military uniform. Yet the more subversive reading of General Patton's character was probably inevitable. "If they want to make a film glorifying him as a great American hero, it will be laughed at," remarked Francis Ford Coppola, a screenwriter on the film. "And if I write a film that condemns him, it won't be made at all" (Lev 2000: 109).[5]

The most important antiwar films of the early 1970s, including *Catch-22* (Mike Nichols 1970), *M * A * S * H* (Robert Altman 1970), and *Slaughterhouse-Five* (George Roy Hill 1972), all suggest that dark comedy allowed auteur filmmakers unprecedented freedom to critique the US military. The tragic incident at Kent State University on May 4, 1970, when members of the Ohio National Guard killed four antiwar protestors, demonstrated to some that the atrocities being committed abroad had come home to roost. Emboldened by the shocking revelation of the My Lai massacre one year earlier, and now by the incident at Kent State, the antiwar movement acquired a similar kind of moral authority that had made Civil Rights one of the most effective social movements in US history. Dark comedy gave directors freedom to advance this newly legitimized antiwar agenda, which would become even more pronounced in later films such as *The Deer Hunter* (Michael Cimino 1978) and *Apocalypse Now* (Francis Ford Coppola 1979).

Hollywood studios were more receptive to forceful critiques of the military for a variety of reasons: the galvanized antiwar movement and its growing popular support, the revelations of military atrocities, and a desire on the part of many within the film industry to be more *relevant*. The film industry was, by 1970, in the midst of an economic recession from which it would not recover until *Jaws* (1975) and *Star Wars* (1977) gave rise to the era of summer blockbusters. Struggling to find an audience in a country divided along generational and ideological lines, Hollywood studios desperately wanted to replicate the box office magic that made *Easy Rider* (1969) such a success. With a screenplay by Terry Southern, the acknowledged purveyor of dark comedy who had also worked with Kubrick on *Dr. Strangelove*, *Easy Rider* encouraged studios to adopt a relatively a new strategy: courting controversy rather than avoiding it.

*M * A * S * H* – an acronym for "Mobile Army Surgical Hospital" – proved that Kubrick's great dark comedy formula could be duplicated. Critics hailed the young Altman, age 35 at the time, as a promising new voice in American cinema. One of the most acclaimed and successful films of the New Hollywood, $M^\star A^\star S^\star H^\star$ became the third highest grossing film of the year and won the Palme d'Or at Cannes. Dark comedy was the secret to its popular and critical success.[6]

Pauline Kael famously gave $M * A * S * H*$ high praise as "the best American war comedy since sound came in," and she put her finger on what made the film such a hit with the counterculture:

> It's a sick joke, but it's also generous and romantic – an erratic, episodic film, full of the pleasures of the unexpected ... . The picture has so much spirit that you keep laughing – and without discomfort, because all the targets *should* be laughed at. The laughter is at the horrors and absurdities of war, and, specifically, at the people who flourish in military bureaucracy. (Kael 1994: 347–8)

Less dark than *Dr. Strangelove* but similar in many other respects, $M^\star A^\star S^\star H^\star$ retains a sort of "surreal innocence" that lightens the mood and tone, making it a "cheery 'black' comedy" in Kael's curiously oxymoronic phrase. With $M^\star A^\star S^\star H^\star$ you don't get the "feeling that there's nothing to do but get stoned and die," she writes: "It's hip but it isn't hopeless" (Kael 1994: 347–9).

Set in an army hospital during the Korean War, $M^\star A^\star S^\star H^\star$ follows a group of profane yet skilled doctors who goof off, play pranks on one another, have sex with nurses, and generally have a raucous good time, even as they show tremendous competence and even élan in treating wounded soldiers coming in from the front lines. Although "explicitly about the Korean War," Lev (2000: 209) points out, the film "can be read as an indirect commentary on America's involvement in Vietnam." Twentieth-Century Fox acknowledged as much in promotional materials, using an image of a woman's legs in high heels forming a peace sign, invoking the symbol of the antiwar movement and thereby courting a countercultural audience. Combining vulgarity, full-frontal nudity, and scatology, $M^\star A^\star S^\star H^\star$ revels in what Bakhtin (1984) calls the carnivalesque.[7]

Mike Nichols' *Catch 22* (1970), made the same year as $M^\star A^\star S^\star H^\star$, is another important dark comedy although it flopped at the box office, earning $9 million on a relatively large budget (at the time) of $18 million, suggesting that the days of big-budget antiwar films were numbered. In part because of the spectacular success of his previous film, *The Graduate* (1967), the studio had been willing to back Nichols' ambitious if commercially risky followup: a film adaptation of Joseph Heller's World War II novel *Catch-22* (1961). Despite an extraordinary ensemble cast (Alan Arkin, Richard Benjamin, Art Garfunkel, Anthony Perkins, Martin Sheen, Jon Voight, and Orson Welles) and a screenplay by Buck Henry, *Catch-22* did not resonate with viewers the way *Dr. Strangelove* and $M^\star A^\star S^\star H^\star$ did.[8] The film does, however, develop a similar critique of the madness of the military industrial complex, which Nichols is a form of institutionalized insanity. Desperate to get out of flying any more bombing missions, the film's would be rebel Yossarian (Alan Arkin) tries to convince Colonel Cathcart (Martin Balsam) that he is crazy, but Doctor Daneeka (Jack Gilford) explains that his actual mental condition is irrelevant (the "Catch-22" of the novel's title): "He would be crazy to fly more missions and sane if he didn't, but if he was sane he'd have to fly them. If he flew them he was crazy and didn't have to; but if he didn't, he was sane and had to." As Morris Dickstein (2007: 113–14) observes, "Yosarian seems perilously close to the Sterling Hayden character in *Dr. Strangelove*, the general who fears that women are sapping his vital bodily fluids. The insanity of the system, in this case the army, breeds a defensive counter-insanity." For audiences disillusioned with the Vietnam War, the point about just how delusional and misguided our military leaders were no longer seemed controversial. On the contrary, it was more or less taken for granted that our military leaders had lost their marbles.

"I think the Vietnam War freed me and other writers," Kurt Vonnegut (2006: 20) recalls, "because it made our leadership and our motives seem so scruffy and essentially stupid." When Vonnegut undertook to write about his own experiences during World War II in *Slaughterhouse-Five*, he realized he could approach the subject of war in a serious way through comedy: "And what I saw, what I had to report, made the war look so ugly" (Vonnegut 2006: 20). The Allied bombing of Dresden, which Vonnegut had witnessed firsthand as a prisoner of war, was a ghastly "military experiment to find out if you could burn down a whole city by scattering incendiaries all over it … Why my fellow prisoners of war and I weren't killed I don't know" (Vonnegut 2006: 18). In his memoir *A Man Without a Country* (2006), the last book he wrote before his death, Vonnegut (2006: 3) poignantly comments on how comedy can be deployed even in the most horrible situations: "Any subject is subject to laughter … . I saw the destruction of Dresden. I saw the city before and then came out of an air-raid shelter and saw it afterward, and certainly one response was laughter. God knows, that's the soul seeking some relief." Far from trivializing it, dark comedy "becomes Vonnegut's means of protecting himself from the horror he has witnessed" (Horton 2005: 85).

Slaughterhouse-Five invokes both Vonnegut's own survivor guilt and the Vietnam War in a scene where Billy Pilgrim's son Robert, back from his first tour of duty in Vietnam, visits his father while on leave from the army. "God, Dad, to think that you lived. It's a miracle. Well, like, one time when a chopper got hit by Charlie just outside our camp. It came down like a stone, but the door gunner walked away." The analogy brings home the fact that *Slaughterhouse-Five* revisits the Dresden bombing retrospectively, through a lens colored by antiwar sentiment. In this scene, *Slaughterhouse-Five* invokes widespread public opposition to the Vietnam War. "Everybody knows it's a lousy war," Robert tells his father, "but sooner or later it's going to be us or the Communists; we've got to stand up to 'em somewhere." His defense of the war recalls the domino theory that was used to justify America's continued involvement in Southeast Asia, but of course the dramatic irony of the scene depends upon the audience disagreeing with him. The film adaptation of *Slaughterhouse-Five* thus preserves Vonnegut's strong antiwar message. "Shot in 1971 while the Vietnam War was still raging," writes Andrew Horton (2005: 83), *Slaughterhouse-Five* reflects an anti-war agenda that indirectly indicts "the futility of Vietnam."

In one of the most forceful indictments of war ever made, *Apocalypse Now* (1979), a film otherwise notable for its visceral realism, Francis Ford Coppola also makes use of dark comedy in a justly celebrated sequence that begins with a helicopter attack on a village – sensationally edited by Walter Murch – and then turns into dark comedy when Lieutenant Captain William "Bill" Kilgore (Robert Duvall) insists on going surfing in the midst of explosions and enemy fire. Ostensibly the purpose of their mission was to drop off Captain Benjamin L. Willard (Martin Sheen) at the mouth of the Nung river, but Captain Kilgore apparently has an ulterior motive: surfing what are reported to be double breaking waves at the point known as Vinh Dinh Drop, especially when he learns that a former professional surfer, Lance Johnson (Sam Bottoms), is in Willard's boat crew. Captain Kilgore's name is Kubrick-like in its suggestive irony, of course, and Robert Duvall's extraordinary performance captures the maniacal hubris of the US military, a dominant theme in dark comedies about war. When one of the captain's officers urges caution, reminding him that attacking a village widely known as "Charlie's point" will almost certainly put the lives of his men at risk and incur too much collateral damage, Captain Kilgore dismisses the suggestion in the first of his two unforgettable lines, "Charlie don't surf!"

Although revered by the men in his Ninth Cavalry Regiment for his aura of invincibility, Captain Kilgore courts danger for the sake of his frivolous obsession with surfing. His attack on the village seems destructive and misguided at best, immoral at worst, and the sequence can be read as a miniature allegory of the Vietnam War as a whole, with the United States cast in the role of imperialistic aggressor against a people who evidently do not want them there. Despite one woman who, seemingly a civilian, assists the Vietcong by throwing a grenade inside a helicopter, the whole scene deliberately invokes the My Lai massacre, which was a turning point in the antiwar movement when it was brought to light in late 1969, more than a year-and-a-half after the actual incident. "The most important thing I wanted to do in the making of *Apocalypse Now*," Coppola remarks, "was to create a film experience that would give its audience a sense of the horror, the madness, the sensuousness, and the moral dilemma of the Vietnam war ... And yet I wanted it to go further, to the moral issues that are behind all wars" (Hagen 1998: 230). The culmination of a trend toward explicit critiques of the military that began with *Dr. Strangelove*, Coppola's virulently antiwar film would have been virtually inconceivable 20 years earlier.

Dark comedy largely disappeared from American screens during the Reagan and Clinton years, with notable exceptions, though the two that come to mind, Martin Scorsese's *After Hours* (1985) and Robert Altman's *The Player* (1992), were both made by New Hollywood directors. To understand why dark comedy went into decline, only to be resurrected in a more postmodern vein by the Coen brothers and by Quentin Tarantino's *Pulp Fiction* (1994), it may be useful to consider King's (2002: 107) distinction between satire and parody: "The target of satire is social and political. Some kind of reference is implied, more or less explicitly, to the real world, a fact that is responsible for its potentially more serious modality. The target of parody tends to be formal or aesthetic. Familiar conventions, representational devices or modes of discourse are the subject of humorous assault or exposure." With the turn towards parody in postmodern cinema, satire's political edge was either blunted or else so obscure as to be virtually unrecognizable, as if dark comedy had been appropriated by the commercial mainstream in much the same way that political dissent was co-opted (Frank 1997). Just as they had in 1967, when Hollywood studios were savvy enough to appropriate the exciting, rebellious sensibilities of *Bonnie and Clyde* and *The Graduate*, the studios again quickly moved to commercialize and incorporate – literally, by acquiring smaller production companies – the short-lived independent cinema of the late 1980s.

The Dude Abides

In two Coen brothers' films of the 1990s, *Fargo* (1996) and *The Big Lebowski* (1998), dark comedy re-emerged in the context of a new, auteur-oriented independent film movement, albeit with less political consequence than in the 1970s. The Coens have flourished in a climate where considerable cultural capital is at stake in their cynical brand of dark comedy. What's at stake politically is less clear. Comparing the independent film movement unfavorably to the New Hollywood, Emanuel Levy (2001: 5) bemoans the "lack of radically political and avant-garde visions." Although their films are marked by a certain "hipness" and "knowingness," he complains, they seem "devoid of serious themes or ideas," as if "brilliant style" alone "will somehow lure viewers into uncritical acceptance" of their work (Levy 2001: 223). Their brand of dark comedy at times seems like a self-conscious exercise in allusion without a target – in short, not so much satire as comedy for comedy's sake.

Fredric Jameson (1992: 82–3) has influentially identified pastiche, rather than parody, as "the price to be paid for a radically new aesthetic system ... in which energetic artists who now lack both forms and content cannibalize the museum and wear the masks of extinct mannerisms," such that "the quest for a uniquely distinctive style and the very category of 'style' come to seem old-fashioned." The Coen brothers tend to rely on audiences well versed in the sort of arcane cultural knowledge that seems necessary to decode their obscure allusions and ironies. The opening credit sequence of *Fargo*, for instance, in which Carter Burwell's portentous score plays over a long shot of a bleak, snowy landscape just as an undistinguished car of American make breasts the horizon, may well pay homage to Kubrick's ironic use of music. Recall the opening credit sequence of *Dr. Strangelove*, where an instrumental version of Harry M. Woods's "Try a

Little Tenderness" plays over images of military aircraft like the B-52 bomber, or the opening aerial montage at the start of *The Shining* (1981), where medieval choral music re-orchestrated for synthesizer by Wendy Carlos and Rachel Elkind establishes, as Kubrick himself put it, "an ominous mood during Jack's first drive up to the hotel – the vast isolation and eerie splendor of high mountains, and the narrow, winding roads which would become impassable after heavy snow" (Ciment 2011). Like Kubrick, the Coens enjoy studio financing while working somewhat at a distance from, if not outside, the studio system. Yet their highly allusive style might be described as post-auteur in that they constantly quote other films and film genres.

Jameson's term "genre pastiche," which he uses in a reading of *The Shining*, is arguably even more applicable to the Coen brothers, whose films confound genre expectations, bending and blending genres rather than conforming to viewer expectations. When "even the possibility of the traditional genre film breaks down," Jameson (1992: 83) says, you get metageneric films. In keeping with this tendency in postmodern cinema, the Coen brothers' hybrid genre films are nothing if not metageneric. *The Big Lebowski* (1998) is at once a send-up of the classic film noir *The Big Sleep* (1946, Howard Hawks), a hyper-revisionist western, a pastiche of Busby Berkley musicals, and a picaresque romp in the tradition of *Gulliver's Travels*, though the political import that was so integral to Swift's eighteenth-century social satire has seemingly all but disappeared. R. Barton Palmer (2004: 12) observes that *"The Big Lebowski* seemed to many of their admirers an exercise in postmodern pointlessness, with its wacky mixture of genres and huge inventory of quotations both literary and cinematic not adding up to much." The blank parody of pastiche may be, in Robert Stam's phrase, a subversive pleasure, but it is a far cry from the kind of subversion embraced, however naively, by the oppositional politics of the counterculture.

While I don't feel the need to defend the Coen brothers against such charges – one could argue that pointlessness is, after all, precisely the point – I contend that their films are apolitical in a historically specific way. As the ultimate slacker film, *The Big Lebowski* in some respects resembles Richard Linklater's *Slacker* (1991) and *Dazed and Confused* (1993), both films about young people whose apathy, aimlessness, and lack of ambition are portrayed as a form of civil disobedience, if not a coherent philosophy. "The dictionary defines slackers as people who evade duties and responsibilities," Linklater once declared. "Slackers might look like the left-behinds of society, but they are actually one step ahead, rejecting most of society and the social hierarchy before it rejects them" (Kopkind 1993). One character in *Slacker* sums up the salient difference between fellow travelers and slackers as follows: "You know how the slogan goes, 'Workers of the world, unite?' We say workers of the world, relax."

Similarly, *The Big Lebowski* captures a historical moment in the late 1980s and early 1990s when the oft-mentioned political apathy of Generation X distinguished them from the putative radicalism of their baby boomer parents. To be sure,

The Big Lebowski confounds easy contextualization, not least because the Dude, far from being a Generation Xer, is in fact an unrepentant radical (more on that below). If the Dude points forward to the slacker generation – he speaks their lingo and clearly struck a chord with them – he also points backward to the 1950s, if only because from all appearances his sole occupation in life is bowling. Director Joel Coen remarks that the bowling scenes in *The Big Lebowski* were "important in reflecting that period at the end of the Fifties and the beginning of the Sixties. That suited the retro side of the movie, slightly anachronistic, which sent us back to a not-so-far-away era, but one that was well and truly gone nevertheless" (Allen 2006: 102).[9]

What makes *The Big Lebowski* especially relevant for my purposes is that it also hearkens back to the heady days of the Hollywood Renaissance, when dark comedy became for a time one of the most effective means of political satire. The Coen brothers graft themselves into that dark comedy tradition first volubly, in the prolific swearing of their two intrepid antiheroes, and then more subtly, in the distinctive cowboy twang of Sam Elliot's voiceover narration, which evokes the antiwar ethos of earlier dark comedies by calling our attention to the first Gulf War:

> Now this story I'm about to unfold took place back in the early nineties – just about the time of our conflict with Sad'm and the Eye-rackies. I only mention it 'cause sometimes there's a man – I won't say a hero, 'cause what's a hero? – but sometimes there's a man … and I'm talkin' about the Dude here – sometimes there's a man who, well, he's the man for his time 'n place, he fits right in there – and that's the Dude, in Los Angeles. (Coen and Coen 1998: 4)

Even if he "fits right in there" during his time and place – Los Angeles, *circa* 1990 – the Dude also connects *The Big Lebowski* to the counterculture; he is in one sense a walking anachronism. To begin with, he swears a lot. "D'ya have to use so many cuss words?" the Stranger complains. Of course, part of the pleasure for viewers of *M*A*S*H** and *The Last Detail* was their flaunting of longstanding taboos against profanity in the movies: "People laughed at the profanity in Robert Altman's *M * A * S * H**," recalls Kael. "It felt good, like loosening your tie" ("Into the Kaelstrom" 1994). By the 1990s, of course, the f-word no longer carried the same weight of transgression. Because black humor is all about "affronting taboos" and indeed "giving offence," as Dickstein (2007: 100) points out, dark comedy "became an aspect of the libertarian, idol-shattering side of the sixties." "Eventually things reach the point," he continues, "where scarcely any taboos were left to be assaulted" (Dickstein 2007: 101).

Yet Jeffrey Lebowski has another connection to the counterculture besides profanity, for it turns out that he is based on a friend of the Coen brothers named Jeff "The Dude" Dowd. At one point, the Dude makes a surprising claim that he was one of the authors of the Port Huron Statement, a document drafted by the Students for a Democratic Society (SDS) at their 1962 national convention meeting at Port Huron, Michigan: "I was one of the authors of the Port Huron

Statement – the original Port Huron Statement, not the compromised second draft. And then I, uh – ever hear of the Seattle Seven?" Although Jeff Dowd did not help write the Port Huron Statement – he was only 13 years old in 1962 – he *was* a member of the Seattle Liberation Front (SLF), founded in 1970 by Michael Lerner a year after the SDS had formally disbanded. Seven members of the SLF – dubbed the Seattle 7 in homage to the infamous Chicago 7 – were charged with "conspiracy to incite a riot" for organizing an antiwar protest that quickly turned violent outside the Federal Courthouse in downtown Seattle in 1970. Dowd briefly went to jail for contempt of court in the wake of the indictments. Far from being the slacker that his cult following has generally perceived him to be, the Dude was in fact based on a bona-fide former revolutionary who hails from the late 1960s. Tenuous as his connection may be, the Dude's claim that he helped write the original Port Huron Statement – not, he boasts, the "compromised second draft" – puts him right back at the scene where the hippie movement was born, as it were. Put another way, it makes him something like the missing link between Kubrick and the Coens.

But there is another countercultural connection that is worth exploring in more detail. Following the Desert Storm context mentioned in the opening voice-over monologue, *The Big Lebowski* later recalls a rather charged political moment when then President George H.W. Bush had to decide whether the United States would respond to Saddam Hussein's invasion of neighboring Kuwait. In unprepared, off-the-cuff remarks at the White House on August 5, 1990, President Bush condemned Iraq's "brutal, naked aggression" against Kuwait and proceeded to make what some commentators at the time insisted was nothing less than a declaration of war: "This will not stand. This will not stand, this aggression against Kuwait" (This Aggression 1991). In a show of presidential resolve, Bush saw fit to repeat these lines some months later in his January 1991 State of the Union Address: "Saddam Hussein's unprovoked invasion – his ruthless, systematic rape of a peaceful neighbor – violated everything the community of nations holds dear. The world has said this aggression would not stand, and it will not stand" (Bush 1998: 136).

I rehearse this interesting buildup to Desert Storm because footage of Bush's speech is shown and heard on a television screen as the Dude stands at a cash register in a supermarket. The Dude then repeats Bush's words after two thugs working for a pornographer named Jackie Treehorn assault him in his home, mistaking him for the "big" Lebowski, a millionaire whose wife Bunny owes him money. Adding insult to injury, one of them urinates on the Dude's rug, doubly insulting because the rug, as he puts it, "ties the room together." The Dude tracks down the Big Lebowski in his mansion and lodges a complaint about the ruined rug: "This will not stand, man" (Coen and Coen 1998: 18). His response to an unprovoked invasion of his home deliberately echoes, in other words, George H.W. Bush's response to Saddam Hussein's invasion of Kuwait. Left to his devices, the Dude would likely have done nothing in response, but

Walter's more aggressive instincts ultimately win the day; some kind of retaliation (or recompense) is required. "We're talking about unchecked aggression here," Walter fumes. "I'm talking about drawing a line in the sand, Dude. Across this line you do not ... " suddenly changing the subject until he picks up the train of thought a bit later in the scene, "and there is no reason, no fucking reason, why his wife should go out and owe money and then pee on your rug. Am I wrong?"

Early in *The Big Lebowski*, the Coens stage another miniature allegory in which Walter, who likely suffers from post-traumatic stress disorder, pulls a gun on his friend Smokey (Jimmy Dale Gilmore) for crossing over the line at the bowling alley. "Over the line!" Walter screams. "This is not 'Nam, this is bowling. There are rules!" According to Todd A. Cormer (2005: 99), "here, we have in miniature the Persian Gulf War: A border has been crossed, rules have been violated, and violence results." Nowhere is the Coen brothers' homage to New Hollywood dark comedy more apparent than when they invoke the political context surrounding the Gulf War. Although he claims at one point that he once "dabbled in pacifism," Walter is the ultimate hawk. He goads the Dude into seeking compensation for the rug from Big Lebowski; he persuades the Dude to keep the $1 million ransom and deliver a fake one instead to the people who supposedly kidnapped Lebowski's wife, Bunny; he insists that they track down the person who stole the Dude's car (with the money in it); and finally, he destroys a brand-new Corvette parked outside the home of a kid named Larry Sellers, which in fact belongs to a neighbor. The wrecked Corvette is, in effect, collateral damage incurred as a result of Walter's aggression. As John Goodman himself told an interviewer: "Walter is strictly Manifest Destiny" (Haglund 2008).[10]

Interpreting everything through the lens of his Vietnam War experience, Walter's propensity to use violence rather than diplomacy adds a politically self-conscious dimension to the film and links it to a long line of antiwar dark comedies. Walter recalls General Ripper and General Turgidson, not to mention Robert Duvall's Colonel Kilgore in *Apocalypse Now*, whose most memorable lines ("Charlie don't surf"; "I love the smell of napalm in the morning") have entered the lexicon in much the same way that Walter's and the Dude's have. A variation on that staple of film comedy, the odd couple, these characters embody not only the trauma of the 1960s but also the ideological impasse and polarization of today's national politics, with the Dude representing a residual liberalism that survived the demise of the New Left and Walter standing for the neoconservative movement of the Reagan era and beyond. Still obsessed with their experiences during the 1960s and 1970s, both are stuck in a rut from which they can't escape.

The wrenching climax of *The Big Lebowski*, involving the death of their bowling partner Donny (Steve Buscemi), suggests that he, too, is a form of collateral damage, since he dies from an apparent heart attack during a confrontation with a group of skinhead neo-Nazis. These are the same neo-Nazis who had earlier tried to extort a million dollars from the Big Lebowski by falsely claiming to have kidnapped his wife. Now they accost the Dude, Walter, and Donny outside the bowling alley and demand a million dollars. The Dude informs them matter-of-factly that Bunny is still alive, as if he can avert violence simply by reasoning with them. When one of the nihilists complains, "It's not fair," Walter retorts, "Fair? Who's the fucking nihilist here? What are you, a bunch of fucking crybabies?" "For us," Joel Coen once remarked, "the nihilists are the bad guys" (Allen 2006: 105). Yet Walter is the one who resorts to violence here, beating them up in retaliation for burning the Dude's car, which in turn triggers Donny's heart attack.

"We know a guy who's a middle-aged hippy pothead," Joel Coen admits, "and another who's a Vietnam vet who's totally defined by, and obsessed with, the time he spent in Vietnam. We find it interesting for our characters to be products of the sixties in some way, but set in the nineties .... What you can say with certainty is that the movie leads to a reconciliation between the Dude and Walter despite their difficult relationship'" (Allen 2006: 95, 105). *The Big Lebowski* ends with a scene, at once darkly comic and touching, where one's laughter is likely to catch in the throat. On a cliff overlooking the beach, the Dude and Walter scatter Donny's ashes from a Folger's coffee can; the wind blows their late friend back in their faces, as if in richly deserved retribution for their roles, albeit unwitting ones, in Donny's death. This scene is intensely funny, macabre, and poignant all at once, a testament to what the Coen brothers at their best can to do with their distinctive brand of dark comedy. Despite what has been perceived as a rather soulless postmodern cynicism, they sometimes manage to convey heartfelt emotion or else moral approbation – recall the moment when a very pregnant sheriff Marge Gunderson (Frances McDormand) admonishes the taciturn killer Gaear Grimsrud (Peter Stormare) in the back of her police cruiser at the end of *Fargo*. When the Dude and Walter, seeking some kind atonement, scatter their friend Donny's ashes, the scene reveals, through its exquisite dark comedy, a beating heart at the center of *The Big Lebowski* that should make us hopeful for the future of the genre.

One of my epigraphs refers to a scene in which the Big Lebowski tells Jeffrey Lebowski, "Your revolution is over, Mr. Lebowski. Condolences." This pronouncement strikes me as premature at best, deluded at worst, for although a backlash against the cultural revolution was inevitable, countercultural values have been largely assimilated into the mainstream, as evidenced by the widespread acceptance of profanity, for instance, or by a reflexive distrust of government (Jenkins 2006). One measure of just how entrenched – and commercialized – countercultural values have become is the extraordinary cult phenomenon of *The Big Lebowski*. Arguably the biggest cult film since *The Rocky Horror Picture Show* (1975), *The Big Lebowski* has spawned its own subculture of Dude-lookalikes who flock to conventions called Lebowski Fests, its own scholarly industry that each year produces a volume facetiously titled *The Year in Lebowski Studies*, and its own religion, the Church of the Latter-Day Dude. Thus predictions of the revolution's demise turn out to have been, as it were, greatly exaggerated. The Dude abides.

Figure 15.2   Walter Sobchak (John Goodman) gives a eulogy before scattering Donny's ashes from a Folgers coffee can, with Jeffrey "The Dude" Lebowski (Jeff Bridges) looking on, from *The Big Lebowski* (1998; director, Joel Coen; producer, Ethan Coen).

When the cowboy narrator shows up again at the bowling alley in the final scene, he provides a sort of reflective coda to the movie:

> The Dude abides. I don't know about you, but I take comfort in that. It's good knowin' he's out there, the Dude, takin' her easy for all us sinners ... . Well, that about does her, wraps her all up. Things seem to have worked out pretty good for the Dude 'n' Walter, and it was a pretty good story, don't ya think? Made me laugh to beat the band. Parts, anyway. Course – I didn't like seein' Donny go. But then, happen to know there's a little Lebowski on the way. I guess that's the way the whole durned human comedy keeps perpetuatin' itself, down through the generations.

The Mark Twain-like voice here alerts us to the fact that we have exited the noir world of the nihilists and come back again to the comedic world of the Dude. It is no coincidence, of course, that the cowboy echoes Preston Sturges' defense of comedy in *Sullivan's Travels*, "There's a lot to be said for making people laugh. Did you know that's all some people have? It isn't much ... but it's better than nothing in this cockeyed caravan." The Coen brothers' next movie, as they surely already knew then, would be a loose adaptation of Homer's *The Odyssey* whose title, *Oh Brother, Where Art Thou?*, mischievously alludes to the film within a film of *Sullivan's Travels*.

As the genre best suited to irreverent or downright subversive critiques of our institutions of power, dark comedy would appear to recommend itself at a time when (as of this writing) two wars drag on, such that being "a nation at war" has come to seem like a normal state of affairs – has indeed become the status quo. Why do the wars in Afghanistan and Iraq, or the war on terror, appear to be incompatible with comedy?[11] We may wonder if the necessary conditions for dark comedy have changed somehow, yet given the genre's rich tradition of cultural critique, surely someone will attempt to revive it.

Notes

1. In an interview published six months before the film's release, titled "How I Learned to Stop Worrying and Love the Cinema" (1963: 12), Kubrick relates that he was "struck by the paradoxes of every variation of the problem from one extreme to the other – from the paradoxes of unilateral disarmament to the first strike." Although he had envisioned the film as a "straightforward melodrama," he soon realized that it would only work as a dark comedy (Southern 1995: 140).

2. I am indebted to Edward Sugden for this point about fascism as a sort of sublimated presence within the US military, which, for Kubrick, belies its commitment to American democracy.

3. In *The Paranoid Style in American Politics* (1996), first published in *Harper's* magazine the same year as *Dr. Strangelove*, historian Richard Hoftsadter worried that the fluoridation conspiracy theory was symptomatic of a disturbing new trend: "the movement against the fluoridation of municipal water supplies has been catnip for cranks of all kinds, especially for those who have obsessive fear of poisoning" (Hoftsadter 1964: 5–6). According to Deborah Nelson (2002: 114), Kubrick "tracks with remarkably little exaggeration the inflamed rhetoric in debates about fluoridation that circulated in the American press during the 1950s."

4. Jonathan Schell's bestselling book *The Fate of the Earth* (1982) would later speculate about the "consequences for the world, insofar as these can be known, of a full-scale nuclear holocaust." Like Kubrick, Schell (2000: 4, 196) pointed out "the circularity at the core of the nuclear-deterrence doctrine; we seek to avoid our own self-extinction by threatening to perform the act."

5. Scott shifted his stance toward the Vietnam War in the five years between *Dr. Strangelove* and *Patton*. In 1965, he visited South Vietnam and wrote an article in *Esquire*, titled "Sorry About That," in which he more or less supported US involvement, whereas in 1970 he infamously called the Vietnam War an obscenity (Lev 2000: 109). Scott refused to accept the Oscar for Best Actor at the Academy Awards in 1970, as did Marlon Brando in 1973.

6. David A. Cook (2000) has called *M * A * S * H* an "irreverent antimilitary comedy" whose "subversive blend of humor and gore" and "contemporary stylization" made it "a hit with the counterculture," since it "was widely perceived in the youth market as a covert antiwar movie" (Cook 2000: 89). Edward D. Berkowitz (2006) attributes the film's appeal to the way it combines realism and satire: "*M * A * S * H* was a comedy that portrayed the military bureaucracy with contempt and did not cover up the gore that was a daily product of war" (Berkowitz 2006: 182). Notably, the screenplay was written by the great comic writer Ring Lardner, Jr., whose career had been in jeopardy when he was blacklisted as one of the Hollywood Ten. Lardner got the last laugh for his work on *M*A*S*H* by winning an Oscar for Best Adapted Screenplay.

7. No unfashionable prude herself, Kael observes that Altman, "taking full advantage of the new permissive rating system," managed to make a film that is not just foul-mouthed but "blessedly profane. I've rarely heard four-letter words used so exquisitely well in a movie, used with such efficacy and glee. I salute *M*A*S*H* for its contribution to the art of talking dirty" (Kael 1994: 348).

8.   Writing in *The New York Times*, Vincent Canby (1970) argued that *Catch-22* was too surrealist for contemporary tastes and should not "be confused with what is all too loosely referred to as black comedy." Geoff King agrees with this assessment in his book *Film Comedy* (King 2002), saying that *Catch-22* is "far more absurd and darkly surreal" than *M * A * S * H*￼ and failed to connect with audiences, not because it isn't dark enough, but because it isn't very funny (King 2002: 105).

9.   Harvard sociologist Robert D. Putnam's well-known study *Bowling Alone* (2000) supports my point that bowling is meant to be anachronistic in the film; the decline of bowling leagues since the 1950s reflects a parallel decline in political engagement, which he believes "plunged … to an all-time low for a presidential election year in 1996" (Putnam 2000: 38).

10. "Watching *The Big Lebowski*," writes David Haglund (2008), "it becomes clear that appreciating Walter is essential to understanding what the Coen brothers are up to in this movie, which is slyer, more political, and more prescient than many of its fans have recognized." He continues: "the Dude and Walter are on opposite sides of the American divide that opened during the 1960s. And while the Dude is the movie's hero, more or less, it's Walter who drives the plot," because the "Dude's pacifist leanings are no match for Walter's assertiveness."

11. Surveying the recent movies that have been made about Iraq and Afghanistan (*Body of Lies, Fair Game, Green Zone, The Hurt Locker, In the Valley of Elah, Jarhead, The Kingdom, The Messenger*), we must ask: where are the comedies? Even anomalies such as *The Tiger and the Snow* (Roberto Benigni 2005), *The Men Who Stare at Goats* (Grant Heslov 2009), and the British black comedy *Four Lions* (Chris Morris 2010) seem to prove the general rule that the current conflicts do not, for whatever reasons, lend themselves to satire.

References

Allen, W.R. (ed.) (2006) The Coen Brothers Interviews, University of Mississippi Press, Jackson, MS.

Bakhtin, M. (1984) *Rabelais and His World*, Indiana University Press, Bloomington, IA.

Berkowitz, E.D. (2006) *Something Happened: A Political and Cultural Overview of the Seventies* Columbia University Press, New York, NY.

Boyer, P.S. (1996) *Dr. Strangelove*, in *Past Imperfect: History According to the Movies* (ed. M.C. Carnes), Henry Holt, New York, NY, pp. 266–9.

Buhle, P. and Wagner, D. (2003) *Hide in Plain Sight: The Hollywood Blacklistees in Film and Television, 1950–2002*. Palgrave Macmillan, New York, NY.

Bush, G. (1998) The hard work of freedom, in *The Geopolitics Reader* (eds. G.O. Tuithail, S. Dalby, and P. Rutledge), Routledge, New York, pp. 136–138.

Canby, V. (1970) "*Catch-22*," *The New York Times*, June 25, http://movies.nytimes.com/movie/review?res = EE05E7DF1738E760BC4D51DFB066838B669EDE (accessed May 19, 2012).

Ciment, M. (2011) "Kubrick on *The Shining*." Interview, http://www.visual-memory.co.uk/amk/doc/interview.ts.html (accessed May 17, 2011).

Coen, J. and Coen, E. (1998) *The Big Lebowski*. Screenplay, Faber & Faber, London.

Cook, D.A. (2000) *Lost Illusions: American Cinema in the Shadow of Watergate and Vietnam, 1970–1979*, Scribner's, New York.

Cormer, T.A. (2005) " 'This aggression will not stand': myth, war, and ethics in *The Big Lebowski.*" *SubStance*, 34 (2), 98–117.

Crowther, B. (2006) *Dr. Strangelove*, in *Screening America: United States History Through Film Since 1900* (ed. J.J. Lorence), Pearson Longman, New York, pp. 141–2.

Dickstein, M. (2007) *Gates of Eden: American Culture in the Sixties*, Harvard University Press, Cambridge, MA.

Doherty, T. (1993) *Projections of War: Hollywood, American Culture, and World War II*, Columbia University Press, New York, NY.

Eisenhower, D.D. (2010) "Farewell Address." 17 January 1961, http://www.h-net.org/~hst306/documents/indust.html (accessed May 19, 2012).

Frank, T. (1997) *The Conquest of Cool: Business Culture, Counterculture, and the Rise of Hip Consumerism*, University of Chicago Press, Chicago, IL.

Gelmis, J. (1970) *The Film Director as Superstar*, Doubleday, New York, NY.

Hagen, W.M. (1998) *Apocalypse Now* (1979): Joseph Conrad and the television war, in *Hollywood as Historian: American Film in a Cultural Context*, revised edition (ed. P.C. Rollins), Kentucky University Press, Lexington, KY, pp. 230–45.

Haglund, D. (2008) Walter Sobchak, Neocon: The Prescient Politics of *The Big Lebowski*, *Slate*, September 11, see http://www.slate.com/articles/arts/dvdextras/2008/09/walter_sobchak_neocon.html (accessed May 15, 2012).

Harris, M. (2008) *Pictures at a Revolution: Five Movies and the Birth of the New Hollywood*, Penguin, New York, NY.

Henriksen, M.A. (1997) *Dr. Strangelove's America: Society and Culture in the Atomic Age*, University of California Press, Berkeley, CA.

Hofstadter, R. (1996) *The Paranoid Style in American Politics and Other Essays*, Harvard University Press, Cambridge, MA.

Horton, A. (2005) *The Films of George Roy Hill*, McFarland, Jefferson, NC.

Into the Kaelstrom (1994) *Entertainment Weekly* (November 18), http://www.ew.com/ew/article/0,,304537,00.html (accessed May 18, 2012).

Jameson, F. (1992) *Signatures of the Visible*, Routledge, New York, NY.

Jenkins, P. (2006) *Decade of Nightmares: The End of the Sixties and the Making of Eighties America*, Oxford University Press, New York, NY.

Kael, P. (1970) The Man Who Loved War. *The New Yorker*, January 13, p. 73.

Kael, P. (1994) *For Keeps: 30 Years at the Movies*, Plume, New York, NY.

Kernin, A.B. (1965) *The Plot of Satire*, Yale University Press, New Haven, CT.

King, G. (2002) *Film Comedy*, Wallflower Press, London.

Kolker, R. (2000) *A Cinema of Loneliness: Penn, Stone, Kubrick, Scorsese, Spielberg, Altman*, 3rd edn, Oxford University Press, New York.

Kopkind, A. (1993) Slacking toward Bethlehem. *Grand Street*, 44, 177–88.

Kubrick, S. (1963) How I learned to stop worrying and love the cinema. *Films and Filming*, 9 (June), 12.

Lev, P. (2000) *American Films of the '70s: Conflicting Visions*, University of Texas Press, Austin, TX.

Levy, E. (2001) *Cinema of Outsiders: The Rise of American Independent Film*, University of New York Press, New York, NY.

Lewis, J. (2008) *American Film: A History*, Norton, New York, NY.

Maland, C. (1979) *Dr. Strangelove* (1964): nightmare comedy and the ideology of liberal consensus. *American Quarterly*, 31 (5), 697–717.

May, E.T. (1986) Explosive issues: sex, women, and the bomb, in *Recasting America: Culture and Politics in the Age of the Cold War* (ed. L. May), University of Chicago Press, Chicago, pp. 154–70.

Monaco, P. (2001) *The Sixties, 1960–1969*, University of California Press, Berkeley, CA.

Morrison, J. (2008) 1964: movies, the Great Society, and the New Sensibility, in *American Cinema of the 1960s: Themes and Variations* (ed. B.K. Grant), Rutgers University Press, New Brunswick, NJ, pp. 110–29.

Mumford, L. (1964) Letter. *New York Times*, March 1, p. 25.

Naremore, J. (2007) *On Kubrick*, British Film Institute, London.

Nelson, D. (2002) *Pursuing Privacy in Cold War America*, Columbia University Press, New York, NY.

Palmer, R.B. (2004) *Joel and Ethan Coen*, University of Illinois Press, Urbana, IL.

Putnam, R.D. (2000) *Bowling Alone: The Collapse and Revival of American Community*, Simon & Schuster, New York, NY.

Schell, J. (2000) *The Fate of the Earth*, Stanford University Press, Stanford, CA.

Schulman, B.J. (2001) *The Seventies: The Great Shift in American Culture, Society, and Politics*, De Capo Press, New York, NY.

Sontag, S. (1990) *Against Interpretation and Other Essays*, Anchor, New York, NY.

Southern, T. (1995) Notes, in *Screening America: United States History Through Film Since 1900* (ed. J.J. Lorence), Pearson Longman, New York, NY, pp. 140–41.

Stam, R. (1989) *Subversive Pleasures: Bakhtin, Cultural Criticism and Film*, Johns Hopkins University Press, Baltimore, MD.

This Aggression Will Not Stand (1991) *The New York Times*, March 1.

Thompson, K. (1999) *Storytelling in the New Hollywood: Understanding Classical Narrative Technique*, Harvard University Press, Cambridge, MA.

Vonnegut, K. (2006) *A Man Without a Country: A Memoir of Life in George W. Bush's America*, Bloomsbury, London.

Wainwright, L. (1964) The Strange Case of Strangelove. *Life*, March 13, p. 15.

Winston, M. (1972) *Humour noir* and black humor, in *Veins of Humor* (ed. H. Levin), Harvard University Press, Cambridge, MA, pp. 269–84.

Part V

Comic Perspectives on Race and Ethnicity

16

Black Film Comedy as Vital Edge

A Reassessment of the Genre

Catherine A. John

Black Comedy is one of the great reservoirs of truth. (Michael Eric Dyson)

If I can make a babe laugh, I'm over like a fat rat! (Mars Blackmon in Spike Lee's
She's Gotta Have It!)

This chapter is an analysis of black film comedy at this historical moment. In his 1993 text *Redefining Black Film*, Mark Reid summarizes the history of black comedic stereotypes within the American film industry. Black and white writers as well as early black performers geared their art towards white audiences who demanded "non-threatening African American humor" (Reid 1993: 23). This laid the foundation for blackface minstrelsy and what Reid calls "hybrid minstrelsy" and "satiric hybrid minstrelsy" (Reid 1993: 19). Reid's analysis, while an effective portrait of the negative stereotype fails to make distinctions between the black stereotype and what he calls "urban black folk humor." In this chapter I reassess the genre.

The challenge of this subject is the breadth of the material. Using Reid's chapter as a point of departure, I will do several things: (i) Assess the continued influence of white stereotypes of blackness in film; (ii) Address black reactions to the work of Tyler Perry; (iii) Analyze Spike Lee's *Bamboozled* (2000) and Tim Story's *Barbershop* (2002). One of the goals of this chapter is to expose a euphoric and rejuvenating element of African American ethnic humor – one that is a central part of *the experience* of black film comedies at their best. This element involves ingroup versus outgroup codes of interpretation of the films and their meanings as well as issues connected to the social and ideological perspectives of the writers and directors. These alternative readings are calculated to address often subconscious and under-explored facets of film reception as well as film-viewing experiences.

A Companion to Film Comedy, First Edition. Edited by Andrew Horton and Joanna E. Rapf.
© 2013 John Wiley & Sons, Inc. Published 2016 by John Wiley & Sons, Inc.

Humor is a central part of most cultures' everyday praxis and it is infused into almost all aspects of African American life. It is a large part of both African and African American storytelling traditions and this helps to explain why many black comedians choose this art form as a way of life. The Jamaican proverb "tek bad tings mek laugh" translates as "find humor in a difficult situation." This is an excellent example of the power behind the comedic craft of Richard Pryor. Considered a genius by many, a large part of his secret was his ability to translate the pain in his life into the joy of laughter. It may well be that humor of some sort is a key part of the foundational matrix of many a culture. As University of Oklahoma film student Jason Quaynor observed, many mainstream American film comedies such as the recent *Get Him to the Greek* (2010) or the now 23-year-old *Bill and Ted's Excellent Adventures* (1989) are often premised on "screwball" scenarios that are hilarious, fantastic, and unlikely to happen. On the other hand, ethnic comedies such as *My Big Fat Greek Wedding* (2002), Spike Lee's *She's Gotta Have It* (1986), or the Jewish humor implied in the films of Woody Allen are premised on frequently ordinary events in the everyday lives of people within these various cultural communities. In fact it may well be that the loss of a collective sense of humor as well as a distinctive food culture signals the loss of ethnicity. It is therefore difficult to address black film comedy without addressing the role of humor in black culture generally and the role of black comedians within their communities on one hand and within American popular culture on the other.

In Robert Townsend's documentary *Why We Laugh* (2009), black female comic Sommore states, "If you want to know what's going on in our communities, watch our comedy." Comedian Bill Bellamy adds, "Comedians, we are healers; we go around the country and we make people laugh." However it is Walter Fauntroy who makes the documentary's most profound observation when he says, "Black comedy is what I call tools of the spirit, by which we cut a path through the wilderness of our despair." This is a deeply consequential statement. It suggests that far from being mere entertainment, black comedy functions as a highly sophisticated instrument; one that, like the blues tradition, offers itself as an emotional repository in which the individual or the collective can place trauma, and in that manner salvage their psyches from retraction and collapse. While for some, references to African Americans' skill as musicians, comedians, and dancers is a restrictive stereotype, the statements made above indicate that within the community these skills have been utilized as powerful internal sources of collective affirmation. How does this power function outside the black community? I am arguing that it is the residual and watered down elements of this cultural characteristic that the dominant society both desires and desires to contain.

The American Film Institute's list of the top 100 film comedies includes no black films and only one film with a black star. This film, *Beverly Hills Cop* (1984), starring Eddie Murphy, is ranked 63rd. On the other hand, Hollywood.com's list of the top 25 most profitable film comedies lists *Beverly Hills Cop* as the top grossing comedy of all time, with its sequel ranked ninth. Eddie Murphy is popular; his *Coming to America* (1988) and *Trading Places* (1983) rank 21st and 24th, respectively. It is interesting to ponder for a moment the significance of this. In the AFI's list there are no black films at all because even *Beverly Hills Cop* is just a film with a black star. On the other hand, at the box office certain genres of black humor have always been popular. It seems then that black independent filmmakers' work like Charles Burnett's *To Sleep with Anger* (1990), Spike Lee's *She's Gotta Have It* (1986) and *Bamboozled* (2000), Malcolm Lee's *Best Man* (1999), *Roll Bounce* (2005), and *Welcome Home Roscoe Jenkins* (2008), Rick Famuyiwa's *The Wood* (1999), *Brown Sugar* (2002), and *Our Family Wedding* (2010), Theodore Witcher's *Love Jones* (1997), and Jennifer Sharp's *I'm Through with White Girls: The Inevitable Undoing of Jay Brooks* (2007) are all but ignored by both ends of the spectrum.

But what does it mean that historically, many of the top-grossing films in the United States, have had black stand-up comedians who subsequently became film stars in central or leading roles? Martin Lawrence's *Big Momma's House* (2000) and its sequels were quite profitable, as were Will Smith's *Hitch* (2005) and Queen Latifah's *Bringing Down the House* (2003). Will Smith's genre of comedy, popularized on the sitcom *The Fresh Prince of Bel-Air*, translated well into commercial box-office appeal. *The Fresh Prince* watered down and capitalized upon the then growing popularity of Hip Hop and almost anticipated its dominance on the American scene. The part of Axel Foley in *Beverly Hills Cop* was originally contracted to Mickey Rourke and then offered to Sylvester Stallone but the substantial commercial success of the film is entirely due to Eddie Murphy's talent as a stand-up comedian. Online summaries of production indicate that hundreds of takes were ruined because the cast and crew were laughing as Murphy improvised both dialogue and scenes where the script failed. Thus, there seems to be an integral relationship between comedic films succeeding and the talent of African American stand-up comics, even when they occupy relatively minor roles.

Whoopi Goldberg's *Jumpin' Jack Flash* (1986) is another example of this. In the film Goldberg plays Teresa Doolittle, a computer programmer who also does financial bank transactions. She receives a message from a "Jumpin' Jack Flash," one that she needs to decode and act upon. The script is weak because, among other things, there is no accounting for why Goldberg's character would go so far to solve a mystery from which she gains nothing. Her ethnically black female comedic style sells an otherwise all-white film comedy. The evidence of a type of minstrelsy is suggested here when African American humor carries a storyline that is unrelated to the group specifically. There is nothing *wrong* with this theoretically and the actors are innocents who are happy to use their talents to reach a broader audience and make a living. But it is important to acknowledge and realize what is happening and why these films are successful. Frequently the ethnic style or humor of the specific comedian is at the heart of the film comedy's pace, flow, and success. This is noteworthy because of the number of films, proportionately speaking, that depend on this formula and specifically on African

Americans as leads, sidekicks or as minor comic relief. It suggests that there is a centrally intertwined if not dependent relationship between American identity and African American comedians. The reverse is not true. African American film comedies do not need white actors or comedians to be successful. In fact the inclusion of a token white actor in an all-black film comedy, like Salim Akil's recent film *Jumping the Broom* (2011), frequently feel like a "post-racial" accommodation strategy rather than an organic development.

The Specter of Amos 'n' Andy and the Anxiety about Minstrelsy

While there is a critical mass of texts written about comedy and black comedians, the list shrinks considerably when considering black film comedy. As a subgenre of film comedy its history is implicated in the story of American racism and race relations while also being an integral part of the formation of this nation's cultural sensibility and identity. Mark Reid links the birth of black film comedy with what he calls "American race humor." But while black film comedy may emerge from American race humor it is worth noting that black *humor* in and of itself does not. In his chapter "African American Comedy Film" from *Redefining Black Film*, Reid defines the genre as any comedy whose narrative is focused on the black community (Reid 1993: 19). By this definition, Eddie Murphy's *Beverly Hills Cop* series, *Jumpin' Jack Flash* as well as most of the films of Whoopi Goldberg would not qualify. Most of the films starring Will Smith such as *Hitch, Men in Black* (1997), and *Bad Boys* (1995) would not qualify. On the other hand, films like *Coming to America, Boomerang* (1992), *Barbershop*, and *Friday* (1995) would all qualify. The films of Tyler Perry and other black romantic comedies would also fit in.

Mark Reid states, "In order to understand how African American film comedy was shaped between the 1960s and 1980s one must understand traditional elements of ... American race humor" (Reid 1993: 19). He analyzes "blackface minstrelsy," and coins the terms "hybrid minstrelsy," and "satiric hybrid minstrelsy" in order to classify and categorize what he sees as "the most pervasive subtypes" of this comedy. Reid defines blackface minstrelsy *as* "an early popular form of American race humor." White actors Edwin P. Christy and Ben Cotton helped to create it. As Reid argues, "the minstrel comics objectified African American oral traditions, physiognomy, dress, dance and song ... [which] allow[ed] whites to take pleasure in the 'hostile or sexual aggressiveness of blacks' while the white race escape[d] the harm that such dramas assign[ed] to the African American community" (Reid 1993: 19–20). I would amend Reid's commentary to say that what the white population took pleasure in was its own projected and distorted stereotypes of blacks, which used exaggerated fragments of African American culture acontextually. Why this form of humor has historically been funny to this population enters into deeply complex socio-psychic terrain.

The objectification of the culturally different and phenotypically African subject as an object is clearly a carryover from the psychological landscape created under slavery. The "slave" was a possession that could be used as a beast of burden or object of exploitative pleasure, be it sexual or sadistically humorous. The original "need" may have stemmed from the oppressed (poor) whites who during the period of slavery and reconstruction had only their whiteness and whatever sense of superiority cruel jokes would allow, to remind themselves that their place in society was more secure and privileged than the black subject/object. As African Americans, we respond with shame and anxiety to these objectified and demeaning representations of blackness, thinking they say something about our worth when they do not.

Reid continues by addressing the 1928 creation of the *Amos 'n' Andy* radio show, which focused on "two aspiring Black men who migrated from Georgia to Chicago; later … their place of migration was changed to New York's Harlem" (Reid 1993: 20). It aired six nights per week and by 1930 it was "more popular than any other show on the air, and its two white stars were the highest paid performers on radio … To gain popularity, Freeman Gosden and Charles Correll (the creators of *Amos 'n' Andy*) used minstrel caricatures and avoided any portrayal of the socioeconomic effects of unemployment, segregated housing and inadequate healthcare in African American communities" (Reid 1993: 20). One could easily argue that this has set the precedent for the American public's lack of substantial interest in any comedy or drama that depicts the social ills of the community rather than isolating its comedic elements. The radio show's immense popularity spawned a film *Check and Double Check*, which failed at the box office, seemingly because the white audience was destabilized by white characters in blackface rather than "genuine negroes" playing the roles. When the show made the transition to television, black actors were hired to perform the major roles (Reid 1993: 21–2).

Reid defines "hybrid minstrelsy" as the use of black performers to do "blackface" roles that had previously been created and popularized by whites. Reid states, "This hybrid humor resulted from the fact that black and white writers as well as black performers concentrated on satisfying the expectations of white audiences, which demanded a non-threatening African American humor." Furthermore, he continues, "The industry exploited the function of the black presence in minstrel comedy to minimize criticism against its racially tendentious product" (Reid 1993: 23–4). Reid states that rather than criticize black actors for their participation in what he sees as minstrel-oriented comedies, "critical analysis should examine how socioeconomic forces determine where and when blacks participate in American popular culture" (Reid 1993: 24). This is an excellent point and it is one that has continued relevance.

While much of Reid's analysis is persuasive, the weakness of his argument lies in his obscuring of the issue of authentic representation. What this means is that when African Americans actually have the freedom to write, create, and perform characters that emanate from their individual and communal experiences, these depictions, no matter how "low down" the representations, are no longer "minstrelsy" in an exclusive sense. Langston Hughes in his 1928 essay "The Negro Artist and the Racial Mountain," suggests that the black underclass or "low down folk" are the source of black cultural innovation, resilience, and identity. By contrast the middle class and upper-class elite usually imitate the dominant society in its stereotyping of the black masses (Hughes 2003: 1268–70). Hughes' argument maintains its relevance today as seen by the range of critical reactions to the representations of blackness from both within and outside the community.

Mainstream society, according to Reid, has historically essentialized certain depictions of black people and projected those that were negative into the forefront of representation. Humorous images of the people that Hughes refers to as "the low down folk" came to represent the population as a whole in a way that minimized the complexity of African American culture. This has kept a hierarchical world order in place, particularly when these representations are removed from the socioeconomic and historical forces that created them. When the black elite or white intelligentsia decry certain representations as stereotypes, it usually means that the "low down folk element" is dominating representation and, truthful or not, these images are viewed by the gentry as derogatory and anti-progress.

In the final sections of Mark Reid's chapter he analyzes black film comedies that he categorizes as "hybrid minstrelsy" or "satiric hybrid minstrelsy." These are films written and directed by African Americans with a fully black cast, such as Ossie Davis's *Cotton Comes to Harlem* (1970), Sidney Poitier's *Uptown Saturday Night* (1974) and *Let's Do It Again* (1975), Michael Schultz's *Car Wash* (1976), Robert Townsend's *Hollywood Shuffle* (1987), and Keenan Ivory Wayans' *I'm Gonna Get You Sucka* (1988). Reid rightly argues that "financial success and mainstream audience approval are not the most important criteria for determining the quality of an African American comedy film" (Reid 1993: 31). He is critical of these films, suggesting that they use as a point of departure for the humor, the same formula that was developed by the white actors in blackface so long ago. He classifies Townsend's *Hollywood Shuffle* and Wayans' *I'm Gonna Get You Sucka* as "satiric hybrid minstrelsy" asserting that although these films satirize the stereotypical roles that blacks have historically been offered in Hollywood films, they now require a stereotypical white subject to be the object of ridicule and therefore one set of stereotypes have simply replaced another. This is not entirely true and there are some weaknesses in the logic of Reid's analysis of these films.

Under the "satiric hybrid minstrelsy" category, Reid briefly addresses Robert Downey's 1969 film *Putney Swope*. Produced, written and directed by whites, the film's plot tells the story of a Wall Street advertising firm whose board of directors is all white except for one black member, Putney Swope. Swope is accidentally elected as the next chairperson and he fires most of the white board members and creates a predominantly black board. "The firm adopts an urban black language style, namely black power rhetoric, and retains the capitalist motives and racist attitudes of the deposed white board members" (Reid 1993: 35). Reid's point is that despite white writers, the film exhibits similar kinds of racial reversals that black films within this genre have done. He uses the film to demonstrate the weaknesses of viewing "satiric hybrid minstrel" films as purely progressive. Yet the analysis of *Putney Swope* seems particularly misguided. While overt satires like *Hollywood Shuffle* and *I'm Gonna Git You Sucka* humorously overdramatize the very minstrel-like roles that have historically limited black actors, *Putney Swope*'s plot reads like a white racist stereotype of what black power would entail. There is not a ring of authenticity anywhere in this description. Furthermore, the notion that "[an] urban black language style [and] black power rhetoric" would be adopted by someone in Putney Swope's position demonstrates an absurd ignorance of the social characteristics of the African American middle class. While Reid may be well aware of these distinctions, the film certainly is not. On the other hand, the films by Townsend and Wayans are spoofing white stereotypes about blackness. They are actually suggesting that these depictions don't really have anything to do with black people in addition to limiting dramatically the ability of black actors and actresses to get roles that demonstrate the breadth of their skills.

Ultimately, Mark Reid's assessment of black film comedy shows that the real struggle is about the lack of range in the commercial representations of blackness and the pigeon-holing resulting from Hollywood's fear of any black humor that threatens box office returns. But the "low down folk" experience is the scapegoat despite the fact these representations are not untrue. Reid essentially asks why certain comedies have been commercially successful and have become mainstream models for black authenticity. Further, what does it mean that the films and depictions that show black characters as deeply flawed, rather than noble, are the most popular? Despite his failure to make a distinction between black stereotypes produced and imagined by whites, and ingroup black humor that is a product of the culture itself, Reid raises very valid questions. His use of the term "hybrid" and "satiric" suggests that something has changed from the days of pure minstrelsy, but he is still critical of Wayans and Townsend's films since as he states, "the traditional purpose of Black humor has been to resist and subvert humor that ridicules members of the Black community" (Reid 1993: 31). This is a rather narrow definition of black comedy. Another purpose it serves is "making us laugh at ourselves," and, at its best, it rejuvenates the spirit of the laugher in self-reflexive ways.

Killing the Messenger: Tyler Perry and the Crisis of Black Representation

Coming to the attention of the mainstream viewer in 2005 with the release of *Diary of a Mad Black Woman*, Tyler Perry's first film caught Hollywood off guard with its box office success in the opening weekends. Based on his successful "Chitlin Circuit" gospel plays Perry's films have a large appeal to black audiences worldwide, and southern black audiences in particular. This seems due to storylines about the black extended family, familiar characters, Tyler Perry playing the black female character Madea (a phonetic version of M'dear [my dear] – a term used historically in the black community to refer to senior mother figures), and plots that always involve vice and tragedy, followed by salvation and redemption.

White audiences may be primarily attracted to Madea as a man in drag – one who makes sense within the context of Martin Lawrence's role in *Big Momma's House*, or Dustin Hoffman cross-dressing in *Tootsie* (1982). Madea may also fit into a farcical buffoonery that is associated with the humor of the minstrel show and/or a vaudevillian history that includes cross-dressing. On the other hand, to a southern black audience, University of Oklahoma student Terrance Jones has observed, "Madea is representative of a real family member that everybody has who is over the top and crazy but who has the ability to bring people together." This gets to the heart of one of the crucial differences between mainstream and "ingroup" viewership of these films. It is what I call internal versus external spectatorship. For viewers of these films who have no organic relationship to the community and the issues represented, Madea's antics may be the primary, if not only, appeal. This is borne out by the fact that the films without Madea such as *Daddy's Little Girls* (2007) and *The Family that Preys* (2008) are all but unknown to many mainstream viewers with a similarly reflective drop in box office returns. But the notion of internal spectatorship is not simply about superficial identification. It involves an ability to read and interpret the storyline through historical codes rooted in the experiences of the community. This is explored in more detail in my analyses of the films *Bamboozled* and *Barbershop*.

Within the black community, the controversies surrounding Perry's work are aggressive and charged. In June of 2010, Aaron McGruder, writer of the black political cartoon series *The Boondocks* satirized Perry as a latent homosexual with a homoerotic cult built around a white Jesus. While McGruder is known for his slicing and clever satire, this episode was suspect in terms of its larger implications. Perry chose, wisely it seems, to ignore the whole thing and simply stated categorically that he had no intention of suing McGruder as online gossip sites had suggested. Spike Lee on the other hand levied clearer and more specific criticism of Perry, openly calling his television sitcoms minstrelsy. In his May 28, 2009 interview with Ed Gordon on *Our World with Black Enterprise*, Lee says:

> Each artist should ... pursue [his or her] artistic endeavors but ... a lot of stuff out today ... is "coonery" and buffoonery. I know it's making a lot of money ... but we can do better ... I see these two ads for these two shows [Tyler Perry's *Meet the Browns* and *House of Payne*] and I am scratching my head ... Tyler's very smart .... We shouldn't think that [he] is going to make the same film that I [would] make ... As

African Americans, we're not one monolithic group … but at the same time, for me, the imaging is troubling and it harkens back to *Amos n Andy*.

In an October 25, 2009 *60 Minutes* interview with Byron Pitts, Perry responds directly to Lee's comments.

I would like to read that to my fan base. Let me tell you what: Madea, Brown, all these characters are bait – disarming, charming, make you laugh bait. So I can slap Madea in something and [use her] to talk about God, love, faith, forgiveness, family – any of those things you know? So that pisses me off; it is insulting. Its attitudes like this that make Hollywood think these people [don't] exist and that is why there is no material speaking to them – speaking to us.

While Lee might respond by saying that Hollywood has produced many films that address this kind of material, Perry would obviously disagree. At stake are differing interpretations of "folk" realism and authenticity. In the interview with Pitts, Perry subsequently stated that he himself is a bit tired of Madea and only continues with her because of his fan base's enthusiasm for the character; he jokingly said it would be his joy to create a film called *Madea's Funeral*.

MSNBC correspondent Goldie Taylor's interview on April 21, 2011 NPR's *All Things Considered*, said that while Perry's work did not speak to her, it spoke directly to "[her] mother, [her] sister, [and her] cousins … meeting them at their point of need." Complementing this statement, Issie Lapowsky in the October 26, 2009 issue of *The New York Daily News*, quotes Oprah Winfrey as saying, "I think [Perry] grew up being raised by strong, Black women. And so much of what he does is really in celebration of that … Madea is a compilation of all those strong black women … And so the reason it works is because people see themselves." On the other hand, Spike Lee's cousin, Malcolm Lee, said of Perry's work:

I have to admit, I enjoy some Madea … the morality tales, I could do without. Just bring me more Madea! [His films are] not as terrible as people say … but [they are] not as good as the box office numbers. Just because something makes money doesn't mean it's good, it's … popular; it taps into something people respond to … [Tyler's] not interested in art, he's interested in turning out a product. There is value in that, building up a studio and being independent. I wish he would get better as the movies go on … I don't think that is his focus right now. (Interview with Clay Cane, BET, February 18, 2011).

Coming from the same generation as Perry, Malcolm Lee comments prove that Madea has a black fan base and is not just a product of white attachment to excessive black humor. Furthermore, he makes a distinction between "turning out a product" and "creating art." While Perry may see himself as doing both, Malcolm Lee's comment suggests that in a capitalist economy Perry's approach has allowed him to become financially independent of Hollywood – and this has value for the black filmmaker. In the ideal world, there would be collaboration between Perry and other filmmakers thus creating more of a market for a wider variety of black films than Hollywood has thus far allowed.

The question as to whether or not Tyler Perry's films and television shows border on minstrelsy gets to the heart of the issues unearthed by Mark Reid – issues that have plagued black representation for quite some time. The fans that appreciate his work see themselves and their families in the representations and his dramas address situations that are ignored or fleetingly portrayed in Hollywood cinema. These are issues such as black women's pain when they are abandoned by their partners for women who are considered more desirable (*Diary of a Mad Black Woman* and *Why Did I Get Married*), the tensions in relationships between professional women and working-class men as well as the challenges of being single fathers (*Daddy's Little Girls* and *Meet the Browns*), children who have been abandoned by their parents and who are raised instead by members of the black community (*I Can Do Bad By Myself*), physical abuse and domestic violence in marriages and generationally transmitted experiences of emotional abuse in mother-daughter relationships (*Madea's Family Reunion* and *The Family that Preys*).

Perry's success may also make it difficult for filmmakers like Julie Dash, director of *Daughters of the Dust* (1991) who are already fighting an uphill battle to introduce other types of black characters who are equally authentic but aesthetically and culturally unfamiliar to Europeans and segments of the black population. Additionally there is a black north versus black south split in terms of Perry's fan base, as well as a "low down folk"/middle-class divide. Despite having southern roots, Spike Lee is both twelve years Perry's senior and speaks from the northeast black bourgeoisie. He was educated at Morehouse, an elite black college, and he was one of very few African Americans at the time to attend film school at NYU. Tyler Perry on the other hand dropped out of high school and lacks both formal education and film training. His success is also a kind of unwelcome morality tale for the black elite since it shows that the vast majority of black viewers, similar to their white counterparts, are humble people who like stories that address their experiences simply and directly. With an empire now valued at $350 million, the child from a broken home who survived molestation and abuse managed to turn his pain into something beautiful – morality plays with all black casts.

Bamboozled: Spike Lee's Political Satire of the Black Image in the White Mind

Spike Lee entered cinematic discourse with a bang in 1986 with the release of his film *She's Gotta Have It!* (see Figure 16.1). What was innovative about Lee's first film and his whole perspective was the pointed and culturally specific introduction of black, urban middle-class life from the United States' northeast corner onto the big screen. It was funky, fresh, controversial and clear. It was an

Figure 16.1   The picture of Tracy Camila Johns as Nola Darling from *She's Gotta Have It!* (director and producer, Spike Lee).

independent perspective that spoke to a cross-section of the black population that had previously been ignored by Hollywood. As a 19 year-old college student, I was entranced by *She's Gotta Have It!* I was able to see, for the first time, a film on the big screen that spoke in a cinematic vernacular that was familiar to me; one that depicted the humor particular to black east-coast rituals of courtship and romance. It was an "ingroup" film that had "outgroup" appeal. His first six or seven films had real significance to people like me. To those of us who came from the worlds that he was trying to describe, his films felt "authentic" – meaning they registered internally as a truthful representation of elements of our own lived experiences.

Since the days of *Amos 'n' Andy* the "black image in the white mind" has influenced American racial humor (see Jordan 1968; Frederickson 1971; Reid 1993). While this humor borrowed from African American folk forms, it was not a product of the experiences of black people, nor was it specifically designed to express their joy and pain. It was something else. Lee's films did this in a fresh new way from a specifically black middle-class perspective. Almost all of his early films became "cult classics" and spawned "ingroup" dialogue and conversation. Outsiders could also peek in on what Vorris Nunley would call "African American Hush Harbor Rhetoric;" they could be privy to conversations that usually happened outside their presence (Nunley 2010: 1). However, Lee's films required some knowledge of the culture in order to interpret the "ingroup jokes"; without this they functioned as strident discourses on race and difference in American society (see *Do The Right Thing* 1989).

With *Bamboozled*, Lee covers ground that addresses both "ingroup" and "outgroup" codes of meaning and interpretation at the same time. The film is a racialized re-make of Sidney Lumet's 1976 Academy Award winner *Network*. In the original, anchorman Howard Beale's statement that he will kill himself "live" on the final airing of his canceled show boosts the network's ratings and prompts the head executives to create a whole show around his mental illness and sensationalism. The head of the network's programming department convinces the executives to manipulate the show's content to increase ratings at the same time that they are producing a docudrama about a "radical terrorist" group, the Ecumenical Liberation Army. When Beale shifts his message from a populist rant of sorts to moralizing about the dehumanization of society, ratings drop. In the end, the executives hire the Ecumenical Liberation Army to assassinate Beale on the air, setting the stage for the second season of their docudrama entitled, *The Mao-Tse Tung Hour*.

Bamboozled uses *Network's* premise as a template but focuses instead on the exploitation of demeaning black stereotypes to boost ratings and entertain. The soundtrack begins with Stevie Wonder singing, "We should never be a misrepresented people." This establishes the target audience as that element of the black population that spends time thinking about the social and political implications of how race and culture are represented visually. The story revolves around Peerless Dothan (Damon Wayans), a black producer at CNS Network, which is headed up by Thomas Dunwitty (Michael Rapaport). Peerless (who has pretentiously changed his name to Pierre De la Croix), is the stereotype of a petit bourgeois African American whose name change and affected speech patterns are indicative of his desires to acquire status and assimilate.

The film opens with Dunwitty stridently chastising his staff for producing shows with low ratings. He singles out De La Croix to stay behind and discuss potential new programs. De La Croix's show ideas highlighting the challenges of integration for the black middle class are ridiculed by Dunwitty who states that while *The Cosby Show* was brilliant, "people [just] want to be entertained." A key exchange happens between them at this stage. Dunwitty, a "Black white boy" who claims to have more street credibility than De la Croix, says: "I grew up around Black people all my life – truth be told, I probably know niggers better than you. Now don't go getting offended by my use of the word nigger. I got a Black wife and two biracial kids so I feel I have a right. I don't give a goddamn what that prick Spike Lee says, Tarantino was right. Nigger is just a word." The multi-layered nature of Lee's satire is established from the get go since Dunwitty's statements reminds the literate viewer of the feud between Quentin Tarantino and Spike Lee over the frequent use of the word "nigger" in the former's films. Lee's film thus moves beyond satire and into the ideologically charged space of race and film production. Given the hierarchy of white privilege in the film industry, Dunwitty's dialogue takes a jab at the type of white person who feels they have the insider knowledge and authority on blackness to make decisions about what is authentic and what should be popular. His lines are funny in a bold-faced, shocking kind of way due to his delivery and the bombastic nature of his claims.

In retaliation, De La Croix decides to make the most racist show possible. He hopes it will prove so offensive that he will be fired and freed of his contract or that black backlash will destroy CNS's credibility. With the use of his assistant Sloan Hopkins (Jada Pinkett Smith) he decides to hire Manray (tap dancer Savion Glover) and Womack (comedian Tommy Davidson), a tap-dancing street performer and his promoter, to star in the show. Previously De La Croix barely condescended to speak to them although they frequently asked him to use his connections to get them a legitimate show. Another subplot within the film involves Sloan's brother, Julius Hopkins, a.k.a. Big Black African (played by rapper Mos Def), who has a musical group called The Mau Mau. They spout black revolutionary rhetoric, thumb their noses at the bourgeoisie, and incidentally are also hoping to get a show on CNS. They function as the script's double for the Ecumenical Liberation Army in *Network*.

In preparation for the meeting with Dunwitty, the viewer is privy to Peerless studying and taking notes on old episodes of *Amos 'n' Andy*. Peerless and Sloan, however, lie to Manray and Womack about the shows aims and content, stating that it is supposed to be a satire that promotes racial healing. Peerless asks Manray to change his name to "Mantan" after black character actor Mantan Moreland, notorious for playing buffoonish black characters based on white stereotypes. Lee puns on the fact that both Manray and the uneducated viewer will not get the joke. Manray and Womack are taken aback when they learn that *Mantan: The New Millennium Minstrel Show* is supposed to be about two characters whose main personality traits are their "ignorance, laziness, dull-wittedness and bad luck." The supporting cast of characters includes: Honeycut, Topsy, Rastus, Sambo, Little Nigger Jim, and Aunt Jemima, all negative black stereotypes from early American popular culture or film. Womack discovers during the meeting that Peerless has given the character he is to portray the name "SleepNEat," another historical reference to a black actor who, like Mantan Moreland, was similarly typecast.

Dunwitty, who loves the whole idea, states jubilantly, "Every week these two Alabama porch monkeys are going to make us laugh and cry and feel good to be Americans." Sloan is now horrified, suspecting that they've gone too far but Peerless goes further, announcing that the whole show will be set in a water-melon patch and that the actors will wear blackface makeup. Womack begins to mount an objection, but is unceremoniously cut off by Dunwitty who insists on an impromptu preview of Manray's tap-dancing skills. A comment needs to be made here about the further significance of Dunwitty. If Lee's films have functioned as a space where the outsider to black culture can have access to "hush harbor rhetoric" then with Dunwitty, Lee creates a kind of white racist hush harbor, i.e., Dunwitty says things that a cross-section of the mainstream may think or feel but which it is terribly taboo to say out loud. This is both wickedly humorous and clever on Lee's part since he manages to make uncomfortable through humor the type of viewer who would previously have had no reservations about the kind of black humor he or she consumed.

Manray jumps onto the conference room table and does an amazing routine thus establishing his talent as the key performance around which the show will revolve. This is a crucial moment. Spike Lee casts Savion Glover as Manray at a moment when Glover was renowned for his exceptional and unorthodox tap dancing style. Within the context of the movie, Manray the character is able to ignore and block out any derogatory aspects of the minstrel show by focusing on the authenticity of his own tap-dancing. More than once within the film he says, "As long as the hoofing is real, I'm cool." When he performs for Dunwitty, his tap dancing is so exceptional that for a moment, the seductive power of his performance shifts the film's focus. For a moment it is no longer a satire about the exploitation of black stereotypes but is instead a genuinely moving performance – the very thing that the dominant society both desires and desires to contain. The genius of Manray's tap dancing makes an interesting point: an element of cultural authenticity, acontextually presented in a nonthreatening format, is an essential part of the process of appropriation for the purposes of profit. Forms of cultural expression that are the least familiar to the dominant society but which have that ability to move the spirit are the most co-opted and consumed since artistic expression has replaced the vacuum previously fulfilled by the sacred in modern and postmodern Western society.[1]

Within the context of the film, Lee satirizes two types of white viewers. First he satirizes the white subject who presumes an inside knowledge of the culture's secrets and on the other hand, he caricatures those unfamiliar with "authentic" representations of blackness, "signifying" on the fact that they cannot tell the difference between the stereotype and the real thing. "Signifying" here refers to the black vernacular tradition of having a laugh at the expense of another. The first of these two stereotypes is most dramatically evident with his portrait of Thomas Dunwitty but is also addressed when Dunwitty hires both a Swedish director and a white female attorney with a PhD in African American Studies from Yale University to protect the show from lawsuits. The lawyer creates "The Mantan Manifesto," which, among other things, manipulates the way the content of the show can be interpreted. Her oversimplification of fairly complex racial issues horrifies Sloan, Peerless, and the socially aware viewer. The second white stereotype is mobilized when Peerless hires a cast of white writers with one or two token Asian Americans to script the dialogue for the minstrel show. They admit that their sole reference points for creating the show's material are sitcoms from the 1970s such as *The Jeffersons* and *Good Times*. With this move, Lee gets in a few laughs at the expense of the non-black viewer whose knowledge of black culture may be a product of television. What Lee also does with these representations is expose the racial illiteracy of the generic mainstream. The absurdity of the racial assumptions of the white characters in the film is laid bare and clearly functions as an allegory for the way these positions operate in both the world of Hollywood cinema as well as in American social and political life.

Mantan: The New Millennium Minstrel Show is ironically a smashing success. As things progress, the audience is encouraged to show up in blackface and the character Honeycut goes around with a microphone asking audience members of

Figure 16.2   Damon Wayans as Peerless Dothan—surrounded by black caricature figures circa 1900 near the end of *Bamboozled* (director, Spike Lee; producers, Spike Lee and John Kilik).

whatever race to all communally identify as "niggers." Dunwitty is ecstatic and Peerless, forgetting his original agenda, is now seduced by stardom and is simply overjoyed to have a hit show. Another subtle joke that only certain black viewers would get is made when Peerless receives the equivalent of an Emmy Award for the show and does a "buck and wing dance" before accepting the award while yelling, "Show me the money!" This is a swipe at the commonly held stereotype within the black community that most of the black roles that receive Oscars are given to actors playing demeaning rather than noble characters. On the other hand Damon Wayans performance when he accepts the award is a caricature of Cuba Gooding's performance when he received the award for his role in the film *Jerry McGuire* – a performance that was commented on within black circles as unnecessarily buffoonish (see Figure 16.2).

To commemorate his success, Sloan gives Peerless one of the racist objects from the turn of the century, "a jolly nigger bank," as a present. It is a black figurehead with a hand in front of the mouth in which a coin is placed before the mouth swallows. Lee's *mise-en-scène* in the scenes in Peerless's office depicts an environment increasingly taken over by racist paraphernalia from a previous era. Students of this film may enter into interesting dialogues about what this means both literally – within the context of the film – and symbolically. Does it prove that similar to Dunwitty's view of the slur "nigger," these objects are just things and any negative sentiment attached to them is in the eye of the beholder? Does it make a statement about the horror of normalizing forms of symbolic violence as humorous? Should viewers be encouraged to think about why they laugh? Are certain forms of humor implicitly premised on hierarchical relationships of power?

Ultimately, *Bamboozled* suggests that the psychic costs of the minstrel show are not worth it. While this issue is a subsidiary part of the plot in *Network*, the cost of these types of representations, particularly for the black community is at the heart of *Bamboozled*. Womack, demoralized by the hollow humor and degrading blackface makeup, quits the show and loses his friendship with Manray. Peerless forgets his original goal of destroying stereotypes and "sells his soul" for fame and money. Manray, on the verge of quitting, comes out on stage without blackface makeup and encourages the studio audience to resist cooptation by shouting, "I am sick and tired of being a nigger." Dunwitty furiously marches on stage, instructs the cameramen to stop filming, and unceremoniously pulls Manray off the air. Manray is forcibly ejected from the building, and as he leaves he is kidnapped by the revolutionary Mau Mau who send a message to CNS stating that they plan to assassinate him at a particular date and time. The networks collectively decide to broadcast the execution.

The Mau Mau name the execution "The Dance of Death" and on the appointed day, they shoot at Manray's feet and eventually kill him. After Manray's execution, the Mau Mau are in turn shot and killed by the police as they exit the warehouse. Unlike the Ecumenical Liberation Army in *Network*, their rhetoric is not depicted as cooptable. The film ends with a disheveled and hysterical Sloan shooting Peerless in his apartment, while blaming him for all that has transpired. Although it is implied that the minstrel show will continue, Lee ends the actual film with footage and film clips of black actors in early American cinema. He seems to be suggesting that these images were derogatory yet influential despite the fact that they are now by and large unknown to contemporary viewers. Historical amnesia has allowed history to repeat itself and the footage is a reminder of the way things used to be.

One statement that is clearly made by Lee's film and Lumet and Chayevsky's is that corporate driven capitalism will respond with violence to anything that threatens its expansion. Within the context of the film, CNS's profits, exploitative black images, and the American appetite for them are interconnected. Manray is beloved as long as he consents to tap dance and wear blackface makeup but he is pulled from the air once he protests and has the ability influence the public. The ideological critique offered up by certain black representations makes them both unpopular and unprofitable – similar to Howard Beale's drop in popularity in *Network* once he changes his message. The Mau Mau's gunning down by the police symbolizes the state's reaction to radical attempts to overthrow the status quo. Spike Lee's film is coded in subtle ways to respond to issues that are part of ongoing "ingroup" dialogue within the black community. In so doing, Lee accomplishes several things: (i) He satirizes the industry's exploitation of racist stereotypes for profit; (ii) He comments on the type of black humor that becomes popular; (iii) He allows the socially conscious viewer to have a laugh at the expense of the politically naïve, benignly racist consumer of black humor; (iv) He satirizes the black response to the white commercial exploitation of black humor and culture; (v) He also addresses the ingroup issue of colonization or seeing oneself through the eyes of dominant society.

With this film Spike Lee explicitly exploits the black image in the white cinematic mind. When I taught this film in a 2010 class on Spike Lee, several of the white students honestly stated that they were confused about when it was and was not appropriate to laugh. This is a comedy with both a serious message *and* comedic value. As a comedy, the film is funny to both a black "ingroup" audience as well as an audience that is literate in the racially and culturally coded conversations that the film addresses. Some of the jokes, puns and satirical references may be lost on viewers who are unfamiliar with black nationalist politics of the 1960s and their continued relevance, the complexity of class divisions within the black community, racist stereotypes from an earlier era of American popular culture, as well as having a basic familiarity with the history of black television and film.

Barbershop as Both an Internal and External Spectator Film

CALVIN PALMER (Ice Cube): My father died broke and frustrated.

EDDIE (Cedric the Entertainer): Your father died rich because he invested in people!"
(Barbershop)

Unlike *Bamboozled*, the 2002 film *Barbershop* starring Rapper Ice Cube and directed by Tim Story was a commercial success. While Vorris Nunley in *Keeping It Hushed* is critical of the film's commercial exploitation of the concept of the "hush harbor," from the standpoint of film comedy, what the film accomplishes is nevertheless worthy of discussion.[2] Despite its commercial success, I maintain that *Barbershop*, in different ways than *Bamboozled*, activates both "ingroup" and "outgroup" codes of interpretation and meaning for black and non-black audiences. Additionally, like many black movies it functions, par excellence, as what I would call a black group spectator film (BGSF). This is a film in which the communal "ingroup" viewing taps into collectively experienced "structures of feeling" and opens up spaces of shared consciousness within the viewers. This is possible particularly when such viewers are part of a conscious and unconscious lived community of references and experiences.

In *Barbershop*, Rapper Ice Cube plays the role of Calvin Palmer who inherits from his father a barbershop that is behind on the property taxes and is in danger of foreclosure. The barbers and hairstylists who make their living at the shop are unaware of his financial crisis and since some of them have worked there since his father was in charge they also function as a *de facto* community. Calvin's pressure is further increased because his wife is pregnant. In a desperate moment, he accepts money from a gangster businessman in the community who treats the exchange as a binding contract. Calvin has an unreasonably short time to double the borrowed money or lose the shop, which the mobster plans to transform into a strip club. In saving the shop, Calvin is also saving the family network of barbers and workers who are a symbolic reservoir of the culture and traditions within the larger African American community. The film and the story are brought to life by the dialogue, conversation, issues and dynamics between the barbers and customers. While Reid would probably classify this film as "hybrid minstrelsy" because of its formulaic reliance on certain modes of humor, it has several layers which situate it within both "ingroup" and "outgroup" codes of meanings and interpretations. A surprisingly diverse range of characters is depicted; some serious issues are addressed; and it enables collective spectatorship communities that are both internal and external to the African American community.

For mainstream American audiences the film used familiar tropes. These included two famous rappers (Ice Cube and Eve), black comedian Cedric the Entertainer, as well as several other actors who achieved a degree of commercial success. There is also a certain amount of slapstick humor. Anthony Anderson and Lahmard Tate play amateur thieves of a new ATM machine that has no cash in it, but which they unwittingly spend the entire film trying to open. There is nothing unique or exceptional about how the film is shot, and there are relatively predictable twists and turns engendered by the aspects of the plot connected to the shop's fate. There are enough "types" in the film who end up in absurd scenarios or who have superficially comedic exchanges to keep the viewer who is not a cultural insider, but who just wants to be entertained, quite happy. Additionally, what Vorris Nunley would see as the *faux* "hush harbor" dynamics in this film would entice "outgroup" viewers into feeling as if they were experiencing authentic and hidden aspects of African American culture. On the other hand, while many of the jokes in the film would be funny to a fairly wide cross-section of viewers, as I will show, the nature of some of the jokes and the reasons why "ingroup" and "outgroup" spectators would find the same jokes funny may vary widely.

In terms of "ingroup" realism, the range of the cast of characters and the relative authenticity of their depictions would have a particular draw for a black audience, especially when the film is collectively viewed. Ice Cube plays Calvin Palmer who is "the average brother." He is a black man who is not from the educated black bourgeoisie depicted in Spike Lee's *School Daze* (1988) but neither is he the petty gangster "Doughboy" that Ice Cube himself plays in John Singleton's *Boyz N the Hood* (1991). Calvin's father owned the barbershop, so he is somewhat economically privileged, but in tastes, affect and speech he is connected to the everyday black experience and would thus engender the identification of the run-of-the-mill black male spectator. Cedric the Entertainer as Eddie plays a "countrified old head" – one whom a white audience may view as a semi-literate humorous curmudgeon. For a black southern audience, however, like Perry's Madea, he may conjure up a concrete family member or community elder. Within the film Eddie is the repository for, and the vehicle through which, the transmission of ancestral cultural values occurs. Anthony Anderson plays J.D., an unschooled criminal who lives with his mother, and Lahmard Tate plays Billy, his even more naïve sidekick. While their stealing of the ATM machine would evoke a standard buffoonery that is generically humorous to an "outgroup" audience or viewer, their discussion of one of their peers as being from a broken home (because he doesn't know his mother) while they are in the process of stealing, and Lahmard Tate's interruption of their crime in order to pursue someone who owes him a mere five dollars pushes the "ingroup" audience and viewer into fits of hysterical laughter since these scenes and dialogue conjure up familiar life scenarios.

In the online summary of the film's plot, the description of Sean Patrick Thomas's character, Jimmy James, is indicative of an "outgroup" interpretation of his role. He is described as "a recent college graduate and academically-astute young man who sees his job at the barbershop as nothing more than a temporary stop on his way to a real 'job.'"[3] To an ordinary black audience, however, he would be viewed as a "mis-educated smart ass," a familiar type in the community who lauds his seeming intelligence over others, but who is not actually as smart as he thinks he is. Michael Ealy plays Ricky Nash who, unlike Jimmy, plays the film's real "organic intellectual," one who does not showboat the way Jimmy does but whose intelligence is grounded and humane despite being an ex-con. The online description of his role however simply states that he is a "two time loser employee at the barbershop." This is significant since these descriptions demonstrate the extent to which different interpretations of the characters and their actions are operative for different audiences.

Leonard Earl Howz plays Dinka, a Nigerian immigrant, who is also a soft-spoken poet. His inclusion further expands the diversity of the film's represen-tation of blackness. Isaac Rosenberg, played by Troy Garity, is a character who identifies more with African American culture than his own Jewish roots and who, similar to Thomas Dunwitty in *Bamboozled*, functions as the "black white boy" in the crew. None of the black clients wants him to cut their hair since there is a stereotypical presumption that he has "no skills." The twist at the end of the film, however, endows him with an "authentic pass card" when he skillfully shapes up Jimmy James' "fro." Rapper Eve plays Terri Jones who is described online as "a hostile young woman" but whose general anger and frustration result from both her cheating boyfriend and her hard-knock life. Her character resounds with familiarity to a black female audience. The other minor characters in the film include an Indian shopkeeper who flouts stereotypes and demonstrates uncharacteristic transethnic brotherly love towards Calvin, and then there are some older black men who pass their time at the barbershop simply for the cultural camaraderie.

With this cast of characters and while maintaining the comedic edge, surpris-ingly serious issues are also addressed. Much of the humor is communicated in the cleverness of the dialogue between the barbers, and it is brought to life by the facial expressions and mannerisms of the cast. The serious issues addressed include: reparations, education and social status, the relationships of whites to black culture, the rehabilitation of criminals, a critique of abusive relationships, brotherhood both within and across ethnic lines, the importance of respecting cultural traditions and cultural diversity within blackness. While Vorris Nunley's critique of the film's staging of "hush harbor" rhetoric has real legitimacy what is interesting nevertheless is that real "hush harbor" rhetoric is expressed. At one point in the film, in the midst of a barbershop argument, Eddie decides to state publicly three popularly discussed "ingroup" views when he says, "Rosa Parks simply sat down, O.J. Simpson murdered his wife, and Martin Luther King Jr. was a womanizer." Many average black people have been part of "ingroup" discussions at one point or the other about these issues, although discussing them in interracial circles has functioned as largely taboo. Finally, another "ingroup" functional feature is the cacophonous nature of the dialogue in the barbershop. Multiple speakers often speak at once; while this may sound like noise and confusion to an "outgroup" viewer, the nuances and complexity of the dialogue during these interactions would not be lost on an "ingroup" viewer. In an "ingroup" context, the collective viewing of this film would function as rejuvenating and validating in the sense described by Walter Fauntroy as "tools of the spirit cutting a path through the wilderness of our lived despair."

Conclusion

I hope that this chapter has demonstrated that, under the rubric of black film comedy, a wide-ranging and complex variety of negotiations are taking place. Ironically, humor is serious business both at the level of affect as well as financially. This is made plain by both the money that black actors make *for* the film industry as well as the emergence of Tyler Perry. This chapter has also delved further into the complexity of old issues of "authenticity." For outsiders to a group, what is frequently considered authentic is the aspect of the group's culture that is the most foreign or different from that of the outsider. In a society where uniqueness is idealized but assimilation is the norm, cultural difference has great profit-making potential in the eyes of the free market. As Spike Lee demonstrates with his use of Savion Glover's tap dancing in *Bamboozled*, this type of cooptation has been normalized, and is simply seen by some as the American way. His film is a morality tale, emphasizing the dangers of this narrative.

On the other hand, one of the most crucial issues addressed here includes recognition of the differing ways that humor is interpreted *within* black communal circles rather than outside of them. Understanding this lays a foundation for much more nuanced interpretations of social relations in the society at large. There is a "vital edge" within that is part of the lifeblood of African American cultural expressiveness and psychic survival. I have tried to show that the hunger for the humor and talent of black comedians as evidenced by their role in American films and their popularity in everyday life demonstrate that an element of this "vital edge" has become an unacknowledged part of what the larger American society also needs and desires. Maybe this power within the culture has more to offer the outside world than is often acknowledged. Maybe the ability to make people laugh at their pain is a gift of the highest order. Maybe humor has the ability to confront in disguised form issues that are too traumatic for direct address. Maybe our comedians are bridge-builders and hope bringers with the symbolic machinery that maintains it all.

Notes

1. For another example of a culturally unfamiliar art form that is ripe for mainstream consumption and appropriation, see the dancing in the documentary *RIZE*. I explore in depth the concept of African American culture as "moving the spirit" in John (2010). I deduced the notion of art as replacing the sacred in Western society from the way in which Staniszewski (1995) discusses the Western consumption of indigenous art in.
2. In his chapter, "Commodifying neo-liberal blackness: faux hush harbor rhetoric in *Barbershop*" Vorris Nunley (2010) states, "the first *Barbershop* movie that was ostensibly about a hush harbor and African American Hush Harbor Rhetoric (AAHHR) was precisely not a hush harbor movie because its commodified neo-liberal versions of AAHHR was oriented towards making non-African Americans comfortable, thereby producing a more consumable blackness" (Nunley 2010: 8).
3. See the Wikipedia summary of this film. The Wikipedia source here is important since it may reflect a popular interpretation of the film.

References

Frederickson, G. (1971) *The Black Image in the White Mind: The Debate on Afro-American Character and Destiny 1817–1914*, Harper & Row, New York, NY.

Hughes, L. (2003) The negro artist and the racial mountain, in *The Norton Anthology of African American Literature* (ed. H.L. Gates Jr.), W.W. Norton & Co., New York, NY, pp. 1268–71.

John, C. (2010) The man in the gutter is the god-maker: Zora Neale Hurston's philosophy of culture, in *Inside Light: New Critical Essays on Zora Neale Hurston* (ed. D.G. Plant), Praeger Press, Santa Barbara, CA, pp. 165–80.

Jordan, W. (1968) *White Over Black: Attitudes Towards the Negro 1550–1812*, University of North Carolina Press, Chapel Hill, NC.

McCluskey, A.T. (2008) *Richard Pryor: The Life and Legacy of a "Crazy" Black Man*, Indiana University Press, Bloomington, IN.

Nunley, V. (2010) *Keeping It Hushed: The Barbershop and African American Hush Harbor Rhetoric*, Wayne State University Press, Detroit, MI.

Reid, M.A. (1993) *Redefining Black Film*, University of California Press, Berkeley, CA.

Staniszewski, M. (1995) *Believing is Seeing: Creating the Culture of Art*, Penguin Books, New York, NY.

Further Reading

Haggins, B. (2007) *Laughing Mad: The Black Comic Persona in Post-Soul America*, Rutgers University Press, Piscataway, NJ. This text, making a similar argument as sections of this chapter, examines the persona of the black comic in mainstream American popular consciousness. It examines the role of the black comic in both American comedy and popular culture.

Palmer, J. (1994) *Taking Humor Seriously*, Routledge, New York, NY. While this text does not deal with issues of African American comedy or humor, it may be of interest to students who wish to examine the role of humor in society more generally. It looks at humor from the vantage point of various disciplines, claiming that none has a monopoly on the phenomenon.

Ross. K. (1996) *Black and White Media: Black Images in Popular Film and Television*, Blackwell, Oxford. Situating her text near the turn of the twenty-first century, Karen Ross juxtaposes analyses of blackness in Hollywood cinema and television with representations coming from the black independent cinema in the United Kingdom and the United States. In this text, "blackness" is broadly defined and refers to African Americans, Afro-Caribbeans and South Asians from the United Kingdom.

Stark, S. (2000) *Men in Blackface: True Stories of the Minstrel Show*, Xlibris Corporation, Bloomington, IN. This text explores the ethnically diverse range of performers who participated in blackface minstrel shows. Early Irish and Jewish performers' relationship to this art form is addressed.

17

Winking Like a One-Eyed Ford

American Indian Film Comedies on the Hilarity of Poverty

Joshua B. Nelson

When the dance is over, sweetheart
I will take you home with my one-eyed Ford

49 song

Hey-yah-hey. So we're all clear, a 49 is an American Indian social gathering, an after-powwow party, a time when people get together to sing, dance, and snag without the emcee's repeated reminders about the interconnectedness of this and the sacredness of that. Indians are spiritual people, sure, but we also know how to have a good time. You might not guess it by the replete images of stoic warriors, torturing savages, and bedraggled or slithering women that Hollywood westerns churned out, but American Indians have been known to tell a joke or two. Some of them are even funny. The jokes, that is. Well, yes, some of the people, too. The 49 songs are like classic jokes: everybody knows them and their histories, which have their own set of references and distinct contexts. They're the Indian equivalent of two guys walking into a bar. Because songs and their lyrics are often owned by families and can't be performed without the cultural rights to them, songs in the Indian public domain use vocable syllables for lead-off verses and later slip in some English lines. These unexpected turns from what initially sound like any other Indian song to the unfamiliar ear sneak in like understated punch lines that play off both the Indian and English contexts of which they are simultaneously a part and apart. Many American Indian films like Chris Eyre's popular *Smoke Signals* (1998) and Sterlin Harjo's *Four Sheets to the Wind* (2007) echo this movement inside and outside of expectations and frames of reference, offering jokes that general audiences will understand but that have farther-reaching resonance for

A Companion to Film Comedy, First Edition. Edited by Andrew Horton and Joanna E. Rapf.

Indian viewers. Indian comedic film takes aim at mainstream misrepresentations and their tried-and-true caricatures of Indians. Fashioned not just in film but also in academic, political, and other discourses, these cardboard cutouts include noble warriors, drunken degenerates, vicious dog eaters, wise old storytellers, lascivious maidens, and heavily burdened drudges in films like *Dances with Wolves* (Kevin Costner 1990), *The Battle of Elderbush Gulch* (D.W. Griffith 1913), and even *Peter Pan* (Clyde Geronimi, et al. 1953). To its dubious credit, Hollywood has cranked out thousands of films with this impoverished cast of characters, although skilled Indian performers like Will Rogers, Chief Dan George, and Gary Farmer managed to bring some humanity to the characters they played. American Indian comedic films and performances lampoon the falsity of early representations and question the hostility motivating and perpetuated in their construction, apologist claims of their harmlessness notwithstanding.

Indian comedy crucially does not stop at critiques of mainstream misrepresentations, however. Insofar as the folks we call in shorthand "American Indians" are made up of several million people from more than 500 different nations, they represent a diverse group: some rich, some poor, some male, female, urban, rural, educated, not, ordinary, and so forth. They – we – are a pluralistic bunch of humans with characteristics as ranging as any group's. One key dimension for the films I'd like to discuss here concerns access to power and resources, and the lack thereof. This question cuts right to Indian peoples' material wellbeing, which seldom concerns mainstream culture or its representations of Indians. Neither, however, do American Indian cultures themselves everywhere work towards material improvement. It is surely fair to say that some aspects of Indian life are complicit with the imperialist projects of keeping Indian voices quiet and keeping Indians consistently at the bottom of America's socio-economic scale. Although racism, poverty, and associated social problems like alcoholism, unemployment, and cultural alienation don't much seem like ingredients in a recipe for hilarity, many comedic moments in films take just these conditions as their set-ups for the one-eyed Ford punch lines.

Indian humor is often thought synonymous with dark comedy, yet the much of the comedic critique in Indian film is distinctly bronze, an alloy of recognition of difficulty and spirit of survival. Writers like James Welch, Gerald Vizenor, and Sherman Alexie have long emphasized this dimension of Indian humor, dedicated to the continuance of Native communities in the face of colonialist legacies of poverty and misrepresentation. Whereas mainstream dark comedy tends to treat ironically the existential angst of the individual, often bourgeois subject, the target of Indian comedy is more often the this-world suffering of the contemporary Indian cultural context: poverty, racism, alcoholism, and the impending threat of foreclosure upon our cultural past and future. This last might seem a little dramatic, but Indians can see at every turn a mean-spirited mascot, a Jeep Cherokee, a Crazy Horse 40-ouncer, or a classroom of children reenacting Oklahoma's land runs, each a reminder that others have staked claims to our lands and ideas of self.

In presenting the gross inequalities facing Native Americans, Indian directors, screenwriters, and performers have developed a keen sensibility less concerned with identification of absurdity than in an affirmative irony. Like the dilapidated one-eyed Ford, American Indian comedic films hijack the mainstream filmic medium and steer it to their own destinations. This chapter traces major moments in American Indian comedic cinema beginning with films not Indian by much measure but featuring game-changing performances like those by Rogers in *Judge Priest* (John Ford 1934), George in *Little Big Man* (Arthur Penn 1970) and Farmer in *Powwow Highway* (Jonathan Wacks 1989). I then turn to works with greater degrees of Indian control over production, like *Return of the Country* (Bob Hicks 1982), *Harold of Orange* (Richard Weise 1984), *Smoke Signals*, and *Four Sheets to the Wind*. Even as the latter films protest poor material conditions, they simultaneously affirm Indian identity in cultural dispositions, history, and community connections. Crucially, they also embrace representation itself despite the spotted history of Indians in film. In an intriguing turn, as American Indian filmmakers have furloughed hackneyed savage characters, they have reworked middle-class protagonists into strongly subversive figures, a trend Alan Velie has identified in literature as well (Velie 1992: 264–8). American Indian female directors like Valerie Red-Horse and Jennifer Wynne Farmer with their film *Naturally Native* (1998) have made powerful statements in this regard.

Setting out to discuss American Indian film begs important initial questions: first, what makes someone American Indian, and how does whatever that is translate into a feature film, so much a collaboration among potentially hundreds of Natives and non-Natives? Identity theorists have spent considerable effort trying to answer the first question without coming to a definitive answer. Most measures include some combination of recognition of Indianness on the part of the individual, communities of other Indians, communities of non-Indians, and an official body (such as a tribal nation or the US government, which measures the dubious concept of blood quantum). Culturally or sociologically speaking, some theorists have suggested components of this recognition include elements such as speaking a tribal language, geographic residence, kinship with other Indians, phenotype, and ceremonial participation (Garroutte 2003: 14–98). Suffice it to say that for present purposes, I consider as Indian those people who understand themselves and are understood by others as such, and I deploy the same practical if imperfect strategy with the films.

Given the ambiguities of the first question, of course, the second – how Indianness makes its way into a film – is made no easier. I treat as American Indian films those that concern Indian subject matter and that involve Indians both in front of and behind the camera in some capacity, say, as director, screenwriter, or author of a source work. Whatever definition we use for "American Indian film," however, important works will be left out of the mix. Besides categorical troubles, space precludes discussion of many films that could well have been included here, such as Sterlin Harjo's *Barking Water* (2009), Sherman Alexie's *Business of*

Fancydancing (2002), Chris Eyre's *Skins* (2002), or *Medicine River* (Stuart Margolin, 1993), which was based on the novel by Thomas King (Cherokee), all of which have hysterical moments. Having Indians in the cast and production crew of a film about Indians by no means guarantees a representative take, but it has shown us viewpoints more Indian than we have gotten from even the most sympathetic of westerns.

On occasion, American Indian actors like Rogers, George, and Farmer featured in movies having little concern for Indian perspectives and brought such presence to their performances that they transcended the narratives that preferred to keep them as landscape ornaments. Except for a brief run during the silent era, most early roles for American Indians were played by non-Natives aided by a little skin-bronzer, for whom realistic portrayals were not a priority. Jeff Chandler, for instance, starred in heavy makeup and dusty wig as the Apache leader Cochise in three films, most notably *Broken Arrow* (Delmer Daves, 1950). Many grunting Indian roles went to Iron Eyes Cody, a.k.a. Espera de Corti, a son of Italian immigrants who fabricated an Indian identity in a peculiar instance of life imitating art (Raheja 2010: 102–44). Why audiences and the industry tolerated (and still tolerate) ethnic substitution with Indians but would hardly stand for such regular and obvious put-ons with other ethnic groups is due to several causes. Some film scholars like Edward Buscombe (2006: 152) argue that employing non-Indians was simply the way things were done given the paucity of American Indian actors, and that "Indians had simply not acquired the star power believed necessary for the film's box-office success.".

In fact, a great many Indians worked as extras, and there were full-fledged organizations of Indian actors in Hollywood that filmmakers could easily have called upon to develop Indian celebrities (Deloria 2006: 105). Few mainstream scholars have questioned deeper, if more uncomfortable, reasons why Indian actors weren't much used, which might well concern prevalent racist attitudes and a desire of filmmakers to avoid having their misrepresentations challenged by Indian people whose lives they touched (Wiegman 1998: 158–68). Once Indian actors finally began appearing in leading roles, they not only demonstrated incredible skill and range, which commanded the sympathies of Native and non-Native audiences, but they also began to carve out a place for Indians in the cinematic world at large. Their demonstrated onscreen success, perhaps convinced producers of the viability of Indian stories, just as it inspired Indian spectators to begin telling them once they overcame their surprise at seeing recognizable representations.

One of the first Indian superstars was Cherokee humorist, author, and actor Will Rogers, who starred in some 70 films in the silent and talkie eras, and in the mid-1930s was Hollywood's number-one male box office draw for his easy-going, improvisational wit. While his films, some of which he wrote and produced, have little to do overtly with Indian subject matter, this very mainstream orientation ironically positions him as a subversive native performer, insofar as he publically foregrounded his Cherokee heritage but refused to play run-of-the-mill Indian roles. Some of his best turns came in collaboration with the master of the Indian stereotype, John Ford. In features like *Stagecoach* (1939), Ford had John Wayne's characters wiping out Apaches by the wagonload. He established a benchmark for savagery in *The Searchers* (1956), and attempted to make amends in *Cheyenne Autumn* (1964) by casting Ricardo Montalban, Gilbert Roland, and Sal Mineo (none of them Indian) in the lead Indian roles. Rogers and Ford worked together on three films, *Doctor Bull* (1933), *Judge Priest* (1934), and *Steamboat 'round the Bend* (1935), all of which enjoyed box-office success, and the men reportedly established a positive working relationship. In *Judge Priest*, which has garnered the most critical attention of any of Rogers' movies, his down-home demeanor further endears audiences already familiar with his nearly ubiquitous persona created through his radio addresses, newspaper columns, and films (Yagoda 2000: 259–65, 305–13).

Based on short stories by Irvin S. Cobb, *Judge Priest* nostalgizes the post-Civil War south in its story about wily magistrate William Priest's machinations to defend Bob Gillis, a taciturn blacksmith charged with assaulting Flem Talley, the neighborhood cad, to set his nephew Rome up with his love interest, the orphaned Ellie May, and to deflate his bombastic antagonist, former senator Horace Maydew. Some decades after the war, the film opens on a comic courtroom scene with Maydew (played by Ford regular Berton Churchill) grandiloquently making the state's case against African-American Jeff Poindexter (played by "Stepin Fetchit"/Lincoln Perry), an alleged chicken thief. The judge, more interested in the funny papers than Maydew's oration, incites an impromptu debate among the veterans in the galley, one of them still in uniform, over what variety of chicken figured in a shared war exploit. After the bickering, Poindexter offers his alibi that he was off catfishing and so couldn't have been stealing chickens at the time. In an abrupt cut from the courtroom, the next shot finds Priest and Poindexter ambling off with their cane poles and a jug of whiskey. Though they have only just met, the two appear as erstwhile if unequal companions throughout the picture (see Figure 17.1). The conflict gets underway after Gillis defends fatherless Ellie May's honor by slugging Flem. During Gillis' trial, Mayhew as prosecutor questions Priest's objectivity and insults him by asking for a recusal, whereupon Priest becomes Gillis' counsel. By film's end, we learn from former-captain and present-preacher Ashby Brand (played by Henry Walthall, *Birth of a Nation*'s Little Colonel) of Gillis' earlier homicide conviction and pardon through his confederate service, and that he is in fact Ellie May's father. Brand narrates these courtroom revelations in a scene orchestrated by Priest and Poindexter.

As familiar as Rogers was to American audiences, they would have been aware of his background, of which he often spoke, as a Cherokee from Oolagah and Claremore in Indian Territory, and of his distinct brand of political humor. His self-effacing delivery gave him free license to ironize the most serious problems of the day and to satirize the most powerful people in America, often with them in the audience. Rogers cut his teeth on this brand of humor growing up on his father's

Figure 17.1 *Judge Priest*; producer Sol Wurtzel; director, John Ford.

ranch on the plains side of Cherokee country at the turn of the twentieth century. Raised by Cherokee parents, surrounded by Cherokees, in a place thoroughly
Cherokee, Rogers developed a kindly humor and embodied mannerisms, so much
a part of his comedy, that bear an indelible stamp of Indian influence. We needn't
take recourse to oral traditions to account for Rogers' comedic aura, looking for
the customary ethnological marks of the trickster as Kenneth Lincoln is wont to
do in his analysis of Indian humor (Lincoln 1993: 21–2), but instead can look to
the more immediate if more prosaic circumstances of his early life on an Indian
cattle ranch. That lifestyle was rooted in a populist agrarianism that informs the
direction of the comedic critique in much of Rogers' work on- and off-screen. In
Rogers' films, as with many of Ford's, the hero is a common man who, even if he
does not rank among the lower classes, maintains sympathy for them and stands
in many respects apart from the upper echelons, members of which are generally positioned as antagonists and catch the bulk of the ironic jabs. In *Judge Priest*,
the self-righteous prosecutor Maydew represents what's crustiest about the upper
crust. At the film's climax, we celebrate his comeuppance as his railroading of
Gillis disintegrates upon the revealing of Gillis' heroic military service, which leads
to a patriotic rejuvenation – a pointedly *confederate* rejuvenation of an ostensibly
inclusive community spirit.

On this point the film would like to have it both ways, nostalgizing a pastoral
South devoid of racist exclusionary practices. Tag Gallagher (1986: 103) rightly
points to the affinities between Priest and Jeff Poindexter, both in terms of their
friendship and their characters' shambling resemblances. In a scene in which the
judge looks to run off Flem, who has obnoxiously come courting Ellie May, Priest
hides behind some bushes and stages a phony conversation between himself and

Poindexter about an angry father pursing Flem with a shotgun. He impersonates Jeff's voice and also overplays his own, hinting at the theatricality that Priest brings to his public persona and that Rogers brings to his role as Priest (and to some extent to his role as Will Rogers, as an enormously wealthy man speaking as a common man). Here an Indian imitates a white imitating a black in a staged sketch within a movie that playfully, if momentarily, encourages identification across boundaries. The scene establishes in dialect what others showing them gone fishing illustrate visually – that Judge Priest's closest counterpart in demeanor and character is Jeff Poindexter, far more so than his nearest professional corollary, Senator Maydew. Priest also twice joins in song with black characters, which no other character does. Though Priest's relationships with black characters are marked by inequality and the film certainly traffics in facile stereotypes, as Rogers occasionally did in other performances, the intricate textures of race within the film, and especially its suggestion that race is something more performed than inherited, complicate any attempt to dismiss the film as simply reflective of its times' dominant racial attitudes. Though *Judge Priest* flirts with progressive affinities, it never seriously questions hegemonic racial politics, with the crucial exception of casting an American Indian in the lead role – a role that called not for feathers and war cries but for wit and poignancy.

Through the next several decades, as the western genre enjoyed its greatest popularity, American Indian actors were largely retired to the scenery, although the revisionist western saw some developments, especially with a watershed performance by Salish actor Chief Dan George in *Little Big Man*. With the incomparable dignity, tenderness, and humor he brought to role of Cheyenne chief Old Lodge Skins, George manages to upstage even so accomplished an actor as Dustin Hoffman. The film's major revision to the genre is its realignment of the story of western conflict towards the Cheyenne point of view, culminating in the 1876 defeat of General Custer at the Battle of the Little Big Horn, which is here told as triumph rather than tragedy. Aged 71 when the movie was made, George earned an Oscar nomination for Best Supporting Actor. Some critics have pointed out the stereotypical quality of his role, a wise, sachem-like figure whose critique of imperialism is defanged by his kindly, welcoming manner and the film's 1960s' counterculture sympathies (Georgakas 1972: 29–30; Kasdan and Tavernetti 1998: 130–4; Kilpatrick 1999: 84–94). For many American Indian spectators and for critic Michael Greyeyes (2008: 110–28), however, George's performance powerfully reminds them of people they know – their fathers, grandfathers, uncles, and friends. His humor, voice, pantomiming, and all his embodied mannerisms went further toward establishing American Indian audiences' identification with him than every preceding non-Native actor in redface combined.

In one of his funniest moments, he treks up a mountain at the film's close with the determination to challenge death and affect his own passing, having settled on the best "good day to die." He thanks the Creator for his victories and defeats in a somber and touching monologue. The most sympathetic character in the film, he lays down to die with ultimate dignity–only to get jarred back into reality by a rainstorm. He asks of his adopted grandson, the title character played by Dustin Hoffman, "Am I still in this world?" Finding that he is, he drops his head to the ground and groans, "Eehh … I was afraid of that." Stuck with a long walk home, we groan and chuckle along with the realization that beautiful rhetoric doesn't secure humans any control over such affairs. Trudging down the mountain, he tells Little Big Man of his new wife, comparing her to mythic figures with whom her people are affiliated: "The only trouble with snake women is they copulate with horses, which makes them strange to me. She says she doesn't; that's why I call her, 'Doesn't Like Horses.' But of course, she's lying." The film bathetically declines, or at least qualifies, the tragic close Hollywood reserved for Indian narratives, opting instead for a comic overturning of expectations, both with a joke and a suspended ending. Quite possibly for the very first time, many Indian spectators saw another Indian on screen playing a character smart and not stupid, dignified and not degraded, sage and not savage, and imagined from Dan George's performance the prospect that American films so often *about* Indians could finally say something worthwhile *to* them. Even Hollywood casting agents caught on.

In subsequent years American Indians would increasingly take over Indian roles. Will Sampson (Muscogee-Creek) in *One Flew over the Cuckoo's Nest* (Milos Forman 1975) played Chief Bromden with great composure and wit alongside Jack Nicholson's character R.P. McMurphy. Sampson enacts an Indian man institutionalized in a mental hospital, mute until near the end when he accepts a stick of gum McMurphy offers and mutters, "Ahh … Juicy Fruit," just before he undergoes punitive, involuntary electro-shock therapy. Despite the shortage of lines, he plays the character with impressive sensitivity and surgical comedic timing.

Gary Farmer (Cayuga) set the benchmark for a major Indian comedic role in his turn as the trickster/dreamer/physical comic Philbert Bono in *Powwow Highway*. Like George, Farmer controls the screen when he appears, not just through his size, although he can indeed dominate spaces and frames, but ironically through his portrayal of Philbert's decidedly undomineering, wide-eyed enthusiasm for powwows, blue-plate specials, and human fellowship. In this film, based on the novel by David Seals, Cheyenne almost-friends Philbert and Buddy Redbow drive across country to break Buddy's sister out jail after she's been framed, diverting Buddy's attention from a vote on an exploitative mining project he opposed on his home reservation. Philbert acquires his wheels just at the film's beginning. Upon viewing a commercial featuring a war-bonneted used-car salesman hawking Mustangs, Pintos, and Broncos in Tonto-speak, he is inspired to secure transportation of his own, and so lumbers down to the salvage yard. Surveying the littered landscape, he sees not a junkyard but a vision of beautiful, galloping ponies. Earnestly announcing to the proprietor, "I want to buy one of your fine ponies," he trades a little whiskey and a little weed for a '64 Buick LeSabre, a rustbucket he christens "Protector the War Pony," complete with a removable driver's side window – one of the finest Indian cars to wobble out of Detroit. After a brief struggle, the engine coughs to life, Philbert unceremoniously discards the plastic Jesus riding on the dashboard, and he sputters off to meet new trials and tribulations as Buddy musters him into his rescue operation (Anderson 1998: 137–52).

Their road trip becomes a modern vision quest that seeks to resolve the form and function of Indian traditions in the modern world, with its pro-liferate misrepresentations of Indians and their beliefs. During the climactic escape-from-the-cops scene, Buddy has a vision similar to Philbert's, seeing himself as a Cheyenne warrior leaping into battle, defiantly hurling his tomahawk at the attacking enemy; back in the narrative, he detaches the Indian car's window and flings it at a pursuing cop car. The car crashes, havoc ensues, and the heroes make their escape. With an Indian car relegated to the mainstream world's scrapheap, the film finds Indians reconciling modernity with tradition by turning technology to their own ends, which are here focused not on consumption of all things shiny and new but on the survival and maintenance of family and community.

A notable short film released in 1982, *Return of the Country*, further set the stage for American Indian-produced comedies. Bob Hicks, a Creek-Seminole Indian from Oklahoma, wrote and directed the parody in connection with his attendance at the American Film Institute (Singer 2001: 44–5). Like *Powwow Highway*, the film pokes fun at the legacy of filmic stereotypes of Indians but more strongly implicates those representations in ongoing political practices that exploit the resources and silence the voices of Native people. It opens to a buxom Indian maiden half-heartedly fleeing a pursuing brave. Both wear grotesque wigs and generic Indian garb, and lack grammatical facility with articles. An abrupt edit reveals this scene to be a clip of a film that is being shown on a talk show, whose guests are the blond-haired, blue-eyed actors portraying the Indians. The lead actress chatters proudly about her Cherokee princess grandmother. The next guest on the show, another pulchritudinous blonde woman, is Georgina Armstrong, the newly appointed Commissioner of Indian Affairs. She is a crony of the President who admits to having no experience working with Native Americans. She explains her plans to hold a powwow for the President where she will present him an eagle feather war bonnet and have him adopted as an honorary Indian. Her dilettantish affinity for American Indians parallels that of the actress, a resemblance reinforced by their physical similarities. The film thus puts cultural dalliances in cinema on a par with those in politics.

The main narrative follows her preparations for the President's visit, as a Buffalo Bill-lookalike producer aids her in staging a political cultural spectacle. Things fall apart when the contracted Native performers collectively refuse to participate in the display, citing the sacrilegious use of the war bonnet. As Commissioner Armstrong enters panic mode with the President on the way, a Muscogee-speaking medicine man named Ya-Dee-Ga, played by Woodrow Haney, appears and conducts a ceremony that presents her with three visions of an alternative world in which Indians rule politics and media, creating racialized images according to the same underdeveloped ethos that the mainstream has used with Indians. Framed against a black background and looking much like a movie spectator, the commissioner witnesses in the first vision an elaborate song-and-dance number in the Fred Astaire tradition, replete with gowned and top-hatted dancers done up in whiteface. This scene too takes an abrupt turn when the medicine man again intrudes, now as a film director calling for more authentic "white" behavior from his Native performers and a lowering of their cheekbones by the makeup artists.

Hicks turns cinema's ethnological fascination with Indian dance on its head in this sequence, offering an ironic commentary on film's preoccupation with high ceremonial spectacle dating back to Thomas Edison's filming of Lakota dancers in Buffalo Bill's wild west show. In the next vision Armstrong observes a press conference at which Ya-Dee-Ga as President announces his appointment of Native bureaucrat and glad-hander Mr. Black Elk to the post of Commissioner of White Affairs. Armstrong tries to raise an objection, but is told she cannot make it in English. The satire on language segues to the last vision, which takes place in a classroom setting with Native children sitting around a fire. A white child dressed in a Boy Scout uniform enters, whereupon he is told he cannot speak English, is stripped, dressed in Indian clothing, and compelled to throw the Bible he carries into the flames, recapitulating the historical political assaults on Native language, religion, and culture attempted by assimilationist policies.

The film closes with Commissioner Armstrong back in her office, dazed as she walks toward the theatrical shebang she has planned. As Ya-Dee-Ga softly sings a Native song contrasting with the brass strains of *Hail to the Chief* issuing from another room, she falters in a doorway, her face half-obscured by the jamb, suggesting in this moment of decision the half-truths and partial tellings of politicians and producers to which Indian people have long been dubious heirs. The film's positioning the commissioner as spectator, however, crucially affirms that non-Native audiences – some of them potentially in positions to influence public policy – also get much of what they think they know from movies that have systematically silenced Native voices. While it's only fair to note that the commissioners and secretaries of Indian Affairs in the United States have in fact been Indian since the mid-1960s, the same cannot be said for leaders in other powerful positions, such as legislators on Indian Affairs committees, academic institution and department heads, health service administrators, and more. The repeated structure of Hicks' *Return of the County*, which interrupts narratives with politics and politics with narratives, jarring viewers into an awareness of cine-matic falsification, reminds us of the hegemonic social attitudes produced by the intimacies between film and policy, and it presciently intervenes in their collusion.

Somewhat better known than *Return of the Country* is prominent Ojibwe author Gerald Vizenor's short film, *Harold of Orange* (Richard Weise 1984) starring Oneida-Cree-Mohawk comedian Charlie Hill, which Vizenor wrote in connection with a regional media project. The film bears his stamp of postmodern playfulness and trickster humor as it satirizes the culturally performative dimensions of philanthropy, following Harold Sinseer and his "Warriors of Orange" in their scheme to secure a foundation grant to raise imaginary coffee beans on the reservation. Harold convinces his friends that they need to put on a real show to endear themselves to the foundation and secure their "pocket change," so they dream up a naming ceremony in which board members draw "dream names" like "Connecticut" and "Baltic" from a stack of Monopoly cards, and join a softball game in which they play on the "Indians" team and the warriors play for the "Anglos." As Robert Silberman (1985: 12) astutely notes, for all the play in Harold's machinations, "the imaginative power that literally saves the day is always qualified by the fact that the material power, quite simply the money, is not under Harold's control." Silberman identifies in Vizenor's own dependence on foundation money to finance the film its sharpest irony. Perhaps for Vizenor, cultural money games, like the softball game, are generally won by the whites dressed and labeled as Indians, but that prevents neither him nor Harold from having fun playing by their own rules, gaming the system, and in the process changing it a little at a time.

Smoke Signals (1998), directed by Cheyenne filmmaker Chris Eyre and based on the short story collection *The Lone Ranger and Tonto Fistfight in Heaven* by Coeur d'Alene-Spokane author Sherman Alexie, who also wrote the screenplay, heralded some of the biggest changes in media representations of Indians. In its early stages of development, the film won the Audience Award and the Filmmaker's Trophy at the Sundance Film Festival. It met with relative success at the box office and became an instant classic among Indian audiences. It was marketed as the first major motion picture starring, written, directed, and co-produced by American Indians to gain a major theatrical distribution.

The more we discover about the roles of American Indians like James Young Deer (Hochunk), Will Rogers, and Edwin Carewe (Chickasaw), however, the harder it will be to sustain such claims of originality. Young Deer wrote several silent films, directed nearly two dozen, and starred in still more during his time at Pathé. Carewe, born Jay Fox, also a writer and actor, directed more than 50 films in the silent era and up to the beginnings of the talking era. My research corroborates Angela Aleiss's (2005: 180) assertion that Carewe's brothers Wallace Fox and Finis Fox were also Chickasaw (all three appear on the Chickasaw Dawes Rolls) and worked for decades in Hollywood, writing, directing, and producing scores of films, including many B-westerns, East Side Kids flicks, and horror movies featuring the likes of Bela Lugosi.

While these forerunners and their films are important to the history of American Indian film and also to American Indian identity in relation to artistic production, *Smoke Signals* stands apart for its positioning American Indian concerns at the heart of its story. Central to the film's appeal is the relationship between the two lead characters. Handsome, cynical Victor Joseph, played old-then-young by Adam Beach (Saulteaux/Ojibwe) and Cody Lightning (Cree), and nerdy, naïve Thomas Builds-the-Fire, played by Evan Adams (Coast Salish) and Simon Baker (Cree-Haida-Squamish), travel from their home reservation in Washington state to Arizona to retrieve the ashes of Victor's father, an alcoholic who abandoned his family years before. Victor and Thomas slowly unravel their shared history of loss as they go. The film playfully contrasts these endearing characters through multiple filmic codes that belie their similarities, judiciously dramatizing and sensitively mocking the failings of both. In a subtle magic realist style, the film's editing similarly embraces contradiction as it employs multiple match cuts that incrementally put events told in flashback into conversation with the central narrative, generating a dialectic that the film understands and depicts as fully present in the present (Kilpatrick 1999: 228–32). The deliberate oscillations between Thomas and Victor, like those between past and present, echo *Smoke Signals'* major movement between comedy and tragedy, the latter occasioned not by fated repetition but by concrete social problems like alcoholism, the colonialist genealogies of which reverberate across generations.

The film opens with several looks at what a title screen tells us is the Coeur d'Alene Indian reservation. Juxtaposed against widespread mountainous and beautiful country are shots of broken down cars and dilapidated trailer houses, one labeled "KREZ" in large, hand-painted letters. From here, local disc jockey Randy Peone (John Trudell, Santee Sioux) broadcasts, checking in periodically with Lester FallsApart (Chief Leonard George, Coast Salish, and son of Chief Dan George). FallsApart offers traffic reports from his vantage atop a broken-down van. Lester's update, delivered with impeccable timing, ranks among the greatest of Indian film comedy moments: "A couple of cars went by earlier. You know ol' missus Joe? She was *speeding*. And, uh, Kimmy and James, they went by in a yellow car and they was arguing... Ain't no traffic really." The singular rhythms here belong to "Indian time," unfolding at their own pace, in their own directions. Speaking of which, we also encounter two Indian women driving another fine Indian car – one that goes only in reverse, a condition that goes unremarked in the movie.

Though not without certain resources, every character suffers from a lack of liquidity, and this same impoverishment requires that Victor accept Thomas' offer of financial help to get to Phoenix. This road trip forms the primary plot, aided by two other strands told in flashback, all of which conspire to reveal the narrative as fragmented and subjective. The first takes place when Victor and Thomas were infants and tells of a Fourth of July party that ends in a house fire – a heartbreakingly fitting ending to the Indians' unselfconsciously ironic celebration of an American holiday that has very little to do with Indian independence. As silhouettes haunt an infernal background, Thomas melodiously recounts in voiceover narration how his parents, unable to escape, tossed him from the second story of the burning house, and how Victor's father, Arnold Joseph (played by Gary Farmer), caught him in an inadvertently heroic moment. The morning after, the camera finds Arnold shuffling uneasily between his wife who holds young Victor and Grandma Builds-the-Fire who cradles Thomas. Distraught over the deaths of Thomas' parents, she nevertheless praises Arnold: "You saved Thomas. You did a good thing." Embarrassed, perhaps bewildered, he squirms and earnestly exclaims, "I didn't mean to." Arnold's response, an unwittingly comedic reply to a tragic loss, resolves the scene in equivocation, suspending him between two families in the *mise-en-scène* and in the story.

Set a dozen years later, on another Fourth of July, the second flashback strand centers on the Joseph family's dysfunction, especially Arnold's physically abuse. Rather than capitulate to the demands of his wife (played by Cree actress Tantoo Cardinal) that they stop drinking, Arnold elects to desert his family. He leaves behind Victor, who has grown into a handsome and guarded boy, and then in the film's present, a caustic young man. Thomas has grown up to be a dork, but one possessed of a poetic sensibility. The film establishes their differences in myriad ways, from Thomas's attentive posture to Victor's slouch, Victor's cowboy boots and jeans to Thomas' three-piece suit, Thomas' ubiquitous squinty grin to Victor's truculent sneer. These and others indicate the deeper-running differences in attitude that generate the film's most prevalent tension. The two are fundamentally at odds, for instance, over how Indians should generally comport themselves. In a revealing exchange, Victor chides Thomas for his metaphoric loquaciousness in which Thomas is "always trying to sound like some damn medicine man or something," affecting his persona from repeated viewings of *Dances with Wolves*. Encouraging Thomas to toughen up and act more masculine, he ironically embraces another Hollywood stereotype, that of the ferocious brave, when he tells Thomas, "First of all, quit grinning like an idiot ... Get stoic .... You gotta look like a warrior. You gotta look like you just came back from killing a buffalo." Thomas objects, "But our tribe never hunted buffalo; we were fishermen." Victor is incredulous: "What?! You wanna look like you just came back from catching a *fish*? This ain't 'Dances with Salmon,' you know." Victor knows as well as the film does that acting out the warrior stereotype is no more an accurate way to be a real Indian than pretending to be a wise shaman, but the former posture has provided him with the armor he believes he requires. On the question of how Indians actually behave, what they are more accurately like, the film itself makes the superior intervention in its depiction of complex characters who experience the full range of human feeling–even such dubious desires as wishing the world were more like the movies.

Once they arrive in Arizona, Victor develops some sympathy for Thomas when he learns from his father's mysterious neighbor Suzy Song (played by Inupiat-Cree actress Irene Bedard) of Arnold's admission that it was he who accidentally started the fire that killed Thomas' parents. Realizing that his father's guilt played a role in both his drinking and his leaving leads Victor to some measure of empathy and forgiveness, tempering his aggression. In this movement, Victor draws closer to Thomas' openness with others, although Thomas is not in fact the paragon of empathy that his differences from Victor suggest he is. Besides the nuisance of his constant chatter, Thomas himself displays a lack of empathy with his incessant stories about Arnold taking him to Denny's (because while in *Little Big Man* it might be a good day to die, in *Smoke Signals*, "it's a good day to eat breakfast"), competing in a frybread eating contest, and so on. Fully aware of Victor's anger towards his father and his desire *not* to talk about him, Thomas presses Victor to open up and reminisce. Such willful disregard more closely resembles Victor's aloofness than it does Thomas' more characteristic amicability. What Victor remembers, as the flashbacks reveal, is Arnold's drinking, abuse, and abandonment. The film doesn't give up on empathy, though, and near the end, Thomas asks Victor once more if he knows why his father left him. Rather than repeat an earlier response and smash Thomas in the face, knowing now that Arnold was fleeing the guilt he felt at having been responsible for the deaths of Thomas' parents, Victor instead echoes his father's earlier equivocation, "He didn't mean to, Thomas," sparing Thomas the anger and resentment to which he was heir and sacrificing his own penchant for brutal honesty.

Such unfolding of the past in the present plays out visually through the editing that moves among the flashbacks, flash-forwards, and the film's present. In one instance, through a match-on-action cut, we see young Victor chasing his father and then, outpaced by a passing bus, on which the adult Victor rides. For an instant the two appear to be together in the same frame or at least linked in the same moment, a joining edit replicated some four times: this bus scene, when Victor exits the reservation store, when he enters his mother's house, and when a basketball appearing in a story told by Arnold and recalled by Suzy rolls into the frame where she and Victor are talking. Often, Thomas's questions about Arnold and Victor's past spark these memories jostled by the unfolding plot. The net effect of the past intimately intertwined with the story's present, particularly with the match edits that call into question whether the present characters might in reality be contemporaneously interacting with or re-experiencing the past, gestures towards magic realism, although the characters do not consciously confront magical moments as they do in a work such as Alfonso Arau's *Like Water for Chocolate* (1992). Even though magic is referenced several times in *Smoke Signals*, it is not produced in any real measure by Arnold, the film's chief "magician," as both Arlene and Suzy refer to him. As Thomas explains early on, Arnold's greatest trick, his disappearance, he practices through drinking and finally pulls off in desertion. There is nothing in his routine at which to marvel. The film's own stylistic innovations and its poignant representations of American Indians as funny, angry, sad, weird, and human offer a far greater sense of wonder.

Equal parts comedy, romance, drama, and political statement, *Naturally Native* came out in 1998, the same year as *Smoke Signals* and also screened at Sundance. The Mashantucket Pequot Nation financed the production, making it the first feature-length film funded by Native sources, although because it failed to find a theatrical distribution deal, too few audiences have had the opportunity to see it. Valerie Red-Horse wrote, starred, and co-directed with Jennifer Wynne Farmer (Shinnecock). Red-Horse claims Cherokee heritage but not citizenship. The film's credits indicate that she is Cherokee and Sioux, but her website at the time of this writing omits any mention of Sioux affiliation (*Valerie Red-Horse* 2011). The movie tells the story of three California-based Morongo-Viejas Band of Kumeyaay sisters' personal challenges and their difficulties in securing funding to start a health and beauty product business, a metaphor for general troubles American Indians often encounter when they enter into ventures that require large capital, such as making films. While the film at times struggles to maintain viewers' attention with its static camera, drab sets, and didacticism, its troubles were surely not aided by the budget that came in under $1 000 000.

The film nevertheless gives voice to subjective positions of contemporary American Indian women, significantly including those not at the bottom of the socio-economic scale, who rarely have their stories told in mainstream films. Indeed, if films depict nothing but poor Indians, they do not go far enough in combating stereotypes but instead reinscribe stereotypical assumptions from which poverty may be inducted as a product of some essential deficiency. Much in the way it blends comedy, drama, and romance, *Naturally Native* combines its intellectual messages on the vagaries of Indian identity politics and on the structural obstacles facing Indian entrepreneurs with affective scenarios that not only personalize the strong female leads but that also poke gentle fun at the contradictions of contemporary Indian life and dramatize the private effects of public policies, conditions, and expectations that collude to maintain American Indians' disempowered social status. The narrative locates this confluence in the sisters' separation from their parents and culture through their mother's alcohol-related death and their adoption by non-Native parents, which resulted in their ineligibility for federal recognition as Indians. This marginalization excludes them from governmental programs, separates them from Indian communities, and estranges them from understanding themselves as Indians–serious troubles the film nevertheless manages with humor.

The sisters relate to their Indian heritage in distinct ways. The eldest, Vicki Bighawk (portrayed by Red-Horse) offers the favored attitude with her politicized consciousness and embrace of cultural markers (prominently shown in props like dreamcatchers, drums, and mandalas that decorate Vicki's home, and especially in her costume, which is overtly urban Indian with tailored, fringed buckskin jackets, and beaded or turquoise jewelry). The middle sister, Karen Lewis, played by Kimberly Norris Guerrero (Colville-Salish), accepts her Indian identity, though for her it plays a secondary role to her aspirations to succeed in business marketing. The youngest sister Tanya Lewis, played by Irene Bedard (Inuit-Métis), struggles the most with being Indian, exclaiming at one point, "What did being Indian ever mean to us anyway, huh? I mean, our mom was a drunk, our dad was dirt poor ... " She blames herself for their mother's death and believes alcoholism and poverty are essential features of being Indian. For each, however, the greater problem concerns the attitudes of the non-Indian financiers for whom the sisters, by turns, lack official sanction, take their traditions too seriously, or are compromised by their affiliation with distasteful gaming enterprises.

In one attempt, they approach an associate who has access to big-money investors but also has an uncomfortably liberal idea of cultural access – she's a new-ager who believes she was an Indian in a previous life. She begins their meeting by waggling a smoldering sage bundle around, chanting, and unexpectedly barking, to the sisters' astonishment. To get the sisters' feet in the door, she suggests they help her with a special sundance she is putting on for wealthy clients, a proposal Vicki rejects with much righteous indignation and a jeremiad on the infungibility of Indian traditions. Despite its didacticism, the scene is among the film's funniest, as the charlatan in her fortune teller garb goes on about how the sisters can help run religious ceremonies despite their unfamiliarity with them. "We're Presbyterian," Tanya deadpans in reply. Though hesitant to approach their father's tribe based on warnings they've received against trying to horn in casino profits, the women find unexpected, if perhaps too-easy, success in their final attempt when they return to their tribal home.

The film attempts a great deal, with its genre blending and its running through a litany of topics of social and political concern to American Indians, including plot segments and sound bites on poverty, mascots, fetishization, violence against women, conflicts between traditional and western medicine, religious syncretism, alcoholism, and Indian hiring preference, among others. At times the film reproduces clichéd representations like mystic-sounding Indian flute music over explanations of traditional beliefs. *Naturally Native* nevertheless represents a major accomplishment in American Indian film, not least because it is likely the first feature film written and directed by an Indian woman, and the first financed by Indian money. On the whole it crafts an engaging and clever story of sympathetic characters, especially women, who bear little resemblance to Hollywood's drudges and objects of colonialist desire. On the contrary, the characters, and especially Red-Horse's production itself, offer examples of empowerment and self-expression that will improve future opportunities for Indian women in front of and behind the camera. Cherokee producer Heather Rae, Cree director and actress Georgina Lightning, Abenaki documentary director Alanis Obomsawin, and others number among the American Indian women in film who continue the crucial enterprise of telling in their own ways their own stories of Indian women recognizable to other Indians.

Sterlin Harjo, a Creek-Seminole from Holdenville, Oklahoma wrote and directed the 2007 feature *Four Sheets to the Wind*, which debuted at Sundance, and took inspiration from several of its forerunners. It borrows from Red-Horse a strong characterization of Indian female characters, from Eyre and Alexie a focus on personal development, and from all of them a sly comedic approach. As in *Smoke Signals*, opportunities for growth are explicitly cast as travel and movement, both literal and metaphorical, as Harjo builds a deceptively complex and rhythmic flow of exit and return among its characters from his subdued narrative of an Oklahoma Indian family coping with the father's suicide. More than an antagonistic battle between opposites, movements to and away from home are represented as both positive and negative depending on the needs of the characters. Similar cycles emerge with the film's major themes of silence and conversation, and grief and humor, all of which are reinforced through two key visual elements: first, the camera's movement from gorgeous views of Oklahoma's rural landscapes to the energetic if at times dilapidated backdrops of urban Tulsa, and second, the progressions in color from muted blue-grays, which surround characters in moments of despondency, to warm reds and oranges, which signal genuine human connections and hopeful possibilities. Harjo crafts touching depictions of young Indians struggling with loneliness, privation, and outlooks for only mediocre futures, and of their parents unsure how to improve their children's opportunities in the Oklahoma land they surely belong to, but where not everyone's doing fine. Perhaps in the film's greatest achievement, it unflinchingly explores these somber themes but remains so dedicated to its comedic sensibility that even its central rumination on death also becomes its running gag.

The film establishes its off-beat humor from the very first. *Four Sheets* opens on a blue-gray dawn as young Cufe Smallhill (pronounced Chuffie, Creek for "rabbit," portrayed by Cody Lightning) unceremoniously drags his father's corpse down a dirt road until he reaches a local farm pond, where he sinks his father's body. In a voiceover narration with English subtitles, a man speaking Creek tells a story of a rabbit tricking a bear into his stomach, which kept him full for a good while. Though connecting the dots between the narrative and the film's themes is not easy, it is clear the film, through the narrator, wants us to be on guard for the unexpected, and the wryly comic. This narrator introduces us to Cufe and what he's up to. During Cufe's conversation with his mother Cora, played by Jeri Arredondo (Apache), as he attempts to explain to her what he's done, we learn that the father, who did not want a funeral, committed suicide. Together with a cousin, they devise a plan to hold services without the body, leading to a wonderfully funny funeral scene, to be discussed below.

Following the burial, Cufe takes a big step when he decides to leave his small-town home of Wewoka to visit his sister Miri in Tulsa. (For her portrayal of Miri, Ojibwe actress Tamara Podemski won the Sundance Special Jury Prize for Acting and was nominated for an Independent Spirit Award.) While there, he witnesses Miri's alarming drinking and her relationships with distasteful, culturally insensitive men, but he also meets Miri's neighbor, Francie, who takes him to hipster parties and posh lounges. Cufe grows increasingly self-aware during his time in Tulsa, thinking about what sort of style he would like to have, the places he would like to visit, and the social skills he feels he lacks.

Despite being out of his element in the urban environment, in Francie's warmly lit apartment, Cufe is able to open up to her, leaving behind the blue-grey hues that engulfed him at the film's beginning. These same muted tones characterize Miri, from the color of her sheets and car, to the lights of the bars where she spends too much of her time. He thereby avoids the risk he runs of becoming, like his father, an agreeable-enough sort of character, but one whose reticence threatens not just to obscure his sense of self but in fact to define it, perpetually keeping him from establishing relationships of any depth, a danger recognized by both his mother and sister. Following a brief return home, Cufe and Cora learn of Miri's suicide attempt, motivated by a constellation of difficult circumstances and destructive behaviors. Once Miri is back home, Cufe takes Francie up on her offer to go travelling, enabled by his mother's financial help, and the film closes with him heading out in another Indian truck, 20 years old and 20 per cent inoperable.

Quietness and reserve typify several of *Four Sheets'* characters, but it would be a mistake to see these qualities as reinforcing the stoicism of the noble savage stereotype. The film and its characters are acutely conscious of non-Natives' misperceptions about Indians and at times work that ignorance to their advantage, playing "old Indian tricks" to get what they're after. They invoke invented traditions, such as when Cufe's cousin Jim convinces an undertaker that, in Seminole tradition, non-Natives are forbidden to see the bodies of the deceased so they can disguise the absence of a corpse; Cufe allows a presumptuous psychiatrist to go on thinking his "Creek name" means "great white warrior" rather than "little penis," which the subtitles clue us into. The film itself might even be pulling one of these OITs with its quick reference to Creek and Seminole beliefs in an alternative, supernatural underwater world, to which Cufe has aided his father's passage.

I don't know much about Creek or Seminole beliefs in this regard, so they may well structure the narrative in ways invisible to me, but it at least seems clear that they do not pertain to the degree that they do in Creek author Craig Womack's novel *Drowning in Fire*, in which traditional symbols, the stomp dance religion, and Creek political history, take center stage thematically and also provide much of the underlying structure. *Four Sheets*, on the other hand, invokes just enough tribal specificity to register the film as Seminole, but it puts some questions and answers above our cultural security clearance or simply outside the narrative at hand. We should not read this tactic as indicative of some inauthenticity or shallowness, but rather as another narrative trick, for the film doesn't set out to theorize Seminole-ness, but lets it emerge naturally from the landscape and the presentation itself as it tells the story it wants to tell, the coming-of-age of a young man who is unselfconsciously Indian.

Such sly manipulations of cultural differences set up the film's funniest moments, especially the early funeral scene where grief and comedy come closest together. Tragedy approaches farce when Cora's friend Sonny appears to offer his condolences and aide. He emotionally explains that he has a coffin that he would be proud to donate to the Smallhill family – a coffin that he helped "fix up" for a play but that would nevertheless be ideally suited to help Frankie on his "final journey." Increasingly resigned to absurdity, Cora accepts. To add a little

Figure 17.2 *Four Sheets to the Wind*; director Sterlin Harjo; producers Chad Burris, Cheyenne Fletcher, and Ted Kroeber.

realism, Cufe and his cousin Jim weigh the casket with several watermelons, one of which has a cartoonish face drawn upon it. The real joke, however, is the coffin itself, which Jim good-naturedly derides as having "warpaint and shit all over it." Sonny – a heavy-set, densely red-bearded, effusive, and phenotypically white character who identifies himself as "a halfbreed… well, actually, I'm one-eighth Cherokee" to several recognizably Indian women – takes great pride in his creation, a stark baby-blue number emblazoned with hackneyed Indian symbols like lightning bolts and handprints. Amid the solemn dignity of the Creek hymns sung during the service, the gaudy empty shell of Indianness, a Hollywood pretense of culture, stands out as absurdly as Sonny's musing to the mourning Indian women, "I find art comes naturally to our people, don't you? You guys tried the corndogs?" (See Figure 17.2.)

The film clearly positions Sonny as a goofball foil, but it just as clearly refuses to leave him there, as it sympathetically develops Cora's relationship with him. Although Cufe insinuates the match follows hard upon his father's death, we see Cora and Sonny going on dates, enjoying each other's company, and conversing freely, all of which we gather were not habits of her marriage to Frankie. In any case, the film handles the fact of an Indian and a non-Indian in a romantic relationship with uncommon ease, simply declining the racialized anxiety that has beleaguered mainstream cinema (and wiped out scores of Indian female characters) for over 100 years, a pattern thoroughly detailed by M. Elise Marubbio (2006: 1–21). Francie's character is also important in this regard, insofar as her ethnicity is ambiguously coded. The subject does not come up between her and Cufe, suggesting a cultural atmosphere that obtains in much of Oklahoma – though decidedly not everywhere – in which American Indians and non-Natives move easily across racial boundaries.

Cufe looks to bring such fluidity to other parts of his life, particularly in travelling to California with Francie, which figures as escape for him. Looking at Francie's pictures in her apartment, he is dumbfounded at the very prospect of leaving for other places. When he tells Francie about Miri's failed attempt to become an actress and her aborted move to California that lasted only two weeks, we sense his trepidation and acceptance of the idea that his world might only consist of a very circumscribed idea of home. Even though it is Miri who sleeps beneath a map (recalling Arnold Joseph in *Smoke Signals*, another weary traveler), Cufe is the character most in need of a getaway. In a classic comic mode, his leaving circumvents the psychic and material obstacles that would impose a tragic ending, no less closed for its protraction. This openness of the ending, long a feature of comedy, suggests the possibility that the constrictive home society might be transformed upon the expected homecomings of the increasing number of travelers. Miri ranks among these but, unlike Cufe, she requires return, not further escape – or more accurately, further escapist behavior (Wood 2008: 126–7). Just as the film blends comedy and drama, it combines leaving and coming home without privileging one over the other. By qualifying apparent contradictions, *Four Sheets to the Wind* begins to represent the complex and many responses through which American Indians navigate their diverse, contemporary lives.

In an early scene in John Ford's western classic *The Searchers*, John Wayne's character, Ethan, reappears on the Jorgensen family's settlement. He takes a seat next to Martin Pauley, an adopted mixedblood Cherokee played by Jeffrey Hunter whom he knew as a child but now doesn't recognize. A war veteran and possible renegade, Ethan is also an Indian expert, and so knows how Indians look, knows where they are to be found, and that's not sitting next to him at a white family's dinner table. He knows what Indians are like: savage, stupid, and stoic. He does not expect them to have, for instance, a sense of humor. To borrow Charlie Hill's line, maybe so Indians never thought he was too funny, either. But, we can still find humor in the Hollywood Indian milieu – take the 49 song that Victor improvises in *Smoke Signals* after being intimidated out of his bus seat by a racist hillbilly. Thinking about cowboys and Indians, Victor muses to Thomas about why audiences never get to see John Wayne's teeth, which makes him suspect. Victor is inspired to sing:

> John Wayne's teeth, hey ya
> John Wayne's teeth, hey ya hey ya hey
> Are they false, are they real?
> Are they plastic, are they steel?
> Hey ya hey ya hey.

Like 49 songs, like Indian cars, American Indian film comedies take what little they've got to work with and subversively tear it down, rebuild it, and get it running again. They manage this innovation with the hybridist, energetic artistic impulse that Homi Bhabha (1994: 7) describes as "a sense of the new as an insurgent act of cultural translation," working in always challenging and ever unstable ways. The repeated ambivalent gesture at the ridiculous Indian car points also to the set-up for the joke: the even more ridiculous conditions of Indian poverty. The hysterical ridicule of John Wayne's teeth scoffs, too, at the very unfunny racist images that paid Hollywood's salaries for decades. Indian comedies are telling new Indian stories about communities cohering despite forces that would corrode them – stories with conclusions hopeful rather than foregone. Telling them, they are introducing fully human Indian characters – John Wayne wouldn't recognize them, or get their jokes. But that's exactly what makes him the perfect butt.

References

Aleiss, A. (2005) *Making the White Man's Indian: Native Americans and Hollywood Movies*, Praeger, Westport, CT.

Anderson, E.G. (1998) Driving the red road: *Powwow Highway* (1989), in *Hollywood's Indian: The Portrayal of the Native American in Film* (eds. P. Rollins and J. O'Connor), University Press of Kentucky, Lexington, KY, pp. 137–52.

Bhabha, H.K. (1994) *The Location of Culture*, Routledge, New York, NY.

Buscombe, E. (2006) *'Injuns! Native Americans in the Movies*, Reaktion, Bodmin.

Deloria, P.J. (2006) *Indians in Unexpected Places*, University of Kansas Press, Lawrence, KA.

Gallagher, T. (1986) *John Ford: The Man and His Films*, University of California Press, Berkeley, CA.

Garroutte, E.M. (2003) *Real Indians: Identity and the Survival of Native America*, University of California Press, Berkeley, CA.

Georgakas, D. (1972) They have not spoken: American Indians in film. *Film Quarterly*, 25 (3), 26–32.

Greyeyes, M. (2008) He who dreams: Reflections on an indigenous life in film. *Theatre Research in Canada*, 29 (1), 110–28.

Kasdan, M. and Tavernetti, S. (1998) Native Americans in a revisionist western: *Little Big Man* (1970), in *Hollywood's Indian: The Portrayal of the Native American in Film* (eds. P. Rollins and J. O'Connor), University Press of Kentucky, Lexington, KY, pp. 130–4.

Kilpatrick, J. (1999) *Celluloid Indians: Native Americans and Film*, University of Nebraska Press, Lincoln, NE.

Lincoln, K.R. (1993) *Indi'n Humor*, Oxford University Press, New York, NY.

Marubbio, M. E. (2006) *Killing the Indian Maiden: Images of Native American Women in Film*, University Press of Kentucky, Lexington, LY.

Raheja, M.H. (2010) *Reservation Reelism: Redfacing, Visual Sovereignty, and Representations of Native Americans in Film*, University of Nebraska Press, Lincoln, NE.

Silberman, R. (1985) Gerald Vizenor and "Harold of Orange": from word cinemas to real cinema. *American Indian Quarterly*, 9 (1), 4–21.

Singer, B.R. (2001) *Wiping the War Paint off the Lens*, University of Minnesota Press, Minneapolis, MN.

Valerie Red-Horse (2011) Curriculum Vitae, http://www.valerieredhorse.com/cv.cfm (accessed May 18, 2012).

Velie, A.R. (1992) American Indian literature in the nineties: the emergence of the middle-class protagonist. *World Literature Today*, 66 (2), 264–8.

Wiegman, R. (1998) Race, ethnicity, and film, in *The Oxford Guide to Film Studies* (eds. J. Hill and P. Church Gibson), Oxford University Press, New York, NY, pp. 158–68.

Wood, H. (2008) *Native Features: Indigenous Films from Around the World*, Continuum, New York, NY.

Yagoda, B. (2000) *Will Rogers: A Biography*, University of Oklahoma Press, Norman, OK.

Further Reading

No book-length treatments exclusively on American Indian film comedies exist, and, unfortunately, there aren't many on Native film in general. The good news is that a handful have been recently published and more are in the works.

Kilpatrick, J. (1999), *Celluloid Indians: Native Americans and Film*, University of Nebraska Press, Lincoln, NE. This includes careful analyses of films that substantially contributed to Indian stereotypes, and to a lesser extent, discussion of early Indian films including comedies like *Harold of Orange*, *Smoke Signals*, *Naturally Native*, and *Medicine River*.

Raheja, M.H. (2010) *Reservation Reelism: Redfacing, Visual Sovereignty, and Representations of Native Americans in Film*, University of Nebraska Press, Lincoln, NE. Michelle Raheja carefully analyzes the ambiguities of Indian actors "redfacing" in productions from the silent era up through contemporary, Native-made films that cultivate an Indian visual aesthetic.

Rollins, P. and O'Connor, J. (1998) *Hollywood's Indian: The Portrayal of the Native American in Film*, University Press of Kentucky, Lexington, KY. This contains excellent essays on representations of Indians, including *Little Big Man*, *Powwow Highway*, and *Dances with Wolves*, though it lacks discussion of Indian-made films.

Singer, B.R. (2001) *Wiping the War Paint off the Lens*, University of Minnesota Press, Minneapolis, MN. Beverly Singer looks at oral traditions in visual media as an expression of cultural sovereignty in her short readings of a great many films, including many shorts like *Return of the Country* and *Harold of Orange*. While the treatments are somewhat brief and the attention to comedy is incidental, the material on production background is helpful.

Wood, H. (2008) *Native Features: Indigenous Films from Around the World*, Continuum, New York, NY. Houston Wood's close readings of indigenous films from all over the world includes solid readings of comedic highlights, as well as thoughtful discussion of notables like *The Doe Boy* and *The Business of Fancydancing*.

18

Ethnic Humor in American Film
The Greek Americans

Dan Georgakas

Ethnic humor has always been double edged. To what degree, for example, is laughing at fractured language laughing *with* or laughing *at* the speaker? Is mis-apprehension of some aspect of mainstream American culture a laugh at the newcomer's foibles or mainstream smugness? What gives these concerns value beyond film or humor studies is that most films reflect the prevailing norms of the time. By reproducing them for a mass audience, cinema reinforces those views. Films with ethnic characters, therefore, actually tell us more about American society and its relationship to ethnic cultures than the actualities of any specific ethnic culture.

Scholars can be misled by the images in any single film as those images may simply reflect a special set of circumstance, plot needs, or some personal views of a specific director, producer, scriptwriter, or star. Even a cluster of films is not very decisive as Hollywood is infamous for indulging temporary thematic fads. Genuine cultural patterns only emerge by looking at how they manifest themselves over a very long period in a multitude of films.

A problem that immediately arises in speaking of ethnic films is the very definition of *ethnic* and then the definition of a particular ethnic subgroup. Quite often, the term *ethnic* is applied almost exclusively to groups such as Native Americans, African Americans, Asia Americans, and Hispanic Americans, who are seen as racial minorities or more generically "people of color." There tends to be minimal breakdown within an ethnic category so that woodlands Iroquois culture is equated with corn-growing Pueblo culture.[1] Another ethnic category consists of non-Christian minorities, most often Jews. Subdivisions within religions usually get more play than subdivisions within language/geographical cultures.

A category that is often bypassed or slighted in these considerations is the specific cultures of the millions of Europeans who immigrated to the United States throughout the twentieth century. Further complicating any historical

A Companion to Film Comedy, First Edition. Edited by Andrew Horton and Joanna E. Rapf.
© 2013 John Wiley & Sons, Inc. Published 2016 by John Wiley & Sons, Inc.

analysis is that during the studio era, Hollywood policy was to "disappear" such groups or relegate them to "local color" status in an industry-wide effort to give cinema a Main Street ambiance. The post-studio era has had more Euro-ethnic images, but only marginally so.

The major exception to the slighting of Euro-ethnics is the treatment of Irish Americans. There are literally hundreds of films that deal with every aspect of Irish culture and feature a wide range of persona. This plethora of images far exceeds any European other group and excluding some genres may be greater than all the other European groups combined. The genre exceptions involve gangster and boxing films where the number of ethnic characters, including non-Europeans, is significant. A final exception is independent filmmaking, which often has a significant ethnic component. Independent filmmaking, in this case does not refer to the "boutique" divisions of major studios, but to independently produced films, hereafter referred to as Indies.

When *My Big Fat Greek Wedding* (2002) became a box office smash, in a review in *Cineaste*,[2] I expressed my exasperation about what seemed to be a paucity not simply of films featuring Greek Americans but the general paucity of films about European immigrants to America. To determine if my sense of exclusion was correct I resolved to ascertain exactly how many Hollywood films contained Greek American characters.[3] To give more meaning to the numbers, I decided to rank each film from GGGG to G. This was not a quality rating but an indication of how important the ethnic dimension was to the film.[4]

That the humor patterns found in films about Greek Americans is similar to that of other Euro-ethnic groups, much less non-Euro ethnic groups cannot be assumed. Nonetheless, the humorous treatment of Greek Americans provides a specific case study against which depictions of other ethnic groups can be compared. The differences may be as telling as the similarities.

The Greeks: Language

A decisive marker for immigrant culture is language. Imperfect English usage is inevitable. How that usage is treated in terms of accent, logic, and grammar serves to define the speaker. At one extreme the language may simply acknowledge the speaker is a newcomer, at another, it may imply he or she is a fool. In the 1930s, two Greek American characters, Gus Paryakarkus and The Greek Ambassador of Good Will, both noted for their speech patterns, were comedic fixtures first on radio and then in the movies.

Paryakarkus ("park your carcass" or "sit down") was the creation of Harry Parke[5] and was a recurring character in 11 feature films and at least four two reelers (see Figure 18.1). Paryakarkus made 39 appearances on Al Jolson's radio show without ever quite managing to pronounce Jolson's name correctly, terming him Joly, Jolston, and the like. Paryakarkus went on to even greater

Figure 18.1 Parkyakarkus.

fame with appearances on the Eddie Cantor radio show. Parkyakarkus pulverized English, but he was often taking the meaning of a sentence or idiom literally rather than figuratively. In *Paint Her Pink*, Paryakarkus boasts he can tear a phonebook in half. Cantor says "not likely". Paryakarkus then does as he boasted but by tearing each page individually! In that sense, the laugh might be on the English-language speaker. Parkyakarkus frequently expressed frustration at American usage, suggesting his interpretations were more logical than his supposed linguistic betters.

Although Paryakarkus was obviously the typical American greenhorn, he was sometimes shown as quite assimilated to American culture and society. In *A Yank in Libya* (1943), for example, Parkyakarkus is inexplicably masquerading as an Arab and utters Parkyakarkusims in an outdoor bazaar. When a lost American asks for help, Parkyakarkus reveals he is also an American and instructs his countryman on how to deal with Arabs. The lost American is quite relieved and treats Paryakarkus as one of "us" rather than as an Other.

The Greek Ambassador of Goodwill created by George Givot moved from vaudeville to the Jimmy Durante radio show. Given that Durante drew many laughs for his own mispronunciations and misuse of English, the Greek Ambassador was on the same linguistic ground as the star of the show. Although he often introduced himself as "Me, Greek," the Greek Ambassador was fond of highly rhetorical language and often ended with his punch line, "How d'ya like that?"

One of the often cited pseudo-profundities originating from the Greek Ambassador was "Those who go to college and never get out are called professors. How d'ya like that?" The Greek Ambassador appeared in feature films, two reelers, and comic phonograph records. Unlike Harry Parke who became so identified with the Parkyakarkus identity that he even tried to make it his legal name, Givot subsequently played a wide variety of ethnic and non-ethnic characters, comedic and dramatic, in thirty motion pictures and then various television shows.

The one time Parke and Givot appeared in the same film was in *Roast Beef and the Movies* (1934), a short comedy featuring Jews who played various ethnicities. Neither their Jewish identity nor their comic language alienated Greek Americans. Their brand of slapstick humor, in fact, was standard in Greek language films of the time and continues to be a staple of Greek humor to the present day. In the 1930s, the incredibly prolific Greek American producer Tetos Demetriades issued comedy records that mocked the pompous language of the Greek elites, particularly politicians, in a manner similar to that of the Greek Ambassador of Goodwill. Demetriades was the legendary producer of bouzouki music that he recorded in trips to the Near East where he often recorded music that was out of favor with a political regime due to its drug references and/or the use of a non-national language. Demetriades also produced the first two Greek language films ever made: *I Grothia de Sakati* (1930) and *Afti Eine I Zoi* (1931). Both melodramas were shot and edited in New York City. More generally, the Greek sense of humor found in the comedy records issued by Demetriades was shared by many immigrant groups, as can be seen by visiting the large room in the Ellis Island Historical Museum. There is an entire wall displaying records and cartoons in the Parke-Givot mode. These were created in the native languages of various immigrant groups living in the United States for sale to immigrants.

The name Parkyakarkus is cute rather than offensive. Such cannot be said of the use of Poupi Kakas as the name for the male romantic lead in *My Life in Ruins* (2009). In case the audience did not grasp the scatological nature of the name, a wisecracking American tourist (Richard Dreyfuss) milks it for laughs for a bus-load of fellow English-speaking tourists. What is puzzling here is that producer Rita Wilson strongly indentifies with her Greek heritage as does Nia Vardalos, for whom the script was created in hopes of repeating the fabulous success of *My Big Fat Greek Wedding*. Later the bus driver who bears the name and has a nephew who bears a variation of kaka shaves his ugly beard and emerges as a handsome poet who will help the uptight Georgia (Nia Vardalos), a Greek American, find her "Greek soul." The best that can be said for this nomenclature is that perhaps it was possible to have such witless and tasteless naming due to the fact that, by 2010, Greek Americans had developed such a positive image in American society that the name could be seen as harmless ribbing. Greek Americans and Greeks in Greece, however, were not amused. Nor was the general public. The humor throughout the film was generally seen as witless as the name bit. *My Life in Ruins* was a huge bomb and a top contender for Worse Film of the Year lists.

A Greek name gets a humorous treatment with political bite in *Charlie Wilson's War* (2007). One of the main characters is CIA maverick Gust Avrakotos (Philip Seymour Hoffman). Although not much is made of his Greek ethnicity, Avrakotos makes a point of emphasizing the "t" at the end of his first name. Congressman Charlie Wilson struggles until he gets the name right, but a know-nothing colleague is indifferent to repeated corrections. The script slyly suggests this linguistic indifference parallels the character's repeated confusion of Pakistan for Afghanistan. For him, it would seem all foreign names more or less sound alike, and it doesn't make any difference if anyone is offended.

Name changes are often cited by theorists as a cultural defeat for the immigrant, a denial or loss of identity. Quite often, however, real life plays a different hand, a situation that is handled with genuine grins and smiles in the final scenes of *America, America* (1963). Stavros Topouzoglou (Stathis Giallelis), the film's main protagonist has finally managed to enter the United States by assuming the name of an Armenian named Hohannes, who has committed suicide. When Stavros gives his assumed name to the immigration officer at the final point of entry, the official genially suggests that he will do better in the United States if he Americanizes his name. "Arness" he suggests, "Joe Arness." Rather than being angry, Stravros is delighted with his new name. He tilts his new straw hat at a jaunty angle and repeats with great bravura, "Joe Arness." This image is a striking contrast with the scenes at the onset of his journey, when a dour, formally dressed Stavros Topouzoglou, wearing a traditional fez, stands with folded arms aboard a flimsy raft ferry in the badlands of Anatolia. The hat, the name, the folded arms, the expression, and the clothing represent the old world of ethnic cultural oppression and political subjugation characteristic of Ottoman society. In the Ellis Island scene, the new name is liberating, a joyous creation of a new personality displaying a new modern hat and a new facial expression as he enters a new and better life that he has freely chosen.

When the Greek language is used in films, it almost always serves a humorous purpose. Quite typical is the comedy bit in *My Big Fat Greek Wedding* in which the American suitor of a Greek American asks her brother to coach him on how to give a dignified formal greeting to her parents. The brother obliges by teaching him to solemnly declare in Greek, "I have three testicles." In a number of gangster films, when the Greeks speak in Greek to non-Greeks, they usually are making insulting remarks that are translated as pleasantries. Far more positive is a scene in *Fifteen Minutes* (2001) which stars Robert De Niro as an ace New York police detective. We chuckle as we listen to De Niro constantly practicing how to properly pronounce "Sa agapo" ("I love you") to television reporter Nicollete Karas (Milena Karakaredes).

What is usually absent from Hollywood fare is a genuine Greek American accent or the use of Gringlish. Greeks do not have an obvious linguistic marker, such as the Germanic *V* sound for *W* or the difficulty that Chinese have with double *L*, which make for many movie yuks. Nonetheless, there is a distinctive

Greek American accent, but it is usually only heard when the actor happens to be a Greek immigrant and there usually is no comic punch. The most apparent aspect of Gringlish[6] to non-Greek speaking is that it often features adding a vowel to an English noun, creating entities such as *caki*, *caro*, *blankita*, *frigidara*, and *blocko*. Greeks themselves find Gringlish amusing. A top Greek-language hit song of the 1930s was titled *To Sigaretto* (The Cigarette). Gringlish, however, is rarely heard in films, mainly because it was confined primarily to early immigrants and so few Hollywood script writers have Greek heritage. What usually passes as Greek immigrant usage is Hollywood Immigrant Speak, a tongue that bears little relation to the native language of the speakers. That brand of fabricated pidgin, for example, is used by Edgar G. Robinson who plays Nick Venizelos, a Greek barber-gambler in *Smart Money* (1931). The name is significant in that Venizelos was the Greek Prime Minister (1910–1920, 1928–1932) best known in the West and highly respected for this wit and intelligence.

Comic Persona

Spike Lee has observed that The Three Stooges are funny, but they would not be if The Three Stooges were the sole image of white people in American film.[7] That's a good standard for looking at buffoon images with ethnic content. Are they chronic, transitory, or particular to a specific film? In the case of the Greeks, Parkyakarkus might be seen as a buffoon, but he usually holds his own linguistically and even bests those with whom he speaks. A stronger candidate for buffoonery is Joe Skopapoulos, the Wrestling Hercules (Ned Pendelton), a central character in *Swing Your Lady* (1938).

Swing Your Lady opens with the Wrestling Hercules looking for bouts in the Ozarks. The car in which he and his manager, Ed Hatch (Humphrey Bogart) are riding gets stuck in the mud. They are pulled free by Sadie Horn (Louise Fazenda), the local Amazon who is the town's blacksmith. Hatch thinks a sure moneymaker would be a bout between Hercules and Sadie. The comedic plot takes a romantic turn when Hercules falls in love with Sadie and then finds himself in competition with a local strong man. Adapted from a Broadway play, the film also features."country" tunes such as "Mountain Swingeroo," "Hillbilly From Tenth Avenue," and "Dig Me a Grave in Missouri." *Swing Your Lady* ends happily for Joe. In a brief epilogue, we see he has wed Sadie, become the town's new blacksmith, and fathered a happy family. By equating immigrants and the people of the Ozarks, the Greek immigrant is made the equal of one strain of quintessential native-born American. On the other hand, Joe Skopapoulos is a slow-witted muscle man who becomes part of a society that is routinely mocked in American film. Humphrey Bogart expressed great regret at being in this film and director Raoul Walsh teased Bogart about his role by placing a billboard poster for

Swing Your Lady into a highway scene in *High Sierra*. Ronald Reagan appears very briefly as a sportscaster. None of *Swing's* songs made the Top 1000 Music charts.[8]

The polar opposite of the buffoon is the suave cosmopolitan. No less a gallant than Cary Grant plays Joe Bascopoulos in *Mister Lucky* (1943). Joe is yet another Greek gambler and in this instance, he is also a draft dodger intent on swindling wealthy socialite Dorothy Bryant (Laraine Day) with a phony charity scheme. Grant makes no effort to Hellenize his character so the winning Grant personality just becomes Greek Grant for this particular film. Joe begins to change when he finds himself falling in love with Dorothy. The critical transformation in his character, however, occurs when he receives a letter written by his mother in Occupied Greece. He takes it to a Greek Orthodox priest for translation and learns of the horrors the Nazis have brought to Greece. Joe becomes a Hollywood good guy and a patriotic American by eschewing the swindle, declaring his love for Dorothy, and signing up to serve in the merchant marine which means service in the perilous waters of the North Atlantic where German submarines stalked all convoys.

A less recognized Greek cosmopolitan is Nick Charles of The Thin Man series. In the novels by Dashiell Hammett, the Greekness of Charles is well established. Not so in the films. The only Greek marker is Nick's Anglicized Greek last name. The first of The Thin Man films was released in 1934. In short, from the early 1930s and to the early 1940s, there is already a diversity of comic images including a very clever Nick Venizelos in 1931, the slow-witted Wrestling Hercules of 1938, an irate, ice-cream vendor in *My Lucky Star* (1938), and a sophisticated Greek Grant of 1943.

Later Greek American comedic characters added even more diversity. In *A Dream of Kings* (1969) Anthony Quinn plays Leonidas Matsoukas, an American Zorba who is a family man but survives through gambling and an unconventional consulting agency billed as the Pendar Counseling Service. As a counselor, he offers sexual advice to an older Greek man fearful he cannot sexually satisfy a much younger woman. Quinn successfully calms his client's fears with a strong dose of sexist language and chauvinist assumptions. His later attempts in the same mode to seduce a female Greek baker played by an ill-cast Inger Stevens is meant to be charming but will strike most viewers as laughable, if not offensive. Matsoukas is far more surprising and winning when a mother brings him her son whom she has found masturbating. Rather than traditional warnings replete with notions of sin and the medical consequences of "self-abuse," Matsoukas takes the boy on the roof for a man-to-man chat under the stars. He genially explains masturbation is a common and natural practice, but it is best his mother not know the nature of his counsel. Upon returning to the office where the mother waits, the lad solemnly concedes he will do nothing that is not natural.

In *Only the Lonely* (1991), a comic vehicle for John Candy, Quinn returns as Nick Acropolis an aging Greek bachelor living in Los Angeles, a kind of retired Zorba. His next door neighbor Rose Muldoon, a role written specifically to lure an aging Maureen O'Hara out of retirement, is filled with Irish-style xenophobia that she freely expresses with great gusto and vulgarity. Her ethnic chauvinism often makes life difficult for her gentle policeman son, Danny Muldoon (John Candy). The salty Maureen minces no words when John becomes involved with Theresa Luna (Ally Seedy) who is of mixed Polish and Sicilian ancestry and works in her father's funeral parlor. Nick tries to intercede on behalf of John, but mainly he wants to bed Rose. When she tells him she doesn't date Greeks and that Greek don't bathe, a clear reference to the "dirty Greek" canard, Nick refuses to take offense and informs Rose she will not be happy until she is sexually liberated. That, he informs her, will also free her from the racism that mars her life and is not reflective of her true nature. The film is filled with a host of ethnic jokes and insults and ends in a huge climatic comedic debacle involving a smorgasbord of ethnicities. This cinematic situation comedy, of course, must end happily. Indeed, John marries Theresa, and Rose, beginning to shed her racism, literally flies off in the company of Nick Acropolis.

Less laudable humorous treatment of Greek male chauvinism is found in *The Tempest* (1982). Philip Dimitrius (John Cassavetes), a prominent New York architect, turns to his father, with whom he has been estranged to discuss the crisis in his marriage. They meet in a Greek pastry/coffee shop in Astoria, a section in New York's borough of Queens that has a large Greek American community and is considered the "most Greek" of any neighborhood in the United States. Philip's father is sympathetic to his son's problems and is dismissive of women. Their conversation is cut short by a Greek waiter who assures them that women needed to be battered a bit from time to time. Neither Cassavetes nor his father take issue with or are upset by the waiter's intervention. Later, they casually cross the street to make some bets at an Off Track Betting parlor. Whether director Paul Mazursky and scripter Leon Capetanos meant the moment to be funny or pathetic, they take it for granted that spousal abuse is acceptable even to Greek American males of the upper middle-class who can joke about it matter-of-factly.

Far more sophisticated sexual humor is found in the Indie *Everything For a Reason* (2000), which takes place on the Jersey shore. Twenty-something Manny Papadopoulos (Dominica Comperatore), a second-generation Greek American and his black friend go bar hopping. When they find two women obviously distressed by the attention of some unruly men, they intervene, much to the women's relief. Manny is immediately attracted to Eva (Erin Neill), one of the two women. Manny is surprised to learn that the last name of the woman to whom he is attracted is Stephanopoulos. Eva, in turn, is equally surprised that Manny is Greek. Manny opines that all the Greek women he knows are usually light-headed, whale-like creatures; Eva responds that all the Greek men she meets are spoiled mamma's boys with more pride than brains. The first date which evolves after the usual does-he(she)-really-like me angst is filled with comic mishaps such as gum in the hair, belching, and inadvertent bodily slaps. Eva doesn't want to have sex before marriage and respects Manny for not pressing her, not knowing, at first, that Manny is far more interested in finishing his film script than finding love, but he doesn't want to be dateless on weekends. Both Manny's brother and Eve's sister, in contrast, are sexually active in a dating scene that includes various sometimes predictable comedy complications such as a groom who discovers he is gay, lovers taking elaborate measure to hide their trysts with others, and a man who thinks no sex act is complete without a sharp slap on a woman's derriere. Ultimately, Manny discovers he is more interested in winning Eva's hand than winning cinema fame; and the couple emerges as the only one in their crowd to survive all the sexual shenanigans to actually find happiness. As in *Swing Your Lady* and *Only the Lonely*, the Greek wins a very strong-willed woman, who in this instance is also Greek. An extra plus of the film is that the handful of scenes with Manny's mother are right on target. She has totally adapted to American life yet retains aspects of Greek culture such as lighting candles at the family's ikon to obtain celestial marital assistance for Manny. And of course she is a good cook whose pastries allow for additional ethnic humor.

A Perfect Couple (1979), set in California rather than New Jersey, has quite a different comic resonance than *Everything For A Reason*. Alex Theodopoulos (Paul Dooley) meets Marta Heflin (Sheila Shea) through a computer dating service. Alex is from a very traditional and wealthy Greek family in the antiques trade. Marta is a singer in a boisterous rock group and lives in a communal loft. Their first date is a rain-soaked fiasco that is followed by a series of comic mishaps and misunderstandings. At one point when the couple manages to have sex in Alex's bedroom, they are discovered by the entire Theodopoulos clan headed by a stern father (Titos Vadis) and an even sterner sister (Dimitra Arylis). Alex eventually leaves his family circle to go on the road with Marta, but the sex and drug atmospherics of her social world do not work for him. Just as Alex has to break with his patriarchic family, Marta realizes that to be happy she will need to break with her charismatic band/commune leader. They each finally manage to sever their patriarchic bonds, and the apparently unlikely lovers are revealed to be a "perfect couple," just as Robert Altman has signaled in his title.

Like the indie *Everything for a Reason*, the Indies *Do You Wanna Dance?* (1997) and *It Could be Worse* (Zach Stratis 2000) score high on authenticity and offer ethnic humor of a kind not common in mainstream Hollywood cinema. *Do You Wanna Dance?* is the first film to feature a Greek Orthodox priest who is not a distant figure with a long beard, knotted John-the-Baptist hair, stove pipe hat, and black robes. Father Chris (Robert Constanzo) comes in modern garb and a modernist demeanor that could easily pass as Unitarian. Father Chris works with a Chicago governmental agency that allows first-time youth offenders to do public service rather than jail time. Father Chris takes in Billy Duncan (Robert Krantz) to perform public serve, Billy, who stole a car for a joy ride, is a professional dancer. When Billy learns that Father Chis wants him to run a dance class, he protests that he doesn't know anything about Greek dancing, Father Chris kindly informs him that he doesn't need an Irishman to teach Greek dancing to Greeks; his seniors want to learn to rumba and tango! The Greek elders quickly win over Billy with their good spirits. Additional plot spice evolves as Billy becomes romantically attracted to Alexia (Patricia Keriotis), a beautiful and modern woman plagued by parents who insist on an arranged marriage with Mr. Halikas (William Zane), a person to whom she is not attracted. Billy manages to stage some comedic musical mishaps to thwart the romance. We also learn that Father Chris is a Chicago Cubs groupie and sometimes cuts short the liturgy to get to a game on time. One of his altar boys happens to be an African American, a circumstance never given any exposition. Rather than a comedic Hellenic waterfall, *Do You Wanna Dance?* offers substantial character development and social commentary in a humorous format. If Alexia's parents are predictable ethnic types, the Greek seniors are not. Father Chris in turn, is not an Americanized Oriental cleric but a jovial guy who could hang out in the local diner as comfortably as he performs rituals at an Orthodox altar. Krantz (nee: Harlambos Karountas) directs as well as starring as Billy. The film's Father Chris is based on Father Chris Kerhulas, who led a parish in Chicago. The black choir boy in the film is played by the son of one of the few African Americans who worship at the real Father Chris Greek Orthodox church.

It Could Be Worse is a virtual home movie written, directed, and cast by Zach Stratis. In a film being made within the film, a Greek American is "coming out" as gay to his family. In the course of the fictional action, however, the real filmmaker decides to use the fictional filmmaker and his now fictional/real film "to come out" to his real family, who happen to be playing the fictional family. Adding to the humor is that the family's singing and dancing is in that delicious realm of being good by virtue of their being so bad. Given the way the film is scripted and shot, however, we are always laughing with them. The film's ironic title is the jocular way Zach presents his sexual orientation to all concerned. *It Could be Worse* is an entertaining tongue-in-cheek riposte to the supposed universal denial or rejection of gay members by ethnic families. Their acceptance of the homosexual son/brother does not come readily or without some regret, and the film takes on other sexual issues with candor, but the atmosphere always remains one of carnival, not angst.

The over-the-top Greek personality most notably portrayed by Anthony Quinn and Harry Parkes finds slightly more muted expression even in dramatic films. A notable example is Nick Dennis' character in the film noir classic *Kiss Me Deadly* (1955). Dennis is Mickey Spillane's only pal, and he always greets the private eye with a resounding "Va-va voom!" This is a reference to the time he disabled a bomb placed in Mickey's car and also portends the film's legendary explosive ending. When the effervescent Dennis is murdered by thugs, an enraged Spillane embarks on a murderous revenge quest. Exuberant as Dennis may be, he is definitely not a buffoon, but a jovial sidekick to the very American Mickey Spillane.

Nick Dennis is also involved in what may be an ethnic in-joke in the film version of *A Streetcar Named Desire* (1951). Dennis plays Pablo Hernandez, one of Stanley Kowalski's poker buddies. In a brief sequence in which Blanche DuBois and Stella walk past him, Dennis appreciatively notes that they are a pair of pretty birds. But he speaks in Greek, not Spanish or English. The scene does not occur in the stage production where Dennis originated the role. There are two credible explanations for this inappropriate use of Greek. Dennis may have become so immersed in Stanislavskyian identification with his character that he spoke Greek inadvertently. More likely, he spoke in Greek to amuse Kazan. What is inexplicable is why Kazan did not edit out the Greek. Perhaps Kazan was mocking the linguistic shortcomings of both the popular and artistic audience. To my knowledge, no Kazan critic has commented on this inappropriate linguistic moment. On the other hand, Stratos Constantinidis and other Greeks have commented on it. Some, knowing that Dennis was Greek sometimes, assumed his character also was Greek.

It's Greek to Me

Certain sequences in films contain humorous incidents specifically linked to Greek cultural traits, real and assumed. At polar opposites in respect for Greek culture are *Side Street* (1950) a Hollywood B-noir and *Dark Odyssey* (1957), perhaps the best of the Greek American Indie productions. In *Side Street*, when the chief detective is informed that an autopsy shows a murdered woman had eaten okra, egg plant, and lamb kabob dressed with olive oil on the night of her death, he disgustedly comments, "Only Greeks and Syrians eat that junk!" Such a comment would never occur in the age of the Mediterranean diet, but at the onset of the 1950s it was thought to be worth a knowing yuk. The derisive "greasy Greek" epithet is only a breath away. In a follow-up scene at the Les Artistes Restaurant, the owner and his waiter chat in Greek and when asked if he remembers the victim, the waiter explains, "Of course, her date left a small tip." The same American working-class audience that probably agreed with the food comment can easily identify with the waiter on the matter of tips, so the Greeks are again kept from being totally exotic.

Dark Odyssey features Yannis Martakis (Athan Karras), a Cretan who has come to America to avenge the sexual molestation of his sister. The story gets complicated when Martakis falls in love with Niki Vassos (Jeanne Jerrems), a second-generation Greek American. Martakis has to decide whether to continue with the vendetta rituals of the old world or take on the life and values of the new. Niki's mother is thrilled with the idea of her daughter being attracted by and attractive to a Greek. There is a lovely scene about treating Martakis to cognac that has comic aspects. Later, when the mother has to deal with the American suitor of her other daughter, cognac again serves as a metaphor – this time for disapproval. The father of the family is quite congenial and makes numerous humorous remarks about having his life ruled by the needs of Greek woman, but they are kindly and appreciative remarks rather than disdainful. Martakis also gets into a tussle with the American suitor of Niki's sister due to Martakis not understanding American mores. Other sequences involving subtle humor of various kinds mark a film that has become a favorite among Greek American audiences. The accents, costuming, and grammar are authentically Greek and the film is mainly shot on location.

In a Sonje Heine vehicle titled *My Lucky Star*, a Greek ice cream peddler fearlessly denounces Heine for not buying his ice cream, First, its pistachios are from his home island in Greece, making them the best possible, and secondly, stingy people like her just perpetuate the economic ills of America. One can read the scene as an immigrant still overly attached to his homeland and at sea about how to peddle his wares in America to a well-assimilated Norwegian immigrant.[9] An alternative reading is that the immigrant is so confident of his American status that he is not ashamed to wed it to his ethnic roots. Moreover, it is the Great Depression which gives his outburst a different flavor than it might in have in a different decade.

A scene perfectly suited to its plot and not meant to be comical at the time may strike contemporary viewers as humorous. In *Tribute To A Bad Man* (1956), Irene Papas plays a Greek immigrant woman in a rough-and-tumble 1870s' Colorado. At a certain point, she sings a Greek love song to none other than Jimmy Cagney. Not exactly a Home on the Range moment, but definitely not a moment meant to distance the two principals from the viewing audience.

Various Greek foods often figure in films. Apparently all Greek American gangsters are genetically programmed to be aficionadas of Greek coffee. Invariably, an American guest is informed this is real coffee and on occasion there is the stern warning not to call it Turkish coffee. Less charming is a moment in *Bullethead* (2000) in which a Greek criminal explains he will slice a man as neatly he slices his feta cheese. In *Shelter* (1997), a Greek thug celebrates the murder of a fellow gangster with a few steps of Greek dancing. Most references to Greek culinary markers are far more benign, dealing with sticky fingers from pastries and hangovers from drinking ouzo.

In a category of its own is Elia Kazan's casting of Arthur Miller in *Boomerang* (1947). Perhaps Kazan is ribbing his audience by casting the already respected play-wright about to become nationally renowned with the stage production of *All My Sons* as a vagabond brought into a police lineup to identity the killer of a priest. In the same film, Kazan casts his uncle (listed as Joe Kazin in some credits), the model for the main character in *America, America*, as Paul Lukash, a man of Eastern European descent, perhaps a sly comment about how all European accents sound more-or-less alike to mainstream American ears. Of course, both choices could be no more than the usual chum casting in minor roles often associated with filmmaking.

Traditional Greek music and bouzouki are frequently used to establish Greek identity or nuance. This generally is done with some respect but with the underlying idea of "Oh those Greeks dance like crazy and loved to break dishes." In fact, historically, Greeks did not break dishes when they danced. That was a fashion begun in the bouzouki clubs of the ports of Greece following the Greek expulsion from Asia Minor in 1922. The dancers wanted to show their contempt for bourgeois society, not their joyful spirits. Most Americans became acquainted with dish-breaking through *Never On Sunday* (1960).[10] The film's fabulous success established bouzouki music and glass breaking as talismen of Greek identity. When non-Greeks are introduced to Greek American society they invariably end up having to learn to dance Greek. Dance serves as a double ethnic marker in *The Deep End of the Ocean* (1998). An Italian boy who has been kidnapped but then raised by a Greek unaware of the boy's true status finally is reunited with his biological family. When asked if he knows how to folk dance, he says of course. The family expects him to do an Italian *tarantella*, the boy performs a Greek *tsamiko*.

Greek music, booze, and a traditional Orthodox priest even show up in Korea. In *The Glory Brigade* (1953), an American unit led by a Greek American has to go into a risky behind-the-battle-lines action with a brigade from Greece. Before the shooting begins, Hollywood manages to provide the Greek brigade with full ethnic attire. The Americans get to drink Greek booze and then watch their new comrades dancing Greek-style, with all the sound that involves, and then receive a formal blessing with a Greek priest in traditional garb. Although Victor Mature who plays the Greek American brigade leader expresses great pride in being of Greek heritage, he is so well assimilated to American culture, that his superior officers do not know he is Greek. In one of the earliest scenes, when Mature is asked if he knows any Greeks, he replies "Well, there's my father."

My Big Fat Greek Wedding

Hovering over any discussion of Greek humor in American film is the sensationally successful *My Big Fat Greek Wedding* (2002). Although often referred to as an independent production, *My Big Fat Greek Wedding* was a not an Indie but the product of Hollywood-based production company working on a substantial $5000 budget and featuring a number of well-known Hollywood and television faces. In addition to its domestic audience, the film found a large audience in Greece and abroad. Rather than opening a new door on ethnic humor or even commenting on the Greek America of its era, however, *My Big Fat Greek Wedding* is more of a reprise or encore of a century of generic ethnic humor. In this respect, the film's true progenitors are not other films so much as classic ethnic radio programs such as Duffy's *Tavern*, *The Life of Riley*, Abbie's *Irish Rose*, *Life with Luigi*, and the *Molly Goldberg* show. Amos and Andy might be included in that group as well.[11] Some of these radio hits had subsequent television incarnations. Among sit-coms originating on television, the closest to the characterizations in *My Big Fat Greek Wedding* might be the very ethnic Uncle Tanoose (Lebanese) of *The Danny Thomas Show*. Also relevant is *I Love Lucy* where the casting of Desi Arnaz and his Cuban accent and culture as Lucy's husband was originally opposed by network executives as too culturally provocative. They wrongly believed that Americans were not ready to "see a Cuban in their living room."

The visual grammar of *My Big Greek Wedding* is a lexicon of ethnic predictability: a culturally conflicted father, an earth mother, a daffy aunt, an obedient younger sister, an irreverent brother, a demented grandmother, an American Prince Charming, and a 30-something gal badly in need of a makeover and a sex life. What appears to be a series of cultural conflicts between the old world and the new world and between mainstream America and Greek America mask what is ultimately a very familiar and comforting celebration of cultural assimilation.

Descendents of the immigrants of the Great Migration of 1880–1924 can easily identify with the humor of *My Big Fat Greek Wedding* as a genial homage to the memories of their parents. For contemporary immigrants, there is the pleasure of seeing their problematic language and marital woes as long-established immigrant patterns in America.

The film was generated by the real life experiences of writer/star Nia Vardalos and producer Rita Wilson. Vardalos was born and raised in Winnipeg, Canada. Later she moved to Chicago where she performed in comedy clubs. Her signature piece became a routine in which her father becomes apoplectic over her desire to marry a non-Greek. Vardalos eventually moved to comedy clubs in Los Angeles. Like many California-bound artists, she came complete with a screenplay based on her routine.

Rita Wilson, who is of Greek ancestry and speaks Greek fluently, saw Varadalos performing at a comedy club. She immediately identified with the situation, especially the baptism of a non-Greek Orthodox groom. She had lived the scenario with the conversion of husband Tom Hanks to Greek Orthodoxy. Wilson had recently started her own production company and the Vardalos script seemed a perfect starting vehicle. Worth noting is that the Vardalos-Hanks relationship is closer to what is seen on the screen than the events in Vardalos' real life. Vardalos' non-Greek groom was of Puerto Rican heritage, a heritage slightly different from that associated with a decidedly White Anglo-Saxon Protestant groom.

The film centers on Toula Portokalos (Nia Vardalos), a young woman first seen decked in very frumpy clothes, wearing awful glasses, and looking overweight. Her father, Gus Portokalos (Michael Constantine) is concerned she is going to become an "old maid" and not find the happiness of his younger daughter Athena (Stavroula Logothettis) who has married a Greek and is raising a family. Rather effortlessly Toula quickly transforms herself into an attractive young woman, leaves her job at Dancing Zorba's (the family restaurant), takes college classes, and falls in love with Ian Miller (John Corbett), a handsome high school teacher. In terms of authenticity, the Greeks of 2002 bear little resemblance to this social portrait. Greek American women, in fact, are notorious consciously of fashion, are quite aware of the Greeks who had emerged as gurus of high fashion Greek American publications have celebrated the achievements of women such as Patricia Field (Nominated for *The Devil Wore Prada* 2006) and Emmy winner for *Sex and the City* (2000); Mary Zophres, nominated for *True Grit* (2011), and the legendry Theoni Aldredge Oscar winner for *The Great Gatsby* (1974) and winner or nominee for a score of Tony and Drama Desk Awards Greek American women also are among the highest percentage of ethnic women holding college degrees.

To be sure there are still Greek fathers like Gus Portokalos who are intent are using any and all means to have their daughter marry a Greek. Also abstractly, Greeks often opine that like marrying like has the best option for happiness. The reality, however, is that the outmarriage rate for Greek women is at least 80 percent and has been so for decades. Given that outmarriage is an ethnic norm, Gus is at least 30 years out of date.[12] More typical is Gus's pride in the Greek language. He consistently explains why one or another English word has origins in Greek. He explains, for example, that *kimono*, a word that everyone thinks is a Japanese import, actually stems from *himona* (he-mo-na), the Greek word for winter. Absurd, to be sure, but somewhat charming and something of a break from most of the film's unimaginative stereotypes. Gus also states that his last name is rooted in the Greek word for orange and Miller stems from apples. That, he explains to the elder Millers. means that the union of their families is a matter of mixing apples and oranges, ingredients that are decidedly different but make a delicious salad. Although the salad metaphor is often used by sociologists to replace the idea of a melting pot, unique to the film is Gus' belief that Windex glass cleaner has medicinal powers. This seemingly inane notion could be linked to a bluish alcoholic liquid used in Greece. That connection, however, is not made in the film. Thus, using Windex to treat cuts and skin irritations becomes an absurdist standing gag that strives for a final chuckle when Ian declares he's used the spray as directed and his new father-in-law is right: it was curative.

My Big Fat Greek Wedding offers such a complete and confident closure to an era of ethnic humor that it brazenly incorporates a parody of WASPs. The non-Greek elders do not become "barbarians" in the traditional Greek terminology, but they are reduced to semi-buffoonery. They drink too much of that ouzo stuff, which looks like water and tastes like licorice. There are gags about Bundt cake compared to Greek pastries. If Gus seems loveably daffy in matters of culture, the WASPs are mainly multiculturally clueless. Rather than immigrants assimilating to WASP traditions, the WASPs assimilate to Greek traditions. Ian gets a full baptismal immersion from a priest who does not look like or behave like Father Chris of *Do You Wanna Dance*. On the wedding day, the bridesmaid's dresses are hideous and Toula gets a zit on her lip, a kind of reprise of *Father of the Bride* in ethnic drag.

Curtain Calls

The most unexpected finding in this chronicle of comedy films with Greek American characters is that the tone is overwhelming one of acceptance and assimilation rather than hostility and rejection. Moreover, this trend begins with the onset of talking pictures and not as an aftermath of the Civil Rights Movement of the 1950s. Whether assimilation is contrary to multiculturalism and whether that is desirable or is debatable. What is not debatable is that European immigrants wanted to have equal status with native-born Americans. The film images of the 1930s indicate this was happening much earlier than often assumed, at least for Greek immigrants. The early images of assimilated or assimilating Greek are strikingly different than the Hollywood images rendered of African Americans, Hispanics, and Asians, particularly in the first 30 years of the talkies.

Even comic nicknames for Greeks eventually take on an equalitarian aspect. In *Man from Diner's Club* (1963), for one, Telly Savalas is a Greek gangster who is called "Teddy Two Legs," because each of his legs is a different size. This physical oddity is shared with Danny Kaye, the film's star, and is a key plot element. In short, the immigrant and the native-born American are now even physically equal (or unequal) in the same manner. Names usually have a distinctly honorable Classic past such as Nick Acropolis – or long last names, such as Skopapoulos, Bascopoulos, Matsoukas, Papadopoulos, and Stephanopoulos, come with a comforting first name such as Joe, Gregory, Manny, and Eva.

Another strong sign of early and continued cultural acceptance is that in almost all of the comedies, the Greek guy gets the non-Greek gal in the final reel. This begins as early as 1931 and continues unabated through to the twenty-first century. Nor are there any films in which the Greek suitor is a sweet but dull Ralph Bellamy-like character who steps aside for a better man as in the typical screwball comedy.

Even more than other film genres, comedies generally use ethnic culture as colorful costuming and wallpaper rather than treating it as inscrutable Otherness or as a respectable alternative, much less an enhancement of American culture. Breaking glasses, drinking Greek coffee, and listening to bouzouki music are just window dressing. Even the Greek-Must-Marry-Greek imperative is reduced to a plot gimmick that is resolved cordially with acceptance by the parents of a non-Greek spouse. None of the Greeks or Americans declare "If you marry that not-us, you no longer exist." Greek language usage is related to cheap word gags, mobster chit-chat, bad grammar, and family bantering rather than as a language that since World War II has produced two Noble Laureates in literature: Giorgos Seferis (1963) and Odysseus Elytis (1979). This preference for Ethnic Culture Lite is just another aspect of the assimilationist assumption that immigrants and their immediate offspring are more like than unlike the native-born. The most frequent manifestation of this view is the Greek diner, which is found in well over a third of all films with Greek American characters. The diner is not a menacing members-only club as in Italian mob movies. Nor is it part of a formidable Chinatown syndrome or a quaint ethnic-cooking site. Instead, the diner is usually a working class hangout where "real" Americans linger. This reaches absurdist heights in *Fletch Lives* (1989) where Chevy Chase, an amateur sleuth disguises himself as a waitress to work in a Greek diner. His moniker is affably bicultural: Peggy Lee Zorba.

Comedy films also do not lock Greek American images into a single class or culture, but offer a generous range of occupations that roughly parallel the shift of the majority of Greek Americans from unskilled working-class workers and peddlers to middle-class professionals with a large dollop of millionaires. Rather than the Stepin Fetchit and "Sleep 'n' Eat"[13] characters that righty affront African Americans, even Greek fools are part of a larger assortment of images and often have some saving grace. Perhaps it is also significant than well-known Hollywood actors showed no reluctance to play Greek Americans. In addition to those already named, their number also includes Gene Kelley, Al Pacino, Dane Clark, Richard Conte, and Jay Leno. Actors of Greek ancestry, in turn, are not limited to portraying Greeks, but often play Italians, Hispanics, and mainstream Americans.

Certainly characters like Parkyakarkus are buffoons, but something that occurs in films about Greek Americans may be different than what happens in most other ethnic films. In *16 Fathoms Deep* (1948), a tale of Greek sponge divers, the buffoon is an American, not a Greek. In this case the buffoon is Arthur Lake, famed for his Dagwood Bumstead roles. The Greek sponge divers are the norm who tolerate the outlandish and rather silly outsider. Lake, for instance, tries a hand at cooking and sponge diving, which the amused Greeks tolerate with the sense of "he means well." During a crucial scene at the sponge exchange, the Greek auctioneer has to indicate the action Lake needs to take five times before Lake understands what he has to do to keep an ill-timed auction from taking place. As already noted, in *My Big Fat Greek Wedding*, it is the Millers who are buffoonish.

What becomes apparent when considering all of the above is the virtual absent of comedic roles for women of actual or fictional Greek ethnicity. Before *My Big Fat Greek Wedding* and *My Life in Ruins*, no Greek American females are found at the center of film comedies. There are no Greek American Mae Wests, Betty Huttons, Judy Hollidays, Lucille Balls, Carmen Mirandas, Molly Goldbergs, Dorothy Lamours, or Marilyn Monroes. And there are no non-Greek women who have created recurring comic Greek figures a la Harry Parke. Like Greek males, Greek females also usually come out romantic winners, but more often than not, they are the passive partner. Another category is made of the sisters, wives, and mothers in the typical Greek family. They are used as another kind of ethnic wallpaper, non-challenging types rather than persons with real individuality.

This lack of female comedians is not due to Hellenic culture. In the national cinema of Greece, women starred in the musical comedies of the 1950s and 1960s, which regularly topped the list of most attended Greek films. More recently, one of the leading directors of Greek comedy has been Olga Malea, who often has women at the center of her work. The lack of comedic roles involving Greek American females would seem to be a combination of American and Greek American views on the propriety of dealing with ethnic-based gender issues in a humorous fashion. *Elektra* (2005) is a comic book creation but except for being campy or kitschy Elektra Natchios is far more lethal than she is humorous. With the exception of *Everything for a Reason*, even the Greek American Indies have not included starring comic roles or powerful comic moments for Greek women. Perhaps one of the attractions of *My Big Fat Greek Wedding* was its belated spotlight on Greek women.

Ethnic historians agree that ethnic music, food, and drink are the last cultural tastes to go. So, too, in ethnic comedy films. There are still no films in which a

Greek American individual dislikes Greek music, doesn't dance well, or rejects Greek cooking. Nor do we see individuals who struggle with Greek Orthodoxy the way so many Irish Catholic characters struggle with Catholicism and cultural Jews struggle with Judaism. This reluctance to go counter to expectations has left numerous humorous opportunities untapped.

A strong difference between mainstream and Indie films is that the mainstream films generally present the immediate past and are agreeable to having that reality recycled, while Indies focus on the present and a potentially different future. For example, *My Big Fat Greek Wedding*'s take on sex, class identification, Americanization, and language reflects patterns far more common at least 20 years before its release, and the film ultimately finds the status quo acceptable. Indeed, in *My Big Greek Wedding* it is the American groom who becomes like the Greek father and accepts a place literally aside the patriarch, however genial the arrangement might be. In contrast, films like *It Could Be Worse, Dark Odyssey, Everything for a Reason*, and *Do You Wanna Dance?* focus on the need for a cultural change that is exactly on their current ethnic time line. The reason for this different seems to be that of most of the Indies with ethnic characters are made by filmmakers (mainly directors, actors, producers, and scriptwriters) who have some Greek ancestry. Most mainstream films are not made by such individuals and even though mainstream filmmakers of Greek descent tend to make more interesting ethnic film than their non-Greek mainstream colleagues, for the most part they succumb to the usual industry pressures to opt for the perceived ethnic norm that is most pleasing to all concerned.

Given that Greek immigration is not associated in the American imagination with any specific political, social, or economic crisis, images of Greek American, comic and dramatic, are probably like those of other Euro-immigrant groups immigrating in the same period. By far the most troubling aspect of this 80-year pattern is that are simply so few films about a significant portion of the American population. Unlike images of Native Americans, Asian Americans, Arab Americans, and African Americans, the problem for Euro-ethnics is not so much the nature of representation but the lack of representation.[14] For Greek Americans, even counting films with the most marginal Greek American characters, during the entire sound era the number of films with Greek American characters is slightly over 100. That averages three films every two years. And that is not funny.

Notes

1. The mistitled *The Encyclopedia of Ethnic Groups in Hollywood* (Parish 2003) is typical in that the only listings are for African Americans, Asian Americans, Hispanic Americans, Jewish Americans, and Native Americans.
2. See Georgakas (2003: 36–7).
3. "Greek American" refers to persons of Greek origin who immigrated permanently to America and any offspring who self-identify in some manner as Greek. I am excluding films with Classic Greek figures such as Alexander the Great and Hercules. I am also excluding, the handful of films set in contemporary Greece

unless they include Greek American characters. Thus, *Boy on a Dolphin* (1957) and *Captain Corelli's Mandolin* (2001) are not included but *Eleni* (1985) and *Guns of Navarone* (1961) are as they include Greek American characters. An annotated filmography of these films can be found at *American Cinema: An Annotated Filmography* at www.lsa.umich.edu/modgreek/windowtogreekculture/cultureandmedia (accessed May 4, 2012).

4. GGGGG indicates a film in which Greek ethnicity is the central element. GGGG indicates that a major character or plot element involves Greek Americans. GGG indicates a film where ethnic identity is not vigorously explored. GG indicates a character whose Greekness is barely noted. G indicates a very minor character who could be of any ethnicity and those cases in which Greek American characters in a novel or play were given a change of ethnicity when the work was brought to the screen.

5. His birth name is Harold Einstein and some of his credits bear that name or a variation. Parke is father of comedians Albert Brooks and Bob (Super Dave Osborne) Einstein.

6. The funniest examples of Gringlish involve a unique combination of Greek, English, and odd hybrids that would only be funny for Greek speakers.

7. See Crowdus and Georgakas (2001). Lee talks about black imagery in Hollywood films on the occasion of his release of *Bamboozled*. This is followed by a critical symposium discussing the film and related issues. Participants were Saul Landau, Armond White, Michael Rlogin, Greg Tate, and Zeinabu Irene Davis.

8. The connection with American country music and Greek music had an interesting manifestation in 2009 when a video circulated on the Internet showing Laurel and Hardy dancing Greek style. The video was a fake. Greek music was used as a soundtrack to a dancing scene from *Way Out West* (1937). The apparent Greek moment is so credible that it received wide distribution. The actual soundtrack is a country-western melody.

9. An example of this analysis is found in Negra (2001: 99).

10. *Never On Sunday* is not usually included in lists of Greek films even though made in Greece. It is viewed as a film about Greece by a phil-Hellenic who lived in Greece as an expatriate. Writer/director Jules Dassin concurred with that view, even though he was wed to Melina Mercouri, Greece's most famous star and eventually an exceptional Minister of Culture.

11. *The Amos and Andy Show* poses a unique circumstance in which the comedic situation was quite similar to other ethnic sitcoms but the original actors were white. African Americans have expressed mixed feelings about characters who were indeed humorous. They were played quite ably by black actors on television, yet the characters represented a troubled Blackface history.

12. There was an influx of Greek immigration from 1965–80. Many had traditional views but generally they were far more urban and sophisticated than the early waves of massive immigration. Their outmarriage rate has not been significantly different from other Greek Americans. Gus could be of that generation but he is atypical of even that cohort.

13. "Sleep 'n' Eat" was played by William Best and Stepin Fetchit by Lincoln Theodore Monroe Andrew Perry. Best appeared in 124 films and Perry in 57. Often they were

uncredited; at other times they were listed by their comedic name and occasionally they were credited by their given names.

14. In this regard it is instructive to note that the demeaning images associated with Perry's Stephin Fetchit and Best's "Sleep 'n' Eat" appear in 191 films, a total greater than all Greek American images during the entire era of talking movies. Best, in fact, alone played the black buffoon in more films than the total of all Greek American images. Moreover, these were only two of the many African Americans presented in demeaning images. A similar syndrome is found in films focusing on Native Americans, Latinos, Hispanics, and Asians.

References

Crowdus, G. and Georgakas, D. (2001) Thinking about the power of images: an interview with Spike Lee, *Cineaste* 26 (2), 4–9.

Georgakas, Dan (2003) My big fat Greek gripes, *Cineaste*, 28 (4), 36–7.

Georgakas, Dan and Lambropoulos, Vassili (2011) *The Greek American Image in American Cinema: An Annotated Filmography*, http://www.lsa.umich.edu/modgreek/windowtogreekculture/cultureandmedia (accessed May 4, 2012).

Negra, Diane (2001) *Off-White Hollywood: American Culture and Ethnic Female Stardom*, Routledge, London.

Parish, Robert James (ed.) (2003) *The Encyclopedia of Ethnic Groups in Hollywood*, Facts on File, Inc., New York, NY.

Further Reading

Cripes, Thomas (1977) *Slow Fade to Black*, Oxford University Press, New York, NY. An excellent guide to African American images during the most negative and inaccurate period in American film.

Demakopoulos, Steve (2000) *Do You Speak Greek?* Seaburn Books, New York, NY. An authoritative discussion of Gringlish.

Fisher, James T. (2009) *On The Irish Waterfront*, Cornell University Press, Ithaca, NY. A close look at Irish images in a major film.

Garcia, Roger (ed.) (1999) *Out of the Shadows: Asians in American Cinema*, Olivares/Asian Cine Vision, Locarno. Traces the images of Asians from the silent era through to the 1990s.

Kallas, John L. (1991) *Growing Up As A Greek American*, KAV Books, Uniondale, NY. Humorous vignettes about Greek American life that reached a wide ethnic audience that can serve as an example of ethnic humor against which cinematic humor in popular cinema can be compared and contrasted.

Rollins, Peter C. and John E. O'Connor (eds.) (1998) *Hollywood's Indian: The Portrayal of the Native American in Film*, University Press of Kentucky, Lexington, KY.

Shaheen, Jack (2009) *Reel Bad Arabs*, revised edition, Olive Branch Books, Northampton, MA. The author summarizes images in nearly a thousand films.

Part VI

International Comedy

19

Alexander Mackendrick

Dreams, Nightmares, and Myths in Ealing Comedy

Claire Mortimer

Alexander Mackendrick's Ealing comedies of the 1940s and 1950s, *Whisky Galore* (1949), *The Man In The White Suit* (1951), *The Maggie* (1953), and *The Ladykillers* (1955), are set in a world that is like but unlike the real world – a dream world, even a nightmare at times – where ineluctable forces operate against, or on the behalf of, the characters. The world of dreams, nightmares, and fables never seems far away in these films. These British comedies depict a society frozen at the cusp of fundamental change, unable to adjust to the downscaling of the Empire and the demands of a new world order – an in-between, liminal society, hovering in a moral and existential no-man's land. An ambiguity shades the characters and narratives reflecting a world view that is questioning and uncertain.

Mackendrick joined Ealing Studios at the start of its most celebrated period, marked by the string of postwar comedies which have come to define the work of the Studio. Diverse film-making talents converged on the Studio at the end of the war, attracted by the benevolent working ethos presided over by Michael Balcon. Balcon had worked in the British film industry since 1919, having taken over Ealing Studios with the aim to make films "projecting Britain and the British character," as was later inscribed on a plaque to mark the closure of the Studios, reflecting his own deep patriotism. George Perry describes the Studio as "basically a middle-class institution of a mildly radical disposition … Balcon cast its members, for all their idiosyncrasies in his own mould" (Perry 1981: 111).

Charles Barr has observed that a typical Ealing comedy functions as a daydream being "a fantasy outlet" for "individual drives and desires for self-fulfilment" which are "rightly" inhibited by society, whereas Mackendrick's comedy *is* a dream,

A Companion to Film Comedy, First Edition. Edited by Andrew Horton and Joanna E. Rapf.
© 2013 John Wiley & Sons, Inc. Published 2016 by John Wiley & Sons, Inc.

playing out the conflicts as they in fact are (Barr 1980: 117). The comic safety net cannot be relied on in Mackendrick's films – as dream turns to nightmare, and the community is defended, at whatever cost. A trace of satire runs through the veins of his comedies, emerging most prominently in *The Man In The White Suit* yet being implicit in the social commentary within the other films.

Mackendrick inhabits the Ealing formula, delivering comedy narratives that superficially conform to its trademark themes, hinging on the unstoppable strength of the community and the triumph of the underdog. Yet he is a rebel who works to subvert the comedy in subtle ways, creating characters and narratives that reflect an ambiguous vision of the world. He harnesses the force of myth and dream to portray an enduring study of human frailties, straining the comic form to incorporate the nightmare, shadowing laughter with a sense of impending loss. Ultimately his comedies can be interpreted as contemplations on identity by a director whose own identity straddles different worlds.

Mackendrick brought a sensibility to Ealing Studios, which reflected the fractured times in the wake of World War II, with shifting populations having lost their roots and connections, seeking to forge identity and a future in the new postwar world. His parents were Scottish, yet he was born in Boston, Massachusetts. His father died when he was six, and his upbringing was handed over to his grandparents back in Scotland. Mackendrick later declared that his "blood is Scots, and the temperament is Scots and I feel Scots, although I am indeed one hundred per cent American" (McQuarrie 1986). Family, dislocation, identity, and the tensions between the community and the outsider were to become central themes in Mackendrick's films. Under the auspices of the Ministry of Information, his wartime duties required him to bear witness to the horrors of warfare and the devastation wreaked on communities, producing propaganda and documentary footage, including a film of the aftermath of a massacre in German-occupied Rome. Far from the reassuring comforts of many Ealing comedies, his films are distinguished by an ambivalent tone, rejecting consensus in favor of barbed, satirical and acerbic commentary on a nation that seems to be incapable of entering the modern era. The Britain at the heart of these comedies is in stasis, repelling change and the agents of change.

Each of Mackendrick's Ealing comedies summons up mythical references, building on the structures and references of fables and mythical characters in creating a framework for a comedy that reaches beyond the contemporary to embrace perennial themes and tensions. For Mackendrick the power of myth is central to storytelling, believing that "stories, even in the contemporary context of mass entertainment" are successful when they "fulfil … an archaic need … something that audiences may not even be aware of" comparing them to "the original function of rites and myths" (Mackendrick 2004: 10–11) in helping "the primitive mind take hold of a mystery." Mackendrick quotes Levi-Strauss in asserting that "art lies halfway between scientific knowledge and magical and mystical thought" (Levi-Strauss 1972: 22), seeing the original purpose of the myth as functioning "as a poetic explanation of concepts that are beyond the limited intellectual capacities of the listeners to deal with" (Mackendrick 2004: 10). The myth articulates beliefs and truths in order to reassure and to educate the listener.

Myths and dreams lie at the core of the narrative of Mackendrick's first film, *Whisky Galore*, contributing to a pervading sense of ambiguity in the comedy. Mackendrick was not the first choice for directing the project, for the adaptation was already in development under the leadership of producer Monja Danischewski. Another key contributor was Ealing director Charles Crichton who was volunteered to re-edit the film in order to "save" it, as a dismayed Michael Balcon did not believe the first edit was fit to be a feature film in its own right. Nevertheless Mackendrick was central to the creative process, making the film his own in re-working the screenplay in collaboration with Danischewski. The film proved to be a huge success for Ealing, primarily because of its popularity in America.

Whisky Galore is based on Compton Mackenzie's novel inspired by real life events in the Scottish Isles. The remote island of Todday is in decline after running out of whisky – the life blood of the community. A ship carrying a cargo of whisky is wrecked close by, leading the islanders to go to elaborate lengths to rescue its cargo, in the face of opposition from Captain Waggett, an Englishman with a deep sense of duty, who wishes to return the cargo to the authorities.

Whisky Galore is typical of Mackendrick's comedies in its evocation of a tension between myth and reality in the portrayal of the idyllic island community of Todday. In many respects *Whisky Galore* is true to Ealing values in using location filming and featuring actual islanders in many scenes. The key note is that of authenticity, made clear in the parodic documentary style opening of the film, accompanying the portentous voiceover with a montage to establish the nature of this isolated community. The tone of the voiceover creates the feel of a travelogue portraying the islanders as a remote, strange and fascinating people, before the seriousness is undercut by the bawdy implications of the "few simple pleasures" described as the camera slowly drifts from an ageing couple indulging in traditional occupations to the procession of children emerging from the doorway of their cottage. Gordon Jackson, who starred in the film, subsequently recalled that Mackendrick worried that he was "not making a comedy, but a documentary of island life" in a crisis of confidence three-quarters of the way through the filming (McQuarrie 1986).

The film may be rooted in a sense of realism, yet its narrative crosses over to the world of myths and dreams that coheres around this isolated community. Todday remains distant from 1940s' Britain, as signified by its strict adherence to the Calvinist creed in respecting the Sabbath, even though they are desperate to rescue the whisky from the wreck. The opening of the film establishes a timeless feel to the narrative, depicting the islanders' bucolic existence, with no sign of modern times. Repeated long shots of the sea, beaches and landscape emphasize the remote wildness of the setting, and a sense of the natural forces that drive the lives of the islanders. The film's structure is punctuated by repetition of these images, reiterating how the tension and conflict on the island is framed within eternal natural forces. In a literal sense these forces drive the narrative, a deep fog resulting in the shipwreck of SS Cabinet Minister, and thence bringing salvation to the island in the form of the cargo of whisky.

The narrative space of Mackendrick's films assumes the mythic resonance redolent of the "green world" of the New Comedy, as identified by Northrop Frye. Frye observed that comedy has a utopian dimension, hinging on the possibility of renewal in terms of the essential narrative cycle. For Frye "the theme of the comic is the integration of society" noting that Shakespearean comedy revolves around "the repressive and the desirable societies [making] a struggle between two levels of existence, the former like our own world or worse, the latter enchanted and idyllic" (Frye 1957: 43–4). Kathleen Rowe has noted that comedy represents "A world wilting under repressive law is liberated through a temporary movement into a dimension Bakhtin would call the carnivalesque, Victor Turner the liminal, and C.L. Barber 'the green world' of festivity and natural regeneration" (Rowe 1995: 47). The whisky becomes the means of rescuing a Todday which has been "wilting", although this merciful release is threatened by English bureaucracy in the form of Captain Waggett. Todday has the potential to be an "enchanted and idyllic" realm, but only by asserting its freedom from the "repressive" law of the outside world – the world of petty rules and austerity.

A mythical resonance pervades the narrative, touching on perennial themes and situations familiar from folk tales. Thus we have the lovers who need to prove their manliness in order to be rewarded with their brides, their quest being to rescue the whisky in order to revive the community. The brides' wily father manipulates the two young men in this respect, making clear to Sergeant Odd that no wedding can take place without a reiteach (betrothal), and the reiteach cannot take place without whisky. We have the foolish young man, George Campbell, who needs to defy his imperious mother in order to release himself from her shackles – redolent of Jack and the Beanstalk, except whisky is the reward, rather than golden eggs.

At the heart of the narrative is the misguided Captain Waggett, who resists the possibility of liberation by seeking to impose redundant strictures on the islanders, and who is ultimately removed from the island after his powers have been persistently eroded. Waggett is the villain of the piece in terms of seeking to block desires, but his villainy is dissipated by his foolishness, rendering him an ambiguous figure. Just as George is empowered by embracing the natural order and proving his manhood, Waggett is emasculated and exiled from the island. A residual sympathy for the hapless exile can be detected in the film, he becomes increasingly isolated by his stubbornness, abandoned even by his wife. Philip Kemp observes that "Mackendrick's moral universe is essentially relative" where there is no simple opposition between "unambiguous good or evil" (Kemp 1991: 28). In consequence the balance of sympathy shifts in the course of *Whisky Galore*, as in the other Mackendrick comedies, to the point where we ultimately want the islanders to have the whisky, and for the couples to be married, but we also develop a lingering understanding of the plight of Waggett.

The central premise of the film is the mystical status of whisky for the islanders, being regarded as an elixir, the absence of which results in the decline of the island, even death. The voiceover informs us that "in Gaelic they call it the water of life, and for the true islander life without it is not worth living," whilst seeing a despairing elderly man passing away, rather than face life without whisky; the camera gazes high into the heavens, showing the sun behind the clouds, suggesting a spiritual force dimmed by the absence of whisky.

The sense of the Western Isles being a magical, space which is outside of time and the "real" world, is not unique to *Whisky Galore*. The British horror film *The Wicker Man* (Robin Hardy 1973) is set on the remote Summerisle, which has its own pagan rituals and customs that ultimately destroy the God-fearing outsider for the greater good. Sergeant Howie is the outsider who comes to investigate the disappearance of a child but is being lured into a terrible trap by the wily villagers. Philip Kemp compares Sergeant Howie's fate to that of Captain Waggett: "Howie is appalled by the islanders' exuberant paganism. Like Waggett, he makes no attempt to explore their beliefs, which he treats as self-evidently misguided and immoral" (Kemp 1991: 39). Both figures represent the patriarchal structures of the "real" world, seeking to control and contain the "exuberant" energies of the islanders, fuelled by beliefs beyond their understanding.

Powell and Pressburger's *I Know Where I'm Going* (1945) is a film that is overtly concerned with myths and dreams. Both films represent the Scottish isles as transformative spaces, taking the outsider away from the realms of reality, and testing their deepest selves. Tom Gunning declares in his essay about *I Know Where I'm Going* "Most commentators ... note its echoes of fairy tales and the oneiric ... The drama of transformation that takes place on the island of Mull ... depends on invoking and – ultimately – overcoming the primordial force of dreams and myths" (Gunning 2005: 97–8). Gunning goes on to compare this "magical" space to the "dark forest that must be crossed in fairy tales and romances," a space in which heroes are tested whilst endeavoring to complete their quest, taking them out of real time into "primordial space and time." The earlier film is a love story, with a definite sense of resolution – the English heroine endures and overcomes the mythical to find true love on Mull – whereas Mackendrick's film is a comedy with a more ambiguous ending.

Captain Waggett is defeated by the combined power of community and place, culminating in the breakdown of his marriage, whereas George and Sergeant Odd successfully complete their quests and are rewarded with enduring love. The final shot of the film, a bird's eye view of Sergeant Odd and "his Peggy" walking across the beach, locates the distant figures back in the heart of their natural environment, now that conflict and obstacles have been overcome. This aspect of the ending carries the hallmark of the fairy story with requited love suggesting a happy ending, after the completion of the quest, but also fulfilling the essential

Figure 19.1 *Whisky Galore* (producer, Michael Balcon): The reiteach: euphoria and enchantment marks the return of whisky to the community.

commitment of all comedy in delivering the new society, with the promise of renewal after the removal of the blocking forces of the repressive regime.

Two other key sequences contribute to the oneiric nature of the film, combining a strong sense of ritual and mythology, and creating a dreamlike space within the narrative. These two scenes affirm the utopian dimension of this comedy, in common with the narrative dynamic of the New Comedy "the appearance of this new society is frequently signalized by some kind of party or festive ritual" (Frye 1957: 163). The public celebration of renewal and rebirth of the community is central to the comedy narrative, which forms a "cycle of renewal." The mouth music (a Gaelic tradition, creating music using only the mouth, to replicate the sound of instruments) and reiteach scenes mark the return of the life-enhancing whisky to Todday, resulting in celebration and exuberance in contrast to the preceding scarcity and suffering. In these sequences the narrative is suspended, entering a surreal world beyond modern concerns, yet this is also the realm of the documentary, portraying indigenous traditions, and using actual islanders as extras. The mouth music sequence is a montage of images of glasses, bottles and euphoric drinkers, linked together by the strangeness of the mouth music itself, which rises from a murmur to a crescendo. The link between the whisky, the community, and the natural environment is made clear as the sequence cuts to images of the sea and the voiceover drunkenly declares "When the dawn rose that memorable morning it found a changed island … Todday was hardly recognisable!" (see Figure 19.1).

The reiteach is another scene of celebration, intensity and energy – verging on the hallucinogenic – the camera weaving around the dancers, fixing on

Peggy's blissful expression, drawing the audience into the heady euphoria and enchantment of the occasion. Just as Sergeant Odd is transported by his love for Peggy, and subsequent acceptance into this other-worldly community, the audience is also brought into the dance. The mouth music and reiteach scenes possess a mythic and utopian intensity, paying homage to ancient traditions and beliefs that are the bedrock of this community. Mackendrick wrote of the importance of "primitive magical rituals" in *On Film-making* when considering the origins of narratives, adding how "rhythmic movement, repetitive gesture and musical noise" helps unify and give clarity to "some otherwise disturbing and fearsome mystery" (Mackendrick 2004: 10–11). These rituals within *Whisky Galore* reveal the bonds and beliefs that bind together this community, shoring it up against adversity, or the intrusion of an interfering outsider like Captain Waggett.

Mackendrick's next film, *The Man In The White Suit*, also revolves around mythic resonance, again straddling two worlds, locating a fairy tale within a northern mill town. The timeless feel to *Whisky Galore* is enhanced by its remote setting, in a community that is essentially unchanged by the modern world, whilst, in contrast, *The Man In The White Suit* is set firmly within an industrial context, a satire that targets the contemporary concerns of scientific progress, industrial unrest and labor relations, delving into darker realms to make its point. The plot centers on maverick scientist Sidney Stratton, played by Alec Guinness, who invents a new textile that can never wear out or get dirty, but subsequently finds that the industry bosses and workers wish to suppress his invention, fearing that it threatens their livelihoods.

Whereas *Whisky Galore* relied on dreams and a strong sense of natural rhythms and traditions, *The Man In The White Suit* creates a nightmare world, full of sinister shapes, threats and deceit, suggesting the sinister forces that lie at the heart of industrial progress – the world of the satire, exploring folly and vice through humor. Indeed Mackendrick's films are characteristic of what Frye terms "ironic comedy" where the demonic world is never far away. The threat of disaster, or even death, is a constant presence, the comedy coming "as close to a catastrophic overthrow of the hero … and then reverses the action as quickly as possible" (Frye 1957: 178). Philip Kemp notes that the film doesn't fit "easily within the Ealing canon … the snarl shows too clearly beneath the grin" (Kemp 1991: 67). The satiric resonance of the film is reinforced by a sense of claustrophobia, with little of the open landscapes and freedom that prevails in *Whisky Galore*. Expressionist lighting, with pronounced menacing shadows, angular shapes and claustrophobic spaces help to create a dark, entrapping world. Daphne Birnley, the mill owner's daughter who befriends Sidney, speaks of her longing to escape: "I'm sick of the Birnley Mills and everyone connected with them and the sooner I leave home the happier I will be." At the end of the film Daphne has failed to leave, her fiancé has betrayed her, and Sidney was not the hero she hoped he would be; whereas Sidney does escape, wandering off to create more havoc in his pursuit of scientific knowledge. Daphne is stuck in her nightmare, yet Sidney still has his dreams.

Mackendrick intended the film to be a satire – not just of the textile industry: "Each character in the story was intended as a caricature of a separate political attitude" (Davies 1953). The characterization is structured as in a fairy tale, with characters fulfilling specific roles in developing the moral of the narrative. The thrust of the satire is embodied in the figure of Sir John Kierlaw, the sinister textile baron at the heart of the nightmares that encircle the world of *The Man In The White Suit*. Kemp observes how Kierlaw is "summonsed" by the mill bosses, driven to tap into "Mephisthophelean" dark forces to overcome the threat posed by Sidney (Kemp 1991: 57). Mackendrick builds suspense as Kierlaw speeds his way north, constructing a sense of evil and menace around him. A low-angle shot builds the sense of impending doom as it shows the dark cars speeding through the night, with just a claw-like hand visible amongst furs, redolent of Gothic horror. A low-level shot tracks Kierlaw shuffling along the corridors towards Birnley, casting dark angular shadows to build the tension. Mackendrick builds a caricature of pure evil, weaving together fairy tale villains and nightmare imagery, withholding the image of Kierlaw's wizened, death mask face in order to create a suspense that is prolonged to create comic effect. In this respect Kierlaw is a departure for one of Mackendrick's comedies, in terms of being a character who is beyond any ambiguity in his evil. Despite Sidney and Kierlaw appearing to be polar opposites with conflicting goals, they are more than a match for each other in terms of their single-minded determination. Both of them will go to any lengths to obtain their goal – Kierlaw is disappointed when Sidney survives being knocked on the head during the tussle in the board room, and will happily use Daphne as bait to ensnare him.

Mackendrick subverts the expected character roles of the fairy tale. For example, Sidney is needed to be a hero, by both Daphne, and Bertha, the union representative, who each assign noble motives to his work, yet he fulfils the comic role of the trickster and exploiting the faith that the other characters place in him. Bertha believes he is heroic in his struggle with the bosses whereas Daphne compares him in his white suit to "a knight in shining armor," explaining to the bemused Sidney that "millions of people all over the world living lives of drudgery, fighting an endless losing battle against shabbiness and dirt – you've won that battle for them, you've set them free! The whole world is going to bless you." Daphne projects her desires and idealism onto Sidney, just as Bertha imparts her own socialist principles to him whereas Birnley is persuaded to bankroll Sidney's experiments through the dream of gaining total domination of the textile industry.

Sidney's suit possesses a strange magical and other-worldly luminescence, helping to enhance his status as a hero. Charles Barr observes that the sheer whiteness of Sidney's suit symbolizes "purity, innocence and the disinterested truth of science" adding that "the suit is the emblem of Sidney's angelic innocence" and that he "is an angel put down among the family of England" (Barr 1980: 135–40). Sidney certainly seems to have appeared from nowhere, unnoticed whilst he ekes out a space for his experiments in the heart of the textile industry, just as he leaves the Mill ignominiously at the end of the film, although with the ominous suggestion that his experiments will not end there. He is a mysterious figure. The whiteness of his suit is symbolic of the strange innocence of Sidney's motivations in contrast to the dark suits and cars of the industrialists, who flock together to suppress his invention in order to preserve their wealth and power.

Mackendrick's comedy gathers a satirical force with the representation of Sidney as a persecuted messianic figure, who is turned on by the mob, with only Daphne and Bertha able to perceive his true worth. The climactic scene in which his suit is ripped apart by the furious crowd certainly builds on this, being the culmination of a nightmare with the alleyways of the town closing in on Sidney; his escape is thwarted, and he is unable to share his discovery with the rest of the world. Mackendrick takes the comedy to the verge of tragedy, creating a moment of genuine catastrophe and threat, the defining characteristic of Frye's "ironic comedy"; Sidney is cornered by the baying mob, yet strikes comic figure, left standing, exposed to the public, in his underwear. The film features many such scenes that draw on slapstick conventions, providing a comic energy that underscores the nightmare world of the satire.

Sidney is no messiah, although an undoubted genius, he is also a fool, whose only concern is to prove his scientific genius, not to make the world a better place. Consequently the film denies any narrative drive towards the happy ending associated with the romantic comedy, in the form of romantic union. Any suggestion of romance between Sidney and Daphne is an impossibility, since he cannot care for anything beyond his experiments. He exploits his landlady's generosity and Bertha's misguided goodwill, as one person after another makes sacrifices to aid his cause. Mackendrick creates comedy out of Alec Guinness's performance, wavering between the extreme lengths he is prepared to go to in order to develop his dream, and his innate dysfunctionality as he proves himself unable to engage with other people. Sidney does not understand anything beyond his experiments; everything he does is solely to promote his goal of creating the perfect fabric. Inevitably, his dedication to science causes mayhem, whether it be crashing into doors with overladen trolleys or steadily demolishing the laboratory with his experiments, incidentally inflicting minor injuries on anyone unlucky enough to be close by.

As a satire, the film forms a fable of greed and foolishness, that Mackendrick intended as an allegory for the nuclear industry, attacking "the so-called disinterested scientist, totally reckless and totally inconsiderate of the consequences of his action" (McQuarrie 1986). Far from being a hero, Sidney is a threat and a fool. He pursues his dream, only for it to become everybody else's nightmare, as the different factions realize the true implications of the invention. Momentarily it appears that Sidney can learn from his mistakes when his landlady, Mrs. Watson, confronts him: "Why can't you scientists leave things alone? What's to become of my bit of washing when there's no washing to do?" Sidney appears stunned by her words yet finishes the film back where he started, deep in thought plotting his next attempt to develop his invention. Nevertheless, he is revealed as the fool he really is when he is finally caught by the mob and his suit disintegrates, proving his invention to be a failure.

The fool is a key comic archetype, figuring large in myths and fables, serving to test the values and moral fiber of the community. Andrew Stott asserts that the fool is a "symbol of contradictions and quandaries," explaining how his role is to affirm the importance of folly in qualifying human pretension, and to be "an ironic and paradoxical identity assumed for the purposes of social commentary and satiric attack" (Stott 2005: 46–7). Sidney's character encompasses a satiric attack on scientific solipsism alongside his role in exposing the duplicity and greed of others. Yet his character has shades of the trickster, another comic archetype, not far removed from the fool, serving the same purpose through trickery and practical jokes. The scene in which Sidney is cornered by the mob encapsulates the mythical resonance of the narrative, calling to mind Hans Christian Anderson's satirical fairy tale *The Emperor's New Clothes*. Two trickster tailors con the vain emperor by promising him the finest suit of clothes ever known to mankind, although with the twist that only people of merit and intelligence will see the clothes. The emperor is thus unable to confess that he cannot see the outfit, and is humiliated in public when sporting his new clothes, when a child calls out that he has no clothes on. *The Man In The White Suit* subverts the fairy tale as Sidney is both the maker of the clothes and the wearer – he is both the conman and the fool. He had convinced Birnley, the emperor, of his ability to create this magical cloth, but is humiliated in public when the suit disintegrates. Both Birnley and Sidney are punished for their pride and egotism – yet Sidney walks free at the end, just like the tailors in the fairy tale.

The catalyst of the action is a sought after substance with magical qualities – as is also the case in *Whisky Galore*. The cloth is magical, with its powers of indestructibility; the thread saves Sidney when it assists him in escaping from captivity in the Birnley mansion, only to betray him to the mob when they espy the luminous whiteness in the dark of the night (see Figure 19.2). In *Whisky Galore* the whisky restore harmony and even health, bringing the community together in happiness, whereas in *The Man In The White Suit* the cloth leads to a breakdown in order and threatens the stability and welfare of all echelons of society.

Sidney is not the hero but the harbinger of chaos, a false hero in seeming to bring the promise of great things, but turning out to be a threat. In this respect, the film steps firmly into the world of the satire, where dreams become nightmares, and where fools and tricksters threaten the community. There is no happy ending or sense of reconciliation at the end of the film – normality has returned to the textile mills yet there is uncertainty with Sidney still at large. Moreover, no one has attained their dream. The mill owners have retained their empires but their greed and foolishness has been exposed in their panic in the face of change. The narrative conforms to a "phase of comedy" identified by Frye, "in which the hero

Figure 19.2   *The Man In The White Suit* (producer, Michael Balcon): Sidney's suit possesses a strange magical and other-worldly luminescence.

does not transform a humorous society but simply escapes or runs away from it, leaving its structure as it was before" (Frye 1957: 180). Frye elaborates that in this phase the hero is "usually himself … a comic humour or mental runaway" and that the central dynamic of the comedy can be that of the "clash of two illusions."

Mackendrick has portrayed another community that lies between two worlds, in this case creating a satire exploring the dichotomy between the interests of science and the community, and the workers and their bosses. These tensions are articulated through the medium of dreams and nightmares, myth and reality, and thus locates contemporary issues within a framework of perennial themes of greed, transgression and ambition. Sidney is the maverick who blazes a trail through normality, a purveyor of dreams and magic, which ultimately turn to nightmare and dust. The ensuing cataclysm exposes the true identities of all the protagonists: Sidney's fixated selfishness, Daphne's need to escape, the mill owners' capacity to do anything to protect their profits.

Whereas *The Man In The White Suit* was another box office success for Mackendrick, the response to *The Maggie* was more muted. Mackendrick returned to Scotland for his next Ealing comedy, *The Maggie*, a film that fuses the business world of *The Man In The White Suit* with the mythical Scotland of *Whisky Galore*. Both *Whisky Galore* and *The Maggie* build an image of the Celtic world which echoes a "dream Scotland" in embracing a sense of otherness, mythical resonance and liminality – offering the promise of an alternative to the repressive reality of our own society, the promise of a new, free society which is the bedrock of the comedy format. Colin McArthur's critique of *Whisky Galore* and *The Maggie* takes the position that both films are typical of the ethnic discourse he labels the "Scottish Discursive Unconscious," a highly ideological representation of Scotland, constructing "the Scots ... as having an essential identity different from – indeed, and in many respects the antithesis of – the Anglo-Saxon identity exemplified by (a certain class of) Englishmen and Americans" (McArthur 2003: 8). McArthur goes on to observe that the discourse evokes "a dream Scotland which is highland, wild, 'feminine', close to nature and which has, above all, the capacity to enchant and transform the stranger" (McArthur 2003: 12). For McArthur the representation of Scotland in the two films is an ideological construct that has been widely perpetuated. *Whisky Galore* centers on a community situated at the far extremes of the British Isles, seemingly at the edge of the known world, in a liminal space where dreams and myths are woven with reality, ultimately shoring up communal identity against threats from the outside.

The narrative dynamic of *The Maggie* hinges on the collision between the old world of the Scottish coastal communities and the new world of global commerce and economic imperatives, embodied in the airline executive Calvin Marshall. *The Maggie's* dual nature had a personal resonance for the director: "it's very much about me ... the story of the American who is an executive in industry and the story of the wee boy mucking about on the Clyde, both of them are myself" (McQuarrie, 1986). The audience is caught between a growing sense of sympathy for the American as his life disintegrates, and engagement with the mischievous innocence of Dougie the cabin boy, who battles to save his master's livelihood.

Geoff King comments how the Ealing comedies are "a product of the time and national context, blending elements of comic fantasy and documentary-style naturalism to explore difficult postwar issues" (King 2002: 158). This is certainly true of *Whisky Galore* with its concerns with austerity and bureaucracy and *The Man In The White Suit*, dealing with scientific progress and labor relations. *The Maggie* reflects concerns about the swamping of indigenous culture and industry by the United States. This tension is articulated through the classic comedy dynamic of inserting the outsider as an interloper into an alien culture, creating a clash in values and consequent questioning of identity. Marshall needs to ship a valuable cargo to Kintyre, but his agent accidentally gives the contract to the crew of a dilapidated Clyde puffer, *The Maggie*. The American realizes the mistake and desperately tries to retrieve his cargo, only to be thwarted repeatedly by Captain Mactaggart and his crew. The comedy centers around culture clash, much like *Whisky Galore*, as the wily crew outwits the outsider, who descends from a state of confidence and self-assurance to self-doubt and despair.

The puffer transports the central characters away from the modern world through wild seascapes and timeless villages, back into the realms of myth and tradition, the oneiric world of *Whisky Galore*. This is the world which exists in parallel with the modern world, representing a simple agrarian lifestyle dominated by tradition and strong family and community values. Northrop Frye observes that the comic narrative is driven by the rebellion of "the hero's society ... against the society of the *senex* ... the hero's society is a Saturnalia, a reversal of social standards which recalls a golden age in the past" (Frye 1957: 171). The world of the puffer, with its simple pleasures, traditions and close community stands in contrast with the bustle and pressures of the business world. The "green world" is characterized by carnival pleasures, representing release from the strictures of the normal world. The crew of *The Maggie* thus have a different agenda and time frame from Marshall, adapting their voyage to optimize the opportunities for drink and pleasure. As Mactaggart observes when Marshall makes yet another frantic telephone call: "I've never seen such a man for the telephone. It'll be the American way, everything in a rush. Ay, but he's not a man that's at peace with himself." The shortcomings of the modern world are epitomized by "the American way," personified by Marshall's brusque business dealings, his need to have control, and the assumption that money will solve any problem, even his marriage, as is made evident in the valuable cargo of household goods with which he intends to furnish the new house to surprise his wife.

Marshall is drawn into the heart of the Western Isles, trying to take control of the situation on board *The Maggie* only to find himself effectively hijacked by the crew. He becomes helpless in the face of invisible forces that test his resolve and resilience, drawing him into the "green world." As in *Whisky Galore* even nature conspires against the outsider as the fog, tides and rocks impede his efforts to gain control. Marshall finds himself pulled into the very heart of the community when Mactaggart forces him into his friend's 100th birthday party, in a celebratory sequence which serves to encapsulate the energy, strength and exuberance of the community and the power of ritual. Marshall is pulled into the dance, just as he has been pulled into the party and taken to the village against his wishes; the force of the community is unstoppable. The whole sequence echoes the carnival pleasures of the reiteach featured in *Whisky Galore*: the point of view shot positioning the audience in the heart of the dance, facing a pretty girl, the Gaelic tongue, the crowd shots in contrast to the isolation of Marshall, the whisky and the swirling traditional music. Marshall is offered refreshment, pleasure, and the admiration of a young woman, signaling the open generous nature of this timeless community; it is a dream world which could take him away from the cares of his normal life, in contrast to the broken phone call in the previous scene when Marshall begs his wife to come and meet him, only to have the phone put down on him. The everyday world has become a nightmare for him that he desperately tries to remedy, with his repeated attempts to communicate with his wife. Ultimately he is a trapped man who is returned to his nightmare at the end of the film as he trudges away to his broken marriage, having lost the contents of his new house. He turns his back on the dream-world of The Maggie and the broader community within which it sails, and thus it too becomes a nightmare for him, blocking his desires.

The Scottish isles offer a mythical world of pleasure and freedom in both *Whisky Galore* and *The Maggie*. For Marshall the journey with *The Maggie* offers a way forward in his life, testing his values and making him reflect on his priorities.

This is made clear in the series of encounters with indigenous characters who are "true" to themselves in pursuing their desires: Mactaggart, Dougie the cabin boy, the girl at the birthday party. The opposing forces of the narrative reflect the dialectic at the heart of much film comedy: the opposition between the world of play, liberation and childish pleasures and the adult world of responsibilities and constraint. Marshall represents the world of the adult, in contrast to the world of Mactaggart, which centers on pleasure and childlike pursuit of gratification. He travels into a timeless world on the edge of reality, much as the film itself hovers between elegy for the director's past and the material concerns of the present day, between adult and child, myth, and reality. Marshall's journey becomes a journey into his psyche, leading him to question his own identity as he is forced to recognize he has no control over events in this "other" world. After *The Maggie* destroys the quay, removing all hope of him being able to transfer his cargo to another boat, he is asked by the captain if he is Mr. Marshall. Standing impassively, overwhelmed, and staring into the chasm that was once the quay, he replies, "I am no longer absolutely sure."

Marshall's identity wavers from this point onwards, as *The Maggie* become a floating communal island transporting the villagers and assorted animals to the birthday party. He continues to try to maintain contact with the outside world through repeated telephone calls, yet he changes his clothes at the next port, and starts to look like a crew member. For Marshall his plight becomes a nightmare, having to confront the fact that he has no alternative but to go along with The Maggie at the pace Mactaggart dictates, that he is in another realm where reason, business and money have no bearing on events, but community and tradition must be respected, or else the forces of nature will work against you. He becomes trapped on *The Maggie*, his attempts to get control being repeatedly blocked – to the extent that the Dougie, the cabin boy, believes that he has killed Marshall having rendered him unconscious after Marshall announced he had bought *The Maggie*.

Northrop Frye recognizes the similarities between comedy and tragedy, observing that "comedy contains a potential tragedy within itself" when the hero teeters on the brink of destruction as a result of his shortcomings, yet is transformed and reintegrated into the social fold by the end of the narrative (Frye 2002: 106). Marshall comes close to redemption but turns his back on the crew at the end of the film, a defeated man wandering off to an uncertain future. He is not transformed or reintegrated – he remains unchanged, in this respect being much like Sidney walking away at the end of *The Man In The White Suit*, although there is a sense that Sidney's single mindedness renders him undiminished by his humiliation, whereas Marshall has seemingly lost his way. The Maggie emerges as the hero. It eludes its demise to gain a new lease of life, courtesy of Marshall having rescued it from the rocks and providing the money for its repairs. Certainly *The Maggie*, and its crew, come perilously close to destruction in the course of the film, most notably when the engine fails and it hits the rocks.

In common with the preceding two Mackendrick comedies, the film reaches an ambiguous conclusion, mainly due to the problematic nature of the character of Marshall. The clarity of the characterization of the "green world comedies" is subverted by Mackendrick's vision, in which there is no clear dichotomy between good and bad, hero and villain; it is a world of ambiguities. Mackendrick set out to characterize Marshall as a hard-nosed, ruthless executive, who lets nothing stand in his way, but Douglas's performance creates a more sympathetic character as he is constantly outmaneuvered by *The Maggie*'s crew. He is a man whose undoubted prowess in the business world has compromised his hopes for personal happiness, as he struggles to save his cargo, his marriage, and his dream of domestic bliss in the Scottish islands. For him the green world is a nightmare g where he has no place, yet his life in the normal world is also a nightmare: he is a doomed man.

Northrop Frye's analysis of Shakespeare's comedies demonstrates how "the action … begins in a world represented as a normal world, moves into the green world, goes into a metamorphosis there in which the comic resolution is achieved, and returns to the normal world" (Frye 2002: 107). The action of *The Maggie* commences in the heart of Glasgow, but then moves to the "green world" of the Scottish isles and coast. Here the action sees Marshall brought to the brink of transformation, yet the ending precludes any conclusive sense of metamorphosis; after having capitulated to the crew, he turns his back on them. In the course of the journey he has ultimately helped salvage the boat by sacrificing his valuable cargo and fixing the engine, proving an ability to think beyond his own interests. Yet there is no final sense of redemption and transformation for his character, when he trudges away from *The Maggie* and her crew, a diminished man who has paid a heavy price for his folly. Marshall shares Captain Waggett's fate in *Whisky Galore* in that both characters are outsiders whose values are ultimately irreconcilable with this mythic world that lies beyond modern Scotland, and both are driven to turn their backs on the community, after paying a heavy price for their folly and temerity.

The story turns full circle in the final scene where we see the puffer returning to the normal world, making its way up the Clyde to ply for business once again. Much like Sidney at the end of *The Man In The White Suit*, Mactaggart and his crew remain on the loose, ready to take on new "victims," both films having seen these hapless agents of destruction wreak havoc, taking on powerful yet flawed adversaries from the modern world of commerce. At the journey's end The Maggie's crew are triumphant. Having resisted Marshall and reached their destination, they have also saved the future of their boat, for the time being.

The puffer crew is proud and stubborn but, too often, "like children, they're easily distracted by immediate gratification," having to be saved by timely interventions from Dougie, the wily cabin boy, Mactaggart's disgruntled sister and ultimately even Marshall himself (Kemp 1991: 98). The crew have much in common with Andrew Stott's definition of the comic type of the "trickster," "a shiftless opportunist" often responsible for "quasi-criminal" activities, testing the limits of society and thus contributing to the process of social renewal and reconciliation (Stott 2005: 51). Geoff King notes how the trickster is often characterized by childlike "unsocialised, uncontrolled and apparently instinctual drives to gratify desires for food, drink and sex" (King 2002: 88). We see this in Mactaggart's crew's commitment to pleasure over business, each voyage being arranged around opportunities to drink and party. The trickster is not confined by boundaries and can travel between worlds, much as *The Maggie* plies her trade between the modern "normal" world of Glasgow and the "green world" of the Scottish coast and islands, the new world of postwar industrial Britain and the old world of traditional and a pastoral way of life.

The crew is wily, effectively conning Marshall, not bothering to correct the agent's mistake in confusing *The Maggie* with a much more seaworthy boat and persisting in misleading and ensnaring him, even to the extent of letting *The Maggie* destroy the quay (due to be demolished anyway) so that he could not transfer his cargo. Dougie the cabin boy commits petty theft, poaching pheasant and committing assault on Marshall, knocking him out when he discovers Marshall's intentions to buy the boat. Ultimately we are encouraged to regard them as benign tricksters, who exploit Marshall's foolishness in order to preserve their way of life. The survival of *The Maggie* is their motivation, and with it the survival of an older way of life and community.

The Ladykillers was to be Mackendrick's last film for Ealing, and it was the last commercial success for the Studio. The film takes the Ealing comedy to the extremes of its signature style, teetering on the cusp of fantasy in its characterization, narrative and *mise-en-scène*. Mackendrick commented: "I knew that I was trying to work on a fable. The characters are all caricatures, fable figures; none of them is real for a moment", describing his film as "an enclosed, fabulous world" (Keating 1986). Professor Marcus (Alec Guinness), an eccentric criminal mastermind, rents a room from the unwitting elderly Mrs. Wilberforce (Katie Johnson). The professor's disparate gang, masquerading as musicians to fool the old lady, use the room as a base for a heist. Mrs. Wilberforce accidentally discovers their crime, and ultimately the gang destroy themselves despite their efforts to kill her.

Here the tricksters become a threat to the community, in their plot to carry out their robbery and subsequently to dispose of Mrs. Wilberforce who inadvertently discovers their crime. As in *The Maggie*, the tricksters travel between worlds, in this case from the normality of 1950s' London, into the 'green world' of Mrs. Wilberforce's house - a relic from a bygone age, a true manifestation of Frye's idea of a "golden age" that has been usurped by the "normal world". The gang travels in a different direction from the trickster crew in the previous film. In *The Ladykillers* they are the outsiders who seek to impose their control on the green world, but are defeated, and destroyed. In this respect the gang has much in common with Waggett (in *Whisky Galore*) and Marshall: the intruders who cannot survive in this "other" world having dared to believe that they have the power to have their way.

Frye describes the green world of Shakespeare's comedies as containing "fairies, dreams, disembodied souls" adding that even though "it may not be 'a real' world ... there is something equally illusory in the stumbling and blinded follies of the 'normal' world" (Frye 2002: 109). The world of *The Ladykillers* is the stuff of dreams, if not nightmares, populated by the lost souls of the gang, who have strayed away from their normal milieu into a world where unstoppable forces result in their destruction. The dark comedy of the film is typical of Frye's "ironic comedy," where the demonic world closes in, threatening death and destruction: "the fear of death, sometimes a hideous death, hangs over the central character to the end, and is dispelled so quickly that one has almost the sense of awakening from a nightmare" (Frye 1957: 179). Mrs. Wilberforce (her name suggesting righteous beliefs and goodness, evoking William Wilberforce, campaigner for abolition of slavery) is the channel for these powerful forces, her frail frame belying her indomitable strength of will and her fearsome belief in "doing the right thing." Once the gang cross her threshold they have entered this other world, never to leave alive.

Professor Marcus, sinking further into madness, realizes their fate towards the end of the film: "There were only five of us ... But it would take 20 or 30 or 40 perhaps to deal with her, because we'll never be able to kill *her*, Louis. She'll always be with us, for ever and ever and ever, and there's nothing we can do about it." This sense of helplessness in the face of the force of innocence, community and bygone values is experienced by Marshall when *The Maggie* destroys the quay and his hopes of gaining control, and by Waggett in the face of the islanders' wiliness in hiding the whisky and repeatedly foiling his personal crusade to restore order.

"The stumbling and blinded follies" of the "normal" world are epitomized in the comic ineptitude of the police, the supposed representatives of order and authority. The film begins and ends at the police station, where the avuncular police, a benign yet incompetent presence throughout the film, steadfastly dismiss Mrs. Wilberforce's tales, to the extent of even transporting the gang's case of money back to Mrs. Wilberforce's house in total ignorance. The robbery takes place on the streets of the normal world, where we see a society rife with petty crime and foolishness, populated by caricatures such as the Irish thief with his silver hoard at the railway station, and the belligerent market trader whose argument with Mrs. Wilberforce snowballs, drawing in bystanders and destroying his stall.

Because the majority of the film takes place in the surreal decaying surrounds of Mrs. Wilberforce's house, a museum piece commemorating a bygone age, *The Ladykillers* takes the sense of an enclosed world even further than in the other comedies. Mackendrick wrote that it was important that the majority of the scenes should take place within the house in order to maintain a "comic tone" consistent with a film which "had to perch on the edge of fantasy." For him, the comedy of the film is situated in a liminal world where "all the main characters are exaggerated cartoon-like characters and when set against natural backgrounds, interacting with real persons, they were in danger of losing conviction" (Mackendrick 2004: 207). The set design paid homage to an expressionist style in utilizing disorientating angles to create a surreal world.

The opening shot of the film is an extreme high angle shot of the house, a fairy-tale cottage marooned in an urban landscape, dated and isolated – much like Mrs. Wilberforce, and everything she represents. The house is claustrophobic; the gang struggles to find space within its cramped Victorian confines, comically jostling with Mrs. Wilberforce and her many "replicants" in the hallway, being overwhelmed by little old ladies. The gang is engulfed by the tiny house. Both house and owner are aged and fragile, yet simultaneously resilient and indestructible; the house leans precariously as a result of bomb damage, prompting One Round affectionately to christen its owner "Mrs. Lopsided," yet she manfully wields a hammer to sort out the plumbing. The house suffers some peripheral damage whilst the gang self-destructs, yet nevertheless appears miraculously unscathed in the final aerial shot, much as its owner is also untouched.

Forces that work alongside the unwitting Mrs. Wilberforce to overcome the gang animate this "other" world. The film involves episodes of slapstick comedy with objects and physical entities undermining the gang at every turn. In the extended scene when the gang attempts to recapture the parrot, a chair entraps One-Round (Danny Green), Harry (Peter Sellers) is bitten by the bird, and Louis (Herbert Lom) gets stuck on the roof. The gang's attempt to escape with the money is thwarted by the house itself, when the front door shuts on One-Round's cello case strap, resulting in the case falling open and exposing the money to Mrs. Wilberforce. Finally Professor Marcus himself, having killed Louis, is foiled on the brink of triumph, when he is hit over the head by the railway signal and falls neatly into the passing goods wagon.

Kemp describes the film as "England reduced to the charm, and the cruelty, of a fairy-tale" (Kemp 1991: 119). Mrs. Wilberforce is the vulnerable old lady alone in her quaint cottage but protected by unassailable forces. Combining her innocence with an indomitable integrity, she remains oblivious to the terrible events that take place within her realm. Her fragility is emphasized in the high angle shots of her surrounded by the gang in the tight spaces of her cottage. As in a fairy tale, good is threatened by evil when the gang decides that the only way they can get away with the money is to kill Mrs. Wilberforce, thus the whimsical charm of a "sweet little old lady" is threatened by murder.

The clarity of this moral outrage is clouded by an ambiguity which is typical of Mackendrick's Ealing comedies. Raymond Durgnat believed that the film has "a quality of moral paradox" due to "the to and fro of [Mrs. Wilberforce's] invincibly ignorant benevolence, and [Professor Marcus's] seething, impotent malice which we can't but share" (Durgnat 1970: 38). The gang endears itself with its utter foolishness. Its perfectly formed plan disintegrates; the gang members are never a true threat to Mrs. Wilberforce. One by one they prove themselves far from hardened criminals when confronted with the prospect of having to kill Mrs. Wilberforce. The gang is helpless and Mrs. Wilberforce is indestructible; we are positioned to understand the scale of their frustration and desperation in the face of such an apparently harmless foe. From the opening scene we have been shown the disruptive impact of the Mrs. Wilberforce on other lives; a baby screams when she peers into its pram, the police groan with despair faced with another of her eccentric visits, and later on we see the carnage resulting from her decision to upbraid the market stall holder for his treatment of the horse that has been eating his wares. The market stall holder is incredulous when he discovers that she is known to the police, and that they "let her out on the loose" after his stall was wrecked because of her intervention.

Mrs. Wilberforce's house becomes a battleground whilst the normal world, in the shape of the criminals, struggles to extricate itself from this "other" world, a world of forces from which they cannot escape, as if the house is charmed. It is significant, and ironic, that Mrs. Wilberforce, seemingly charmed and thereby removed from the sordid crimes going on around her, sleeps through the night while the gang members gradually destroy each other. This is the world of black comedy, where laughter is conflated with death, the slapstick nature of each death negating horror in favor of humor. As darkness falls, a nightmare is unleashed in the shadows and darkness around the cottage, accompanied by periodic screeches of the steam trains. The film verges on horror with a sequence of desperate murders. One by one the bodies are thrown (or fall) into the goods wagons, towed away by the endless procession of steam trains, as if evil is removed from the world of Mrs. Wilberforce, and ceremoniously returned to the "normal" world. Frye observes that "the principle of the humor is the principle that unincremental repetition … is funny" (Frye 1957: 168). The excessive nature of the repeated deaths generates laughter, enhanced by the slapstick of the action; the threat of the demonic world is turned on itself, resulting in self-destruction. An impermeable shell of morality and principle surrounds this remnant of a bygone age, repelling any threat or suggestion of change which might dissipate the comic effect, and ensuring that "stable and harmonious order" will be restored.

The Ladykillers weaves together nightmares and dreams more than any of Mackendrick's preceding comedies. William Rose, who wrote the screenplay, had conceived the original story in a dream. Mackendrick commented that "The fact that it was something that Bill had quite literally dreamed up really entranced me. Dreams are a marvellous source of imagery for movies" (Keating 1986). The narrative framework encourages the viewer to speculate about the possibility that the whole story of the gang is actually Mrs. Wilberforce's dream, and that the police are actually correct in persistently disbelieving her. The repeated images of her sleeping whilst the night unfolds invite this interpretation, as does the opening scene in the police station where her reputation for delusion and fantasy becomes clear. She has come to explain the truth to the police behind her friend's sighting of a spaceship in her garden: "She never saw it in the first place … . On Wednesday in Children's Hour they were doing a little play called, errr, 'Visitors From Other Worlds'. Amelia had her wireless on .... Well, it's obvious. She dropped off to sleep. The whole thing was just a dream. Amelia was so embarrassed she quite refused to come here and tell you herself. " Amelia's experience, or her imagined experience, has clear parallels to what happens during the course of the film.

On one level it is absolutely typical of Mrs. Wilberforce to take it upon herself to assist her friend and carry out her duty in explaining the misunderstanding. Yet on another level it establishes a narrative framework of an elderly lady being visited by beings "from other worlds," who have dematerialized in the course of the night. Indeed Mrs. Wilberforce wonders aloud to the Sergeant whilst she is ushered off the premises: "I must say if there are any beings on other worlds, I can't think why they would want to come to our world, can you?" Her question becomes ironic in the course of the next scene when she sets out on her journey home, only to be stalked by a "being" from another world, who has trespassed into the innocence of the "green" world. The camera tracks Professor Marcus using evocative gliding movements to convey a sense of the supernatural and the surreal.

The disruption and threat represented by Professor Marcus is highlighted by the dramatic change in the weather conditions, signaling his intrusion into Mrs. Wilberforce's world. The apparition of his sinister silhouette is greeted by an abrupt downpour, which empties the high street, accompanied by an increasingly ominous soundtrack. Suspense mounts whilst he trails Mrs. Wilberforce back to her house, circling the building as if stalking his prey, whilst she remains oblivious to the threat. This sequence establishes the proximity of the nightmare world of the ironic comedy, juxtaposed with the innocence of the "green" world at an early stage of the film, employing conventions more familiar from darker genres, in particular the horror film. Frye notes how comedy typically has a "ternary form": "a stable and harmonious order disrupted by folly ... and then restored" (Frye 1957: 171). He likens the middle action to winter. In *The Ladykillers* it is signified by the abrupt change of weather with the arrival of Professor Marcus. With restored order the sun returns to the world of Mrs. Wilberforce, the street becomes busy again and she is able to leave her umbrella behind at the police station.

Mrs. Wilberforce is untouchable, possessing powers that put her beyond any threat posed by the nightmare world. She lives within dreams of the past, constantly referring to her memories and past events, her consciousness hovering between reverie and reality. In this respect she is a manifestation of Victorian values that endure within the community. She is inviolable because she is beyond the reach of the present. Hence she is humored by the police whilst she weaves a trail of disruption within the community before retreating to her domain, her time capsule cottage at the far reaches of the cul-de-sac.

The mythic world of Mackendrick's comedies becomes a place where community and identity are tested, resulting in the revelation of the essential nature of the characters – whether it is the misplaced integrity of Captain Waggett in trying to enforce the rule of law, the greed of the bosses of the textile mills, the personal crisis that lies behind Calvin Marshall's business success, or the indestructible moral certainties of Mrs. Wilberforce. The narratives result in the expulsion of agents of change in favor of retaining established values and social cohesion, yet Mackendrick leaves a lingering sense of uncertainty because our sympathies are skewed and resolution is undermined. The happy ending expected of film comedy is tempered by ambiguity, typically leaving a lingering sense of unfinished business. The status quo is maintained, but at a cost that borders on the tragic for some of the characters. For the audience the characterization can prove ambiguous, in the face of the expected polarity and clarity of the comedy: villains evoke sympathy while heroes are flawed and blinkered. Charles Barr goes so far as to describe the characters as "robustly Machiavellian … undermining the Ealing polarisation of nice and wholesome and harmless versus coarse, tough and brutal" (Barr 1980: 118). Philip Kemp wrote of Mackendrick's "dual vision, the split perspective of the half-assimilated outsider … the ambivalence of his regard that sets up the moral tensions within his films" suggesting that this essential ambiguity hinges on the director's own position straddling worlds: Scotland and America, within and without the war (Kemp 1991: 246).

Although Mackendrick was able to flourish as a director at Ealing he was never really comfortable within the benign constraints fostered by Michael Balcon's paternalistic regime. Mackendrick's Ealing films are permeated by a tension between nightmares and the Ealing vision of Britishness. His comedies increasingly subverted the Ealing spirit, veering away from the reassuring messages of unity and communal triumph, questioning consensus and social constraints, probing the nature of postwar Britain and ultimately taking comedy to the brink of darkness, with the satirical vision of *The Man In The White Suit* and the black comedy of *The Ladykillers*. The influence of his body of work continues to be felt, most explicitly in Bill Forsyth's *Local Hero* (1983), effectively paying homage to *Whisky Galore* and *The Maggie* in its evocation of the Scottish idyll, and in the Coen brothers' remake of *The Ladykillers* (2004).

Mackendrick's time at Ealing was just an interlude in his career, spanning five films (including the melodrama *Mandy*) before he traveled to Hollywood. *The Ladykillers* finished Mackendrick's journey through the psyche of a nation. He moved back to his birthplace – America – and to the challenges of Hollywood, while Ealing Studios stuttered to an end. His first American film *The Sweet Smell of Success* (1957) was a critical and box office success that he struggled to build on, ultimately becoming an acclaimed film teacher and author of an influential book *On Film-making*.

References

Barr, C. (1980) *Ealing Studios*, The Overlook Press, New York, NY.
Davies, D.J. (1953) As I see it. *Film Teacher*, 10 (Spring), 8–12.
Durgnat, R. (1970) *A Mirror For England*, Faber & Faber, London.

Frye, N. (1957) *Anatomy of Criticism: Four Essays*, Princeton University Press, Princeton, NJ.

Frye, N. (2002) The argument of comedy, in *Narrative Dynamics: Essays on Time, Plot, Closure, and Trames* (ed. B. Richardson), Ohio State University Press, Columbus, OH, pp. 102–9.

Gunning, T. (2005) On knowing and not knowing, going and not going, loving and not loving, in *The Cinema of Michael Powell* (ed. I.A. Christie), British Film Institute, London, pp. 97–8.

Keating, R. (1986) *Omnibus*, British television program, BBC, May 2.

Kemp, P. (1991) *Lethal Innocence*, Methuen, London.

King, G. (2002) *Film Comedy*, Wallflower Press, London.

Levi-Strauss, C. (1972) *The Savage Mind*. Oxford University Press, Oxford.

Mackendrick, A. (2004) *On Film-making*, Faber & Faber, London.

McArthur, C. (2003) *Whisky Galore! and The Maggie*, I.B. Tauris, London.

McQuarrie, D. (1986) *Mackendrick: The Man Who Walked Away*, British television program, STV, August 21.

Perry, G. (1981) *Forever Ealing*, Pavilion, London.

Rowe, K. (1995) Comedy, Melodrama and Gender, in K.B. Karnick, *Classical Hollywood Comedy*, Routledge, New York, NY, p. 47.

Stott, A. (2005) *Comedy*, Routledge, New York, NY.

Further Reading

Barr, C. (1998) *Ealing Studios*, 3rd edn, University of California Press, Berkeley, CA. Barr has been deemed the absolute authority on Ealing Studios since the original publication of this study, back in 1977. This survey of the life and times of the most celebrated of British film studios is informed by inimitable research, involving interviews with key players and authorities on the subject, many of whom have since passed away. It is a very accessible account, giving a wider social and cultural context to the films.

Frye, N. (2000) Anatomy of Criticism, Princeton University Press, Princeton, NJ. The third essay "Archetypal criticism: theory of myths" provides a critical framework for the study of comedy. Frye develops a framework for literary criticism, aligning comedy with spring, and satire with winter. Frye's schema offers fascinating insights into the mythic potential of comedy.

Kemp, P. (1991) *Lethal Innocence: The Cinema of Alexander Mackendrick*, Methuen, London. The first, and only, comprehensive study of Mackendrick's work, extending beyond Ealing to cover his Hollywood career. This is an indispensable guide to Mackendrick, informed by interviews with Mackendrick, his colleagues and family.

King, G. (2002) *Film Comedy*, Wallflower Press, London. King gives a very useful overview of the comedy genre, including a chapter on satire and a section on the representation of Britishness in Ealing films. This is a wide-reaching study of the forms, and socio-historical contexts of film comedy.

Mackendrick, A. (2004) *On Film-making*, Faber & Faber, London. Frequently acclaimed as the greatest book on filmmaking, this is a distillation of Mackendrick's teachings from his quarter of a century at the California Institute of the Arts in Los Angeles. Mackendrick makes reference to his own films, giving invaluable insights into his vision and techniques. The foreword is written by Martin Scorsese. The editor, Paul Cronin, maintains a website dedicated to Mackendrick's work, http://www.thestickingplace.com/alexander-mackendrick/ (accessed May 4, 2012), and is working on a follow up to *On Film-making*, putting together further writings and interviews.

McArthur, C. (2003) *Whisky Galore! & The Maggie*, I.B. Tauris, London. McArthur's guide to Mackendrick's two Scottish films develops a detailed analysis of the wider socio-cultural context, alongside insights into Ealing Studios and the contemporary reception of the films. McArthur's perspective is critical of the representations of Scottishness in the films, offering a "rethink" of the films.

20

Tragicomic Transformations

Gender, Humor, and the Plastic Body in Two Korean Comedies

Jane Park

Introduction

As a Korean American exchange student in Seoul in the early 1990s, I accepted many free packets of tissue from smiling salesgirls. It was always good to have these on hand because toilet paper wasn't yet available in the public restrooms. I never bothered to read what was printed on the packets until one day, I noticed with horror and shame that they were almost all advertisements for fat farms and weight-loss programs.

Rather than supporting my resistant feminist critique, friends and relatives encouraged me to try the programs, telling me how much prettier I would look if I lost the excess weight. The only people who seemed to find me attractive at the time were older, grandmotherly women, who often stopped me in the street to remark on my beautiful, round *boksileoun* (lucky) face. They obviously didn't realize that the plump features once prized in the hungry, war-torn country of their youth were no longer considered desirable – let alone "lucky."

In this chapter I focus on two South Korean (hereafter, Korean) films that explore the abject, angry, and aspiring forms of humor inspired by such incidents as the personal one described above, of women failing to meet dominant codes of beauty and femininity in contemporary Korean society. *200 Pounds Beauty* (Kim Young-hwa 2006) and *301, 302* (Pak Cheoul-su 1995) follow the plight of single women who are punished for their failure to conform to these codes and who attempt to transcend the limited gender roles allotted them by actively changing their bodies. In the former, an obese 20-something woman has radical plastic surgery to win the love of her indifferent crush object. In the latter, two

A Companion to Film Comedy, First Edition. Edited by Andrew Horton and Joanna E. Rapf.

obsessive-compulsive female neighbors forge a sadomasochistic association that revolves around their perverse relationships to food. The characters all undergo painful physical and psychological transformations, which require certain forms of symbolic death that, in turn, help to facilitate ambiguous scenes of self-reconciliation.

200 Pounds Beauty can be classified as a popular film for its three-act structure, character-driven narrative, and formulaic plot as well as for its commercial success in Korea and the Asian region. Meanwhile, *301, 302*, which received critical accolades at home and abroad, falls squarely into the art house category with its highly experimental narrative and formal style. In contrast to the male-focused action, thriller, and gangster genre films that have gained international popularity since 1999, both movies offer female-focused hybrid comedies, which ambivalently depict the experiences of single, modern women in post-democratic Seoul by focusing on the relationships of the protagonists to their volatile bodies.

While these films foreground female pain and suffering, they also elicit laughter – a laughter that for me and I suspect many female viewers, is tinged with a number of contradictory, sometimes overlapping emotions, including disgust, anger, recognition, anxiety, and elation. As a way of exploring the complexities of this laugher, I want to look at how different kinds of humor – dark and perverse, silly and slapstick – help to frame the narrative development of the protagonists. In particular, I am interested in how popular notions of femininity are addressed, critiqued, and validated through these comedic forms.

For instance, in *200 Pounds Beauty* slapstick humor frames the protagonist's journey and encourages the audience ultimately to identify with her whereas in *301, 302* dark humor does the opposite, precluding the audience from identifying too closely with either character. I want to consider how these processes of identification or distance, prompted by different forms of humor, might be read beyond a simple celebration or critique of so-called normative femininity.

Comedy became a popular genre in South Korea in the 1950s and early 1960s, during the golden age of Korean cinema. Jinsoo An provides a working definition of the genre as "a body of narrative films that feature laughter-producing situations and a happy ending," which can be used to characterize the various comedy cycles since the golden age (An 1998: 31). Transnational, hybrid slapstick films reigned in the late 1950s during the tumultuous period after the Korean War, followed by melodramatic family comedies in the early 1960s when President Park Chung Hee institutionalized the film industry as part of the massive economic restructuring of the nation (Kim, C 2010: 46–118). With the imposition of strict censorship laws, comedy films were necessarily depoliticized, resorting primarily to physical humor in the gender-bending B-film comedies of the late 1960s and youth comedies in the 1970s (Kim, C 2010: 169–201; An 1998: 34–6). Finally, with the 1988 Olympic Games and the emergence of a civilian government in 1993, censorship and regulation were relaxed, allowing comedies to perform social satire as in *Two Cops* (Kang Woo-suk 1993). The form of comedy that came to dominate in the 1990s, however, was the romantic comedy imported through

Hollywood and successfully hybridized for local audiences in the hit film, *Marriage Story* (Kim Ui-seok 1992) (An 1998: 36–8).

The romcom dominance continued in the 2000s, epitomized by the success of films such as *My Sassy Girl* (Kwak Jae-young 2001) and *200 Pounds Beauty*, even as generically hybrid comedies such as *Attack the Gas Station!* (Kim Sang-jin 1999), *My Wife is a Gangster* (Cho Jin-gyu 2001), and *Save the Green Planet* (Jang Joon-hwan 2003) gained national and international recognition. Given the significant presence of comedy in Korean commercial cinema, surprisingly little has been written in English with respect to its formal, narrative, or the historical aspects (An 1998; Ablemann and Choi 2005; Kim, C 2010). Within this already small body of scholarship, Korean women as objects and subjects of humor – rather than of tragic melodrama – have been even less theorized (Choi 2010 85–115; Park, J. 2010).

I seek to help fill this gap by examining how different kinds of humor operate in two films that were marketed as comedies in the United States. What images do *301, 302* and *200 Pounds Beauty* present of urban Korean women? What kinds of physical and emotional transformations do the protagonists undergo, and what effect do they have on how the women perceive themselves and are perceived by others? Most significantly, how is humor deployed to critique the social institutions that fuel the characters' desire to change their bodies? In particular how is it used to help them come to terms with their bodies and the histories of trauma that they bear?

Before answering these questions, it is important to provide some background on conceptions of beauty and femininity in contemporary South Korea.

Remaking Korean Female Bodies

According to an article in the Singapore-based newspaper, *The New Paper*, it took two hours to apply the cosmetic equivalent of 92 pounds on Kim Ah-Jung, the 106-pound actress who plays the before-and-after versions of the protagonist, Hanna, in *200 Pounds Beauty*. When Kim saw herself in the fat suit and makeup for the first time, she was in shock as were her girlfriends who "cried when they saw me, but … couldn't explain why" and her male co-star, Joo Jin-mo, who "asked her weakly, 'are you all right?'" ("Friends Cried When They Saw me in Fat Suit" 2007).

In another article from the same newspaper, Kim confesses "When I first looked at myself after the special effects makeup, I was really shocked and cried when nobody was looking… until the seventh shooting, I couldn't focus on acting". However, she was ultimately able to "immerse herself in the character and even drew strength from nasty comments from passers-by who whispered they 'felt sick' to see her filming in the streets" ("Acting Heavyweight" 2007).

Such extreme aversion to larger female bodies is a relatively new phenomenon in Korea. Historically, full-figured women were valued over their skinnier counterparts for their physical assets, which were seen as more likely to fulfill traditional female expectations, i.e. to produce healthy sons, perform domestic labor, and effectively manage the family. In fact, until the mid-twentieth century and even later in the countryside, beauty was considered a detrimental trait in "proper" women due to its association with their less proper, marginalized counterparts, *kisaeng* (prostitutes and courtesans) (Kendall 1996: 100).

This changed as the country modernized, first with the introduction of Western-style technology and capitalism under Japanese colonization (1910–1945), then with rapid industrialization under the martial government of President Park Chung Hee and his successors (1961–1992), and finally, with the implementation of a civilian government in 1993. Partly in response to higher living standards and the heavy influx of foreign media images, dieting became a national trend among young middle-class women in the early 1990s, and eating disorders such as anorexia and bulimia, previously unheard of in Korea, began to be diagnosed and treated for the first time (Efron 1997).

Cosmetic surgery became popular during this period, and has since become so common, that according to ARA Consulting, which specializes in the industry, a conservatively estimated 30 percent of Korean women aged 20 to 50, had some kind of procedure performed in 2009 (Fackler 2009). The percentage among young women is even higher, according to an Internet poll conducted the same year by the Korean newspaper *Chosun Ilbo* in which almost 60 percent of the 20–30-year-old female participants who were looking for marriage partners said they had had some form of plastic surgery done, and 90 percent said they would if they had the financial resources (90 Percent 2009). Furthermore, going under the knife in Korea is quickly becoming a global phenomenon – included in the growing medical tourism industry dubbed "Medical Hallyu" – which is attracting regional and international clients to the country for such popular procedures as double eyelid surgery, nose implants, and increasingly, jaw reduction as part of a larger entertainment tour package.

The ostensibly Western-inspired aesthetic that result – characterized by fair skin, a tall, thin, busty body, and a small, oval face with large eyes and sharply defined features – seems to emulate the global standard of white female beauty that has been exported through American popular culture, especially Hollywood movies. Yet Asian women who aspire toward this aesthetic end up resembling the female characters of Japanese *manga* and *anime* more than those of American films, and it is the hybrid, Eurasian aesthetic of the former that is promoted in numerous ads and magazines targeting Asian women around the world. Ruth Holliday and Jo Elvfing Hwang emphasize the limitations of reading this aesthetic simply as the imposition of Western beauty codes on Korean women and men who uncritically internalize and reproduce them. They point out that in South Korea "successful surgery with no expense spared, should look 'natural', where natural is importantly defined as enhancing *Korean* features." This is in telling contrast to "unsuccessful surgeries often defined as producing an unnaturally 'Western' appearance" (Holliday and Hwang in press). They go on to add that shifts in aesthetic ideals cannot be reduced to Korea's relationship with the West but must also take into account its "strong sense of nationalism, as well as its national relationship with other regional powers" such as Japan (Holliday and Hwang in press).

Given the complex entanglements of recent transcultural flows with the ongoing legacies of Japanese and American colonialisms, contemporary beauty norms in South Korea seem to gesture toward a global fantasy of feminine beauty, which melds ideal "Western" and "Eastern" features. This racially and culturally hybrid aesthetic marks Korean – and to some extent, Asian – modernity as a complex cultural and aesthetic modification written on the usually young and malleable female body for local and international consumption. Remaking bodies, in this instance, implies both imitation and appropriation and a certain amount of creative agency on the part of those whose bodies are modified. A thorough analysis of this syncretic process is beyond the scope of this paper; however, I attempt to outline its contours in the realm of film comedy.

Interestingly, plastic surgery as an explicit trope or theme rarely appears on the big screen, with three noteworthy examples in *Shiri* (1999) directed by Kang Je-gyu, and *Address Unknown* (2001) and *Time* (2006) both directed by Kim Ki-duk. In these films, the decisions of the female protagonists to change their faces serve as a metaphor for the costs of serving the patriarchal systems of nationalism, US imperialism, and heterosexual romance, respectively. This leads to the death of the protagonist at the hands of her partner in the first case, her self-mutilation in the second, and her insanity in the last – noncomic endings that follow a well-established pattern in Korean cinema, of punishing women for stepping outside the roles of the good Confucian wife and mother.

In contrast, the women in *200 Pounds Beauty* and *301, 302* are not punished by external forces. Instead they live and suffer, knowing they must abide by and appease these forces – the sexist norms that define them as objects of and caregivers for men – in order to gain social visibility and power. Rather than escaping the patriarchal order through death or losing agency by wholly succumbing to it, these characters actively remake themselves, physically and psychologically. In the following sections, I show how these makeovers are presented in a broadly comic register. And I argue that the effect of this comic touch is to expose the constructed nature of the normative femininity, which the protagonists simultaneously resist and desire.

"It's Tough Being Beautiful": The Pain and Labor of Beauty

200 Pounds Beauty whose original title translates to "it's tough being beautiful," focuses on the timely topic of plastic surgery but with a light, comedic touch and a sympathetic, down-to-earth female protagonist who not only survives but also succeeds in reaching her goals.

The musical romcom chronicles the trials and tribulations of Hanna, an unattractive woman graced with a beautiful voice and a heart of gold, who sings backstage for the hot yet hopelessly untalented pop star Ammy (Ji Seo-yun) and moonlights as a phone sex operator to pay for her institutionalized father's medical bills. In her free time, she eats and drinks voraciously with her best friend, Jeong-min (Kim Hyeon-sook), also a backup singer; fantasizes about fitting into stylish clothes; and pines for Sang-jun (Ju Jin-mo), her workaholic boss and Ammy's producer and ex-boyfriend. After a humiliating experience in which she learns Sang-jun is not interested in her, Hanna blackmails one of her sex phone clients – a prominent plastic surgeon – to transform her from head to toe so that she can win Sang-jun's affection.

After the surgery, Hanna reinvents herself as "Jenny," a Korean American ingénue who replaces Ammy and paradoxically gains fame for being an innocent and "natural" beauty. Rather predictably, her new identity and the benefits of being beautiful go to Hanna's head, leading her to cut ties with Jeong-min and her father while growing ever more anxious about being found out as a fraud by Ammy, Sang-jun, and her fans. The anxiety escalates until the climax when Hanna reveals her past identity on stage to a stunned audience, who slowly begin to chant *kwaench'ana* ("it's all right") as she weeps and mourns for her former fat, abject self. In that moment, she dramatically and publicly reconciles who she was with who she has become. The movie ends on an upbeat note with Jenny's death and the rebirth of a new, thin, and confident Hanna – a successful and independent woman for whom Sang-jun now pines.

Adapted from the manga, *Kanna-San, Daiseikou Desu (Kanna's Big Success)* by Suzuki Yumiko, this updated Ugly Duckling meets Little Mermaid story proved to be a surprising hit, selling 6.5 million tickets and earning $45 million at the Korean box office (Paquet 2006). It went on to win the Grand Bell Award for best actress and best cinematography in 2007, was adapted into a successful stage musical in 2008, and spawned a less successful sequel in 2010. The film also performed well in the region, hitting the number one spot in Hong Kong and Singapore (Lee, H-W 2007). Finally, it catapulted Kim Ah-Jung, the actress who plays Hanna, to *hallyu* fame, eclipsing Jun Ji-hyun's popularity from *My Sassy Girl* five years earlier.

At first glance, the film seems to fit all the requirements of the post-feminist narratives epitomized in the *Bridget Jones Diary* and *Sex and the City* movies along with makeover reality TV shows such as *The Swan, From Ladette to Lady,* and *What Not to Wear*. Hanna learns, post-op, that being a "beautiful girl" goes beyond appearances. It involves learning how to *act* beautiful and in so doing, *become* properly desirable and feminine. That this never-ending process of *becoming*, with all of its consumerist pleasures, also restricts women's abilities to reach their full potential as active human subjects is by now a well-known feminist critique in the West (Wolf 2002; Bordo 2004; Tasker and Negra 2007).

A careful reading of films like *200 Pounds Beauty* can add a nonwestern perspective to this discussion by showing how seemingly similar messages of achieving female empowerment through beauty and sexuality are actually grounded in and express very different notions of womanhood in relation to self, family, and society.

For instance, empirical studies on eating disorders among Korean and Korean diasporic women indicate that their desires to be thin cannot be reduced to the simple imitation of a Western fad (Ko and Cohen 1998; Gordon 2005; Jackson et al. 2006). Instead, Neo-Confucian values, which emphasize the family unit and social conformity play a role equally if not more important than that of exposure to Western culture, in shaping the changing norms of modern Korean femininity (Kim, T. 2003). Indeed, Seungsook Moon and Sang-un Park have discussed how an indigenous example of female aspiration is inscribed in the very origin myth of the nation.

In the myth, Koreans trace their ancestor to Tan'gun, the hybrid child of the sky god Hwanung and a female bear. This bear becomes a human woman after she diligently follows the sky god's instructions to eat only garlic and mugwort in a cave for one hundred days. Hwanung pities the Bear Woman because she is single and childless, takes her for his wife, and impregnates her with the future of Korea. According to Moon, this myth "suggest[s] that woman's only contribution to the creation of the Korean nation was the provision of a proto-nationalist womb ... In addition, the transformation of a bear into a woman carries the deep social meaning of womanhood epitomized by patience to endure suffering and ordeal" (Moon 1998: 41). Yet as Park argues, the Bear Woman's persistence also allows her, albeit within the terms of patriarchy, to transform herself physically and thus transcend her animal fate (Park, S. 2007: 46). As mentioned earlier, Neo-Confucianism did not and does not intrinsically value beauty; what Park and Taeyon Kim suggest is that the increasingly important role of beauty in contemporary Korean society – and the idea that one must suffer to attain beauty – is aided and to some extent, intensified through existing Neo-Confucian modes of female socialization which stress conformity and subservience to men. At first glance, *200 Pounds Beauty* appears to endorse a similar kind of aspirational structure in which Hanna must endure emotional and physical suffering to gain male attention. Yet ultimately it celebrates a talented and single career woman who is so successful that she doesn't need a man. What do we make of these seeming contradictions?

The film opens with Hanna's visit to a male fortune-teller who tells her to give up trying to change the fate "written on her face." Hanna respectfully protests and keeps asking for his help to get Sang-jun to love her. The disgusted fortune-teller finally gives her what is clearly a worthless amulet, and in her gratitude, Hanna bows, knocking over and breaking several valuable objects. Her unconscious clumsiness along with other stereotypes associated with fat people such as sloth, gluttony, and stupidity construct her, in the first half of the film, as the literal butt of the joke. Unlike Kathleen Rowe's figure of the "unruly woman," Hanna as a fat woman, cannot critique or counter the male gaze that refuses to acknowledge

Figure 20.1   Hanna negotiating with the plastic surgeon (*200 Pounds of Beauty*; director, Yong-hwa Kim; producer, Park Mu-Seung).

her (Rowe 1995: 31–43). Instead, she retreats to melancholia – internalizing her emotional pain and frustration and responding to male rejection by trying to kill herself. Tragic loss becomes comedic survival, however, in the first major turning point of the film. Hanna is attempting to gas herself after giving up hope of ever attracting Sang-jun, when she is interrupted by a call from one of her top clients, a plastic surgeon desperate to hear her sexy voice singing his favorite song, a Christian hymn.

It is important to note here that Hanna's power as a subject stems from what she can do with her voice, which comes to stand for emotional authenticity both in her backup singing and phone sex work. As an unattractive woman, she is necessarily marginalized in a "lookist" society where women's appearances matter more than their abilities. Yet the film also suggests that in a highly neoliberal society like South Korea, talent matters more than beauty insofar as it can provide the economic means through which one can improve one's appearance. The subsequent scene in which Hanna blackmails the plastic surgeon by playing him a recorded tape of one of their sessions mirrors the opening scene with the fortune teller, replacing and linking traditional magical practices with the magic of modern medical science. It is also the scene in which we first see her breaking fat stereotypes by being clever and resourceful, if not yet angry (see Figure 20.1).

Skinny Unruliness, Fake Innocence, and a Happy, Unromantic Ending

Hanna is not allowed to express anger at men for the way they have treated her and other unattractive women until she herself is attractive. After a painful year of enduring multiple plastic surgery procedures and disciplining her body at the gym – a process condensed into montage – she emerges as a new woman, thin, gorgeous and utterly unrecognizable, even to her best friend. (see Figure 20.2). In contrast to the first half of the film, she wields enormous power over men

Figure 20.2 Post-op Hanna as a "beautiful girl" (*200 Pounds of Beauty*; director, Yong-hwa Kim; producer, Park Mu-Seung).

with her beauty, and the humor of these scenes lies in her unconscious ability to manipulate them into doing what she wants. This is made even more comic – and tragic – when compared with how she is treated before plastic surgery. The humor also rises from scenes in which Hanna sympathizes with a stalker (because like him, she understands unrequited love) and violently beats up the doting salesman who swindles Jeongmin (because like her best friend, she too, has been used by Lotharios). While the anger in these scenes is cathartic for Hanna and the audience, it is bewildering to those around her since her newfound beauty discredits her ability to empathize with the suffering of the ugly.

The only time the film does not trivialize her anger is when she confronts Sang-jun after he tells her that he knows her secret. Crying, she rages:

> It's scary, so I'm only a product. Hanna is worthless but Jenny is worth a fortune. Is that it? … It's been so hard. Now I see I was a big fool … . My having plastic surgery made me repulsive? [She takes down photos of herself and accidentally cuts herself] I'm fine. It doesn't hurt. It's nothing compared to what I've been through. I cut off my bone and skin. Lying on the table do you know who I thought of? I thought that was painful. But this is worse. You broke my heart. Tissue won't fix it. (*200 Pounds Beauty*, 2006)

Tissue doesn't fix it, but Hanna's decision to reveal herself as a fake a few scenes later, miraculously does. In the film's climax, performed by a weeping Kim, Hanna confesses her true identity to her fans as Sang-jun plays footage of the old Hanna singing a song she composed. Interestingly, this is the only Korean song in the movie – all the rest are retro American pop songs by Blondie and Janet Jackson – and it is sung here and earlier, when Hanna auditions as Jenny. This song could be read as emblematic of national and cultural authenticity in contrast to the covers of US songs, and this authenticity is further highlighted in its repetition here, when Hanna's cover is willingly blown (see Figure 20.3).

The film's stance on plastic surgery, much like that on the role of beauty in romantic love, is ambiguous. Jeongmin tells Hanna that women who get plastic surgery are monsters; the plastic surgeon has turned to phone sex because he

Figure 20.3 Jenny tearfully revealing herself as Hanna to a stunned audience (*200 Pounds of Beauty*; director, Yong-hwa Kim; producer, Park Mu-Seung).

no longer desires his made-over wife; and Sang-jun likes Hanna's alter-ego for her supposed innocence and purity. But plastic surgery is ultimately condoned and accepted as a necessary step for achieving personal and professional success. Hanna originally transforms herself in order to get Sang-jun to love her. After the operation, however, she is driven less by her desire for him and more by the determination to realize her new self as a "beautiful girl" and a rising star. What begins as a desperate measure ends up as a smart career move.

What is fascinating, here, is that Hanna's innocence, characterized by the purity of her voice and heart, is built on inauthenticity. In pursuit of money, love, and fame, she commits a number of seemingly deceptive acts. As a backup singer, she perpetuates the fraud that Ammy is actually singing. As a phone sex operator, she helps men commit virtual adultery. Even her relationship with her father has incestuous overtones as she pretends to be her mother whose unexplained death he clearly has not accepted. Hanna's role as substitute for her own mother is also significant insofar as it inverts the normative temporal narrative of young (thin) adolescent girl to matronly (fat) middle-aged wife, thus fulfilling the unnatural dream of eternal youth promised through plastic surgery.

However, Hanna is exonerated of blame in all of these cases because her *intentions* are innocent: she lies in order to help and support *others* as per the Neo-Confucian model of ideal, selfless womanhood. For Ammy and Sang-jun she provides the valuable commodity of talent in an entertainment industry characterized by illusory trends; for her phone sex clients she weaves erotic fantasies that supplement their loveless marriages; and for her father, she sustains the romance of marriage, which she herself curiously eschews at the end of the film for a career.

In this sense, her purity is based on impurity; rather than liberating herself from the androcentric nation through death or reproducing it as a mother, Hanna chooses an alternate route of survival. Perhaps this is one of the reasons the film was so popular not only in Korea but all over Asia – because more than the sacrificial female figures of earlier melodramas, the tragicomic experiences of young, aspiring female characters, provide, for younger audiences, a different relationship to gender, sexuality, and the nation that speaks to the rapid transformation of their countries and cultures, and their own aspirations to become rising stars in the new world order. As a star, Hanna becomes an icon, a commodity whose process of construction is anxiously displayed in the form of her past, natural self, which functions as backdrop to her present, modified self when she comes out to the audience in her last concert as Ammy. In this scene the film provides a fantasy of ultimately painless female transformation – from fat to thin, ugly to beautiful, invisible to visible – that is accepted, and even celebrated, in the public sphere. The key term here is fantasy. It is important to stress that such a scenario remains a fairy tale in present-day South Korea where celebrity suicides following depression, episodes of public shaming, and sexual harassment have become disturbingly routine (Veale 2008; McCurry 2009). This feel good movie thus plays down the continued existence of a highly patriarchal culture in which women, particularly those in the entertainment industry, are still seen primarily as sex objects for men.

Feminist Black Humor in *301, 302*

The neoliberal dream of public female self-empowerment in *200 Pounds Beauty* finds its nightmarish private counterpart in *301, 302*, released a little over a decade earlier and the first Korean film to be distributed internationally. A commercial failure, it was a critical success, winning the Grand Bell Award for Best Film in Korea in 1995 and chosen as the official selection for the Sundance Film Festival, Berlin International Film Festival South Korean nominee for Academy foreign-language film in 1996 (Carson 2007: 267). Unlike *200 Pounds Beauty*, which elides the psychological and physical pain of self-transformation, *301, 302* foregrounds the violence that accompanies women's efforts to change their bodies both in order to conform to and escape from normative codes of womanhood.

The handful of English-language academic articles on the film provides fairly straight feminist readings of how it critiques patriarchy through its representation of the two women and their relationships to food and sex (Kee 2001; Lee, H. 2005; Carson 2007). None, however, notes the ways in which black humor is used to perform this critique, especially with regard to 301's multiple physical and psychic transformations throughout the course of the film. This will be the focus of the reading that follows.

The term "black humor" was coined in 1945 by French surrealist writer and poet André Breton in his edited collection, *Anthology of Black Humor*, which featured a number of short stories by a wide range of writers, philosophers, and artists, including Jonathan Swift (credited by Breton as the originator of this comic form), Lewis Carroll, Friedrich Nietzsche, Arthur Rimbaud, Franz Kafka, and Marcel Duchamp (Breton 2001: 3). In his introduction, Mark Polizzotti summarizes black humor as "the opposite of joviality, wit, or sarcasm. Rather, it is a partly macabre, partly ironic, often absurd turn of spirit that constitutes the 'mortal enemy of sentimentality'" (Breton 2001: vi).

Black humor deals with taboo issues and events, especially death, in a satirical or ironic way even as it maintains their seriousness. Whether appearing in literature, popular media, performance, or everyday life, the intent of such humor is to shock and unsettle the audience, drawing out an uneasy, slightly horrified laughter, which, rather than conforming to and reproducing dominant ideologies, sharply critiques them. In the process, black humor reveals both the powerlessness of human beings caught in an absurd and unjust universe and their strength and resilience as conditionally free agents (see also the material on *Dr. Strangelove* in this volume).

While *301, 302* does not strictly qualify as a comedy, I would argue that, in its incongruous melding of horror and comedy, its ambivalent treatment of taboo topics such as anorexia, death, sexual abuse, and cannibalism, and its campy, masquerading performances of femininity, it is rife with black humor. Both protagonists are single, middle-class women in their late twenties or early thirties, characterized by their compulsive attitudes toward food and by the minimalist, ultramodern apartment spaces where almost all of the action takes place. The plump divorcee in unit 301, Song-hee (Pang Eun-jin), lives to cook and eat while the ascetic writer in unit 302, Yun-hee (Hwang Sin-hye) is nauseated by the sight of food and cannot keep anything down. While the characters are given names, the film usually refers to them by their apartment numbers. This lends them an urban anonymity that aligns them with global capital rather than situating them within familial networks, i.e. as somebody's wife, mother, or daughter, which is still the prominent mode of address for women in Korea (Lee, H. 2005: 12).

The uncomfortable humor of the film derives from the ever more sadistic attempts by 301 to force feed 302, not in a compassionate effort to save her life but to fatten her up so that her gauntness, which 301 desires, no longer poses a threat to her own corpulent femininity (see Figure 20.4). These increasingly violent attempts are intercut with flashbacks of the characters' traumatic pasts, which link their attitudes toward food to sexual abuse and pathology and which culminate in the merging of the two characters when 302 seems to ask 301 to kill, prepare, and eat her. A sardonic twist on the female buddy film, the two women who begin by embodying opposite poles of womanhood (fat, oversexed, excessively domestic versus skinny, celibate, anti-domestic) end in the confidently androgynous persona of 301. A gourmet cannibal and liberated single woman, 301 is finally shown sleeping on the couch where she is pleasantly haunted by her former adversary and now friend, 302, who has literally become a part of her.

The film opens with a male detective visiting 301 to investigate the mysterious disappearance of her neighbor. Through 301's narration, we learn that 302 rejected food, men, and life and desired above all else, to "disappear." Her eating disorder and avoidance of intimacy stem from being abused as a teenager by her stepfather, a butcher whose sex acts are crosscut with the seemingly nurturing act

Figure 20.4   301 attempting to forcefeed her anorexic neighbor (*301, 302*; director and producer Cheol-su Park).

of feeding her meat at the dinner table. There is nothing funny in the scenes that constitute 302's back story: the repeated rapes, shot in a hellish red filter with jarring, industrial music in the background; the dysfunctional conversations between 302 and her neglectful, materialistic mother; and the accidental death, inadvertently caused by 302, of a neighborhood girl, who is found frozen in the shop's refrigerator (a scene that foreshadows the final shot of 302's head frozen in 301's refrigerator).

Quotidian sequences of 302 in the recent past as a depressed writer, swathed in chic, form-hiding black clothing, working on her computer, popping pills, and ceaselessly vomiting are also intentionally heavy, monotonous, and humorless. Due to the relentlessly repetitive way in which these are filmed and the listless, automaton-like way that the character is performed, it is difficult to feel much identification with her, outside of the moral obligation to sympathize with a victim of sexual abuse.

In contrast, the tragicomic story of 301's marriage, its breakdown, and her transformation from victim to victimizer to survivor is much more engaging and provides a useful counterpart to the easy makeover narrative in *200 Pounds Beauty*. 301's marriage paradoxically fails from her extreme efforts to be the model wife, expressed through the elaborate meals she cooks for her husband. In a stylized, somewhat awkward dinner sex scene at the beginning of the marriage, the couple's culinary and erotic appetites are explicitly linked, and we learn that 301 associates her husband's desire for her food with his desire for her.

As Joan Kee points out, "Although 301 supposedly toils for the benefit of her home and thus her husband, it is necessarily a self-centered series of acts intended to appease her own dependency on the unattainable wife-mother ideal"

(Kee 2001: 456). In other words, cooking symbolizes 301's simulacral desire to be the ideal wife and therefore, woman. This desire is rooted in narcissism: 301 wants to construct and inhabit a fantasy of perfect domesticity in which she plays the role of the sexy young wife. When her husband refuses to play the counterpoint role of the appreciative husband, she grows despondent and gains weight, using food to assuage her feelings of rejection.

From Abject Housewife to Liberated Cannibal: 301's Volatile Body

In *200 Pounds Beauty* the fat suit is worn in the first half of the film to distinguish pre-op from post-op Hanna, whose radically different new body is narratively constructed as stable and sustainable; except for a few moments in the tanning booth and in Sang-jun's arms when she is nervous that her silicon breasts might explode or feel unnatural, Hanna experiences no physical side effects from the surgery. Nor does she fundamentally change her lifestyle to maintain her new body. The fat suit paints her as a sympathetic clown who fulfills all the stereotypes of fat people then disappears after the surgery, to be seen only once again as a ghostly mediated presence in a public performance. In contrast, the fat suit in *301, 302* underscores the volatility of 301's constantly transforming body – one that we watch morph into various versions of the character at various points in the film. These, along with changes in her clothes and behavior, mirror her psychological state and serve to cement key events in her life (see Figure 20.5).

First introduced as an elegant thin woman with short hair when she greets the detective, we then see 301 in flashback as a plump and loudly dressed woman on the day she moves into her apartment. This is followed by a montage sequence where she resolves to lose weight and goes on a strict diet and workout routine, which leaves her thinner but with a slightly protruding belly. A second flashback reveals her degeneration from a svelte young wife to an increasingly larger and tackier version of herself as the marriage deteriorates. With green-tinted makeup, a bad perm, and frumpy, matronly clothing, 301 looks the most monstrous during this phase of her life. Finally, we return to the recent past in which she is dining on 302, looking radiant in a white dress and long, wavy hair. This is the last time we see 301 with long hair as the final shot is of her on the couch, appearing the same as when we first see her in the film.

The remainder of this section examines two scenes that combine slapstick and black humor to articulate 301's growing feminist rage and consciousness. While Hanna can only express her anger after she has lost weight and gained popularity, 301 does so at her most abject, after she has gained weight and lost faith in her marriage. Interestingly, this is when she stops trying to be the perfect wife who feeds and cares for her husband and instead decides to satisfy her own excessive appetites.

Figure 20.5 Newly divorced and liberated 301 on a diet (*301, 302*; director and producer Cheol-su Park).

The first scene opens with 301 preparing a huge meal, absurdly complete with a wedding anniversary cake, to eat by herself while watching a variety show on TV (see Figure 20.6). The young male members of then popular hip hop band, Seo Taiji and the Boys, are asked what they seek in a wife. They respond that she needs to be pretty and thin. At this point a huge female comedienne is brought on stage, and everyone bursts into laughter. 301 glares at the screen, eats more cake, and marvels at the woman's bravery. The phone rings. It's her mother excitedly telling her about a new super diet juice that she has just ordered for her. When 301 does not respond positively, she chastises her daughter for letting her body go and unwittingly destroying her marriage. Unable to take the incessant criticism, 301 screams, "I don't know, Mom! Just hang up!" and cuts her off. Later, she is settling back into the couch when she hears something rip. The camera cuts to a close-up of a large tear in the seat of her skirt. She spends the rest of the day eating, imagining her husband having an affair, and bathing Chong Chong, their little pet dog. When the husband comes home late and drunk, he chastises her for leaving the dog in the bathtub and almost downing it, then proceeds to heap attention on Chong Chong and ignore his wife.

Hyangjin Lee notes that both 301 and 302 reject their mothers and by extension, motherhood – a "denial [that]... claims back the female body from the patriarch ... [and becomes] the symbol of her new sexual identity" (Lee, H. 2005: 10). The only mother to appear on screen is 302's who sacrifices her daughter's wellbeing for the comforts of a petit-bourgeois existence while 301's mother is reduced to a nagging voice on the phone. Both mothers also are significantly absent in the jarring pre-credit sequence, which juxtaposes voiceovers of 301 and 302 as little girls talking about how they don't like their mothers' food.

Figure 20.6   Hanna as a fat and unhappy housewife, watching television and talking to her mother on the phone (*200 Pounds of Beauty*; director, Yong-hwa Kim; producer, Park Mu-Seung).

Later we see 301 standing precariously on a stool, chopping a zucchini while 302 hides furtively in the corners of the butcher shop. When the women reject their mothers, they also reject the ideological role of the "modern wife" embodied by women of their mothers' generation, the first to move to the city, live in nuclear families, and aggressively manage the family's finances and children's education (Cho 2002: 172–9).

In the second scene, 301 defies all her mother's expectations for her to succeed in this role, which requires sublimating erotic and emotional desire for the husband to rearing children and successfully orchestrating the household. While 301 cooks breakfast, her husband tells her he would rather eat fast food since it is more modern and convenient. She responds by asking if he would also like to buy women on the street, conflating the consumption of food with that of sex, and accusing him of having an extramarital affair. As he splutters, 301 calmly declares, "Today's meal is the last I cook for you. I used your favorite ingredient. I need money. I'm going to cook better and live the way I want."

The next shot is an extreme close up of Chong Chong's head boiling in the pot. A clear allusion to the scene in which Alex (Glenn Close) cooks the pet family bunny in *Fatal Attraction*, this act codes 301 as crazy and foreshadows her murder of 302. What complicates this reading, though, is the fact that *boshintang*, the soup that 301 makes out of Chong Chong, is a dish that is not coded as "modern" or cosmopolitan in South Korea. It is also often associated with enhancing virility in men. Hence by feeding her husband their dog and symbolic child, 301 responds to her husband's critique of her cooking and by extension, her domestic performance, and effectively severs the marriage.

Later, as a newly single woman, she diligently goes on a diet and works out, following the advice that 302 writes in a women's magazine. She loses weight but then finds life dull and decides to cook lavish meals again, this time for her neighbor who comes to stand as a substitute for her ex-husband with her indifference to 301 and her preoccupation with work, i.e. her writing, which unlike 301's cooking, is consumed in and by the public. A number of scenes follow in which 301 violently tries to feed 302 until she learns about 302's trauma and subsequent illness, at which point she begins to treat her like a surrogate child, cooking her soft food and bathing her.

In a perverse inversion of pregnancy, 301 finally ingests 302, an act that seems to help her achieve equilibrium between the two poles of feminist resistance that the two embodied, namely excessive masquerade and disengagement. Kee notes that "Pak undermines the treatment of 301/302 as a horror film by infusing the dinner scene in which 301 presumably dines on the body of 302 with an almost reverent quality" reminiscent of the Holy Communion (Kee 2001: 454). The head of 302 in the fridge becomes an object of worship, and 301 plays the role of "reverent priestess rather than culpable murderer" (Kee 2001: 454).

I would suggest that the scene, which provides a different kind of "happy ending," is also infused with the campy humor that characterizes the film's overall treatment of domestic femininity as controlled masquerade. This is epitomized in 301's interaction with the detective, where she plays the innocent divorcee whose extraordinary culinary skills he blithely enjoys but which we know have more dangerous potential. Furthermore, the detective is incapable of interrogating 301 because she strategically deploys the (private) housewife role in a similar way that Sang-jun cannot interrogate Hanna because she seamlessly performs the (public) female star. 301's obsessive compulsiveness, which would be coded as psychotic were she a man, is instead coded here as the normalized female condition of hysteria. Funnily enough, this is what allows her to get away with murder.

Conclusion

On the surface *301, 302* and *200 Pounds Beauty* are very different films, stylistically (art house versus commercial), temporally (preglobal Korean film versus postglobal Korean film), ideologically (feminist versus post-feminist), and comically (black humor versus slapstick). Perhaps the most important difference is that whereas Hanna publicly confesses her secret – and thereby gains approval from and conditional power within the patriarchal order – 301 withholds the secret indefinitely, arguably displaying a greater power in her subversive ability to overplay the rules of the game. Both, however, describe a similar process of marginalized women attempting to gain agency and power by modifying their bodies. For Hanna this means getting plastic surgery to become visible in a society that fails to see her; for 301 and 302 this means using food to imagine an alternate space in which their identities are no longer defined by and through men.

More specifically, the films chronicle the psychological transformations of Hanna and 301 through their physical transformations. The processes and effects of these changes are tragicomic: the protagonists experience pain, loss, and suffering yet ultimately survive and/or find peace. The characters all attempt to live outside the normative gender roles of wife/mother, primarily through their professional identities. Hanna and 302 distinguish themselves through their singing and authorial voices, respectively, and 301 actively gets out of her marriage to pursue her cooking. Perhaps more significantly, these characters blur the boundaries between work and life. Hanna's "home" shifts from her apartment to hospital to the music studio as her identity and body changes. The apartments of 301 and 302 reflect their "work" – characters comment that one looks like a restaurant, the other, a library.

Both films clearly critique motherhood and by extension, the bourgeois nuclear family structure, primarily through absent, negligent, or critical mothers. These inadequate mother figures find their complements in weak, abusive, or workaholic patriarchs: Hanna's demented father, 302's abusive stepfather, Sang-jun, and 301's husband. As a substitute for the breakdown of familial networks, the films feature strong, if ambivalent, bonding among female friends. Jeongmin, Hanna's best friend, functions as a surrogate sister, giving her advice and taking care of her as well as her double, attempting suicide after male rejection, and also opting to get plastic surgery. Meanwhile, what begins as a contest of wills between two antipodal women in *301, 302* dissolves into a culinary merging that sparks their friendship after 302's death.

Finally, both films use female bodies to represent the complex palimpsest of Korean modernity to international audiences. As such they supplement and extend the existing English-language scholarship on Korean cinema, which has focused either on the figures of sacrificial and/or transgressive women in melodramas of the golden age or the role of men in more contemporary, especially post-1999 Korean cinema, which consists primarily of action and gangster films. By injecting melodrama and horror with different kinds of comedy, these films project another image of a contemporary Korea in which women carve out alternative spaces for themselves as subjects by actualizing their fantasies.

The fact that very little critical literature exists on comedy in Korean cinema has to do with the fact that in South Korea, as in the United States and other parts of the world, comedy has been considered inferior to other genres, targeted as low culture, and feminized. It also has to do with filmmakers being unwilling to take a risk in targeting female audiences, although this is changing with the success of romcoms such as *My Sassy Girl* and *200 Pounds Beauty*. However, this success is still limited to the Asian region, which begs the question of cultural specificity that comedy inevitably poses. As Kristine Karnick and Henry Jenkins remind us, "like all cultural practices, laughter has a history, a history that reflects tensions of class, race, gender and sexuality, a history that needs to be central to our attempts to understand film comedy" (Karnick and Jenkins 1995: 269).

A joke is funny only if the audience has the cultural literacy to decode it. This literacy can come from a lived knowledge of the culture in which the joke originates, the formal and narrative conventions through which the joke is structured and told, or a combination of both. In an era of cross-cultural flows and flows of people, intensified through ever more advanced media and transportation technologies, what is considered funny, how, why, for whom and in what contexts are important questions that can help us understand the ways in which these flows are changing our notions of identity and community.

In 2009 Pak Cheoul-su was slated to direct an independent US remake of *301, 302* into a Hollywood film titled *10A/10B* starring Marisa Tomei and Liv Tyler (McNary). And in 2011, an American reviewer of *200 Pounds Beauty*, echoing the sentiments of many US viewers, wrote "there's nothing in here that feels distinctly Korean, and the amusing bits wouldn't be out of place in a particularly warm-hearted romantic comedy from Hollywood" (Kratina 2011). These films seem to be seen as having universal appeal for women, but neither will be remade anytime soon, perhaps due to the unsuccessful reception of similar remakes in the United States such as *My Sassy Girl* and *The Lakehouse* (Park, J 2010: 13.3–13.4). If and when they and other women-centered comedies from Korea do break into the US market, it will be interesting not only to see how the humor translates over (or not) but also how it reconfigures the ways in which women, as objects and subjects of laughter, appear on the big screen.

Acknowledgements

This work was supported by the Academy of Korean Studies Grant (AKS-2011-R15). Many thanks to Joanna Rapf and Andy Horton for kindly inviting me to contribute to the volume and their extraordinary patience with me through the editing process. I presented different versions of this chapter in 2011 at the Association for Asian Studies, the Cultural Studies Association of Australia, and the Korean Studies Association of Australia and received helpful comments from the audiences. I especially want to thank Soyoung Kim, Hyaeweol Choi, and Joanna Elfving-Hwang for their excellent suggestions and advice.

References

90 Percent of Korean Women Would Have Plastic Surgery, Poll Shows (2009) *Chosun Ilbo*, (October 26).

Ablemann, N. and Choi, J. (2005) "Just because": Comedy, melodrama and youth violence in *Attack the Gas Station*, in *New Korean Cinema* (eds. C. Shin and J. Stinger), New York University Press, New York, NY, pp. 132–43.

Acting Heavyweight (2007) *The New Paper* (January 16).

An, J. (1998) Anxiety and laughter in Korean comedy films, in *Post Colonial Classics of Korean Cinema* (ed. C. Choi) University of California Press, Irvine, CA, pp. 31–8.

Bordo, S. (2004) *Unbearable Weight: Feminism, Western Culture, and the Body*, 10th edn, University of California Press, Berkeley, CA.

Breton, A. (2001) *Anthology of Black Humor* (trans. and introduced by Mark Polizzotti), City Lights Publishers, San Francisco, CA.

Carson, D. (2007) Transgressing boundaries: from sexual abuse to eating disorders in *301/302*, in *Seoul Searching: Culture and Identity in Contemporary Korean Cinema* (ed. F. Gatewood), SUNY Press, Albany, NY pp. 265–82.

Cho, H. (2002) Living with conflicting subjectivities: Mother, motherly wife, and sexy woman in the transition from colonial-modern to postmodern Korea, in *Under Construction: The Gendering of Modernity, Class and Consumption in the Republic of Korea* (ed. L. Kendall), University of Hawaii Press, Honolulu, HI, pp. 165–97.

Choi, J. (2010) *The South Korean Film Renaissance: Local Hitmakers, Global Provocateurs*, Wesleyan University Press, Middletown, CT.

Efron, Sonni, Women's Eating Disorders Go Global (1997) *The Los Angeles Times*, October 18.

Fackler, Martin, Economy Blunts Korea's Appetite for Plastic Surgery (2009) *The New York Times* (January 2).

Friends Cried When They Saw me in Fat Suit (2007) *The New Paper* (April 20).

Gordon, R. (2005) Eating disorders east and west: A culture-bound syndrome unbound, in *Eating Disorders and Cultures in Transition* (eds. M. Nasser, M. Katzman, and R. Gordon), Taylor & Francis, New York, NY, pp. 1–21.

Holliday, R. and Elfving-Hwang, J. (in press) Gender, globalization and cosmetic surgery in South Korea. Forthcoming in *Body and Society*.

Jackson, S., Keel, P., and Lee, Y. (2006) Trans-cultural comparison of disordered eating in Korean Women. *International Journal of Eating Disorders*, 39 (6), 498–502.

Karnick, K. and Jenkins, H. (1995) Introduction: Comedy and the social world, in *Classical Hollywood Comedy* (eds. K. Karnick and H. Jenkins), Routledge, New York, NY, pp. 265–81.

Kee, J. (2001) Claiming sites of independence: Articulating hysteria in Pak Ch'l-su's *301/302*. *Positions: East Asia Cultures Critique*, 9 (2), 449–66.

Kendall, L. (1996) *Getting Married in Korea: Of Gender, Morality and Modernity*, University of California Press, Berkeley, CA.

Kim, C. (2010) South Korean Golden-Age Comedy Film: Industry, Genre, and Popular Culture (1953–1970). Dissertation. Department of East Asian Languages and Cultures. University of Illinois at Urbana-Champaign.

Kim, T. (2003) Neo-Confucian body techniques: Women's bodies in Korea's consumer society. *Body and Society*, 9 (2), 101–2.

Ko, C. and Cohen, H. (1998) Intraethnic comparison of eating attitudes in native Koreans and Korean Americans using a Korean translation of the eating attitudes test. *The Journal of Mental and Nervous Disease*, 186 (10), 631–6.

Kratina, A./Comic Book Bin (2011) 200 Pounds Beauty at the Fantasia Film Festival, http://www.comicbookbin.com/200poundsbeauty001.html (accessed May 18, 2012).

Lee, H. (2005) Representing sex and sexuality: Requiem for mother. *Gender and Sexuality*, 1, 7–28.

Lee, Hyo-won (2007) *200 Pounds Beauty* Charms Overseas Film Fans. *Korea Times* (May 30).

McCurry, Justin (2009) Storm in South Korea over Jang Ja-yeon's Suicide. *Guardian* (April 1).

McNary, Dave (2009) Marisa Tomei, Liv Tyler Team to Thrill: Chul-soo Park to Direct 10A/10B. *Variety* (May 7).

Moon, S. (1998) Begetting the nation: The androcentric discourse of national history and tradition in South Korea, in *Dangerous Women: Gender and Korean Nationalism* (eds. E. Kim and C. Choi), Routledge, New York, NY, pp. 33–65.

Paquet, Darcy/Koreanfilm.org (2006) *200 Pounds Beauty*, http://koreanfilm.org /kfilm06.html (accessed May 18, 2012).

Park, J. (2010) Remaking the Korean romcom: A case study of *Yeopgijeongin geunyeo* and *My Sassy Girl*, in *Complicated Currents: Media Flows and Soft Power in East Asia* (eds. D. Black, S. Epstein, and A. Tokita), Monash University E-Press, Melbourne, pp. 13.1–13.12.

Park, S. (2007) "Beauty will save you": The myth and ritual of dieting in Korean society. *Korea Journal*, 47 (2), 41–69.

Rowe, K. (1995) *The Unruly Woman: Gender and the Genres of Laughter*, University of Texas Press, Austin, TX.

Tasker, Y. and Negra, D. (eds.) (2007) *Interrogating Postfeminism: Gender and the Politics of Popular Culture*, Duke University Press, Durham, NC.

Veale, Jennifer (2008) South Koreans are Shaken by a Celebrity Suicide. *Time* (October 6).

Wolf, N. (2002) *The Beauty Myth: How Images of Beauty are Used Against Women*, Harper Perennial, New York, NY.

Further Reading

An, J. (1998) Anxiety and laughter in Korean comedy films, in *Post Colonial Classics of Korean Cinema* (ed. C. Choi), University of California Press, CA, pp. 31–8. To date, Jin-soo An's work on South Korean comedy films remains the only historical survey of the genre written in English. An traces how these films illuminated and redefined ideas of family, domesticity, and gender roles during the tumultuous socioeconomic changes in South Korea from the late 1950s to the early 1990s. Subgenres examined include the melodramatic family-based comedies of the late 1950s, the gender-bending slapstick movies of the 1960s, the college youth films of the 1970s, and the romantic comedies of the 1990s.

Choi, J. (2010) *The South Korean Film Renaissance: Local Hitmakers, Global Provocateurs*, Wesleyan University Press, Middletown, CT, pp. 85–115. Jinhee Choi provides a comprehensive overview of the growth of the South Korean film industry in the past decade, linking close readings of blockbusters with their industrial production contexts. Her chapter on such popular romance films as *My Sassy Girl*, *Art Museum by the Zoo*, and *Asako in Ruby Shoes* is one of the few essays in English, to date, on this genre in contemporary Korean cinema.

Kim, S. (2005) Questions of women's film: *The Maid*, *Madame Freedom*, and women, in *South Korean Golden Age Melodrama: Gender, Genre, and National Cinema* (eds. K. McHugh and N. Abelmann), Wayne State University Press, Detroit, MI, pp. 185–200. In this groundbreaking work, Soyoung Kim provides a genealogy of "women's film" in South Korea from the 1950s to 1990s. She begins by tracing the multilayered ways in which such classic films as *The Maid* and *Madame Freedom* (http://uk.omg.yahoo.com/news/victoria-beckham-knows-shes-successful-spice-girl-110222418.html) constructed notions of modern womanhood in the 1950s. Kim then goes on to draw links between figures of female military sex workers in the melodramas of that period and in independent cinema of the 1990s, showing how the genre of women's film continues to evolve, both aesthetically and politically.

Rowe, K. (1995) *The Unruly Woman: Gender and the Genres of Laughter*, University of Texas Press, Austin, TX. Kathleen Rowe's study of "unruly women" shifts the feminist lens from melodrama to comedy in order to look at the multiple strategies that such strong, funny, and rebellious women characters and performers as Miss Piggy and Roseanne Barr deploy to critique the patriarchal institutions and ideologies that try to contain them. The book is particularly useful for its emphasis on the female body as a site of potential transgression and transformation.

21

Comedy "Italian Style" and *I soliti ignoti (Big Deal on Madonna Street, 1958)*

Roberta Di Carmine

FERRIBBOTTE *(Tiberio Murgia): Sono sempre i piùmeglio che se ne vanno.*

DANTE CRUCIANI *(Totò) Ebbè: oggi a te (indica Ferribbotte), domani a lui ...* *(indica Capannelle)*

FERRIBBOTTE: *The best are always the ones to go.*

DANTE CRUCIANI: *Well, today your turn (pointing at Ferribbotte) tomorrow his ... (pointing at Capannelle) (Mario Monicelli, I soliti ignoti)*

Comedy "Italian Style"

Cinema has always had a vital role in Italian society. Between the 1930s and the 1970s, Italian cinema attracted the largest audience in Europe, a goal reached primarily because of its ability to appeal to people with stories related to the Italians' life experiences (Gundle 1990: 195–224). A popular genre in Italian cinema, comedy responded more than other genres to Italian audience's expectations to find entertainment and escapism in cinema thus establishing its influence in the transformation of Italian social and cultural reality.

Considered by many to represent both a movement and a genre, "Italian style" comedy (*commedia all'italiana*) generally includes comedies produced between the late 1950s and the late 1970s (Giacovelli 1990: 7–12; Fournier Lanzoni 2008: 1). Some of the most popular "Italian style" comedies include *La grande guerra*

A Companion to Film Comedy, First Edition. Edited by Andrew Horton and Joanna E. Rapf.
© 2013 John Wiley & Sons, Inc. Published 2016 by John Wiley & Sons, Inc.

(*The Great War*) (Mario Monicelli 1959), *Tutti a casa* (*Everybody Go Home*) (Luigi Comencini 1960), *Il mantenuto* (*His Women*) (Ugo Tognazzi 1961), *Divorzio all'italiana* (*Divorce Italian Style*) (Pietro Germi 1961), *Il sorpasso* (*The Easy Life*) (Dino Risi 1962), *I mostri* (*Opiate '67*) (Risi 1963), and *Sedotta e abbandonata* (*Seduced and Abandoned*) (Germi 1964). Depicting their respect for traditional beliefs and morals and mocking Italian life with irony and often without pity, the characterization of the Italian's faults and taboos unsettled the foundations of Italian society by openly showing its hypocrisy and pettiness.

These comedies define an "Italian" style because they expose social and political changes that involve Italian popular culture – a culture influenced by the Catholic Church but also transformed by the phenomena of urbanization and industrialization during the years of the economic miracle. In the aftermath of World War II, and with the proclamation of a democratic republic, Italy had to face the challenges of rebuilding a society destroyed by the war, but also find a balance between the historical heritage left by fascism and the uncertainty given by a new political direction following the victory of the Christian Democratic Party in 1948. This unstable phase deeply affected Italy as it shifted from a mostly agricultural and traditional society to an industrial and modernized one in which the nation's economy successfully explored foreign markets.

In this chapter, I wish to offer insights on "Italian-style" comedy and its role in Italian film culture by looking at Mario Monicelli's *I soliti ignoti* (*Big Deal on Madonna Street* 1958). Considered to be the prototype of this new comic style, *I soliti ignoti* best exemplifies the "Italian style" by offering a comic and yet pungent analysis of the cultural changes that characterized Italy in the late 1950s. Thanks to this film, director Monicelli, with the collaboration of screenwriters Age, Scarpelli and Suso Cecchi D'Amico, launched a comic style that points out, pitilessly and nastily, the absurdities of cliché and commonplaces found in the Italian culture.[1] As Monicelli eloquently says, comedy "Italian style" better than any other genre responded to a criticism of manners, an indication of a disposition to say things "with a little tongue-in-cheeks, or at least with a satirical intention, with a desire to ridicule" because, he admits, "Comedy is nasty; even better, it is cruel" (Gili 1980: 63; Mondadori 2005: 15).[2]

Although inclined to provoke laughter, "Italian-style" comedy offers a dark portrayal of the illness of society. Maurizio Grande sees in this aspect one of the main reasons for its popularity as it portrays Italy in a negative yet humorous way, a society that is "deaf, distracted, cynical, indifferent, blind, bold, aggressive, amoral, scornful, chameleon, greedy for success and ready to pay it at any price" (Grande and Caldiron 2003: 53). It is by avoiding sugar-coated depictions of the Italian reality that comedies became successful among audiences as they criticized a society that, because of the country's greater wealth, became more individualistic but neglected the needs of individuals. Laughing at somebody else's expenses has been very effective among Italian audiences whenever films were meant to expose viewers to a society characterized by hypocrisy and prejudices.

Together with Monicelli, a number of directors (among others, Germi, Risi, Comencini), screenwriters (such as Age and Scarpelli, Cecchi D'Amico, Ruggero Maccari, Rodolfo Sonego) and actors (Marcello Mastroianni, Vittorio Gassman, Alberto Sordi, Monica Vitti, and Anna Magnani) shared their views, with irony and some malice, on a period characterized by economic and social transformations. Political and social reforms and unequal wealth distribution, increasing clashes between lower and upper classes, housing shortages, and increasing unemployment account for the socio-economic aspects depicted in "Italian-style" comedy.

Contrary to the remarks often made by scholars and critics who see Monicelli as the "father" of the *commedia all'italiana*, the Italian director rejects this label because, he claims, the style has always been part of film comedy as it originated from *commedia dell'arte* (Monicelli *et al.* 2001: 54). He insists, however, in stressing the fundamental role of actors, such as Totò, Gassman and Sordi, whose brilliant comic performances resemble the ridiculousness of the stock characters of the *commedia dell'arte*. In portraying the good qualities as well as the faults of ordinary people, the characterization given by Totò in films such as *Totò cerca casa* (1949) and *Guardie e ladri* (1951) exemplify the attention given by comedy films to a society distressed and profoundly shaken by the war.

In the past few years, the work of some scholars, such as Rémi Fournier Lanzoni, has provided a critical background to evaluate more effectively and, consequently, appreciate the historical and artistic place of "Italian style" comedy in Italian cinema. Fournier Lanzoni speaks of "Italian style" comedy as a response to the bourgeois comedies of the postwar era, and includes in this movement "comedies from approximately 1958 to 1979 that share a common denominator: a new type of ruthless social satires through the lenses of cynicism and the grotesque" (Fournier Lanzoni 2008: 8). Gian Piero Brunetta comments on how, in "Italian-style" comedy, the need to denounce old and new problems of a society deeply affected by two world wars, fascism, the Resistance, and the economic miracle, is embodied by versatile performances of comic actors (Brunetta 1995: 312).

I soliti ignoti: Monicelli's Comedy "Italian Style"

I soliti ignoti tells the story of a group of unskilled but amiable thieves who try to commit the perfect heist by robbing the safe of the *Monte di Pietà* (charitable pawnbroker) located in *Via delle Madonne* (on Madonna Street) (see Figures 21.1–21.3). The idea comes from Cosimo (Memmo Carotenuto) who, at the beginning of the film, is sent to jail for attempting to steal a car. Once in prison, he learns about the possibility of robbing the safe by breaking through the wall of a vacant apartment. This last heist would allow him happily to retire. Capannelle (Carlo Pisacane), the eldest of the group, and Norma (Rossana Rory), Cosimo's girlfriend, in order to

Figure 21.1 *I soliti ignoti* (1958; producer, Franco Cristaldi). Capannelle (Carlo Pisacane), Tiberio (Marcello Mastroianni), Peppe (Vittorio Gassman) and Ferribbotte (Tiberio Murgia), eating pasta and beans after failing the "big deal."

get Cosimo out of jail, find in Peppe (Vittorio Gassman), an unsuccessful boxer, ironically nicknamed "the Panther," the one who can take Cosimo's place for the attempted theft.

The other thieves involved in the heist include: the goodhearted Mario (Renato Salvatori), the youngest of the thieves, who ends up stealing baby carriages because, he says, "they are the only ones left without an alarm"; Ferribbotte (Tiberio Murgia), a possessive Sicilian who keeps his sister, Carmelina (Claudia Cardinale) locked in their apartment because he does not want to compromise his Sicilian "man's honor" as she is engaged and about to be married; and Tiberio (Marcello Mastroianni), a former photographer who is taking care of his son while his wife is in jail serving time for smuggling cigarettes.

The story develops when Peppe is out of jail because of an amnesty. After learning about the safe from Cosimo, Peppe convinces the others to do the job. They begin studying each detail of the robbery, from searching for the best spot in order to get into the vacant apartment to taking lessons on how to break into a safe from a respectable and renowned thief, Dante Cruciani (Totò). The "scientific method," as Peppe calls this big hit, is carefully prepared, beginning with a movie filmed by the thieves to show the inside the apartment where the safe is located.

The core of the movie follows the unlucky heroes as they learn how to break a safe from their master, Dante, while Mario falls in love with Carmelina and Peppe befriends Nicoletta (Carla Gravina), the maid employed by two elderly ladies who live in the apartment next to the pawnshop. Prior to the thieves breaking into the

Figure 21.2 *I soliti ignoti* (1958; producer, Franco Cristaldi). Tiberio (Marcello Mastroianni), Ferribbotte (Tiberio Murgia), Mario (Renato Salvatori), Capannelle (Carlo Pisacane), Peppe (Vittorio Gassman) meeting with the renowned master thief, Dante Cruciani (Totó).

Figure 21.3 *I soliti ignoti* (1958; producer, Franco Cristaldi). Learning how to break into a safe with master thief Dante Cruciani (Totó).

now vacant apartment, Cosimo is out of jail but, rather than collaborating with the others on this robbery, decides to work on his own but ends up dying tragically. In the attempt to mug an older woman, he is run over by a tram while trying to avoid getting caught by the police.

The end of the film focuses on Peppe, Capannelle, Tiberio and Ferribbotte in the vacant apartment. Mario is the only one to give it up as he decides to find an honest job in order to marry Carmelina. Viewers follow the thieves as they heroically overcome some more comic obstacles on the way to carry out their big deal. Once they finally break through the wall, they realize that the scientific method, the favorite definition used by the stammering Peppe, failed as they hit the wrong wall. In the end, dirty and disheartened, the protagonists sit in the kitchen, eating pasta and beans and discussing their loss and their unhappiness, yet still willing to move on with their unfortunate lives. Leaving the apartment almost bursting into flames while Capannelle reheats a bowl of pasta, Ferribbotte and Tiberio go back to their respective homes, Peppe is mistaken as a worker while entering a factory, and Capannelle wanders in the streets of the outskirts of Rome. The last shot is of a newspaper article that states: "Persons unknown bore a hole to steal pasta and beans" (*I soliti ignoti: col sistema del buco rubano pasta e fagioli*).

In offering an ironic denunciation of the 1958 society, *I soliti ignoti* establishes one of the main traits of "Italian style" comedy: social satire. It also successfully mirrors an historical epoch characterized by postwar reconstruction, economic development and a personal awareness of social changes. The peak in the growth of Italian national economy was reached between 1958 and 1963, a period of five years commonly defined by historians as the economic boom. As implied by its definition, "boom" underlines the sudden economic thriving, the economic miracle that renovated the national economy of a society that rapidly became urbanized and industrialized.[3]

The portrayal of a small group of Italian petty thieves reflects this unique economic climate, a time characterized by contradictions provoked by consumerism which deeply affected the social structure of Italy. Thanks to the unforeseen acclaim received by *I soliti ignoti*, comedy "Italian style" gained extraordinary popularity among national and international audiences and critics.

The film was born under bizarre circumstances. As noted by Enrico Giacovelli, when Monicelli was asked by producer Franco Cristaldi to make use of the expensive sets created for Luchino Visconti's *Notti bianche* (*White Nights*, 1957), he decided to make a parody of one of his favorite genres, the American crime films, and of the French caper film Jules Dassin's *Rififi*. In fact, following the popularity of the 1955 French film, he initially thought of an Italian comedy titled *Rufufù* to poke fun at the criminals' personalities but then decided to set a story of a group of "unknown individuals", in a poor Roman neighborhood, which would speak of Italian humankind, something he felt comfortable describing (Giacovelli 1990: 45).

Also, a few artistic components of the film suggest the effects of its popularity on other famous films of the period. The quick pace of the film's opening, which introduces the film's "criminals," sustained by a jazzy soundtrack, seems to be reminiscent of the opening sequence of Billy Wilder's *Some Like It Hot*, released in 1959. Monicelli, like Wilder, mixes conventions and codes of traditional American crime films and comedy to entertain viewers while at the same time inviting them to reflect upon the absurdities of societal expectations and norms.

Nominated for the 1959 Academy Award's Best Foreign Film, *I soliti ignoti* became the most recognized of the new genre. The sequels of *I soliti ignoti*, *Audace colpo dei soliti ignoti* (*Fiasco in Milan*) (Nanny Loy 1960) and *I soliti ignoti vent'anni dopo* (*Big Deal on Madonna Street 20 Years Later*) (Amanzio Todini 1985) failed to reproduce the comic and ironic depiction accomplished by the 1958 film (Giacovelli 2002: 95; Fournier Lanzoni 2008: 42). The originality of the 1958 film lies in its ability to reflect so effectively the socio-economic context of a very unique period. By having characters whose personalities are defined by dialects and by clothing style, Monicelli emphasizes Italy's geographical and cultural diversity. Comic dialogue serves to convey humor because it relies on the unique cultural value of the dialect. Monicelli has pointed out that "Italian-style" comedy was mostly defined by the presence of dialects, another reflection of the social reality of the 1950s when the Italian language as a unified language had not been formed but was divided by its many dialects (Mondadori 2005: 29).

The variety of dialects in *I soliti ignoti* includes the Roman dialect of Tiberio, Peppe, Mario, Cosimo, and Norma, the Neapolitan of Dante, the Sicilian of Ferribbotte and Carmelina, the northern dialects from Veneto of Caterina and from Bologna of Capannelle and, finally, the dialects of supporting characters such as Carmelina's fiancé, from Abruzzo, Caterina's soldier-boyfriend, from Puglia. They suggest the existence of a microcosm of poor devils, each of them embodying the clichés and commonalities of both Northern and Southern Italians and emphasized to unmask their ridiculousness and to stress the authenticity of the film's narrative. For example, the actress Carla Gravina, in her role as a maid speaking the dialect of Veneto, mimics a role and a dialect traditionally related to the eighteenth-century Venetian playwright Carlo Goldoni. Monicelli intentionally refers to the character's social status and also to the traditions of the *commedie*, a mix of wit and humor typically found in Goldoni's plays. The dialect is reminiscent of another cinematic tradition of Italian neorealism, an indication of the comedy's appreciation of stories that viewers could relate to as if they were "real."[4] Jean A. Gili (1998) claims, the uniqueness of *I soliti ignoti* as an "Italian-style" comedy can be found in its ability to convey the artistic expression left by Italian neorealism, such as its social realism, into a new cinematic movement (Gili 1998: 176).

As Sebastiano Mondadori (2005) points out, "Italian style" comedy emphasizes how humor relies on the peculiarity of the moment, of a specific period and place, a "generational sensibility" successfully expressed in Monicelli's film (Mondadori 2005: 65–6). The comic lines, however, reflect the individual's drama in adjusting to an evolving society and lifestyle. Capannelle, the eldest of the group, exemplifies this comic formula. One of his wishes is to get a mistress when he gets the money from the "big deal." His comic attempts to eat whenever he comes across some food, combined with his desire for a mistress in his life, embody the contradictions stereotypically assigned to the average, traditional Italian man. This is also the paradox commonly found in "Italian style" comedy and established here by the contrast between needs (food) and desires (mistress).

In *I soliti ignoti*, the comic situations function to underline the struggle of the lower social classes in the late 1950s. This comic style successfully spoke to Italian viewers of a reality characterized by laughter but, as pointed out by Massimo Moscati (2003), also by harsh social relationships, the inequity of the Italian legal system, and the intrusiveness of bureaucracy (Moscati 2003: 214). The film's representation of Cosimo in jail is especially worth mentioning because it reveals one of the components of the formula of the comedy "Italian style:" the "art of getting by" (*l'arte di arrangiarsi*). Cosimo and Capannelle's failure in stealing the car is balanced by their engagement in finding a solution, a way out, for Cosimo who is caught by police. An example of the "art of getting by" can be seen in the sequence when Cosimo, in jail, advises his lawyer on the appropriate sections of the criminal code to present in front of the judge to get him out of prison.

The "art of getting by" finds in Totò its best representative. Antonio de Curtis, known as Totò, a Neapolitan actor and a prince by adoption, during the 1950s was renowned as the "Prince of Laughter" thanks to his popular characterizations fully integrated into the tradition of the Italian comedy. In *I soliti ignoti* Totò, in the role of master thief Dante Cruciani, delivers some of the best comic lines when, at Cosimo's funeral, the thieves gather in memory of the poor fellow. Commenting on Cosimo's death, Ferribbotte says, "the best are always the ones to go" and Dante replies: "Well, today your turn (pointing at Ferribbotte) tomorrow his (pointing at Capannelle)."

Film comedy, like any other cultural manifestation, stems from the society that produces it. It aims to generate laughter, and often laughter is a reaction to an uncomfortable situation, like at a funeral, or an unlikely one or a release from the awkwardness of a moment. Cosimo's expertise in legal matters contrasts with the conventional codes found in the characterization of criminals, therefore playing with viewers' expectations and provoking laugher. In this way, the *commedia all'italiana* lets the audience accept unrealistic situations as likely. The spectator at the same time witnesses the positive outcomes of the "art of getting by" while unveiling the bizarre viewpoint of a society apparently functional. By speaking indirectly about the contradictions of the Italian penal code of the late 1950s, *I soliti ignoti* shows how effective comedy "Italian style" can be in unfolding the absurdities of bureaucracy and the incongruities of a system that affects the individual as much as the community.

The film's irony reaches its climax when Cosimo speaks about the possibility of robbing the *Monte di Pietà*, the charitable trust also known as *Banco dei Pegni*. This is an institution that follows Christian principles, such as charity, and gives loans to the poor in exchange for goods. The choice of an organization based on traditional values exposes the viewer another paradox of life. The thieves' attempt to rob from the safe in the *Monte di Pietà*, which provides help to people in need, reflects the bizarre undertone of absurdities and contradictions found in society and so forcefully highlighted by "Italian-style" comedy.

The thieves' failure mirrors the failure of individuals to become part of a society that slowly moves away from their morals and needs. Monicelli finds in the outskirts of Rome the symbol of the struggle of the lower socio-economic class who, like the thieves in this film, are fundamentally good-natured but are also driven to commit small crimes to fulfill their desire for a wealthy, happy life. These characters' honesty and good nature combined with the irony shaped by the absurd situation are best illustrated by Tiberio's remarks on money. While trying to break through the wall, Tiberio dreams of getting the money from the safe to have a house and a bank account for the kid "so when he grows up he remembers all the sacrifices his father made for him."[5] Dialogue such as this reminds the viewer of the real nature of people like him, poor devils who were not likely even to become rich or successful. As pointed out by Giacovelli (1990), Monicelli's film represents prototypical Italians dealing with the economic miracle and foresees their failure precisely because the dream of the working class to reach the bourgeoisie appears easy but proves virtually impossible (Giacovelli 1990: 45).

The representation of women is another social component that adds to the formula of "Italian-style" comedy Maggie Günsberg (2005: 60–95) notes how "Italian-style" comedy centers its concerns on masculinity leaving femininity to a representation from a male viewpoint. "Italian-style" comedies, although primarily made by men, targeted an audience who could readily identify women defined by the traditional roles of wife and/or mother, and by femininity that conformed to a Catholic mentality, which consumerism had dramatically changed in the era of the economic miracle. In *I soliti ignoti* we see this change in the depiction of marriage ironically portrayed in the characterization of the only married couple in the film, Tiberio and his wife, Teresa. Traditional gender roles are provocatively reversed in the film, with Tiberio, the husband, an unemployed photographer but responsible parent who is taking care of the baby while the wife has a job (although illegal) and provides for the family. The end of the film, though, reinstates the emphasis given to marriage from a traditional male standpoint with Mario taking a honest job to marry Carmelina.

Closeup on Comedy "Italian Style"

One way to distinguish "Italian-style" comedy within the Italian comedy genre is its realistic approach to comic situations, an Italian response to the American traditions of the slapstick comedies offered by Charlie Chaplin and Buster Keaton. Hollywood cinema has influenced Italian film culture since the fascist years. This helps explain the popularity of genres, such as early silent comedies and crime films, that are subtly referenced in Monicelli's *I soliti ignoti*, whose reverence for the early comedies is recognized in the intertitles used in his 1958 film. American movies were popular in the 1920s and 1930s to the extent that they "Americanized" the Italian movies of the period; however, in the years of the economic miracle Italian audiences preferred to watch comedies that spoke of an Italian rather than an American reality.

In the slapstick comedies, characters usually find themselves overcoming situations and obstacles with no physical harm or deadly consequences, suggesting how some sort of extraordinary power leads to an ordinary man's social acceptance and recognition. In the "Italian style" comedies, on the contrary, characters do not have special powers but experience trouble and failure in their efforts to achieve happiness and success promoted by the economic miracle. Similar to American slapstick comic characters, Italian characters face obstacles but these are mostly provoked by the clash between commodities and ideals generated by the sudden wealth Italians experienced between the 1950s and 1960s.

The years of the economic miracle increased the disparity between the middle class and the working class and underscored the unequal distribution of wealth. National incomes doubled, exporting operations increased, and a significant migration occurred from the rural south to the northern urban areas. Italians' lifestyles changed drastically from being traditionally supported to a modernized style characterized by commodities such as television sets, cars, radios, dishwashers, holidays, and vacation homes. These commodities are used in the *commedie all'italiana* to depict a society affected by the economic miracle – a society that is torn between material wealth and traditional values. The agricultural south is barely influenced by the economic miracle, but is strongly attached to traditional values, such as an honor code. The differences between the lifestyles and economic status of the industrial north and the agricultural south are often employed by the directors of the "Italian style" in order to mock the economic miracle considered to be a phenomenon which contributed to make Italy one of the most industrialized nations in the world (Forgacs 1996: 273–90).

In the rapidly evolving economic climate of the 1950s, Italian cinema, and most significantly Italian comedy, maintained an essential role in shaping national culture. In the 1950s, cinema also became the most popular form of entertainment in Italy and one that successfully brought together peoples from different social classes (Gundle 1990: 201). Enrico Giacovelli (1990: 8–9) stresses that at the core of "Italian-style" comedy there is a society in which ordinary lives are depicted with harsh realism to show how the illusion of a happy life full of commodities clashes with people's struggles to achieve genuine happiness.

During the 1960s, "Italian-style" comedy reached its darkest moment in films such as Germi's *Divozio all'italiana* (*Divorce Italian Style* 1961) and *Sedotta e abbandonata* (*Seduced and Abandoned* 1964), when, thanks to an *eccesso comico* (comic excess), they reached popularity because they were successfully staged the weakness, hypocrisy, masked cowardice, and ignorance of provincial Italy (Grande and Caldiron 2003: 55).

In *Divorzio all'italiana*, Mastroianni plays the role of a Sicilian nobleman who, secretly in love with his cousin (Stefania Sandrelli), kills his wife and marries his beloved. By way of the honor code of the Sicilian tradition, the nobleman, when freed from prison, can openly marry the young cousin. The film's ending, like most of the endings of "Italian-style" comedies reflects on how life resembles a farce in which people are deceived or left unaware of the consequences of their actions. The last shot shows the newly wed on a yacht: while they kiss, the young bride is flirtatiously playing with the young skipper's feet, a conclusion that rejects the happy tone of traditional comedies but underlines the irony of the comic style.

Germi treats serious social problems with a black humor, addressing divorce, for instance, in a country when it was not yet legalized. Screenwriter Furio Scarpelli claims how Germi's films have been successful in showing the problematic role justice and law have had in Italy so that, paradoxically, a man, like Mastroianni's character in *Divorzio all' italiana*, has to commit a crime to be able to leave his wife and marry another woman (Scarpelli 2006). In his *commedie*, Germi depicts a male-dominated society in which men play either shallow, narrow-minded characters or are associated with an honor code that is ridiculed to expose society's hypocrisy and backwardness. An example of this structure is the character of the Sicilian father of a 15-years-old impregnated daughter in another Germi film, *Sedotta e abbandonata* (*Seduced and Abandoned* 1964).

The importance of Germi in the Italian-style comedy lies in his ability to reproduce a critical image of the Sicilians. Germi lets audiences reflect not only on the absurdity of traditions and cultural norms but also on sexuality and eroticism – subjects that, at that time, were unlikely to be discussed on screen. Similarly, Monicelli points out how screenwriters and directors of the *commedia all' italiana* succeeded in getting rid of both censorship and self-censorship, often going against those producers and distributors who were not willing to take financial risks for films that revealed society's hypocrisy and disillusionment (Pintus and Biarese 1985: 153).

Furthermore, central to Germi's comedies was the presence of witty, vibrant dialogue that voiced the clash between liberal and progressive beliefs and old-fashioned, conservative principles, and reflected the impossibility for many of achieving the lifestyle evoked by the economic boom (Giacovelli 1990: 45).

The introduction of television in the mid 1950s in Italian households, and the social transformations that followed contributed to the formation of a consumer society that, despite growing economic wealth, struggled to maintain a balance between traditional values and modern lifestyles. By 1964, the national economy had collapsed, forcing consumers to limit their expenses and spending on discretionary items. One of the reasons for the economic crisis was the lack of participation from the State. Without the State regulating the evolution of the economy and the production of goods, there was chaos. Far from being organized, like other European nations, in providing equal distribution of wealth and salaries and better infrastructures for its citizens, Italians suffered from contradictory values celebrated by consumerism. One of the most successful portrayals of this crisis is given by Luigi Zampa in his 1968 *Il medico della mutua* (*Be Sick … It' s Free*). Zampa's satire on the inefficiency of the Italian healthcare system stands out as one of the most successful "Italian-style" comedy films of the 1960s for its portrayal of the young medical doctor who is eager to get rich at the expense of his patients – a reminder of the devastating effect of social climbing (Giacovelli 2002: 104).

The introduction of private television in the late 1970s resulted in a general social and cultural transformation, and, with the deregulation of state television, which first broadcast on one channel in 1954, cinema lost its primary role as a popular phenomenon in Italian culture, fully replaced by mass media, television and radio.[6]

Although "Italian-style" comedy has been popular with audiences, some scholars, film critics and directors have questioned its definition, classification and even its artistic quality (Quaglietti 1986). Can artistic quality, for example, be found in comedies whose distinctive feature relies on a judgmental and cruel portrayal of Italian society? Following a 1985 roundtable on the *commedia all' italiana*, some of the most notable screenwriters, directors, actors and producers of "Italian-style" comedy commented on the originality of the comedy while others denounced its harsh view of Italian society.[7]

Most of the criticism of the *commedia all' italiana* revolved around the lack of seriousness and reliability in the way the comic style neglected the realist component that was successfully defined by Italian neorealism. Some critics even believed that comedy's popularity was responsible for overlooking the social problems that were affecting Italy during these years (Bondanella 1990: 145). Giacovelli suggests that those who initially criticized the *commedie all' italiana* for derogatory representations of the Italians, while acknowledging the performances given by outstanding actors such as Totò and Sordi, revised their position once comedies gained recognition. Some other critics even suggested the elimination of the term "Italian style" from its definition, a radical idea that reinforced their rejection of such comedies (Giacovelli 1990: 12). Despite the criticism, *commedie all'italiana* has been successful in challenging viewers to reevaluate moral and social values by ridiculing their relevance in society. The primary function of comic characters, as noted by film scholar Gerald Mast, is to use antisocial behavior to challenge society's norms (Mast 1973: 23). The characters of the *commedia all'italiana* desperately try to become part of the new, modern society, but they inevitably fail. They simultaneously want to belong while resisting complete assimilation in the consumer reality where looks and gadgets count more than moral values and traditions.

The Beginnings of *commedia all'italiana*

From the Cretinetti film series of the silent period, performed by the French actor André Deed, and the *teatro di varietà* (staged variety shows) with Ettore Petrolini to the comedies of the fascist period (known as *telefoni bianchi*) and those of the post-World War II period known as the *neorealismo rosa* (pink neorealism), the Italian audience was exposed to a variety of comic styles and performances. Fournier Lanzoni looks at the history of the Italian comedy and finds that, despite its popularity, comedy encountered some obstacles, one being the Italian language. According to this scholar, the popularity of comedy films of the silent period diminished mostly because of the presence of many Italian dialects. Once the intertitles translated the dialect into the vernacular language, they inevitably overlooked the cultural meanings tied to the dialect. Only with the advent of the sound did the different regional dialects help Italian comedy regain popularity. Peoples were able to identify with and follow the story in the dialect as the *battuta* (the comic line) functioned as "a catalyst for popular audiences to remember a film for its memorable line rather than physical feats of skills" (Fournier Lanzoni 2008: 11).

The *teatro di varietà* (staged variety shows) and the *avanspettacolo* (comic shows performed live in between feature films) are two of the most significant cultural moments in the mid-1900s that had an impact on "Italian-style" comedy. During this period, comic actors such as Ettore Petrolini and Totò greatly influenced the formation of "Italian-style" comedy. Petrolini, a forerunner of the *avanspettacolo*, "developed an artistic significance with the long neglected farce genre reminiscent of the *commedia dell'arte*." Because of his mocking style, comedy was able to overthrow the censorship imposed by the fascist ideology of the late 1920s and early 1930s.

Totò's ability to visualize the drama of the average man who, while making fun of societal traditions and customs, strives to succeed in life contributed to the popularity of the comedy "Italian style." In some of his most successful films–*Totò cerca casa* (*Totò Looks for a Place*) (Monicelli 1949), *Guardie e ladri* (*Cops and Robbers*), co-starring Aldo Fabrizi (Monicelli and Steno 1951), *Napoli milionaria* (*Side Street Story*) (Eduardo De Filippo 1950), *Totò e Carolina* (*Totò and Carolina*) (Monicelli 1954), comedy found in his uniquely comical persona the best characterization of the ordinary (and broke) man.

During the fascist period, Benito Mussolini exerted his influence on Italian cinematic culture. From the proclamation in 1922 that cinema was the strongest weapon of the State, to the establishment of the *Cinecittà*, the cinema studios in 1937, he influenced the production of Italian comedy, making it difficult for other genres, such as drama, to compete in celebrating fascist ideals. Most of the films produced during this period projected nationalistic and patriotic ideals to promote the image of Italy as a powerful European nation. Despite Mussolini's involvement, because of the regime's ban on imported films, some filmmakers supported the production of more national comedies. Only a few comedies became commercially successful. Among them were Mario Camerini's comedies, *Darò un milione* (*I'll Give a Million*, 1936) and *I grandi magazzini* (*Department Store*, 1939) starring Vittorio De Sica who later gained international fame for directing the neorealist masterpiece *Ladri di biciclette* (*Bicycle Thieves*, 1946). The short but popular period of comedies produced between 1937 and 1941 is referred to as *telefoni bianchi*. This genre reflected the glamorous life style of middle-class Italians and the white telephones used in the film's settings symbolized "wealth and elegance as opposed to the common, ordinary black telephone" (Fournier Lanzoni 2008: 14).

Only later in the 1940s, and influenced by the international critical acclaim of Italian neorealism, did Italian cinema find in comedy a distinctive artistic site for a discussion of the social contradictions found in post-World War II Italy. During the 1950s, a new genre, *neorealismo rosa*, produced comedies in response to the critical postwar years and to the neorealist films whose bleak narratives, unlike comedies, attracted an international rather than national audience. *Neorealismo rosa* was neither a subgenre of neorealism nor a style that strictly adhered to neorealist principles. A commercially successful genre, pink neorealism moved away from neorealism by privileging sentimentality and laughter over sad depictions of poverty, social injustices, unemployment and postwar healing. But it is worth noting that a comic vein was already present in many of the neorealist masterpieces, such as in *Roma, città aperta* (Rossellini 1945) when one of its leading characters, Don Pietro, while hiding some weapons from the fascist soldiers who are searching for partisans, hits the head of an old man lying in a bed with a frying pan to silence him and make it look like he is administering him his last rites (Bondanella 1990: 39). Influenced by both the traditions of the Italian comedy from the silent period and of the comedies of the *telefoni bianchi* and of *neorealismo rosa*, comedy "Italian style" finds in the late 1950s a fertile ground to attract national audiences by transforming the conventional comedy into an innovative artistic form.

In addition to the lack of traditional comic conventions such as an established ending and a critical view of societal expectations, another innovative element of "Italian-style" comedy is the presence of dramatic events like death. Monicelli remembers that in *I soliti ignoti*, despite the initial resistance from the film's producer to let one of the characters' die, the inclusion of death was instrumental in breaching the conventional rules of traditional comedy films (Codelli 1986: 64).

I wish to conclude this section by examining the role of *commedia all' italiana* in Italian popular culture. The Italian definitions of "culture" and "popular" reflect a specific linguistic and ideological structure that dates back to fascism. During the fascist years, *cultura popolare* was used to delineate a national culture which was opposed to the American "mass culture." This distinction between mass and popular reflected a political ideology meant to underline the national trait of the Italian people in contrast to a capitalist value found in the mass culture. Only later, in the 1970s and 1980s, did the division between mass and popular culture end, caused mostly by the deregulation of Italian television (Baranski and Lumley 1990: 12). A positive effect of television on Italian culture consisted of bringing rural communities closer to urban centers and facilitating the formation of a national identity unified by a common Italian language. *Cultura* is "coupled to the epithets *popolare* and *di massa* to refer, respectively, to activities developed by the people for their own use, and to mass-produced forms and their consumption" (Barański 2001: 9). The peculiar configuration of *cultura* in Italy derives from diverse subtexts that culture and cultural experiences have as they change from north to south, from region to region, and from city to country. The media, most significantly cinema, have often represented Italy as a country full of cultural differences and contradictions, as previously discussed, from a heavily industrial north to a mostly agricultural south. Popular culture and, in particular, films have often been studied through high-cultural lenses. Geoffrey Nowell-Smith (1990) notes *commedie*, which are representatives of popular culture, are often overlooked because of the dominant roles played in Italy as well as abroad by Italian art cinema and Hollywood cinema (Nowell-Smith 1990: 52). In this observation one might find a possible explanation of why so many of the popular "Italian-style" comedies have struggled to find a larger international audience. The recent DVD releases, in the US market, of popular comedies such as Monicelli's *I soliti ignoti*, Germi's *Sedotta e abbandonata* and *Divorzio all' italiana*, and Alberto Lattuada's *Il Mafioso* are only a few examples of the problems associated with the distribution of popular comedies outside Italy. This contrasts with the popularity of the neorealist films made by De Sica and Rossellini and the art cinema films by Federico Fellini, Michelangelo Antonioni and Luchino Visconti. Sequels and remakes indicate the popularity of Monicelli's film, the most recent being the US production *Welcome to Collinwood* directed in 2002 by the Italian-American brothers Anthony and Joe Russo who set their story in the working class neighborhood of Cleveland.[8]

The Final Stages of Comedy "Italian Style" and its Heritage in Italian Film Comedy

Despite the many controversies expressed over the years by some directors, like Comencini's (1985) denial to find an artistic heritage of "Italian-style" comedy, and by some critics who have attacked it for being too naïve and escapist, *commedia all' italiana* documents one of the most significant events in the twentieth-century Italian film culture. In roughly 20 years, comedies produced with a distinct "Italian style" proved to be successful in combining the comic with a social criticism with a well defined sarcastic tone. Its main goal – to laugh at human weaknesses and show the cruelty of mockery by portraying treacherous individuals – resulted in a style that is influenced by past literary traditions and a generation who conceived comedy as the best way to narrate stories.

However, by the 1980s, Italy had changed drastically into a modernized country more inclined to individualistic consumption than to collective experience, and the popularity of comedy "Italian style" came to an end. For some, its end was inevitable and occurred even earlier, in the late 1970s, with the increasing number of private television channels and the inevitable drop in moviegoers that had changed film culture in Italy. The innovative, uniquely popular component of comedy "Italian style" -its dark and cynical tone- had disappeared (Fournier Lanzoni 2008: 230). During the 1980s and 1990s, the influence of television on the Italian film culture resulted in the production of comedies often too conformed to television models, lacking the original artistic expression found, on the contrary, in the post-war years (Brunetta 1995: 381–6). As Monicelli pointed out, since the late 1970s, not only comedy but also Italian cinema was facing an ideological crisis, when terrorism and student uprisings transformed the ways Italian cinema looked at the social reality (Mondadori 2005: 47).

Monicelli modifies comic "Italian style" in two of his films of the late 1980s and early 1990s: *Speriamo che sia femmina* (*Let's Hope It's a Girl*, 1986) and *Parenti e Serpenti* (*Dearest Relatives, Poisonous Relations*, 1992). As Italian society changes, Monicelli tries to maintain a balance between tragedy and comedy but leaves behind the aggressiveness that prevailed in his comedies of the 1950s and 1960s.

Between the 1980s and 1990s, Italian cinema released a number of diverse comic styles, from the comically wretched stories of the misfortunes of an unlucky man, Fantozzi (Paolo Villaggio), to the shallow comedies directed by the brothers Vanzina often regarded by critics to be the "trash" of Italian comedy. Successful comedies, such as *Nuovo Cinema Paradiso* (1988, by Tornatore) and *Mediterraneo* (1991, by Salvatores), which were acclaimed by both critics and viewers, privileged a nostalgic look at the past in their attempt to find their own cinematic style, breaking away from the traditions of "Italian-style" comedies.

Two representatives of this new generation of filmmakers who, to some extent, embrace some of the main traits of "Italian style" comedy are directors/actors Carlo Verdone and Roberto Benigni. Verdone's early films, *Un sacco bello* (*Fun is Beautiful*, 1980) and *Bianco, rosso e Verdone* (*White, Red and Verdone*, 1981) and Benigni's internationally acclaimed *La vita è bella* (*Life is Beautiful*, 1997) define two distinct comic styles, showing ways of telling stories about Italians' flaws, like in the 1950s and 1960s comedies, but echoing personal reactions to contemporary reality. The goal of comedy has therefore shifted from being a social satire to a bittersweet view of the Italians' weaknesses but without the merciless tone that characterized "Italian style" comedies.

Thanks to worldwide artistic recognition and the high praise *La vita è bella* received from audiences, Benigni is often celebrated as a new comic persona who unifies tragedy and comedy to speak about the Holocaust, inviting viewers to appreciate a comic style that relies on tragic elements in order to unfold evil as a collective illness. The artistic reputation Benigni also gained for other popular films – *Johnny Stecchino* (*Johnny Toothpick*, 1990) and *Il piccolo diavolo* (*The Little Devil*, 1988) – reflects his playfulness and his ability to suggest rather than blatantly show society's dramatic reality (Borsatti 2001: 76). Lacking the pungent, merciless approach of the comedy "Italian style," Benigni's comic style speaks of social faults with a lighter tone than Monicelli. Yet in *La vita è bella* Benigni is an example of how the horrors of war and laughter function together to provide a comic relief in a narrative that speaks of anti-Semitism during World War II.

Similarly, Verdone explores in his successful *Bianco, rosso e Verdone*, a wide range of stereotypical male figures, from the low-class macho to the inflexible high-school teacher, gaining national celebrity similar to that received by his mentor Alberto Sordi, one of the most popular comic actors of "Italian style" comedy. The caricatures in Verdone's cinema also function as reminders of the important role of comic actors in the comedies of the 1950s and 1960s in illustrating, with devilish humor but also decency, the contradictions of an unique epoch.

Despite their stylistic and thematic differences, Benigni and Verdone invite people to laugh at the tragic silliness of life. The screenwriters and directors who contributed to the popularity of "Italian style" comedy worked during postwar reconstruction and were greatly influenced by neorealism, whereas the generation of comic directors and actors like Benigni and Verdone established a comic vein in a time defined less by the socio-economic effect of the economic miracle but more by the changes in film culture and in Italian society.

In 2010, thanks to comedies that focus on contemporary social issues (such as gay relationships in the traditional south; the north-south separation, and corruption), Italian comedy has fully emerged as a versatile genre.[9] Its increasing popularity has contributed to reinforce the major role of comedy in Italian cinema, a presence greatly established by Monicelli's *commedia all'italiana*.

"Italian-style" comedy functioned as a cinematic lens through which an epoch's unique combination of values and traditions were displayed. Socio-economic changes together with the responses given by individual directors such as Monicelli in *I soliti ignoti* show how cinema could subvert conventional categories but also challenge moral principles and speak of ambivalent and complex Italian identities, torn between the uncertainties of a new era and traditional values. Monicelli eloquently points outs that cinema is destined to transform itself and to adjust to both a culture and audience that change inevitably (Mondadori 2005: 240). Cinema, as a medium through which feelings are expressed and stories are told, will never cease to exist and Monicelli's "Italian-style" comedy will always occupy a special place in Italian cinema.

Notes

1. The collaboration between the Italian director and a group of screenwriters was influential in establishing a "cinema of screenwriters," a characteristic of comedy "Italian style," a collaboration that made it possible for Monicelli to share social and cultural concerns.

2. "La commedia è cattiva, anzi è spietata." The translations are mine unless specified.

3. For a detailed analysis of the Italian economic miracle, see Crainz (2003).

4. During the casting for *I soliti ignoti*, Monicelli discovered Tiberio Murgia (who plays the Sicilian Ferribotte) working in a restaurant. Carlo Pisacane (who plays the

Bolognese Capannelle) was found while acting in street theaters. Both were dubbed because their appearances, but not their native dialects, suited the characterization of these two men. Murgia was originally from Sardinia, and not Sicily, and Pisacane from Naples and not Bologna. In addition to that, Monicelli notes that Vittorio Gassman, at that time known for his dramatic roles, was chosen as Peppe despite the producer's protest. Other actors who became famous thanks to *I soliti ignoti* include Carla Gravina, a young actress originally from Veneto, here at the beginning of her career, and at that time an unknown Claudia Cardinale. A native of Tunis, when hired for this film Cardinale did not speak Italian but was nonetheless chosen because her appearance typified the dark beauty of southern Italian women (Mondadori 2005: 30).

5. See the original script of *I soliti ignoti* (Pallotta and Sirianni 2002: 23).

6. By the late 1950s, several movie theaters had closed throughout Italy mostly due to the high taxes imposed on films and an increasing number of movie theatres in the Catholic parish halls. See Lizzani (1979), Wagstaff (1996), Nowell-Smith (2001).

7. In 1984, the Italian organization called *Federazione Italiana dei Circoli del Cinema*, led a project on "Italian-style" comedy in order to confront its many controversies. This contributed to initiate an important dialogue with those directly involved with the *commedie all'italiana*. See Pintus and Biarese (1985).

8. Other remakes include: Louis Malle's *Crackers* (1984); *Palookaville* (1995) by Alan Taylor, and a musical, *Big Deal*, staged only briefly and directed by Bob Fosse (Mondadori 2005: 28).

9. See the two reviews on Italian comedy films written by Nick Vivarelli in *Variety* (2010 a,b). He mentions the following comedies released in 2010 for their significant contribution to a revival of film comedy: Nina Di Majo's Tuscany-set *Matrimoni e altri disastri* (*Marriage and Other Disasters*), Ferzan Ozpetek's *Mine Vaganti* (*Loose Cannons*), Gabriele Salvatores' *Happy Family*. One might also add to this brief list the 2011 comedy *Che bella giornata* (*What a Beautiful Day*) starring the new face of Italian comedy, Checco Zalone, who has won public attention with his politically incorrect views on the Italians' vices and prejudices.

References

Barański Z.G. (2001) Introducing modern Italian culture, in *The Cambridge Companion to Modern Italian Culture* (eds. Z.G. Barański and R.J. West), Cambridge University Press, Cambridge, pp. 1–15.

Barański Z.G. and Lumley, R. (eds.) (1990) *Culture and Conflict in Postwar Italy. Essays on Mass and Popular Culture*, St Martin's Press, New York, NY.

Barański Z.G. and West, R.J. (eds.) (2001) *The Cambridge Companion to Modern Italian Culture* Cambridge University Press, Cambridge.

Bondanella, P. (1990) *Italian Cinema: from Neorealism to the Present*, Continuum, New York.

Borsatti, C. (2001) *Roberto Benigni*, Il Castoro Cinema, Milan.

Brunetta, G.P. (1995) *Cent'anni di cinema italiano*, vol. 2, Laterza, Rome.

Codelli, L. (1986) *L'arte della commedia*, Dedalo, Bari.

Comencini, L. (1985) Intervista, in *Commedia all'italiana: Parlano i Protagonisti* (eds. P. Pintus and C. Biarese), Gangemi, Rome, pp. 43–5.

Crainz, G. (2003) *Storia del miracolo italiano*, Donzelli, Rome.

Forgacs, D. (1990) *Italian Culture in the Industrial Era: 1880–1980*, Manchester, UK: Manchester University Press.

Forgacs, D. (1996) Cultural Consumption, 1940s to 1990s, in *Italian Cultural Studies: An Introduction* (eds. D. Forgacs and R. Lumley), Oxford University Press, Oxford, pp. 273–90.

Forgacs, D. and Lumley, R. (eds.) (1996) *Italian Cultural Studies: An Introduction*, Oxford University Press, Oxford.

Fournier Lanzoni, R. (2008) *Comedy Italian Style: The Golden Age of Italian Film Comedies*, Continuum, New York, NY.

Giacovelli, E. (1990) *La commedia all'italiana: La storia, i luoghi, gli autori, gli attori, i film*, Gremese Editore, Rome.

Giacovelli, E. (1999) *Non ci resta che ridere: Una storia del cinema comico italiano*, Lindau, Torino.

Giacovelli, E. (2002) *Breve storia del cinema comico italiano*, Lindau, Torino.

Gili, J.A. (1998) *Italian Filmmakers: Self-Portraits: A Selection of Interviews*, translated by Sandra E. Tokunaga, Gremese Editori, Rome.

Grande, M. and Caldiron, O. (2003) *La Commedia all'italiana*, Bulzoni, Rome.

Gundle, S. (1990) From neorealism to Luci Rosse: cinema, politics, society, 1945–85, in *Culture and Conflict in Postwar Italy: Essays on Mass and Popular Culture* (eds. S.G. Barański and R. Lumley), St. Martin's Press, New York, NY, pp. 195–224.

Günsberg, M. (2005) *Italian Cinema: Gender and Genre*, Palgrave Macmillan, New York, NY.

Lizzani, C. (1979) Il cinema italiano alla fine degli anni cinquanta, in *Il cinema italiano 1895–1979*, Editori Riuniti, Rome, pp. 248–72.

Mast, G. (1973) *The Comic Mind: Comedy and the Movies*, Bobbs-Merrill Company, Indianopolis, IN.

Mondadori, S. (2005). *La commedia umana: Conversazioni con Mario Monicelli*, Il Saggiatore, Milan.

Monicelli, M. and Borghini, F. (eds.) (2002) *Autoritratto*, Polistampa, Florence.

Monicelli, M. and Codelli, L. (eds.) (1986) *L'arte della commedia*, Dedalo, Bari.

Monicelli, M., Sabatini, M., and Maerini, O. (eds.) (2001) *Intervista a Mario Monicelli: La Sostenibile Leggerezza Del Cinema*, Edizioni Scientifiche Italiane, Napoli.

Moscati, M. (2003) *Breve Storia del Cinema*, Bompiani, Milan.

Nowell-Smith, G. (1990) Italy: Tradition, backwardness and modernity, in *Culture and Conflict in Postwar Italy: Essays on Mass and Popular Culture* (eds. Z.G. Barański and R. Lumley), St. Martin's Press, New York, NY, pp. 50–62.

Pallotta, A. and Sirianni, S. (eds.) (2002) *I soliti ignoti*, Un mondo a parte, Rome.

Pintus, P. and Biarese, C. (eds.) (1985) *Commedia all'italiana: parlano i protagonisti*, Gangemi, Rome.

Quaglietti, L. (1986) Le "vere" e le "false" commedie all'italiana, in *Commedia all'italiana: Angolazioni controcampi* (ed. R. Napolitano), Gangemi Editore, Rome, pp. 65–73.

Scarpelli, F. (2006) Interview featured in the Criterion Collection DVD release of *Divorzio all'italiana*. Dir. Pietro Germi. Perf. Stefania Sandrelli, Marcello Mastroianni, Lando Buzzanca, Leopoldo Trieste, Daniela Rocca. Produced by Franco Cristaldi.

Vivarelli, Nick (2010) Local Comedies Click in Italy. Market Share Strong, Even as Holly-wood Fare Scores. *Variety*, May 15, p. 7.

Vivarelli, Nick (2010) Italian Pix Laugh to the Bank. *Variety*, May 17, p. 6.

Wagstaff, C. (1996) Cinema, in *Italian Cultural Studies: An Introduction* (eds. D. Forgacs and R. Lumley), Oxford University Press, pp. 216–32.

Further Reading

d'Amico, M. (1985) *La commedia all'italiana: Il cinema comico in Italia dal 1945 and 1975*, Mondadori, Milan. Gives an overview of comedy "Italian style" and Italian comedy film.

Forgacs, D. (1990) *Cultural Industries, Politics and the Public*, St. Martin's Press, New York, NY. Provides a compelling study of postwar Italian culture.

Giacovelli, E. (1999) *Non ci resta che ridere: Una storia del cinema comico italiano*, Lindau, Torino. Gives a detailed analysis on the history of Italian film comedy.

Ginsborg, P. (1990) Family, Culture and Politics in Contemporary Italy, in *Culture and Conflict in Postwar Italy: Essays on Mass and Popular Culture* (eds. Z.G. Baranski and R. Lumley), St. Martin's Press, pp. 21–49. Offers an interesting examination of leisure time activities in postwar Italy.

22

"Laughter that Encounters a Void?"

Humor, Loss, and the Possibility for Politics in Recent Palestinian Cinema

Najat Rahman

> *Palestinian cinema provides … a visible incarnation of Palestinian existence in the years since 1948 … by trying to articulate a counter narrative and a counter identity. These films represent a collective identity. (Edward Said, Preface, Dreams of a Nation)*

In Scene 2 of Hany Abu-Assad's *Paradise Now* (2005), a framing of Said, one of the main characters, in a photo shop in Nablus, anticipates and calls attention to the framing of the film, and that of Palestinians. We see Said in a close-up profile against a synthetic, kitschy background image of what looks like a New England town with a tree in the blooming colors of the autumn season surrounding his profile. Said's face looks serious in contrast to the zealous photographer who insists that he smile for the photo as he adjusts Said's position against this imposed background. The stubbornness of both (Said who refuses to smile, and the photographer who refuses to take the photo without one) elicits a comic tension. A matter-of-fact conversation follows about picking up the photo; a photo that will later serve to identify him after his suicide mission, we subsequently find out. Somehow all is arranged. The photo and the film come to life in a space of dissension.

While recent films directed by Palestinians have often addressed subjects centered on loss, violence, death, they have often strikingly employed humor in its various forms (parody, irony, the absurd, dark humor), to complicate and nuance their representation, as if to portray first and foremost a fundamentally human experience and to reclaim and salvage selves long lost to given representations and tired meanings. They do so also to mark a certain death that inhabits those lives

A Companion to Film Comedy, First Edition. Edited by Andrew Horton and Joanna E. Rapf.
© 2013 John Wiley & Sons, Inc. Published 2016 by John Wiley & Sons, Inc.

the films depict, both from the violence that delivers it and from the deadening daily routines of oppression. Humor emanates precisely from this death, from the mechanical that generates it; it seems to call for a work of mourning and gestures towards art as a refuge for politics. Analyzing films from the last ten years, I wish to explore the modalities of humor and the effect of representation on the possibilities for *politics* in recent Palestinian cinema. I focus on three films that were produced under Israeli occupation: *Laila's Birthday* by Rashid Mashrawi (2008), *Divine Intervention* by Elia Suleiman (2002), and *Paradise Now* by Hany Abou Assad (2005).

In *Laila's Birthday*, Abu Laila, a judge turned cab driver, has strict rules for his passangers but faces a typical day of chaos, contradictions, and lawlessness under occupation when he finally breaks down, assumes his judicial role, and passes judgment. In *Divine Intervention*, an image of a Palestinian fighter used as target practice is transformed into a flying female ninja that wages a mythical battle against Israeli Defense Forces, spanning the history of the struggle in a replay reminiscent of video games and popular global films. In *Paradise Now*, two friends are preparing for a suicide mission. The first one to be videotaped in a typical fashion with a prepared speech, is frustrated when he discovers that the video recorder has broken down and did not record his solemn speech; on the third retry, he interrupts his delivery and advises his mother instead on the best place to buy water filters.

These films consciously reflect on the act of representation, on its aesthetic and political dimensions. In representing what seems to defy representation, humor plays a key role, pointing the way to the possibilities and limits of cinematic representation. Humor resists any foregone conclusion or easy interpretation. It also renders the situation depicted all the more haunting. Humor sometimes reaches an aporetic function, in constructing and deconstructing meaning, all the more to bear witness to the grave historical reality. The following questions will concern us: Can humor, and cinematic art, allow for an overcoming of "deadening political realities" and offer an "emancipatory aesthetic" (Dabashi 2006: 144)?[1] If, according to Jacques Rancière in *Dissensus*, very little if any politics exists today, is art (and specifically film) the displaced space for it?[2] To what extent does humor and loss, often present in Palestinian films, open unto politics? Are these filmmakers reconfiguring what is meant by art as (true) politics? And if it is, is it no longer art? How do the senses of the individuals under occupation get affected? How do these films signal this? To what extent do they reproduce, counter, or reconfigure this assault on the senses? These questions are not, of course, limited to Palestinian artists *per se*. As I will show in these films, humor evokes a promise of a new communal life, even as it signals limited freedom.

Films have been providing a certain visibility to Palestinians in the face of their historical invisibility as well as of the distorted and imposed representations of their identity. It is this contested collective identity rather than a lack of film production that has contributed to the invisibility of Palestinian cinema and to "a lack of a comprehensive film history" (Chan 2007: 8–9). Writing about the Oscar nomination of *Paradis Now* in 2006, Felicia Chan indicates that the controversy around the film "dramatises the tensions in operation as a cultural identity seeks a political one" (Chan 2007: 9). Palestinian identity is in fact mostly a political one, given the scattering of a nation. Recent films by Elia Suleiman and Hany Abu-Assad, along with others, have gained international recognition.[3] As co-productions, often financed by European nations, they complicate the notion of "national cinema" and starkly reveal the tensions between national narratives and transnational forces.

Hamid Naficy maintains that Palestinian cinema is "one of the rare cinemas in the world that is structurally exilic ... made either in ... internal exile in an occupied Palestine or under the erasure ... of displacement and external exile" (Naficy 2006: 91). This heterogeneous corpus nonetheless shares a quest for "nationhood" (Chan 2007: 9). Dabashi (2006: 10) writes about its *statelessness*, what he calls "geographical absence," which haunts its history to become "the creative core of Palestinian cinema, what has made it thematically in/coherent and aesthetically im/possible." This diversity is also reflected in form. While I focus on three features, the cinematic production has ranged from documentaries to experimental films to art video and video installations, and so forth (Naficy 2006: 91).

Is Film a Refuge for Politics?

If politics is "a struggle to have *one's voice heard* and *oneself recognized* as a legitimate partner in debate," and if speech is the ground for all historical instances of politics, can film then become a space for politics in its absence elsewhere (see the introduction by Corcoran to Rancière (2010: 9), my emphasis)? How does humor in film contribute to this? Films, which present different Palestinian voices, counter the erasure that has not only been of the people, but of the condition of the political that Palestinian filmic art henceforth frames. A double erasure ensues: erasure of the political and erasure as history. Rancière (2010: 145) writes: "the shrinking of political space has conferred a substitutive value on artistic practice ... art is starting to appear as a space of refuge for dissensual practice." In a *geography that is also shrinking*, where increasingly there is no place for the Palestinian, art becomes that place. This chapter follows from Rancière's work, which argues that a shift has taken place that has led to a general depoliticization and a change in artistic practice, where politics may increasingly be found in art. As he insists, however, this is not an argument for art as the place for politics (Rancière 2010: 20).

Politics conceived as *dissensus* produces internal difference in a society through "the intervention in the visible and the sayable" (Rancière 2010: 37). As such, could we not conceive of humor as precisely that which also intervenes in "the visible and the sayable"? Art and politics, as forms of *dissensus*, can possibly "disrupt forms of domination," in "reorienting general perceptual space and disrupting forms of belonging" (Rancière 2010: 15, 2). Marking this shift to the disappearance of politics, and interrogating aesthetic practices in this context, Rancière signals that these forms, which include film and other visual arts, may create new "political subjectivation"; however they remain fundamentally aesthetic, as such creation cannot be simply willed; the aesthetic process may not yield what is intended (Rancière 2010: 151). Art therefore cannot be simply collapsed into politics, nor can it be completely separated from it. Rancière (2010: 133) states: "Aesthetic art promises a political accomplishment that it cannot satisfy … those who want it to fulfill its political promise are condemned to a certain melancholy." And yet, the way he defines politics shows the affinity between art and politics.

> What really deserves the name of politics is the cluster of perceptions and practices that shape this common world. Politics is first of all a way of framing, among sensory data, a specific sphere of experience. It is *a partition of the sensible, of the visible and the sayable*, which allows (or does not allow) some specific data to appear; which allows or does not allow some specific subjects to designate them and speak about them. It is a specific intertwining of ways of being, ways of doing and ways of speaking. (Rancière 2010: 152, emphasis mine)

Rancière interrogates the significance of the "and" in art and politics. *Poiesis*, is, after all, making in art, making in politics. However, with the aesthetic, "this knot between *poiesis* (a way of doing) and *aisthesis* (a horizon of affect) is undone … the loss brings … a promise of a new form of individual and community life." This possibility for new communal life is the opening onto politics. Rancière highlights the democratic nature of art that potentially addresses itself to anyone (Corcoran 2010: 16).

These films propose that art is life. More than that, they propose an art of death, as the art itself evokes the death of politics. Already the art image of Mona Hatoum, *Negotiating Table*, is emblematic in this sense. It reveals a dead corpse shrouded and laid on the surface of a wooden table, murdered, possibly tortured, and absent figures missing on the opposing empty chairs; it announces art as preoccupied with death, in its violent, contemporary forms. Humor, as we will see in the next section, emanates from and signals a certain death.

In this context, what if we were to willingly read Hegel's famous proclamation, "art is a thing of the past," not as an eclipsing of art as it has existed in Europe, so that all art is subject to the history and demarcations of Western aesthetics, but rather as art that enacts a tension with the past. What is taking place today in Palestinian art is the reinscription of a historical loss and an art that makes a claim on the present.

Humor, a Divine Intervention?

According to Henri Bergson (1912) the comic also has to be considered within "the nature of art" and its relation to life, including to politics. For Bergson, the comic cannot be entirely situated in either the realm of art or of life (Bergson 1912: 135). It is utilitarian in so far as it aims for improvement; and it is aesthetic in so far as the comical emerges from a certain freedom "when the society and the individual freed from the worry of self-preservation, begin to regard themselves as works of art" (Bergson 1912: 20). Others such as George Meredith and P.B. Shelley also argued that freedom was essential for the comic. And yet, what happens when there is no such fundamental social or political freedom?

While laughter signals "a slight revolt on the surface of social life," it nonetheless focuses our attention on mechanical gestures rather than on intentional acts, on missed freedoms (Bergson 1912: 200).[4] It is precisely the "breakdown" of these gestures into free acts that the films open up and that we will consider in this paper.

Laughter, which is not necessarily subject to will, and which is fundamentally *human*, as Bergson has noted,[5] is more significantly a response to a certain mechanism that we witness or that we elicit. The comical is characterized first and foremost by *"mechanical inelasticity"* (Bergson 1912: 10, emphasis in the original) whether "introduced into nature" or into "regulation of society" (Bergson 1912: 47). He writes, "a really living life should never repeat itself ... This deflection of life towards the mechanical is here the real cause of laughter" (Bergson 1912: 34). So we laugh when someone living resembles something mechanical or when something mechanical is at the heart of someone living. Ultimately, all humans are prone to rigid habits that turn them against themselves and others (Bergson 1912: 130).

Laughter, then, which can signal a certain aesthetic, in sharing with it the principles of equality, expressiveness, and *indifference*, also signals a certain *anesthetic* in that it appeals to intelligence, not to emotion. Bergson speaks of an *"absence of feeling"* which usually accompanies laughter," a laughter that "demands something like a momentary anesthesia of the heart" (Bergson 1912: 4, 5, his emphasis). Indifference and a social environment are prerequisites for it, even when this social complicity is imaginary: "Our laughter is always the laughter of the group" (Bergson 1912: 6).

If humor's aesthetic qualities open it to the political, in the sense of disrupting the consensual, its social dimension seems to do so as well: "Laughter must answer to certain requirements of life in common. It must have a *social* signification" (Bergson 1912: 8). Humor, however, proves aporitic. This same social aspect seems to close it from it, however, in demanding conformity and consensus. For while a social environment inevitably creates difference, this difference is corrected by laughter in a society that insists on conformity. Social maladaptation and *"a growing callousness to social life"*, are sources for laughter (Bergson 1912: 133–4). Laughter inevitably implies a relation to power: "Laughter cannot be absolutely just ... Nor kind-hearted either. Its function is to intimidate by humiliating" (Bergson 1912: 198). At least since Aristophanes, then, laughter has touched on politics and society. Since then, too, comedy has also been connected to aesthetic expression and to fantasy.

Figure 22.1   Rashid Mashrawi, *Laila's Birthday* (2008; producers, Mohamed Habib Attia, Rashid Masharawi, and Peter van Vogelpoel).

Rashid Mashrawi's *Laila's Birthday* (2008)

Rashid Mashrawi's film (Figure 22.1) is not simply a "social satire" that aims to expose and to correct; it is also "laughter (that) … encounters a void" (Bergson 1912: 85). The film was lauded and described as "cinema of the absurd and sociological exposé" (Feinstein 2008), an "exasperated fidelity to a chronically malfunctioning city" (Ella Taylor, *Village Voice*), and a "dark urban comedy" (Holden 2009) – one that does not "address politics or document holy war" (DVD Back Cover). In all these accounts, the film is rendered in a depoliticized urban space, and its comic aspects separated from any politics, as if Ramallah simply suffers from municipal mismanagement rather than from occupation and continued dispossession of a nation, as if the film is simply a study of a social group in a random urban setting. In the face of such erasure of the political, it is as if the film itself can be credible and worth watching only if it showed the Palestinians not as occupied people but as people trying to survive amongst corruption, not attributed to anyone in particular. Such mystification is also evident in the translation of the film, which turns the political prisoner, who appears in different scenes as a protester, witness and emblem of a larger conscience, into a "convict." It is important to distinguish clearly between the social and the political, as Rancière does: "between those who are regarded as capable of taking care of common problems and the future, and those who are regarded as being unable to think beyond private and immediate concerns. The whole democratic process is about the displacement of that boundary" (Rancière 2010: 58).

The figure of Abu Laila seems to represent a political subject who is able to attend to the common problems (and what they indicate for the future) as well as to the more personal daily matters. The film's events take place in one day, implicitly representing a "typical day." Asked by his wife how his day was at the end of the film, the main character, Abu Laila, responds, "as usual." And thus his trials signal an extended existence under a singular occupation that neither resembles classical colonialism nor sovereign statehood. Already his name, Abu Laila, signals a comic tension: rather than his given name of "Jalal," which means reverence, he chooses Abu Laila, a suggestive parody on the patriarchal practice of taking on the name of the first born son. The feminine name of Laila evokes the nocturnal world of fantasy. In the film, Abu Laila awakes before dawn to a shattering noise, an intrusion from the outside into his home, where evidently he cannot find full refuge. He takes stock of his silent surroundings, opens the balcony and surveys the quiet city, anticipates another day, walks to his daughter's bedroom, returns anxious as he looks at the camera, a mirror image of himself appears, before the bustling of the new day begins with preparation for work and school in a familial setting, announcing Laila's birthday celebration in the evening, where the father is expected and will oblige.

The day begins with the useless ritualistic morning visit to the Ministry of Justice, after the dropping off of the daughter at school. We learn that the entire ministry has recently been replaced, although the concern remains with the decorative aspects of justice, as evidenced by the preoccupation with the replacement of office curtains. As a judge, a "returnee" seeking to help build a nation, Abu Laila is now a taxi driver. The figure of the returnee reminds us of those who have not returned and highlights how the nation is "partially scattered," and by extension that "rights and obligations extend beyond boundaries of nation states" (Butler 2010). He establishes strict laws for his taxi counter to the times where essential lawlessness, injustice, chaos and uncertainty reign in Ramallah where he lives with his family. These laws, constituting the basis for the comical situations, include not going to the checkpoint, not allowing smoking in his taxi or weapons, not letting amorous teenagers just loiter in his car for the lack of a private space. Some of the absurdities he encounters include getting stopped by a policeman simply because the policeman wants to purchase his taxi for extra income. He renders service within a very limited area, bound by checkpoints, revealing the constrained life under occupation.

In our consideration of art and politics, and how both redistribute the field of the sensible, the film shows how the senses of individuals under occupation are assaulted and saturated, especially by sounds of shelling, helicopters, gunfire, traffic, cell phones, and so forth. Laughter is a release that counters this assault. The assault on the senses heightens some senses but not others, signaling a process of dehumanization, an effort at survival, and an eclipsing of the political. The film alludes to this in many different episodes. One such scene of disorientation is when the main character watches the TV news in a café with a group of men. All are listening and begin to speculate about the scene of destruction presented to them, about who the soldiers are and where the event is taking place. Is this the work of the Israeli occupation, the American occupation of Iraq, and so on? More than a sign of solidarity and a sense that all occupations are alike, this scene seems to point again to the mystification of political oppression through representation, even to those undergoing occupation. Ironically, a scene of mayhem breaks out amidst the viewers when shelling occurs in the immediate vicinity, coinciding with their speculations. This shelling breaks down the divide between their reality and the representation on TV that distances them from themselves, framing the limits of representation and the errors of misrecognition. Again, even as they take shelter under a table while they hear more shelling, speculation ensues about whether the shelling is from the Israelis or from factional internal fighting, forcing a sordid and violent collapse between the event and its representation. As Judith Butler (2006: 144) points out, "for representation to convey the human, then, representation must not only fail, but it must *show* its failure." All this culminates in Scene 6 of the film, where the regime of representation and humor breaks down.

In this scene, located at a gas station where the main character stops, Abu Laila emerges from his absurdly decorated for a wedding taxi. The appearance of the cheerful car contrasts with the grim toll on him. Standing in a distracted fashion, as the curious worker who fills his car with gasoline watches, Abu Laila becomes increasingly conscious of how his senses are assaulted by the chaos around him, by the previous shelling, and the ordeals of a day under occupation. As traffic noise, the sounds of blaring horns and of helicopters in the sky become intolerable, he takes a loud speaker, significantly from a police car that is also filling up, to speak out and address his fellow compatriots and occupiers. He loses control, as the tragic seems to coalesce with the comic. He tells two men in two cars who are holding up traffic and creating a traffic jam to move along; he tells the pedestrians to move onto the sidewalks; he tells the young men carrying arms that they are neither soldiers nor policemen and that if they want to carry arms their place is with the resistance and not amongst women and children. He does not forget the Israeli helicopters and bitterly lauds their military might. He "breaks down" in protest, to deliver a judgment, to breach an opening onto something new.

The "breakdown" transforms the mundane space of the gas station into a scene of political protest, of dissensual speech, of judgment. The main character finally passes a judgment and assumes his role as judge. His pronouncement brings temporary order. The quest for freedom is articulated, freedom from flying Israeli helicopters, from chaos, from the dysfunctionality of the everyday in a condition of occupation where authority has signaled simply policing the everyday. The scene counters this daily assault on the senses (among other things) with its own assault: first with speaking out and rupturing the "normalcy" of the abnormal, then with the return to the domestic, harmonious sphere. It sets up a new sense of the aesthetic as political.

On the one hand, the return to the familial sphere becomes an active way to resist the assault on the senses; on the other hand, instead of pursuing the possibilities of this breakdown, the film privatizes it into a family simply coping with the everyday and trying to survive under singular political circumstances, as if the struggle has been reduced to one simple form: to endure each day. Andrew Horton and Joanna Rapf write in this *Companion to Film Comedy* that comedy, which reflects complex socio-political problems, "celebrates the human capacity to endure rather than to aspire and suffer." Humor in this film is connected to daily endurance. The scene of the "break down" also suggests that humor lends dignity and complexity to those subjected to a condition that robs them of both. In *Divine Intervention's* regime of the fantastic or in *Paradise Now's* regime of contingencies, failures are pursued to their logical end. All three films, however, insist on the absurd, that which is disharmonious and out of joint with propriety or reason. This conception of the absurd is close to that of dissensus, which Rancière defines as a disruption of consensus.

In this geography, the reduction of politics to policing is evident. Palestinians, a plural proliferation, abiding by no principle of unity except for political claims and historical grievances that promise to extend into the future, are caught between the policing of the Israelis and that of their leadership, as well as that of the Arabs. The scene of the "breakdown," however, momentarily transforms this space from one of policing to one of politics, albeit a threatening transformation, as evidenced by the reaction from Abu Laila's fellow men. Rancière (2010: 37) states: "The police ... say[s] ... there's nothing to see and so nothing to do but move along ... Politics, by contrast, consists in transforming this space of 'moving along', of circulation, into a space for the appearance of a subject: the people, the workers, the citizens. It consists in re-figuring space."

Politics in this film emerges as intimately linked with justice, and with a particular speech act performed as a breakdown of all oppression, provisional as this may be, when those excluded or subordinated speak out (Rancière 2010: 6). This speech act is significantly humorous, a corrective and an index for a life torn apart. Humor insists on common speech. In order to get anyone's attention Abu Laila has to use a loudspeaker, competing with the helicopter noise, the blaring horns, and the numbing indifference, lest his voice be crowded out. Humor here mitigates the pathos that all too often defines that reality and that becomes the all too common representation of the victim. As Rancière indicates, politics is not simply about governance or the proclamation of the "Rights of Man":

> Politics begins when those who were destined to remain in the domestic and invisible territory of work and reproduction, and prevented from doing "anything else," take the time that they "have not" in order to affirm that they belong to a common world. It begins when they make the *invisible visible*, and make what was deemed to be the mere noise of suffering bodies heard as a discourse concerning the "common" of the community. Politics creates a new form, as it were, of *dissensual* "commonsense." (Rancière 2010: 139, emphasis mine)

Like aesthetics and politics, humor creates new realities, "invents ways of ... seeing, and saying, engenders new subjects, new forms of collective enunciation" (Rancière 2010: 7). However, the danger of retreating into the private realm is to deny Palestinians the status of political beings, to relegate them to a domestic space as a group:

> If there is someone you do not wish to recognize as a political being, you begin by ... not understanding what he says, by not hearing what issues from his mouth

as discourse ... . Traditionally, in order to deny the political quality of a category –
workers, women and so on – all that was required was to assert that they belonged
to the "domestic" space that was separate from public life. (Rancière 2010: 38)

Before the scene of the breakdown, Abu Laila takes a woman who has just lost
her husband home from the hospital: it is a scene of silent grief juxtaposed with
the later scenes of the wedding celebration, the anticipated celebration of Laila's
birthday, and with the many comic scenes. Comedy and tragedy intermingle, as
they do in life. The comic, then, is linked to loss and allows for the maintaining
of a certain dignity, precisely the first casualty of occupation, rather than falling
into banality, senselessness or being overwhelmed by the injustice. Associations of
loss and mourning are reinforced throughout the day: the birthday cake to Laila is
originally a gift from the wife to her dead husband whom she thought was simply
recovering in the hospital. The structure of substitution and continuation around
loss evokes solidarity and community in the face of dispossession. Such a scene
of mourning structurally opens onto the possibility of politics in the breakdown.
Humor and mourning are both responses to loss.

Judith Butler, in "Violence, Mourning, Politics," an essay in *Precarious Life:
The Powers of Mourning and Violence*, argues that mourning, which necessitates
an acceptance of a transformation, may open onto politics: "It is not that
mourning is the goal of politics, but ... without the capacity to mourn, we lose
that keener sense of life we need in order to oppose violence" (Butler 2006: 21,
xviii). Butler argues that grief is not simply a private state; rather it provides a
sense of community: "If my fate is not originally or finally separable from yours,
then the 'we' is traversed by a relationality that we cannot easily argue against"
(Butler 2006: 22–3). The experience of loss and mourning is one that could
inspire solidarity and justice. Adressing those of us *"beside ourselves,* whether
in ... passion, or emotional grief, or political rage," she addresses those undone
by loss: what is lost is not simply a place or an other, but something in that place
or that other that cannot be altogether known; something of the self is lost as
well for the self is constituted by its attachment and relation to an other (Butler
2006: 24). In the experience of dispossession, a certain relation to the self and to
place, to things, a certain tie whose nature remains enigmatic, is lost (Butler 2006:
22). As Rancière (2010: 16) also argues, loss promises a "new form of individual
and community life" through an art that could be available to everyone. And the
art that engages loss also holds a promise, in that it is democratic. The promise
of "political accomplishment" can never altogether be fulfilled, however, and
aesthetics remains distinct from politics (Rancière 2010: 133).

Humor also faces loss in these films. It does so to pierce through oppressive
realities and open the possibilities for new oppressions. Like Mashrawi's film,
Suleiman's *Divine Intervention* creates new ways of seeing a colonial structure
visible in its effects which are painfully absurd. Humor allows for seizing the
tangible in the everyday in its most profound truth. The human struggle to

survive is both elevated and held to unforgiving scrutiny. This poignant chronicle of love and pain, as Suleiman subtitled his film, is a testament to the power of the imaginative in the fantastic that elicits the film's most memorable humor, to imagine beyond the violence.

At the Limits of Representation: Elia Suleiman's *Divine Intervention*

The effect of humor on representation can be seen compellingly in the fantastic in Elia Suleiman's *Divine Intervention*. By its humorous fantastic imaginings, it stages and complicates cinematic representation and the national narrative. The introduction of fantastic elements seems to highlight through dark humor, irony, and parody, a socio-political reality marked by the absurd, where the absurd is thenceforth an index for power and for violence, a manifestation of the state of occupation. Suleiman's film starkly reveals the tensions between national affirmations of identity and globalized representations of them. Inspired by global cultural influences – the film is often evoked in relation to the work of Buster Keaton and Jacques Tati in its negotiation of the serious and of humor, in its reflection on humor and its place – the film represents the political in the mundane and insists on transnational cultural connections in the face of internal rifts in the relations between the self and others.

The film asks the following questions: How does one represent differently? "How does the diasporic inform/disrupt ideas of the national?" (Butler 2011). One also asks along with the film scholar Gonul Dönmez-Colin, is memory enough when making a film about "people and places that are disappearing"? (Dönmez-Colin 2007: 177).

Presented as a chronicle, *Divine Intervention* is a mosaic where events seemingly lack coherence, and happen without any context, which creates a poignant effect, both comical and alienating, and which the introduction of the fantastic amplifies. The visual narration, the use of a static camera and wide shots, suggest stifling tedium in Palestinian life, creating the effect of the absurd that the film depicts as everyday socio-political reality. Everything is in a liminal state, since the present is one of struggle and continual loss. Such a state is ritualized into everyday social interaction, so that all relations between the self and the other are violently constrained within this state's bounds. The narrator, E.S., portrayed as a filmmaker and a silent witness to his own life, has to meet his lover at the Ram checkpoint, since they live on different sides of it. As such, they both witness, and therefore endure, daily Israeli harassment of Palestinians. The film begins in his birthplace, Nazareth and ends in Jerusalem, encapsulating his own life and that of Palestinians from the Nakba of 1948 to the occupied present.

Suleiman's work significantly appeals to fantastic images, eclectically borrowed from video games and films, seemingly escaping the confines of Palestinian

Figure 22.2 Ninja image: Elia Suleiman, *Divine Intervention* (2002; producer, Humbert Balsan).

national identity only to reaffirm them. Three scenes constitute the intervention of humor through the fantastic. The first shows E.S. driving to see his ailing father. As he finishes off an apricot, he throws the pip out the window, striking and blowing up a military tank with it. The second shows his female friend crossing the Ram checkpoint on foot against the orders of the Israeli soldiers, which causes the guard tower to fall. The scene I am concerned with is the "climax" of these episodes, and also for the film. It involves a female "ninja" figure facing Israeli armed men (see Figure 22.2). The image of the Palestinian that serves as target practice is transformed before the eyes of the attackers into a fighting and flying ninja, "essentially casting the Israelis in the role of Goliath" (Porton 2003: 124–7).

The incorporation of the fantastic is significantly a humorous staging of representation.[6] If the fantastic is what presumably departs from the real and calls it into question, the real itself has become in the film a theater of the fantastic. In this final scene, the fantastic consists of a representation, an image coming to life and becoming a reality. It is this incongruity of a flying ninja in this typical West Bank landscape juxtaposed with the familiar militarized figures that elicits the laughter and is emblematic of the absurd. The frame of the ninja scene, which begins with an image of a female ninja and returns to that same image, after the confrontation, presents the conflict and face off as one of representation, and hence of political existence: who has the power to represent, who creates images of others, who diffuses these images. In a parody of multiple genres, the escalation of the violence spans the history of the conflict. The ninja, head-covered in a kuffiyeh, and in black, begins in response by throwing stones, then Molotov cocktails, and then throws an Islamic crescent at her opponents who are using heavy military weapons. Everything is mediated by the image. The scene stages dominant representations about Palestinians that justifies more violence against them. When the image of that same Palestinian serves as a target of violence and comes to life as a female ninja figure, it shows the effect of representation on reality. At the same time it presents the struggle of Palestinians against overwhelming force in affirming a national identity. At the end of the scene, the Israeli commander stands alone in a desolate landscape, oblivious to the image of the Palestinian as militant that he installed in the ninja. More than simple testimony to what is absent, the image becomes part of a struggle, challenging representations on the ground, as it were, and participating in forging a different space. The ninja scene becomes the focus for the disparate elements of the film, rupturing the representation and its violence that are imposed on Palestinians.[7] The real and the imaginary connect the mundane and the historical, where film offers a memory that begins from a particular Palestinian standpoint, draws on shared myths, and is addressed to a more global community through film.

The fantastic highlights Suleiman's cinematic language, which "juxtaposes two versions of reality – one present and the other absent, each concealing yet exposing the other" (Gertz and Khleifi 2008: 181). The tendencies of the fantastic seem to also be those of dark humor. Dark comedy, which characterizes the work of Elia Suleiman, involves using irony to attack an apparently absurd universe. It employs violent images, where there is little sense of hope, as we witness in the ending of this scene and the ending of the film. It is through the fantastic that Suleiman achieves a dark humor, allowing him to focus attention on the process and consequences of representation, on how representation serves as an essential component of the political conflict and as a challenge to his cinematic endeavor.

We see this tendency of dark humor in the use of symbols in this scene, such as the map of Palestine, the colors of the flag, the crescent and star, the halo of bullets. Nutith Gertz and George Khleifi argue that Suleiman's use of symbols is double-edged, introducing the historical symbols of the struggle and placing them in a virtual space. While Suleiman "exposes ... the fictitious status of these symbols through the use of parody, absurdity, and humor, he also searches for the truth behind them and renews their lost significance" (Gertz and Khleifi 2008: 180–1). Through these symbols, the intervention of the fantastic presents Palestinian struggle and affirms national identity.

In borrowing from Biblical myths and visual popular culture, Suleiman articulates an ironic expression of identity that escapes the narrow confines of nationalism but manages a necessary articulation of self in the face of an aggressive negation and appropriation. Besides being the most spectacular and the most sophisticated scene in the film, the "ninja scene" testifies to violence under occupation, to its forms and its responses.

The fantastic also becomes a way to face the anguish of loss. Sobhi al-Zobaidi (2008) argues that "poetic and imaginary means ... provide Palestinians with the virtual worlds they need in order to negotiate their loss and confinement ... [they are] driven towards virtual worlds in search of continuity." It is this unexpected distance from reality, or the collapse of reality into the fantastic – where an apricot pit, for example, is able to blast a military tank, and where the driver continues on nonchalantly – that elicits the laughter. The all too real violence of every day military occupation is reworked and transformed through the imaginary into a virtual response that calls it into question and defies it.

The fantastic – and dark humor – attempts to achieve what is impossible in reality, to bring together what has been torn asunder: "to break down the stifling blocked borders … to reunite the fractured space and to rejoin the divided identity" (Gertz and Khleifi 2008: 178). In response to Gertz and Khleifi, Zobaidi compellingly notes, however, that it is not simply a question of breaking down road blocks but also of facing the effacement of Palestinians and their claim to the land. "Palestinian cinema … goes beyond 'roadblock movies' around which identities clash, power is practiced, and struggles take place … it is not the roadblock that presents the crisis, but memory itself " (Zobaidi 2008). Through humor and fantasy, *Divine Intervention*, with a foreboding ending that amplifies the seriousness of the Palestinian predicament under occupation, allows for the possibility of overcoming cinematic obstacles in creating another space.

Suleiman enacts a nuanced and compelling cinematic representation by means of the introduction of humor and the fantastic. In going against prevalent narrations of Palestinian identity, the film emerges as a true possibility of politics in the face of continued fragmentation of the geography, the people, and the memory. In this act of representation that borders on testimony, Naficy (2001: 18) writes, "Suleiman … gives voice to the film – with all the muteness, inarticulateness, and trauma of coming into language that are the hallmarks of his work." It is in this innovative cinematic endeavor that Suleiman offers fantastic humor to *present* what eludes *re/presentation*.

Hany Abu-Assad's *Paradise Now* (2005)

Paradise Now takes place during the second Intifada in Nablus, from 2000 to 2005. Nablus, of course has always been a key historical site of resistance to the Israeli occupation.[8] The film tells the story of two friends, Said and Khaled, who have signed up for a suicide mission together. Living under occupation and working in a garage to support their families, their present is revealed as precarious, and their future uncertain. Said is haunted by his father's past, executed presumably for being a collaborator when Said was only ten. Khaled's father's past also looms large for the son who perceives his father as capitulating in his struggle against the Israelis in the first Intifada. The two young men undergo a change and come to radically different decisions regarding the suicide mission. Whereas one was wavering and the other convinced, a reversal takes place with the introduction of a contingency. Together the two positions constitute a chiasmus and a political impasse.

The heart of the film is the possibility of contingency, which becomes the source of humor and its unraveling: something inexplicably goes wrong. The contingent leads to the breakdown of representation and of the operation itself in Scene 7. Yet it also allows for them. This contingency allows for an innovative aesthetic and for politics. Politics, as Rancière has suggested, is predicated on a "radical contingency" (Rancière 2010: 21).

Scene 7 introduces contingency in representation through its malfunctioning, when the video recording fails leading to other complications. This humorous and sober scene is a deconstruction of a genre of representation around suicide bombing. (Here one thinks of the theme song of $M * A * S * H$, "Suicide is Painless.") The scene opens with a photographer facing us, the viewers, as if he is about to take a photo of us. Behind him are a group of men watching, including Said and Jamal, the facilitator of the mission. We are situated by the camera in the place of Khaled who is about to give a speech, before he carries out his mission. Then the photographer takes a video camera and begins recording. The camera now frames Khaled. There is a gradual close up of Khaled as Said looks on gravely. Khaled begins his speech solemnly with familiar recitations from the Qur'an; he addresses his father and mother in formal Arabic, which is itself incongruent and deflates the solemnity. When he has finished, he asks, "So how was it?" This nave concern about his performance given the reality of death that waits is both comical and startling. The photographer indicates nonchalantly that the camera had not recorded anything. Something went wrong. Repetition ensues, this time with an audience eating sandwiches. It is a repetition that deflates blind discourses of heroic action. In this repetition, we are being photographed and videotaped again. In the second performance of Khaled, there is a stop. The camera is not working again. In the third try, we now see the back of Khaled and the front of the video photographer. We are still in the film, framed on the side of Khaled. Khaled suddenly stops once he launches into his prepared speech and offers his mother some advice about the best place to buy water filters, as mentioned earlier. It is as if this faltering performance will unhinge many things, among them the resolve of Khaled.

The breakdown of representation is highlighted in the film, indicating representation's power and shortcomings as well as the need for alternative visions. Late in the film, Said tells his story in an effort to convince the organizer to let him carry out his mission. He represents himself against what he perceives and what he proclaims as the occupier occupying all roles, leaving none for the occupied.

Said's recorded performance is much more solemn, as if to signal how humor also risks falling into the senseless, risks robbing the dignity of living beings. Said's words launch the visual preparations of the body with the participation of the sounds of Quranic recitations. The camera moves in a continuous circle, which seems to be in harmony with the space in which Said and Khaled find themselves. As it circles, a shift signals the advancing of the purification ritual to prepare the bodies for burial (usually performed after the bodies are dead). The camera creates a visual rhythm to the sounds of the Quranic recitation that come to a closure with an image reminiscent of the Last Supper in Bunuel's *Viridiana*. We see a large wooden table with Said and Khaled at the center and the group of men next to them sitting for lunch. The idea of the martyr (and witness) in this scene transcends their religious identities. The scene is highly aesthetic with its visual tableaux, rhythmic Arabic of the Qur'an, circular and continuous camera movement, juxtaposition of Said's solemn words and images of the purification rites for the dead. A recurrent motif in the film is that "life is death under occupation": "Under occupation we are already dead"; "In this life, we are dead anyway," reiterate Said and Khaled.

Said describes occupation as "life imprisonment." Among its crimes, he states, is that, "it breaks any resistance, it ruins families, it destroys morals and people." It is in this sense that collaboration is the principal drama in the family life of Said and of the others. The popular consumption of videos of execution of collaborators, as we see in Scene 15, is indicative of this. In addition to showing the abject violence of occupation, and of some of the responses to it, it shows how the struggle is political first and foremost. No one can maintain a neutral position, not even the viewer who is framed at several instances within the bounds of the film and who is confronted by the gazes of the characters in the last scene. The viewer is not allowed the luxury of the aesthetic distance. In this emphasis on the ravages on the family, the film differs from the resilient vision in *Laila's Birthday*, where the family is the bedrock that allows the individual to endure.

What strikes one about the film that treats such a thorny political issue is its subtle aesthetic (especially its visual elements). One can see this in the way it portrays two different worlds, the old city of Nablus, with its Ottoman stone houses and ravaged vestiges from the violence of occupation, juxtaposed with images of modern Tel Aviv, which is less than an hour away, and the prosperous semblance of a "normal life." This separation of political narrative and aesthetic is deceptive. A complex relation exists between them, as evident in the many scenes.

Scene 5 of *Paradise Now* presents what seems like a sardonic reflection on cinema and the Palestinians, in a film that is not only a "buddy story" but has elements of a "romantic comedy." As Suha asks Said about his hobbies, she wonders if he likes to go to the cinema. Said explains that there is no cinema in Nablus, that they burned Cinema Rivoli ten years ago in protest against Israel for not allowing Palestinian workers into Israel. Suha asks: "Why Cinema?" Said responds: "Why us?" Said asks a question that has politically plagued Palestinians from the beginning, but it had not found a hearing or public forum: "Why us?" The question implies that the regime of politics has been Western, with Israel as its agent, and the Palestinians bearing the burden of history.

As she continues her questions about his possible preferences in cinema, she asks, "What genre?" He responds, "The kind that frustrates." She: "Like what?" He: "Like life." While art always takes on a life of its own, not being solely bound to external constraints, excising life from Palestinian art is not innocent. A discussion follows around struggle and the many ways of resistance. For Suha resistance should always be "non-violent"; for Said, the forms of violence that are imposed always already determine the nature of the struggle. There are different positions in the film regarding how to struggle. Khaled tells Suha that she is changing a political struggle into an ethical one: "You want to change the struggle into morals; Israel doesn't have morals." He seems to concede to her point of view later in the film when he becomes skeptical about the suicide mission. A distinction between the political and the ethical, however, need not lead to a political struggle that negates ethics.

Warner Independent Pictures, which distributed the film, has yet again depoliticized an historical struggle and transformed it into an urban conflict. The trailer describes the film in cultural terms as "a culture searching for its place." It tentatively ventures into political terrain by conceding it as "a call for peace." The trailer concludes however by taking a political position itself: "Sometimes the most courageous act is not to act."

Austere in its aesthetic, with elegant shots, the effect that the film produces is nonetheless that of a political nature rather than simply of the pleasurable, technically innovative, or of the beautiful. It is an art of experience rather than an art of expression. Like the other films I have discussed, it sets up a new sense of the aesthetic beyond pleasure and beauty: it sets up a scene of politics, reframing the aesthetic as political. In fact, the film announces this. Said worries that the effect of his story may be "entertaining people whose lives are a little better." Said wonders, "The world watches indifferently."

In the final scene, each principal character looks at the camera, looks at us finally, then a close up of Said's eyes is revealed looking at us. Then white. It is a scene that captures *dissension*, an innovative aesthetic that breaks the regime of representation and reconfigures the field of the sensible: it looks back, implicates us, and refuses to entertain or to continue the violence.

The three films, like other recent films not discussed in this chapter, use humor as a critical lens through which to assess daily life under occupation and as an index for a political impasse. More than that, humor, in its ability to "partition the sensible … the visible and the sayable," can be aligned not only with aesthetics, as Bergson has argued, but with politics as Rancière demonstrates.

Such humor proliferates and has received a warm welcome from its audiences, following the literary tradition of Palestinian authors such as Emile Habiby, and there is no indication that such filmic engagement with humor is fading out, given the recent shorts of Abu-Assad and Suleiman's latest film, *The Time that Remains* (2009). One notes a proliferation of programs on Palestinian television incorporating humor as well, along with the fact that Israeli cinema has produced successful comedies such as *The Band's Visit* (Eran Kolirin 2007). This film, despite its successful international reach, has its limitations. It erases Palestinian presence while embracing the Egyptian/Arab in a venture of cultural tolerance. The only Palestinians in the film are some of the actors present in a landscape of a cultural exchange free of them or of their political reality.

While Palestinian film may not be the most viable arena for politics, it has significantly allowed for it in its absence elsewhere. It has emerged as a space of dissent – one with multiple voices and visions. Through the filmmakers' innovative (if provisional) dismantling of a familiar regime of representation, the films discussed in this chapter push through humor and beyond humor to reconfigure the assault on senses and lives delivered by occupation and by discourses that maintain it, to an aesthetic that neither harmonizes the violence into a simple effect of the beautiful nor falters on its innovative possibilities. In pushing through aesthetic, the films provide an uncompromising terrain for politics. And in pushing through the aesthetic, it pushes through humor as humor opens into a space of critique and of affirmation of the self's aspirations for freedom.

Notes

1. I am grateful to Prospero Saiz and Livia Monnet for the lucid, engaging, and challenging discussions around the issues of humor, aesthetics, and politics. I would also like to thank Andrew Horton and Joanna Rapf for reading and commenting on my article with thoughtfulness, humor, and profound insight.

2. We follow from Hamid Dabashi and others in considering Palestinian cinema to be one made by Palestinian filmmakers (Dabashi 2006: 144). Jacques Rancière (2010: 37) conceives of politics as *dissensus*, or the manifestation of "two worlds in one," for we are in the order of consensus, according to him, which establishes hierarchies and separation between the social and the political, art and culture, proper and improper activity or speech.

3. This recognition is most notable in the Cannes Jury Prize for *Divine Intervention* in 2002 and in the Golden Globe award for Best Foreign Language Film and Oscar nomination for Hany Abu-Assad's *Paradise Now*, 2005.

4. Bergson (1912: 143) defines gestures as "the attitudes, the movements and even the language by which a mental state expresses itself outwardly without any aim or profit, from no other cause than a kind of inner itching."

5. For Bergson (1912: 3) the comic is *human*, both in the sense of not being shared by other species and as a mark of our humanity and its limits.

6. Various reviewers of the film saw the incorporation of the fantastic as one of wish fulfillment, not for change but for vengeance. One critic asks if this is "acquiescence or violent desire for revenge": "Is Suleiman sidestepping serious questions about the tactics of the Palestinian intifada ... by portraying anti-Israeli violence as harmless fantasy?" (Ventura 2003).

7. The question of representation has preoccupied the work of Suleiman from the beginning. See, for instance, *Introduction to the End of An Argument* (1990), with Jayce Salloum, which takes up the depiction of Arabs in Western media. Suleiman's most notable films include *Chronicle of Disappearance*, which received the Venice Film Festival Award in 1996 for Best First Film, and *The Time that Remains* (2009).

8. Other films by Hany Abu-Assad include *Rana's Wedding* (2002), *Ford Transit* (2002), *Nazareth 2000* (2001), and *Sanctuary* (2002). Like the other two films, and many others Palestinian films, this is a co-production (Palestine/France/Germany/the Netherlands/Israel). Conditions around filming were harrowing and included kidnapping of a group member by a Palestinian faction, shelling by Israelis near filming location,

German members of the crew who left work. The location of filming was changed from Nablus to Nazareth after that. Note also that the words "martyr" and "witness" are linked in Arabic (*Shaheed* and *Shahed*, respectively).

References

Abu-Assad, Hany (2005) *Al Janna al-an* (Paradise Now), Warner Home Video, Burbank, CA.

Bergson, Henri (1912) *Laughter: An Essay on the Meaning of the Comic* (trans. Clousdesley Brereton and Fred Rotwell), Macmillan, New York, NY.

Butler, Judith (2006) *Precarious Life: The Powers of Mourning and Violence*, Verso, New York, NY.

Butler, Judith (2010) What Shall We Do without Exile, Sixth Annual Edward Said Memorial Lecture, The American University in Cairo, November 7, http://www.youtube.com/watch?v = MLgIXtaF6OA (accessed May 18, 2012).

Chan, Felicia (2007) What dreams may come: (Palestinian) cinema/nation/history. *Variant*, 30, 8–9.

Dabashi, Hamid (2006) *Dreams of a Nation: On Palestinian Cinema*, Verso, New York, NY.

Dönmez-Colin, Gönül (2007) *The Cinema of North Africa and the Middle East*, Wallflower Press, London.

Feinstein, Howard (2008) Laila's Birthday. *Screen International*, September 7.

Gertz, Nurith and Khleifi, George (2008) *Palestinian Cinema: Landscape, Trauma, and Memory*, Indiana University Press, Bloomington, IN.

Holden, Stephen (2009) Navigating Ramallah, An Eye Out for the Absurd. *New York Times*, May 27.

Naficy, Hamid (1998) *Home, Exile, Homeland: Film, Media and the Politics of Place*, Routledge, New York, NY.

Naficy, Hamid (2001) *An Accented Cinema: Exilic and Diasporic Filmmaking*, Princeton University Press, Princeton, NJ.

Naficy, Hamid (2006) Palestinian exilic cinema and film letters, in H. Dabashi (ed.) *Dreams of a Nation*, Verso, New York, pp. 90–104.

Porton, Richard (2003) Notes from the Palestinian diaspora: an interview with Elia Suleiman. *Cineaste*, 28 (3), 24–27.

Rancière, Jacques (2010) *Dissensus: On Politics and Aesthetics* (ed. and trans. S. Corcoran), Continuum, London.

Taylor, Ella (2009) Laila's Birthday is Mashrawi's Day in the Life of Ramallah. *Village Voice*, May 27.

Ventura, Elbert (2003) Ghost World. *Pop Matters*, 20 February, http://popmatters.com/film/reviews/d/divine-intervention.shtml (accessed May 18, 2012).

Zobaidi, Sobhi (2008) Tora Bora cinema, *Jump Cut: A Review of Contemporary Media* 50, http://www.ejumpcut.org/archive/jc50.2008/PalestineFilm/index.html (accessed May 18, 2012).

Zubaidi al-, Kais (2006) *Palestine in Cinema*. Institute for Palestine Studies, Beirut.

Further Reading

In addition to the key contributions on Palestinian cinema (Nacify 1998, 2001, 2008; Dabashi 2006; Gertz and Khleifi 2008), see:

Ball, Anna (2008) Between a postcolonial nation and fantasies of the feminine: the contested visions of Palestinian cinema. *Camera Obscura: A Journal of Feminism, Culture, and Media Studies*, 23 (69), 1–33. A very informative article that focuses on the question of gender in Elia Suleiman's *Divine Intervention* and Michel Khleife's *Wedding in Galilee*.

Bourlond, Ann (2000) A cinema of nowhere: an interview with Elia Suleiman. *Journal of Palestine Studies*, 29 (2), 95–101. An early but seminal interview with Elia Suleiman.

Bresheeth, H. and Hammami, H. (eds.) (2006) The Conflict and Contemporary Visual Culture in Palestine and Israel. *Third Text*, 20 (nos. 80/81), n.p. A special double issue on Palestinian and Israeli art, literature, architecture and cinema.

Butler, Linda (2003) The Occupation (and Life) through an Absurdist Lens. *Journal of Palestine Studies*, 32 (2), 63–73. A concise introduction to Elia Suleiman and his films.

Dickinson, Kay (2000) The Palestinian road (block) movie: everyday geographies of second intifada cinema, in *Cinema at the Periphery* (eds. Dina Iordanova, David Martin-Jones and Belén Vidal), Wayne State University Press, Detroit, MI. An illuminating essay on recent Palestinian cinema.

Ginsberg, Terri and Lippard, Chris (2010) *Historical Dictionary of Middle Eastern Cinema*, The Scarecrow Press, New York, NY. An indispensable companion to the study of Middle Eastern cinema, insightful and erudite.

Khatib, Lina (2006) *Filming the Modern Middle East: Politics in the Cinemas of Hollywood and the Arab World*, I.B. Tauris, New York, NY. One of the very few studies on the subject, informative.

Stein, Rebecca and Swedenburg, Ted (2005) *Palestine, Israel, and the Politics of Popular Culture*, Duke University Press, Durham, NC. This important work incorporates studies of Palestinian cinema and situates it within a general trend of other arts and cultural expressions.

White, Rob (2010) Sad times: an interview with Elia Suleiman. *Film Quarterly*, 64 (1), 38–45. A more recent interview with Elia Suleiman that discusses his most recent work.

Yaqub, Nadia (2007) The Palestinian cinematic wedding. *Journal of Middle East Women's Studies*, 3 (2), 56–85. An illuminating article that examines the films of George Khleifi and Hany Abu-Assad's in light of the trope/theme of wedding and its significance in Palestinian culture.

Part VII

Comic Animation

23

Laughter is Ten Times More Powerful than a Scream

The Case of Animated Comedy

Paul Wells

I was once asked to speak in Poland about the ways Polish animation was viewed from other national and cultural perspectives. It was perhaps not the wisest of decisions to tell the assembled dignitaries, filmmakers, and scholars – in a place embedded with Catholic practices, and mere miles from Auschwitz – that I knew Poland through its jokes. "Why did the bride think she had the most elegant wedding in Poland?" I advanced, "Her veil practically covered her overalls!" Now leaving aside this joke's baggage of social stereotypes, and the fact that I compounded the error by mentioning recent British documentaries about "Bobski the Builder" and "Lena the Lap Dancer," commentaries on the influx of Polish workers in the United Kingdom, I saved myself by noting that I had learned the "truth" about Poland through the bleak, absurdist humor of its animation. Everyone smiled and chuckled with recognition, but this was no joke.

For many years, of course, brought up on Disney features and Saturday morning cartoons, I assumed that cartoon "anarchy" of the golden era shorts from New York and Hollywood studios between 1928 and 1945, defined "comedy" in animation. Like most other forms of expression, though, it is actually the case that humor in the animated film is historically, culturally, and contextually specific. In his astute analysis of aspects of British comedy, Andy Medhurst (2007: 12) warns we should be "simultaneously taking care to locate comedies in their specificities of time and place, while also considering how they relate to broader histories and traditions of what is deemed to be funny, though of course such histories are never straightforwardly linear and such traditions are constantly open to contest and contradiction." Indeed, it is clear that whatever form of comedy is taking place, it is rooted in contexts in which all things – identity, community, nation, language, politics, culture etc. – are open to question and interpretation, and no

A Companion to Film Comedy, First Edition. Edited by Andrew Horton and Joanna E. Rapf.

analysis is free from the sense of humor and intervention of the author. With this in mind, I can only declare my white, left-leaning liberal, semi-reconstructed male, London-centric Englishness as the key credentials underpinning this discussion; and the fact that I have written about animation for some time, shared my views in over 30 countries; written and directed (comedy) scripts for TV, radio, and theater in various nations; and left Poland in one piece.

Crucially, while animation shares many techniques of comic construction with other kinds of comedy writing and performance, it does offer particular and distinctive forms of visual and verbal "gags." These gags have helped to define some of the unique aspects of the language of animation *per se*, and further, provided a specific platform and outlet to address alternative points of view and to create challenging and subversive visions (see Wells 1998: 127–86). This discussion will, therefore, offer a brief, comparative analysis of the core comic tendencies and principles in animation, focusing on the United States, the former Soviet bloc, Poland, England, and Japan, offering some thoughts about the "universal" aspects of animated comedy, and examples where the comic is functioning in complex political circumstances.

Although, in the first instance, this approach may seem too general and simplistic, it is clear that animation within a variety of nations is often rooted in visual cultures working in opposition to mainstream forms of representation. It positions itself in a way that often gives a clear purpose to the comic through the seemingly intrinsic metaphoric qualities of the animated form. As Estonian animator, Priit Pärn has remarked, by creating animation you are already indicating that you are thinking differently, and this in itself, is the first step in having a comic point of view.[1] This point remains fundamental, in that a certain perspective characterizes all comedy, and it is important to delineate who determines this outlook, since comic material of any sort is defined through the additional factors of its execution and performance, and further, how effective its reception is for any given audience. These variables make "comedy" very difficult to apprehend. Equally, claims for comedy's ability potentially to bring down governments are also overstated, but it may represent and encourage particular forms of resistance. What is crucial in this discussion, though, is that if there is to be the suggestion that there are distinctive credentials for animated films within specific national contexts, then it should be assumed that animation filmmakers work with, and consciously signify their social and cultural knowledge as the subject and object of their humor, *and* also rely on the viewer's understanding of animation itself as the medium of its delivery.

"I'm a Toon. Toons are Supposed to Make People Laugh"

In this defining comment about the assumptions *American* audiences have of "cartoons," Roger Rabbit in Robert Zemeckis's *Who Framed Roger Rabbit?* (1989), recognizes that the codes and conventions of the form in the dominant tradition in the United States have largely been predicated upon the construction of visual jokes and comic events. In essence, this process in itself was informed by the influence of the graphic idioms of comic strips and vaudevillian performance modes. On the one hand, graphic invention found a vehicle in Otto Mesmer's "Felix the Cat" cartoons (1919–1936), in which, for example, Felix's tail at any one point could become an exclamation mark, an aircraft propeller or a banjo neck. On the other hand, refinements in performance found an early peak in Winsor McCay's creation of *Gertie the Dinosaur* (1914), implicitly insisting that comedy in animation worked most successfully when mediated through a particular "personality," a perspective taken up and advanced for many years at the Disney Studios. As Neale and Krutnik (1990: 32) point out, however, "The animated short is, of course, a particularly rich field for examples of the illogical, the impossible, and the absurd. Explicit motivation is usually lacking. Motivation here tends to be generically implicit: all kinds of improbable things simply happen in this kind of comedy."

Crucially, then, animation operates as a vehicle by which normal expectations can be ignored, subverted and re-interpreted, but rather than motivation being in some way absent or arbitrary, it is highly specific, evidenced both through what is achieved technically, and more significantly here, how the animation filmmaker is positioned within or hidden by the text. Effectively, the language of animation operates either to *dilute* representative forms – it is only paint, puppets, or pixels after all – or *amplify* them – this is so different, extreme, and unusual, it will be even more noticeable. Ultimately, then, the animation filmmaker, whether using more formalist strategies to manipulate the spatial orthodoxies of the cartoon form, playing with the dynamics and flexibilities of character, or indeed, the moral, political, and cultural mores of any one nation, finds comedy through *rhetorical play* (see Telotte 2010).

In the United States, this was at first based on the comedy of the silent clowns – Chaplin and Keaton for example – and an engagement with the changing conditions of the modern era (see Goldmark and Keil (eds.) 2011). Raymond Durgnat also stresses the role of Mack Sennett in drawing upon the influence of French comedies, and evolving the early comic preoccupations of American cinema, *per se*: "By 1912 he was beginning to establish the unholy trinity of American screen comedy: parody (of other films), ridicule (especially of noble virtues and lofty sentiments) and visual knockabout (which he lifted, by insistence and inventiveness, to the level of poetic fantasy)" (Durgnat 1969: 68).

Though this was not lost on the pioneering animators in the United States, it is interesting to note that once the techniques in making animation evolved, they were an intrinsic aspect of creating specific gags that could not be executed in the live action form, *and* prompted a quasi-theoretical approach in understanding how animation communicated particular ideas. E.G. Lutz's *Animated Cartoons*, written in the 1920s, was the first extended manual that described how animation was made, and was used by Disney and others. It included a section on "humorous effects," which stressed the "universality of pantomime," where "gesturing is understood by all races," and argued "that there are some forms of motion productive of laughter that do not imitate actions natural to the human organism, but seem to acquire their power of risibility from their resemblance to mechanical motion," referencing the theories of Henri Bergson (Lutz 1920/1998: 228–9). Bergson's now seminal dictum, that "the attitudes, gestures and movements of the human body are laughable in exact proportion as that body reminds us of a mere machine" (Bergson 1911/2002: 14) is resisted by Lutz, however, on the basis that the humor in animation does not emerge from comparison between organic and mechanistic forms, but because animation can literally translate the organic into the mechanical – "there is no need to consider physiological impossibilities of the human organism, the artist can make his characters spin as much as possible" (Lutz 1920/1998: 231). Lutz stresses repetition in, and the physical agitation caused by, the very "constructed-ness" of the motion of the animated cartoon as the key in prompting amusement, clearly calling attention to the self-evident artifice in the form as its comic novelty. Arguably, at this stage in the development of the animated cartoon this was much more observable, as the heights Disney reached in the fluidity of motion itself were a long way off, and cartoons were much more reliant on cutting between gags, and limited movement cycles. Nevertheless, in many senses, it is this focus on the *naturalizing* of "impossible" actions and conditions in the cartoon which simultaneously speaks to the sometimes radical and aspirant change in the modern era, but equally, an underpinning suspicion, that whatever humankind may achieve, it is still characterized by its own tendency to render itself as *failing* in some way. This tension, thereafter, informs the animated comedy of modern America.

The animated cartoon in the United States has featured in a number of analyses that see it as an almost intrinsically "Modernist" form (see Klein 1993; Leslie 2002; Wells 2002), and in relation to comedy, Michael North has argued,

> the machine age seems to have brought, along with all its other dislocations, a new motive for laughter and perhaps a new form of comedy ... If there is something inherently funny in mechanical reproduction, then it is also possible that modernity itself is governed by a comic rhythm, even when it is not particularly amusing. (North 2009: 5)

In America, the animated cartoon was arguably the embodiment of this rhythm, ultimately moving beyond the early pioneers, to the sophistication of Disney's physical and situational comedy in "personality" animation, the Fleischer's more sensual, sexual and primal approach, embodying the new immigrant humor, Warner Bros' urban, knowing and ironic stance on American mores and the language of animation itself, and UPA's (United Productions of America) focus on a more literate whimsy. Mickey Mouse, of course, has become an iconic figure; the embodiment of the Disney brand. His initial persona was predicated on broad, barnyard, almost vulgar physical comedy, but his reinvention over time positioned him more as a "straight-man" in comic situations where he was merely foil to the 'dumb' or confused actions of Pluto and Goofy, or the anger and misdirected urgency of Donald Duck. Pluto, Goofy and Donald often broke the rules, mostly inadvertently, and it became Mickey's job to play peacekeeper, regulator or apologist.

Tex Avery, Chuck Jones and Bob Clampett at Warner Bros' "Termite Terrace," the termite-riddled studio the animators worked in, were to reinvent the cartoon by extending its parameters, making it faster, more brutal, more surreal, and more self-consciously interventionary, playing upon the increasing conservatism of the Disney *oeuvre* as it embraced a lyrical, sometimes sentimental, and archetypically gothic engagement with its folk and fairy tale narratives. Disney had argued that the animated feature could not sustain itself on gags alone, and this inevitably prompted a different approach to storytelling, which necessarily diverted the studio from its increasing sophistication in the development of the sight gag. The most renown of Disney's "nine old men" of the classic era, Ollie Johnson and Frank Thomas, suggest "the personality of the victim of a gag determines just how funny the whole incident will be," noting mime artist, Marcel Marceau's idea that "if a dignified man slips on a banana peel, it is funny. If it happens to a man who is down and out, it is not" (Thomas and Johnson 1981: 32). While this merely suggests that an audience may like to laugh at the undermining of authority, status and self-regard, it also points to the notion of how the sometimes seemingly arbitrary brutalities of the American cartoon may function, since it is not the action itself that is amusing alone, but the relationship with, and reaction by, the character to what has happened. This both points to what is funny, and extends the narrative situation. In relation to early animation, "the audience was drawn into the picture through the types of gags and sprightly business … People were delighted by cycles and other tricks to make the impossible look plausible" (Thomas and Johnson 1981: 74) but Disney essentially believed that an audience needed to know how a character felt in order to determine their own response to the humor. This naturally led to character-centered humor, and the play on the dominant characteristics of individual figures as the subject of the gag – Donald Duck's frustration, Goofy's ineptitude, Pluto's curiosity – which ironically, was advanced further in Warner Bros' characters, with Bugs Bunny's wise-ass reposts, Daffy Duck's inevitable slide into surreal indignity and madness, and Coyote's humiliation and defeat. The most literate and articulate of the Warner Bros. directors, Chuck Jones, has remarked though that this is also nuanced by the sensibility of the director who worked with the character: "Friz [Freleng]'s Bugs would be more of a scamp, and Tex Avery's more a controlled lunatic. Bob Clampett's was a thoroughly amoral lunatic … All these characters – Bugs, Daffy, Pepé, Porky – in a way are like the multiplications of our own foibles. And if they weren't … they wouldn't be funny" (Furniss 2005: 129).

Jones informally theorized his approach to animation throughout his career (see Jones 1990, 1996) and constantly stressed "the fun lay in the marriage of oddities: a French skunk in a perfume shop; a male rabbit singing Brunnhilde's role against a mighty eighty piece symphony orchestra; a singing frog driving a simple man into diabolical frustration" (Jones 1990:123). The "marriage of oddities," or what comedy theorists call "incongruity," was the essence of the American cartoon, but in a spirit that ran the gamut from stupidity to surrealism. In essence, many of the dominant characteristics of the key American cartoon characters connect with the ways in which "stupidity" is made manifest in conduct and behavior. Davies (1996: 28) notes that "jokes about stupidity inevitably flourish in modern societies based on competition, rational calculation, and technical innovation, for stupidity means failure and the downfall of self and others alike." In many ways, American cartoon characters constantly battle against their own fears of failure, and from this comes the comedy of witnessing how they behave because of their fear, and the consequences when they inevitably fail. While Disney for the most part retained the integrity of the situation in which his characters appeared, Warner Bros. constantly subjected their characters not merely to character conflict and chase scenarios, but the vicissitudes of the cartoon form itself. Tex Avery's characters, for example, were just as likely to run off the edge of the screen, break the "fourth wall" and speak to the audience, and find themselves physically distorted beyond recognition, as they were to be trapped in everyday storms, flypapers or clocks.[2]

Durgnat remarks of Avery's *The Cat Who Hated People* (1948), in which a cat flies to the moon to escape his treatment on earth (he gets hit with a broom and a boot, shot at, and humiliated by babies), that "Objects-gone-mad, processes-run-amok, all following their own autonomous logic, devoid of any human discrimination, inflict upon [the cat] every sort of indignity, and finally, we see him back on earth, wrapping the pavement round him like cozy bedclothes, kissing it and crying 'I love people ... ' as hurrying crowds walk on him, tread on him, walk on him, tread on him" (Durgnat 1969: 185). It is Avery, of course, who gives the seemingly arbitrary autonomy of the action its inherent logic, a logic that suggests that the everyday world is a literal nightmare, while the psychological one – essentially represented by the cat's time on the moon – may be much worse. The cat returns to New York, in "the good ol' U.S. of A" as the consequence of a golf swing, supposedly relieved to be home, even though he is continually walked over. For the viewer, this is a relief. The world has been made into a place of un-relieved chaos and unbounded agency, but the viewer is permitted to laugh – this concept of "permission" I will return to in a moment. It is only the comic inflection of this approach that detracts from the view that this is an act of surrealist art.

In 1933 Salvador Dali had his first one-man show in New York, and, sponsored by Pablo Picasso, visited the United States a year later, familiarizing himself with American culture and meeting what were in his view, the three great American surrealists: the Marx Brothers, Cecil B. DeMille and Walt Disney. Only in 1945 did he begin work with the Disney studio on a specifically surrealist piece, *Destino*, which was ultimately resurrected, completed and released in 2003. In many senses, it is a pity that Dali did not identify Bob Clampett at Warner Bros' "Termite Terrace" as America's fourth great surrealist, as his cartoons are testament to the choreographic and comic influence of Harold Lloyd in his "Thrill" comedies, the landscapes of William Burroughs, and the unconscious paranoia of the modern world, identifiable in his persistent engagement with insanity, senility and suicide. Clampett's cartoons – and most specifically, the Looney Tune, *Porky in Wackyland* (1938), a clear influence on *The Cat That Hated People*–are the surrealist masterpieces of the golden era.

Inspired by a *New York Times* article about an expedition to Africa in search of the rare dodo bird, Clampett transports Porky Pig to Wackyland in "darkest Africa," styled partly after Lewis Carroll's "Wonderland," and the work of Dali, and illustrator and comic book artist, Milt Gross. A place where "it can happen here," "populated by 100 nuts and a squirrel," is both a summation of irrational nonsense humor and a reflection of contemporary anxiety and alienation – figures are both monstrous and cute, elastic and broken, malleable and malformed. Porky's pursuit is essentially a sideshow to a *tour-de-force* de-construction of two-dimensional animation conventions and the invention of left-field grotesques. The banana-footed, retractable armed, sub-Daffy, Dodo, can manipulate the cartoon environment, drawing its own exits and changing the material space to destabilize Porky's attempts to capture him. A Carroll-esque peacock with playing-card plumage emerges along with a convict carrying his own prison bars, demanding freedom; a cross-eyed rabbit plays on a swing suspended from his own extended ears; a cat/dog creature chases its own tail; a bird made from a car-horn "honks" its own head; a three-headed figure based on the Three Stooges, whose mama was "scared by a pawnbroker's sign," beats itself up; a candle-headed, multidirectional information sign, gives Porky access to the Dodo's underworld castle; and the Dodo, himself, perhaps not quite the last of its kind, and the ultimate in cartoon flexibility, teases and humiliates Porky, surprising him with extended "woo-ing."

Clampett simultaneously reinvents the chase cartoon, anticipates the modernist minimalism of the later UPA shorts, and depicts fears and phobias as literal character constructs. Porky's pursuit is as much Clampett's quest to test the boundaries of cartoon narrative, and to reframe the freedoms of the jazz age as the creative permission to abstract popular idioms as the expression of artistic concerns and perverse social commentary. Like André Breton and Dali in Europe, Clampett's imagery reveals the unconscious of late American Modernism and the symbols of a nation coming to terms with nature in the new (and quasi-apocalyptic) machine age. Avery and Clampett were not merely engaging with *rhetorical play*, but what I wish to term the *permissive filter* of animated comedy. The very artifice and craft orientation of animation, and its common presence as children's entertainment, have often been used to cite animation as a language of the innocent and innocuous. This has always been an anomaly as animation has always been made by adults with an adult sensibility, even when making films that might entertain children. The very language of animation serves as a mask, a veneer, and an illusion because in not being in any way literal, it is inherently subtextual, metaphorical, and analogous; and it is in this that I believe it offers a distinctive approach to comedy. This permissive filter offers both permission for, and a *carte blanche* approach to, any form of joke making, which defies conventional notions of coherence and veils the implied author.

Writing in 1990, Neale and Krutnik argue that animation "can provide both isolated and systematic examples of 'self-awareness' and 'self-reflection,' of what the Russian formalists called *ostranemie* – estrangement, foregrounding, the exposure of the poetic or aesthetic device" (Neale and Krutnik 1990: 90). Though much has been made since of this Brechtian-style alienation in the form, it is actually the permissive filter which has been enabling for the animation film-maker working in comedy, because it foregrounds the self-conscious nature of the joke, and the attitude informing the joke, rather than a traditional aesthetic effect or a clear act of orthodox authored art-making (though, as I imply above, and throughout this discussion, there is obviously a clear case for the argument that this is also so). This is one of the reasons why Avery, Clampett and others were not acknowledged in their time for their achievement, but the comedy itself – essentially optimistic for all its brutalities and violence – was viewed as satisfyingly relieving and very entertaining in its sheer visual invention. Such work survives in the new millennial era. Pixar has embraced the classical storytelling of the Disney studio, enhancing narrative complexity through a commitment to explore contemporary themes, for example environmental issues in *WALL-E* (2008). This is a darker edged absurdist comedy, however, emerging from audience recognition of humankind's seemingly inevitable decline into alienation, obesity, and consumer complacency. Dreamworks, Pixar's leading competitor, in making features like *Shrek* (2001), and its sequels, has adopted a similar stance to Warner Bros. in the 1930s and 1940s. These are smart, "gag"-led movies, topical and knowing, deliberately playful and glib, less earnestly satirical, emphasizing entertainment before commentary, glee before glum. The popularity of such features has seen animation at the center of mainstream American (Western) culture. There is some irony in the fact that such films apparently provide a comforting façade as family fare, but actually, evidence insight, interrogation and investigation of contemporary mores. A similar approach is used – more self-conscious and purposive – in non-American contexts, which could use the form for highly amusing affects but often remain unchallenged in their implied critique.

A Patient in a Lunatic Asylum

If the American cartoon tradition still refers much to its golden era between 1928–1945, in the work of figures like Bill Plympton, essentially a "Deadpan" Avery, and Canadian, John Kricfalusi, a more "gross out" Clampett, approaches elsewhere draw on different social sources and work in different ways. When asked to describe what animation is, master Russian animator, Yuri Norstein, who made *Tale of Tales* (1979), often regarded as the greatest animation ever, replies with a joke: "There is a patient in a lunatic asylum, writing a letter, observed by his friend, who asks 'What are you doing?' The letter writer replies, 'I am writing a letter to myself,' to which his friend asks, 'What are you writing?' He looks up and answers, 'I don't know, I haven't received it yet.'"[3] Norstein effectively summarizes the often "mad" insularity of the animator, and animation as a form that can support complex ways of expressing personal perspectives and visions.

Ironically, if Avery's cat wanted to come home to the "good ol' U.S. of A" for its supposed openness and democratic principles, perhaps the characters in animation from other more repressive and interventionist political regimes have a different kind of comic register. This is obviously most common in the nations of the former Soviet bloc, which experienced the repressions of Russian communist government. This situation had mixed consequences for the role and function of comedy, and often reflects the insularity, ambivalence and irony of Norstein's joke. As I am seeking to suggest through the examples I have already given and through the concepts of rhetorical play and the permissive filter, I view animated comedy as a state of mind, one ably visualized through the distinctiveness of the form in re-inventing not merely what is said, but how it is said.

In his study of Communism through its jokes, Ben Lewis (2008: 82) has suggested that "historians of facts like to say that Communists 'tolerated no dissent' or denied 'free speech.' The historian of jokes knows that this was not the case. The unofficial jokes show that it is always impossible to eradicate free speech; the official ones show that certain kinds of criticism could be spoken."

Particularly effective was the political cartoon, which since the 1930s epitomized a certain kind of tolerated dialectic of dissent, always foregrounding its status as "a joke" and something that should not be taken overly seriously. The "visual" discourse of comic practice as played out in animated films had the added advantage of using the "permissive filter" at least to obfuscate or make ambivalent particular kinds of resistance to the party line. An unofficial Communist joke will help reveal how this was achieved: "What's the difference between Impressionism, Expressionism and Socialist Realism?" Answer: "The Impressionists paint what they see; the Expressionists paint how they feel, and the Socialist Realists paint what they are told to." Animation had the advantage of mixing Impressionist and Expressionist tropes into modes of Socialist Realism. Charles Eidsvik has written of the presence of "mock realism" in Eastern European films, predominantly those from the former Czechoslovakia, stressing that film comedy is already more overtly politicized than in the West. He notes, "What creates the comic effect is that allusions to the real world of the viewer allow the viewer to react in terms of an imagined world suggested by the film – one that *is* incongruous and funny" (Horton 1991: 93). This, then, is not merely the incongruity of ideas and concepts, or material experience and psycho-somatic experience, but one about "reality" as conceived and represented *as if* it operated on the terms and conditions defined by the State, but which actually bears no relationship to the "real world" lived in by the people. The outcome, of course, is a depiction of the world that the authorities cannot refute, but which becomes the subject and object of ridicule in the minds of the viewers – a pleasurable recognition and relief shared by all in the face of ideological and sometimes militarist oppression.

Chris Robinson, in his study of Estonian animation, picks up upon this approach when he looks at the work of Rein Raamat, whose films, he suggests, "are notable for their meticulous drawings, philosophical themes, and lack of humour," but while acknowledging his achievements within an oppressive system, he nevertheless argues that "reality is not as logical and rational as Raamat's art imagines it to be" (Robinson 2006: 67, 78). Raamat's attempt not to offend the State by using more universal archetypes of good versus evil, rich versus poor, and so forth, in seeking resolution in his films proved insufficiently in touch not merely with social reality but also with what animation could achieve by using its Impressionistic and Expressionistic possibilities.

It was this that was not lost on Priit Pärn, who has since become one of animation's most significant filmmakers. Pärn successfully circumnavigated the expectations of the State, neither servicing "Socialist Realism" nor creating anti-American propaganda, but using both as part of his own personal approach to animation. Steve Lillebuen, wrote of Pärn's film, *Time Out* (1984), suggesting that it was a "Yellow Submarine" world, reminiscent of a Warner Bros. cartoon, with its bookending curtains, working as "a morbid combination of *Monty Python* and *Ren and Stimpy*," but eventually conceding that "this is about as far from the *Bugs Bunny* and *Tweety Show* as you can get" (Lillebuen 2005: 16). Pärn is a careful to use the particular language of animation to resist dominant forms of graphic and narrative expression, while at the same time recalling and revising them. Master Russian animator, Fedor Khitruk, has suggested that animation is an art that distils "emotions in a concentrated form"; " ... it is caricature, but not because it has to be funny, but because caricature means bringing out what is characteristic. That's why I consider animation to be a synthesis of caricature and poetry."[4]

Pärn is careful to use his caricature to oscillate between ironic observation and poetic idioms, normally referring to dream states, fantasy, or personal modes of consciousness. He is therefore bringing out what is "characteristic" in the people and situations he depicts, but equally, foregrounding his own characteristics as an observer. This means that his work is naturally Impressionistic and Expressionistic, while still remaining grounded in "Socialist Realism" expected in Eastern European text. In resisting the "cute," "big-eyed," "squash 'n' stretch" tradition of character animation in the American or Japanese style, preferring instead what seem to be puppet-styled grotesques from a Western perspective, Pärn is only really engaging with the reality of physical ordinariness – the "warts 'n' all" unattractiveness of humankind, rather than the construction of idyllic, innocent, and appealing human forms. Pärn has no desire to reach a mass audience familiar with such tropes, but instead, he looks to those who may engage with his vision and its national and cultural reference points. Further he is refreshing what have become, to a certain extent, exhausted vocabularies of representation in classical animation, particularly in the American context, changing some of the aesthetic, metaphoric and ideological assumptions at its heart.

His film *Breakfast on the Grass* (1987) was submitted to the authorities in 1983 but refused production until the thaw of *perestroika* in 1986. The narrative begins with a dedication "to the artists who did everything that they were permitted to do," a double-edged acknowledgement of the efforts of artists to sustain freedom of expression in the light of the oppressions of totalitarian government. The narrative is divided into five episodes, featuring four characters – Anna, Georg, Berta and Eduard – who unbeknownst to each other, share the similar bleak terrain of life determined by an impoverished but authoritarian regime. They are referenced in each other's narrative, with the implication that all are only defined by the moment in which they live, their lack of identity in the midst of the mass, and the minimal achievements in merely surviving. Pärn begins the film with a car accident, an extended scream, and a goldfish bowl crashing to the floor in Anna's apartment, as she rushes to prepare when she realizes she is late for work. This is not merely anxiety but a genuine fear about engaging with the outside world, as her umbrella blows away in a rainstorm, a grotesque mass of people mocks her, people compete aggressively for a place on a bus, and she must defend herself from potential sexual assault. Pärn exposes the irony of a tyrannical regime in which there seems to be the superficial order of oppressive routine, habit, and service to the State, but which is actually characterized by a venal culture fighting in whatever way possible for pleasure and resources. A shopping trip is a competitive trauma, for example, where Anna loses apples to opportunist children and is tricked by a black marketeer into getting an apple in return for sexual favors.

Pärn felt he had explored the formal principles of metamorphosis and the mutability of form for comic purposes in his early film, *And Plays Tricks* (1978), so he deploys this approach to more ironic effect in this film. He uses metamorphosis to show a sense of physical and material dissolution in the characters' worlds that therefore have a sense of inexplicable temporariness and passing ephemera. This is especially the case in the episode that begins with Georg's fantasy of himself as a bourgeois intellectual, versed in the fine arts and possessing material wealth. This literally dissolves, becoming a place in which everything is black, rotting and broken. Pärn points up the ironic notion that to attain these quasi-Western values and culture Georg must attain the status of a senior government bureaucrat. His pursuit of an appropriate jacket projects him into an absurdist farce. In order to get an appropriate jacket he must help all the people whom he asks to help him. He must get a pair of glasses for the tailor, for example, but is confronted by a queue of blind men blocking his way to the opticians. He becomes party to the fact that Soviet life is actually an oppressive mechanism, where power resides

with those who manipulate others, and kills those who do not conform. Once he
finally puts on the jacket, however, he is content to accept the implicit status quo.

There has now been a generation born since the Berlin Wall came down, and
some contemplation on the part of Eastern Europeans about their experience.
While many have seen benefits, and there have been many changes, there are
people who feel disadvantaged by the fact that their work is now not State
supported and their endeavors have been subject to the most exploitative aspects
of Western capitalism, no preparation for market culture, and a lack of investment
in a competitive infrastructure. Fundamentally, many believe that their efforts to
live under Soviet law left them better placed and happier than under the vestiges
of a market economy. Much to the incomprehension of some Western ideologues,
many people were content in the Soviet system simply because they had learned
to live within it. This is Berta's story, the third episode in Pärn's narrative. Even
though Berta is faceless and feels she has literally to construct her identity by
drawing on her face – another referential aspect of animation itself – she reconciles
her domestic life by caring for her children on the unofficial terms and conditions
the culture has developed. She gives her daughter balloons by exchanging them
for an apple; the sexual resonance of this act, implied from Anna's story. Pärn
even invests this with an ambivalent eroticism, itself part of a representational
system in his work that sometimes offends Western moral sensibilities.

This is perhaps exacerbated most in Eduard's story, in which a surreal cab ride
results in his humiliation and literal diminution at the hands of hierarchical bureau-
crats and obese prostitutes. The limitations of the system are best represented in
two visual gags: one, where a one-eyed senior administrator blinds himself with
the spoon in his cup of tea and another where a bust of a leader on a plinth disso-
lutely flows away down its pedestal, only to be replaced by an exact replica. In the
film's final episode, Eduard gains access to the "paradise" of a park, and is joined by
Anna, Georg and Berta, who assemble in the tableau pose of Manet's masterpiece,
Déjeuner sur l'herbe. It is in this that Pärn consolidates the meaning of his film, aligning himself with Manet's work, which scandalized Paris because it was viewed as
both crude in its technique and its subject matter, exactly the same response that
attended Pärn's approach to non-Disney styled animation, and his direct, uncompromising depiction of the Communist regime. Equally, Manet's painting does not
wholly reject academic painting or official taste, referencing Raphaël and Titian in
the way Pärn suggests the graphic anarchies of Terry Gilliam or Bob Clampett.
By using irony in this way, both point to a certain venality and vulgarity embedded in humanity despite the social, cultural and political conditions that manage
and define them. Further, they foreground the absurd brutality of the hierarchies
that determine how life should be led, and what tastes, postures and ambitions
humankind should supposedly pursue.

This is far from the "gag" comedy of the American model, of course, prompting
different kinds of visceral and cerebral responses. Pärn's version of "mock realism,"
however, may seem like a "laugh-riot," to coin a phrase, compared to the works

of Polish animators like Daniel Szczechura, Ryszard Czekela, and Stefan Schaben-beck, artists I wish to describe as "graphic symbolists,"[5] whose passion, poetry and puns are bound up in a Bressonian enigma. Robert Bresson is not known as a "gag" man, and indeed, on the occasion that he does mention "humor," he cites Montesquieu: "its difficulty consists in making you find in a thing a new feeling which nevertheless comes from the thing" (Bresson 1986: 127). Bresson's spare, intense, fragmentary "realism" is echoed directly in much Polish animation, and the normally black absurdist humor that arises from these films is perhaps the inevitable consequence of a nation negotiating the tensions between embedded Catholicism, the dark resonance of the Holocaust, and the enduring impact of Soviet communism. Particular kinds of repression mix freely with the legacies of oppression, and from this spiritual and political fusion emerges a primal, sometimes paranoid, yet passionate engagement with life. Comedy in this context, then, is essentially philosophical. To understand the pleasures of the joke is to engage with the pleasure of understanding an idea, a puzzle, a metaphor; it is to be amused by the method and process by which the bleak meaninglessness of human existence might be denied or triumphed over. It is the new feeling found within the thing itself.

Daniel Szczechura, for example, shows the building of a complex machine, made up of many parts and built by many men, which is then revealed as a pencil sharpener in *The Machine* (1961). This could be a satire of the waste, inefficiency, and ineptitude of the State, the limited output from an overblown infrastructure, or simply a surreal reversal of expectation, in that something so complex makes something so basic. Either way, the metaphor is used to shock or surprise, and this is a key motif in Szczechura's work. It emerges again when he provides an abstracted overhead perspective on the machinations in a congregation to attain the President's seat in *The Chair* (1963). Similarly, we see it in the endless flight of a ski-jumper, who enjoys the freedoms of sharing his skis with a friend on his travels, and by-passing falling parachutists, finally only records a meager jump length in the competition, in *First, Second, Third* (1964). Yet again, we experience surprise in the carefully crafted controlled routine of a man before he leaps from a window in *Jumping* (1978). These are in effect, intellectual "jokes"; observational vignettes of black humor, in which some "new feeling" is recovered from a potentially predictable scenario.

This concept is taken further by Stefan Schabenbeck, whose film *Everything is a Number* (1966) (Figure 23.1) finds a man in conflict with a range of numbers and geometric shapes, and ultimately, hundreds of other men like himself disgorged from a mathematical machine. He becomes cloned and absorbed within them—literally another number. It is a surprisingly prescient critique of humankind being overtaken by data and technology, isolated, alienated, and lost while supposedly part of a larger community.

In *Exclamation Mark* (1967), Schabenbeck takes this preoccupation with the individual, the mass and the symbolism of graphic expression to another level, rendering individuals as a mass of dots seen from above, literally going about the

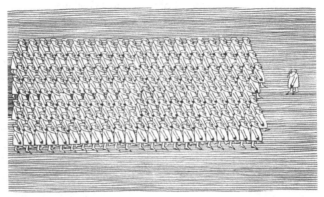

Figure 23.1 *Everything is a Number* (directed and produced by Stefan Schabenbeck) graphically delineates both literally and metaphorically the role of the individual and the mass, and with it comments upon issues of conformism, alienation, social immersion, and notions of resistance.

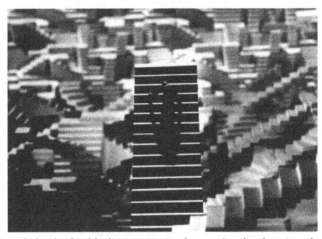

Figure 23.2 Schabenbeck's bleak exposition of a man's relentless Sisyphean existence in *The Stairs*, which he directed and produced, insists upon an absurdist rejection of the apparent meaninglessness of contemporary life.

instrumental business of making shapes and forms. This ultimately results in their construction of a perfect sphere. In a Sisyphean effort, a group of figures pushes the heavy globe up a hill, listening to the instructions of a single figure standing atop the ball. Inevitably, the ball rolls backwards crushing all the pushing figures and the figure on top, leaving the shape of an exclamation mark in the ground. The camera zooms out to discover numerous exclamation marks across the land, marks of shock, surprise, indignation, fixed forever. In essence, Schabenbeck depicts a mass graveyard, the consequence of meaningless work, mindless authority, and a lack of genuine purpose or identity. Yet at the same time he produces an almost entirely abstract work. *The Stairs* (1968) is a 3D riff on the same theme, following a man as he negotiates endless flights of stairs, until tired and exhausted, he lies down at the very top and becomes a stair himself (see Figure 23.2). This, like the absurdist works of Samuel Beckett and Eugene Ionesco, becomes an epic extemporization upon the meaninglessness of existence, an extrapolation of a philosophic principle that calls upon the audience to acknowledge, accept, and find solace in the comfort of common fate.

Schabenbeck's final absurdist masterpiece of this period is *The Drought* (1969), which was initially banned for apparently overtly showing "a wall" that the authorities believed represented "the Iron Curtain," and would be interpreted as a critique of the politics of the Soviet Union. However, the film's meaning runs much deeper. Figures unsuccessfully seek to breach huge chasms in a barren, dried-out landscape, consistently failing in their bridge building and bids to connect. It is Schabenbeck's final irony that the film concludes with a torrential storm and a flood, which with the blackest of humor, unifies them all.

From a Western perspective, this may seem unredeemingly bleak, and at one level it is, but it is also a way in which art can function as a mechanism by which all of life's vicissitudes and injustices are rendered as a joke in the grand scheme of either absent, indifferent, playful, or vengeful gods. This moves "humor" from being a localized or culturally specific idiom, and uses it as a vehicle for universal perspectives. Avner Ziv has suggested that there are four basic functions of humor: to achieve group solidarity, to reduce conflict and malice, to engage with and either perpetuate or challenge prevailing (stereo)typologies, and to induce pleasure (see Ziv 1988). If applied to the work of Schabenbeck and his ilk in the Eastern European context, there is clearly the representation of the group as an abstract mass, the reduction of conflict through acceptance of life's existential malaise, the elimination of typologies by rendering every individual's fate as common and universal, and the pleasure derived from knowing that life's fundamental lack of meaning can be laughed at and laughed about. Humankind literally has the last laugh. This is permitted through the very abstraction animation allows, and the metaphysical purchase embedded in its visual codes and conventions.

Girls' Nights Out

If this discussion so far, and film culture overall, has been dominated by men, it is worthwhile taking into account the comic work undertaken by women, and the fact that women have found animation to be a particularly conducive medium in which to work, embracing its authorial control, and its opportunities for personal expression. The form has also afforded women an opportunity to find original comic perspectives. Czech animator, Michaela Patlatova, for example, in films like *Words, Words, Words* (1991) uses the comic convention of "speech bubbles" to demonstrate the limits of human verbal communication. Men whisper and conspire, at one point addressing "the elephant in the room," made literal in ani-mation. The elephant is fluid enough to pass into their heads and through each other's ears. A man and a woman seek to complete a "jigsaw-puzzle" composed of colorful utterances that have taken the shape of puzzle pieces. A seemingly arbitrary figure of a yellow dog consumes everyone's drinks as they dramatize exis-tence through words, words, words. Patlatova resists the "Politics" embraced by figures like Pärn and Schabenbeck, preferring the "politics" of the personal. This is typical of women animators who, for the most part, seek to base their humor on personal experience and close observation, noting the nuances and non sequiturs of experience as the "windows" by which the human condition is understood. A long-held debate all over the world is whether male and female humor is signifi-cantly different, and clearly, there is no consensus about this, but it does seem clear in the English context that women animators have emerged, not merely as artists with a distinctive vision, but as successful visual comediennes.

It has often been suggested that the English have a particular predisposition to joke (see Fox 2004), partly as a way of brokering communication with oth-ers, partly as a defense mechanism, partly as a way of dealing with embarrass-ment and unease. As in all nations there are many traditions of humor but British animation predominantly finds its antecedents in the political satire of Hogarth, Gilray, Cruickshank, Tenniel and Low (see Geipel 1972) and the broader defin-ing principle of what I wish to call "wit," which is primarily understood as an intellectual form of humor. It should be stressed here, too, that although "Bri-tish Animation" remains a convenient overarching term for films produced in Britain, I will actually be discussing the characteristics of "English" humor in ani-mation. (It might be further noted that some of the best exponents of British animation are from "abroad" anyway. Bob Godfrey, for example, is Australian, Terry Gilliam is American, Richard Williams is Canadian, John Halas is Hungar-ian, and so on.) Carl Hill has identified English "wit" as speaking to "common sense" and an "egalitarian tendency," and working as an "instrument of social and moral discipline." Hill also notes, however, that there is sometimes an "ideologi-cal duplicity" in the nature of English wit because of a tension between its "critical and conformist" functions, when "it represents the rule of reason and the forces of progress and innovation, [yet] is ready to turn to the irrational intimidation of ridicule should reason overstep its bounds and threaten social anarchy." Hill fur-ther argues that "wit mediates between the ruling elite and the general populace, keeping the elite in check even as it gives it a mandate to govern" (Hill 1993: 20–3). These factors—ideological duplicity, codes of moral, social and artistic discipline, egalitarian purpose, and the mediations of reason and ridicule within the English social context, become the subject matter of much British animated comedy. Such wit finds particular expression, for example, in the short films of Candy Guard, and especially her animated "sit-com," *Pond Life* (1996). Wit is also exemplified in Sarah Kennedy's *Crapston Villas* (1995), Alison Snowden and David Fine's *Bob and Margaret* (1998), based on the exemplary short, *Bob's Birthday* (1993) (perhaps the definitive film about English embarrassment), and specifically, in the work of Joanna Quinn, based on scripts by her partner, Les Mills (see Kitson 2008; Wells 2008).

In *Girls Night Out* (1986), Quinn neatly reversed the assumptions of patriarchal cinema by using a male stripper as the subject of the "female gaze" of her key character, Beryl, simultaneously parodying the macho bravura of masculine sensibilities and the phallic imperatives of cinematic conventions. Quinn's extraordinary draughtsmanship, fluid imagery, and dynamic use of satirical caricature readily capture the energy of the characters and make a pointed statement about femininity, female identity, and feminist idealism played out through "the everyday." Beryl, a middle-aged factory worker who is taken by her work colleagues to a male strip show, hilariously pulls the stripper's thong off, revealing the difference between phallic presumption and power and its physical counterpart, the small penis. Where the American cartoon essentially makes the body, plastic, arbitrary and a space for physical play, and Eastern European animation uses the body to engage with political reality (social role, labor, psychosomatic identity), animation in an English setting focuses the body as a site of self-consciousness and cultural judgment. This becomes the subject of Quinn's *Body Beautiful* (1988), which sees Beryl pestered by sexist factory lothario, Vince, and teased and criticized by her female workmates concerning her weight. Recalling a lifetime's worth of feeling guilty and persecuted about her size, Beryl responds by taking up a fitness regime at the local gym and training with a rugby team in order to enter the factory "Body Beautiful" contest. Competing against Vince, and other lithe contestants, Beryl performs a routine that rejects everyone's constant criticism and the inherent sexism and pressure to conform that she experiences. Quinn cleverly uses the freedoms of animation to configure Beryl's body as a musical instrument and as a newly muscled form that nevertheless speaks to the dimensions of a middle-aged woman, proud of her own body and sense of being. The factory's Japanese owners vote Beryl the winner of the contest, and her victory represents more than a personal triumph, operating as a critique of male assumptions about women, and the social and cultural infrastructures that repress them.

Dreams and Desires—Family Ties engages more specifically with one of the underlying themes of all three films: Beryl's deep-seated romantic and spiritual desire. Always viewed through her body and society's dismissal of the middle aged, Beryl harbors erotic feelings and a need to be defined through achievement. She becomes obsessive about using her home video camera, and invests in reading about film to improve her skills, all of which she wishes to use when recording her friend Mandy's wedding. In her desire to achieve distinctive *verité*, persuasive tracking shots (tying the camera to a man's broken leg in a wheelchair) and *Kino pravda* (attaching the camera to a rampant dog), Beryl manages to wreck Mandy's wedding and reception. Quinn's *tour-de-force* graphic renditions of amateur video making, with its unintentional views of feet, ceilings, and corridors, and extraordinary drawing skills in capturing Beryl's drunken dreams and well intentioned blunders speak to a quality of observation that signifies a currency of "cleverness" as well as "comedy" in the narrative and representation. This simultaneous presence of knowing "intelligence" and self-conscious "joke making" is the very definition of English animated "wit," seen also in the work of Chris Shepherd, Phil Mulloy, Run Wrake, Let Me Feel Your Finger First, and Bunnage and Link (see Norris 2008).

Taigu and Laughing Gods

Master Japanese animator, Hayao Miyazaki, has noted, "Unlike the foreign countries, where people may argue about whether Christ ever laughed or not, Japanese gods are basically laughing gods. It's like the weather in Japan: there may be harsh times, but basically the sun shines on us" (Miyazaki 1996: 367).

This essentially optimistic perspective on Japanese culture is effectively grounded in a social conservatism based on a politeness and decorum that underpins most aspects of Japanese society. Japanese identity is predicated fundamentally on its familial, group and generational closeness, and notions of duty, honor and service, rather than the solipsistic perspectives of Western celebrity culture, satirized in British shows like *2DTV*. Inevitably, postwar Japanese culture has been inflected by Western influence, manifest in Japanese anime in the way that the design is based on Western representational idioms. This occurred because Japan drew upon Western conceptions of modernity, and as such, white, blonde, large-eyed heroines and classical, young, egocentric heroes became the focus of animated narratives, even though the sources for these were often drawn from indigenous manga stories. For many people in other countries, therefore, there is often some confusion, and unintended humor emerges from reading an anime on Western terms and conditions. Even some of the conventions that anime uses to distinguish its storytelling—speeding graphic lines, shapes and colors in the background at moments of emotional intensity, a large sweat drop signifying stress, nosebleeds at points of sexual arousal, and extensive head-scratching in moments of embarrassment—sometimes seem to provoke amusement for non-Japanese audiences. The success of anime in the West has meant that audiences have slowly learned these conventions and have become more aware, too, of comic strategies that are constructed for, and meaningful to, the Japanese, and which ultimately, have their source in the cultural terrain described earlier.

Perhaps it is inevitable that a conservative culture encouraging the acceptance of a certain hierarchical order and models of collectivism and homogeneity, should have art forms that offer oppositional points of view, and sometimes prioritize "individualism" in its own right as a vehicle for alternative perspectives. The "lone wolf" outsider figure featured in numerous dramatic narratives, but inevitably in comic anime, is a fool—*taigu*—mostly, characterized by a sense of frustration and powerlessness in the face of desire and the everyday execution of life's tasks. Susan Napier (2001: 77–8) has suggested that in more sensually and erotically charged stories, this is the "comic voyeur," a young male laughed at because he cannot fulfill the fantasies that emerge from the privilege of his male gaze. Unlike, Beryl in Joanna Quinn's films, he cannot break the rules, and in many senses, this figure is emblematic of where humor emerges in Japanese animation. The rules, limits and expectations of Japanese culture are so pronounced, that response to this is often excessive and aggressive. As Napier (1996: 235–64) has noted of dramatic vehicles, this prompts an "imagination of disaster," or in game shows, features perverse and physically demeaning challenges, or in hentai, pornographic extremes. In comic anime, it is a playful exaggeration of how convention confounds and misrepresents individual sensibilities.

Urusei Yatsura (1981–1986) is a good example of the way many Japanese Romantic comedies use a mix of registers to facilitate incongruous humor and physical slapstick. Based on Rumiko Takahashi's popular manga, the story begins with the arrival of the Alien, oni (elsewhere understood as a demon, but in this context, wholly ironic), intent on invading earth. Among their number is the cute, green-horned, Lum, daughter of the Alien leader, who is chosen by her kind to compete with hormonal male teenager, Ataru Moroboshi, in a game in which, should Ataru touch her horns within the week, he wins the right to retain the Earth, preventing the invasion taking place. Ataru's girlfriend, Shinobu, promises to marry him if he succeeds. In a scenario, predicated on farce structures, Ataru steals Lum's bikini top, and while she is protecting her modesty, Ataru touches her horns, gleeful that now he will be able to get married. Lum, however, misunderstands this, and believes he means to marry her, accepting his "proposal" on live television, and eventually moving in with him! Their relationship is at the center of the series, which employs mythic elements and folk idioms, as well as a kind of "magic realism" reminiscent of US sitcoms like *Bewitched, I Dream of Jeannie*, and *The Flying Nun* in which the supernatural and the everyday mix freely and create unusual, and equally farcical storylines. Ataru falls for numerous high-school and other-worldly girls, which offends Lum, and earns Ataru electric shocks, but this kind of exchange, while reflecting tensions and conflicts in romantic bonds, is contextualized within more excessive situations. The Moroboshi family, for example, is subject to an atomic bomb-styled explosion, which completely wrecks their house, and in Tex Avery "King Size Canary" fashion, a huge swallow, growing ever bigger through Lum's magic candy, ends up wrecking Tokyo in a Godzilla-type blitz. Whereas in Western comedy, a *deus ex machina* is often imposed to resolve a narrative, or to refocus its moral agenda, these casually apocalyptic comedies are left as inconclusively as the narratives of arbitrary destruction of a Laurel and Hardy or a Buster Keaton film. Rather than being left as deadpan codas, however, they imply a chaotic and anarchic response to the highly sensitive codes and conventions of Japanese culture. Further, every freedom of working in animation is exploited to create impossible fantasy situations and performative spectacle. This approach has become a convention at a narrative level through deliberately overextended scenarios, and crucially, through the use of "parody" drawing, stressing the "super-deformity" of expressions, reactions, body shapes, and so on. Simply, the animation itself signals its exaggeration as a way of laughing at the rules embedded within, and expectations of, any given situation.

In the independent sector, this is probably best epitomized in the work of Yoji Kuri, who emerged in the 1960s as one of the Animation Sannin ko nai (Animation "Gang of Three"), making animated film, both in the spirit of speaking to the freedoms of the "cartoon" and as an *avant-garde* art practice. This was not new in animation. As Michael North notes of early production in France:

> There were also animated cartoons making the new art movements into subjects for humor. Emile Cohl, who had started his creative life among the Incoherents, produced several of these, including the *Le Peintre néo-Impressioniste* and *Le Cubiste*. In fact, the work of artists such as Cohl, who produced lampoons by and of the *avant-garde*, shows how difficult it could be to distinguish these two kinds of humor and to determine just who was more successfully mocking whom. (North 2009: 21)

This collapsing of a "fine art" sensibility and a "joke-making" facility is common in much animated humor. Kuri's work freely demonstrates this in the way that he exploits the visual metamorphoses and symbolic abstraction of the form, and uses a minimalist soundtrack, often composed of a single sound (a violin note in *G String* (1969)) or incongruous noises (counterpoint sounds in *The Room* (1967)) recalling the dramatic vignettes of action in Noh theatre. The best example of an *avant-garde*, quasi-Fluxus tendency with a playful soundtrack in Kuri's work, is *Human Zoo* (1962), a zany series of rapid vignettes featuring a large woman's sado-masochistic treatment of a series of small men, set in a cage, merely accompanied by male shouts of reaction and pain. The woman pulls a man like a dog, pokes one with an umbrella, another with a broom, sits on a man's head and bottom, attacks a man with an extending bosom, crushes a man between her breasts, and pokes another as if he were a budgie. The men are, in essence, pets, but treated with fetishistic disdain. Again, every social convention about the polite subservience of Japanese women in the face of authoritarian men is violated, but with no small hint of the excesses that then go on in private as a reaction to inhibited and habitual social mores. The film's sparseness and anti-narrative repetitions, however, render this as much "art" as "animation," the comic innovation of the *avant-garde*.

That May Not Be All, Folks!

In Pixar Animation's *Monsters Inc.* (2001), Sulley, a giant turquoise monster, is but one of a number of supposedly frightening creatures who emerge at night to scare children, collecting their screams "to power" the alternative world of Monstropolis in which they live. Sulley's trainer is Mike Wazowski–"That's Mike with

One 'I'"—a green, single-eyed, bowling-ball character, who discovers that, as well as screaming with fear, children scream with laughter, and "laughter is ten times more powerful than a scream." Animation often draws its comedy from the very tension that characterizes that "scream"—exploiting anxieties, fears, assumptions and expectations that might be personally, culturally and socially harmful in any one national context, but instead, creating often cathartic humor. As I have suggested throughout this discussion, this has been achieved largely through the permissive filter embedded in the overt illusionism of the animated form, and the ways this defines a seemingly alternative realm of expression that allows a temporary release from both realist conventions of representation, and by extension, the realities of the everyday world. This new site of expression—self-consciously artificial, unconventional, subjective—allows the possibility of rhetorical play, in which a comic approach affords the possibility of comment, critique, and above all, implied "change." As Sheri Klein has suggested, the artist has a range of devices and techniques to provoke laughter, including "association, transposition, transformation, exaggeration, disguise and appropriation" (Klein 2007:19). Such processes all indicate models of change, but it is surely the comic invention of animators, who succeeded long before Duchamps and his ilk, and long after, too, in revising both the perception of art, and the modern world, not merely in aesthetic and conceptual terms, but in the representational construction of "a modern world" itself. Animation in all its forms, and in all national contexts, has succeeded in prompting fresh associations, material transpositions, physical transformations, visual exaggerations, authorial disguise and metaphysical appropriation. But, in its comic idioms it has been especially indicative in the ways it laughs at the foibles and follies of humankind, that there are always alternative points of view, and metaphysically charged representations of "modern worlds" hinting at other kinds of preferred existence. The hilarious anarchies of the animated form worldwide, should not merely be taken at face value. Their distinctiveness, insight and difference always suggests that might not be all, folks.

Notes

1. Personal interview with the author, November 2010.
2. These gags feature in Warner Bros. and Disney cartoons and are addressed in various texts. See Adamson (1974), Peary and Peary (1980), Pilling (1984), Sandler (1998).
3. Personal interview with the author, June 2002.
4. Quoted in *The Spirit of Genius: Fedor Khitruk and his Films*, a documentary written and directed by Otto Alder (1998).
5. I have written about Polish animation in the forthcoming second edition of *Understanding Animation*, identifying five key typologies of animation in Poland. These are "Proto-surrealists," "Plastic Formalists," "Graphic Symbolists," "Iconoclasts of Consciousness," and "Aesthetic Reconstructionists."

References

Adamson, Joe (1974) *Tex Avery: King of Cartoons*, Da Capo, New York, NY.

Bergson, Henri (1911/2002) *Laughter: An Essay on the Meaning of the Comic*, Kessinger Publishing, Whitefish, MT.

Bresson, Robert (1986) *Notes on the Cinematographer*, Quartet Books, London.

Davies, Christie (1996) *Ethnic Humor Around the World*, Indiana University Press, Indianapolis, IN.

Durgnat, Raymond (1969) *The Crazy Mirror: Hollywood Comedy and the American Image*, Faber & Faber, London.

Eidsvik, Charles (1991) Mock realism: the comedy of futility in Eastern Europe, in *Comedy/Cinema/Theory* (ed. A. Horton), University of California Press, Berkeley, CA.

Fox, Kate (2004) *Watching the English*, Hodder & Stoughton, London.

Furniss, Maureen (2005) *Chuck Jones Conversations*, University Press of Mississippi, Jackson, MS.

Geipel, John (1972) *Cartoon: A Short History of Graphic Comedy and Satire*, David & Charles, Trowbridge.

Goldmark, Daniel and Keil, Charlie (2011) Funny pictures: animation and comedy, in *Studio-Era Hollywood*, University of California Press, Berkeley, CA.

Hill, Carl (1993) *The Soul Of Wit: Joke Theory From Grimm to Freud*, University of Nebraska Press, Lincoln, NE.

Jones Chuck (1990) *Chuck Amuck*, Simon & Schuster, London.

Jones Chuck (1996) *Chuck Reducks*, Time Warner, New York, NY.

Kitson, Clare (2008) *British Animation: The Channel 4 Factor*, Parliament Hill Publishing, London.

Klein, Norman (1993) *7 Minutes; The Life and Death of the American Cartoon*, Verso, London.

Klein, Sheri (2007) *Art and Laughter*, I.B. Tauris, London.

Leslie, Esther (2002) *Hollywood Flatlands: Animation, Critical Theory and the Avant Garde*, Verso, London.

Lewis, Ben (2008) *Hammer and Tickle: A History of Communism Told Through Communist Jokes*, Weidenfeld & Nicolson, London.

Lillibuen, Steve (2005) *The Animated Films of Priit Pärn*, Metro Cinema Publications, Toronto.

Lutz, E.G. (1920/1998) *Animated Cartoons*, Applewood Books, Bedford, MA.

Medhurst, Andy (2007) *A National Joke: Popular Comedy and English Cultural Identities*, Routledge, London.

Miyazaki, Hayao (1996) *Starting Point 1979–1996*, Viz Media, San Francisco, CA.

Napier, Susan (1996) Panic sites: the Japanese imagination of disaster from *Godzilla* to *Akira*, in *Contemporary Japan and Popular Culture* (ed. John Whittier Treat), Curzon Press, Richmond, pp. 235–64.

Napier, Susan (2001) *Animé: From Akira to Princess Mononoke*, Palgrave, New York, NY.

Neale, Steve and Krutnik, Frank (1990) *Popular Film and Television Comedy*, Routledge, London.

Norris, Van (2008) "Yeah, looks like it n'all..." the "live action" universe and abridged figurative design and computer animation within modern toss. *Animation: An Interdisciplinary Journal*, 3 (3), 231–49.

North, Michael (2009) *Machine Age Comedy*, Oxford University Press, Oxford.

Peary, Gerald and Peary, Danny (eds.) (1980) *The American Animated Cartoon*, E.P. Dutton, New York, NY.

Pilling, Jayne (ed.) (1984) *That's Not All Folks! A Primer in Cartoonal Knowledge*, BFI, London.

Robinson, Chris (2006) *Estonian Animation: Between Genius and Utter Illiteracy*, John Libbey Publishing, Eastleigh.

Sandler, Kevin (ed.) (1998) *Reading the Rabbit: Explorations in Warner Bros. Animation*, Rutgers University Press, New Brunswick.

Telotte, J.P. (2010) *Animating Space: From Mickey to WALL-E*, University Press of Kentucky, Lexington, KY.

Thomas, Frank and Johnson, Ollie (1981) *Disney Animation: The Illusion of Life*, Abbeville Press, New York, NY.

Wells, Paul (1998) *Understanding Animation*, Routledge, London.

Wells, Paul (2002) *Animation and America*, Rutgers University Press, New Brunswick.

Wells, Paul (with Quinn, Joanna and Mills, Les) (2008) *Drawing for Animation*, AVA Academia, Lausanne.

Ziv, Avner (1988) *National Styles of Humor*, Greenwood Press, Westport, CT.

Further Reading

Goldmark, Daniel and Keil, Charlie (eds.) (2011) *Funny Pictures: Animation and Comedy in Studio Era Hollywood*, University of California Press, Berkeley, CA. An exemplary collection of essays (I modestly bar my own from that view, of course), addressing the comic approaches of the Disney and Fleischer studios, the figures of, among others, Charlie Bowers, Tex Avery and Frank Tashlin, and analysis of the meaning and impact of cartoon comedy.

Jones, Chuck (1990) *Chuck Amuck*, Simon & Schuster, London. Chuck Jones' amusing engagement with his craft, stressing the importance of character, and advancing certain conditions in which he believes animation best succeeds and humor flourishes, especially in the case of the "Roadrunner" cartoons.

Klein, Norman M. (1993) *Seven Minutes: The Life And Death of the American Cartoon*, Verso, New York, NY. An insightful reading of the "golden era" of the American animated cartoon, addressing the evolution and status of "the gag" and looking at how cartoon narrative evolved to embrace the changing nature of the modernist era in the United States. Klein investigates how the properties of the cartoon speak to the machine age, the emergence of melodramatic forms and contexts, and offer significant perspectives on American society and culture.

Leslie, Esther (2002) *Hollywood Flatlands: Animation, Critical Theory and the Avant Garde*, Verso, London. A perceptive and detailed analysis looking at the place of animation as a modernist form of expression, and in relation to the critical and intellectual perspectives of the avant garde, as it engaged with contemporary America. Drawing upon the work of Adorno, Benjamin, Eisenstein and Kracauer, Leslie presents a treatise on animation as a philosophical and ideologically charged art form in populist guise.

Peary, Danny and Peary, Gerald (eds.) (1980) *The American Animated Cartoon*, Dutton, New York. An engaging collection of essays, which explores the early history of animation in figures like Winsor McCay, assesses the Disney legacy and the comic anarchy of the

Warner Bros. studio that challenged it, and offers an overview of cartoon characters, in a combination of analytical pieces and interviews with figures like Chuck Jones and Bob Clampett.

Robinson, Chris (2005) *Unsung Heroes of Animation*, John Libbey, Eastleigh. Robinson, an idiosyncratic, often polemical and highly informed writer, here, and in a further collection, *Animators Unearthed*, champions the work of independent animators worldwide, focusing in some cases on the more alternative comic visions of figures like Phil Mulloy, Mati Kütt, Priit Pärn, JibJab, PES, Don Hertzfeldt and Joanna Quinn.

Telotte, J.P. (2010) *Animating Space: From Mickey to WALL-E*, University of Kentucky Press, Lexington, KY. An investigation of the way animation manages and uses notions of "space" in the construction of its narrative spectacle and gag construction, perceptively taking in the shift from traditional drawn animation to computer generated imagery, and stressing the role of technology in facilitating (comic) animated forms.

Thomas, Frank and Johnson, Ollie (1997) *Too Funny for Words: Disney's Greatest Sight Gags*, Abbeville Press, New York, NY. Continuing the work of the seminal *Disney Animation: The Illusion of Life*, Thomas and Johnson, two of Disney's renown "Nine Old Men," explain and illustrate various approaches to creating the "sight gag," addressing issues of character, timing and context.

Wells, Paul (1998) *Understanding Animation*, Routledge, London. Includes an extensive breakdown and definition of approaches to comic practice, and gags in animation, using examples from a range of films from a variety of global contexts.

24

Theatrical Cartoon Comedy

From Animated Portmanteau to the *Risus Purus*

Suzanne Buchan

Introduction

Animation film directors have created some of the most memorable comedic moments and characters of the last century. Audiences watching an animated cartoon generally expect to laugh, and this expectation raises a number of questions. Why do we have comic expectations when we watch an animation film? What is the relationship between how jokes and wit are expressed in animated film and the laughter and smiles they evoke? Does this film form treat humor differently to the way a live-action film does, and if so, how? What are the formal, stylistic, and narrative elements that contribute to its humor, and in what way, if any, is this unique to animated film? This chapter is an attempt to provide insights into these straightforward but immensely complex questions.

I will examine the historical origins and development of "funny" animation in relation to the joke in language, specifically the relationships between humor in the spoken and written word and animated films. This is supported by a framework of observations on humor made by Henri Bergson in *On Laughter* (1900) and Sigmund Freud's *Jokes and their Relation to the Unconscious* (1905) along with some excursions into the later texts of James Joyce to propose analogies between text-based and animated visual language. I will also posit some theoretical concepts of humor to suggest what is funny and why, and how this is stylistically, culturally, and/or formally determined or not. In doing this I am undertaking "serious play," and close analysis can undermine the effect of surprise, an important element of comedy. But a close analysis of the joke and its development towards the comic in the cartoon genre can illuminate how it functions on screen.

A Companion to Film Comedy, First Edition. Edited by Andrew Horton and Joanna E. Rapf.
© 2013 John Wiley & Sons, Inc. Published 2016 by John Wiley & Sons, Inc.

My focus will be on films made for theatrical distribution up to the 1950s that were made for mixed audiences and meant to be experienced in cinemas, before television usurped these short films as content filler. I will briefly begin with comic strategies that emerged in Early Cinema, concentrating on graphic works of French artist Émile Cohl. I then turn to the refinement of comic narrative in North America around the advent of sound, in "conventional" cartoons made in film studios or commercially oriented companies. Finally, I will explore the golden age of Hollywood cartoons and their close relationship with studio feature productions, and finish with observations on satirical and socio-critical comedy up to the mid-1950s. The films discussed are chosen for three reasons: they are exemplary for a particular comedic strain or genre of cartoon, they are widely available, and because they serve to illustrate the theoretical and aesthetic framework I am proposing.[1] My celluloid, cartoon-based corpus leaves out many films, including the recent boom in feature-length and 3D animation. Yet as I address form, characters and comedic strategies that are independent of technique and technologies, I hope the reader will find what I am proposing in many other animation films.[2]

Preamble: Definitions, the Human and Metamorphosis

Before turning to the films, I want to clarify terms and introduce some concepts with which I will work. First, my use of the very broad term "animation": pure, arts-based animation (distinct from increasingly prevalent digital animation) uses a wide variety of artistic media. This chapter is exclusively concerned with graphic, or 2D animation made with drawing or inked and painted cels and shot on film stock. This type of animation is distinguished first and foremost as a graphic form of narrative, in contrast to photoindexical representation in live-action filmmaking. While it is photoindexical – as a chemical process of recording what is in front of the camera – it is also mimetic.[3] This material distinction is important because, with the exception of three-dimensional object or puppet animation, animators mimetically create entirely unique visual realms with their art. This style of animation is the dominant form during the pre-digital commercial period.

The main character in Tex Avery's *Big Heel-Watha* (1944) tells the audience that "in a cartoon, you can do anything." The visual realm of 2D animation is inherently full of surprises; nothing is implausible or impossible; transformations, spatial transpositions without a transition or cut, actions impossible according to laws of physics, exaggeration, unnatural proportions, non-human forms endowed with anthropomorphic characteristics. These formal attributes have a particular function in the development of cartoon humor because they can represent extreme caricature and exaggerated figures. Fantastic graphic and plastic universes serve to underpin and enhance these figures, often taking on the form of the cartoon character's thoughts and subjective cosmogonies. Bergson, however, provides a challenge to Avery's claim with an important observation about what we laugh at that implicates the animation artist/director:

> the comic does not exist outside the pale of what is strictly *human* ... You may laugh at an animal, but only because you have detected in it some human attitude or expression. You may laugh at a hat, but what you are making fun of, in this case, is not the piece of felt or straw, but the shape that men have given it, – the human caprice whose mould it has assumed. (Bergson 2003: 3)

Animator Alexander Alexeeff agrees with Bergson: "Contrary to live-action cinema, animation draws the elements of its future works from a raw material made *exclusively of human ideas*, those ideas that different animators have about things, living beings and their forms, movements and meanings" (in Bendazzi 1994: xxii).

Here we have a further key between human and animated humor – the figures, the decors, the gags and actions which make us laugh or smile are a graphically expressed product of an artist's imagination, and "the shape [she has] given it, – the human caprice whose mould it has assumed" has a human source.

There is also a formal element of comedy in animation that is central to its effect. Bergson suggests that "we regard [laughter], above all, as a *living thing* ... Passing by imperceptible gradations from one form to another, it will be seen to achieve the strangest *metamorphoses*" (Bergson 2003: 2–3, emphasis mine).

In animation, these gradations are not imperceptible – on the contrary, though they can be breathtakingly fast, and they offer rich arrays of surprising visual transformations to the viewer. Metamorphosis is the fundamental principle and effect of much drawn and painted animation; individual static images, each slightly different than the previous one, are photographed on a roll of film. When projected, these images give the illusion of unity and movement, and effect a transition in form over a period of time. Animated characters and forms are not living things – they are made of paper, pencil and paint.[4] But the animation technique and its underlying effect of metamorphosis create an illusion of sentience, intent, movement and existence, all of which can be central to developing the comic. The viewer's experiential factors that diverge from accepted norms of "reality" play a central role in her ability to comprehend the impossible on screen, an impossible that becomes plausible, and often hilariously funny.

The Joke in Language

Animation's fundamental ability to express metamorphosis is a primary feature of the film form; as I have proposed elsewhere, "metamorphosis is not limited to the visual arts" (Buchan 1998: 24). In terms of the comic it is available in spoken and written language, Bergson notes a difference between two types of the comic in language that is fundamental to what I will propose: "We must make a distinction, however, between the comic *expressed* and the comic *created* by language. The former could, if necessary, be translated from one language into another .... But it is generally impossible to translate the latter. It owes its entire being to the structure of the sentence or to the choice of the words" (Bergson 2003: 45).

I'd like to explore aspects of translation of the comic "*created* by language" as a formal transmutation from text-based literature into the visual art of animation. Freud suggests a number of jokes techniques that are used in language, and I will introduce three in this chapter that offer compelling comic possibilities, summarized here: 1. condensation (a) with formation of composite word, (b) with modification; 2. multiple uses of the same material (c) as a whole and in marts, (d) in a different order, (e) with slight modification, (f) of the same words full and empty; and 3. double meaning (g) meaning as a name and as a thing, (h) metaphorical and literal meanings, (i) double meaning proper (play on words), (j) *double entendre* (Freud 1966: 41–2). I will also explore a metamorphic style that evokes "animated" transitions in the reader's mind – where words are reconstructed to produce new meanings. James Joyce, with his wittily inventive creation of word combinations and neologisms, is a particularly good example of a metamorphic stylist. Joyce's texts are also very funny: Richard Ellmann suggests that "comedy was [Joyce's] true mode" (Ellmann 1978: xi). This is especially true for *Ulysses* (1922) and *Finnegan's Wake* (1939), and I will be working mainly with the single word in these two texts. Bosinelli and Whitsitt's comments are useful here as they emphasize the humor to be found at this level. "The comic side of Joyce's writing, his humour, irony and parodic attitude are not the first things that come to mind when reading this author ... even the smallest item of Joyce's prose, the word, has more often than not a laugh or a smile inscribed into it, and once one begins to see this aspect of his writing, then reading Joyce can be great fun" (Bollettieri Bosinelli and Whitsitt 2010: 158).

I will show how the fun of Joyce's linguistic play can be "translated" into equivalent imagery in animation. By literally moving beyond the single artwork – the original form of the "cartoon" – to a series of images, animation introduces time and movement to drawings presenting one or more "shots" to form short sequences of images.[5] It is through this simultaneity of multiple meanings within the image combined with movement over time that the comic is achieved so effortlessly. We will see that there are many funny moments in animation that use analogous, image-based, rather than semantic, language-based methods.

Much has been written about animation's relationship with Vaudeville / *Variéte* and emerging comic strategies in Early Cinema. According to Henry Jenkins (1990: 5), there was "a large scale commodification of the joke ... the number of joke books published in the United States had grown from 11 in 1890 to 104 in 1907." This explosion had a parallel in film comedy productions, and animation shares with it an element of its early origins that lies in the transition from the spoken or written word to illustrations and photographic imagery.[6] Sigmund

Freud's seminal book on the joke, coextensive with Vaudeville, is concerned with language and speech. I will adapt some of his concepts on the joke to explain the transition from written/spoken humor to its animated counterpart. Freud cites Theodor Lipps (2005: 80) to define a first feature of jokes, brevity: "The account given by Lipps ... of the brevity of jokes is significant: 'A joke says what it has to say, not always in a few words, but in *too* few words – that is, in words that are insufficient by strict logic or by common modes of thought and speech' " (Freud 1966: 13).

We can ask ourselves how this observation of linguistic economy translates into animated graphic imagery. If we consider the single frame satirical newspaper cartoon and comic as a painterly or graphics-based art form, it can "say" what it has to say by compressing into a single image what a joke can take many words to express. Time-based animation can increase this with duration, metamorphosis and movement.

Animated Portmanteau

Many of Early Cinema's animated films had minimal plot or narrative and were usually a compilation of variations on one or more familiar gags using stop trick and single frame animation. Bodyless heads strung up as musical notes (Georges Méliès, *Le Mélomane* (*The Melomaniac*), 1903) a comb styling a woman's hair (Segundo De Chomon's *El Hotel Electrico* (*The Electric Hotel*), 1908) – these object-based tricks showed animated *movement*. The films from French artist Émile Cohl were the first films to use graphic animated metamorphosis, a technique that has prevailed through to contemporary animation productions They were also a welcome exception to the standard animated gag that was predominant in most North American cartoon animation to the end of the 1920s. Intelligently conceived in their design, humor, format and movement, his films were the first to achieve something close to perfection of the metamorphosis of the simple line. Donald Crafton describes Cohl's films as "extraordinary in their outrageousness, their outlandishness, and, frequently, in their incomprehensibility. They do not imitate the physical knockabout gags of the Vaudeville stage ... they rely instead on a peculiar dry, cerebral wittiness that make his films stand alone in pre-World War I cinema" (Crafton 1990: 257).

Wit is a specific form of humor that requires creative engagement from both the witty person and the recipient of wit.[7] William Hazlitt makes a distinction between wit and humor: "Humour is the describing of the ludicrous as it is in itself; wit is the exposing of it, by comparing or contrasting it with something else ... [wit] is the product of art and fancy" (Hazlitt and Keynes 2004: 425)

For Freud, wit is the capacity of a person capable of:

> joke-work ... [that] is not at everyone's command, and altogether only a few people have a plentiful amount of it; and these are distinguished by being spoken of as

having "wit" and we must therefore presume the presence in these "witty" people of
special inherited dispositions or psychical determinants which permit or favour the
joke-work. (Freud 1966: 140)

Cohl's films are replete with illogical events that could be described with Joyce's
"an intrepidation of our dreams" (Joyce 1968: 338), a clever portmanteau with
direct allusion to Freud's *Interpretation of Dreams* that adds the humorous meaning of "intrepid" to "interpretation." The first of Freud's joke techniques mentioned in the section "the Joke in Language" – condensation (a) with formation
of composite word – is a technique of the portmanteau word, a central feature
of Joyce's later works. Portmanteau refers to the fusing of two or more words or
lexemes to produce a new, composite word with a different meaning, transforming the source words into a new semantic expression. Portmanteau words require
the reader's co-creational engagement to comprehend this merging and resulting
new meaning. Witty examples from Joyce include: "jogjaunty" (Joyce 1984: 222),
"contransmagnificandjewbangtantiality" (Joyce 1984: 32), "pornosophical" (Joyce
1984: 353), "doggybowwowsywowsy" (Joyce 1984: 143), "shis," and "hrim" (Joyce
1984: 440).

The condensation of portmanteau is highly useful for interpreting Cohl's animated, metamorphic graphic images. His animated wit is analogous to linguistic transformations and shifts in meaning found in Joyce's writing – what I call
Joyce's metamorphic textual cineantics – but the shifts in meaning are visual and
take place during animated metamorphosis. In the following I compare some of
Joyce's portmanteau words with scenes from Cohl's films. In *Fantasmagorie (Fan-
tasmagoria)* (1908), a cinemagoer is subject to a "crossex*animation*" (Joyce 1968:
339, italics mine) by a woman's huge feathered hat; with a breathtaking tempo
her head expands, is "ballooned" (Joyce 1968: 339), and a puppet figure appears in
it. It grows and gestates like an embryo in a placenta, explodes and from a white
blur the figure is pieced together in "symphisis" (Joyce 1968: 92). The main puppet
figure undergoes a number of charming metamorphoses as the "comedy nomina-
tor" (Joyce 1968: 283), is stuck in a bottle "absintheminded" (Joyce 1968: 464), and
as the bottle morphs into a flower he "reamalgamerge[s]" (Joyce 1968: 49).[8] In *Le
cauchemar de Fantoche (The Puppet's Nightmare)* (1908) the main figure is awakened
in a black space of "noughttime" (Joyce 1968: 349), is "whirrld" (Joyce 1968: 147) in
an endless void as a spiral twines around him. In these films, Cohl's animated line
shares creative techniques with Joyce's syntactic innovations: ellipsis, simultaneity, mindscreen, compression, displacement, and appeal to intelligence. The witty
"funantics" (Joyce 1968: 450) in his films are generated by his inventive metamorphosis, abstraction of figures and forms and incisive transformations of the figures'
"environment" – an autonomous graphic universe determined by metamorphosis
and animated portmanteau.

Animated portmanteaus are disruptions of form in space and time. Joyce
expert Fritz Senn coined the term "dislocution" as a "spatial metaphor for all

manner of metamorphoses, switches, transfers, displacements" (Senn 1984: 202).
He muses that dislocution "might even stand for all those effects that make us
respond, spontaneously, with laughter" (Senn 1984: 211). He points out that
"it is, of course, the reader who – potentially – executes all the mental shifts"
(Senn 1984: 209). However, in the animated film, the viewer does not execute
these "mental shifts" because the concreteness of the visual image provides her
with a visual representation of metamorphosis. Cohl's combination of wit and
graphic metamorphosis pushes the gag and joke into visual portmanteau and
subsequently into the comedic. His films are exemplary visual dislocutions, full
of animated portmanteaus. Many later animation films use these principles,
from Pat Sullivan and Otto Messmer's *Felix the Cat* (1919–1936), Max and Dave
Fleischer's *Out of the Inkwell* series (1918–1929) to Tex Avery's hyperbolic Classic
Hollywood cartoons (1935–1957).

The Advent of Sound and Sonic Portmanteau

Kristin Thompson points out that "in the late 1920s comedic animation
increasingly drew from live-action comedy – vaudeville, burlesque and slapstick"
(Thompson 2005: 141), yet until the advent of sound, animated cartoons lagged
behind popular cinema's increasing concern for narrative coherence and its use of
refined strategies that invited a more absorbed attention from the spectator. The
long-familiar gags didn't keep pace with technical and aesthetic developments.
Sound and music improved the somewhat sketchy and broken comic narrative
and allowed a wider repertoire of gags. The Fleischer Brothers' *Song Car Tunes*
(1924–1927) were screened with recorded sound using the Phonofilm system,
and when *Steamboat Willy* (Ub Iwerks), the first of Disney's Silly Symphonies,
was released in 1928, contemporary reports describe the audience response to
the cartoon as electric (Maltin 1987: 34–5). Driven by sound-oriented gags, it
exploited the possibilities of sound synchronization, often to slapstick comic
effect: a goat's tail becomes a music box crank, a goose squeezed by (a rather
nasty) Mickey, a honking bagpipe, and as the tails are pulled of piglets suckling,
their squeaks sound like a xylophone. Musical synchronization of movement
(Mickey-Mousing) was to become a dominant sound technique, and to the
present day, music remains a driving force for animated movement.

Music thus became a significant generator of comedic moments, and it
refreshed animation with new comic opportunities. In one of the early Warner
Bros. Merrie Melodies, the Academy Award nominated *It's Got Me Again* (1932),
gags and pranks are not just set to music – they interact with it, and are inspired by
it. Some of them are drawn to be visual representations of the originating source
of the music. Thompson offers a number of features of sound as it is specifically
used in animated comedy: "Sound could be isomorphic, having the same shape
as the visual image. It could metaphorically accentuate movement, with a slide

of chords on a xylophone as a character falls over, or a cymbal clash when a character is hit on the head with an object" (Thompson 2005: 140).

Part of this film's humor – and many others of the time – lies in the mice's usurpation of musical instruments to serve their needs: a tuba becomes a tunnel up to a tabletop, a violin a slide to the floor, a drum a trampoline, an accordion a lift down to the floor, a record the dance platform, a metronome a catapult. Another part originates in an enjoyable effect of surprise and astonishment of the animated figures' performances: mice as we have never seen them, singing, dancing, playing instruments, a fluid, undulating grandfather clock. These examples of metaphorical sound from *It's Got Me Again* relate to a certain pleasure to be had watching such films. Freud suggests that

> The philosophers, who count jokes a part of the comic and who treat the comic itself under the heading of aesthetics, define an aesthetic idea by the condition that in it we are not trying to get anything from things or do anything with them … but that we are content with contemplating them and with the enjoyment of the idea. (Freud 1966: 95)

It's Got Me Again's dancing and rhythmically pulsating instruments, mice and objects elicit this aesthetic pleasure. This film is exemplary for many that followed. One that self-reflexively makes fun of the synchronization of animated figures and music is Friz Freleng's *Rhapsody in Rivets* (1941) in which a building crew creates the music using their tools while erecting a skyscraper to Liszt's Hungarian Rhapsody (conducted by the foreman). An example of Thompson's of isomorphic sound is used in the *Screwy Truant* (Tex Avery 1945). A truant officer (an anthropomorphized dog) steps on tacks while running; we hear an explosion, the sound of a rolling flat tire as he slows down and stops, and the sound of air escaping as his "foot" deflates. Then he opens a hatch in his backside that has a "spare foot."

I'd like to expand Thompson's taxonomy of animated sound with a new feature that incorporates some of Freud's comic concepts and Joyce's portmanteau words. While he is not specifically referring to the portmanteau technique, comparing other theoretical concepts of jokes (Emil Krapelin, Lipps), Freud cites Heymans (1896) who "explains how the effect of a joke comes about through bewilderment being succeeded by illumination" (Freud 1966: 12) This is exemplified with what Freud considers "a brilliant joke of Heine's who makes one of his characters, Hirsch-Hyacinth, a poor lottery-agent, boast that the great Baron Rothschild had treated him quite as his equal – quite 'famillionarely' " (Freud 1966: 12–13). The neologism at the core of this joke is "famillionarely," a portmanteau word that combines, the words "family," "familiar," "familiarly" and "millionaire." It uses Freud's joke techniques of condensation with modification (family and millionaire), and double meaning/*double entendre* (treating someone familiarly,

Figure 24.1 Top row: an example of visual and sonic portmanteau in the Fleischers' *Dizzy Dishes* (1938; producer, Max Fleischer). Bottom row: Three examples of comic non-compossibility and visual portmanteau in Bob Clampett's original *Porky in Wackyland* (1938; producer, Leon Schlesinger).

i.e. as a member of the family, but also with class and wealth-based sarcastic distance between a millionaire and a poor lottery agent).

As I suggested with reference to Cohl's films, this joke technique can also function on *a graphic level*, and it is often enhanced through combination with sound. The fragmentation and recombination of lexeme word fragments to create a new a word with multiple meanings can take on visual form in drawn animation, when animated figures are created out of composite unrelated fragments. I will illustrate this with an example of a new sound feature, what I call comedic sonic portmanteau. It is based in Freud's joke technique of "the multiple use of the same material" (Freud 1966: 41), in this case a sound, and it bridges and merges two unrelated, contrasting objects. In the Fleischer Brothers' *Dizzy Dishes* (1930), a waiter prepares food in the back kitchen for an angry, hungry customer. Using two cleavers, he hacks a collection of meat on a chopping block. In time with this the sound of the chopping – a snare drum – increases to a frenetic pace as the waiter chops faster (see Figure 24.1). He moves to a shelf, leaving the cleavers to chop furiously in time with the drum, returns, throws plates and a clock into the mess, and takes hold of the cleavers again. Over the space of a few seconds the cleavers hack the meat and the chopping block into a crumbled pile that transforms into a miniature train, the chopped meat now coal in the coal bin behind the engine. Just before we see the engine emerge from the pile, a bell dings (the clock?) like the bell of a train crossing. The sound remains the same – a snare drum – but with the images, it transforms from the sound of cleavers to the pumping noise of a steam engine. The snare drum we hear throughout this sequence is not isomorphic; it does not "have the same shape as the visual image" (Thompson 2005). As the graphic metamorphosis of the butcher block and cleavers into a miniature train develops, "bewilderment [is] succeeded by illumination." The continuous sound of the snare drum effectively shifts as a sound bridge, a sonic portmanteau, from hacking cleavers to a chugging steam engine – transforming the gag into a ingenious merging of sound and animated metamorphosis.

Cartoon Anarchy and Noncompossibility

During the Classical Hollywood period (1930–1945) the major studios refined the narrative content of their films. For the early comedy of this era, Jenkins describes "two competing aesthetic systems: one governed by a demand for character consistency, causal logic, and narrative coherence, the other by an emphasis on performance, affective immediacy, and atomistic spectacle" (Jenkins 1990: 4). A similar development happened within animation. Disney's attraction for audiences increasingly depended "more on the classical dramatic patterns (suspense, choreography, 'romantic movements'), than on dreamlike imaginative qualities created by animated drawings" (Bendazzi 1994: 65). Dominated by the classical unities of time, place and action, Disney's films mark a move away from the comic potential in cartoon animation defined by its inherent capacity for disruption, disunity and chaos. Comic inventions within the increasingly narrative cartoons continued to be drawn from gags, situations and accidents, but much less from metamorphoses or the sudden activation of inanimate objects. Other cartoons of the period generally adhered to live action conventions of space, narration and character, but exploited their potential to surprise and disrupt the physical realm. Many of the Hollywood studio animation artists had learned their craft at Disney, but they were able to exercise greater creative comic freedom, and a different aesthetic system, at the other major Hollywood animation studios (Warner Bros., MGM, Universal).

Porky in Wackyland (Bob Clampett 1938)[9] is a cartoon that pushed the comic potential of disruption, disunity and disorder to an extreme, in a similar way Joyce did in the 14th "Circe" chapter of *Ulysses*, an unparalleled attempt at expressing visual transformation through the written medium of symbolic language. It uses a "technic" of hallucination and alludes to the brothel, intoxication, and memory. The excerpt here is one of the many italicized directions throughout the chapter that have a theatrical, and I would claim, animated cinematic, quality:

> *(Bloom walks on a net, covers his left eye with his left ear, passes through several walls, climbs Nelson's pillar, hangs from the top ledge by his eyelids, eats twelve dozen oysters (shells included), heals several sufferers from the king's evil, contracts his face so as to resemble many historical personages, Lord Beaconsfield, Lord Byron, Wat Tyler, Moses of Egypt, Moses Maimonides, Moses Mendelssohn, Henry Irving, Rip van Winkle, Kossuth, Jean Jacques Rousseau, Baron Leopold Rothschild, Robinson Crusoe, Sherlock Holmes, Pasteur, turns each foot simultaneously in different directions, bids the tide turn back, eclipses the sun by extending his little finger.)* (Joyce 1984: U15.1841–51)

Cartoons abound that use analogous visual transformations, and because the animator can create an illusion of life for almost any drawn or painted form, animators can create figures similar to some non-human figures also introduced throughout the "Circe" chapter that assume roles, have speaking parts and perform actions: "The Call," "The Answer," "The Timepiece," "The Gramophone," "The Gasjet," "The Flybill," "The Pianola," and "The Yews."

Porky in Wackyland is full of similar metamorphoses, impossible events and more-or-less anthropomorphic figures composed of fragments and illogical parts. These constructions are an element of film metaphor that work with "noncompossibility" that Noël Carroll describes as "physically noncompossible elements in the filmic array ... [that] have been fused or connected in a way that defies physical compossibility, not in order to represent a state of affairs in the world of fiction, but to *interanimate* the categories the image brings to mind" (Carroll 2001: 215, italics mine).

I have written elsewhere on portmanteau and noncompossibility in the Quay Brothers' puppet animation (Buchan 2011: 129–32). As the films I am discussing are cartoons, Carroll's brief exploration of how cartoons can *visually* "interanimate" these elements includes reflecting on Popeye's arm/anvil, made using drawn and painted cel animation. "A man cannot have an anvil embedded in a working arm ... the spectator cannot rely simply on what the image in isolation shows and on what she knows about science and the world. She must also consider the context in which the image figures as well as the likely intentions of the filmmaker in presenting the image" (Carroll 2001: 216).

Some similar comic examples of animated noncompossibility and portmanteau figures in *Wackyland* include: the sun rising to reveal it is resting on a totem pole-like support of animals, a horn on legs honks itself by squeezing its rubber "head," a seething whirlwind blur settles to be a panting, two-headed- and shared body "catdog," a three-headed "man" (the heads are caricatures of the Three Stooges) arguing with his three "selve" (see Figure 24.1). These animated figures and are visual portmanteaus comparable to Joyce's language in this hallucinatory text from *Ulysses*: The Timepiece cries "Cuckoo" three times (Joyce 1984: U15. 1133–35), The Gasjet lets out "Pooah! Pfuiiiiiii!" (Joyce 1984: U. 2280), The Pianola sings "My girl's a Yorkshire girl." (Joyce 1986: U15. 4115), The Yews cry "*(their silverfoil of leaves precipitating, their skinny arms aging and swaying)* Deciduously!" (Joyce 1984: U15. 3453–4)

But it is not only the figures that are funny; the illogical metamorphosis of forms add to the film's antic humor, as the following examples illustrate. Porky enters a black space in a small box, slides down a tunnel (like Alice down the rabbit hole), is squeezed like a drop through an enormous tap, and 12 doors without walls around them slide open and disappear in sequence to reveal a stage with a castle with a moat. The castle's drawbridge lowers, transforms into a speedboat that the Do-Do gets out of. Its antics are wacky – it runs circles in the air, conjures a pencil from nowhere and draws a door on what seems to be the sky, and instead of opening it, it lifts the bottom like a soft curtain and Porky escapes. Standing in an empty space with an elevator dial on its top, the Do-Do yells "going uuu-up" as the door closes and the "elevator" rises in the air. Running away, it arrives at a cliff, panics, then "lifts" the landscape across from the cliff (a mountain) to reveal a flat plain. Its arms extend to pull a brick wall in front of it that Porky runs into. Porky finally catches the Do-Do, who says "I really am the last of the Do-Dos, ain't I, fellas?" and a gaggle of identical Do-Dos fill the screen. *Porky in Wackyland* creates an animated version of Bergson's "strangest metamorphoses." For the viewer, rather than having to make the intellectual effort of ideation – the conceptualization of a mental image – that Joyce's words require, the cartoon's nonsensical concepts are given visual concrete form and reified in the illusion of projection.

It's All in a Name: Caricature and Parody

As animated comic "stars" developed, spoken dialogues joined music on the sound track. The funny voice was not only used for animated "born inked" stars (designed characters, not human performers), for which the combination of human voice (often Mel Blanc) and anthropomorphized animal characters is also a type of sonic portmanteau. Warner Bros. produced many animated parodies of their feature films and famous actors, and animators took great freedom in poking fun at them. *Hollywood Steps Out* (Tex Avery 1941), set in a dinner club, caricatures some of Hollywood's best known romance and comedy stars – Cary Grant, Clark Gable, Bing Crosby, James Stewart, Oliver Hardy, Mickey Rooney, Harpo and Groucho Marx (most of the voices were done by the less-known Kent Rogers). The animators exploit what Bergson considers the comic element in drawn caricature. He describes the human face as imperfect, with minor distortions, inharmoniousness and possible grimaces, and suggests "the art of the caricaturist consists in detecting this, at times, imperceptible tendency, and in rendering it visible to all eyes by magnifying it" (Bergson 2003: 13). Freud has a similar description of the effect of caricature as Bergson, that it

> brings about degradation by emphasizing ... a single trait which is comic in itself but was bound to be overlooked so long as it was only perceivable in the general picture. By isolating this, a comic effect can be attained which extends in our memory [and is visually on display] over the whole object. This is subject to the condition that the actual presence of the exalted object himself [*sic*] does not keep us in a reverential attitude. (Freud 1966: 201)

Animation can exaggerate human attributes and behaviors and add new ones in a way unthinkable in live action. A few of the many examples of this in the cartoon: Grant's oversize ears, Edward G. Robinson's bulldog face, Johnny Weissmuller's stiff, ballooningly muscular physique, Stewart's huge underlip. These figures are comic because, while we are not "in the presence of the exalted object" (the Hollywood star), the parodies and caricatures of them are so well drawn and when animated, an element of their "presence" is experienced, and they become ridiculous. What is really funny in this film is that "serious" actors – Greta Garbo, Robinson, Bette Davis, Weissmuller, James Cagney, Humphrey Bogart, Peter Lorre – perform actions or say things that would probably never be part of a live-action film role. The voices, remarkably similar to the actors' own, are also subtly performed to emphasize single traits: Stewart's stammer, Lorre's whine, Garbo's basso, slow breathiness. As Bergson comments:

> The art of the comic poet consists in making us so well acquainted with the particular vice, in introducing us, the spectators, to such a degree of intimacy with it, that in the end we get hold of some of the strings of the marionette with which he is playing, and actually work them ourselves; this it is that explains part of the pleasure we feel … a comic character is generally comic in proportion to his ignorance of himself. (Bergson 2003: 15)

Besides the physical caricature, out-of-character situations for the animated counterparts of these "serious" actors are comic because they are designed to be ignorant and unwitting parodies of themselves. Freud observes that parody and travesty "achieve the degradation of something exalted in another way; by destroying the unity that exists between people's characters as we know them and their speeches and actions, by replacing either the exalted figures or their utterances [or appearance] by inferior ones" (Freud 1966: 201).

Cagney, Bogart and George Raft, in character for their Film Noir and gangster roles, heatedly discuss a heist that transpires to be a child's game of them tossing pennies against a wall – bathos instead of crime drama. The haughty, elusive Garbo is a working-class cigarette girl with hooded eyes and enormous feet (which she apparently had), and Clark Gable is forever chasing a woman (he was known as a womanizer in Hollywood). These are either the "vices" Bergson mentions or intimate knowledge of the actors that expose a human element of what lies beneath their constructed star perfection. Sometimes a star is featured as a caricature of generic film roles they actually played: for instance Peter Lorre in two monster cartoons: *Hair Raising Hare* (1946) and *Birth of a Notion* (1947). Hollywood actors' personalities, traits and voices were also widely used as sources for anthropomorphic animal characters, and animators often made use of Bergson's latter notion, that "a comic character is generally comic in proportion to his ignorance of himself": Pepé Le Pew, the French paramour continually foiled by his own skunk stench (unsmellable to himself), Porky Pig's naiveté, Elmer Fudd's Sisyphus hunt for the rabbit and his struggle to articulate the letter "r," Daffy Duck's hubris, Wile E. Coyote's persistently defeated inventiveness.

Names can be funny too; Joyce fully exploited the comic potential of shifts in meaning, blundered euphemisms and figurative use of words in names, as in the following examples (which should be pronounced out loud to reach the full comic effect): Commendatore Bacibaci Beninobenone; Borus Hupinkoff; Grandjoker Vladinmire Pokethankertscheff; Hi Hung Chang (Joyce 1984: U12.

556–66). While not as dense and multilexemed as Joyce's neologisms, some cartoons also use portmanteau names and inversions to great effect, and they also employ Freud's condensation, multiple use of the same material and the third technique of "double meaning" (Freud 1966: 42): Hatta Mari, Babbit and Catstello (Abbot and Costello) Ham and Ex, Bunny and Claude, or Foghorn Leghorn (his loud voice and a breed of chicken). Cartoons were sometimes based on feature films, and film titles were often either portmanteau names or puns. Here are some of many from Warner Bros. Looney Tunes and Merrie Melodies: *Carrotblanca, Tale of Two Kitties, To Duck or Not to Duck, Bacall to Arms, The Big Snooze, The Mouse-Merized Cat, Birth of a Notion, Wise Quackers, The Scarlet Pimpernickel*, and so on. These titles raise an expectation of comic content that draws on puns, colloquial language or play with film and book titles.

Animated Paranomasia, Idiom, and the Parodic Grotesque

We've seen how animated cartoons can visualize portmanteu and exploit the comic potential of animated caricature. I will now explore how animation can quite literally visualize language play, where "the language itself becomes an object" (Senn 1983: 33, translation mine). Discussing the relationship between a concrete object and an abstract relation, Bergson proposes that "a comic effect is obtained whenever we pretend to take literally an expression which was used figuratively" (Bergson 2003: 49–50). Tex Avery famously went to hilarious hyperbolic extremes with quirks and jokes of language. His films literally abound with animated paranomasia (puns, play on words), idiomatic expressions and malaproprisms. To develop this I'll start again with an example from Joyce's *Ulysses*: "Ham and his descendants musterred and bred there" (Joyce 1984: U8. 742). The pun and word play sets up a hilarious epic interlinking Babylon, Hamlet, cannibalism, Dublin pubs, and the growling stomach of a hungry Leopold Bloom. The humor of this phrase is developed through Freud's techniques of multiple use of the same material (the biblical Ham, Hamlet and cooked pork) and double meaning (mustard and musterred; bred and bread). While the reader must perform ideational effort to understand Joyce's pun, Bergson's explanation of the comic in paranomasia comes closer to what Avery achieves in *Symphony in Slang* (1951): "An amusing result is likewise obtainable whenever a symbol or an emblem is expanded on its concrete side, and a pretence is made of retaining the same symbolical value for this expansion as for the emblem itself" (Bergson 2003: 50).

In Avery's film, the play on words is coextensive with animated visualized concretization of words, and it also uses Freud's joke techniques of multiple use of the same material and of double meaning/*double entendre*. A few examples: a young man (who speaks the slang of the time) arrives in heaven and isn't understood by St Peter, who takes him to the angel Noah Webster (cf. the

Figure 24.2   Top row: visual puns from Tex Avery's *Car of Tomorrow* (1951; producer, Fred Quimby). Bottom row: Daffy breaking the "fourth wall" and scenes of comic *risus purus* (Chuck Jones's *Duck Amuck*, 1953; producer, Edward Selzer).

eponymous dictionary). As the man narrates the story of his life, his words are imagined by the angels, who take him literally, and events unfold as animated visual concretizations of puns. A few examples from the film: "born with a silver spoon in my mouth," "cutting the mustard" at a job, being "beside myself," "making some dough," being "all thumbs," a girlfriend with "nice pins," and "her hair done up in a bun," "going to pieces," "feeling blue" when it was "raining cats and dogs." The cartoon ends when he "dies laughing." In these examples, and many others I hope readers will recall from his other films, Avery literally visually concretizes an expression used figuratively, and because they take place concurrently in the cartoon – the phrase spoken as the images are animated – the viewer does not need to perform ideation, and experiences comic pleasure in purely visual and aural terms.

In the post-World War II period, popular entertainment also made fun of the (forced) redomestication of women, workplace situations, and burgeoning consumer culture. Bergson notes that "certain professions have a technical vocabulary: what a wealth of laughable results have been obtained by transposing the ideas of everyday life into this professional jargon" (Bergson 2003: 54). Avery's *Car of Tomorrow* (1951) is one of a short series of cartoons he made that satirized popular consumerism of the times.[10] Avery merged technical vocabulary with car-salesman colloquialisms to create visual puns. A new car's motor "still has a few bugs in it" (the hood opens to show insects crawling on the engine), and another has new "seal beam headlights" (the headlights open and two seals bark). In a self-reflexive moment where even Avery seems to thinks he went too far with visually literalizing puns, the narrator's voice says "oh, no!" and a drawn cartoon artist's hand enters the frame and crosses out the seal headlights. We hear "no more parking problems if you own this little number" and a man gets out of the car and packs it up into the size of a wallet. For "a powerful little job" with "200 horsepower," the sequence shows many galloping hooves under the car body, and a "hill climber special" has wheels that transform into toilet plungers to walk up a hill (see Figure 24.2). While some of these are a bit too literal, and even "corny," comic pleasure arises again from economy of expenditure upon ideation, as the images provide us with concrete examples of colloquial language.

A discussion of cartoon comedy without the chase genre is almost unthinkable, as it is an enduring motivation for gags and comic situations. A superb example that transforms the straightforward chase into a rollicking animated conceit is Tex Avery's *King-size Canary* (MGM 1947). Norman Klein suggests that Avery's characters were "enigmas who lived outside the rules of plot, space and time," which had the clear purpose "to undermine the restrictions of cartoon melodrama," and that his working methods were based on "the shock of the improbable" (Klein 1993: 172–3). I will concentrate on three elements in *King-size Canary*: repetition and progression, exaggeration, and the comic grotesque.

A starving alley cat, frustrated in many attempts to get a meal, ends up with a scrawny canary on a plate. The canary pitifully squeaks, "I've been sick." The cat sees a bottle on a shelf labeled "Garden Jumbo Gro" with a before and after image of a small, then large, flower, has a "brain storm" (lighting and thunder included), looks at the bottle again and the image changes to a "before" (small) and "after" (large) canary. He force-feeds the canary, and it starts to grow. He gets it on a table, plucks feathers and salts its leg, and looks up to see an enormous bird whose head touches the kitchen ceiling. The cat meekly puts the feathers back and sneaks away. The canary realizes it is huge, strong and, wanting revenge, it runs after the cat and the pursuit begins. The rest of the film is a series of chases involving cat, canary, bulldog (the canary's protector), and a mouse (which sides with the cat). Besides this repetition, there is a canonical progression in each chase – one animal drinks Gro-More and gets bigger than the last largest character.

This is an example of Freud's joke technique of multiple use of the same material; it is heightened by what Bergson describes as "an effect which grows by arithmetical progression, so that the cause, insignificant at the outset, culminates by a necessary evolution in a result as important as it is unexpected" (Bergson 2003: 35). But this is not only a progression; it is a systematic one that includes exaggeration, a technique that Bergson suggests "is always comic when prolonged, and especially when systematic ... It excites so much laughter that some writers have been led to define the comic as exaggeration, just as others have defined it as degradation" (Bergson 2003: 53).

The combination of repetition, progression and systematic exaggeration results in what Torben Grodal calls the parodic grotesque that "underlines the patterned and thereby the mechanical elements of the features they exaggerate and deform, for instance by upscaling certain features or by simplifying certain schemata of thoughts and actions" (Grodal 1999: 202). This is a feature of many Hollywood cartoons of the 1940s and 1950s, a zenith perhaps being Tex Avery's surreal and absurd distortion of body parts and his character's actions in *King-Size Canary*. Grodal (1999: 192) refines this to suggest, many comic grotesques are not expressions of mysterious and irrational phenomena, but expressions of the pleasure of accepting the shock-like "incomplete irrationality," and rejecting a serious calculation of the problems involved.

The film is animated, so it is not an irrational phenomenon – it is a series of imaginative drawings in a cartoon world. The viewer does not have to engage with comparisons with a schemata based in the real, physical world, and can enjoy the comic events on offer. Although he is referring to a live-action screwball comedy, Grodal's description of the audience's reaction to chase scenes is valid for the films I am discussing here:

> When we watch a comic chase scene like the one at the end of [Frank] Tashlin's *The Disorderly Orderly* [1964], in which those involved very quickly lose all control over the outcome, we soon give up our voluntary reactions and our teleological modelling of the events and laugh at them, and in this way bale out of the impossible job of making full, realistic sense of the sequence. (Grodal 1999: 191)

Hugh Kenner, a James Joyce specialist fascinated by animation, and by Chuck Jones in particular, sums up the essence of Avery's humor and particular type of animation: "Tex Avery's sense of the animatable universe was formed in the decade when a dotted line from the eye of Felix the Cat could knock over a chipmunk, and he remained impervious to the claim that animation should strive for the Illusion of Life" (Kenner 1994: 27). By breaking so many rules of the illusion of life, Avery's cartoons generate a different kind of laughter. In some instances the pleasure in the comic that arises from economy in expenditure upon ideation is accompanied by an overload of visual information on screen that generates cathexis (a high concentration of mental energy).[11] Referring to Freud's writing on jokes, Grodal suggests that this kind of laughter seems "to demand a certain switching-off of conscious and voluntary forms of reaction" and proposes that "like other types of automatic response, [laughter] is a reaction to overload, an 'escape-button alternative' to voluntary reactions" (Grodal 1999: 187–8). Avery's animated hyperbole and the visual and sonic portmanteau in many of his cartoons provokes this kind of visual and conceptual overload, a comic overload not possible in live-action film (an exception being perhaps, Frank Tashlin's and Jacques Tati's works). The animated figures and spaces visualize for the reader the dislocutory mental shifts readers of Joyce perform when reading the overload of portmanteau and hallucinatory style, that Senn suggests make us respond spontaneously with laughter.

The *Risus Purus*

Much as been written on North American cartoons from the World War II period including *Bugs Bunny Nips the Nips* (Friz Freleng 1944), *The Ducktators* (Norman McCabe 1942), *Plane Daffy*, (Frank Tashlin 1944), and *Blitz Wolf* (Tex Avery 1943).

These films present a different kind of humor than I have discussed so far, and invoke satire, the grotesque, and often include violent visual metaphors of the ridiculous pathos of the human condition – humor that reflects the threats and dangers of the time. They often use some nastier versions of what Freud suggests are methods that make people comic. Caricature, parody and travesty (as well as their practical counterpart, unmasking) are directed against people and objects that lay claim to authority and respect. They are opportunities for what Freud calls "*Herabsetzung* ["putting down," degradation] as the apt German expression has it" (Freud 1966: 200). These films introduced new, darker kinds of comedy in cartoons, and in the post-War years many retained this shift to black humor, satire and humiliation.

Freud also observed about caricature, parody and travesty that "it is obvious that these techniques can be used to serve hostile and aggressive purposes" (Freud: 189). One of the most brutal – and brutally funny – cartoons that uses most of these and other methods, including unmasking, is Chuck Jones's genial *Duck Amuck* (1953). In the film, Daffy is placed in a range of generic film scenery: a medieval castle (musketeers); a farmyard (farmer), a snowy landscape (skier); a tropical island (beach dress and ukulele). Daffy stoically adapts, changing his costume to suit the scene, but the scenery is ever-changing and increasingly ridiculous. He steadfastly carries on adjusting his performance to his environments, then loses his temper, faces the camera and says to the animation artist, "Buster, this is an animation cartoon, and in an animated cartoon, they have scenery." What follows is a lesson in humiliation. Daffy is erased, turned into a noncompossible freak, put through all kinds of harrowing experiences, the nadir for him (and both shocking and hilarious for us for us) being when the four-sided frame of the animated diegesis collapse on him (see Figure 24.2).

Daffy's direct address to the screen (to the animation artist and to us) erases the sacred "fourth wall" of fictional performance. It makes direct use of Bertolt Brecht's *V-effekt* (Verfremdungseffekt/alienation effect) in theater where the performer "never acts as if there were a fourth wall besides the three surrounding him. He expresses his awareness of being watched" (Brecht 1964). This aims to force audiences to be aware of the artificiality and construction of performance and makes it difficult to experience the narrative and the actors' characters passively as entertainment. Instead, they are made to engage intellectually and empathetically with the mishaps, problems, and larger political consequences of a performance. This alienation device is also apparent in the film's sound design. An example is when Daffy strums a guitar and starts to sing and there is no sound. With a poster, he requests "Sound Please" (see Figure 24.2). He strums again, and we hear a machine gun firing, a horn honk, and when he throws the instrument on the ground it makes the "hee-haw" sound of a donkey. The guitar, independent of Daffy, makes a shuddering movement that like a machine gun being fired that also jerks Daffy's body. Its strings vibrate with the horn honk and its cracked case moves in time to the donkey wheeze, expanding and contracting like an accordion.

A furious Daffy raises his finger and we expect vocal indignation: instead we (and Daffy) hear a rooster crow, a monkey hoot, and a mouse squeak.

Daffy's dilemmas are hilariously comic; but it is an experience of comedy that would not be possible in live action for a number of reasons. Because he is an animated figure, Daffy will not experience the fatal consequences of a fall to earth, of walls collapsing on him, or a bomb exploding in his face. We don't feel the same kind of empathy that we would for a human, and there is less degradation in a cartoon figure, partly because we know it doesn't exist outside projection. There is more scope to enjoy a pleasure that is not critical of another human, and less intellectual effort is needed to balance the conflict of criticism and *Schadenfreude* or degradation with the pleasure of the nonsense and exaggeration. Because we can escape the ethical responsibility of human empathy, we can enjoy the brutality of this utterly absurd humor.

There is thus a shift from laughing *with* Daffy to laughing *at* Daffy, when with the *V-effekt* we become aware of the animation artist and the sadism at play. With this knowledge, we laugh at Daffy's humiliation as we become complicit with the artist (revealed at the end as Bugs Bunny) who is causing Daffy so much grief, and this generates a feeling of superiority. Lipps observes that

> The comic ends in the moment when we ascend the pedestal again, i.e. where we begin to feel superior. The feeling of superiority proves to be the complete opposite of the feeling of the comic, as its classic deadly enemy. The feeling of the comic is possible to the extent that the feeling of superiority doesn't arise and cannot arise. (Lipps 2005: 22)

This superiority both stifles the comic and gives rise to a different experience of humor; while the comedy may end, a smile endures on our faces. Philosopher Simon Critchleys' book *On Humor* (2002) begins with an epigraph from Samuel Beckett's *Watt* – coincidentally published in 1953, the same year *Duck Amuck* was made – of Beckett's subtle *risus purus* (pure smile) described in *Watt* (Beckett 1959: 48). At the end of Critchley's delectable treatise, paraphrasing Beckett's *risus purus*, he concludes: "For me, it is this smile – deriding the having and the not having, the pleasure and the pain, the sublimity and suffering of the human situation – that is the essence of humour. This is the risus purus, the highest laugh, the laugh that laughs at the laugh, that laughs at that which is unhappy, the mirthless laugh ... " (Critchley 2002: 111)

As *Duck Amuck* unfolds, Daffy becomes more and more unhappy, and it is his suffering, humiliation, and our feeling of superiority that elicits the *risus purus*. But this is not to say that this kind of humor is simply cruel; on the contrary, as Critchley further observes: "Yet, this smile does not bring unhappiness, but rather elevation and liberation, the lucidity of consolation. This is why, melancholy animals that we are, human beings are also the most cheerful. We smile and find ourselves ridiculous. Our wretchedness is our greatness" (Critchley 2002: 111).

Chuck Jones was a master of the animated *risus purus*; some of his characters were deeply unhappy: Daffy or the frog in *One Froggy Evening* (1955), or humiliated: Wile E. Coyote (*Beep Prepared* 1961). But Jones was not alone – other directors created similar characters, for instance Tex Avery's prosaic Droopy Dog and ungratified Wolf, and some frustrated and humiliated cartoon characters were animated by different directors and their artists over the years, notably Sylvester the Cat (Friz Freleng and Chuck Jones) and Elmer Fudd (Bob Clampett, Chuck Jones, Friz Freleng).

The comic antithesis to these unhappy characters, Bugs Bunny, also featured in many of these directors' cartoons: Tex Avery, Chuck Jones, Friz Freling, Robert McKimson and Bob Clampett all did films with Bugs. Chuck Jones remarked, "Bugs Bunny is who we want to be. Daffy is who we are" (cited in Graber 2009: 96). Through their cartoons, these animation artists concurrently present us with both the ridiculousness of who we *want to be* and the comic potential of who *we are*. Their remarkable range of comedy and humor, from nave slapstick and hilariously funny antics to satire, black humor, and the *risus purus*, lies in their ability to translate the tragic and comic elements and behaviors of the human – from our dark, unhappy recesses to our fanciful silliness – into their drawn, painted animated characters.

Paul Klee proposed that satire "is not an excess of ill humour, but ill humour resulting from a vision of something higher ... ridiculous man, divine God. Hatred for anything stagnant out of respect for pure humanity."[12] It is fair to say that the artists whose works I've used to explore some of the many forms, styles and techniques of comedy – Cohl's witty metamorphoses, Avery's anarchic visual portmanteau, or Jones's animated *risus purus*– have in common a vision of humanity that finds its best expression in humor. When we laugh at their hapless figures and antics in worlds impossible for us to inhabit, we are also laughing at ourselves. I end this chapter, and my attempt at the impossibility of the task of describing humor in animated cartoons, with a citation from Freud that is also at the end of his book on jokes: "It is only with misgivings that I venture to approach the problem of the comic itself... when the works of a great number of eminent thinkers have failed to produce a wholly satisfactory explanation" (Freud 1966: 188–9). While analysis can explain some features, comedy in theatrical animation is as varied as the personalities, experiences, and histories of its viewers. It is in each of us to discover what is funny in these films and how they enrich our lives, from rolling-on-the-floor laughter to the *risus purus*.

Notes

1. Most of these films are available on film, the Web, VHS or DVD.
2. I must emphasize that while noncommercial, nonconventional animation is not the topic of this chapter, it can also be very funny.

3.   There are, of course, hybrid exceptions to this, including animation that works with collaged photography.

4.   When used to describe an animated character the pronouns "he," "she," and "they" in this chapter refer to the illusory existence and suggested gender on screen of that character.

5.   A shot in cinema is a series of images recorded in a single uninterrupted take of the camera. As animation is shot single frame, every frame is a shot, hence my use of "shot" in quotation marks.

6.   For more on the relationship between print media and animation studio developments, see Thompson (2005: 137).

7.   Editor James Strachey rightly points out the dilemma and terminological difficulties of translating the German *der Witz*, as it has multiple meanings beyond "the joke" as it is generally used in the translated text. Wit "is used both for the mental faculty and for its product – for 'wittiness' and 'the witticism,' to use renderings that have been rejected [in the translation]" (editor's preface in Freud (1966: 7–8).

8.   See Crafton (1990: 258–66) for his analysis and for stills of *Fantasmagorie*.

9.   It was remade in Technicolour 1949 as *Dough for the Do-Do*, directed by Friz Freleng. See also Paul Wells' chapter in this volume for another discussion of the Clampett film.

10.   As with a number of cartoons over history, some sequences poke rather harmful "fun" at gender, ethnicities and nationalities.

11.   To see the artistic imagination that develops over a succession of frames, the reader should take the opportunity to see what Avery's film universe looks like when it is slowed down on a DVD or VHS to the level where single frames are visible. It is possible to see the individual drawings and how the metamorphoses are developed over time on a series of separate drawings before being shot frame by frame.

12.   Cited in Vanderbeek (1966: 337).

References

Beckett, Samuel (1959) *Watt*, Grove Press, New York, NY.

Bendazzi, Giannalberto (1994) *Cartoons: One Hundred Years of Cinema Animation*, Indiana University Press and John Libbey & Co, London.

Bergson, Henri (2003) *Laughter: An Essay on the Meaning of the Comic*, Project Gutenberg E-book, http://www.gutenberg.org/files/4352/4352-h/4352-h.htm (accessed May 18, 2012).

Bollettieri Bosinelli, R.M. and Whitsitt, S.P. (2010) The laughing word of James Joyce, in, *Translation, Humour and Literature* (ed. Delia Chiaro), Continuum, London, pp. 158–70.

Brecht, Bertolt (1964) *On Theatre* (trans. John Willett), Methuen, London.

Buchan, Suzanne (1998) Graphic and literary metamorphosis: animation technique and James Joyce's *Ulysses*, *Animation Journal*, 7 (1), 21–34.

Buchan, Suzanne (2011) *The Quay Brothers: Into a Metaphysical Playroom*, University of Minnesota Press, Minneapolis, MN.

Carroll, Noël (2001) *Theorizing the Moving Image*, Cambridge University Press, Cambridge.

Crafton, Donald (1990) *Emile Cohl, Caricature, and Film*, Princeton University Press, Oxford.

Critchley, Simon (2002) *On Humour*, Routledge, London.

Ellmann, Richard (1978) *Ulysses on the Liffey*, Oxford University Press, Oxford.

Freud, Sigmund (1966) *Jokes and their Relation to the Unconscious* (trans. J. Strachey), Routledge & Kegan Paul, London.

Graber, Sheila (2009) *Animation: A Handy Guide*, A&C Publishers, London.

Grodal, Torben (1999) *Moving Pictures: A New Theory of Film Genres, Feelings, and Cognition*, Clarendon Press, Oxford.

Hazlitt, William and Keynes, Geoffrey (ed.) (2004) *Selected Essays of William Hazlitt 1778 to 1830*, Kessinger Publishing, Whitefish, MT.

Jenkins, Henry, III (1990) "Fifi was my mother's name!": anarchistic comedy, the vaudeville aesthetic, and diplomaniacs. *The Velvet Light Trap*, 26, 3–27.

Joyce, James (1968) *Finnegan's Wake*, Faber & Faber, London.

Joyce, James (1984) *Ulysses: The Corrected Text* (ed. Hans Walter Gabler), Penguin, London.

Kenner, Hugh (1994) *Chuck Jones: A Flurry of Drawings*, University of California Press, Berkeley, CA.

Klein, Norman M. (1993) *7 Minutes: The Life and Death of the American Animated Cartoon*, Verso, New York, NY.

Lipps, Theodor (2005) *Komik und Humor: Eine psychologisch-ästhetische Untersuchung*, Hamburg und Leipzig: L. Voss. Project Gutenberg E-Book, http://www.gutenberg.org/ebooks/8298 (accessed May 18, 2012).

Maltin, Leonard (1987) *Of Mice and Magic: A History of American Animated Cartoons*, Penguin Books, New York, NY.

Senn, Fritz (1983) *Nichts Gegen Joyce: Joyce Versus Nothing. Aufsätze 1959–1983*, Haffmanns Verlag, Zürich.

Senn, Fritz (1984) *Joyce's Dislocutions* (ed. J.P. Riquelme), Johns Hopkins Press, Baltimore, MD.

Thompson, Kirsten (2005) Animation, in *Comedy: A Geographic and Historical Guide, Vol. 1* (ed. Maurice Charney), Praeger Publishers, Westport, CT, pp. 135–152.

Vanderbeek, Stan (1966) RE: vision. *The American Scholar*, 35 (2), 337.

Further Reading

Critchley, Simon (2002) *On Humour*, Routledge, New York, NY. This is a wonderful introduction to the philosophy of humor that takes the reader though histories of wit, comedy, the joke and literature. A brilliant contextual companion to the darker sides of Hollywood cartoons, Critchley's book manages to avoid the danger that "a theory of humor is not humorous," and includes dozens of examples that can evoke laughter in the reader.

Kenner, Hugh (1994) *Chuck Jones: A Flurry of Drawings*, University of California Press, Berkeley, CA. Kenner's delectable book opens up a new way of thinking about Chuck Jones' cartoons, and it simultaneously offers new ways of thinking about classic Hollywood cartoons. A scholar of literature, including James Joyce, Kenner's deep readings of the inspirational sources, drawing and ideas behind Jones's works is also generously sprinkled with personal anecdotes and helpful facts.

Klein, Norman M. (1993) *7 Minutes: The Life and Death of the American Animated Cartoon*, Verso, New York, NY. The Classic Hollywood cartoon period is incisively and respectfully deconstructed into an incisive study of the American theatrical cartoon.

With observations on comedy throughout, it offers both a historical review and specific insights into the production contexts and sociocultural influences. See especially Chapter 2: The Gag (pp. 19–31).

Maltin, Leonard (1987) *Of Mice and Magic: A History of American Animated Cartoons*, Penguin Books, New York, NY. The "granddaddy" of animation history and production, this early publication offers a plethora of information on the main North American studios, personalities, technical innovations and films from the silent film period to the 1970s.

Thompson, Kirsten (2005) Animation, in *Comedy: A Geographic and Historical Guide, Vol. 1* (ed. Maurice Charney), Praeger Publishers, Westport, CT, pp. 135–52. Thompson's nonchronological review of comedy in animation includes reflections on specific techniques of comedy in animation, from caricature and slapstick to rubberhosing, and a number of analyses that relate earlier animation to contemporary works.

Index

Note: "n." after a page reference indicates the number of a note on that page